DICTIONARY OF

TWENTIETH CENTURY CULTURE

Hispanic Culture of
Mexico, Central America,
and the Caribbean

DICTIONARY OF

TWENTIETH CENTURY CULTURE

Hispanic Culture of Mexico, Central America, and the Caribbean

Edited by

Peter Standish

Associate Editors

| Jan Michael Hanvik | Stephen M. Hart | Nancy L. Ruyter |
| Florencia Bazzano Nelson | Maureen E. Shea | Robert L. Smith |

A MANLY, INC. BOOK

GALE

an International Thomson Publishing company I(T)P®

Printed in the United States of America

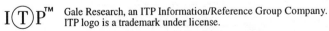
I(T)P™   Gale Research, an ITP Information/Reference Group Company.
          ITP logo is a trademark under license.

10 9 8 7 6 5 4 3 2 1

TABLE OF CONTENTS

TOPICAL TABLE OF CONTENTS

NEWSPAPERS AND MAGAZINES

PHOTOGRAPHY

EDITORIAL PLAN

Culture is a broad term that has different meanings for different people. It is a word that is used variously to describe how we are alike, how we are different, and what we should aspire to know and appreciate. Thus the title of this work was the subject of careful deliberation by the advisory board at the initial planning meeting in 1990. At issue were basic definitions that determined the fundamental elements of the editorial rationale.

The consensus was that the *Dictionary of Twentieth-Century Culture (TCC)* should undertake to provide a ready reference for the vocabulary of culture, which the board defined as the broad language drawing on shared knowledge used by people of similar backgrounds to communicate with one another. A standard dictionary of language records the definitions of words used in verbal discourse; the advisory board agreed that such dictionaries are inadequate to define more complicated structures of meaning that *TCC* addresses. Communication is frequently extraverbal, drawing on shared experiences, common concepts, communal notions about celebrities, and universally construed messages conveyed by certain images. Culture embraces all aspects of life, from the mundane to the sublime, from the knowledge of grocery-item brand names and the images they connote to a familiarity with classic works of literature, music, and art.

Culture broadly construed is an unmanageable topic for a dictionary-type reference work. Comprehensive coverage would fill a large library. For practical reasons, it was necessary to narrow the scope of *TCC*. The advisory board elected to restrict the series to entries on people, places, terms, art forms, and organizations associated with creative expression in the humanities, those forms of creativity that seek to describe and interpret the human condition. Certainly physicists, chemists, physicians, mathematicians, jurists, and legislators are as creative in their own ways as writers, artists, actors, dancers, and musicians. But as specialists, they view the world from different, though no less important, perspectives than creative artists in the humanities do. Because we cannot do justice to all these worldviews in a single series, we have limited ourselves to the rich world of art, music, literature, drama, radio and television performance, movies, and dance. The advisory board elected not to include entries on individual works because works are described in entries devoted to their creators. Both high and low art that meet the qualification of having made a lasting impression on society will be covered. Endurance is a matter of editorial judgment, and it will be left to volume editors and the editorial board to make the necessary decisions about inclusion.

Obviously it is a distortion to suggest that creative expression occurs in isolation. Most art is not about art but about people from all walks of life and the ways they act, individually and in the company of others. The people, events, and ideas outside the arena of creative expression that stimulated artistic responses have a special significance in culture, and entries are provided to describe certain specific social and historical forces and the creative responses they prompted.

The purpose of *TCC* is not to prescribe what people should know about modern culture; rather, *TCC* attempts to describe and define what people have collectively thought was significant. The purpose of *TCC* entries is definition rather than analysis. Entries are concise, in some cases as brief as a few sentences. In rare cases does an entry exceed one thousand words.

The decision to organize *TCC* volumes geographically was a difficult one, determined by practical considerations and by assumptions about the readership for the series. In fact, of course, there are several distinct cultural groups in most countries, defined sometimes by religion, sometimes by ethnicity, sometimes by socio-economics. Careful attention is due separate cultural groups around the world, but that responsibility must be left to another work. *TCC* is devoted to cultural commonality, not cultural diversity.

Related to the decision to take the broad view of distinct cultures is the advisory board's perception of the audience for *TCC*: American high-school and college students and the patrons of American public libraries. The board has assumed a certain ethnocentrism among the audience, and thus *TCC* will be disproportionately American in character. Other volumes will, in most cases, concentrate on the dominant cultures of a country. Unarguably, comprehensive coverage of the topic is the work of lifetimes.

Certainly many significant entries could be added to those included here. Almost as certainly, entries that should have been included are inadvertently omitted. Significance is a subjective judgment, determined in large part by the cultural background to which the editors themselves are bound. There is some comfort in the anticipation that *TCC* will be a living project that continues its evolution after publication of this volume.

Richard Layman
Columbia, South Carolina
18 April 1994

DICTIONARY OF TWENTIETH-CENTURY CULTURE PUBLISHING PLAN

American Culture After World War II
American Culture Before World War II
Russian Culture After World War II
Russian Culture Before World War II
German Culture
African-American Culture
Arab Culture in the Middle East
Arab Culture in Northern Africa
French Culture
Hispanic Culture of South America

Hispanic Culture of Mexico, Central America, and the Spanish Caribbean
Italian Culture
British Culture After World War II
British Culture Before World War II
Native American Culture
Japanese Culture
Chinese Culture
African Culture South of the Sahara
Eastern European Culture
South East Asian Culture

ACKNOWLEDGMENTS

This book was produced by Manly, Inc. Karen L. Rood is senior editor. Ann González was the in-house editor. She was assisted by associate editors Julie E. Frick and L. Kay Webster.

Production coordinator is James W. Hipp. Photography editors are Julie E. Frick and Margaret Meriwether. Photographic copy work was performed by Joseph M. Bruccoli. Layout and graphics supervisor is Penney L. Haughton. Copyediting supervisor is Laurel M. Gladden. Typesetting supervisor is Kathleen M. Flanagan. Systems manager is George F. Dodge. The production staff includes Phyllis A. Avant, Ann M. Cheschi, Patricia Coate, Joyce Fowler, Stephanie C. Hatchell, Kathy Lawler Merlette, Jeff Miller, Pamela D. Norton, Laura Pleicones, Emily R. Sharpe, William L. Thomas Jr., and Allison Trussell.

Walter W. Ross and Steven Gross did library research. They were assisted by the following librarians at the Thomas Cooper Library of the University of South Carolina: Linda Holderfield and the interlibrary-loan staff; reference-department head Virginia Weathers; reference librarians Marilee Birchfield, Stefanie Buck, Stefanie DuBose, Rebecca Feind, Karen Joseph, Donna Lehman, Charlene Loope, Anthony McKissick, Jean Rhyne, Kwamine Simpson, and Virginia Weathers; circulation-department head Caroline Taylor; and acquisitions-searching supervisor David Haggard.

FOREWORD

As the century closes, Spanish ranks fourth among the world's most widely spoken languages — after Chinese, English, and Russian — and the number of Spanish speakers is growing. This is the second of two volumes in the *Twentieth-Century Culture* series to be devoted to the culture of the American countries where Spanish is the predominant language. The previous volume dealt with South America — that is to say, with territories from Colombia to Tierra del Fuego, at the southern tip of the continent; the present one deals with Mexico, Central America, and the Hispanic Caribbean. All the Central American countries except Belize (formerly British Honduras) are covered — as are Cuba, the Dominican Republic, and Puerto Rico in the Caribbean. Although latino culture in the United States is outside the scope of this volume, the geographical proximity of the United States, the history of U.S. intervention in area affairs, the status of Puerto Rico as a U.S. territory, and the fact that so many Hispanic people have lived and worked in North America are all factors that have made some transnational coverage inevitable. Overall, it will be evident that the field encompassed in these volumes is a vast one, and that coverage has had to be selective.

The Spanish American countries share much in common in view of their colonial past, but there are also major cultural differences among them because they were subject to outside influences apart from that of Spain and because some of them enjoy the added richness that comes from having a significant indigenous heritage. So far as the areas covered in the present volume are concerned, it is illustrative to compare countries such as Costa Rica (whose population is predominantly European in origin), Guatemala (where Indians are still a majority of the population), and Cuba (where African elements are strong).

The Spanish exploration of the Americas radiated out from the Caribbean. During the first of his four voyages to the Americas, Christopher Columbus founded a colony on the island that was named Hispaniola (the home of present-day Haiti and the Dominican Republic), but it was another island, Cuba, that became the base of operations for the Spaniards, and it was from there that many of the explorations of other territories were launched, including the one that led to the dramatic conquest of Mexico in 1521. For years, in successive probings along the Central American isthmus, the Spaniards tried to find a way to the Orient until they eventually realized that what they had found was in fact another continent. As it happened, Cuba was the last colonial American possession to be lost by Spain (in 1898) and has consequently occupied a particularly significant place in the history of Spanish America.

In 1992, five hundred years after Columbus first made landfall in the Bahamas, there was much controversy surrounding the term "New World." It was argued that this term reflected the arrogance of the European conquerors, who had, in fact, encountered and largely destroyed some highly developed civilizations that were in some ways more advanced than those of the "Old World." A modern Central American writer, Augusto Monterroso, has a fable that illustrates the point; it tells of a Catholic friar, captured by Indian warriors and about to be sacrificed on the local pyramid. Confident in his knowledge that an eclipse is due, the friar boasts to the Indians that, if they do not release him, he will cause the sun to be covered; minutes later, he lies dead, while his captors recite the dates on which eclipses are due.

Just as some indigenous peoples had a sophisticated knowledge of astronomy, there were some who were also advanced in social organization. Whether deliberately or inadvertently, the arrival of the Spaniards, rather than preserving what was valuable, brought disease and destruction. In the Caribbean territories the effect was to all but wipe out the Indians. Elsewhere, especially in southern Mexico, Honduras, and Guatemala, indigenous cultures have survived into our day. We see evidence of them, for example, in music and dance, where forms or practices survive more or less intact, or by fusion (syncretism) with imported cultural manifestations. There have also been conscious movements to extol things indigenous in art and literature, sometimes confused with political motives; and there are increased signs of respect for indigenous cultures, in the form of official bodies charged with their protection.

The defense of Indian interests may be said to have its beginnings in the writings of Fray Bartolomé de las Casas, who in 1542 published his *Brevíssima relación de la destruyción de las Indias* (Brief Account of the Destruction of the Indies), dedicated to Philip of Spain and denouncing the treatment of the Indians by the Spaniards; thus was born the "leyenda negra," the "black legend" of Spanish cruelty. In fact not all the Spaniards were evil; in general, however, the Indians were badly treated and exploited. In some circumstances, where the Indians could not survive or do the work demanded of them, African slaves were imported. Especially in the Caribbean territories, the importation of slaves (which las Casas actually advocated, although he later

xvii

came to regret it) grew with the rise of the sugar and tobacco trades. Thus, the cultural mix was further complicated. There is some reason to believe that these slaves in the Spanish colonies were better treated than were their counterparts in North America, but thousands became runaways (*cimarrones*) and fled to areas bordering the Caribbean, including Belize, Panama, and the northern coast of South America. There and on the Caribbean islands the African-based cultural presence remains strong. The cultural mixture of Indian, African, and European elements was matched by a racial one, despite prejudices and class distinctions, and the result is that a great many Spanish Americans are the product of an intermingling of races.

Just as the Spaniards brought new diseases to America, so they took others back; syphilis for example. A more positive result of the "encounter" of these different cultures (to use a more fashionable term than "discovery") was the arrival of the previously unknown horse in America and of the potato (an Inca staple) in Europe. An extensive process of crossfertilization had begun. From the point of view of the Europeans, a "New World" it most certainly was, for (rather as we might talk of discovering a "new planet") they had previously lived in ignorance of America's existence. The "Indians" were so called precisely because Columbus thought he was in the Far East. It is also important to realize that what motivated Spain was not only greed. Like others before and since, the Spaniards were driven by an insidious combination of greed and the absolute belief that they had their God on their side. Spain itself had suffered invasion by other crusaders, the "Moors," who had occupied much of the Iberian peninsula since 711. By the late fifteenth century, its various kingdoms were coming together. The "Catholic Monarchs" Ferdinand and Isabella had expelled not only the Moors but also the Jews, and it seemed logical to continue the Catholic crusade in combination with economic and political expansion. Spain did profit handsomely from the New World in wealth, prestige, and power, while the part of religion in shaping Spanish American culture is not to be underestimated. From a religious standpoint the Indians had to be "shown the light"; yet somehow indigenous beliefs and practices have survived, often by assimilation with Catholic ones. In modern times Indian beliefs are subject to other, largely Protestant, missionary pressures.

During the colonial period there was little interest in preserving the cultures of indigenous peoples such as the Incas; the aim was to convert them to European ways, and the main responsibility for doing so lay with the church. In the eighteenth century, however, the powers of the church in the colonies were somewhat compromised when the Jesuits — whose role as educators and missionaries had been so vital — were expelled from the Americas because Charles III of Spain found them too active in politics. After the Jesuits turned their energies against Spain, the Inquisition retaliated with more-effective repression in the rebellious colonies. Then, against the background of the Napoleonic Wars in Europe, Spanish America began to shake off the Spanish yoke, and the new republics started to emerge. By the third decade of the nineteenth century the greater part of Spanish America had been liberated from Spain. There followed a new era of immigration to various countries, one which reached massive proportions in certain areas, particularly in the southern core of South America in the early decades of the twentieth century. (The flow was later revitalized by the two world wars.) Hence, somewhat as in the United States, one finds names as diverse as O'Gorman, Poniatowska, Carpentier, Kahlo, and Belli alongside those of Spanish origin. All have served to enrich the culture of Spanish America, while the Spanish language remains the vital link between so many diverse peoples.

As the new republics took shape during the second half of the nineteenth century, they became anxious to define their separate identities. Consequently, art, music, and literature often display a marked emphasis on the peculiar characteristics — such as the flora and fauna, and the indigenous elements — that were not to be found in the Old World. Yet somewhat paradoxically the artists, writers, and musicians who devoted their energies to such ends often employed European forms of expression. Criollism in literature, Indigenism in literature and art, and Nationalism in music all relate to this need to discover an independent identity. Eventually there evolved less nationalistic, more mature and sensitive artistic attempts to capture the complexities of the New World, to portray the worldview of the indigenous peoples, and to explore the contradictions of a region unified to a great degree by language yet composed of countries proud of their own distinctiveness and equivocal in their attitude to the United States (the new colonial power) and to Europe (the colonial power of the past and still the continent that exerts a considerable pull for Latin American intellectuals).

The political course of the twentieth century has not been easy for many of these countries, victims of economic hardship, dictatorial regimes at home, and interference by their powerful neighbor to the north. Two countries have dominated the political and cultural scene: Mexico and Cuba. Mexico, along with Argentina, has been something of a cultural and economic powerhouse for Spanish America at large. The 1959 revolution that brought Fidel Castro to power in Cuba became an obsession for the United States, while providing a cultural rallying point and stimulus for many artists and intellectuals, whether sympathetic to the revolution or not. In many places the repression that characterized most of the colonial period has been replaced by new forms of intolerance and censorship, with the result that many creative artists, whether by choice or of necessity, have sought exile in other countries, often in Europe or the United States. Ironically, repression has in fact been the driving force behind much creative activity, and the result has sometimes been works of impressive quality, deeply felt indictments of injustice realized in artistic forms that show no signs of compromising aesthetic considerations. How an artist can and should protest has itself been a polemical issue among intellectuals, some of whom regard as traitors not only those whose creative work is not overtly committed to social and political reform but also those whose creative works are cosmopolitan rather than rooted in the day-to-day realities of Latin American life. Yet cosmopolitanism and exile are two factors that have contributed to a new awareness of Spanish American culture on the part of people in other countries. In the twentieth century Latin American artistic activity has come into its own, has grown beyond the imitative style and the provincial theme, and has won respect among the cultural powers that once dominated.

It is evident that all the cultural manifestations of the many different Spanish-speaking countries, countries that function in a Latin American cultural context, cannot be fully covered in reference works such as these. These two volumes cover the major writers, artists, and performers, as well as the most significant background events, personalities, cultural phenomena, and organizations, that have made the most lasting contributions to twentieth-century culture, both elevated and popular.

The state of knowledge regarding different cultural activities varies a great deal; at one extreme, literature, documentary by nature, is also highly documented and has attracted wide critical attention during the second half of the twentieth century. At the other extreme, dance is a subject about which documentation is more sparse or less accessible. Therefore, the literature entries are the result of ruthless sifting and selection, involving many omissions of writers whose reputations may well last beyond the century, whereas the dance entries are sometimes tentative attempts to map that particular area of cultural activity. Other broad subject areas fall between these two extremes: art is quite well documented, music, cinema, and the media less so. Certain motion pictures have entries of their own. They are milestones in an industry that remains small, especially by comparison with the power and scale of Hollywood: in 1993, for example, only about thirty feature-length movies were produced in the whole of Latin America.

While the Spanish language is a convenient rallying point, and political boundaries are a tempting means of classification, the fact is that cultural activities sometimes "speak" through gestures or visual means that are not language-bound and not always inclined to respect political boundaries. Much of what is covered in the ensuing entries can therefore be described as Latin American (involving French and Portuguese-speaking countries, as well as Spanish). Painters, dancers, musicians, and filmmakers collaborate, exhibit, and perform in ways that often frustrate the wishes of nationalists (and compilers of reference works). Even literature — in which regional vocabulary or a concentration on local settings and themes has often been used in an attempt to forge a distinct national tradition — has become internationalized: the Colombian writes in expectation that the Mexican (or Spaniard, come to that) will read his work. Furthermore, many a Hispanic creative artist has contributed to the culture from a base outside the home country.

This book contains several background entries, including a few long entries designed to provide an overview of subject areas, sometimes with essential historical background; examples are those titled Art, Radio and Television, Dance, Fiction, Poetry, and Music. Within entries, a word or group of words in **bold** indicates that an entry on that topic exists in this same volume. Finally, those readers who are unfamiliar with the structure of Spanish names should note the following: two surnames (family names) are normal, the first being inherited from one's father and the second from one's mother. These surnames are often used both together, and if not, it is normal to use only the first: thus Guillermo Cabrera Infante could be referred to as simply Guillermo Cabrera (but not as Guillermo Infante). Some confusion has been generated through the misuse of Spanish names by English speakers: for example, Gabriel García Márquez, the Nobel Prize winner from Colombia, is often referred to as "Márquez" in the English-speaking world, but in the Spanish one he is always García Márquez.

— P.S.

TWENTIETH CENTURY CULTURE

Hispanic Culture of
Mexico, Central America,
and the Caribbean

Timeline: Selected Works and Events

1898

Historical and Political Events
Spain loses Cuba, its last possession in the Americas.

Literature
Mexicans Amado Nervo and Jesús E. Valenzuela found the avant-garde journal *Revista Moderna,* which they continue to edit until 1911 with the participation of Julio Ruelas, Saturnino Herrán, and Alfonso Reyes.

1900s

Literature
Modernismo in vogue

Art
Symbolist Art, Impressionism, and Post-Impressionism emerge in Latin America.

1900

Literature
Urguayan José Enrique Rodó publishes *Ariel,* one of the most influential essays in Latin American cultural history.

1901

Historical and Political Events
The Platt Amendment, passed by the U.S. Congress and subsequently appended to the Cuban constitution, authorizes the intervention of the United States in the internal affairs of Cuba.

1902

Art
Painter Wifredo Lam is born in Cuba.

Literature
Poet Nicolás Guillén is born in Cuba.

Photography
Photographer Manuel Alvarez Bravo is born in Mexico City.

1903

Historical and Political Events
Backed by the United States, Panama declares its independence from Colombia and subsequently grants the United States the rights to build the Panama Canal.

The University of Puerto Rico is founded through the expansion of the Normal School at Río Piedras.

1904

Art
Julio Ruela paints *La iniciación de Don Jesús Luján a la Revista Moderna* (The Initiation of Don Jesús Luján to the Revista Moderna).

Cinema
Actor-director Emilio "El Indio" Fernández is born in Mexico.

1905

Art
Puerto Rican Ramón Frade paints *El pan nuestro de cada día* (Our Daily Bread).
Muralist Juan O'Gorman is born in Mexico.

Cinema
Actress Dolores del Río is born in Mexico.

Literature
Publication of *Cantos de vida y esperanza* by Nicaraguan poet Rubén Darío marks the end of the heyday of Modernismo.
Novelist Alejo Carpentier is born in Cuba.

Theater
Playwright-diplomat Rodolfo Usigli is born in Mexico.

1906

Art
Puerto Rican Miguel Pou founds the Academia Miguel Pou in Ponce. He directs the art school until 1950.

1907

Historical and Political Events
Pre-Columbian murals are discovered in Teotihuacán, outside Mexico City. Artist Saturnino Herrán works as a draftsman copying frescoes in Teotihuacán for the Museo Nacional of Mexico.

Music
Twelve-year-old Cuban composer Ernesto Lecuona writes the danza *La Comparsa,* one of his first compositions.

1908

Literature
Poet Juan Antonio Corretjer is born in Puerto Rico.

1909

Art
Dr. Atl founds the Centro Artístico (Artistic Center), where he advocates the creation of a national Mexican art.

Literature
The anti–Porfirio Díaz Ateneo de la Juventud (Youth Atheneum), an intellectual society, is established in Mexico by Alfonso Reyes, José Vasconcelos, and others.

1910s

Art
Rafael Yela Gunther promotes Indigenism in Guatemalan art.

Music
Nationalism begins to predominate in Latin American music.

1910

Historical and Political Events
The Mexican Revolution breaks out. The most violent period lasts until 1920.

Art
With government support Dr. Atl organizes an exhibition of Mexican artists.

Music
The corrido, a popular form of Mexican song, becomes a major means of communicating and recording events of the Mexican Revolution.

1911

Historical and Political Events
Porfirio Díaz is ejected from the presidency. Francisco Madero is elected to replace him.

Art
Mexican artist José Clemente Orozco produces cartoons for the newspapers *El Universal* and *El Hijo del Ahuizote.*

1912

Historical and Political Events
U.S. Marines intervene in Cuba to put down a revolt and invade Nicaragua to oversee the presidential election and protect U.S. financial interests.

Music
Manuel Ponce composes "Estrellita" and *Canciones Mexicanas.* His Piano Concerto No. 1, which has its premiere in this year, is the first major composition to incorporate elements of Mexican folk music.

1913

Historical and Political Events

With assurances of support from the United States, Gen. Victoriano Huerta seizes control of the Mexican government from President Francisco Madero.

Art

Mexican printmaker José Guadalupe Posada dies.

1914

Historical and Political Events

World War I begins in Europe.
The Panama Canal opens.
The Constitutionalists, led by Venustiano Carranza, seize control of the Mexican government.

Art

Dt. Atl directs the pro-Carranza newspaper *La Vanguardia* at Orizaba, including illustrations by José Clemente Orozco and David Alfaro Siqueiros.

1915

Historical and Political Events

Gen. Victoriano Huerta resigns the presidency of Mexico and is replaced by Venustiano Carranza.

Art

Out of favor after publishing a caricature critical of the Carranza presidency, José Clemente Orozco is forced to live as an outcast in the poorest neighborhoods of Mexico

1916

Historical and Political Events

The United States seizes control of the Dominican Republic and installs its own military government.

1917

Historical and Political Events

Federico Tinoco seizes the presidency of Costa Rica but resigns under threat of a U.S. invasion; Julio Acosta García is elected president.
U.S. troups occupy Cuba to protect U.S. business interests.

1918

Art

Saturnino Herrán paints *Nuestros dioses* (Our Gods).

1919

Theater

Playwright and fiction writer René Marqués is born in Puerto Rico.

1920s

Art

Muralism, Indigenism, Estridentismo, and graphic art dominate Mexican art. Impressionism, Post-Impressionism, and post-Cubist figuration predominate in Cuba.

Impressionist painter Ramos Martínez founds the first Escuela de Pintura al Aire Libre Barbizón (The Barbizón Open-Air School of Painting) in Mexico.

Music

Ernesto Lecuona is awarded a Gold Medal at the Cuban National Conservatory.

Carlos Mérida returns from Europe to Guatemala and begins to depict indigenist themes.
The Escuela Barbizón is closed.
In Paris Jean Charlot produces his first woodcut, and Diego Rivera meets Pablo Picasso.

Literature

Mexican writer Alfonso Reyes publishes his essay *Visión de Anahuac* (translated as *Vision of Anahuac*).
Poet Octavio Paz is born in Mexico.

City and paints his watercolor series *Los marginados* (The Outcasts).

Literature

Mexican novelist Mariano Azuela publishes *Los de abajo* (translated as *The Underdogs*), portraying the excesses of the Mexican Revolution.

Literature

Manuel Gamio publishes *Forjando patria.*

Art

Mexican artist Diego Rivera paints his Cubist work *Paisaje zapatista* (Zapatista Landscape).

Literature

Poet Julia de Burgos is born in Puerto Rico.

Literature

Writer Juan José Arreola is born in Mexico.

1920

Historical and Political Events
The most violent period of the Mexican Revolution ends as Alvaro Obregón is elected president.

Art
David Alfaro Siqueiros founds the magazine *Vida Americana* in Barcelona.

Dr. Atl is appointed director of the department of fine arts of the Secretaría de Educación Pública (Department of Public Education).

Literature
Mexican poet Amado Nervo publishes one of his best-known works, *La amada inmóvil* (1920; The Motionless Beloved).

1921

Art
Dr. Atl, Roberto Montenegro, and Xavier Guerrero receive the first commission to paint murals at the Colegio Máximo de San Pedro y San Pablo.

Painter Rufino Tamayo is appointed head of the Departamento de Etnografía (Ethnography Department) at the Museo Nacional de Antropología (National Museum of Anthropology) in Mexico City.

Artists Diego Rivera and Jean Charlot arrive in Mexico.

The Estridentismo movement begins.

Literature
President Obregón of Mexico appoints José de Vasconcelos head of the Secretaría de Educación Pública.

Music
Carlos Chávez composes *El fuego nuevo*, a ballet inspired by an Aztec theme.

1922

Art
In Mexico City, at the Escuela Nacional Preparatoria (National Preparatory School), where Frida Kahlo is a student, Diego Rivera paints the encaustic mural *La creación* (Creation), with the assistance of Jean Charlot, Guatemalan Carlos Mérida, and Xavier Guerrero.

Charlot and Fernando Leal, both of whom join Estridentismo, run a printmaking workshop at the open-air school of Coyoacán.

David Alfaro Siqueiros returns to Mexico from Europe, where he has been since 1919.

Music
Ernesto Lecuona and Gonzalo Roig found the Orquesta Sinfónica de la Habana, the first Cuban symphony orchestra.

1923

Art
Cuban painter Wifredo Lam settles in Spain.

Diego Rivera and other Mexican Muralists establish the Sindicato de Obreros Técnicos, Pintores, y Escultores (Union of Technical Workers, Painters, and Sculptors).

David Alfaro Siqueiros, Ramón Alva de la Canal, José Clemente Orozco, and Silvestre Revueltas paint murals at the Escuela Nacional Preparatoria (National Preparatory School), including Siqueiros's *Entierro de un martir obrero* (Burial of a Martyred Worker).

Rivera begins murals at the Secretaría de Educación Pública.

Dr. Atl publishes *Artes populares de México* (Popular Arts of Mexico).

Music
Amadeo Roldán's *Obertura sobre temas cubanos* incorporates African elements into Cuban art music.

Photography
Tina Modotti and Edward Weston arrive in Mexico.

1924

Art
Under the Mexican minister of education, José Vasconcelos, the muralists Diego Rivera, José Clemente Orozco, and David Alfaro Siqueiros use nationalist, popular, and dramatic themes to paint the walls of Mexico City.

José Clemente Orozco paints the fresco *Fuerzas reaccionarias* (Reactionary Forces) at the Escuela Nacional Preparatoria (National Preparatory School). Riots break out in the school in reaction to Orozco and Siqueiros's art, resulting in the mutilation of some of their murals and the dismissal of the muralists.

The first estridentista exhibition is held at the Café de Nadie (Nobody's Coffee Shop) in Mexico City.

Literature
Manuel Maples Arce publishes *Urbe: Poema bolchevique en 5 cantos,* illustrated by Jean Charlot.

Photography
Photographers Lola Alvarez Bravo and Manuel Alvarez Bravo settle in Oaxaca and become interested in the photo documentation of the indigenous culture of that area.

1925

Art
Estridentistas settle in Jalapa, receive official support, and publish the avant-garde magazine *Horizonte*.

Ethnology
José Vasconcelos, the Mexican minister of education, publishes *La raza cósmica* (translated as *The Cosmic Race*), in which he maintains that the mixture of Spanish and Indian blood in Latin America has created a fifth race, the mestizo.

Literature
Poet and religious leader Ernesto Cardenal is born in Nicaragua.
Poet and novelist Rosario Castellanos is born in Mexico.

Music
Rafael Hernández forms the Trío Borinquen, one of the earliest trios of voices and guitars.

1926

Historical and Political Events
Augusto César Sandino begins guerrilla warfare against U.S. Marines occupying Nicaragua.
The Cristeros (Followers of Christ) react to anticlerical measures introduced by the Mexican government, launching a civil war that continues until 1928.

Art
Allowed to complete his commission at the Escuela Nacional Preparatoria (National Preparatory School), José Clemente Orozco paints *La trinchera* (The Trench) and *Cortés y Malintzín* (Cortés and Malintzín).

Diego Rivera travels to the Soviet Union and in the same year paints frescoes at the Escuela Nacional de Agricultura (National School of Agriculture) in Chapingo.

Luis Arzubide publishes *El movimineto estridentista* (The Estridentista Movement).
Mexican artist Francisco Goitia paints *Tata Jesucristo* (Father Jesus Christ).

Literature
Fiction writer José Luis González is born in Puerto Rico.

1927

Art
Cuban avant-garde artists Víctor Manuel García and Antonio Gattorno return to their home country from Europe and exhibit their work, the first exhibition of modern art in Cuba.

The Cuban Generation of 1927 initiates a rebellion against traditional academic art and publishes the avant-garde magazine *Revista de Avance*.
The Estridentistas disband.

1928

Historical and Political Events
Mexican president Alvaro Obregón is assassinated. He is succeeded by Plutarco Elías Calles.

Art
Costa Rican avant-garde artist Teodorico Quirós organizes the first of several exhibitions at the Salón Nacional (National Salon), usually dominated by regionalist art.
The Mexican League of Revolutionary Writers and Artists (LEAR) is founded.
The Mexican artists group "30–30" is formed.

Cinema
Director Tomás Gutiérrez Alea is born in Cuba.

Journalism
Two major newspapers, *La Prensa* and *El Nacional,* are established in Mexico.

Literature
Mexican novelist Carlos Fuentes is born in Panama.
Contemporáneos magazine begins to circulate in Mexico.
Martín Luis Guzmán publishes *El águila y la serpiente* (translated as *The Eagle and the Serpent*), a novel of the Mexican Revolution.

Music
Carlos Chávez is founding director of an orchestra that becomes the Orquesta Sinfónica de México in 1929.
Amadeo Roldán's *La rebambaramba* ballet evokes scenes of Afro-Cuban cult music.

1929

Art and Architecture
Mexican artist and architect Juan O'Gorman designs his own residence, among the earliest Functional buildings in Mexico.
Artist Diego Rivera is appointed director of the Instituto Nacional de Bellas Artes (National Institute of Fine Arts)

in Mexico City. Later this year he marries artist Frida Kahlo, and the two leave for the United States.
Mexican painter María Izquierdo has her first individual exhibition and shares a studio with artist Rufino Tamayo.
Artist Alberto Gironella is born in Mexico.

Music
Silvestre Revueltas returns to Mexico to become assistant conductor of the Orquesta Nacional de México and professor of violin at the National Conservatory.

Alejandro García Caturla's symphonic work, *Tres Danzas Cubanas,* is performed at the Ibero-American Symphonic Festival as part of the International Exhibition of Barcelona.

1930s

Art
Regionalism predominates in Costa Rican art from the 1930s until the 1950s.

1930

Historical and Political Events
Rafael Leonidas Trujillo takes power in the Dominican Republic. He remains its military dictator for the next thirty-one years.

Art
José Clemente Orozco paints murals at Pomona College in Claremont, California, and at the New School for Social Research in New York City.

A graphic art workshop is established at the Escuela Nacional de Bellas Artes in Mexico City.

Music
Silvestre Revueltas composes his first major work for orchestra, *Cuauhnahuac.*

Radio and Television
Radio XEW, La Voz de América Latina, begins broadcasting *La hora íntima de Augustín Lara.*

1931

Architecture
Juan O'Gorman designs the house-studio of Diego Rivera at Pedregal San Angel.

Art
Rivera paints murals at the San Francisco Stock Exchange and the California School of Fine Arts.
Mexican artist David Alfaro Siqueiros is imprisoned for his political activities.

Literature
The Cuban negrista poet Nicolás Guillén publishes *Sóngoro Cosongo: Poemas mulatos.*

Music
Ernesto Lecuona forms the Lecuona Cuban Boys, a touring rumba/bolero group.

Photography
Manuel Alvarez Bravo produces the photograph *Parábola óptica* (Optic Parable).

1932

Historical and Political Events
After a rebellion in El Salvador, government troops acting under orders from Salvadoran president Maximiliano Hernández Martínez kill thousands of peasants, an act that becomes known as La Matanza (The Massacre).

Art
Rufino Tamayo is appointed head of the Departamento de Artes Plásticas (Department of Plastic Arts) of the Secretaría de Educación Pública in Mexico.
Diego Rivera has a restrospective exhibition at the Museum of Modern Art in New York and works on murals at the Detroit Institute of Art.

David Alfaro Siqueiros leaves Mexico and paints the mural *Tropical America,* criticizing U.S. imperialism, in Los Angeles. He is deported from the United States in 1933, and the mural is subsequently covered with whitewash.

Literature
Poet Heberto Padilla is born in Cuba.

Music
Amadeo Roldán becomes conductor of the Philharmonic Orchestra of Havana.

1933

Historical and Political Events
Under pressure from a peasant army led by Augusto César Sandino, U.S. Marines withdraw from Nicaragua.

Art
Rufino Tamayo paints a large mural at the Conservatorio Nacional de Música (National Conservatory of Music).

Diego Rivera works on a mural at Rockefeller Center in New York City. Controversial because it includes a portrait of V. I. Lenin, it is later destroyed.

Music
Carlos Chávez composes his neoclassical *Sinfonía de Antígona* and his *Cantos de México,* which employs indigenous instruments.

1934

Historical and Political Events

Led by Anastasio Somoza García, the Nicaraguan National Guard assassinates Augusto César Sandino. Somoza and his dynasty rule the nation as dictators until 1979.

Art

Artist José Luis Cuevas is born in Mexico.

Photography

Manuel Alvarez Bravo produces the photograph *Obrero en huelga, asesinado* (Striking Worker, Assassinated).

1935

Art

The Primer Salón Nacional de Pintura y Escultura (First National Salon of Painting and Sculpture) of Cuba includes avant-garde artists working on Cuban themes.

The Galería de Arte Mexicano, the first art gallery in Mexico, is founded.

Literature

Mexican writer Gregorio López y Fuentes publishes *El indio*.

Music

Silvestre Revueltas begins composing incidental music for the Mexican film industry.

Pianist Jorge Bolet makes his European debut.

1936

Historical and Political Events

Military dictator Jorge Ubico assumes power in Guatemala.

Cinema

Allá en el rancho grande, directed by Fernando de Fuentes, premieres.

Music

Amadeo Roldán becomes director of the Conservatorio Municipal de Música del Ayuntamiento de la Habana (Havana Municipal Conservatory), later renamed the Amadeo Roldán Provincial Conservatory.

Popular Culture

The first strip of the Mexican comic *Los supersabios* is published.

1937

Art

The Taller de Gráfica Popular (Popular Graphic Workshop) is established in Mexico.

David Alfaro Siqueiros paints *Echo of a Scream* and participates in the Spanish Civil War on the side of the Popular Front government.

Literature

Puerto Rican poet Luis Palés Matos publishes *Tuntún de pasa y grifería*.

Music

Roque Cordero wins the National Prize of Panama for his carnival march "Reina de amor" (Spirit of Panama).

Jorge Bolet makes his U.S. debut with the Philadelphia Orchestra and wins the Naumberg Prize for piano.

Alejandro García Caturla's *Obertura Cubana* receives first prize in the Cuban National Music Contest.

Theater

Mexican dramatist Rodolfo Usigli publishes *El gesticulador* (The Impersonator). A controversial satire of Mexican politics, it cannot be performed publicly until 1947.

1938

Art

El Segundo Salón Nacional de Pintura y Escultura (Second National Salon of Painting and Sculpture) of Cuba includes works by a second generation of avant-garde artists.

José Clemente Orozco paints frescoes at Hospicio Cabañas, and Rufino Tamayo works on a mural at the Museo Nacional de Antropología in Mexico City.

Literature

French Surrealist André Breton visits Mexico.

Music

José Ardévol is awarded the National Prize for Cuban Chamber Music.

1939

Historial and Political Events
World War II begins in Europe.

Art
The Instituto Nacional de Bellas Artes (National Institute of Fine Arts) is established in Cuba.

David Alfaro Siqueiros returns to Mexico and begins the mural *Retrato de la burguesía* (Portrait of the Bourgeoisie).

Frida Kahlo paints *Las dos Fridas* (The Two Fridas).

1940s

Art and Architecture
Internationalist trends begin to emerge.

1940

Historical and Political Events
Fulgencio Batista is elected president of Cuba.

Art
Exposición internacional del surrealismo (International Surrealist Exhibition) is held in Mexico City. The Ateneo Puertorriqueño opens an exhibition gallery.

Art and Literature
Wilfredo Lam illustrates André Breton's *Fata Morgana*. Lam, Breton, and anthropologist Claude Lévi-Strauss travel to Martinique and meet poet Aimé Césaire.

Cinema
Mexican actor Cantinflas stars in *Ahí está el detalle.*

Dance
The Ballet Jooss and the Ballets Russes du Colonel de Basil tour Latin America.

Ethnology
Cuban Fernando Ortiz Fernández publishes *Contrapunteo cubano del tabaco y azúcar* (Cuban Counterpoint Between Tobacco and Sugar).

Music
Mexican Carlos Chávez composes *Xochipilli-Macuilxochitl,* which employs Aztec instruments.

1941

Cinema
Cantinflas stars in *Ni sangre ni arena* (Neither Blood nor Sand).

1942

Historical and Political Events
Mexico declares war on the Axis nations.

Art
Surrealist Leonora Carrington arrives in Mexico.
Puerto Rican artist Lorenzo Homar fights in World War II.

Music
José Ardévol helps to found and becomes leader of the Grupo de Renovación Musical (Group for Musical Reform) in Cuba.
Conductor Eduardo Mata is born in Mexico.

1943

Art
Wifredo Lam paints *La jungla* (The Jungle).
Diego Rivera paints the mural *Sueño de una tarde de domingo en la Alameda Central* (Dream of a Sunday Afternoon at the Alameda Central).

Cinema
Movie actress Dolores del Río returns from Hollywood to Mexico, where she stars in *María Candelaria,* directed by Emilio Fernández.

Literature
Novelist Reinaldo Arenas is born in Cuba.

1944

Historical and Political Events
Fulgencio Batista "retires" from Cuban politics and goes to live in Florida. He is succeeded by Ramón Grau San Martín.
Juan José Arévalo becomes head of the Guatemalan government and begins efforts to democratize the nation.

Art
Alfredo Gálvez Suárez paints murals at the Palacio Nacional in Guatemala City.
Frida Kahlo paints *La columna rota* (The Broken Column).

Literature
Wolfgang Paalen begins publishing the magazine *Dyn* in Mexico.

Music
José Ardévol is awarded the Cuban National Symphonic Prize.

1945

Historical and Political Events
World War II ends.

Architecture
Mexican architect Luis Barragán begins work on the residential development Los Jardines del Pedregal (Pedregal Gardens).

Art
Diego Rivera and David Alfaro Siqueiros work on murals at the Palacio de Bellas Artes (Fine Arts Palace) in Mexico.

1946

Art and Cinema
The Taller de Cinema y Gráfica of the Comisión de Parques y Recreos Públicos (Film and Graphic Art Workshop of the Commission of Public Parks and Recreation) is founded in Puerto Rico.

Journalism
La Nación begins publication in Costa Rica.

Literature
Miguel Angel Asturias publishes his novel *El señor presidente* (translated as *Señor President*), the main character of which is based on Guatemalan dictator Manuel Estrada Cabrera (in power 1898–1920).

Music
Olga Guillot is acclaimed as the most popular vocalist on Cuban radio.
Roque Cordero's *Panamanian Overture No. 2* has its premiere.

1947

Art
Costa Rican painter Francisco Amighetti begins a series of murals in public buildings.
The Taller de Gráfica Popular publishes the portfolio *Estampas de la revolución mexicana* (Images from the Mexican Revolution).
María Cenobia Izquierdo paints *La Virgen de los Dolores* (The Virgin of Sorrows).

Cinema
The Mexican movie *María Candelaria*, starring Dolores del Río and directed by Emilio "El Indio" Fernández, wins first prize at the first Cannes Film Festival.

Literature
Mexican novelist Agustín Yáñez publishes *Al filo del agua* (translated as *At the Edge of the Storm*), a novel set during the Mexican Revolution.

1948

Historical and Political Events
The Organization of American States (OAS) is founded.

Cinema
Olga Guillot appears in *La Venus de Fuego,* the first of sixteen films in which she has parts.

Literature
Cuban novelist Alejo Carpentier's influential essay on magical realism is published.

Music
Mexican composer Manuel Ponce dies.
Julián Carrillo publishes "Sonido 13" in *Fundamento científico e histórico.*

1949

Art
The División de Educación de la Comunidad del Departamento de Instrucción Pública (Division of Community Education of the Department of Public Instruction) of Puerto Rico begins producing educational posters.

Cinema
Matilde Landeta directs *La negra Angustias* (Angustias the Black Woman).

Literature
Mexican poet Octavio Paz publishes *Libertad bajo palabra* (Liberty on Parole).

Music
José Ardévol receives the Ricordi International Symphonic Award.

Theater
Mexican dramatist Xavier Villaurrutia publishes *Invitación a la muerte* (translated as *Dancing with Death*).

1950s

Art

Artists react against Muralism and Indigenism in Mexico and Regionalism in Central America, as abstract art and neofiguration emerge throughout the region.

Music and Dance

Frank "Machito" Grillo, Tito Puente, and Tito Rodríguez touch off an explosion in the popularity of Latin dance music in New York.

Dámaso Pérez Prado's recordings convert the mambo into an international dance craze.

1950

Architecture

Mexican architect Mario Pani builds the large apartment complex Multifamiliar Presidente Juárez (destroyed in 1985).

Pani, Juan O'Gorman, and others design the campus of the Universidad Nacional Autónoma de México (National Autonomous University of Mexico).

Art

David Alfaro Siqueiros works on new murals at the Palacio Nacional de Bellas Artes in Mexico City.

The Centro de Arte Puertorriqueño (Center for Puerto Rican Art) is founded to support graphic art.

Cinema

Luis Buñuel directs *Los olvidados* (*The Young and the Damned*) in Mexico.

Literature

Octavio Paz publishes his essays *El laberinto de la soledad* (translated as *The Labyrinth of Solitude*).

Radio and Television

XHTV, the first Latin American television station, begins broadcasting in Mexico City.

1951

Architecture

Félix Candela publishes *A New Philosophy of Structures,* which increases the popularity of structures built from reinforced concrete throughout Latin America.

Music

José Ardévol is awarded the Cuban National Symphonic Prize.

1952

Historical and Political Events

Puerto Rico becomes a Free Associated State to the United States, achieving commonwealth status.

Fulgencio Batista seizes power in Cuba.

Architecture

Cuban architect Max Borges designs the Cabaret Tropicana in Havana.

Art

Guatemalan artist Carlos Mérida works on mural reliefs for the Multifamiliar Presidente Juárez apartment complex in Mexico City.

Mexican artist Alberto Gironella helps to found the Galería Prisse.

Art and Architecture

Cuban architect Aquiles Capablanca builds the Office of the Comptroller, which features a ceramic mural by Amelia Peláez.

Cinema

Alberto Gout directs *Aventurera*.

Music

Olga Guillot and Panart records revolutionize the Cuban recording industry with their 45 rpm recordings of "Miénteme" (Lie to Me) and "Estamos en paz" (We Are at Peace).

Theater

Puerto Rican writer René Marqués publishes his play *La carreta* (The Oxcart).

1953

Art

Frida Kahlo has her first one-woman show in Mexico.

José Luis Cuevas exhibits at the Galería Prisse.

Literature

Cuba novelist Alejo Carpentier publishes *Los pasos perdidos* (translated as *The Lost Steps*).

Music

Roque Cordero is named director of the Panama National Institute of Music.

José Ardévol receives the National Prize for Cuban Songs in the Martí Centennial Competition.

1954

Historical and Political Events
After confronting the United Fruit Company, which had dominated Central America for a half century, by appropriating more than four hundred thousand acres of its land to implement his program of agrarian reform, President Jacobo Arbenz of Guatemala is overthrown by a CIA-led coup. Thirty-two years of Guatemalan military dictatorships begin.

Art
Frida Kahlo dies.

Mexican artist Remedios Varo has her first one-woman show.

Mexican artist José Luis Cuevas speaks out publicly against Muralism.

The Centro de Arte Puertorriqueño (Puerto Rican Art Center) is closed.

Cinema
El mégano (The Charcoal Worker) is directed by Julio García Espinosa and Tomás Gutiérrez Alea.

Music
Olga Guillot is acclaimed as the "Best Popular Vocalist" in Cuba.

1955

Art
Mexican artist José Luis Cuevas begins to gain international recognition.

Art and Architecture
Guatemalan architects Pelayo Llerena and Roberto Aycinema design the Palacio Municipal (City Hall) in Guetemala City. The building features a mosaic by Carlos Mérida and reliefs by Guillermo Grajeda Mena and Dagoberto Vásquez.

Literature
Mexican novelist Juan Rulfo publishes his best-known work, *Pedro Páramo.*

1956

Architecture
Felix Candela designs the Iglesia de la Virgen Milagrosa in Mexico City.

Art
Alberto Gironella founds the Galería Proteo in Mexico City.

Literature
Octavio Paz publishes *El arco y la lira* (translated as *The Bow and the Lyre*), a controversial essay on the poet's role in society.

1957

Architecture
Luis Barragán and Mathias Goeritz collaborate on the design of the Las Torres de Satélite in Mexico City.

Félix Candela designs the restaurant Los Manantiales in Xochimilco, Mexico.

Art
Diego Rivera dies.

Literature
The Premio Biblioteca Breve is instituted.

Music
Pablo Casals founds the Casals Festival, the Puerto Rican Symphony Orchestra, and the Puerto Rican Conservatory of Music.

Argeliers León composes *Yambú, Bolero y guaguancó,* and *Akorín.*

1958

Art
Primera Bienal Interamericana de Pintura y Grabado (First Inter-American Biennial of Painting and Engraving) in Mexico includes many works by Abstract Expressionists.

The Museo Nacional de Arte Moderno (Naitonal Museum of Modern Art) is created in the Palacio Nacional de Bellas Artes (National Palace of Fine Arts) in Mexico City.

Art and Architecture
Roberto Aycinema and Jorge Montes Córdova design the Instituto Guatemalteco de Seguridad Social (Guatemalan Institute for Social Security), which includes a mosaic mural by Carlos Mérida as well as wall reliefs by Roberto González Goyri.

Music
Panamanian composer Roque Cordero receives the Caro de Boesi Award for his Symphony No. 2 at the second Latin American Music Festival, in Caracas, Venezuela.

1959

Historical and Political Events
Forces loyal to Fidel Castro triumph in the Cuban Revolution.

Cinema
The Cuban Film Institute is established.

Literature
The Casa de las Américas Prizes are established in Cuba.

1960s

Art
The graphic arts are developed in Cuba: posters and illustrations are produced for the Cuban Film Institute; the Casa de las Américas; the Organization of Solidarity with the Peoples of Asia, Africa, Latin America; the magazine *Tricontinental;* and the Departamento de Orientación Revolucionaria (Department of Revolutionary Orientation).

Literature
Major novels of the Boom are published.

Music
Salsa emerges.

1960

Art
An outdoor exhibition at Las Arcadas in San José, Costa Rica, exposes the general public to new abstract trends.

The Costa Rican Grupo Ocho (Group Eight) is formed and dominates the local art scene until the 1970s. Most of its members are abstract artists who studied abroad.

David Alfaro Siqueiros is imprisoned in Mexico for "social dissolution." In protest several artists boycott the Mexican Segunda Bienal Interamericana de Pintura y Grabado.

Mexican critic Luis Cardoza y Aragón uses the term *la ruptura* to designate a group of young artists who publicly reject the School of Mexico.

Alberto Gironella, a member of La Ruptura Generation, paints *Reina Mariana* (Queen Mariana), an early work in his long series based on works by Veláquez.

Rafael Ferrer's exhibit at the Universidad de Puerto Rico causes a scandal because of the aggressive, spontaneous, and sexually explicit nature of his paintings.

Cinema
Cantinflas stars in *Pepe.*

Literature
José Ardévol receives first prize in the Amadeo Roldán Contest sponsored by the Cuban National Library.

La Onda generation emerges in Mexico.

1961

Historical and Political Events
Cuban exiles trained and armed by the United States fail in their attempt to invade Cuba at the Bay of Pigs.

Dominican Dictator Rafael Trujillo is assassinated.

Art
The avant-garde Grupo Taller is formed in Costa Rica.

Calling themselves *Los Interioristas,* the Nueva Presencia group exhibits in Mexico for the first time.

Puerto Rican artist Luis Hernández Cruz exhibits abstract pieces at the Instituto de Cultura Puertorriqueña (Puerto Rican Culture Institute).

Art
The Costa Rican government begins national awards in art, literature, and journalism.

Cinema
En el balcón vacío (On the Empty Balcony) is directed by Jomi García Ascot.

1962

Historical and Political Events
The U.S. Navy blockades Cuba to prevent the Soviet Union from establishing missile bases there. Soviet premier Nikita Khrushchev agrees to abandon his plans and in return President John F. Kennedy promises that the United States will not invade Cuba.

Literature
Mexican novelist Carlos Fuentes publishes *La muerte de Artemio Cruz* (translated as *The Death of Artemio Cruz).*

Mexican novelist Rosario Castellanos publishes *Oficio de tinieblas* (Rites of Darkness).

Cuban novelist Alejo Carpentier publishes *El siglo de las luces* (translated as *Explosion in the Cathedral*).

Music
Roque Cordero's Violin Concerto commissioned by the Koussevitzky Foundation has its premiere at the Third Inter American Music Festival in Washington, D.C.

1963

Historical and Political Events
President Juan Bosch is overthrown by a military coup in the Dominican Republic.

Art
Leonora Carrington paints *El mundo mágico de los mayas* (The Magical World of the Mayas), a mural for the

Museo Nacional de Antropología (Naitonal Museum of Anthropology) in Mexico City.

The avant-garde Galería Praxis is founded in Managua, Nicaragua.

Literature

Mexican writer Elena Garro publishes her best-known novel, *Recuerdos del porvenir* (translated as *Recollections of Things to Come*).

Mexican writer Vicente Leñero publishes *Los albañiles* (The Stonemasons).

1964

Architecture

Mario Pani designs a massive building complex at Tlatelolco.

Art

The Nueva Presencia group dissolves.

Rafael Ferrer's second exhibition at the Universidad de Puerto Rico features the controversial installation *Tableau*.

1965

Historical and Political Events

U.S. Marines invade the Dominican Republic after dictator Donald Reid Cabral is deposed by forces loyal to former president Juan Bosch.

Art

Puerto Rican artist Lorenzo Homar produces the print *Unicornio en la isla* (Unicorn on the Island).

Cinema

Arturo Ripstein directs *En este pueblo no hay ladrones* (There are No Thieves In This Town) and *Tiempo de morir* (A Time to Die).

Music

Héctor Campos-Parsi's *Duo trágico In Memoriam John F. Kennedy* is performed at the Inter American Festival of Music.

1966

Art

David Alfaro Siqueiros creates the complex mural *Marcha de la humanidad en Latinoamérica* (March of Humanity in Latin America), later installed at the Poliforum Cultural in Mexico.

Cinema

Tomás Gutiérrez Alea directs *Muerte de un burócrata* (The Death of a Bureaucrat).

Humberto Solás directs *Manuela*.

1967

Historical and Political Events

Ernesto "Che" Guevara is executed by government forces in Bolivia.

Anastasio Somoza Debayle becomes dictator of Nicaragua.

Cinema

Julio García Espinosa directs *Las aventuras de Juan Quin Quin*.

The Viña del Mar Film Festival is organized by Aldo Francia.

Literature

Guatemalan novelist Miguel Angel Asturias wins the Nobel Prize for literature.

Carlos Fuentes wins the Premio Biblioteca Breve.

José Emilio Pacheco publishes *Morirás lejos* (You Will Die Far Away).

Cuban novelist Guillermo Cabrera Infante publishes *Tres tristes tigres* (translated as *Three Trapped Tigers*).

Music

The annual Rafael Hernández Festival is established in New York by Peter Bloch.

1968

Historical and Political Events

Military police massacre more than three hundred student demonstrators in Mexico City's Tlatelolco Square.

The Summer Olympics are held in Mexico City.

Gen. Omar Torrijos stages a successful coup in Panama and installs himself as dictator.

Architecture

Mexican architect Ricardo Legorreta designs the Hotel Camino Real in Mexico City.

Cinema

Tres tristes tigres, based on the novel by Guillermo Cabrera Infante, is directed by Raúl Ruiz.

Humberto Solás directs *Lucía*.

Memorias del subdesarrollo (Memories of Underdevelopment) is directed by Tomás Gutiérrez Alea.

The Second Meeting of Latin American Filmmakers is held in Venezuela.

Literature

Cuban writer Miguel Barnet publishes *Biografía de un cimarrón* (translated as *The Autobiography of a Runaway Slave*).

Cuban novelist José Lezama Lima publishes *Paradiso*.

1969

Historical and Political Events

A weeklong war breaks out between El Salvador and Honduras. It is popularly referred to as the "soccer war" because a tumultuous soccer match acted as a catalyst for existing tensions between the two countries.

Art

Puerto Rican artist Rafael Ferrer exhibits the installations *Hay* and *Grease* at the Whitney Museum of American Art in New York City.

Cinema

Manuel Octavio Gómez directs *La primera carga del machete* (The First Charge of the Machete).

Literature

Cuban novelist Reinaldo Arenas publishes *El mundo alucinante* (translated as *Hallucinations* and as *The Ill-fated Peregrinations of Fray Servando*).

Religion

Nicarguan Ernesto Cardenal publishes *El Evangelio en Solentiname* (translated as *The Gospel in Solentiname*), an important contribution to Liberation Theology.

1970

Literature

Oscar Collazos publishes *Literatura en la revolución y revolución en la literatura*, a debate between Latin American writers about politics and literature.

The testimonial narrative genre receives formal recognition in Cuba.

1971

Art

The Primera Bienal Centroamericana de Pintura (First Central American Art Bienial) is held in Costa Rica.

Cinema

Frida Kahlo is filmed by Marcela Fernández Violante.

Tomás Gutiérrez Alea directs *Una pelea contra los demonios* (A Struggle Against the Demons).

Journalism

CANA, the Caribbean news agency, is established.

Literature

Writers and intellectuals worldwide protest the imprisonment of Cuban poet Heberto Padilla for political views that the Cuban government considers incorrect.

Mexican writer Elena Poniatowska publishes *La noche de Tlatelolco* (translated as *Massacre in Mexico*).

1972

Cinema

Manuel Herrera directs *Girón*.

Literature

Cuban novelist Severo Sarduy publishes *Cobra*.

1973

Art

Photo-realism becomes a dominant style in Cuba.

Cuban American artist Ana Mendieta begins her *Silueta* (Silhouette) series in Oaxaca, Mexico.

Cinema

Sergio Giral directs *El otro Francisco* (The Other Francisco).

Photography

Panamanian Sandra Eleta settles in Portobelo and begins to photograph members of the community.

1974

Art
School of campesino painting emerges in Solentiname, Nicaragua.

Cinema
Manuel Octavio Gómez directs *Ustedes tienen la palabra* (Now It's Up to You).

Sara Gómez begins filming *De cierta manera,* completed in 1978.

1975

Art
Cuban Flavio Garciandía creates the photo-realist painting *Todo lo que necesitas es amor* (All You Need is Love).

Cinema
Sergio Giral directs *Rancheador* (Slave Hunter).
Felipe Cazals directs *Canoa*.

Marcela Fernández Violante directs *De todos modos, Juan te llamas* (Whatever You Do, It's No Good).

Literature
Carlos Fuentes is appointed Mexican ambassador to France. He serves until 1978.
Fuentes publishes *Terra Nostra*.
The Premio Miguel de Cervantes is instituted.

1976

Architecture
Luis Barragán designs Casa Gilardi in Mexico City.

Cinema
Jorge Fons directs *Los albañiles* (The Bricklayers).
Raúl Araiza directs *Cascabel* (Rattlesnake).

Jaime Hermosillo directs *La pasión según Berenice* (The Passion According to Berenice).

Literature
Puerto Rican writer Luis Rafael Sánchez publishes *La guaracha del macho Camacho* (translated as *Macho Camacho's Beat*).

1977

Art
A group of Puerto Rican abstract artists forms Frente (Front).

Literature
Alejo Carpentier wins the Premio Cervantes.

1978

Historical and Political Events
The Guatemalan military begins a counterinsurgency war against the largely indigenous population in the country's highlands. By 1985 some 150,000 are massacred.

1979

Historical and Political Events
The Sandinistas depose dictator Anastasio Somoza in Nicaragua.

Art
The Sandinistas establish Centros Populares de Cultura (Popular Cultural Centers) and several public galleries in Nicaragua.

Cinema
The Cuban Film Institute hosts a Latin American movie festival.
Pastor Vega directs *Retrato de Teresa* (Teresa's Portrait).
Sergio Giral directs *Maluala*.
Jaime Hermosillo directs *María de mi corazón* (Darling Maria).

1980s

Art
Neo-Expressionism emerges in Latin America.
A loosely connected group of Mexican artists develops Neo-Mexicanism.

Conceptual Art, Installation Art, and Performance Art become important art forms in Cuba.
A muralist movement develops in Nicaragua, where the Sandinista government strongly supports the arts.

1980

Historical and Political Events
Archbishop Arnulfo Romero is murdered in El Salvador by a government terrorist squad.

Anastasio Somoza is assassinated in Paraguay.

Art
Cuban avant-garde artists organize a festival of performance art, held in a private house.

1981

Historical and Political Events
Panamanian dictator Gen. Omar Torrijos dies in a plane crash and is replaced by Gen. Manuel Noriega.

Art
The Cuban exhibitions Volumen I (Volume I) and Trece Artistas Jóvenes (Thirteen Young Artists) signal the emergence of a new avant-garde generation.

Cuban American artist Ana Mendieta produces her *Esculturas rupestres* (Rupestrian Sculptures) at Jaruco, near Havana.

The Rufino Tamayo Museum of Contemporary Art opens in Mexico City.

Cinema
Diego de Texera directs *El Salvador, el pueblo vencerá* (El Salvador, The People Shall Overcome).

Ana María García directs *La operación* (The Operation).

Marcela Fernández Violante directs *El país de los pies ligeros* (In the Land of Light Feet).

Literature
Octavio Paz wins the Premio Cervantes.

1982

Art
The avant-garde Grupo Hexágono is formed in Cuba.

Cinema
Cecilia Valdés is directed by Humberto Solás.

1983

Cinema
Tomás Gutiérrez Alea directs *Hasta cierto punto* (Up to a Point).

1984

Art
The Primera Bienal de La Habana (First Havana Biennial) is held in Cuba.

Cinema
Juan Carlos Tabío directs *Se permuta* (House Swap).

Oscar Castillo directs *La Xegua*.

Paul Leduc directs *Frida, naturaleza viva*.

Literature
Me llamo Rigoberta Menchú y así me nació la conciencia (translated as *I . . . Rigoberta Menchú*) is published by Rigoberta Menchú and Elisabeth Burgos.

1985

Cinema
The Fundación de Nuevo Cine Latinoamericano (Foundation of New Latin American Cinema) is established in Havana.

Juan Padrón directs *Vampiros en la Habana* (Vampires in Havana).

Jesús Díaz directs *Lejanía* (Parting of the Ways).

1986

Art
José Bedia installs *El golpe del tiempo* (The Beat of Time) at the Segunda Bienal de La Habana in Cuba.

Cinema
The Escuela de Cine y Televisión is founded in Cuba.

Marcos Zuringa directs *La gran fiesta* (The Gala Ball).

1987

Historical and Political Events
President Oscar Arias of Costa Rica wins the Nobel Peace Prize for his efforts to end the civil war in Nicaragua.

Literature
Carlos Fuentes wins the Premio Cervantes.

Photography
Mexican Flor Garduño works on her photographic series *Bestiario* (Bestiarium).

1988

Cinema

Agilberto Meléndez directs *Un pasaje de ida* (One-Way Ticket).

Fernando Birri directs *Un señor muy viejo con unas alas enormes* (A Very Old Man with Enormous Wings), based on a work by Gabriel García Márquez.

Tómas Gutiérrez Alea directs *Cartas del parque* (Letters from the Park), based on a work by García Marquez.

Literature

Mexican writer Angeles Mastretta publishes her first novel, *Arráncame la vida* (translated as *Mexican Bolero*).

Music

Olga Guillot celebrates fifty years of singing boleros and performs in 100 Years of the Bolero, a celebration held in the Dominican Republic.

1989

Historical and Political Events

U.S. troops invade Panama to capture Gen. Manuel Noriega and and take him to the United States for trial on charges of drug trafficking.

Cinema

Old Gringo, based on Carlos Fuentes's novel *Gringo viejo* and directed by Luis Puenzo, is filmed in Mexico.

Jaime Humberto Hermosillo directs *La tarea* (Homework) and *Intimidades en un cuarto de baño* (Bathroom Intimacies).

Photography

Mexican Graciela Iturbide publishes *Juchitán de las mujeres* (Women's Juchitán), a book of her photographs.

1990

Historical and Political Events

The Sandinista government is removed from power in Nigaragua after President Daniel Ortega loses to Violeta Chamorro in the national elections.

Cinema

Nicolás Echeverría and Juan Mora Cattlet direct *Cabeza de Vaca*.

Héctor Veitía, Mayra Segura, Mario Crespo, and Ana Rodríguez direct *Mujer transparente* (Transparent Woman).

Literature

Octavio Paz wins the Nobel Prize in literature.

1991

Cinema

María Novaro directs *Danzón*.

Carlos Carrera directs *La mujer de Benjamín* (Benjamin's Woman).

Alfonso Cuarón directs *Sólo con tu pareja* (Only with Your Partner).

1992

Historical and Political Events

Guatemalan Mayan activist Rigoberta Menchú wins the Nobel Peace Prize.

Guerrilla war ends in El Slavador when the Farabundo Martí National Liberation Front signs a peace treaty with the government.

Literature

Dulce María Loynaz wins the Premio Cervantes.

1993

Cinema

Alfonso Arau directs *Como agua para chocolate* (Like Water for Chocolate).

Tomás Gutiérrez Alea directs *Fresa y chocolate* (Strawberry and Chocolate).

1994

Historical and Political Events

The North American Free Trade Agreement goes into effect among Canada, the United States, and Mexico.

The indigenous population of the state of Chiapas rebels against the Mexican government.

Cinema

Julio García Espinosa directs *Reina y rey* (Queen and King).

Luis Argueta directs *El silencio de Neto* (Neto's Silence).

1995

Cinema

Fernando Pérez directs *Madagascar*.

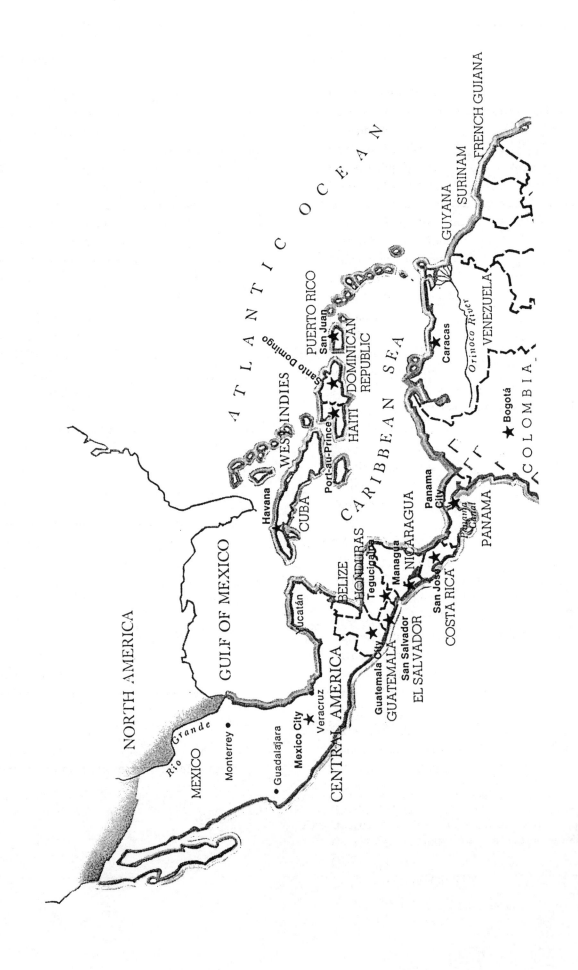

A

ABSTRACT ART

There are two principal types of abstract art: Geometric Abstraction and Informal Abstraction. Geometric Abstraction, which has developed throughout Latin America since the 1940s, generally refers to geometry-based abstract modes, such as hard-edge abstraction, including Concrete Art, Constructivism (or Constructive Art), Generative Art, Op Art, Kinetic Art, and Minimalism, as well as soft-edge abstraction, also called Geometría Sensible. Informal Abstraction emerged in Latin America during the 1950s. This abstract mode, also called Lyrical Abstraction or Informalism, refers to nongeometric abstract styles that emphasize color, loose brush strokes, and textured surfaces.

Geometric Abstraction has often paralleled periods of economic optimism and a utopian desire for modernization, which in the case of Brazil, Mexico, and Venezuela also led to important urbanization projects. While Geometric and Informal Abstraction received broad support in South America, fewer artists worked in these styles in the regions covered by the present volume, and most of those who did were from Puerto Rico, Cuba, Mexico, Guatemala, Nicaragua, and Costa Rica. In these countries abstraction became important in the late 1950s, when many artists rejected the prevalent figurative tendencies of Regionalism, **Indigenism,** and **Muralism.** Like their peers in South America, these artists often perceived Geometric Abstraction as a cosmopolitan language with the power to connect their personal projects to the wider international explorations of abstract art, especially the kind of geometry-based art favored in Europe. Informal Abstraction also has antecedents in Europe, especially in French and Spanish informalism, and to a lesser extent in the Abstract Expressionism of the United States; but it often differs from these movements in its evocation through colors and textures of cultural meanings that relate to Latin America. During the 1950s, 1960s, and 1970s many artists in Mexico, Central America, and the Caribbean were encouraged to turn to abstraction by the prices paid for and attention given to abstract paintings and sculptures in international art contests and exhibitions. International art competitions were often sponsored by multinational corporations such as Esso (Standard Oil), who thought of the dissemination of Abstract Expressionism as a way of expanding U.S. cultural and political influence.

In Puerto Rico the majority of artists rejected Geometric and Informal Abstraction in favor of figurative modes and regional and social themes, because they considered abstraction a form of cultural colonialism. In spite of the predominance of figuration, in the 1960s several important abstract artists emerged in Puerto Rico, including the sculptors Jaime Suárez, Sylvia Blanco, Rolando López Dirube, **Rafael Ferrer,** and Pablo Rubio. In 1977 **Luis Hernández Cruz,** Lope Max Díaz, Antonio Navia, and Paúl Camacho — all of whom had worked with different abstract modes — founded the avant-garde Frente (Front) group in order to encourage an internationalist approach to art. **Olga Albizu** was one of the first Puerto Rican painters to work with Informal Abstraction, also explored by Blanco, Julio Rosado del Valle, Luis Hernández Cruz, Roberto Laureano, Angel Nevárez, Jaime Romano, Noemí Ruiz, and Jaime Suárez. Among the informal abstract painters, Julio Suárez, Wilfredo Chiesa, José Bonilla Ryan, and Raúl Zayas López also worked with Post-Painterly Abstraction, an abstract style that was developed in the United States in the 1950s by painters such as Helen Frankenthaler and Sam Francis. Several Puerto Rican artists preferred to work instead with Geometric Abstraction, including Elí Barreto, Camacho, Rafael Colón-Morales, Max Díaz, Domingo García, Domingo López, and Navia. Seeking creative freedom and a more sympathetic

La isla pasa (1978; The Island Passes) by Rafael Ferrer (Archer M. Huntington Art Gallery, University of Texas at Austin, Barbara Duncan Fund, 1984 [1984.75])

public, many of them lived in New York permanently or for extended periods.

In Cuba abstract art emerged through the activities of the groups Los Once (The Eleven), active during the early 1950s, and Pintores Concretos (Concrete Painters), working during the 1960s. The members of Los Once rejected the sugarcoated nationalism of the regionalist styles prevalent during the 1940s and 1950s in favor of Informal Abstraction, an art they considered free of state propaganda. Their interest in politics was also reflected in their boycott of several official exhibitions and their organization in 1954 of the Anti-Bienal, an alternative art exhibition in protest against the Bienal Hispano-Americana sponsored by the dictatorial governments of Fulgencio Batista (Cuba) and Francisco Franco (Spain). Among the members of Los Once were Hugo Consuegra, Fayad Jamis, Guido Llinas, Raúl Martínez, Tomás Oliva, and Antonio Vidal. Martínez later produced important examples of neofigurative art, Pop Art, poster design, and **graphic**

art. Other Cuban artists working with informal abstract art are Julio Girona, Hortensia Gronlier, Julio Matilla, Raúl Milián, and Juan Tapia Ruano. The earliest Cuban artists to engage in Geometric Abstraction during the 1950s were the sculptor Sandú Darié and the painter Luis Martínez Pedro. Darié's articulated mobile structures, whose multicolored geometric shapes could be changed through manipulation, are comparable to those produced in Brazil by the concrete artist Lygia Clarke. Martínez Pedro and Darié were members of the Pintores Concretos group, which also included Salvador Corratge, Lolo Sodevilla, and José M. Mijares. Other important Cuban geometric abstract artists are Mario Carreño, José Rosabal, and Carmen Herrera.

In Mexico abstraction prevailed over the usually dominatant figuration in the 1960s. Among the first artists to work with abstraction was the Guatemalan **Carlos Mérida,** who had settled in Mexico. During the 1930s and 1940s his work became closer to Informal

Abstraction and **Surrealism**. It combined simplified figures inspired by Mayan art with the treatment of form, texture, and color of Abstract Expressionism. During the 1950s, as Mérida integrated his art into the context of architecture, he turned away from Informal Abstraction toward a stronger use of geometry. Perhaps because Mérida was Guatemalan, he escaped the harsh condemnations that **Diego Rivera** and **David Alfaro Siqueiros** voiced of Mexican artists such as **Rufino Tamayo** and **José Luis Cuevas,** who, like Mérida, favored more avant-garde forms. The 1950s marked the emergence of a loose group of younger artists called **La Ruptura Generation** (The Break). In spite of their diverse styles, ranging from Neofiguration to different types of abstraction, these artists concurred in their denunciation of the didactic, ideological, and stylistic limitations of muralism. Among these geometric abstract artists were the sculptors Manuel Felguérez, Mathias Goeritz, and Helen Escobedo, while the informalists, who were in the majority, included Gabriel Aceves Navarro, Lilia Carrillo, **Pedro Coronel,** Fernando García Ponce, Gabriel Ramírez, Olivier Seguin, and Vlady (Vladimir Kibalchich Rusakov). Others, such as Vicente Rojo and Gunther Gerzso, worked with abstract modes that combined aspects of both Geometric and Informal Abstraction. Many of these abstractionists were supported by Miguel Salas Anzures, director from 1957 to 1961 of the Departamento de Artes Plásticas (Department of Plastic Arts) of the Instituto Nacional de Bellas Artes (National Institute of Fine Arts). Salas Anzures facilitated their participation in important art exhibitions, such as Mexico's Segunda Bienal Interamericana of 1960 and the Bienal de São Paulo of 1961. In spite of the scandal avant-garde art generated and the dominance of the traditional School of Mexico, the creation of new art galleries such as Prisse, Antonio Souza, Proteo, and Juan Martín helped open the international art market to Mexican abstract art.

In Central America most artists interested in abstract art did not completely abandon figuration. In their works they often combined subtle figurative references with Informal Abstraction, which was the dominant abstract mode. In Guatemala the interest in abstract art appeared first in the work of the members of the Generation of 1940, who struggled to open Guatemalan art to more international trends, and, especially since the 1950s, to Informal Abstraction and Neofiguration. **Rodolfo Abularach,** Margarita Azurdia (also known as Margot Fanjul), Rafael Pereira, Efraín Recinos, and Emar Rojas were among those who explored Informal Abstraction, while Luis Díaz and Rodolfo Mishaan worked with Geometric Abstraction. Other artists, such as Roberto Cabrera, Roberto González

Goyri, César Izquierdo, Arturo Martínez, and Marco Augusto Quiroa, produced semiabstract works linked to Neofiguration. On the other hand, Roberto Ossaye favored a semiabstract style in his paintings, one based on geometry, which linked his work to that of the Uruguayan Joaquín Torres-García.

Many of the abstract artists active in Nicaragua during the 1960s also worked with figuration, often combining diverse aspects of Informal Abstraction with subtle figurative and thematic references. Abstract art was introduced by Managua's Galería Praxis, an avant-garde gallery active from 1963 to 1973 and founded by Alejandro Aróstegui, Cézar Izquierdo (from Guatemala), and Amaru Barahona. The Praxis group supported the politics of the FSLN (Sandinista National Liberation Front, see **Nicaraguan Revolution**), which resulted in the imprisonment, torture, and exile of several of its members by the Anastasio Somoza regime. Praxis included abstractionists such as Arnoldo Guillén, Orlando Sobalvarro, and Leonel Vanegas. Other important Nicaraguan artists to explore abstraction include Santos Medina, Javier Orozco Molina, and **Armando Morales,** who achieved significant international recognition. In spite of the variety of informal abstract modes practiced by these artists, they shared a preference for rich, dark colors, dense textures, somber themes, and subtle references to pre-Columbian art. In the 1970s and 1980s, after the Praxis gallery was destroyed in the 1972 earthquake, several other art galleries opened their doors, such as the Galería Fernando Gordillo of the ASTC (Sandinista Union of Cultural Workers) and the Galería Xavier Kantón of ENAP (National School of Plastic Arts). During this period many abstract artists broadened their use of colors and textures that subtly evoked earthy surfaces and natural phenomena. The Sandinista government's strong support for cultural development infused the art scene with a renewed sense of dynamism and an interest in issues of cultural identity and popular outreach.

The first artists to introduce abstraction in Costa Rica were Rafael Angel García, **Manuel de la Cruz González,** and Lola Fernández, all of whom scandalized the public by exhibiting abstract works at the Museo Nacional (National Museum) in the late 1950s. Although the attempt of the outdoor exhibition at Las Arcadas in San José (1960) to bring the new abstract trends to the general public had mixed success, the Costa Rican government, interested in modernizing the country, supported the new art and in 1961 laid down regulations providing for national awards for art, literature, and journalism. In that same year the Grupo Ocho (Group Eight) was formed, including Cruz González, García, Hernán González, César Valverde

Vega, and Néstor Zeledón Guzmán, most of whom had studied abroad and were abstractionists. Although this group dominated the local art scene during the 1960s and early 1970s, many critics believe it failed to produce an art linked to Costa Rican cultural reality.

REFERENCES:

Luis R. Cancel and others, *The Latin American Spirit: Art and Artists in the United States, 1920–1970* (New York: Bronx Museum of the Arts/Abrams, 1988);

David Craven, *The New Concept of Art and Popular Culture in Nicaragua since the Revolution of 1979: An Analytical Essay and Compendium of Illustrations* (New York: Edwin Mellen Press, 1989);

Shifra M. Goldman, *Contemporary Mexican Painting in a Time of Change* (Austin: University of Texas Press, 1981);

Norma Loaiza, *La abundancia y el tiempo* (San José, Costa Rica: Editorial Universidad Estatal a Distancia, 1982).

— F.B.N.

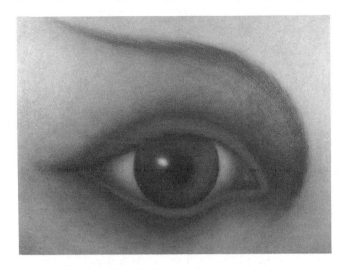

Artemis (1979) by Rodolfo Abularach

RODOLFO ABULARACH

Rodolfo Abularach (1933–) worked with figuration and **Surrealism** and has produced a well-known series of drawings of eye-shaped icons. Abularach studied art in his native Guatemala, in the United States, and in Mexico. In his early works, such as the painting *El choque* (1956; Impact), Abularach depicted bulls and scenes of bullfighting in an expressive, simplified realism, with dark, heavy outlines emphasizing the structure of the composition. During the 1950s Abularach and other Guatemalan artists found the blend of abstraction with figuration to be a reinvigorated way of addressing Mesoamerican and traditional Central American themes, the main concern of the earlier movement of **Indigenism.** In drawings such as *Estela* (1957; Stele), the human figure is immersed in a complex network of abstract organic shapes, while in works such as *Vuelo luminoso* (1959; Luminous Flight) the image of flying birds becomes only a suggestion of wings in motion achieved through the subtle contrast of light and dark abstract shapes. Drawing, which allowed Abularach to work with light in subtle ways, became his favorite medium.

After receiving two Guggenheim fellowships (1959 and 1960), Abularach settled in the United States. Since the 1960s he has concentrated on working with frontal and profile images of the eye, understood as an archetypal symbol of ancient wisdom. His realistic close-up views of eyes often transcend the mundane to acquire spiritual meaning. In *Aparición* (1967; Ap-

parition), from the series *Centros* (Centers), the eye becomes a mandala-like figure with cosmic connotations. Critics have often connected the mysterious and intense appearance of Abularach's disembodied eyes with Surrealism.

REFERENCE:

Lowery S. Sims, "New York Dada and New World Surrealism," in *The Latin American Spirit: Art and Artists in the United States, 1920–1970* (New York: Bronx Museum of the Arts/ Abrams, 1988), pp. 152–183.

— F.B.N.

AFRO-CARIBBEAN DANCE

The story of dance in the Caribbean islands and mainland Caribbean coastal areas cannot be separated from the story of slavery and plantation culture. Europeans colonized the area beginning in the fifteenth century, and African slaves were brought there until the nineteenth century; these slaves often escaped to Central America, carrying their culture with them. African traditional influence in the Atlantic coastal regions of Belize, Honduras, Guatemala, and Nicaragua can be traced back to wrecks of Spanish slave ships off Saint Vincent in 1635; after several uprisings, slaves had been transported from Saint Vincent to Roatán Island, off Honduras. Evidence of the spreading of Afro-Caribbean dance along the coastal region can be seen in the may-pole dance; the tira and chakanari (with instrumental accompaniment); and the punta, wanaragua, hunguhungu, gunjai, sambai, warini, and chumba (all accompanied by singing).

Wherever African and European populations coexisted, the European dances tended over time to take on African features. In Cuba in the 1850s dances based on European forms but modified by Cubans of African descent were more popular among Creoles and foreigners than were the European originals. As a result of migration and acculturation, the traditional folkloric dances of the area are based on both European and African roots, but there have been exceptions to this general syncretism: on the island of Hispaniola (now Haiti and the Dominican Republic) some slaves, even when freed, adopted the dances of their masters exactly as imported from Europe, while others consciously chose to perform dances as brought from their homelands in Senegal, the Gold Coast, Guinea, or the Congo. Still others dressed in European clothing as they danced African steps.

One of the two national dances of Puerto Rico, the **bomba,** is predominantly African. Salient African features include the audience forming a circle within which the dancers perform; the lead singer standing next to the drums, and the chorus behind the singer; the soloist singing the stanza, and the chorus responding with the refrain; and the solo dancer approaching and finally saluting the drums. While this call-and-response, leader-follower dance form is characteristic of much of African dance, it is also common in Spain and Flanders. In Cuba four dances known to have survived from colonial times include the palo (stick), a war dance representing the attempts of slaves to break away to freedom; the yuka, a secular dance representing fertility and sexuality; the makuta, a vigorous dance symbolizing the joy and devotion of the religiously devout; and the ireme, or "little devil," dance, representing the spirits of past generations.

African influence is also strong in dance for the concert stage, especially in Cuba. Soon after its foundation in 1948, the **Ballet Nacional de Cuba** broke with its parent organization, the Sociedad Pro-Arte Musical, an association of upper-class Havana citizens who sought to promote the classical and fine arts. The Ballet Nacional sought instead to draw on all of Cuba as a source of inspiration for its activities, including Afro-Cuban culture. This idea was stressed even more strongly by the founders of the Danza Contemporánea de Cuba company, which chose a work called *Mulato* as one of its three premiere pieces in 1960. So dominant was the presence of African-derived elements in this company's agenda that the dancer Marianela Boán left it in 1988 in order to investigate choreography that did not include African aspects. An example of African-influenced contemporary dance is *Mascando inglés* (Chewing English), by Puerto Rican postmodern choreographer Viveca Vázquez. In this dance a couple dancing to **salsa** music take off their shoes and allow African-based movements to take over,

as if they are returning to a state where national and racial distinctions are blurred.

REFERENCE:

Richard E. Hadel, "Carib Dance Music and Dance," *National Studies: A Journal of Social Research and Thought* (Belize), 1 (November 1973): 4.

—J.M.H.

Afro-Caribbean Music

The music of African slaves and their descendants in the Caribbean Basin constitutes a complex mixture of diverse musical practices. The geographic origins of the slaves, the conditions in which they and emancipated Africans lived, and their low socio-economic status may, however, provide a means of understanding the rebirth of some of their music in the Americas. Deprived of their authentic African instruments and materials with which to build them, slaves reconstructed from memory an array of musical accessories from materials available in their new environment. Caribbean slaves were typically worked from ten to twelve hours per day for six days and were given Sunday as a day intended for rest. On these and other festive days they were encouraged to participate in song and dance entertainments as a means of enlivening their spirits and ensuring their good health. These celebrations drew on a variety of African cultures that were thrown together indiscriminately. Forced to develop a consensus of cultural traditions, a fresh source of future artistic development was born: neo-Africanism. Neo-African musical culture found support in the *cabildos* (black mutual aid societies) and secret male societies, which, from time to time, were outlawed by colonial governments.

Freemen and slaves who promptly adapted to European languages, customs, and comportment were eventually destined to serve patrons in urban areas. Those who developed musical talents were able to parlay their efforts into a valued source of income and a less brutal way of life. Performing music was not deemed an acceptable occupation for the European colonial gentleman; it was, however, an appropriate activity for the lower classes. For the talented freeman and the indentured house servant, playing European music on European instruments became a lucrative alternative to their normally destitute condition. Social and popular music gradually became the province of urban blacks, and not merely from the standpoint of performance. As musical literacy developed, so did the production of arrangements and compositions by black musicians. It was a question of time before neo-African instruments, principally percussion instruments, were introduced into the *conjuntos* (small ensembles) and popular dance bands.

The abolition of slavery in the nineteenth century resulted in a massive migration of former slaves to urban areas in search of work. Unemployed masses found solace in the development of neighborhood entertainments of song and dance that became the **rumba** (Cuba), the **plena** (Puerto Rico), the **merengue** (Dominican Republic), and the cumbia (Panama and Colombia). Stylized versions of these and other acculturated genres became commercially attractive to nightclubs and theaters. By the early twentieth century, developments in tourism and the media (radio, recording, and film) could commercially exploit a flourishing mosaic of colorful, neo-African musical genres.

To develop an allied American front during the early days of World War II, the United States actively encouraged a strengthening of relations with the Caribbean and Latin America. The Hollywood film industry and major recording companies endeavored to renew North American interest in Latin American cultures and to re-interpret those cultures for northern consumption. Scores of movies and recordings, not to mention scholarly research programs, focused on the cultural wealth of the southern neighbors. The Panamerican Union (later the **Organization of American States**), the Alliance for Progress, and the Peace Corps were all intended to create closer cultural and political ties to Latin America. In these endeavors, music became a major means of communication. The more recent civil rights movement in the United States created an enhanced environment for interest in African-American cultures, an interest that extended to black traditions of the Caribbean Basin. As a result, Afro-Caribbean music reached new levels of popularity worldwide via the commercial successes of musics such as **salsa,** merengue, cumbia, and reggae.

REFERENCES:

Alejo Carpentier, *La música en Cuba* (Mexico City: Fondo de Cultura Económica, 1993);

Cristóbal Díaz Ayala, *Música cubana del Areyto a la Nueva Trova,* second edition (San Juan: Editorial Cubanacán, 1981);

Bernarda Jorge, *La música dominicana: Siglos XIX–XX* (Santo Domingo: Editora de la Universidad Autónoma de Santo Domingo, 1982);

Alberto Pérez Perazzo, *Ritmo afrohispano antillano: 1865–1965* (Caracas: Editorial Sucre, 1988).

— R.L.S.

Rosario Aguilar

Born in León, Nicaragua, Rosario Aguilar (1938–) studied in Managua, the United States, and Guatemala. Between 1963 and 1993 she published seven brief novels and a collection of short stories. Her first novel, *Primavera sonámbula* (1964; Somnambulant Spring), portrays the psychological conflict of a young upper-class woman confined to a psychiatric ward. The time spent in the clinic coincides with her sexual awakening. She decides to escape her confinement and face the dangers of reality, managing to overcome her psychological crisis and survive. Several of Aguilar's other novels concentrate on crucial moments in women's lives, when they must make difficult decisions and confront a hostile society that permits sexual exploitation of women and forces them to accept traditional roles they would prefer to avoid. *Rosa Sarmiento* (1964) is based on the life of **Rubén Darío**'s mother, who defies León's upper-class society during the second half of the nineteenth century and flees with her young lover. *Aquel mar sin fondo ni playa* (1970; That Sea Without a Bottom or a Beach) reflects the anguish of a young housewife who fears that any child she bears will be mentally handicapped like her husband's child by another marriage. *Las doce y veintinueve* (1975; Twelve Twenty Nine) depicts the tragedy of the 1972 earthquake that destroyed Managua and affected all of Nicaragua. The novel was written as a tribute to Nicaraguan women, during the International Year of Women in 1975. The catastrophe forever changed the lives of the four protagonists, who come from all walks of life. *El guerrillero* (1976; The Guerrilla) reflects the political realities of Nicaragua under the regime of **Anastasio Somoza.** The protagonist is a rural teacher who falls in love with a guerrilla whom she hides in her house while Somoza's National Guard searches for him. After he leaves, she realizes that his commitment is only to the revolutionary cause, and she undergoes a crisis that is resolved when she also becomes involved in clandestine resistance to Somoza. *Siete relatos sobre el amor y la guerra* (1986; Seven Tales About Love and War) is also about women's participation in the Sandinista liberation movement against Somoza. Many of the women characters die in combat, while others are tortured and raped. In *La niña Blanca y los pájaros sin pies* (1992; The Child Blanca and the Birds With No Feet) the protagonists are characters from the time of the Spanish conquest of the Americas early in the sixteenth century. The suffering caused by the conquest is represented by an Indian princess who is used and abandoned by the Spanish conqueror Pedro de Alvarado. She refuses to continue speaking Spanish, in an attempt to regain her original identity. The other female voices in the novel suffer similar abuse and form a chorus of protest in their native language, Nahuatl. Aguilar's most recent work, *Soledad: Tú eres el enlace* (1995; Soledad: You Are the Link), is a biographical narrative about her mother, based on family interviews, old records, and memories.

REFERENCES:

John Beverley and Marc Zimmerman, *Literature and Politics in the Central American Revolutions* (Austin: University of Texas Press, 1990);

Ann González, " 'Las mujeres de mi país': An Introduction to the Feminist Fiction of Rosario Aguilar," *Revista/Review Interamericana*, 23, nos. 1–2 (Spring–Summer 1993): 61–72.

—N.P.

AGUINALDO

The word *aguinaldo* has several meanings related to the Christmas season; it may refer to a gift or bonus or to a religious folk song. Such songs are prominent in much of Latin America and descend from the Spanish **villancico,** which uses either sacred or secular texts. As a musical folk genre, the aguinaldo has a simple melody, alternating a choral refrain (*estribillo*) and verses (*coplas*) and employing the lively rhythms of other Latin American music.

REFERENCE:

Gerard Béhague, "Latin American Folk Music," in *Folk and Traditional Music of the Western Continents*, by Bruno Nettl (Englewood Cliffs, N.J.: Prentice-Hall, 1990).

—R.L.S.

OLGA ALBIZU

Olga Albizu (1924–) is one of the first Puerto Rican painters to work with **abstract art.** She studied art in Puerto Rico, Europe, and New York, where from 1948 to 1951 she pursued graduate studies under the direction of well-known abstract expressionist painter Hans Hofmann. Albizu's early paintings were figurative, but after she settled in Manhattan in 1956 she turned to Informal Abstraction, a style that was strongly opposed in Puerto Rico. In paintings such as *Crecimiento* (1960; Growth) and *Sin título* (1980; Untitled), Albizu explored the combination of monochromatic backgrounds, subtle blends of bright colors, thick brushwork, impastos (sometimes applied with a spatula), and diverse textures. Her designs for record jackets for contemporary music, such as the bossa nova albums of Stan Getz and João Gilberto, were widely disseminated by RCA and other companies.

REFERENCE:

Marimar Benítez, "The Special Case of Puerto Rico," in *The Latin American Spirit: Art and Artists in the United States,*

Claribel Alegría with Argentinean writer Julio Cortázar, 1979 (photograph by Carlos Franco)

1920–1970 (New York: Bronx Museum of the Arts/Abrams, 1988), pp. 72–105.

—F.B.N.

CLARIBEL ALEGRÍA

Claribel Alegría, who was born in Nicaragua in 1924, considers herself Salvadoran since her family moved to El Salvador when she was an infant and she lived there until the late 1940s. Her poetry, novels, **testimonials,** short stories, and essays reflect the reality she lived as a child in El Salvador, witness to the massacre of (by some estimates) thirty thousand peasants in 1932 at the hands of the Salvadoran military under then-president Maximiliano Martínez. Her belief that a writer has a commitment to reveal the conditions of the oppressed is evident in the political content of her works. She links the oppression of the underprivileged in her society with that of women at all levels. Many of her protagonists are women from the upper classes who suffer physical and psychological violence because of gender. Her novels and testimonials are frequently written in collaboration with her husband, Darwin Flakoll, from the United States. One of their most recognized novels is *Cenizas de Izalco* (1966; translated as *Ashes of Izalco*), which tells of the *matanza* (massacre) of thousands of peasants in El Salvador at the same time as the eruption of the Izalco volcano in January 1932. Although the rebellion was defeated, the ashes of Izalco serve in the novel as a metaphoric representation of the massacred peasants, whose ashes will foster the future revolution against the military-dominated government in El Salvador. This preoccupation with giving voice to the victims and survivors of military violence is evident in the testimonials *No me agarran viva: La mujer salvadoreña en lucha* (1983; translated as *They Won't Take Me Alive*) and *Para romper el silencio: Resistencia y lucha en las cárceles salvadoreñas* (1984: Breaking the Silence: Resistance and Struggle in Salvadoran Jails). *Despierta mi bien, despierta* (1986; Awake, My Love, Awake) and *Luisa en el país de la realidad* (1987; translated as *Luisa in Realityland*) depict a woman's struggle against alienation and oppression through her own creative efforts, a theme that is also prominent in Alegría's essays and poetry. With the bilingual publication of her book of poetry, *Flores del volcán / Flowers from the Volcano* (1982), Alegría became known internationally. Her poems in this collection and in several others, such as *Sobrevivo* (1978; I Survive), also frequently represent the voices of the victims of military oppression and U.S. imperialism in El Salvador, Nicaragua, and elsewhere in Latin America.

REFERENCES:

Sandra M. Boschetto-Sandoval and Marcia P. McGowan, eds., *Claribel Alegría and Central American Literature: Critical Essays* (Athens: Ohio University Center for International Studies, 1994);

Maureen E. Shea, *Undercurrents of Oppression in Latin American Women's Novels* (San Francisco: Austin & Winfield, 1993);

George Yúdice, "Letras de emergencia: Claribel Alegría," *Revista Iberoamericana*, 51 (July–December 1985): 953–964.

— M.E.S.

ALBERTO, ALICIA, AND FERNANDO ALONSO

Alberto, Alicia, and Fernando Alonso were instrumental in the development of stage dance in Cuba, especially through their formation of the **Ballet Nacional de Cuba.** They began their professional studies at the School of Ballet of the Sociedad Pro-Arte Musical of Havana, an organization supported by Havana's upper classes and designed to promote the classical, European fine arts in Cuba. Alicia (1921–) began her studies in 1931, Alberto (1917–) in 1933, and Fernando (1914–) — Alicia's future husband — in 1936.

Alberto Alonso began his performing career in 1935 dancing with the Ballets Russes de Monte Carlo (founded in 1932 by the Russian theater agent Col. Wassily de Basil and René Blum) and later the Ballets Russes du Colonel de Basil. Alonso returned to Cuba at the beginning of World War II and helped create professional Cuban concert-stage choreography. The premiere of his first piece of choreography in 1942 began his mission to breathe new life into stage dance in Cuba, which up to that point had been used primarily as a rite of passage for the daughters of upper-class families and had consisted of restagings of European classics; no incentives or support for creating original works existed in the country.

In the early 1940s, while Alicia Alonso was restaging European ballets such as Pyotr Ilich Tchaikovsky's *Swan Lake* (1876) and Michel Fokine's *Les Sylphides* (1909), Alberto was creating psychological and dramatic works, dances denouncing social ills, and other original works. His *Before the Dawn* (1947) scandalized the Sociedad Pro-Arte Musical, whose socially privileged members were unprepared for a dramatization of the life of the exploited lower classes. The work's groundbreaking stylized choreography of popular and Afro-Cuban dances — the **rumba,** the **bolero,** the *bote,* the **conga,** and the "little devil" dance — was also considered scandalous.

Citing lack of understanding and support, Alberto, Alicia, and Fernando Alonso separated from Pro-Arte and, with help from American Ballet Theatre of New York, founded the Ballet Nacional de Cuba in 1948. While Fernando and Alberto Alonso created choreography and organized the school and company administratively, it was the tremendous prestige of the internationally renowned prima ballerina, Alicia Alonso, that assured the project's viability. Her years of international touring as a star of the American Ballet Theatre made her the ideal representative of Cuba, which was asserting itself as an independent force on the world's stage.

REFERENCE:

Jorge A. González, "Apuntes para la historia del ballet en Cuba," *Revista de Música*, 2 (October 1961): 228–248.

— J.M.H.

LOLA ALVAREZ BRAVO

Lola Alvarez Bravo (1907–1993), an important Mexican photographer, studied at the Escuela Nacional Pre-

Luis Cardoza y Aragón, Frida Kahlo, Jacqueline and André Breton, Lupe Marín, Diego Rivera, and Lola Alvarez Bravo in 1938

paratoria (National Preparatory School), where in 1922 she met **Frida Kahlo.** Later, she associated with members of the leftist intelligentsia, including the main participants in **Muralism.** In 1925 she was introduced to **photography** by her husband, **Manuel Alvarez Bravo.** Her early photographs from the mid 1920s are similar in style to those of her husband, with whom she shared a camera and a darkroom. Because of her interest in Mexican popular types, as opposed to her husband's penchant for poetic and artistic allusions, Lola Alvarez Bravo preferred the documentary approach of the U.S. photographer Paul Strand, whom she met in 1933. Her remarkable black-and-white photo-documentation of the Mexican people emphasized the subtleties of daily life rather than the stylization of posed compositions.

Alvarez Bravo separated from her husband in 1934. She subsequently moved to the house of painter **María Izquierdo,** a popular meeting place for intellectuals that was close to the university and the Instituto Nacional de Bellas Artes. Her first position as a staff photographer was with the monthly *El Maestro Rural* (The Country Teacher), published by the Secretaría de Educación Pública (Ministry of Public Education). She also received assignments from *Vea, Voz, Avance, Futuro,* and *Espacio,* which led her to become a pioneer-

ing force in the field of photojournalism. Her sensitive treatment of rural Mexico and its indigenous people also made her the photographer preferred by artists and intellectuals who embraced **Indigenism.** She photographed not only artists but also their works. While her numerous portraits of Kahlo are among her best-known works, she also photographed several paintings by Kahlo prior to changes made by the artist.

Lola Alvarez Bravo taught at and directed the photography workshop at the National Institute of Fine Arts, curated traveling exhibitions to provincial cities, opened her own commercial gallery in 1951, and became involved in cinematic productions in the late 1960s. Her often-overlooked body of fashion and advertisement photographs was a means of financial sustenance and was of less importance to her than the documentation of Mexican crafts, customs, and pre-Columbian sites. She continued to be an active photographer until the late 1980s, when she lost her sight. Throughout her career Alvarez Bravo was interested in the play between light and shadow, which she expressed in the following ways: as a rigid mechanical pattern in *Unos suben y otros bajan* (1940; Some Go Up and Others Go Down), as an erotic suggestion in the *Tríptico del martirio* (1949; Triptych of Martyrdom), and as a mysterious and tense relationship in the

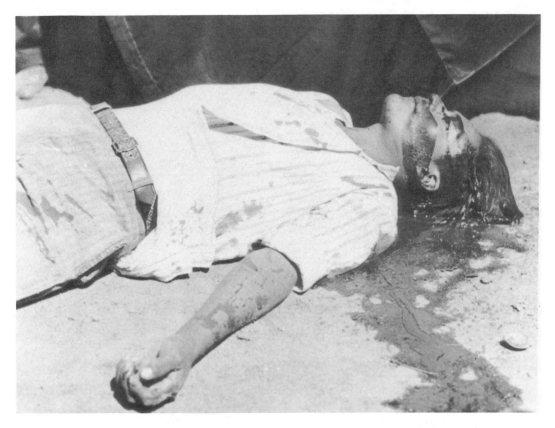

Obrero en huelga, asesinado (1934; Striking Worker, Assassinated) by Manuel Alvarez Bravo

untitled photograph of a masked participant in a 1982 gay rights rally.

REFERENCE:

Oliver Debroise, *Lola Alvarez Bravo: In Her Own Light* (Tucson: Center for Creative Photography, University of Arizona, 1994).

— C.M.

MANUEL ALVAREZ BRAVO

Mexican photographer Manuel Alvarez Bravo (1902–) is among the most important in Latin America. He was introduced to **photography** by Fernando Ferrari Pérez, a botanist and engineer. Ferrari Pérez and German photographer Hugo Brehme ventured across Mexico on several photographic excursions and invited Alvarez Bravo to accompany them. Shortly afterward Alvarez Bravo began to work in Brehme's Mexico City studio while continuing his career in accounting. During this period Alvarez Bravo saw and admired the modernist, nonpictorialist photographs of Edward Weston and Tina Modotti. Transferred to Oaxaca in 1924 by the Oficina Nacional de Contaduría (National

Accounting Office), Alvarez Bravo and his wife, photographer **Lola Alvarez Bravo,** became interested in the photodocumentation of the indigenous culture of that area. He worked with black-and-white photography, recording inhabited spaces. By the late 1920s he had synthesized pure formalism and its frequent concomitant, abstraction, with his interest in **Indigenism.** In 1929 Manuel Alvarez Bravo began to teach photography at the Instituto Nacional de Bellas Artes (National Institute of Fine Arts). He was closely associated with the artists participating in **Muralism;** yet his photographs did not blatantly propagandize their political agenda. He did not become a full-time photographer until 1931, when he made his first sale to the Museum of Modern Art in New York.

While Alvarez Bravo also developed a reputation as a specialist in the reproduction of artworks, his freelance fieldwork earned him prominence as a photographic chronicler of Mexico. His subjects of choice were members of the working and peasant classes, anonymous but heroic in their endurance. Many of his photographs captured what attracted the Surrealists to Mexico: the occurrences of death and dream imagery in everyday Mexican life. For example, the photograph *Parábola óptica* (1931; Optical Parable), which was included in the 1940 exhibition of **Surrealism** that took place in Mexico, is an uncanny image of an ordinary optician's shop decorated with oddly staring eyes.

A full understanding of Alvarez Bravo's photographs is often dependent on knowledge of the titles he gave them. *Obrero en huelga, asesinado* (1934; Striking Worker, Assassinated), his most famous work, must be understood though its title, since the image offers no intrinsic visual explanation of events. Like many of his photographs, *Obrero en huelga, asesinado* creates a spatial intimacy between the viewer and the subject. The angle used to photograph the lifeless but open-eyed subject places the viewer in a kneeling position. This trend continued throughout Alvarez Bravo's career. For instance, the subject of *Niña en su ventana* (1959; Girl at Her Window) leans out into the viewer's space.

Also engaged in the film industry in various capacities from the 1930s, Alvarez Bravo left photography and cinema as professional occupations in 1959, to cofound a publishing house specializing in fine art books.

REFERENCE:
A.D.Coleman, "The Indigenous Vision of Manuel Alvarez Bravo," *Artforum,* 14 (April 1976): 60–63.
                                                        — C.M.

Rafael Aponte-Ledée

Rafael Aponte-Ledée (1938–), born in Guayama, Puerto Rico, is perhaps the most prominent representative of his country's avant-garde composers. At the age of nineteen he received a scholarship from the Puerto Rican government's Department of Public Instruction, enabling him to pursue studies in piano, music theory, and composition at the Royal Conservatory in Madrid. In 1965 he was awarded another scholarship by the Puerto Rican Institute of Culture to attend the prestigious Centro Latinoamericano de Altos Estudios Musicales del Instituto Torcuato di Tella (The Torcuato di Tella Latin American Center for Advanced Musical Studies) in Buenos Aires, where he studied with the eminent Argentinean composer, Alberto Ginastera.

Various institutions in Puerto Rico have commissioned new works from Aponte-Ledée, and he has received prizes from the Athenaeum of Puerto Rico (1967 and 1968) and from the Puerto Rican Institute of Culture (1969). He has participated in numerous festivals of contemporary music in Washington, Buenos Aires, Madrid, Zagreb, Maracaibo, the first Encounter on Aleatory Music in Montevideo, and the Festival

Casals in San Juan. As a founding member of the Puerto Rican Society of Contemporary Music, Aponte-Ledée has been instrumental in promoting contemporary music in Puerto Rico, through public performances with the progressive ensemble Fluxus and through his composition classes at the Puerto Rican Conservatory of Music and subsequently at the Department of Music at the University of Puerto Rico in Río Piedras.

Among his prize-winning works are *Dialogantes* (1967), *Tema y seis diferencias* (1968; Theme and Six Variations), and *Epítasis* (1969). Other important works include *Elegía para cuerdas* (1965; Elegy for Strings), *La ventana abierta* (1968; The Open Window), *Streptomicyne* (1970), and *Los huevos de Pandora* (1975; Pandora's Eggs).

REFERENCES:
Composers of the Americas, volume 17 (Washington, D.C.: Pan American Union, Secretary General of the Organization of American States, 1957);

Compositores contemporáneos puertorriqueños (San Juan: Instituto de Cultura Puertorriqueña, Centro de Investigaciones y Ediciones Musicales de Puerto Rico, 1981).
                                                        — R.L.S.

Architecture

Early-twentieth-century architecture in Mexico, Central America, and the Caribbean was based almost entirely on European precedents. Mexican independence in the early nineteenth century offered little impetus for architectural innovation, but the following periods of French occupation and the Porfirio Díaz dictatorship fully embraced French neoclassical architecture at the expense of both Iberian and indigenous Mexican designs. Although the phenomenon spread somewhat to Central American capital cities, it met with limited acceptance in Mexico's state capitals and even less in rural, agrarian-based communities, where folk interpretations of the elaborate Churrigueresque style imported from Spain continued into the early twentieth century. Major Mexican cities such as Puebla and Zacatecas, which had forged artistic and architectural traditions independent of those of Mexico City, continued to utilize local tile and folk stone-carving traditions and were less enthusiastic than the capital in their reception of neoclassicism. Following the Spanish-American War, Caribbean capitals such as San Juan and Havana quickly recognized the interests of the tourist industry; they perpetuated neocolonial styles, in part for that reason.

Following the **Mexican Revolution** of 1910, the styles of European modernism were introduced first

Las torres de Satélite (Satellite City Towers), Mexico City, designed by Luis Barragán and Mathias Goeritz in 1957

into Mexico and later into Central America. Several architects from this region studied in Europe, and many of those who studied at home also adopted the principles of Le Corbusier's functionalism. The functional structures that first appeared in Latin America in the late 1920s were not merely a bastion of the elite intelligentsia, they were also recognized by practically minded governments throughout the region as an efficient means of housing a rapidly growing population and providing the expanding concomitant social services. The artist and architect **Juan O'Gorman** designed some of the earliest functional buildings in Mexico, such as his own residence (1929) and that of **Diego Rivera** (1931). One of the earliest proponents of socially oriented functional structures, O'Gorman designed many schools commissioned by the Secretaría de Educación Pública (Ministry of Public Education). Also cost-effective was the concrete-shell construction that had become an important feature across the Latin American architectural landscape. One of the early innovators in this technique was the architect **Félix Can-**

dela, a Spaniard who immigrated to Mexico. Although the scientific foundations for concrete-shell construction had been laid in Europe, it was the first twentieth-century architectural development to come of age in Latin America. The plasticity of the concrete shell, which depended on form rather than mass for strength, allowed it to be manipulated into a wide variety of shapes. This architectural form first found popularity in the early 1950s, in structures ranging from Havana's Cabaret Tropicana (1952), designed by the architect Max Borges, to industrial warehouses and Candela's Iglesia de la Virgen Milagrosa (1954–1955; Church of the Miraculous Virgin) in Mexico City.

The International Style, the dominant style during the twentieth century, arrived in Latin America shortly after its European inception, but prior to World War II it was not readily expressed in large-scale vertical structures because of Mexico and Central America's strong tradition of stonemasonry and, more significantly, because of the scarcity of structural steel until the late 1940s. The midcentury International Style buildings in Mexico City, largely the work of the architect **Mario Pani,** greatly influenced construction in other Latin American capitals, as did construction in Caracas and Bogotá. Pani also participated in the design of numerous urban housing projects in the 1950s and 1960s, such as the Multifamiliar Presidente Juárez (1950, destroyed in the 1985 earthquake) and **Tlatelolco** (1964), which adopted a less sophisticated version of the International Style than did his commercial designs. During this period, Pani joined Carlos and Enrique del Moral as chief architects of the Ciudad Universitaria (University City) at the Universidad Nacional Autónoma de México (National Autonmous University of Mexico), one of the most important architectural projects in Latin America during this period, comparable to Caracas's Ciudad Universitaria (begun in 1950; University City) and the city of Brasilia. Although not as successful as the Caracas campus, the designs for UNAM's University City integrated visual arts with functionalist architecture, as in the Biblioteca Central (1949–1951; Central Library), designed by O'Gorman, Juan Martínez de Velasco, and Gustavo Saavedra. O'Gorman was responsible for exterior decoration of the central part of this building, a ten-story tower, covered on its four faces with monumental mosaics, which portray scenes and figures from pre-Hispanic, colonial, and modern Mexico. Another important building in the Ciudad Universitaria is the Estadio Olímpico (Olympic Stadium), one of the largest in the world, featuring a mosaic by Rivera on its facade. The entire campus project covered an area of fifteen hundred acres and included the work of more than one hundred architects.

The 1950s also witnessed an important architectural renewal in Guatemala after the founding of the Escuela de Arquitectura (School of Architecture) at the Universidad Nacional (National University). Among the earliest buildings in the International Style, buildings that, like UNAM, also emphasized the integration of architecture with mural decoration, were Guatemala City's Palacio Municipal (1955–1956; City Hall) and the Instituto Guatemalteco de Seguridad Social (1958–1959; Guatemalan Institute of Social Security). Designed by the architects Pelayo Llerena and Roberto Aycinema, the Palacio Municipal features a large glass mosaic by **Carlos Mérida** on an interior wall and concrete relief murals by Guillermo Grajeda Mena and Dagoberto Vásquez on the exterior walls. The Instituto Guatemalteco de Seguridad Social, designed by Aycinema and Jorge Montes Córdova, also included another large mosaic mural by Mérida and wall reliefs by Roberto González Goyri. Guatemala was one of the areas where experiments were undertaken to provide low-cost rural housing, such as the project designed by the faculty at Germany's Kassel University. The designs incorporated local materials and were based on indigenous and vernacular building traditions that were earthquake-resistant and allowed for owner maintenance. In Cuba, the architect Aquiles Capablanca used the principles of modern architecture to design the Office of the Comptroller in Havana (1952–1954), which features the use of thin pillars for support, a honeycomb facade, and a ceramic mural by **Amelia Peláez.**

While functionalism played a vital role in the architecture of Mexico during the 1950s and 1960s, several architects, such as O'Gorman and **Luis Barragán,** reacted against its influence and adopted the principles of organic architecture proposed by Frank Lloyd Wright. O'Gorman adopted this style for his later structures, including his private residence at La Pedregal San Angel (1956), which incorporated a natural grotto as part of the house and used the rough volcanic rock of the Pedregal as building material. Barragán also masterfully reconciled modern domestic architecture with the environment. His designs were influenced by his belief in the human psychological and spiritual need to connect with nature, as well as by his emphasis on the varying qualities of natural light. Although opposed to the political agenda of the proponents of **Indigenism,** Barragán evoked spaces sculpted by thick walls, limited exterior fenestration, and decorative play between light and shadow, in ways characteristic of both Mesoamerican and Spanish colonial structures. His designs, regarded as timeless classics, influenced several followers later in the century. Younger architects fused the International Style with Barragán's organic and eclectic approach, thereby bringing a previously unknown warmth to monumental structures, such as Ricardo Legorreta's Hotel Camino Real (1968). Mathias Goeritz also challenged the principles of functionalism by designing, in collaboration with Barragán, what Goeritz called "emotional architecture," an example of which is his structure Las torres de Satélite (1957–1958; Satellite City Towers), at the entrance of the Ciudad Satélite neighborhood. This piece consists of five triangular concrete towers with an average height of 156 feet, painted in different colors. Although the towers are not habitable, their size created an urban area closer to architecture than sculpture.

REFERENCE:

Nueva arquitectura en América Latina: Presente y futuro (Mexico City: Ediciones G. Gili, 1990).

— C.M.

JOSÉ ARDÉVOL

José Ardévol was born in 1911 in Spain, where his father, Fernando, served as director of the Instituto Musical de Barcelona (Barcelona Institute of Music) and of the Orquesta de Cámara (Chamber Orchestra). Following an excellent musical education José Ardévol immigrated to Cuba at the age of nineteen. He became a Cuban citizen and immediately established a close relationship with Cuban music and musicians. He founded the Chamber Orchestra of Havana in 1934 and served as its director for eighteen years. In 1936 he began teaching at the Municipal Conservatory of Havana, where his close friend, **Amadeo Roldán**, served as director. He accepted the presidency of the Cuban National Music Commission, which was set up to invigorate Cuban musical activities, and was active in the creation of the National Symphony Orchestra, the National Chamber Orchestra, and the National Conservatory.

The untimely deaths of Amadeo Roldán (1939) and **Alejandro García Caturla** (1940) placed Ardévol in a position of leadership, from which he could guide a group of younger composers in the development of the craft of musical composition and in their understanding of great universal models of the past. In 1942 the Grupo de Renovación Musical (Music Reform Group) was launched by Ardévol with an aspiring group of Cuban composers: Harold Gramatges, Edgardo Martín, Julián Orbón, Hilario González, **Argeliers León**, Serafín Pro, and Gisela Hernández.

Ardévol's emphasis on the craft of composition and on universal values, coupled with an avoidance of

Reinaldo Arenas (photograph by Nestor Almendros)

the exotic, clearly placed him among the neoclassicists. Among his more than ninety varied works are numerous chamber genres (ensemble sonatas, quartets, quintets), orchestral works for full symphony as well as chamber orchestra, concertos, songs, cantatas, a ballet, and incidental music for movies. He won recognition for many of his works, including the 1938 Cuban National Prize for Chamber Music, the 1944 and 1951 Cuban National Symphonic Prizes, an honorable mention in the 1944 Washington Chamber Music Guild Competition, the Ricordi International Symphonic Award in 1949, the National Prize for Cuban Song in the 1953 José Martí Centennial Competition, and first prize in the Amadeo Roldán Contest of the Cuban National Library in 1960. Ardévol's record of service to music is a strong one; he was a tireless promoter of musical activity at the national and international levels.

REFERENCES:

Alejo Carpentier, *La música en Cuba*, second edition (Mexico City: Fondo de Cultura Económica, 1972);

Cristóbal Díaz Ayala, *Música cubana del Areyto a la Nueva Trova*, second edition (San Juan: Editorial Cubanacán, 1981);

Helio Orovio, *Diccionario de la música cubana: Biográfico y técnico*, second edition (Havana: Editorial Letras Cubanas, 1992).

— R.L.S.

REINALDO ARENAS

Reinaldo Arenas (1943–1990), whose first name is sometimes spelled "Reynaldo," was born in Cuba and, like many people of his generation, initially supported the **Cuban Revolution,** only to become disillusioned with it later. Although not of the same generation, he was a close friend and admirer of **Virgilio Piñera** and **José Lezama Lima.** Arenas's homosexuality, together with the fact that he became well-known for books published without the approval of the **Fidel Castro** regime, landed him in jail. His works were suppressed, though, according to the author, he continued to write, if only for the eager readership guaranteed by the censors. After several tries Arenas finally managed to leave Cuba in 1980 and settle in New York. His autobiography, *Antes que anochezca* (1992; translated as *Before Night Falls*), opens with a preface written as he was facing death from AIDS in 1990; in December of that year he committed suicide. Much of *Antes que anochezca* consists of a passionate account of persecution and betrayal of the many Cubans who compromised their integrity under pressure from the revolutionary powers.

Arenas had established his literary reputation with his first novel, *Celestino antes del alba* (1967; translated as *Singing from the Well*), a long monologue revealing the sufferings of a mistreated child. This child turns out to be an imagined companion of the speaker, who is seeking refuge in fantasy from a cruel reality, which Arenas conveys with a harshness worthy of **Juan Rulfo.** Arenas's second novel, *El mundo alucinante* (1969; translated as *Hallucinations* and as *The Ill-fated Peregrinations of Fray Servando*), was well received abroad and proved to be one of the most significant novels ever to come out of Cuba. On one level it is a fictionalized biography of a Dominican friar, Fray Servando, who is persecuted for his religious and political beliefs and spends much of his time fleeing imprisonment. On another level, the novel functions allegorically: life and the self are prisons. Some critics have identified picaresque elements and have spoken of the influence of Voltaire (*Candide*), François Rabelais, Francisco Gómez de Quevedo, and Baltasar Gracián; other critics have seen a more explicit message of disillusionment with a pseudorevolutionary Spanish America. There is no doubt that the Cuban authorities did not like *El mundo alucinante,* even though the novel was written before the regime's repressive tendencies were fully apparent. In *El mundo alucinante* three narrators (the friar in first person, a second-person narrator, and an omniscient narrator) give sometimes contradictory accounts of events. The style of writing is often parodic, while literary and political figures from many periods come into contact with the friar. One such figure is Lezama Lima, thinly disguised under the name of Padre José de Lezamis. Lezama, for his part, devoted some pages of his *La expresión americana* (1969; American Expression) to Fray Servando. In the course of his autobiography, Arenas observes that his own life sometimes seemed to be imitating the trials and adventures of Fray Servando.

Other works by Arenas are *El palacio de las blanquísimas mofetas* (1980; The Palace of the White Skunks); *Termina el desfile* (1981; translated as *The Parade is Over*); and *La vieja Rosa* and *Arturo, la estrella más brillante* (1981, 1984; two short works translated together under the title *Old Rosa*). Another of Arenas's novels, *Otra vez el mar* (1982; translated as *Farewell to the Sea*), had to be rewritten three times from scratch, the first two versions having fallen into official Cuban hands. The third writing was smuggled out of Cuba in the late 1970s. Arenas's books have been highly valued outside Cuba.

REFERENCES:

Reinaldo Arenas, *Before Night Falls,* translated by Dolores Koch (New York: Viking, 1993);

Seymour Menton, *Prose Fiction of the Cuban Revolution* (Austin & London: University of Texas Press, 1975).

—P.S.

RAFAEL ARÉVALO MARTÍNEZ

Born in Guatemala, Rafael Arévalo Martínez (1884–1975) was an important writer of the period following **Modernismo.** His works anticipate the psychological novel that gained importance in Latin America later in the twentieth century. He wrote poetry and novels but is best known for his short stories. His most famous story is "El hombre que parecía un caballo" (1915; The Man Who Looked Like a Horse), which initiated a trend in the Latin American short story that Arévalo Martínez called "psycho-zoological." Characters assume human and animal characteristics, underscoring their similar psychological and physical properties. In "El hombre que parecía un caballo" Arévalo Martínez imaginatively portrays the life of the Colombian poet Porfirio Barba Jacob and the similarities between him and a horse. It is a profound psychological study of the character, revealing his inner consciousness through interior monologue. In "El trovador colombiano" (1914; The Colombian Troubadour) the protagonist is a combination of human and dog, and in "El señor Monitot" (1922) Monitot is equated with the elephant, and many other animals appear, including snakes, doves, tigers, and birds of prey.

Arévalo Martínez's novelistic production is divided into two main categories: the autobiographical and the sociopolitical. In the first are *Una vida* (1914; A Life), *Manuel Aldano* (1914), and *Las noches en el palacio de la nunciatura* (1927; Nights in the Palace of the Nunciature). The second vein includes *La oficina de paz de Orolandia* (1925; The Peace Office of Orolandia), which deals with yankee imperialism in Central America, *Viaje a Ipanda* (1939; Voyage to Ipanda), and perhaps his most fantastic novel, *El mundo de los maharachías* (1939; The World of Special Creatures), in which the world is populated by strange creatures who combine human and animal characteristics, with long, splendid tails that are sensitive organs.

REFERENCES:

Teresa Arévalo, *Rafael Arévalo Martínez: Biografía de 1926 hasta su muerte en 1975* (Guatemala: Oscar de León Palacios, 1995);

Manuel Antonio Girón Mena, *Rafael Arévalo Martínez: Su vida y obra* (Guatemala: Editorial José de Piñeda Ibarra, 1974).

—M.E.S.

MANLIO ARGUETA

Manlio Argueta, born in El Salvador in 1935, spent his formative years in the company of a group of young Salvadoran poets whose intense political activity often resulted in their exile from the country. In 1956, while studying law at La Universidad Nacional (The National University), Argueta helped to form an intellectual group called the Círculo Literario Universitario (The University Literary Circle). The popular Salvadoran poet **Roque Dalton** was also a member of the group, as were **Otto René Castillo** and Roberto Armijo. At a time when Central America lacked a significant number of serious literary critics, intellectual circles aided inexperienced writers by reviewing and helping them perfect their literature.

Early in his career Argueta published only poetry collections, such as *Canto a Huistaluexitl* (1956–1957; Song to Huistaluexitl); *De aquí en adelante* (1967; From Here On); and *En el costado de la luz* (1968; On the Side of the Light), which won him a Central American literary prize. Argueta's poetry is diverse in its topics but maintains an underlying tone of criticism. He later turned from poetry to the novel as his preferred genre for expressing political and social concerns. His first novel, *El valle de las hamacas* (1970; The Valley of Hammocks), can be described as a fictive account of a historic event in El Salvador. In part, Argueta was inspired to write his novel in protest against the 1960 attack on the university by public security forces sent by the unpopular president José María Lemus to eliminate the growing opposition party, the Partido Revolucionario de Abril y Mayo (The April and May Revolutionary Party). The protagonist of *El valle de las hamacas,* Raúl, is a student leader and left-wing politician. The novel begins with some background of Raúl's life and then becomes more political in its message, describing scenes of torture and entering into a discussion of the guerrilla movement. Argueta's style recalls some works of the **Boom** in Latin American literature, because of his use of stream-of-consciousness and rapidly shifting narrators.

Other novels published by Argueta include *Caperucita en la Zona Rosa* (1970; Little Red Riding Hood in the Zona Rosa [a chic area of Mexico City]) and *Un día en la vida* (1980; translated as *One Day of Life*), an important **testimonial** novel narrated in the form of a monologue by a peasant woman who describes life in a countryside seething with the violence of revolutionary and governmental activity. Argueta's *Cuzcatlán donde bate la mar del sur* (1986; translated as *Cuzcatlán: Where the Southern Sea Beats*) is also a testimonial, presenting a variety of peasant voices that reflect on historical situations, from a massacre in 1932

to present-day events. Manlio Argueta lived in exile in Costa Rica from 1972 to 1973, when he was able to return to El Salvador.

REFERENCE:

David Escobar Galindo, ed., *Indice antológico de la poesía salvadoreña* (San Salvador: UCA, 1987), pp. 619–622.
                                                                — D.H. & M.E.S.

JUAN JOSÉ ARREOLA

The Mexican writer Juan José Arreola (1918–) is a contemporary of **Juan Rulfo,** a writer with whom he is sometimes compared. With Rulfo, Arreola shares origins in Jalisco, a perfectionism in writing, and a certain aloofness from the commercial artistic round. Like Rulfo's literary output, Arreola's work is modest in quantity; but unlike him, Arreola is in his own way a humorist and a showman. He was once an actor in a troupe organized by **Xavier Villaurrutia** and **Rodolfo Usigli** and even played small parts at the Comédie-Française in Paris.

Arreola's literature is playful and mimetic, the product of a good ear and a delight in invention. He relies above all on intuition and is suspicious of reason. Arreola's themes advocate a new humanism, often seen as a necessary antidote to an increasingly technological society. His writing has been compared to that of Kafka. Arreola's work consists largely of short stories and other brief pieces, such as aphorisms and stylistic exercises, but there is also one novel, *La feria* (1963; translated as *The Fair*), which won the Xavier Villaurrutia Prize (shared with a work by **Elena Garro**). Arreola is largely self-taught. He has been an important figure on the Mexican literary scene, instrumental in bringing many other writers to public attention through literary publications or television, and influential as a teacher of creative writing.

Apart from his novel, Arreola's most important works are *Varia invención* (1949; Diverse Invention), *Bestiario* (1958, revised 1981; Bestiary), *Confabulario* (1952), and *Palindroma* (1971). *Confabulario,* a key work, has been revised and augmented several times, generating titles such as *Confabulario total* (Total Confabulary) and *Confabulario definitivo* (Definitive Confabulary) as well as much confusion along the way. Surely the best-known of Arreola's stories is one called "El guardagujas" (The Switchman), whose opening recalls Charles Dickens's story "The Signalman." "El guardagujas" alone has probably inspired as much focused critical analysis as the rest of Arreola's works put together, which is evidence both of its intriguing ambiguities and of the general difficulty in coming to grips with Arreola's oeuvre. This story has been read by critics as a satiric critique of the Mexican railway system, as social or political satire, as an exploration of the fantastic and the real, and as a metaphor for human existence. In fact, whatever its wider implications, "El guardagujas" is a relatively rare example of a piece by Arreola with a specifically Mexican setting; in general his writing tends toward the cosmopolitan.

Great as the formal diversity of Arreola's literature is, formal characteristics do not generally pose difficulties for the reader. Arreola's work, however, is not easily characterized or explained in general terms and not always easily understood. As social criticism, it targets such things as commercialism, the technological society, hypocrisy, and bureaucracy. For example, "Baby H.P." is a short, parodic advertisement that tries to sell to the housewife the idea of a device that will harness the energy an infant wastes in apparently purposeless limb movements, enough energy perhaps to run a food mixer for a few seconds. Arreola is also clearly interested in human relationships, even obsessed with the idea of the love triangle, and enigmatic in his presentation of women. In addition, he deals with religious and ethical themes. *Confabulario* opens with "Parturient montes" (The Mountains Shall Give Birth), a title followed immediately by an epigraph taken from Horace that declares that what will be born is merely a ridiculous mouse. The story alludes to the gulf Arreola feels exists between the writer's creative impulse and the end product. These examples illustrate something of the variety of ideas that Arreola clothes in forms that are no less varied. He makes use of allegory, fables, parables, and animalesque caricature (all of which lead one to think of medieval ways of storytelling). His excursions into the fantastic and his advocacy of a new human order invite comparison with Julio Cortázar, while his recasting of earlier tales suggests an affinity with Jorge Luis Borges, the other Argentinean master of short fiction. Yet Arreola is very much his own man, enigmatic and unusual.

REFERENCES:

Bertie Acker, *El cuento mexicano contemporáneo* (Madrid: Playor, 1984);

Emmanuel Carballo, *Diecinueve protagonistas de la literatura mexicana del siglo XX* (Mexico City: Empresas Editoriales, 1965);

Yula M. Washburn, *Juan José Arreola* (Boston: Twayne, 1983).
                                                            — P.S.

ART

The art produced in Latin America during the twentieth century is characterized by a remarkable variety of expressions that reflects differences determined by diverse cultural and racial heritages, as well as historical circumstances. Since colonial times, numerous blends of Indo-American, African, and European cultural heritages have taken place; after the period of independence, as nations consolidated and defined their own identities, other cultural exchanges occurred with the arrival of new waves of European immigrants, who often reinforced the links between Latin America and Europe.

Until the 1960s most Latin American artists of the twentieth century received part of their formal training in Europe, where they adopted classic avant-garde attitudes that led them to reject earlier art, promote formal experimentation, reassess the art of non-European cultures, and explore the role of technology as a means for social progress. They also incorporated characteristics of several different European styles, such as **Impressionism and Post-Impressionism,** Cubism, Futurism, Constructivism, Expressionism, **Surrealism,** and Informalism, selectively choosing formal and thematic strategies according to their personal and regional objectives. After their return home these avant-garde artists disseminated the modern art trends they had encountered in Europe, which were subsequently transformed at the local level into new languages better suited to express the changes caused by urban growth, industrialization, and the political conditions of the various countries. For this reason, while the most important art movements in Latin America until the 1950s were linked to modern art trends in Europe, these trends did not fully determine art developments in Latin America: they were also shaped by national, cultural, and historical circumstances. Therefore, modern movements such as Impressionism and Surrealism must be considered not only in respect to their European history but also in terms of the Latin American context in which they continued to develop.

After the 1950s many Latin American artists began to travel to the United States, especially to New York, which during the 1940s had become the new center of international modernism. Movements such as **abstract art,** Neofiguration, **Conceptual Art, Installation Art, and Performance Art,** and Neo-Expressionism are international expressions with important developments not only in the United States and Europe but also in Latin America, since artists from Latin America were often instrumental in the initial formulation of these styles.

In general terms, the first modernists in Latin America used typical vanguardist tactics in order to disseminate their ideas and defend them from the attacks of older established artists: they formed cohesive groups that often included artists, writers, and in some cases musicians and architects; they published aggressive manifestos and magazines attacking both the status quo and other avant-garde groups; and they held exhibitions and regular meetings where new strategies were planned. The first modern trends to appear in Central America, Mexico, and the Caribbean at the turn of the century were Impressionism, Post-Impressionism, and **Symbolist Art,** introduced by several artists who had studied in Europe or with artists trained in Europe, such as the Mexicans Alfredo Ramos Martínez, Joaquín Clausell, Julio Ruelas, and **Saturnino Herrán;** the Puerto Ricans Francisco Oller and **Miguel Pou;** and the Cubans Víctor Manuel García and Antonio Gattorno, both leading members of the Generation of 1927. Their rebellious rejection of the outdated but still dominant late-academic schools paved the way for later avant-garde developments, especially in Mexico.

After the initial break with Impressionism and Symbolist Art during the years of the **Mexican Revolution,** nonacademic styles continued to appear in the work of several Mexican artists, such as **José Guadalupe Posada**'s popular illustrations and **Dr. Atl**'s Post-Impressionist landscapes of Mexico, as well as **Francisco Goitia**'s and **José Clemente Orozco**'s expressionist depictions of the war. After the revolutionary war the administration of Alvaro Obregón actively supported **Muralism,** perhaps the most influential of the avant-garde movements that emerged in Latin America during the 1920s. Like many of their Latin American counterparts, leading muralists such as **Jean Charlot,** Orozco, **Diego Rivera,** and **David Alfaro Siqueiros** had been abroad and worked with avant-garde styles connected to Expressionism and post-Cubist figuration. On the walls of public buildings made available to them by the government, these artists created a new image of Mexico, one that proposed a more inclusive national identity in accordance with the principles of **Indigenism.**

Muralism has often overshadowed the activities of **Estridentismo,** a parallel avant-garde movement during the 1920s. Under the leadership of Mexican poet Manuel Maples Arce, several writers and artists, such as Charlot and Ramón Alva de la Canal, worked together to produce an art that was revolutionary both in form and content. Their emphasis on formal experimentation is also found in the work of **Amelia Peláez,** one of the pioneers of the introduction of modern art into Cuba during the 1930s. She developed a personal variety of synthetic Cubism, one that challenged the dominant academic tradition. Although Peláez worked in relative isolation, she joined the ranks of the Cuban intelligentsia in their active support for modern trends and their preference for Cuban themes. In spite of

El hombre en llamas (1938–1939; The Man in Flames) by José Clemente Orozco, the central fresco at the Hospicio Cabañas in Guadalajara

their efforts, most Cuban artists, like most artists in the Central American countries, adopted slightly modernized figurative modes while concentrating on landscapes and sugarcoated picturesque scenes, until the 1950s.

During the 1930s Muralism and its emphasis on Indigenism began to spread throughout the Americas, exerting a considerable influence in Guatemala through the paintings of **Carlos Mérida** and in Costa Rica through the sculptures of **Francisco Zúñiga,** as well as in El Salvador. Muralism also influenced the **graphic art** produced in Mexico during the 1930s and 1940s, especially that of the Taller de Gráfica Popular, whose members focused on Mexican themes. Inspired by the earlier graphic tradition of Posada, the Taller brought about a renaissance in the graphic arts, with far-reaching consequences, since it influenced the graphic work of Puerto Rican artists during the 1950s and of Chicano artists after the 1960s. Once Muralism and Indigenism achieved official status as the School of Mexico, several important artists working there during the 1930s and 1940s, such as **Rufino Tamayo** and Carlos Mérida, challenged the ideological and thematic parameters of this dominant school by instead advocating thematic freedom and formal experimentation. A second alternative to Muralism was offered by **Surrealism,** which during this period produced important and complex developments in Mexico and throughout Latin America. There were two different groups of Surrealists in Mexico: artists working independently, such as **Lola Alvarez Bravo, Mario Alvarez Bravo, María Izquierdo,** and **Frida Kahlo,** and artists who had direct connections with Surrealism, including the exiled Europeans **Leonora Carrington** and **Remedios Varo.** Although most Mexican artists traditionally associated with Surrealism developed independently of this movement, their work often featured odd visual juxtapositions while also emphasizing fantasy and dreamlike imagery. Many of these artists were included in the Exposición Internacional del Surrealismo, held in Mexico City in 1940. In the Caribbean, the Cuban **Wifredo Lam** became one of the leading forces in the second generation of Surrealists. He formulated a masterly synthesis of African and Cuban elements with modern styles, including Cubism and Surrealism. Later contemporary artists connected with Surrealism include the Guatemalan **Rodolfo Abularach** and the Mexican **Alberto Gironella.**

Although the preeminence of Muralism began to be challenged in the 1950s, its emphasis on art as a vehicle for political and social commentary was continued by the series of graphic-arts movements in Mexico mentioned earlier and others that emerged in the Caribbean. During the 1950s the development of printmaking in Puerto Rico was initially tied to official public-service campaigns, which relied on **posters** produced by artists hired by the state-supported Taller de Artes Gráficas (Graphic Arts Workshop), whose aim was to convey information about health, political, educational, and cultural issues. Graphic artists such as **Lorenzo Homar,** Rafael Tufiño, and **Carlos Raquel Rivera,** who belonged to the Generation of 1950, favored national and political themes and the use of more-traditional figurative modes over avant-garde styles, which they considered to be a form of U.S. cultural colonialism. The following generation of graphic artists, with **Myrna Báez** as a leading figure, adopted more avant-garde styles while continuing to work with national themes. In Cuba the postrevolutionary administration of **Fidel Castro** also encouraged the development of poster making after the mid 1960s. Cuban printmakers such as Raúl Martínez and Alfredo J. González Rostgaard synthesized eclectic avant-garde styles, including Pop Art, into new ways of expressing

cultural, social, and political contents, achieving a high degree of visual sophistication and winning international acclaim.

The figurative tendencies of Regionalism, Indigenism, and Muralism lost their dominance in Mexico, Central America, and the Caribbean during the 1950s with the emergence of abstract modes, especially Informal Abstraction, which artists considered a more international visual language. They were also encouraged to turn to abstraction by the attention given to abstract works in international art contests and exhibitions, often sponsored by multinational corporations seeking to expand U.S. influence. While abstract modes have received broad support in South America, fewer artists have worked in these styles in the northern regions of Latin America. In Puerto Rico most artists rejected abstraction in favor of figurative modes and regional and social themes, but in the 1960s several important artists turned to abstraction, including Julio Suárez, **Rafael Ferrer, Luis Hernández Cruz,** and **Olga Albizu.** Seeking creative freedom and a more sympathetic public for their avant-garde art, many of these abstractionists settled in New York or lived there for extended periods. In Cuba abstract art emerged through the activities of the groups Los Once (The Eleven), active during the early 1950s, and Pintores Concretos (Concrete Painters), working during the 1960s. Abstract artists such as Hugo Consuegra, Sandú Darié, and Luis Martínez Pedro rejected the sentimental nationalism of early regionalist styles and were instead in favor of Geometric and Informal Abstraction, which they considered free of state propaganda.

In Mexico during the late 1950s, a group of young avant-garde artists came to be called **La Ruptura** Generation (The Break), characterized by a search for greater artistic freedom and the denunciation of the propagandistic bent of Muralism and Indigenism, all of which provoked strong attacks by muralists such as Diego Rivera and David Alfaro Siqueiros and heated public debate. The generation of "The Break" included artists working with a variety of styles and aesthetic philosophies. Manuel Felguérez, Pedro Coronel, Vlady (Vladimir Kibalchich Rusakov), Vicente Rojo, and Gunther Gerzso, among others, worked with different modes of abstract art, including Geometric Abstraction and Informal Abstraction. On the other hand, Arnold Belkin, Rafael Coronel, Francisco Corzas, **José Luis Cuevas,** Alberto Gironella, Leonel Góngora, and Francisco Icaza, all members of the **Nueva Presencia** group, rejected abstraction in favor of Neofiguration, a type of expressionist figurative art inspired by the philosophy of existentialism.

In Central America most artists interested in abstract art did not completely abandon figuration; in their works they often combined figurative references with Informal Abstraction, which was the dominant abstract mode. In Guatemala the interest in abstract art appeared first in the work of the members of the Generation of 1940, who struggled to open Guatemalan art to more-international trends. Similarly, in Nicaragua during the 1960s, several artists combined diverse aspects of Informal Abstraction with subtle figurative and thematic references. Abstract art was introduced by the avant-garde Galería Praxis, which also supported the politics of the Sandinista National Liberation Front, resulting in the imprisonment, torture, and exile of several of its members by the Anastasio Somoza regime. An important Nicaraguan artist who explored abstraction was **Armando Morales,** who soon achieved international recognition. In the 1970s and 1980s the work of the Praxis gallery was continued by other institutions, such as the Galería Fernando Gordillo run by the ASTC (Sandinista Union of Cultural Workers). The Sandinista government's strong support of cultural developments, including an important mural movement, infused the art scene with a renewed sense of dynamism and interest in issues of cultural identity and popular outreach. **Manuel de la Cruz González** was among the first artists to introduce abstraction in Costa Rica in the late 1950s. In 1961 the Grupo Ocho (Group Eight) was formed, including Cruz González and other abstract artists who had studied abroad. Although this group dominated the local art scene during the 1960s and early 1970s, many critics believe it failed to produce an art linked to Costa Rican cultural reality.

During the 1970s figurative modes became prevalent again in Mexico through the work of several artists connected with the so-called School of Oaxaca, such as **Francisco Toledo.** Oaxacan artists favored figurative styles and myth-inspired themes often related to **Magical Realism,** a label that has also been applied to some of the art produced by the Nicaraguan artist Armando Morales. In Puerto Rico different modes of figurative graphic art and painting continued to thrive, while in Cuba artists such as Flavio Garciandía and Tomás Sánchez, concerned with issues of nationality and cultural identity, concentrated on Photo-realism after the mid 1970s. This last style of painting, related to the **testimonial** aesthetic developed in literature, allowed artists to explore popular images, which later became important in the development of Conceptual Art, Installation Art, and Performance Art in Cuba. These modes of radical art, which utilized unorthodox materials and popular images as media for ideological or intellectual commentary, began emerging throughout the United States, Europe, and Latin America in the 1960s and gave rise to some

of the most important contributions to modern art in the latter part of the century.

The most significant developments in Conceptual Art, Installation Art, and Performance Art in Mexico, Central America, and the Caribbean have been in the work of Cubans such as **Ana Mendieta** and **José Bedia.** While Mendieta for the most part worked independently in the United States, Bedia was a leading participant in Volume I, a controversial group of young avant-garde artists who during the 1980s broke with the art of the past and paved the way for radical art modes involving popular art, kitsch, ethnic identity, and other cultural issues. Outside Cuba important conceptual and installation artists include the Puerto Rican Rafael Ferrer (who created several groundbreaking installations in New York in the late 1960s and early 1970s) and the Mexicans Felipe Ehrenberg (who has worked with conceptual installations since the 1970s) and Guillermo Gómez Peña (whose performances have addressed U.S.–Mexican border issues).

In recent years figuration in Latin America has received a new impulse though the work of artists using Neo-Expressionist modes, such as the Cuban **Luis Cruz Azaceta,** the Puerto Rican **Arnaldo Roche Rabell,** and the Mexican **Rocío Maldonado.** Through their bold figurative style, characterized by strong colors, loose brush work, and an emphasis on texture, these artists explore issues of colonialism, violence, and sexual freedom. Azaceta and Roche have developed a lasting interest in self-portraiture, reviving a tradition that also has important examples in the art of other Latin American painters, such as the Mexicans Frida Kahlo, José Luis Cuevas, and **Nahum Zenil.** Both Maldonado and Zenil belong to a loosely organized group of contemporary Mexican artists called the Neo-Mexicanists. Like other members of the group, they question broader traditional cultural and sexual attitudes, signaling a return to ideological issues in Mexican art.

REFERENCES:

Dawn Ades, *Art in Latin America: The Modern Era, 1820–1980* (New Haven & London: Yale University Press, 1989);

Luis R. Cancel and others, *The Latin American Spirit: Art and Artists in the United States, 1920–1970* (New York: Bronx Museum of the Arts/Abrams, 1988);

Gilbert Chase, *Contemporary Art in Latin America: Painting, Graphic Art, Sculpture and Architecture* (New York: Free Press / London: Collier-Macmillan, 1970);

Waldo Rassmusen, Fatima Bercht, Elizabeth Ferrer, eds., *Latin American Artists of the Twentieth Century* (New York: Museum of Modern Art, 1993).

— F.B.N.

MIGUEL ANGEL ASTURIAS

Miguel Angel Asturias (1899–1974) was born and raised in Guatemala City with a three-year interlude at his grandparents' ranch in Salamá, Baja Verapaz. In 1922 he helped found the "Popular University" of Guatemala. In 1923 he was awarded a degree based on his dissertation "The Social Problems of the Indian," a study that has been harshly criticized for its negative stereotyping of the Mayas. His later works, however, indicate that his perspective had changed. Asturias spent ten years in Europe studying and writing, influenced by the pre-Columbian mythology of his homeland and the Parisian surrealist trends in vogue at the time. His first book, *Leyendas de Guatemala* (1930; translated as *Legends of Guatemala*), combines the lessons of the ancient Mayan Book of Counsel, the *Popol Vuh,* with a magical, surrealist vision, a combination that gives Asturias's writings a unique character. He returned to Guatemala in 1933 (shortly after the dictator Jorge Ubico closed the Popular University that Asturias had helped to found) and then served the revolutionary government of Juan José Arévalo in 1945, as cultural ambassador to Mexico. There he published his best-known novel, *El señor presidente* (1946; translated as *Señor President*). Later he moved to Buenos Aires, where he also served as cultural attaché. In 1949 he published his masterpiece, *Hombres de maíz* (translated as *Men of Maize*), and in 1950 *Viento fuerte* (translated as *Strong Wind* and as *The Cyclone*), one of three novels, called the banana trilogy, that detail the impact of the United Fruit Company on the Guatemalan people. Asturias's brief service as ambassador to El Salvador (1953–1954) was interrupted when Arévalo's successor, President Jacobo Arbenz, was overthrown in a CIA-led coup that installed the dictatorship of Col. Carlos Castillo Armas, who deprived Asturias of his Guatemalan citizenship. For the next five years Asturias lived in exile in South America. During that period he published several novels, of which the most important are the second of his banana trilogy, *El papa verde* (1954; translated as *Green Pope*), and *Week-end en Guatemala* (1956). Allowed back into Guatemala in 1959, he published the third book of his banana trilogy, *Los ojos de los enterrados* (1960; translated as *The Eyes of the Interred*), and *El alhajadito* (1961; translated as *The Bejeweled Boy*). He then traveled throughout Europe, and in 1963 he published *Mulata de tal* (The Hybrid Mulatta), a novel that is based on a popular Maya Quiché folktale about a man who sells his wife to the devil and then must pay the consequences. Asturias also published a travel book on Romania, various plays, poetry, and essays. He was awarded the Lenin Peace Prize in 1966 and was named ambassador to France in the same year. In 1967 Asturias became the second Latin American writer to receive the Nobel Prize for Literature.

El señor presidente is most often classified as a **dictatorship novel,** a thematic genre that dates back to the nineteenth century and that saw a revival in the 1970s. The president of the title of Asturias's novel is an evil, omnipresent being with absolute power, one who controls through fear. He knows everything and, with indifference or sadistic pleasure, orders the imprisonment, torture, and death of hapless victims. The plot is complex and contains numerous subplots with seemingly unrelated characters; however, they form a collage of largely weak, greedy, corrupt, and grotesque personages, reflecting the corrosion of a society dominated by terror. A few individuals stand out for their refusal to become accomplices in the president's brutal manipulation of his subjects; they invariably are broken, imprisoned, tortured, and murdered. At this level the president emerges as the victor. On a metaphysical level, however, the main plot of the novel may be read as the struggle between life and death. Miguel Cara de Angel ("Angel Face"), the dictator's favorite henchman, falls in love with the daughter of one of the president's intended victims. Love transforms him and operates as a vital force that opposes the president's power of death, ultimately converting Miguel into the president's antagonist. The final confrontation between the two becomes an enactment of Maya Quiché mythology: the president is seen as Tohil, the rain god who demands human sacrifice, and Miguel Cara de Angel is represented by the hunters about to be sacrificed. Since the latter symbolize fertility, the encounter is between life forces and death. Although Miguel Cara de Angel pays with his life for his disloyalty, his son lives on to represent the love that redeemed him, and in this sense he triumphs over the president's bloodthirsty agenda. In *El señor presidente* Asturias uses an omniscient narrator who, like the president, knows and sees all but does not reveal everything. Therefore, the reader becomes involved in deciphering the various psychological dimensions of the characters as they interact in their social milieu. The novel is a ruthless portrayal of life under a vicious dictatorship, but it is more than that: the power of the narrative imagination is reflected in an onomatopoeic, melodious language laden with metaphors, neologisms, regionalisms, and oral vulgarities spoken by some of the more-crass characters. This rich poetic language transforms some of the harshest elements into another reality; hence the interplay between conscious reality and the subconscious revealed in dreams and nightmares, stream of consciousness, fantasies, memories, sensations, and a mythological world. The interaction between light and dark imagery reflects the forces of good and evil, life and death, linking space and time to an infernal world controlled by a terrifying dictatorship. Today *El señor presidente* continues to be popular, not least because its subject matter reflects continuing Latin American realities.

Asturias's other masterpiece is *Hombres de maíz,* despite a complex, seemingly disorganized structure that renders it almost incoherent to the lay reader. An underlying narrative thread based on Mayan and Aztec mythology connects the different sections in the novel. The title is taken from the Mayan myth of creation related in the *Popol Vuh,* which depicts the failures of the gods in their efforts to create human beings, until they choose maize as the primary element from which to mold them. (Hence the importance of corn as a source of physical and spiritual nourishment to the Mayan peoples). The first part of the novel portrays the struggle of the Mayas to preserve their culture, refusing to grow corn for commercial purposes. It details the struggle between a Mayan warrior and the military, the betrayal of the warrior by his own people, and the repercussions of the curse imposed by Mayan sorcerers on the betrayers and their offspring. The second part describes the trials of a blind man searching for his wife who has deserted him, a story that reappears in the third part as a popular, legendary tale. The third section, intertwined with pieces of the first and second, is the most complex. In it the main character also loses his wife and in his searchings for her encounters spirits that perhaps represent his subconscious and that lead him into an underworld populated by past and future figures, including the warrior of the first section. During this journey he occasionally assumes the form of a coyote, his animal spirit; (the Mayas believe that human beings have another animal form that represents their true nature). In the end, characters of different sections encounter each other, and the various myths are linked to the betrayal and curse imposed by the sorcerers in the first part, lending the novel the unity that it seems to lack at first glance. *Hombres de maíz* is a novel replete with legendary folktales, Indian myths, and surrealist visions that give it a dreamlike quality; many of the scenes are described in a magical manner, blending the imaginary with the real. This novel, like most of Asturias's works, portrays Latin American realities in a unique way, reflecting diverse ethnic and mythical interpretations of epic and daily phenomena.

REFERENCES:

Giuseppe Bellini, *La narrativa de Miguel Angel Asturias* (Buenos Aires: Losada, 1969);

Richard Callan, *Miguel Angel Asturias* (Boston: Twayne, 1970);

René Prieto, *Miguel Angel Asturias' Archaeology of Return* (Cambridge: Cambridge University Press, 1993).

—M.E.S.

DR. ATL

The politically active Dr. Atl (born Gerardo Murillo, 1875–1964) was among the first proponents of a national mural movement in Mexico. Murillo studied at the Instituto Nacional de Bellas Artes (National Institute of Fine Arts) in Mexico City, and in 1897 he received a grant to study philosophy and law in Rome, where he became interested in politics and participated in student revolts and popular strikes in 1900. The following year he worked on two mural projects in Rome and Paris and became one of the first modern Mexican mural painters. Murillo returned to Mexico in 1903 and was appointed professor at the Bellas Artes school. In 1910 he organized an exhibition of Mexican painters and publicly supported the idea of establishing a national school of mural art. To this effect he created a Centro Artístico (Art Center), and for it he obtained a commission to decorate the walls of the Anfiteatro Bolívar at the Escuela Nacional Preparatoria (National Preparatory School). The outbreak of the **Mexican Revolution,** however, halted the project. Murillo, who was popular among the students, supported the 1911 student strike against the outdated teaching methods and academicism of the Escuela Nacional de Bellas Artes.

Murillo returned to Paris in 1911 to study volcanology; there he came into contact with socialist and communist intellectual circles that followed the thinking of Jean Jaurès, who believed that a middle-class urban intelligentsia should take over leadership of society and the socialist movement. Murillo changed his name to Dr. Atl ("atl" meaning "water" in Nahuatl, one of Mexico's indigenous languages) and helped Mexican revolutionaries, including **José Vasconcelos,** in their attempt to win support for Venustiano Carranza. Later Dr. Atl returned to Mexico to join Carranza's forces as head of propaganda. He and other artists and intellectuals were forced to flee to Orizaba when Mexico City was occupied by Pancho Villa's forces. At Orizaba, Dr. Atl set up a printing press at the Church of La Soledad and began issuing pro-Carranza publications, such as *Acción Mundial* and the newspaper *La Vanguardia,* with the collaboration of Ramón Alva de la Canal, **Francisco Goitia, David Alfaro Siqueiros** (who was a captain in Carranza's army), and **José Clemente Orozco.** In 1916 Dr. Atl left Mexico for political reasons, and he stayed in California until 1920.

Alvaro Obregón's administration reestablished peace, and in 1920 Vasconcelos, who had become minister of education, appointed Dr. Atl director of the Department of Fine Arts. Dr. Atl received a mural commission at the Colegio Máximo de San Pedro y San Pablo, together with Xavier Guerrero and Roberto

Self-portrait (1938) by Dr. Atl (from Helen MacKinley, *Modern Mexican Painters*, 1941)

Montenegro (1921–1922). He was also requested to undertake a complete survey of popular arts, which resulted in his book *Las artes populares en México* (1921; Mexican Popular Arts) and in his organization of the first exhibition of this type of art in Mexico; he also founded the Comité Nacional de las Artes Populares. During the 1920s and 1930s, Dr. Atl continued to study and paint images of volcanoes. He also wrote several books about art and volcanology, as well as a series of profascist articles. In the 1940s he produced his best-known images of volcanoes in a style that shares the emphasis on light effects of **Impressionism** and the boldness of the colors and fluidity of the lines of Post-Impressionism. In paintings such as *Amanecer en las montañas* (1940; Dawn in the Mountains), Dr. Atl used a special kind of homemade oil crayon he invented. In 1958 he exhibited a series of *aeropaisajes* (air-landscapes) featuring views of nature seen from the air, such as *Los volcanes* (1950; The Volcanoes).

REFERENCE:

Arturo Casado Navarro, *Gerardo Murillo, el Dr. Atl* (Mexico City: Universidad Nacional Autónoma de México, 1984).

— F.B.N.

ARTURO AZUELA

Born in Mexico City in 1938, Arturo Azuela is part of a long literary tradition continuing through generations in his family and including **Mariano Azuela,** author of *Los de abajo* (1915; translated as *The Underdogs*), one of the most celebrated novels of the **Mexican Revolu-**

tion. Arturo Azuela, however, did not respond to a literary calling until late in life. He studied at the National Autonomous University of Mexico, where he became a professor of mathematics and the history of science. He was also a musician and a journalist and published many articles on his academic specialties. In Mexico City Azuela helped found a group called Literary Encounters, which annually sponsored an international book fair. He held many prestigious positions, such as those of president of the Association of Mexican Writers, literary director of the National Institute of Fine Arts, and president of the Latin American Confederation of Writers.

In Azuela's novels a commonly recurring theme is a concern for diverse social conditions in Mexico City, often linked to the complex process of urbanization. *El tamaño del infierno* (1973; The Size of Hell), which narrates the story of a family's search for the promised land in urban Mexico City following the revolution, received the Xavier Villaurrutia Prize in 1974. *Un tal José Salomé* (1975; One José Salomé) weaves a different tale: a small town bordering the capital is consumed by the process of urban expansion. Azuela received the Premio Nacional de la Novela de México in 1980 for his novel on the 1968 massacre of protesters in **Tlatelolco,** *Manifestación de silencios* (1979; translated as *Shadows of Silence: A Novel*). *La casa de las mil vírgenes* (1983; The House of the Thousand Virgins) reveals the author's continued preoccupation with social issues in Mexico City. In addition to his urban concerns, Azuela continually stressed the need for dialogue between Spanish-language writers, regardless of nationality or ideology.

REFERENCE:

Reinhard Teichmann, *De la Onda en adelante: Conversaciones con novelistas mexicanos* (Mexico: Posada, 1987).

— M.T.

MARIANO AZUELA

Known as the initiator of the novel of the **Mexican Revolution,** Mariano Azuela (1873–1952) was born in Lagos de Moreno in the state of Jalisco. His father was a land proprietor of modest means, and Mariano Azuela spent his childhood fluctuating between the town and his father's ranch outside it. Azuela received a medical degree in Guadalajara in 1899 and practiced medicine until 1911, when he was named political chief of Lagos de Moreno. When in 1912 the country disintegrated into various revolutionary factions vying for power, Azuela served as medic to a band of revolutionaries. Later he fled with the troops to Ciudad Juárez and then on his own to El Paso to escape the onslaught of an opposing revolutionary group. During this period, in the heat, confusion, and violence of a revolution out of control, he wrote his most famous novel, *Los de abajo* (1915; translated as *The Underdogs*). It was first published in serial form in the Spanish newspaper *El Paso del Norte* in late 1915 but did not gain critical acclaim until 1924–1925, when a literary polemic in Mexico propelled Azuela and the novel into the limelight. Returning to Mexico City in 1916, Azuela spent the rest of his life practicing medicine and writing. He won various national honors, including the prestigious National Prize for Sciences and Arts in 1942. He was buried in the Rotunda de Hombres Ilustres (The Rotunda of Distinguished Men).

Azuela's works include theater, biography, criticism, short stories, and novels and may be divided into several phases. The first includes works written before and during the revolution; among them are *María Luisa* (1907), *Los fracasados* (1908; The Failed Ones), and his better works of that period: *Mala yerba* (1909; Weeds), *Los de abajo*, *Los caciques* (1917; The Chieftains), *Las moscas* (1918; The Flies), and *Las tribulaciones de una familia decente* (1919; The Tribulations of a Proper Family). The second stage of Azuela's literary production was influenced by vanguardist movements; it includes *La malhora* (1923; The Bad Hour), *El desquite* (1925; Retaliation) and *La luciérnaga* (1932; The Glowworm), which is considered one of his best novels. The third period is marked by political satire and criticism of people in power as a result of the Mexican Revolution; *El camarada Pantoja* (1937; Comrade Pantoja) and *Nueva burguesía* (1941; The New Bourgeoisie) reflect Azuela's disillusionment with the revolution. Also included in this last phase are *La mujer domada* (1946; The Tamed Woman), *Sendas perdidas* (1949; Lost Paths), *La maldición* (1955; The Curse), and *Esa sangre* (1956; That Blood).

Los de abajo, the most important novel of the Mexican Revolution, adopts the point of view of the underprivileged — the underdogs. Azuela portrays the revolution as a whirlpool that carries everyone away in its eddies of passion, greed, violence, fury, and loathing. In a direct, harsh, and dramatic style Azuela depicts the battles, the looting, the drunken orgies, the rape of women and villages, the casual killing of human beings, and the corruption at all levels of the revolution in its most violent period during the second de-

Mariano Azuela accepting the Premio Nacional de Letras from President Miguel Alemán of Mexico, 1946

cade of the twentieth century. His characters include greedy, violent thieves; self-serving, cynical intellectuals; passionate, jealous men and women; and dreamy idealists. Most of them do not know or care why they are fighting; they have been personally caught up in the intensity of the moment and are unable to stop. Azuela's style is colorful, almost cinematic, painting a mural of individuals and masses in uncontrollable movement. Through ample use of dialogue the personalities of the characters emerge, giving the impression of authentic, psychological depictions of real people in a historic struggle. As a realistic portrait of a revolutionary struggle that reveals the weaknesses, uncertainties, and dilemmas of the participants-characters, the novel has wide appeal and has been translated into numerous languages. *Los de abajo* and his other works make Mariano Azuela one of the most important novelists of Mexico.

REFERENCES:

Stanley Linn Robe, *Azuela and the Mexican Underdogs* (Berkeley: University of California Press, 1979);

Jorge Ruffinelli, *Literatura e ideología: El primer Mariano Azuela, (1896–1918)* (Mexico City: Premia Editora, 1982).

— M.E.S.

B

Myrna Báez

Myrna Báez González (1931–), one of the most important painters and graphic artists of Puerto Rico, is part of a generation of artists who reached artistic maturity during the 1960s. Báez shared her contemporaries' interest in working with more avant-garde styles, as well as their nationalistic opposition to U.S. cultural colonialism, in spite of the fact that her independence-oriented political activism at times had negative repercussions on her employment. Báez studied art in Spain and the United States, acquiring technical virtuosity in many different painting and **graphic art** techniques, such as airbrush, linocut, intaglio, lithography, collography, and silk-screening. In 1957 she joined the Ateneo Puertorriqueño (a cultural association), later becoming one of its officials. She also studied in the Taller de Artes Gráficas (Graphic Arts Workshop) of the Instituto de Cultura Puertorriqueña, directed by **Lorenzo Homar,** a man whose pro-independence orientation and interest in regional themes influenced her art. In the late 1950s and early 1960s Báez produced several landscapes of her native island, such as the print *Yunque II* (1958; Anvil II), as a symbolic affirmation of Puerto Rican culture. During the 1960s Báez changed to a more abstract conception of form and color, turning from realism to an expressionist figuration centered on the human figure. Soon she began to include different textures and figurative styles within the same image, as in *Juego de cartas* (1971; Card Game). In this color print she combines several lacelike patterns with a realistic depiction of the playing cards and an expressionistic representation of the two women playing. Báez experimented with the location of the figures in the picture field, arranging them in opposite directions, as on a face card. In other works she also experimented with placing large figures in constricted spaces or cutting them off with the frame.

El juez (1970; The Judge) by Myrna Báez (Museo de Antropología, Historia y Arte, Universidad de Puerto Rico, Recinto Río Piedras)

During the 1970s and 1980s Báez explored the psychological effects in and of her work. For instance, the painting *El marco dorado* (1982; The Golden Frame) suggests a mysterious and hidden narrative through a complex interplay of gazes, including those of the real observers, the depicted viewer (who is looking at himself in a mirror), and the female model reflected in the mirror. Another group of Báez's works produced during this period deals with images inspired by the history of art and comments on the fact that most Latin Americans learn about European art through reproductions. In prints such as *La Gioconda* (1973) Báez examines the perception of art as a secondhand image while at the same time claiming her right to inherit and continue the tradition of Western art. By the end of the 1970s Báez began to produce works in a style that can be described as lyric, often dealing with the position of women in art. In her silk screen *Georgia O'Keeffe en Puerto Rico* (1980; Georgia O'Keeffe in Puerto Rico), Báez depicts a vast view of the southern desertlike seascape of the island, achieved through an abstract combination of light colors with different textures. In the midst of the empty space stands the small figure of O'Keeffe, an admirer of desert lands and a female artist like Báez herself.

REFERENCE:

Tres décadas gráficas de Myrna Báez, 1958–1988: Exposición Homenaje, VIII Bienal de San Juan del Grabado Latinoamericano y del Caribe (San Juan: Museo de Arte de Puerto Rico, Instituto de Cultura Puertorriqueña, 1988).

— F.B.N.

BALLET INDEPENDIENTE

The Ballet Independiente of Mexico is one of only three contemporary dance companies supported entirely by the government. (The others are the **Ballet Nacional de México** and **Ballet Teatro del Espacio**.) The Ballet Independiente was founded in 1966 by Raúl Flores Canelo, who had studied with **Guillermina Bravo**, José Limón, and Anna Sokolow and danced with the Ballet Nacional de México; his desire was to break with the solemnity he felt was overtaking Mexican contemporary dance. Along with works by such foreign choreographers as Sokolow and Tim Wengerd of the United States and Graciela Henríquez of Venezuela, thirty of Flores Canelo's choreographies form the core activity of the Ballet Independiente. The company includes an influential school and sponsors a choreography competition. After the death of Flores Canelo, Manuel Hiram assumed the positions of artistic director and lighting designer. Both Flores Canelo and Hiram won the highest distinction in Mexican dance, the José Limón Prize, awarded by the government of the state of Sinaloa in conjunction with the Instituto Nacional de Bellas Artes.

— J.M.H.

BALLET NACIONAL DE CUBA

The Cuban National Ballet Company was founded by **Alberto, Alicia, and Fernando Alonso** in 1948 as an offshoot of the Sociedad Pro-Arte Musical of Havana. The company, together with its sister company, the Ballet de Camagüey (founded in 1967), has premiered more than four hundred works, more than half of them by Cuban choreographers. According to prima ballerina Alicia Alonso, a main objective of the company was to respectfully present the great works of the past while recognizing the different needs of twentieth-century artists and audiences. Resulting from this perspective is the company's other principal objective: to present works reflecting the contemporary human condition in its individual and collective manifestations.

The company achieved world-class stature after receiving the imprimatur of **Fidel Castro**'s revolutionary government in 1959. Shortly after the Cuban Revolution, Castro visited the Ballet Nacional studios to consider Alberto Alonso's request for $100,000. Castro was sympathetic to the company's goal of incorporating poor, rural children with no previous access to the arts into the school's training programs, and he liked its plan to use Alicia Alonso's worldwide prestige to represent Cuban excellence in dance on the stages of the world. Reportedly, Castro doubled the sum Alberto Alonso had requested, confident that the company would lend prestige to the Cuban Revolution as one of its flagship enterprises.

One of the Ballet Nacional's aims was to express Cuban social reality through dance, and a means of doing so was the creation in 1975 of the Choreographic Workshop to train the company's dancers in choreography. A measure of the company's success is the fact that it has performed in more than twenty countries of Asia, Europe, and the Americas. It has won the Grand Prix de la Ville de Paris twice, as well as the Anna Pavlova and the Estrella de Oro prizes. Its versions of classical ballets have been staged for national and world-class companies. Despite its international stature, the company has always striven for a distinctive Cuban identity, which is achieved and maintained by the use of Cuban choreographers, legends, popular dances, painting, music, and other elements. At the same time, the company accepts universal aesthetic forms or standards, as exemplified by its adherence to the classical ballet vocabulary and its use of the music conventionally used by ballet choreographers.

Another spin-off of the Ballet Nacional is the Ballet Santiago de Cuba, founded in eastern Cuba in 1990. The three companies share teachers, repertory, and curriculum and depend equally on government support. Two were founded in smaller cities than Havana to ensure that, as far as possible and in keeping with the goals of the revolution, art reached all the people.

REFERENCE:

Jorge A. González, "Apuntes para la historia del ballet en Cuba," *Revista de música*, 2 (October 1961): 228–248.

—J.M.H.

Ballet Teatro del Espacio

The Ballet Teatro del Espacio, founded in 1977, is one of only three contemporary dance companies supported entirely by the Mexican government. (The others are the **Ballet Nacional de México** and **Ballet Independiente.**) It was founded by the dancer-choreographers Gladiola Orozco and Michel Descombey, both of whom were early directors of Ballet Independiente; Descombey had also been a director of the Paris Opera Ballet. Ballet Teatro del Espacio is known for combining a high technical level derived from a classical ballet base with a distinctive critical voice that frequently protests against social and cultural realities. The company maintains its own school and theater in a residential area in the center of Mexico City.

REFERENCE:

Alberto Dallal, *La danza en México en el siglo XX* (Mexico City: Consejo Nacional para la Cultura y las Artes, 1994).

—J.M.H.

Miguel Barnet

Miguel Barnet

Born into a wealthy, white family in Havana, Miguel Barnet (1940–) became interested in black ethnographic studies at an early age. His interest intensified after he met **Fernando Ortiz,** the renowned ethnologist who stimulated interest in Afro-Cuban studies. For six years Barnet, still a young man, studied Afro-Cuban folklore with a focus on religion. During this period he met Esteban Montejo, a 105-year-old former slave who became the source for Barnet's best-known book, *Biografía de un cimarrón* (1966; translated as *The Autobiography of a Runaway Slave*). In this book Montejo narrates his life as a plantation slave, his experience as a runaway hiding in the forest, what life was like after the abolition of slavery when the oppressed conditions for black Cubans largely remained the same, and his own participation in the war to free Cuba from Spanish colonial domination (1895–1898). Montejo's remarkable memory provides invaluable and unusual insights into the life of a black slave, offering rich descriptions of African folklore, including feasts, religious beliefs, witchcraft, courtship rituals, dances, games, food, and drink. His own struggle for survival emerges as that of an isolated, strong individual who learned to trust only himself and preferred to be alone (although he spent various periods living with different women). Montejo's personal experience of what it was like to live as a slave in nineteenth-century Cuba makes *Biografía de un cimarrón* particularly significant.

While there are many slave narratives in the United States, *Biografía de un cimarrón* is one of only two such narratives known to exist in Cuba. (The other is Francisco Manzano's *Autobiography,* which was published by the English abolitionist Richard Madden in England in 1840; in Cuba it was not published until 1937.) Although it received little attention initially, *Biografía de un cimarrón* was eventually acclaimed by the critics and recognized as an invaluable anthropological document that added significantly to an otherwise unbalanced view of history that generally presented only the point of view of the white people. As reflected in the Spanish and English titles, it has been regarded as an autobiography and as a biography, as historical fiction and as documentary. It is best classified as a **testimonial** novel, a genre that gives voice to the unprivileged. Questions of authorial intervention have arisen, and in his introduction Barnet openly explains the editing techniques he employed to make Montejo's life story chronological, less repetitive, and more accessible to the reader. One may conclude, then, that *Biografía de un cimarrón* is the product of a collaboration between Montejo and Barnet. The narrative inspired a dramatic, operatic monologue written by the Swiss composer Hans Werner Henze.

Barnet has written three other life histories that are not as highly regarded as Montejo's story. They are *Canción de Rachel* (1970; Rachel's Song), the story of a music-hall performer; *Gallego* (1981; The Galician), which narrates the experiences of a Galician immigrant to Cuba; and *La vida real* (1986; Real Life), the life of a Cuban who immigrated to New York. He has also written various articles dealing with documentary literature and black culture.

REFERENCES:

Alistair Hennessy, "Introduction and Bibliographical Essay," in *The Autobiography of a Runaway Slave,* by Miguel Barnet and Esteban Montejo (London: Macmillan, 1993);

William Luis, ed., *Literary Bondage: Slavery in Cuban Narrative* (Austin: University of Texas Press, 1990);

Elzbieta Sklodowska, *Testimonio hispanoamericano* (San Francisco: Peter Lang, 1992).

— M.E.S.

LUIS BARRAGÁN

Mexican architect Luis Barragán (1902–1988) was known primarily for his upscale single-family residential structures (see **Architecture**). In the late 1920s Barragán and three other architects from Guadalajara were known as the "Guadalajara Four." They were associated with the conservative Partido de Acción Nacional (National Action Party), which denounced the changes brought about by the **Mexican Revolution** and rejected **Indigenism,** which was then being institutionalized in Mexican art. However, Barragán was not antagonistic toward other cultural influences. His first period of study in Europe in 1925 led to interests in Islamic architecture, African art, and Art Deco, all of which influenced his neocolonial designs of the late 1920s and early 1930s. During the 1930s, after moving to Mexico City, Barragán adopted the style of Func-

tionalism, which was influenced as much by the promotion of rational and economic architecture by the administration of Lázaro Cárdenas as it was by De Stijl's aesthetics and Le Corbusier's design. At this time Barragán produced designs he believed were neither unique nor noteworthy and felt displeased with the constraints placed upon his work.

Barragán reached greater artistic maturity in his combined domestic architecture and residential urban planning, which together allowed him a greater freedom of design. His first widely acclaimed residential development was Los Jardines del Pedregal (begun in 1945). Although in the Pedregal Gardens Barragán followed Frank Lloyd Wright's concept of harmonizing architecture with the landscape, he rejected both Functionalism and International Style. Barragán, a deeply religious man, believed that residential architecture was only successful if it accomplished the spiritual mission of providing an atmosphere of serenity and intimacy. While International Style architecture prescribed walls of glass that visually opened the interior living space to the exterior landscape, Barragán preferred the inclusion of a central garden onto which interior spaces converged. The central garden and largely unfenestrated exterior walls were traditional design features extending back to ancient Mediterranean and Mesoamerican precedents. Such gardens were intended to foster thought and spirituality by providing an interior space sculpted by the changing patterns of light and shadow throughout the day. One of Barragán's masterpieces in Mexico City, the Casa Gilardi (1976; Gilardi House), is a particularly good example of his accommodation of monumental forms to a human scale as well as the transformation of colonial antecedents into modern forms. In this house as in others, by means of thick and textured walls, flat surfaces, an interplay of light and shadow, and a bold use of colors, Barragán evokes the sense of awe and mystery he felt as a child at colonial mission complexes.

REFERENCE:

Clive Bamford Smith, *Builders in the Sun: Five Mexican Architects* (New York: Architectural Book Publishing, 1967).

— C.M.

BARRO ROJO

Barro Rojo (Red Clay), a dance company founded in Mexico in 1982 at the Universidad Autónoma de Guerrero, was originally directed by the Ecuadoran choreographer Arturo Garrido. The university's philosophy at that time was that all of its offerings should relate to the needs of the common people; thus it is not surprising that Barro Rojo's first work, *El camino,* which won the National Dance Prize in 1982, deals with the struggle of the people in El Salvador. Barro Rojo's intention was always to fight elitism in Mexican dance and to provide career opportunities for dark-skinned people from poor neighborhoods. Another of its initial tenets, growing out of Mexico's history of folkloric dance, was to present contemporary dance in plazas, streets, atriums, fields, and even cemeteries. Its themes include revolutionary movements, homosexuality, and Mexican mythology. Barro Rojo later separated from the university and moved to Mexico City. The company is arguably Mexico's best-known and most firmly established independent group — in the sense that although it receives funds from the government, its salaries, rent, and production expenses are not entirely subsidized.

— J.M.H.

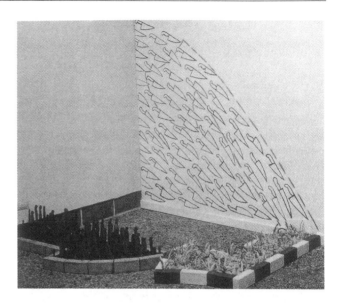

Sarabanda contra siete rayos (1985; Saraband against Seven Flashes of Lightning) by José Bedia, installation at the Amelie A. Wallace Gallery, State University of New York, Old Westbury

JOSÉ BEDIA

José Bedia Valdés (1959–) is a leading contemporary Cuban artist. He studied in Havana's Escuela de Artes Plásticas San Alejandro (San Alejandro School of Plastic Arts) and later at the Instituto Superior de Arte (Advanced Institute of Art). In 1981 he participated in a groundbreaking exhibition, Volume I, which signaled the emergence of a new avant-garde generation, the first in Cuba to have been educated entirely according to the revolutionary ideals of **Fidel Castro**'s government. Many of these young artists, including Bedia, worked with different types of radical art, such as **Conceptual Art, Installation Art, and Performance Art,** often exploring aspects of popular art and kitsch. Bedia's abiding interest in Amerindian and African traditions has had a profound impact on his art. Until the early 1980s he created objects resembling archaeological pieces, which he combined with fragments of authentic artifacts. He soon concentrated on the process of production of such things and on their enduring function over long periods. For instance, in his wall installation *Doce cuchillos* (1983; Twelve Knives), exhibited at the First Biennial of Havana (1984), Bedia placed several knives made of different materials over a tar-painted circle and included labels, written in chalk, explaining their manufacture.

Since the late 1980s Bedia has often integrated ritual forms and symbols of the African Cuban religion Palo Monte (which he himself practices) with visual and mythical elements taken from indigenous cultures of the Americas. In his complex and metaphorical installations, as well as in his drawings, Bedia has affirmed marginalized spiritual systems of belief through the language of contemporary art, making powerful anticolonialist and antirationalist statements while attempting to restore the social and spiritual function of art. In his mixed-media installation for the 1986 Biennial of Havana, *El golpe del tiempo* (1986; The Beat of Time), Bedia represented an Indian chief lancing a crescent moon with a spear that featured, hanging from its horizontal shaft, a series of photocopies of a horse and its rider. Each copy was progressively blurred, symbolizing the marginalization suffered by American Indian groups. Bedia's subject and his expressionistic outline drawing style were inspired by the art of the South Dakota Sioux, with whom he lived in 1985. Another installation, *Segundo encuentro* (1992; Second Encounter), showed the dark outline of a figure holding on its head a small modern warship pierced by numerous arrows. In this work Bedia compared the violence of the European conquerors against the indigenous peoples of the Americas to U.S. aggression against Latin America while simultaneously identifying the destruction of the warship as the action of a Palo Monte spirit.

REFERENCE:

Osvaldo Sánchez, "José Bedia: La restauración de nuestra alteridad. Restoring Our Otherness," translated by Diego Robirosa, *Third Text,* no. 13 (Winter 1991): 63–72.

— F.B.N.

ANTONIO BENÍTEZ-ROJO

Among the writers who came to prominence with the Cuban Revolution, Antonio Benítez-Rojo (1931–) is one of the most important in terms of the short story. His best-known collections are *Tute de reyes* (1967; translated as *The Winning Hand*) and *El escudo de hojas secas* (1968; translated as *The Magic Dog and Other Stories*). For the first of these collections, Benítez-Rojo received a **Casa de las Américas prize,** and for some time he was a high-ranking official in the sponsoring organization. Eventually, however, he joined the army of writers and artists who sought refuge outside Cuba. Benítez-Rojo held several visiting professorships in the United States before settling at Amherst College in Massachusetts.

Benítez-Rojo's stories were highly praised by one of Spanish America's best-known short-story writers, the Uruguayan Mario Benedetti, and are often said to have been influenced by the fiction of the Argentinean writer Julio Cortázar, one of the great figures of the **Boom** and a master of the short-story genre. Benítez-Rojo's themes deal with the failings of prerevolutionary Cuba and the difficulties in adjusting to postrevolutionary life. "Estatuas sepultadas" (Buried Statues), which is one of the stories gathered in *Tute de reyes* and the most anthologized of those Benítez-Rojo has written, illustrates some of the things he has in common with Cortázar: the ability to use a female narrator convincingly, to evoke an adolescent worldview, and to incorporate mysterious elements into a realistic narrative. This story, moreover, has clear antecedents in Cortázar's "Casa tomada" (translated as "House Taken Over"), "Final del juego" (translated as "End of the Game"), and "Los venenos" (translated as "The Poisons"). Whereas in "Casa tomada" Cortázar tells of a house occupied by a middle-aged brother and sister that is being taken over by unidentified forces, those that threaten the house in Benítez-Rojo's story, with its aristocratic family, clearly stand for a new political order. In "Estatuas sepultadas" the neighbors' property has already been turned into an educational institution from which revolutionary marches are broadcast, while the inhabitants of the besieged house have long been without electricity and have otherwise been cut off from the outside world, save for the clandestine nocturnal supplies that pass through the railings. All the while the grass is invading their property from outside. Transparent as the allusions are to both the pre- and postrevolutionary orders, this story is by no means a monolithic political tract; the heavily symbolic "Estatuas sepultadas" is complex and not altogether unambiguous.

In all, Benítez-Rojo has published five collections of stories, a novella, two novels (including *El mar de lentejas*, 1991; translated as *Sea of Lentils*), and several works of criticism.

REFERENCES:

Lucrecia Artalejo, "Creación y subversión: La narrativa histórica de Antonio Benítez-Rojo," *Revista Iberoamericana,* 56, nos. 152–153 (July–December 1990): 127–130;

Julio Ortega, "Los cuentos de Antonio Benítez," in *El cuento hispanoamericano ante la crítica,* edited by Enrique Pupo-Walker (Madrid: Castalia, 1973).

— P.S.

BIARRITZ FESTIVAL

The Biarritz Festival (Festival International de Biarritz) is held annually in southwest France. It began in the late 1970s and rapidly established itself as important for featuring Latin American films. Each year there is an open film competition and a retrospective series of movies from a selected Latin American country. Three prizes are awarded in the film competition; winners have included Ricardo Larraín (Chile) for *La frontera,* Carlos Azpurúa (Venezuela) for *Disparen a matar,* Sergio Cabrera (Colombia) for *La estrategia del caracol,* José Ramón Novoa (Venezuela) for *Sicario,* and Luis Argueta for **El silencio de Neto,** the first feature film produced in Guatemala. In 1995 the most coveted award, the Grand Prix (awarded by a professional jury), as well as the prize for best actress, went to *Madagascar,* by the Cuban director Fernando Pérez. That movie is a study of the relationship between a mother and her daughter. Cuba also captured the other major prize, awarded following an audience vote, with **Tomás Gutiérrez Alea** and Juan Carlos Tabio's *Guantanamera.* Another Cuban director whose work has been recognized in the past is **Julio García Espinosa.** In general, the Biarritz festival has been important in bringing Latin American filmmakers to the attention of a wider public, sometimes providing directors with enough leverage to enable them to have their works shown in their home countries.

Cinema, however, is not the only focus of the festival, whose subtitle is "Cinémas et Cultures de L'Amérique Latine": music, literature, and the plastic arts occupy a smaller part of the program but have been important enough to attract figures such as Fernando Botero and Mario Vargas Llosa. The Cuban writer and painter **Severo Sarduy** had some of his work exhibited at the festival in 1994, and in 1995 Gabriel García Márquez was in attendance while homage was paid to his **Fundación de Nuevo Cine Latino-**

americano and Cuba's film school, founded in 1986. (See also **Huelva Film Festival.**)

—P.S.

BIBLIOTECA AYACUCHO

The Biblioteca Ayacucho, named after a decisive 1824 battle in the struggle for Spanish American independence from Spain, is an ambitious collection of more than 150 classics of Latin American letters; it was begun by presidential decree in Venezuela in 1976. The initial volume comprises the political writings of Simón Bolívar, whose dream was a unified Spanish America, an idea that the Biblioteca Ayacucho takes up on a cultural level. The Ayacucho collection includes works by authors from all parts of Latin America and covers a variety of genres, such as poetry, fiction, and political and sociological essays. The series also includes anthologies of indigenous literatures, Cuban **costumbrismo,** and popular theater. Each volume includes a substantial prologue, a bibliography, and a comprehensive chronology of the relevant period. After 1987 the last section was dropped, and a comprehensive chronology from 900 B.C. to 1985 A.D. was published separately. Modern poets and novelists represented in the collection thus far include Pablo Neruda, Gabriel García Márquez, Julio Cortázar, José Donoso, César Vallejo, **Carlos Fuentes, Juan Rulfo,** and **Alejo Carpentier.**

REFERENCE:

Angel Rama, "La Biblioteca Ayacucho como instrumento de integración cultural latinoamericana," *Latino América,* 14 (1981): 325–339.

—R.G.M.

BOLERO

Not to be confused with the Spanish bolero, with which it has no musical relationship, the Latin American bolero is a moderately paced ballad that first became popular in the Hispanic Caribbean and Mexico and eventually spread to South America. The roots of the bolero may be found in the Cuban **danzón,** which had developed from the French contredanse. In early versions the bolero was accompanied by guitars, but its growing popularity soon demanded more elaborate musical settings. The Latin American bolero is in duple meter and expresses subtle rhythmic syncopation in moderate to slow tempo. Structurally, it consists of a brief instrumental introduction and two sections of sixteen to thirty-two measures each, in which an intimate, romantic text is sung. Typically, the first sixteen-measure section is in a minor key, and the last sixteen-measure section changes to a major key. The elements that most effectively distinguish the bolero from other genres are the romantic lyrics and the slower tempo.

As the bolero developed in Cuba and spread to other parts of the Caribbean basin, it began to acquire regional idiosyncrasies. The strong influence of African musical culture in eastern Cuba, for example, gave a characteristic flavor to Cuban boleros that was most obvious in rhythmic procedures. The merging features of a closely related, but rhythmically more active genre, the Cuban **son,** resulted in the hybrid bolero-son. Among Cuban composers of boleros who gained international recognition through recordings and motion pictures are Osvaldo Farrés (*Acércate más, Acaríciame,* and *Quizás, quizás*); Bobby Collazo (*La última noche* and *Vivir de los recuerdos*); Julio Gutiérrez (*Llanto de luna, Siguiéndote*); Mario Fernández Porta (*Mentiras tuyas, ¿Qué me importa?, No vuelvo contigo*); Pedro Junco Jr. (*Nosotros*); Tony Fergo (*Alma vanidosa, En la palma de la mano, Sonámbula luna*); Juan Bruno Tarraza (*Soy tuya, Soy feliz*); Ernesto Duarte (*¿Cómo fue?*); and Frank Domínguez (*Tú me acostumbraste*).

In Mexico, European music was a much stronger influence than African music. The popularity of Italian opera and the Spanish **zarzuela** led to the development of the lyrical **canción mexicana,** as seen in the works of **Manuel Ponce.** In addition, since the turn of the century the Cuban danza habanera (Cuban dance in **habanera** rhythm) had been established as the most popular dance in the Americas, a position that it maintained for many years, especially in Mexico. It was the peculiar combination of elements from opera, zarzuela, Mexican song, and the **habanera** that produced the lyrical version of the bolero in Mexico. Guty Cárdenas preceded **Agustín Lara** as an early composer of Mexican boleros, but Lara's contributions to the genre early in its Mexican life established the norms that would be followed by generations of successors: Agustín Lara (*Mujer, Solamente una vez,* and *Palabras de mujer*); **María Grever** (*Cuando vuelva a tu lado* and *Alma mía*); Alberto Domínguez Borras (*Perfidia* and *Frenesí*); Consuelo Velásquez (*Bésame mucho, Corazón,* and *Te espero*); Pablo Beltrán Ruiz (*Somos diferentes*); and José "Pepe" Guizar (*Sin ti*), among countless others.

The role of the bolero in Puerto Rico has had much to do with its commercial popularity and the intensity with which it was fixed upon as a marker of cultural identity. In the 1930s Puerto Rico had not yet developed the variety nor the quantity of folk, popular, and commercial musics that Cuba and Mexico could boast. Consequently, in Puerto Rico there was more intense concentration on fewer genres, such as the elegant danza puertorriqueña, inherited genres such as the Spanish **villancico,** and folk genres such as the **plena,** various forms of the **seis,** and **aguinaldos** (Christmas carols). The huge migration of Puerto Ricans to New York following the Spanish-American War in 1898 undoubtedly contributed to an intensely intimate, even nostalgic approach to the bolero. Thousands of dislocated families and separated lovers found consolation in the impassioned lyrics that expressed their isolation and loneliness. **Rafael Hernández** (*Campanitas de cristal, Desvelo de amor, Lamento borincano,* and *Lo siento por tí*) and **Pedro Flores** (*Amor perdido, Perdón, Obsesión,* and *Bajo un palmar*) were prominent among the composers who established the bolero in the community of Puerto Ricans, divided between those who had moved to the United States and those who remained on the island. Other well-known composers from Puerto Rico are Noel Estrada (*Acuarela borincana* and *En mi viejo San Juan*), Myrta Silva (*¿Qué sabes tú?* and *Tengo que acostumbrarme*), Tito Henríquez (*Sollozo*), and Sylvia Rexach (*Nave sin rumbo, Alma adentro, Y entonces*). The romantic and social significance of the bolero, also known as the bolero criollo, was summed up in Pedro Malavet Vega's *Historia de la canción popular en Puerto Rico* (1992), in which he pointed out that it "served for decades to provide an amorous nearness, as the antechamber of matrimony, in times when that musical embrace between man and woman was the only one that was socially acceptable."

REFERENCES:

Néstor Leal, *Boleros: La canción romántica del Caribe (1930–1960)* (Venezuela: Grijalbo S.A. de Venezuela, 1992);

Pedro Malavet Vega, *Historia de la canción popular en Puerto Rico (1493–1898)* (Santo Domingo: Editora Corripio, C. por A., 1992);

Hernán Restrepo Duque, *Lo que cuentan los boleros* (Bogotá: Centro Editorial de Estudios Musicales Ltda., 1992);

Jaime Rico Salazar, *Cien años de boleros* (Bogotá: Centro Editorial de Estudios Musicales, 1987);

John Storm Roberts, "Salsa: The Latin Dimension in Popular Music," in *The Many Worlds of Music,* volume 3 (New York: Broadcast Music Inc., 1976).

— R.L.S.

JORGE BOLET

Jorge Bolet (1914–1990) was born in Havana, Cuba, to parents of Spanish descent. His father had fought in the Cuban War of Independence from Spain, and his mother was from an aristocratic family of plantation owners. His older sister, María Josefa, became his first piano teacher, and his brother Alberto became a successful violinist and was associate conductor of the Orquesta Filarmónica de la Habana (Havana Philharmonic) prior to the **Cuban Revolution,** after which he moved to California and took a position with the Long Beach Symphony Orchestra.

Jorge Bolet appeared as a soloist with the Havana Symphony Orchestra at the age of ten and was known locally as a prodigy by the age of twelve. Shortly thereafter he received a scholarship to study at the Curtis Institute of Music and moved to Philadelphia, where he studied piano with David Saperton and conducting with Fritz Reiner. Later he also studied with Leopold Godowsky (1932–1933), with Moriz Rosenthal (1935), and briefly with Rudolf Serkin (1937).

Following his European debut in Amsterdam (1935) and his American debut with the Philadelphia Orchestra (1937), Bolet won two coveted competitions: the Naumberg Prize (1937) and the Josef Hofman Award (1938). During the next four decades, excluding a period of post–World War II U.S. military service, Bolet combined teaching (the Curtis Institute, Indiana University) with regular appearances as a recitalist in many of the well-known concert halls of the world. In the United States he appeared regularly at New York's Town Hall, Carnegie Hall, Alice Tully Hall, and Avery Fisher Hall in Lincoln Center. Having acquired a more aggressive manager in 1980, the solo concerts, appearances with major orchestras, and recording contracts increased. Bolet was finally acknowledged as one of the last and greatest living interpreters of Romantic piano literature.

REFERENCES:

Teresa Escandon, ed., *Jorge Bolet Memorial Editions: Preludes and Ballades of Frédéric Chopin* (Miami: CPP/Belwin, 1994);

George Kehler, ed., *The Piano in Concert* (Metuchen, N.J.: Scarecrow Press, 1982);

Helio Orovio, *Diccionario de la música cubana: Biográfico y técnico* (Havana: Editorial Letras Cubanas, 1992).

— R.L.S.

BOMBA

Bomba is a generic term covering a group of African-derived song/dance types employing the call-and-response format that is widely dispersed in the Americas. In addition, *bomba* identifies the drum that accompanies such types of song and dance. Although similar song/dance types are found in other parts of Latin America, generally with other names, the bomba has traditionally been associated with Puerto Rico, in particular with the southern coastal region around the city of Ponce and later the eastern region of Loiza Aldea. The bomba in the Ponce region arrived directly with slaves from Guinea, who were brought to work on the sugar plantations of the southern coast. The bomba in Loiza Aldea appears to have arrived with slaves from the French Caribbean, especially Haiti. The bomba began in the seventeenth century as entertainment and a means of expression for slaves; bomba celebrations were held on Saturday nights, at the end of harvest, and for birthdays, weddings, wakes, and the like. Variations on the African characteristics of these dances were contributed by immigrants from France's Caribbean colonies between 1780 and 1815.

Primary among the shared choreographic features of the many varieties of bomba is the challenge between dancer and drummer, in which the drummer tries to match the dancer's improvisational steps. If the dancer tires or runs out of ideas, he retires. If the drummer cannot compete, he defers to a second drummer. Men, women, and couples may challenge, but only one dancer at a time may dance. Common musical features include an improvised verse alternating with a unison refrain accompanied by two bomba drums, one larger (the *burlador*) and one smaller (the *requinto* or *subidor*); two claves (rhythm sticks); and one **maraca** (gourd rattle). The burlador and the claves maintain a repeated rhythmic pattern, while the requinto provides the animation of the song and dance through improvisations. While the instrumental accompaniment tends to provide rhythmic interest through syncopations and cross rhythms, the vocal part proceeds in close agreement with the duple meter.

The bomba, often cited as one of the principal folk genres of Puerto Rico, enjoyed renewed popularity among New York Puerto Ricans when it was included in performances of **salsa** by Frankie Malabe and Willie Colón. (See also **Afro-Caribbean Dance.**)

REFERENCES:

Charley Gerard, with Marty Sheller, *Salsa! The Rhythm of Latin Music* (Crown Point, Ind.: White Cliffs Media, 1989);

Francisco López Cruz, *La música folklórica de Puerto Rico* (Sharon, Conn.: Troutman Press, 1967);

James A. McCoy, "The Bomba and Aguinaldo of Puerto Rico as They Have Evolved," dissertation, Florida State University, 1968.

          — R.L.S. & J.M.H

BONGOS

Closely associated with Afro-Caribbean music, bongos, or in Spanish *bongós*, are small double drums tuned a fourth apart and attached to each other by the barrels. The player holds them between the legs and plays them with the hands. Folk musicians used to make bongo heads from goat skins, but today they are manufactured from synthetic materials. Unlike other percussion instruments, such as the **conga** drums and the

timbales, bongos are not limited to repetitive beats. Instead, they often provide a rhythmic counterpoint.

REFERENCE:

Diagram Group, *Musical Instruments of the World* (New York: Paddington Press, 1976).

          — R.L.S.

BOOM

The Boom marked a turning point for the Latin American novel. The term itself, in use by the late 1960s and popularized by José Donoso in his *Historia personal del "boom"* (1972; translated as *The Boom in Spanish American Literature: A Personal History*), refers to the explosion that took place in Latin American fiction during the 1960s. Latin American novelists began to be recognized internationally, and their works were translated into many languages. Commercial interests undoubtedly promoted the Boom, and its legitimacy as an intrinsic cultural phenomenon has been questioned by nationalists and left-wing critics, who note that not only did most of the Boom novelists write their great works abroad, but also many of these works were published in Spain by Seix Barral. While it was not new for prominent Latin American writers to write and publish major works outside their home countries, the Boom writers made an intentional break with previous novelistic styles — especially the popular **regionalist** and **indigenist** traditions — and they exhibit an obvious fascination with European and North American modernism, specifically authors such as William Faulkner, Ernest Hemingway, Henry James, Virginia Woolf, Thomas Mann, John Dos Passos, and Marcel Proust. The most influential writer for the Boom novelists, however, was Argentinean Jorge Luis Borges. The international success of the Boom writers drew attention to major Latin American novelists of earlier decades, including Carlos Onetti, **Miguel Angel Asturias,** and **Juan Rulfo,** who came to be recognized as precursors of the Boom.

The authors universally designated as the core of the Boom are Mario Vargas Llosa of Peru with several novels, *La ciudad y los perros* (1963; translated as *The Time of the Hero*), *La casa verde* (1966; translated as *The Green House*), and *Conversación en La Catedral* (1969; translated as *Conversation in The Cathedral*); Julio Cortázar of Argentina with his complex and internationally recognized *Rayuela* (1963; translated as *Hopscotch*); **Carlos Fuentes** of Mexico with several novels, most notably *La muerte de Artemio Cruz* (1962; translated as *The Death of Artemio Cruz*); and Gabriel García

Guillermo Cabrera Infante, circa 1971

of the dead, the feelings of natural phenomena and inanimate objects, and the parapsychological, for example. There is also an increasing self-referentiality in the works of Boom writers, and the reader is often obliged to take an active role in constructing the fiction. In contrast **Post-Boom** fiction is less hermetic and often draws on popular art forms.

REFERENCE:

Angel Rama, "El boom en perspectiva," in his *La crítica de la cultura en América Latina* (Caracas: Ayacucho, 1985).

— P.S. & A.G

JUAN BOSCH

Dominican writer and president Juan Bosch (1909–) has spent most of his life in exile battling tyranny, principally the dictatorship of Rafael Trujillo (see **Dictatorship Novel**). After Trujillo was overthrown, Bosch was elected president in 1963, in the first free elections held in the Dominican Republic. He was overthrown a few months later by a U.S.–supported military coup and returned to a life in exile. He ran again for president in 1966 but was defeated by a conservative candidate, Joaquín Balaguer.

Bosch's collections of short stories reflect his commitment to social justice, portraying social conflicts with special sympathy for the downtrodden and marginalized. Despite Bosch's dedication to the struggle for social justice, he does not sacrifice the artistic dimensions of his writings to the political messages he imparts. Most of the plots in his earlier years — for example *Camino real* (1933; Highway) and *Indios* (1935; Indians) — portray life in the Caribbean islands; thus he is considered a regionalist writer. After 1937 he experimented with newer formal trends, allowing him greater freedom in the use of symbolism and the exploration of the realms of fantasy. He achieved a more universal dimension in that the plots could occur in the Antilles or anywhere. These stories appear in *Dos pesos de agua* (1941; Two Loads of Water), *Ocho cuentos* (1947; Eight Stories), and *La muchacha de La Guaira* (1955; The Girl from La Guaira). He also wrote one novel, *La mañosa* (1936; The Shrewd Girl), ostensibly about an earlier era but in fact critical of Trujillo.

REFERENCE:

Bruno Rosario Candelier, *La narrativa de Juan Bosch* (Santo Domingo: Editora Alfa y Omega, 1989).

— M.E.S.

Márquez of Colombia, whose masterpiece *Cien años de soledad* (1967; translated as *One Hundred Years of Solitude*) was critical in garnering international acclaim for Latin American fiction. Cuban **Guillermo Cabrera Infante,** with his novel *Tres tristes tigres* (1967; translated as *Three Trapped Tigers*), should also be included among the essential proponents.

The Boom was most notably associated with **magical realism,** a style that blurred conventional distinctions between reality and imagination by layering formal or aesthetic systems of meaning (myths, allegory, symbolism) and nonordinary realities to produce an original vision of Latin America. In some cases the results came close to approximating the Indian worldview, assimilating aspects of life that seemed out of place in the Western literary tradition — the world

Juan Bosch (center) in April 1965, after an unsuccessful attempt to return him to power in the Dominican Republic (Wide World)

GUILLERMINA BRAVO AND THE BALLET NACIONAL DE MÉXICO

Often referred to as the mother of Mexican modern dance (or sometimes the stepmother, since she took over from **Waldeen** and other pioneers), Guillermina Bravo (1920–) was born in Veracruz. She studied dance and piano at the Academia de Danza and the Conservatorio, where she learned a badly taught classical ballet technique and "duncanisms," movement exercises inspired by American dancer Isadora Duncan. In 1939 Bravo was introduced to the modern dance techniques of the American-born teacher-choreographer Waldeen, who also taught Bravo that dance could be pursued as a professional career and that it should be influenced by the social concerns of the Mexican Communist Party. Bravo danced professionally for the first time in 1940 in the fledgling dance company directed by Waldeen. In 1946 she and her fellow dancer Ana Mérida founded the Ballet Waldeen, the aims of which were to be experimental, to leave behind the technical and ideological limitations of classical ballet, and to use elements of indigenous and mestizo culture to create an art that arose from the heart and expressed the struggles of the people.

In 1947 Bravo founded the Academia de Danza Mexicana within the Instituto Nacional de Bellas Artes, and in 1948 she founded the Ballet Nacional de México, which Waldeen, in an unusual turnabout, joined in 1948 or 1949. In the early years of the Ballet Nacional it was said that one should not ask in which theater Guillermina — synonymous with "Guillermina's company" — was dancing, but in which cornfield, since Bravo's mission was to study life and dance among the peasants and to bring performances to them. From 1957 to 1990 the company toured such places as Russia, China, Romania, France, Italy, Cuba, the United States, Puerto Rico, Great Britain, Spain, Poland, Czechoslovakia, Yugoslavia, Luxembourg, Switzerland, Holland, Finland, Germany, and Bulgaria. The year 1963 began a period of sending company members to New York for ten-week residencies at the Martha Graham School. (The Graham teaching system had long been codified and standardized, whereas the Mexican system was a compilation of techniques and exercises from various sources).

One of the foremost of Bravo's accomplishments was to obtain salaries for dancers. In 1979, for the stability and visibility she had brought to the company over the years, Bravo received the Premio Nacional de las Artes directly from the president of Mexico. In 1991 she founded the Centro Nacional de Danza Contemporánea (CENADAC), comprising two separate entities: a school and a company in Querétaro, a medium-sized city northwest of Mexico City. The company is fully supported by the Consejo Nacional para la Cultura y las Artes (National Council for Culture and the Arts), the Instituto Nacional de Bellas Artes, and the government of Querétaro. The school offers the equivalent of a high-school diploma in dance, which is required to pursue a bachelor's degree in performance, choreography, teaching, research, or production at the CENADAC or comparable institutions.

Bravo's championing of indigenous peoples and of third world guerrilla movements as well as the presence of leftist themes in her work led to threats of government censorship. While she was fulfilling the goals of the **Mexican Revolution** and bringing worldwide recognition to the advanced state of Mexican culture, governments were wary of any incitement to protest against their policies. Bravo's threatened works treat such themes as the guerrilla struggle in Guatemala, workers' strikes and the betrayal of workers by corrupt union leaders, and conditions of Mexican day laborers in the United States. Despite career-long struggles with the authorities who controlled cultural budgets and programs, Bravo won unmatched governmental support for the Ballet Nacional. She never ceased to identify her artistic struggle with the struggle of exploited peoples nor to understand the world through Marxism and not through God. She proclaimed that her greatest teachers were Mexico's Indian peoples.

Bravo created fifty-seven choreographies for the Ballet Nacional. The dance critic and historian César Delgado Martínez divides her work into eight phases: nationalism or realism (1946–1957); experimentation with nonrealistic themes (1958–1963); experimentation with diverse uses of the chorus (1964–1967); exploration of the interior life of man and investigation of stage space through geometric forms (1967–1971); integration of the two previous currents (1972); solo dance (1973–1982); themes of love and death (1977–1982); and a return to origins in order to try to understand the world (1983–   ).

REFERENCE:

César Delgado Martínez, *Guillermina Bravo: Historia Oral* (Mexico City: CENIDI-Danza, 1994).

—J.M.H.

JULIA DE BURGOS

One of Puerto Rico's most prominent poets, Julia de Burgos (1914–1953) was born into extreme poverty in Santa Cruz, in the province of Carolina. She was one of twelve siblings, six of whom died as infants, victims of illnesses caused by poverty. She struggled through childhood and adolescence to educate herself and later support herself with various kinds of jobs. Her life was difficult not only economically but also emotionally, in part because of her commitment to the nationalist cause of an independent Puerto Rico, her strong feminist stance, and the discrimination she suffered as a mulatta both in the Caribbean and in the continental United States, where she lived for some years.

Her books of poetry reflect her major political and social commitments as well as an erotic dimension and an obsession with death, this last being especially prevalent in her later years. Perhaps her most famous poem, "To Julia de Burgos" in *Poema en veinte surcos* (1938; A Poem in Twenty Furrows) reveals the division between the female self constructed to satisfy social expectations and the authentic, creative woman who seeks fulfillment at all levels and emerges triumphant in the struggle against oppressive social norms. In *Canción de la verdad sencilla* (1939; Song of the Unadorned Truth) love predominates as a major theme, while *El mar y tú* (1954; The Ocean and You), published posthumously, reflects a sense of anguish as she became increasingly alienated from society. She was discovered unconscious from the effects of alcoholism on the streets of New York and was pronounced dead on arrival at Harlem Hospital on 4 August 1953.

REFERENCES:

Yvette Jiménez de Báez, *Julia de Burgos: Vida y poesía* (San Juan, Puerto Rico: Editorial Coquí, 1966);

Diana Vélez, "Julia de Burgos," in *Spanish American Women Writers,* edited by Diane Marting (Westport, Conn.: Greenwood Press, 1990), pp. 85–93.

—M.E.S.

C

MANUEL DEL CABRAL

Manuel del Cabral (1907–) is a poet and novelist who was born in Santiago de los Caballeros, in the Dominican Republic. Both **Pedro Mir** and del Cabral were members of the literary group *La Cueva*. Del Cabral traveled extensively through Latin America, North America, and Europe and resided for many years in Argentina, where he published his most important books of poetry, such as *Trópico negro* (1942; Black Tropics), *Compadre Mon* (1943; Godfather Mon), and *Chinchina busca el tiempo* (1945; Chinchina Looks for Time). Together with **Nicolás Guillén** and **Luis Palés Matos,** del Cabral was the initiator of black poetry in the Caribbean. His *Doce poemas negros* (1935; Twelve Black Poems) was published four years after Guillén's well-known *Sóngoro cosongo,* and two before Palés's *Tuntún de pasa y grifería.* In *Doce poemas negros* as well as in *Trópico negro,* del Cabral explores Afro-Caribbean culture and creates a consciousness of the social problems of the region. *Compadre Mon* is a lengthy poem in which mankind sings to the earth in search of its origins, and *Chinchina busca el tiempo* reveals the poet's interest in metaphysics. In 1953 a selection of del Cabral's poems appeared in the anthology *Nueva poesía dominicana* (New Dominican Poetry), published in Spain.

REFERENCES:

Jeanette Bercovici Coin, "Social Aspects of Black Poetry in Luis Palés Matos, Nicolás Guillén and Manuel del Cabral," dissertation, New York University, 1976;

Elmore Joseph DeGrange, "The Poetry of Manuel del Cabral," dissertation, Tulane University, 1969.

— F.V.

LYDIA CABRERA

Lydia Cabrera (1900–1991), well known for her short stories based on oral African folklore, and an authority on the African religions practiced in her native Cuba, was born at the turn of the century into a large family in Havana. She was close to her father, an established writer and publisher, who groomed Cabrera for a literary career from an early age. After her father's death Cabrera began a successful furniture business and then gathered her profits to fund her self-imposed exile in Europe. She lived in Paris as a painter and was influenced by the Surrealist movement there. When her close friend, Teresa de la Parra, the Venezuelan author of *Ifigenia,* became ill with tuberculosis, Cabrera traveled to Switzerland with her to await her recovery.

Cabrera wrote her first collection of short stories, *Cuentos negros de Cuba* (1940; Black Stories from Cuba), at that time. Interest in African folklore had already begun in Paris in the 1930s with the **Négritude** movement, and the French translation of her work, published in 1936, was well received long before the Spanish version was submitted to the presses. Cabrera's stories relate the oral tales she had heard as a child growing up in a household with a black nanny and black servants. The stories in *Cuentos negros de Cuba* are not mere transcriptions of the original African tales; Cabrera inserts her ironic humor and inventiveness into the retelling. It would be hard to argue that these are stories with a moral to them. The apparently simple narratives contain rapid changes in tone, from mythical to superstitious to ironic, that complicate any straightforward reading. The characters, while representing folkloric figures from traditional tales, nonetheless have individual traits that set them apart. Cabrera manages to combine innovative fiction with firmly held traditional beliefs.

María Teresa de Rojas, Lydia Cabrera, Peter Watson, and Wifredo Lam, 1947

fiction works based on the African cultural practices she had studied in Cuba.

REFERENCE:

Ada Ortúzar-Young, "Lydia Cabrera," in *Spanish American Women Writers,* edited by Diane Marting (Westport, Conn.: Greenwood Press, 1990).

—D.H.

GUILLERMO CABRERA INFANTE

One of the most original, important, and controversial writers to have emerged in modern Cuba, Guillermo Cabrera Infante was born in 1929 in a small town called Gibara, where his parents founded the local Communist Party, an action that led to their arrest and the loss of their books. Some years later, Cabrera was himself jailed for publishing a short story with profanities in it (in English). His early years as a writer directly preceded the Cuban Revolution, but, while political and social matters are a major concern in some of his stories and in *Vista del amanecer en el trópico* (1974; translated as *Dawn in the Tropics*), the political uproar of his time scarcely enters the pages of his novels, nor is it much reflected in his essays and screenplays. Eventually, however, he was exiled from Cuba and lived briefly in Spain before settling in London.

Cabrera's early work, written while still in Cuba, consists of various pieces for the journals or papers with which he was associated (mainly *Bohemia, Nueva Generación,* and *Revolución,* an organ of the revolutionary government), movie reviews later collected in the book *Un oficio del Siglo XX* (1962; translated as *A Twentieth Century Job*), and the short stories of *Así en la paz como en la guerra* (1960; As in Peace So in War). (This collection was published in translation in France, Italy, and Poland and nominated for the Prix International de Littérature, but Cabrera was later scornful of the book on the grounds that it reflected rather than created reality).

For a while Cabrera served **Fidel Castro**'s government as director of the Consejo Nacional de Cultura (National Cultural Council) and as an executive in the newly formed **Cuban Film Institute,** but he soon fell foul of official censorship. *Un oficio del siglo XX* not only gathers his film criticism, but it also charts his rise and fall from grace (under the pseudonym of G. Caín). In 1962 Cabrera was sent a safe distance from home, to Brussels as cultural attaché, and by 1965 he had left Cuba for good. An interview three years later in an Argentinean magazine made clear his opposition to the lack of artistic freedom under Castro, while it also helped precipitate the Heberto **Padilla Affair,** for

After her return to Cuba in 1938, Cabrera published two more short-story collections: *¿Por qué?: Cuentos negros de Cuba* (1948; Why?: Black Stories from Cuba) and *Ayapá: Cuentos de Jicotea* (1971; Ayapá: Stories from Jicotea). Her research-based writings are less complex but dense in the amount of information they convey. Some of her investigative works are *El monte* (1954; The Mount), notes on the religion, magic, superstitions, and folklore of the Cuban people; *Anagó* (1957), a vocabulary of Yoruba spoken in Cuba; and *Koeko iyawó* (1980), a treatise on Yoruba rule. Cabrera investigated the three main African tribes in Cuba: the Yoruba, Bantu, and Ewe, and extensively interviewed the people of Pogolotti, a predominantly black community in Cuba.

Lydia Cabrera later moved to Coral Gables, Florida, where she continued to write stories: *Cuentos para adultos niños y retrasados mentales* (1983; Stories for Childish Adults and the Mentally Retarded) and non-

Padilla had spoken up in support of the novel that was bringing Cabrera worldwide recognition but was banned in Cuba: *Tres tristes tigres* (1967; translated as *Three Trapped Tigers*). Although Cabrera had worked to rid that book of anything that smacked of politics, it was not allowed to circulate legally in his country of birth, nor had it met with the approval of Francisco Franco's right-wing regime in Spain, where Cabrera had been working on it. Yet it was in Spain that *Tres tristes tigres* was eventually published. Soon after, it was translated into German, French, and English. (It had also won the **Premio Biblioteca Breve** for 1964, in a different version and under the title he used years later for another book, *Vista del amanecer en el trópico*).

Much of the popularity of Cabrera's novel (though he would himself reject the idea that he writes "novels") is because of his unique talent for playful exploitation of the possibilities of language, especially his mastery of parody and puns. As *Tres tristes tigres* opens, he makes easy transitions between languages, and later there are frequent shifts between different levels of Cuban Spanish. He attempts to portray many elements of Cuban society as well as offer the multiple perspectives of writers who serve as models for his characters. His varied techniques for presenting the tales and memories of the writer/characters in this novel include letters, dialogue (often in the form of disjointed telephone conversations), and stream of consciousness. The characters of *Tres tristes tigres* never clearly take form as individual, dynamic entities but rather merge to give a collective impression of Cuban consciousness, one that also captures the author's view of his homeland through a rhapsodic use of language. The book is consciously artificial, musical, and performed (spoken) by a variety of narrators who seem to improvise in irregular fragments and tend to prove unreliable.

Among Cabrera's other well-known works, *Vista del amanecer en el trópico* is a collection of vignettes of moments in Cuban history from pre-Columbian times to the time of writing, a disturbing work whose anonymous style matches the dehumanizing conflicts suggested in it. *La Habana para un infante difunto* (1979; *Infante's Inferno*) takes its title from a play on Maurice Ravel's *Pavanne Pour L'Infante Défunte* (Pavanne for The Dead Infanta), a playfulness that is typical of Cabrera's linguistic antics. *La Habana para un infante difunto,* an erotic Bildungsroman set in Havana, is a book whose wordplay is based on the literary rather than the colloquial language that informed *Tres tristes tigres. Holy Smoke,* which was first published in English (1985), is no less brilliant in its plays on that language and is a half-serious study of the role of the

cigar in Cuban cultural history. Much of it is parodic, as usual, and funny. Also worthy of mention is Cabrera's screenplay for the movie based on Malcolm Lowry's *Under the Volcano.*

REFERENCES:

Rosemary Geisdorfer Feal, *Novel Lives: The Fictional Autobiographies of Guillermo Cabrera Infante and Mario Vargas Llosa* (Chapel Hill: North Carolina Studies in Romance Languages and Literatures, 1986);

David Patrick Gallagher, *Modern Latin American Literature* (Oxford: Oxford University Press, 1973);

Ardis Nelson, *Cabrera Infante in the Menippean Tradition* (Newark, Del.: Juan de la Cuesta, 1983);

Raymond Souza, *Major Cuban Novelists: Innovation and Tradition* (Columbia: University of Missouri Press, 1976).

— P.S.

NELLIE CAMPOBELLO

Mexican author Nellie Campobello was born in 1900 in the state of Durango and grew up during the most intensely violent moments of the **Mexican Revolution.** Her father died in the fighting, and one of her brothers fought under Pancho Villa. Her experiences as a child in the midst of the turmoil of the revolution later became the focus of her most recognized novel, *Cartucho. Relatos de la lucha en el norte de México* (1931; Cartucho. Tales of the Struggle in Northern Mexico). Considered by some critics to be a collection of short stories, *Cartucho* consists of a series of vignettes narrated in the first-person and depicting the impressions of a young girl living through the daily violence of the revolution. The episodes describe the appearance and disappearance of soldiers from various revolutionary factions, with a marked favoritism for Villa and his troops, as they pass through the town where the narrator lives. Cartucho (Cartridge) is the name of one of the soldiers who disappears and is never heard from again. Campobello's style is stark and vivid, alternating between tender and dispassionate descriptions of perpetrators and victims of violence alike; in fact, Campobello has been criticized for the objective tone in *Cartucho* when describing scenes of brutal torture and murder; some readers have called the account sadistic, finding it especially objectionable in the writings of a woman. Nevertheless, although long ignored, *Cartucho* has gained more and more attention from critics as an authentic and unique depiction of the Mexican Revolution.

Campobello's second novel, *Las manos de mamá* (1937; translated as *My Mother's Hands*), is also a series of vignettes, describing the close relationship between mother and daughter, the former representing stability in a time of tremendous upheavals and violence. Campobello has also written poetry, largely depicting the natural, rural world in which she grew up. Her years as an interpreter and performer of native dances in Mexico City led to the publication of her book *Ritmos indígenas de México* (1940; Indigenous Rhythms of Mexico) in collaboration with her sister.

REFERENCE:

Dale E. Verlinger, "Nellie Campobello: Romantic Revolutionary and Mexican Realist," in *Latin American Women Writers: Yesterday and Today,* edited by Yvette E. Miller and Charles M. Tatum (Pittsburgh: Latin American Literary Review, 1977), pp. 98–103.

— M.E.S.

HÉCTOR CAMPOS-PARSI

Born in 1922 in Ponce, the second largest city of Puerto Rico, Héctor Campos-Parsi first concentrated his studies on biology and psychology at the University of Puerto Rico. Following brief studies in medicine at the National University of Mexico, he returned to Puerto Rico to attend to the family insurance business. During his stay in Mexico he was impressed and influenced by personal contact with the great Mexican composer **Carlos Chávez,** and this revived his earlier interest in music. He subsequently received a scholarship to study at the New England Conservatory of Music, became active in numerous organizations there, and also attended the Berkshire Music Center in Tanglewood, Massachusetts. At Tanglewood he studied composition with Aaron Copland and orchestral conducting with Serge Koussevitzky. His lack of basic training in music led him to leave the New England Conservatory in search of more individualized attention. Following a brief stay at Yale with the German composer Paul Hindemith, Campos-Parsi was encouraged by Copland to study with Nadia Boulanger in Paris. His four years with Boulanger were highly productive; among other achievements, he received the Maurice Ravel Prize, awarded by the American Conservatory, for his Sonata No. 2 for Violin and Piano.

Campos-Parsi's early compositional period was in the nationalistic vein, winning him much affection among his compatriots and international attention in the musical world. Later he became attracted to neoclassicism and then to experimental ventures and avant-garde techniques. His musical life thus reflects the revolutionary nature of music in this century. Among his most successful works are *Oda a Cabo Rojo,* commissioned by the Festival **Casals** in 1959; *Duo trágico In Memoriam John F. Kennedy,* for the

Inter American Festival of Music in Washington, D.C., sponsored by the **Organization of American States** in 1965; and *Petroglifos,* commissioned by the Puerto Rico Institute of Culture for the Third Festival of Latin American Music in Caracas (1966). In addition to his life as a composer, Campos-Parsi served for many years as director of the music program of the Puerto Rico Institute of Culture.

REFERENCE:

Fernando H. Caso, *Héctor Campos en la historia de la música puertorriqueña del siglo XX* (San Juan: Instituto de Cultura Puertorriqueña, 1980).

— R.L.S.

CANA

The Caribbean News Agency (CANA), headquartered in Bridgetown, Barbados, is cooperatively owned by private and government media. CANA was established after Reuters announced in 1971 that it would increase the cost of its services by 63 percent and *The Daily Gleaner,* the major Jamaican newspaper, withdrew from the Reuters consortium. Established by media organizations in Barbados, Guyana, Jamaica, Trinidad and Tobago, and Montserrat, CANA quickly gained a reputation for quality and credibility. It is often considered a model Third World news agency.

The Associated Press, United Press International, Reuters of Britain, Agence France-Presses, Efe of Spain, ANSA of Italy, DPA of West Germany, and Prensa Latina of Cuba all have client newspapers, magazines, and broadcasting stations throughout Latin America. Mexico, Brazil, and Argentina each has a national news service, and since 1970 leading Latin American daily newspapers have cooperatively maintained LATIN, a regional news agency serving papers in every Latin American nation except Cuba.

REFERENCE:

Michael B. Salwen and Bruce Garrison, *Latin American Journalism* (Hillsdale, N.J.: Lawrence Erlbaum, 1991).

— S.M.H.

CANCIÓN MEXICANA

Long under the cultural domination of Spain, the new Mexican Republic of 1823 began a long process of artistic liberation in which other foreign influences were accepted and absorbed. Several prominent factors in the process of acculturation have been identified by experts: the abandonment of the Spanish style of *seguidillas* and *boleras andaluzas,* the fascination with Italian opera and the bel canto style of singing, the popularity of romantic operatic arias and **romances,** and the emergence of romantic poets. These factors were strong influences in the development of the **canción mexicana** (Mexican song genre). An extensive classification of the genre by Vicente Mendoza identifies several characteristics by which such songs may be grouped: musical form, verse meter, subject of text, regional origin, intended use, style of performance, and rhythmic accompaniment. This variety of categories reflects the extraordinary diversity of Mexican song. One of the main subgenres of canción mexicana is **canción ranchera.**

REFERENCE:

Vicente T. Mendoza, *La canción mexicana: Ensayo de clasificación y antología* (Mexico City: Instituto de Investigaciones Estéticas, Universidad Nacional Autónoma de México, 1961).

— R.L.S.

Canción Ranchera

The roots of the canción ranchera, one of the principal genres of the **canción mexicana,** developed in the nineteenth century as Mexicans sought to redefine their national identity. In the late nineteenth century, the period when Mexico opened its cultural boundaries to influences from other countries (apart from Spain), Italian opera, the French *vals,* and the Bohemian polka were absorbed into Mexican musical life. As these foreign sources were adapted to older Spanish styles, musics best described as Mexican began to appear. The poetic and musical properties of the vals, polka, and Italian aria were preserved more faithfully in sophisticated urban centers than in distant rural areas. The ornamentation of the virtuoso bel canto singing style, for example, or the elegant French vals, were appropriate fare for the urban elite, but the tastes of the ranchers and cowhands of the central plateau were less refined; they preferred simplified, straightforward songs.

One means of simplification consisted of reducing songs to two rhymed quatrains and a ritornello that typically featured repetition of part of the verse. Musical elements (melody, harmony, and rhythm) were also simplified. Melodies were confined to a moderate range and proceeded in stepwise motion with leaps arpeggiated to agree with harmonic tones. Harmony was judiciously reduced to two or three chords: the tonic chord (built on the first tone of the scale), the dominant chord (built on the fifth tone of the scale), and the subdominant chord (built on the fourth tone of the scale). Rhythms were based on European traditions in which 3/4, 6/8, 9/8, and 4/4 meters were prominent. The alternation and simultaneous use of 3/4 and 6/8 meters in many songs and dances provided a strong matrix from which lively and complex rhythms were derived.

Following the revolution of 1910, the surge of nationalistic fervor led to greater appreciation of rural genres of music, such as the **corrido** and the canción mexicana. In this period the term *canción ranchera* was adopted to identify a body of music that had been in development for over half a century. Surviving competition from foreign musics such as the Argentinean tango, jazz, and the Spanish **zarzuela,** the ranchera rose to fame through the voices of Pedro Infante, Jorge Negrete, and others in radio broadcasts, recordings, and the products of the Mexican film industry. The ranchera has been featured in numerous motion pictures, serving not only to entertain but also to emphasize national cultural values. As the twentieth century draws to a close, numerous television programs originating in Mexico City maintain a strong presence throughout Latin America, especially in Central America, and in Latino market areas of the United States. Mariachi ensembles performing rancheras and corridos are popular in the southwestern United States, especially in Texas, Arizona, and California, where popular festivals and workshops are annual events.

REFERENCES:

William Gradante, " 'El Hijo del Pueblo': José Alfredo Jiménez and the Mexican Canción Ranchera," *Latin American Music Review,* 3 (Spring/Summer 1982);

Vicente T. Mendoza, *La canción mexicana: Ensayo de clasificación y antología* (Mexico City: Instituto de Investigaciones Estéticas, Universidad Nacional Autónoma de México, 1961).

— R.L.S.

Felix Candela

Félix Candela (1910–) was one of the great architectural innovators in concrete-shell construction (see **Architecture**). Born and educated in Madrid, Candela became particularly interested in the Theory of Plasticity and in laminar structures. For this reason, in 1935 Candela went to Germany to study with concrete-shell specialists. He arrived in Mexico in 1939 as a refugee from the Spanish Civil War. Candela's belief that the form of a structure, rather than its mass, offered durability and stability at first found few supporters in Mexico City, where most architects doubted the stability of Candela's structures in an area known for its poor subsoil and seismic activity. Candela defended his designs in *A New Philosophy of Structures* (1951), which attacked standard architectural theories and stated

Iglesia de la Virgen Milagrosa (Church of the Miraculous Virgin), Mexico City, designed by Félix Candela in 1954–1955

into soaring free-edge forms with seemingly unsupported exterior roof lines. Free-edge forms demonstrated Candela's philosophy of concrete-shell construction, asserting that form, not mass, was the essential element in support systems.

REFERENCE:

Colin Faber, *Candela/The Shell Builder* (New York: Reinhold, 1963).

— C.M.

CANTINFLAS

The Mexican comedian and movie star Cantinflas (1911–1993) was born Mario Moreno. He came to the screen after achieving popularity as a dancer, tumbler, and circus entertainer. His dirty shirt, baggy pants, and worn-out shoes were the hallmarks of his *peladito* character, a picaresque "wise guy" from the slums, who appeared in movie after movie. Cantinflas first appeared in Miguel Contreras Torres's *No te engañes, corazón* (Don't Deceive Yourself, Dear), after which he appeared in *Siempre listo en las tinieblas* (Always Ready in the Darkness) and *Jengibre contra dinamita* (Ginger Versus Dynamite). He became internationally successful with the 1940 movie *Ahí está el detalle* (There is the Detail), his first full-length feature. In a final courtroom scene, Cantinflas makes fun of the social and legal system by completely confusing both judge and lawyers to his advantage. Thus began Cantinflas's huge popular following. His second full-length feature, which proved to be a major box-office success, was released in 1941 under the title *Ni sangre ni arena* (Neither Blood nor Sand), a spoof on the Spanish novel *Sangre y arena* by Vicente Blasco Ibáñez (1909; translated as *Blood and Sand*), which had recently been turned into a movie by Hollywood. Another huge success came with *El gendarme desconocido* (1941; The Unknown Policeman). These two films established Cantinflas as the most famous Spanish-speaking actor in Spanish America. Audiences outside the Hispanic world, however, probably remember Cantinflas best for his roles in two Hollywood films, *Around the World in 80 Days* (1956) and *Pepe* (1960).

that the elasticity of reinforced concrete surpassed previous assumptions. This paper, delivered at Harvard University, increased the popularity of concrete-shell construction in Latin American architecture during the 1950s.

Most of Candela's commissions in the early 1950s came from the business and industrial sectors that had become aware of the relatively low cost of concrete-shell construction. The simplicity of reinforced concrete groin vaults led to the erection of Candela's designs even in rural communities; an example is the school at Ciudad Victoria, Tamaulipas (1951). Such clients did not allow Candela much latitude to realize new formal expressions made possible by concrete. Yet the pursuit of such hyperbolic forms consumed Candela throughout his career. At times the concrete hyperbolic paraboloid was manipulated to mimic traditional forms, as can be seen in the soaring Gothic-inspired verticals of the Iglesia de la Virgen Milagrosa (1954–1955; Church of the Miraculous Virgin) in Mexico City. Among Candela's most elegant works is the Restaurant Xochimilco in Los Manantiales (1957); the groin-vaulted octagonal structure allowed Candela to manipulate the concrete shell

REFERENCES:

Charles Ramírez Berg, *Cinema of Solitude: A Critical Study of Mexican Film, 1967–1983* (Austin: University of Texas Press, 1992);

Carl J. Mora, *Mexican Cinema: Reflections of a Society 1896–1980* (Berkeley, Los Angeles & London: University of California Press, 1982).

— S.M.H. & P.S.

Cantinflas (right) standing behind Mapy Cortés in *El gendarme desconocido* (1941; The Unknown Policeman)

EMILIO CARBALLIDO

Emilio Carballido is one of the most influential dramatists in twentieth-century Mexican theater. He has also produced four novels, as well as a collection of short stories, *La caja vacía* (1962; The Empty Box), often overshadowed by his theatrical prowess. He was born in 1925 in Córdoba, Veracruz, but lived in Mexico City for the next fourteen years. Carballido studied at the National Autonomous University of Mexico and held various important posts, such as instructor at the School of Dramatic Arts of the National Institute of Art, member of the editorial staff of the University of Veracruz, and director of the theater section of the National Polytechnic Institute. Carballido also traveled to New York in 1950 on a Rockefeller Fellowship.

Carballido began his literary career writing one-act plays. He went on to produce full-length plays, ballets, movie scripts, and children's theater. His characters often serve to explore satirical and ironic themes. Many of his plays incorporate provincial realities, as is the case with *Un pequeño día de ira* (1962; A Small Day of Ire), which won a **Casa de las Américas prize** in 1962. Carballido's fascination with provincial topics stems from his experiences after leaving Mexico City for the provinces in 1939 to rejoin his father in Córdoba. Nevertheless, Carballido's theater is not strictly limited to provincial themes; his dramas have

also included colonial themes, for example, in the farce *El relojero de Córdoba* (1960; translated as *The Clockmaker from Córdoba*); mythological themes, including his modern version of the myth of Perseus in *Medusa* (1960); and purely fantastical themes, as in *El día que se soltaron los leones* (1960; The Day the Lions Were Set Free). Carballido's plays have won several important awards in addition to the Casa de las Américas; among them are the Juan Ruíz de Alarcón and Heraldo prizes.

REFERENCE:

Margaret Sayers Peden, *Emilio Carballido* (New York: Twayne, 1979).

— M.T.

ERNESTO CARDENAL

Known as the national poet of liberation, Ernesto Cardenal was born in Granada, Nicaragua, in 1925. He studied in Managua and then earned a degree from the National Autonomous University of Mexico in 1946. Until he returned to Managua in 1950, he studied at Columbia University in New York and traveled throughout western Europe. Upon his return to Nicaragua he joined a revolutionary group which planned the April Conspiracy of 1954 against the dictatorship of Anastasio Somoza. The conspiracy was betrayed; the leaders were executed; and Cardenal was forced into exile. In 1957 he entered a Trappist monastery in Gethsemani, Kentucky, where he studied under the poet-priest Thomas Merton and adopted the latter's philosophy of nonviolence. He left the monastery in 1959 and continued to study theology in Mexico and Colombia, where he came into contact with younger priests influenced by Liberation Theology, a doctrine that calls upon the Catholic clergy to commit themselves to the application of their teachings, modeled on the life of Jesus Christ, and to the struggle for justice and peace in their communities. It was during this period that he wrote his popular epigrams (published in book form in 1972 as *Epigramas*), short, generally highly ironic poetic pieces that play upon language to communicate the frustrations of love or to issue a cry against political repression. He also wrote a series of *salmos* (psalms) and other poetry reflecting Christian themes. The most well known is perhaps "Oración por Marilyn Monroe," a prayer dedicated to the movie star in which he portrays her loss of innocence, her increasing disillusionment, and her appropriation and exploitation by the media, which forces her into an alienation that eventually leads to her suicide. In 1965 Cardenal returned to Nicaragua, was ordained a priest, and went on to found the Christian community of Solentiname in an archipelago in one of Nicaragua's two great lakes. Solentiname was founded on the principle of nonviolence, but as Somoza's repression increased against the people of Nicaragua, Cardenal became more militant and more deeply involved with the Sandinistas. At the height of Somoza's repression in 1977, Cardenal was forced into exile and became a spokesperson for the Sandinistas. When Somoza was overthrown in 1979, Cardenal returned to Nicaragua to become the minister of culture under the Sandinista government. (See **Nicaraguan Revolution**).

One of his most important works, *Hora 0* (1959; *Zero Hour and Other Documentary Poems*), was written after the failed April Conspiracy of 1954. The poem is a history of the efforts of the peasant-hero Augusto César Sandino in his war against the United States Marines, his assassination by Somoza, and parallel events that evolved into the April Conspiracy, which culminated in the assassination of the principal leader of that rebellion, Adolfo Báez Bone. The poem is representative of what Cardenal has called "exteriorism," a narrative poetry that is grounded in historical events and plays upon the past and present to open the possibility of a future revolutionary transformation of Nicaraguan society and a new national identity. It is profoundly influenced by a blend of Christian-Marxist philosophies, offering a symbolic, cosmic, and concrete

Ernesto Cardenal (courtesy of the Organization of American States)

interpretation of Nicaraguan culture. During his years in Solentiname Cardenal wrote several important books of poetry, among them *El estrecho dudoso* (1966; The Dubious Strait) and *Homenaje a los indios americanos* (1969; Homage to the American Indians). They reflect Cardenal's passion for an idealized pre-Columbian past, emphasizing an idyllic and egalitarian way of life characteristic of the Mayan civilization. He also published an important contribution to the philosophy of Liberation Theology, based on his experiences in Solentiname: *El Evangelio en Solentiname* (translated as *The Gospel in Solentiname*).

In 1970 Cardenal traveled to Cuba and was deeply impressed by what he perceived as the Christian basis of the revolutionary transformation of that society. His reflections of his experiences were published in *En Cuba* (1970, 1972; In Cuba). It was following this trip that Cardenal became increasingly involved in the militant struggle of the Sandinistas, although he did not relinquish the ideal of nonviolence until the eve of the overthrow of Somoza. His most important works during this period are *Canto nacional* (1972; National

Song) and *Oráculo sobre Managua* (1973; Oracle over Managua). Both these extensive poems reflect Cardenal's Christian faith combined with Marxist politics, which together serve in the struggle against oppression. The latter poem depicts the disastrous effects of the December 1972 earthquake, which devastated Managua, and the subsequent abuse and corruption of the Somoza dictatorship, which pocketed international aid for personal gain. The earthquake and the consequent increase in the armed struggle against Somoza are seen as the final stage of a long process of history and revolution that would culminate in a transformed society. In 1989 Cardenal pubished *Cántico cósmico* (Cosmic Chant), a vast poem that attempts to describe the universe from an evolutionary perspective. It combines science, history, Christian symbolism, erotic imagery, and cosmic revelations to produce an all-encompassing vision of humanity and the universe based on love.

REFERENCES:

John Beverley and Marc Zimmerman, *Literature and Politics in the Central American Revolutions* (Austin: University of Texas Press, 1990);

Paul W. Borgeson, *Hacia el hombre nuevo: Poesía y pensamiento de Ernesto Cardenal* (London: Támesis, 1984).

—M.E.S.

ALEJO CARPENTIER

One of Latin America's most prominent novelists, Alejo Carpentier (1904–1980) was born in Havana of a French father and Russian mother. He studied architecture, then journalism, music, and anthropology, with a special focus on folklore, in Havana and Paris. He became renowned as a musicologist, giving lectures abroad and writing on musical theory and history; the most important result is *La música en Cuba* (1956; Music in Cuba). He was one of the founders of the vanguardist journal *Revista de Avance* (1927–1930) and during his time in Paris became associated with the Surrealists.

Carpentier was very much involved with political happenings in Cuba. In 1927 he was jailed, and later he was exiled for his protests against the government of the Cuban dictator Gerardo Machado y Morales. While in jail he wrote the first version of *Ecué-yamba-ó,* a novel that reflects the influence of the French Surrealists and that later was published in Madrid, in 1934. An Afro-Cuban historical novel, it depicts the lives of black Cubans, with their magical folklore, rituals, ceremonies, hexes, and celebrations. It also includes a condemnation of the Machado dictatorship and the harsh existence of rural blacks struggling to make a meager living off the land. *Ecué-yamba-ó* is a

prelude to Carpentier's next novel, *El reino de este mundo* (1949; translated as *The Kingdom of This World*), which was published sixteen years later after a visit to Haiti. In this novel he portrays the magical world of the legendary black king of Haiti, Henri Christophe. In the prologue to this book Carpentier coins the term *lo real maravilloso* (the marvelous real), which came to be closely associated with the technique of **magical realism** later made famous by the Colombian 1980 Nobel laureate, Gabriel García Márquez. *El reino de este mundo* takes the reader into the magical world of black slaves, who use their folklore to survive inhumane treatment while subverting the authority of their white masters. Such historical figures as Christophe (king of Haiti at the beginning of the twentieth century), Mackandal and Bouckman (slaves who instigate the rebellions against white slave masters), and Paulina Bonaparte (wife of the French general Leclerc) appear, to complete a historical portrayal of Haitian reality at the turn of the century. Carpentier uses various techniques, such as time dislocation and fragmentation, free association, and mythical allusions, to communicate the disjuncture suffered by black Haitians as slaves and then as theoretically free men and women but in fact people who end up under the domination of a black king.

Carpentier's next novel, *Los pasos perdidos* (1953; translated as *The Lost Steps*), is considered his masterpiece. The protagonist, a musicologist, travels from the United States to the jungles of the Orinoco in search of ancient musical instruments. He encounters a group of natives who are living in the Stone Age and becomes enchanted with their simple and primitive way of life and with what he believes are the authentic origins of music. He leaves for professional reasons and, when he attempts to return, discovers that nature has transformed the jungle, and that it is no longer possible to return to the same world. The end of the novel underscores the futility of the artist's attempt to escape a decadent, modern world by returning to his natural origins in search of cultural and artistic roots. Carpentier's skillful manipulation of symbols and metaphors adds to the rich, baroque descriptions of an exuberant and uncontrollable world in which time is dictated by nature and not regimented artificially as it is in the civilized world. The juxtaposition of the magical, harmonious elements of the indigenous existence with the technological world of the protagonist highlights the blending of the European and indigenous elements that forms the basis of many Latin American societies.

Carpentier's other novels continue in this vein, combining magical interpretations of real events and historical figures with highly symbolic language and a

Alejo Carpentier in Havana, 1962 (photograph by Paolo Gasparini)

manipulation of time sequences. They are *El acoso* (1965; The Persecution), a condemnation of the Machado regime; *Guerra del tiempo* (1958; The War of Time); and *El siglo de las luces* (1962; translated as *Explosion in the Cathedral*), which again focuses on the mythical aspects of the Caribbean world, especially Haiti. In *El siglo de las luces* the principal characters become involved in the aftermath of the French Revolution in the Caribbean colonies. Following a fairly traditional narrative format (chronological, linear time; omniscient narrator), the action and ultimate fate of the disillusioned characters reflect the difficulty in overcoming historical realities in pursuit of revolutionary ideals. *El recurso del método* (1974; translated as *Reasons of State*) focuses on the role of a corrupt and inept Latin American dictator who emulates decadent European models and forgets his native roots; it is an important contribution to the **dictatorship novel** in Latin America.

Carpentier's prose style, often referred to as "baroque," reveals his acquaintance with music and architecture in its occasionally abstruse vocabulary; music has also served as a structuring device for several works: for example, *La consagración de la primavera* (1978; The Rite of Spring) owes something to Igor Fyodorovich Stravinsky's *Rite of Spring,* while *El acoso* is modeled on Ludwig van Beethoven's *Eroica* Symphony No. 3.

Although he lived abroad for many years, as a cultural attaché and diplomat, Carpentier returned to

Cuba after the triumph of the revolution in 1959, accepting an important cultural appointment. He discreetly admired Jorge Luis Borges and was a friend of **Carlos Fuentes,** who, like many others, spoke out against the repressive activities of the revolutionary government in the early 1970s; but Carpentier was careful to avoid conflict with the Cuban authorities. He died in Paris in 1980.

REFERENCES:

Roberto González Echevarría, *Alejo Carpentier: The Pilgrim at Home* (Ithaca, N.Y.: Cornell University Press, 1977);

Donald Shaw, *Alejo Carpentier* (Boston: Twayne, 1985);

Barbara J. Webb, *Myth and History in Caribbean Fiction: Alejo Carpentier, Wilson Harris, and Edouard Glissant* (Amherst: University of Massachusetts Press, 1992).

— M.E.S. & P.S.

LEONORA CARRINGTON

The English-born painter and writer Leonora Carrington (1917–) is one of the most important Mexican Surrealists. Carrington grew up in a wealthy household, but from her youngest days she rebelled against her conventional upbringing. She studied art in Florence and Paris and in 1937 attended the Amadée Ozenfant Academy in London. Her connection with **Surrealism** began the following year when she met the German Surrealist artist Max Ernst in London. They subsequently lived together in Paris and later settled in St. Martin d'Ardèche in France. Carrington became part of the Surrealist movement and began a lifelong friendship with **Remedios Varo.** During the early Parisian period Carrington wrote her first short stories, "The House of Fear" and "The Oval Lady" (which included illustrations by Ernst), and also produced a series of paintings dealing with the theme of childhood, such as *Self-portrait* (1938). Many of her literary and visual works featured whimsical scenes with animals, especially horses, important symbols in the Celtic myths that she had often heard during her childhood.

In 1939 while Ernst was interned as an enemy alien in France, Carrington had a nervous breakdown, after which her family had her placed in a mental institution in Spain, later putting her under the care of a former nanny. Carrington eventually escaped her supervision and married her friend Renato LeDuc, a Mexican diplomat who agreed to a marriage of convenience to help Carrington get to New York. Carrington met Ernst again in Lisbon; he had been released from the French camp but was now in a relationship with the wealthy art collector Peggy Guggenheim, who arranged passage for him to New York as well. Carrington wrote about the dramatic events of this period and her struggle to regain freedom and a renewed sense of self in her book *Down Below*, published in New York in 1944. The Surrealists regrouped there, and Carrington participated in many of their activities, contributing drawings and stories to the magazines *View* and *VVV*.

Carrington and LeDuc arrived in Mexico City in 1942, where they lived near Remedios Varo and her husband, the Surrealist poet Benjamin Peret. They were part of a group of European artists living in Mexico, one that included Luis Buñuel and Enrique "Chiqui" Weisz, who became Carrington's second husband after a friendly divorce from LeDuc. Varo and Carrington had a close and productive friendship; their works in the mid 1940s often show mutual influences.

After 1945 Carrington achieved full artistic maturity. The principal theme in her work has continued to be a search for self-knowledge and spiritual enlightenment expressed through a complex personal iconography employing female sorceresses, animal guides, a knowledge of botany and alchemy, mythology, and Celtic legends. In carefully executed tempera and oil paintings, such as *The House Opposite* (circa 1947) and *Grandmother Moorhead's Aromatic Kitchen* (1975), Carrington redefines the traditional female spaces of the home and kitchen as transcendental sites where spiritual and creative activities come together. Mexican culture influenced Carrington's art in subtle and oblique ways, except in the large mural *El mundo mágico de los Mayas* (1963; The Magical World of the Mayas), painted for the Museo de Antropología in Mexico City and later transferred to the Museo Regional in Tuxtla Gutiérrez, Chiapas. In preparation for this mural Carrington traveled to Chiapas, studied the practices of local *curanderas* (female folk healers), and learned about regional religious festivals, which she recorded with great accuracy.

REFERENCE:

Whitney Chadwick, *Women Artists and the Surrealist Movement* (New York: Thames & Hudson, 1985).

— F.B.N.

Casa de las Américas Prizes

The Casa de las Américas prizes are literary awards instituted in Cuba in 1959 as one of several cultural initiatives taken only a few months after **Fidel Castro**'s revolutionary forces wrested control of the island from Fulgencio Batista. The objective of the awards was to stimulate and publicize Latin American literature and to place the Cuban Revolution at the center of Latin American cultural life. Most of the well-known names

of Latin American literature have either received the prize or have been members of the jury that awards it yearly. By the mid 1990s some 17,000 book manuscripts have been entered; some 500 authors have received awards; and about 1,000 writers had served as members of juries. In the late 1960s the category of **testimonial narrative** was added, endorsing and stimulating the production of this significant genre of Latin American cultural discourse in the subsequent decade. In 1994 prizes were awarded in the categories of fiction, poetry, children's literature, sociohistorical essays, women's studies, Brazilian literature, Caribbean literature in English or Creole, and literature in three Amerindian languages (Mapuche, Aymara, and Mayasense). In the early 1990s a Casa de las Américas prize was worth the equivalent of three thousand dollars, and it was paid in the national currency of the individual winners.

REFERENCE:

Judith A. Weiss, *'Casa de las Americas': An Intellectual Review in the Cuban Revolution* (Chapel Hill & Madrid: Editorial Castalia, 1977).

— R.G.M.

Pablo Casals

Pablo (or "Pau" in Catalan) Casals (1876–1973), the distinguished Spanish cellist, conductor, and composer, was born in Catalonia to a Puerto Rican mother. After studying with his father in Barcelona, he moved on to the Madrid Conservatory. His early career included playing in cafés and theaters in Barcelona and Paris, where his performances were enthusiastically received. In 1897 he began a two-year stint as professor of cello at the Barcelona Conservatory, also giving concerts in Europe, especially Paris and London, and in 1901 he embarked on his first tour of the United States. In subsequent years he became acknowledged as one of the world's foremost cellists, and in 1919 he formed the Casals Orchestra in Barcelona. A fierce opponent of the Francisco Franco regime in Spain, Casals went into voluntary exile in 1939, vowing never to return to the country of his birth while Spain remained under totalitarian rule. He established the renowned Prades Festival in France (1950), where he remained until resettling in Puerto Rico, the birthplace of his mother, in 1956.

Casals was received in Puerto Rico as an illustrious native son, and plans were developed to begin a new festival bearing his name. The year 1957 was a spectacular one for the eighty-one-year-old maestro. He founded the Casals Festival, the Puerto Rican Symphony Orchestra, and the Puerto Rican Conservatory of Music; all were government sponsored. Also in that year he married his young Puerto Rican cello student, Martita Montáñez, to whom he dedicated *Tres estrofas de amor* (1958; Three Love Poems), with text by Tomás Blanco. A special occasion in Casals's last years was the performance of his *Hymn to the United Nations* (1971), which he conducted at the United Nations in New York. In addition, he began an international appeal for peace with his Christmas oratorio *El pesebre* (1962; The Manger).

During his lifetime the Casals Festival attracted the participation of many of the world's most talented musicians. His dedication and tireless activity brought great benefits to Puerto Rico. In the years since his death the Puerto Rican Symphony Orchestra has continued to play an important role in the cultural life of the island. Similarly, the Conservatory of Music together with the Departments of Music at the University of Puerto Rico and the Inter American University of Puerto Rico continue to provide solid academic and performance experiences for young musicians and prospective audiences.

REFERENCES:

Robert Jacobson, "The Casals Centennial," *High Fidelity/Musical America* (October 1976): 33–35;

Alfredo Matilla Jimeno, *De música* (Río Piedras, Puerto Rico: Universidad de Puerto Rico, 1992);

Donald Thompson, "The Casals Festival Question," letter to the editor, *High Fidelity/Musical America* (March 1977): 4.

— R.L.S.

CASAS DE CULTURA

Casas de Cultura are cultural centers located in many villages, towns, and cities throughout Latin America. Largely supported by government funds, Casas de Cultura often house libraries, museums, and schools where children and adolescents study visual art, music, and dance. The centers often serve as springboards for the creation of ballet, modern-dance, and folk-dance companies. The Casa de Cultura preserves and promotes manifestations of traditional arts as well as imported and contemporary forms.

— J.M.H.

ROSARIO CASTELLANOS

A major literary figure, Rosario Castellanos (1925–1974) was born in Mexico City but grew up in rural surroundings in Chiapas, an impoverished area in southern Mexico with a large indigenous Mayan popu-

lation. Rejected by parents who favored her younger brother, Castellanos spent her childhood in relative isolation, raised largely by a Mayan nanny. When her brother suddenly died, her parents' resentment toward her became even more palpable. In 1941 Mexican President Lázaro Cárdenas promulgated a land reform plan intended to redistribute land among the rural poor, especially the indigenous peoples. As a result Castellanos's parents lost their land and moved to Mexico City. The conflict between the wealthy landowners and the impoverished, mostly indigenous, population became an important theme in her novels, short stories, plays, essays, and poetry. Another major theme is the suffering of women because of gender combined with ethnicity and class. Other personal experiences are also reflected in her literature.

Castellanos's first novel, *Balún Canán* (1957; translated as *The Nine Guardians*), describing the life of the indigenous Tzotzil and addressing the problem of land tenure in Chiapas, gained national recognition. It is a semi-autobiographical novel, narrated in part by a seven-year-old girl whose life is overshadowed by a younger brother, her parents' favorite. As a result she is raised by her Tzotzil nanny, who teaches her the ways of the indigenous peoples. The novel is divided into three parts, the first and third narrated by the young girl living with her wealthy family in a provincial town; the second describes the family's trip to their ranch, the conflict between the landowners and the Tzotzil, and the flight of the landed families from the Tzotzil, who rise up in rebellion. In this second part the narrator is omniscient; however, the narration is interspersed with interior monologues of the different characters, who reveal concerns associated with being women, Indians, or orphaned outsiders in a world controlled by wealthy men. A sort of Bildungsroman, the novel ends on a pessimistic note when the girl's younger brother dies and her nanny, who had predicted his death as revenge by the Tzotzil witchdoctors, is banished from the house. The concluding scene suggests that the girl has rejected her nanny's teachings and has learned to adopt the ethnocentric, superior attitude of her parents. Today *Balún Canán* can be read as a novelistic representation of the roots of the indigenous uprising in Chiapas against the national government, beginning early in 1994.

A later book, *Oficio de tinieblas* (1962; Rites of Darkness), focuses on the Chamula Indian rebellion in San Cristóbal in 1867 and is considered an important neo-**indigenist** work. Castellanos's short stories in *Ciudad Real* (1960; Royal City) and *Los convidados de agosto* (1964; The Guests of August) deal with similar themes of ethnic and gender discrimination. Those included in her last collection of short stories, *Album de familia* (1971; Family Album), concentrate more on the alienation of middle- and upper-class Mexican women struggling to find an autonomous identity in the male-dominated space they inhabit. Her "Lección de cocina" ("Cooking Lesson") is an excellent example of the use of language and metaphor to describe woman's confined, domestic reality. Many of her numerous essays are in *Mujer que sabe latín* (1971; Women Who Know Latin), an important sociological and cultural treatise on the difficult conditions under which most women struggle for economic and intellectual recognition. A collection of some of her best-known poetry may be found in *Poesía no eres tú* (1972; You Are Not Poetry), which includes poetry written since 1948. These poems concentrate on the themes found in her other work as well as new themes: for example, the search for the other, an exploration of death, the act of writing, and the struggle to find an authentic voice. Castellanos's best-known play is *El eterno femenino* (1975; The Eternal Feminine), a farce that dramatizes the lives of various Mexican female historical figures and satirizes the hypocrisy of a society that imposes a sexual double standard.

Early in her life Castellanos established herself as a writer and joined the circle of Mexican, Nicaraguan, and Guatemalan writers who became known as the Generation of 1950. She became director of cultural programs in Chiapas and traveled throughout the region with a puppet troupe for two years. It was this experience, together with her upbringing, that enabled her to develop the indigenous themes that are so prominent in her writings. Later, Castellanos held professorships in Mexico and the United States and continued to write for newspapers and journals, always exploring woman's identity and place in culture. In 1957 she married a Mexican professor, but the marriage failed and only accentuated her loneliness. After two miscarriages she gave birth in 1961 to her son, Gabriel, and divorced her husband shortly afterward. At the height of her career, Castellanos was appointed Mexican ambassador to Israel. Her life ended in Tel Aviv, when she was apparently electrocuted while turning on a lamp in her living room.

REFERENCES:

Maureen Ahearn, ed., *A Rosario Castellanos Reader* (Austin: University of Texas Press, 1988);

Frank Dauster, "Rosario Castellanos: The Search for a Voice," in *The Double Strand: Five Contemporary Mexican Poets* (Lexington: University Press of Kentucky, 1987), pp. 134–162.

— M.E.S.

OTTO RENÉ CASTILLO

Otto René Castillo (193?–1967), born in Quezaltenango, Guatemala, became a political activist at an early age. He was forced into exile after the coup

of 1954, when reformist president Jacobo Arbenz was overthrown and replaced by a CIA-chosen army officer. At various times during his life Castillo suffered repercussions because of his political commitment, which is evident in his poetry. Much of Castillo's poetry was seen by his contemporary, the Salvadoran poet **Roque Dalton,** as calling for commitment from the intellectual to match that of the active revolutionary, reflecting Castillo's belief that the individual had an obligation to contribute to the betterment of the masses. Castillo recognized the importance of the Mayan culture and tradition. He was an active supporter of the guerrilla movement, as is reflected in his collection of poetry *Vámonos patria a caminar* (1965: Let's Move Forward, Homeland). In 1967, while fighting against government forces, he was captured and tortured to death.

REFERENCE:

John Beverley and Marc Zimmerman, *Literature and Politics in the Central American Revolutions* (Austin: University of Texas Press, 1990).

— M.E.S.

FIDEL CASTRO AND THE CUBAN REVOLUTION

The charismatic leader of the Cuban revolution, Fidel Castro was born in 1927 in the town of Mayarí in southeastern Cuba. He attended Jesuit schools and graduated with a law degree from the University of Havana in 1950. At the university Castro was a political activist who took up the cause of nationalism, worked with revolutionary groups in other Caribbean territories, and later attempted the overthrow of Fulgencio Batista's corrupt dictatorship. Castro first achieved notoriety with his assault on the Moncada army barracks on 26 July 1953. He was captured, jailed, and released two years later. At his trial he defended himself with a speech known by its closing words, "La historia me absolverá" (History will absolve me), later published in book form and regarded as the founding document of Castro's movement, thenceforth known as the 26th of July Movement. After prison Castro went to Mexico and with the help of Argentinean physician **Ernesto "Che" Guevara** organized Cuban exiles into a small guerrilla army. Castro and his eighty men invaded Cuba in December 1956, and after a disastrous skirmish with Batista's troops, one that considerably thinned the ranks of the rebels, the survivors of Castro's army — among them Fidel's brother Raúl and Guevara — entrenched themselves in the Sierra Maestra. The Batista army failed to dislodge them from this mountain stronghold in spite of a massive offen-

Fidel Castro and Soviet premier Nikita Khrushchev in New York City, 23 September 1960, while attending a session at the United Nations. This public embrace helped to convince U.S. president Dwight D. Eisenhower to impose an embargo on trade with Cuba.

sive. Guevara's *Pasajes de la guerra revolucionaria* (1959; translated as *Reminiscences of the Cuban Revolutionary War*) is an account of the invasion.

As a result of the guerrilla insurgency in the mountains and political pressure in the cities, Batista's government collapsed on 1 January 1959. Castro entered Havana and accepted the office of premier. In December 1961 he publicly declared himself a Marxist-Leninist. In April of that year his government had turned back an invasion by some fifteen hundred Cuban exiles, trained by the CIA in Guatemala, whose purpose was to touch off a mass revolt against Castro. The Bay of Pigs invasion (as it was called) turned into a triumph for the revolution and led to the missile crisis of October 1962, since the Soviets secretly began sending nuclear warheads to Cuba, allegedly to prevent another invasion. The U.S. Navy blockaded the island, but Armageddon was avoided when President John F. Kennedy and Soviet premier Nikita Khrushchev agreed to a deal whereby the Russians would remove their missiles from Cuba in exchange for a promise that the United States would not support further attempts to invade Cuba. Castro then became the target of at least eight assassination attempts engineered by the CIA, one of which involved the resources of organized

crime. As Castro took his revolutionary movement to other Latin American nations and later to Africa, the United States developed an official policy based on economic and diplomatic isolation and designed to weaken Castro's leadership. Despite U.S. efforts Castro remained in power (surviving even the collapse of the Soviet Union) by a combination of charisma, political skill, and determination. However one may judge his revolution, Castro has become a nationalist symbol throughout Latin America and the Third World.

Cuban cultural politics during the 1960s were relatively permissive, but afterward government control grew and became repressive. From the start the revolution aimed at having an international appeal based on the ideals of its two chief leaders, Castro and Guevara. Guevara, during the early 1960s, advocated the idea of the "New Man," and Castro spread the "Bread Without Fear" slogan. The two dimensions of revolution, the political and the moral, were thought inseparable, and Cuba felt the moral responsibility to encourage revolution elsewhere. Hence Guevara led expeditions to the Congo and to Bolivia, in what proved to be a futile attempt to propagate the revolutionary faith. Radio stations beamed the revolutionary message to other parts of Latin America; Cuba welcomed young revolutionaries who came to be trained in guerrilla warfare; revolutionary groups opened fronts in other Latin American countries.

Culture, too, was viewed as having a role to play in the international projection of the Cuban revolution. To this effect **Casa de las Américas** and the **Cuban Film Institute** (ICAIC) were created shortly after Castro took power. Casa de las Américas was and is a publishing enterprise that through its homonymous journal and the annual prize instituted in 1959 soon became a focal point of Latin American letters. Almost all the major Latin American authors published or were reviewed in the journal *Casa de las Américas* or traveled to Cuba to judge the contestants for the annual prize or were themselves awarded the honors. Without the revolution and its international dimension, the **Boom** in Latin American fiction would have been less noisy. The Cuban film industry, furthermore, bloomed in the 1960s and achieved international renown with films such as **Humberto Solás**'s *Lucía* and **Tomás Gutiérrez Alea**'s *Memories of Underdevelopment*.

Castro's interest in cultural matters was evident in June 1961 when he convened a meeting with artists and intellectuals, resulting in the formation of the Union of Cuban Artists and Writers (UNEAC). It was then that Castro proclaimed, "Within the revolution, everything; outside the revolution, nothing." The line dividing the inside from the outside, however, was not precisely demarcated.

In Cuba during the 1960s painters such as **Wifredo Lam** and **René Portocarrero** flourished, and **poster** art became particularly dynamic. Equally significant was the emergence of **testimonial narrative** and of musical performers and composers such as Silvio Rodríguez and Pablo Milanés, who overhauled Cuban rhythms (such as the **mambo, cha-cha-cha, son,** and **rumba**) so popular abroad in prerevolutionary times.

Things went sour when in 1971 the poet Heberto Padilla was accused of having counterrevolutionary views and was obliged to make a public apology when receiving one of the Casa de las Américas prizes. (See **The Padilla Affair.**) As a result, many intellectuals, Latin American and foreign, cosigned a letter of protest to Castro, in which they defended artistic freedom. The 1970s witnessed a decline in artistic creativity and an especially harsh crackdown on theatrical companies for allegedly harboring an inordinate number of sexual deviants. More generally, Castro's cultural politics of the 1970s coincided with a renewed and successful effort on the part of ICAIC to produce films specifically designed for a national audience. (Pastor Vega's *Portrait of Teresa* — which put inveterate Cuban "machismo" on trial — was one of the most popular films of the period.)

The Padilla case showed that in times of crisis a dictatorial regime will resort to repressive tactics that in better times it may not choose to implement. It also served notice that artistic freedom in Cuba was conditional. As time went by, many of the major Latin American intellectuals who had once supported the revolution broke with it, with the notable exception of Gabriel García Márquez, who has said that he still sees it as the lesser of two evils.

Cuba's role as an international provider of culture, however, is not over. In 1985 in Havana, García Márquez established his **Fundación de Nuevo Cine Latinoamericano** (New Latin American Film Foundation), a project to which he donated funds and six film scripts that have already been shot by directors from several Latin American countries and Spain.

REFERENCES:

Edmundo Desnoes, ed., *Los dispositivos en la flor* (Hanover, N.H.: Ediciones del Norte, 1981);

Tad Szulc, *Fidel: A Critical Portrait* (New York: Morrow, 1986).
                                                                                                      — R.G.M. & P.S.

CENIDI-Danza

The Centro Nacional de Investigación, Documentación e Información de la Danza José Limón (José Limón National Center for Research, Documentation and In-

formation on Dance), or CENIDI-Danza, founded in 1983, has been directed by such scholars as Patricia Aulestia de Alba, its founder, and Lin Durán Navarro, a former dancer and renowned researcher. It is located at the Centro Nacional de las Artes (National Arts Center) in Mexico City (completed in 1995), and its aims are to preserve the history of dance in Mexico and to make this information available to as wide a public as possible. The center is a repository for videotapes, audiotapes (largely of interviews with dance personalities), printed programs, posters, photographs, and scholarly publications, and it regularly collaborates in programming panels, conferences, publications, and seminars on such topics as dance and medicine, comparative methods for teaching classical dance, and the Mexican legacy of **Waldeen.**

CENIDI-Danza provides residencies for writers and researchers to examine either topics of personal interest or assigned subjects based on priorities established by the director. Its seventy-three listed publications include bulletins, reviews, books, conference papers, and catalogues that cover figures such as José Limón, Waldeen, Anna Sokolow, Gloria Campobello, **Guillermina Bravo,** and Sergio Franco; contemporary themes such as subsidized companies, independent groups, and dance education; and reports on meetings such as the Primer Coloquio Nacional sobre Danza y Medicina (First National Colloquium on Dance and Medicine) and the Primer Encuentro Nacional de Investigación de la Danza (First National Conference on Dance Research). CENIDI-Danza is a division of the government's Subdirección General de Educación e Investigación Artísticas (Subdirectorate of Artistic Education and Research), which is itself part of the Instituto Nacional de Bellas Artes (National Institute of Fine Arts).

                                                                                                      — J.M.H.

Censorship

Spanish America has a long tradition of censorship. Beginning with the control of information by the Spaniards and the Catholic Church during colonial times, official censorship continued through the independence movements that sprang up just after the turn of the early nineteenth century — a period that also saw the birth of the newspaper in Spanish America — down to the twentieth century, during which those in power in the region often used the media to influence public opinion. The abusive control of information has been dealt with in many works of art, films, and books, including some **dictatorship novels.**

One frequent means of control has been bribery, or the "subsidy" system, through which a government subsidizes the importing or manufacturing of newsprint, printing presses, or broadcasting equipment and in return gains sympathetic coverage. In a majority of the Latin American republics, domestic reporters are usually prevented by their governments from probing deeply or consistently into the malfunctions of the state. It remains for foreign correspondents to uncover such matters, when they are able to do so.

The traditional method of minimizing political opposition was simply to silence the press, a practice often employed by the Latin American caudillos, or strongman presidents, of the nineteenth and early twentieth centuries. Later dictators — most notably Juan Perón in Argentina in the 1940s and **Fidel Castro** in Cuba in the 1960s — have used the mass media to "reeducate" the masses. In the pre-Castro period, Cuban journalism suffered from alternating periods of censorship and bribery, and genuine press freedom was rare. From 1925 to 1933, for example, the dictator Gerardo Machado used overt censorship to control the press. Since the revolution of 1959 all media in Cuba, from daily newspapers to television, have had the primary obligation of encouraging Cubans to identify the Castro regime with the values of the nation. In 1971 the Cuban Education Congress stated: "Radio, television, cinema and the press are powerful instruments of ideological education for the creation of a collective conscience. Mass media cannot be left to chance or used without direction." When a constitution was promulgated in 1975, Castro used the occasion to point out to foreign correspondents that no rival political parties, ideologies, or media criticism would be allowed to undermine the Marxist state. The two most important newspapers in Cuba, *Granma* and *Juventud rebelde,* for example, are funded by the government and express unfaltering progovernment views.

Elsewhere, government intervention has been perhaps more discreet, though no less real. Mexico is one of several nations in the region where the government has legally institutionalized management of the news media though a web of subtle interventions. With its essentially one-party democracy controlled by the Partido Revolucionario Institucional (Institutional Revolutionary Party), or PRI, Mexico is neither authoritarian nor libertarian. While many believe that most newspapers in Mexico either reflect or are directly controlled by vested interests, some publications are firmly independent, including *El Norte* of Monterrey, *La Jornada* of Mexico City, and the weekly newsmagazine *Proceso.* One way in which the Mexican government wields control over the press is by its ownership of Productora e Importadora de Papel, SA

(PIPSA), the business that controls the importation, manufacture, distribution, and sale of newsprint. In 1974 *El Norte* had its newsprint supply cut by 83 percent after President Luis Echeverría Alvarez was angered by its reporting and editorials. The government has little control over the airwaves, however. The leading Mexican television network, **Televisa,** possesses independent economic and political power that makes it difficult for the government to exert much pressure. Although there have been instances in which its news coverage has brought government wrath upon it, Televisa has generally been sympathetic to the policies of the ruling party. In May 1994 Televisa played a major role in publicizing the first-ever Mexican presidential debate, attracting a huge national audience for the debate among Ernesto Zedillo, the candidate for PRI; Diego Fernández de Cevallos, the candidate for Partido Acción Nacional (National Action Party), or PAN; and Cuauhtémoc Cárdenas, the candidate for Partido Revolución Democrática (Democratic Revolutionary Party), or PRD.

Another pattern of censorship has been in evidence in Nicaragua. From 1937 until 1979 the Somoza family dominated Nicaragua. For part of that period (1950–1979) an opposition daily newspaper, *La Prensa,* was sometimes able to express its disagreement with government policy, but at many other times it was subject to government censorship. When the regime of Anastasio Somoza Debayle fell to the Sandinistas in 1979, the new government decided to make a break with the past. On 17 August 1979 the five-person ruling junta announced a "Press Freedom Law," which warned the media not to publish stories against the victorious revolutionary government or in favor of the ousted Somoza forces. In addition to taking over the existing Radio Nacional, the junta also set up its own radio station, Radio Sandino, and used both to promote a positive image of its new policies. Radio Sandino programs were subsequently carried by all other Nicaraguan broadcasting stations. Nongovernment news could be found principally in *La Prensa,* which was associated with the powerful Chamorro family, who were hostile to the new regime. The Sandinistas put pressure on *La Prensa* not to criticize the government, but it did not outlaw the paper, as would have been normal in Castro's Cuba. In 1980 twenty ardent supporters of the government resigned from *La Prensa* to publish their own daily, *El Diario Nuevo,* which united forces with the Sandinista daily, *Barricada,* in providing uncritical and enthusiastic coverage of governmental actions and policies. When the Sandinistas fell from power in 1990 and Violeta Chamorro became president, *La Prensa* predictably came to present a positive view of the new government and its policies. (See **Nicaraguan Revolution.**)

REFERENCES:

Marvin Alisky, "Latin America," in *Global Journalism,* edited by John C. Merrill (New York: Longman, 1983), pp. 249–301;

Alisky, *Latin American Media: Guidance and Censorship* (Ames: Iowa State University Press, 1981);

Elizabeth Fox, ed., *Media and Politics in Latin America: The Struggle for Democracy* (London: Sage, 1988);

Michael B. Salwen and Bruce Garrison, *Latin American Journalism* (Hillsdale, N.J.: Lawrence Erlbaum, 1991).

— S.M.H. & P.S.

CHA-CHA-CHA

In the 1940s new approaches to the third section of the Cuban **danzón** eventually produced several new genres of popular song/dance music, among them the **mambo** and the cha-cha-cha. Antonio Arcaño's **charanga** ensemble, Arcaño y sus Maravillas, revitalized the rhythm of the third section of the danzón by adding complex syncopations. This innovation resulted in the danzón-mambo, a song/dance section that required intricate dance steps. Enrique Jorrín (1926–), a violinist in Arcaño's charanga ensemble, observed that many dancers could not negotiate the difficult choreography of the danzón/mambo. He simplified the music by focusing on singable, danceable melodies in moderate tempo without syncopated counterrhythms in the accompaniment. His innovation, realized in the early 1950s, became the cha-cha-cha, a name said to have derived from the sound of feet shuffling to the choreographic pattern (one-two, one-two-three). Among the charanga ensembles that helped to popularize the new dance were the Orquesta Aragón and José Fajardo y Sus Estrellas. The new dance became one of the most popular in the hemisphere by the mid 1950s. In the United States the cha-cha-cha was typically performed by existing larger bands featuring brass and woodwinds rather than the charanga ensemble. Prominent cha-cha-cha musicians were **Tito Puente** (*Rico vacilón, Pare cochero*), **Tito Rodríguez** (*Me lo dijo Adela, Los marcianos*), and **Frank "Machito" Grillo** (*Quimbombo*).

REFERENCES:

Cristóbal Díaz Ayala, *Música cubana del Areyto a la Nueva Trova,* second edition (San Juan: Editorial Cubanacán, 1981);

Helio Orovio, *Diccionario de la música cubana: Biográfico y técnico* (Havana: Editorial Letras Cubanas, 1992);

Olavo Alén Rodríguez, *De lo afrocubano a la salsa: Géneros musicales de Cuba* (San Juan: Editorial Cubanacán, 1992).

— R.L.S.

CHARANGA

The charanga, a Cuban musical ensemble consisting of two violins, flute, piano, bass, timbales, and **güiro,** emerged in the early part of the twentieth century. Also known as the charanga francesa, this ensemble gained precedence over the older military-style ensemble for performances of the popular Cuban **danzón.** In the 1920s the surge in popularity of the Cuban **son,** accompanied by sextet and septet ensembles, diminished popular interest in the charanga. The sextet included guitar, **tres,** bass or **marímbola, maracas,** and claves; the septet added trumpet. With the introduction of the **cha-cha-cha** by Enrique Jorrín in 1951, the charanga regained its popularity, but the explosion of interest in the **mambo** of the 1950s once again robbed the charanga ensemble of its predominance. Later additions of **conga** drum, more violins, and singers expanded the instrumentation of the charanga, which has been preserved in the contemporary group Los Van Van.

REFERENCES:

Peter Manuel, *Popular Musics of the Non-Western World: An Introductory Survey* (New York: Oxford University Press, 1988);

Rebeca Mauleón, *Salsa Guidebook for Piano and Ensemble,* (Petaluma, Cal.: Sher Music, 1993);

Helio Orovio, *Diccionario de la música cubana: Biográfico y técnico,* second edition (Havana: Editorial Letras Cubanas, 1992).

— R.L.S.

JEAN CHARLOT

The French-born Jean Charlot (1898–1979) participated in Mexican **Muralism** and **Estridentismo** and was one of the main supporters of the **graphic arts** in Mexico. Charlot, who had a Mexican grandmother, was born in Paris and studied art in France. In 1921 he arrived in Mexico, where because of his knowledge of fresco technique he was soon invited to participate in Muralism, first as an assistant on **Diego Rivera**'s encaustic mural painting *La creación* (1922; Creation) in the Escuela Nacional Preparatoria (National Preparatory School). Later, Charlot produced other fresco paintings in a modernized realism influenced by Cubism, such as *La conquista de Tenochtitlán* (1922; The Conquest of Tenochtitlán), located on the staircase of the Preparatoria, and *Cargadores y lavanderas* (1923; Porters and Washerwomen), at the Secretaría de Educación Pública (Ministry of Public Education).

Even more important than Charlot's production as a muralist was his work as a printmaker and teacher

Jean Charlot in 1947 standing in front of a section of *La conquista de Tenochtitlán* (1922; The Conquest of Tenochtitlán), a mural he painted at the Escuela Nacional Preparatoria in Mexico City

of graphic art. Not only did he draw attention to the work of earlier printmakers such as **José Guadalupe Posada,** he also helped revive woodcut technique in Mexico, encouraging its traditional use as a vehicle for representing social themes. In 1921 Charlot joined the Escuelas de Arte al Aire Libre, where he met Fernando Leal, Ramón Alva de la Canal, Fermín Revueltas, and Leopoldo Méndez, all of whom participated in Estridentismo. In 1922 he began to run a print workshop with Fernando Leal in the open-air school of Coyoacán, where he taught woodcut and lithography to Francisco Díaz de León, Gabriel Fernández Ledesma, and Emilio Ameto, who became important contributors to the graphic revival of the 1930s and 1940s.

The woodcut's roughness and expressiveness of texture and line made it the perfect means of introducing the avant-garde art of Estridentismo (1921–1927), with its concern with political and revolutionary issues. Not surprising, most of Charlot's works for Estridentismo consisted of woodcuts produced between 1922 and 1925. These include illustrations in the magazines *Irradiador* and *El Universal Ilustrado,* such as his highly abstract composition *Retrato psicológico de Maples Arce* (1922; Psychological Portrait of Maples Arce), published in *El Universal Ilustrado.* Charlot also produced prints for several of the books published by his fellow Estridentistas, such as Manuel Maples

Arce's *Urbe: Poema bolchevique en 5 cantos* (1924; *Metropolis*). Charlot's woodcuts for *Urbe,* such as *Viaducto* (Viaduct) and *Buque a vapor* (Ocean Steamer), echo the utopian interest in technology that was typical of Estridentismo, as well as the group's interest in avant-garde art.

In the 1930s Charlot turned to **Indigenism** and participated in the Taller de Gráfica Popular (Popular Graphic Workshop). He began producing numerous prints representing indigenous peoples in daily activities, such as the color lithograph *Lavandera no. 8* (1933; Washerwoman No. 8) and the black-and-white lithograph *Lavanderas* (1937; Washerwomen). The style of these prints consistently favored blocky figures with outlines regularized by simplified geometric patterns.

REFERENCE:

Peter Morse, *Jean Charlot's Prints: A Catalogue Raisonné* (Honolulu: University Press of Hawaii, 1976).

— F.B.N.

CARLOS CHÁVEZ

Carlos Chávez (1899–1978), the leading composer, conductor, and music educator of Mexico, was born close to the town of Popotla in the Federal District of

Mexico in 1899. He began piano lessons with his older brother, Manuel, and continued with local teachers who provided a firm understanding of harmony and of European classical and romantic piano literature. At age eleven he began studying with **Manuel Ponce,** whose interest in Mexican folk music exerted a lasting influence over Chávez's musical life. Among other influences were the **Mexican Revolution** and an indigenous heritage from his maternal grandfather.

By the age of nine Chávez was writing small pieces for the piano. By twelve he was teaching himself the essentials of composition through intense study of the works of European composers, especially Johann Sebastian Bach, Ludwig van Beethoven, and Claude Debussy. Chávez pursued these studies not as a dilettante but as an avid analyst of harmony, counterpoint, structure, and orchestration. He did not include most of the music he composed during this early period (to 1921) in his definitive catalogue; it is music that appears to consist of experimental exercises in compositional technique. Only four works from this early period were published: *Extase* for voice and piano (1918); *Imagen mexicana* (1920); *Sonata No. 2* (1921); and *String Quartet No. 1* (1921).

Although vestiges of the Mexican Revolution continued after 1921, a period of reconstruction and rebirth of Mexican culture began in that year. **José Vasconcelos,** the secretary of public education who had supported the creation of murals by **Diego Rivera** and **José Clemente Orozco,** commissioned Chávez to write a ballet inspired by an Aztec theme. Chávez responded with *El fuego nuevo* (The New Fire), the work that inaugurated his first professional period (to 1928). The original version, written for a small orchestra in 1921, was not performed. Revised in 1927, it was not premiered until 1930. During this period he demonstrated more confidence in his technical skill and revealed a commitment to musical values that he perceived as stemming from indigenous sources. Earlier opera composers had dealt superficially with Indian subjects through music that was essentially European. Chávez's extensive personal exposure to indigenous music throughout his early life enabled him to express the essence of indigenous music without resorting to quotations.

The plot of *El fuego nuevo* is based on an ancient Aztec ritual: at the close of each fifty-two-year cycle, the new-fire ritual was performed to beseech the gods not to destroy the empire and to bestow the gift of life for a new cycle. The required orchestra for the revised version was large: sixty strings, fourteen woodwinds, twelve brass, bass drum, six tympani, and a female chorus. In addition, a large number of indigenous percussion instruments were required: three slit drums; small drum; tam-tam; four **güiros** (scraped gourds); cymbals; rattles; and groups of ocarinas in high, medium, and low registers. The persistent, varied, and sometimes violent rhythms; the use of the minor third; the characteristic calls of the conch-shell trumpet; and the use of the pentatonic scale were all reflections of what is sometimes referred to as Chávez's "Indianist" orientation.

In the 1920s, disappointed by the limitations of post–World War I musical life in Europe, Chávez turned to the United States, where he found excitement and innovation in industry and the arts. Back home, Chávez invested an enormous effort to bring Mexico into the twentieth century musically: public concerts and tastes appeared to be locked in the nineteenth century. With the help of **Silvestre Revueltas,** Chávez produced numerous programs of contemporary chamber music featuring works of Claude Debussy, Maurice Ravel, Arnold Schönberg, Béla Bartók, Darius Milhaud, Francis-Jean-Marcel Poulenc, Edgard Varèse, and others. Although the concerts did not achieve their goal, the effort demonstrates that Chávez's interests were not confined to the single issue that occupied nationalist composers. Some years later (1932) he was named knight of the Legion of Honor in recognition of his many performances of contemporary French music.

In 1926 Chávez began two large-scale works that both reinforced his nationalistic image and confirmed his interest in contemporary styles and techniques: *Los cuatro soles* (The Four Ages [of the Earth]) and *Caballos de vapor* (Horsepower). *Los cuatro soles* is based on legendary Aztec beliefs regarding the four stages of creation and destruction of the world: air, water, fire, and earth. *Caballos de vapor* focuses attention on episodes in contemporary life, contrasting life in the tropics with life in the industrialized north and again consisting of four principal movements: The Dance of Man; The Boat; The Tropics; and The Dance of Men and Machines. Given the nature of the work, Chávez takes the opportunity to refer to Mexican popular, folk, and Creole songs and dances: tango, huapango, and sandunga. Both works have been presented as ballets and as symphonic suites.

By 1928 the problems of orchestral organizations and professional musicians in Mexico had reached chaotic proportions. The lack of financial and public support had caused the new Orquesta Sinfónica *Mexicana* to suspend a series of Beethoven symphony concerts. Admired for his success as a composer and for his clear sense of direction and commitment, Chávez was invited by concerned musicians to reform the orchestra and to become its conductor. He accepted the post and the following year changed the orchestra's name to

Orquesta Sinfónica de México. Within a few seasons his dedication and enthusiasm had helped convert this orchestra into a first-class organization. It became a national institution with improved funding from governmental and private sources. Chávez remained as its musical director for twenty-one years, during which time the orchestra became a showcase for international composers and performers as well as an accessible medium of expression for Mexican composers.

In the same year that he assumed the direction of the symphony orchestra, Chávez was appointed director of the National Conservatory. He immediately began to modernize an antiquated and irrelevant curriculum, promoted the performance of chamber music, founded the Conservatory Chorus, founded the Orquesta Mexicana (which incorporated indigenous instruments), initiated a series of Conservatory Concerts to give student musicians and composers a performance venue, and institutionalized courses in composition, orchestration, and historical research. In addition to his other commitments, he insisted on teaching composition, an effort that produced some of Mexico's most active contemporary composers, among them Silvestre Revueltas, Blas Galindo (1910–), José Pablo Moncayo (1912–1958), Salvador Contreras (1912–), Daniel Ayala (1908–), and Luis Sandi (1905–).

Chávez returned to the United States for a brief visit in 1932, and he heard a performance of his symphonic suite *Caballos de vapor* by the Philadelphia Orchestra under Leopold Stokowski. Stokowski took him to the studios of RCA Victor in New Jersey and to the Bell Telephone Laboratories in New York. Impressed by the potential of electronic reproduction of music, Chávez wrote a report for Mexican consumption that was later converted into the book, *Toward a New Music: Music and Electricity*, published by W. W. Norton of New York (1937).

Overt nationalism began to subside somewhat in the works of Mexican composers in the 1930s and 1940s (see **nationalism in music**) as contemporary European influences created interest in more-universal values. One of Chávez's greatest masterpieces was created during this era of aesthetic transformation. In *Sinfonía de Antígona* (1933), a symphonic work based on incidental music composed earlier for a stage production of Jean Cocteau's version of Sophocles' tragedy, indigenous nationalism was replaced by neoclassical procedures. Similar works followed: *La hija de Cólquide* (1943–1944; The Daughter of Colchis), originally a ballet conceived by and for Martha Graham and later revised as a symphonic suite (1947); the *Violin Concerto* (1948–1950); and the *Sinfonía No. 3* (1951–1954).

Carlos Chávez's interest in neoclassicism and contemporary music should not be construed as an abandonment of Mexican nationalism. In the same year that he composed his first symphony (1933) he dedicated *Cantos de México* to Silvestre Revueltas. The instrumentation of this work includes flute, piccolo, clarinet, two violins, tenor drum, and a variety of Mexican instruments: chirimía (an indigenous oboe); **vihuela; guitarrón;** large harp; **marimba;** a variety of drums, rattles and scrapers; **güiro;** and other minor percussion instruments. Further, the music was inspired by native and popular sources. Later works of this type include *La sinfonía india* (1936), also employing indigenous instruments, and *Xochipilli-Macuilxóchitl* (1940), an attempted reconstruction of pre-Columbian music, using Aztec instruments.

After 1936 Chávez returned often to the United States and conducted performances of his works with most of the major orchestras. Following his tenure with the Orquesta Sinfónica de Mexico and the Instituto Nacional de Bellas Artes, Chávez continued to lecture and teach, but, responding to numerous commissions, dedicated most of his energy to expanding his already large catalogue of compositions. Among the outstanding major works produced in his final period were the last four symphonies (Nos. 3–6), the opera *The Visitors,* the cantata *Prometheus,* the ballet *Pirámide,* two works for orchestra (*Clio* and *Resonancias*), and various chamber works.

REFERENCES:

Roberto García Morillo, *Carlos Chávez: Vida y obra* (México City: Fondo de Cultura Económica, 1960);

Otto Mayer-Serra, *The Present State of Music in Mexico* (Washington, D.C.: Panamerican Union Music Division, 1946);

Robert Stevenson, *Music in Mexico: A Historical Survey* (New York: Crowell, 1952);

Herbert Weinstock, "Carlos Chávez," *Composers of the Americas: Biographical Data and Catalogs of Their Works*, volume 3 (Washington, D.C.: Pan American Union, General Secretariat, Organization of American States, 1955).

—R.L.S.

CHICANO LITERATURE

At about the same time as the generation of **La Onda** writers were becoming known in Mexico in the 1960s and 1970s, Chicano literature (literature by Mexicans or Mexican Americans living in the United States, particularly in the Southwest) began to receive international attention. A series of historic events in the 1960s and 1970s marked the period that came to be known as the Chicano movement and gave rise to a literature that focused on Chicano history and culture, emphasizing the socially oppressed condition of the Chicanos. These events included the civil rights movement, the antiwar movement, the evolution of cultural pride in the Chicano community, the unionization of farmworkers led by César Chávez and Dolores Huerta, the creation of the Teatro Campesino (Popular Theater) by Luis Valdez, and the women's movement. The Chicano texts trace a historical evolution in the United States up to the present day with references to Aztec origins in the mythical land of Aztlán, which becomes a metaphor for the Southwest; the Mexican-American war of 1848, in which Mexico lost about half of its territory consisting of what is now Texas, California, New Mexico, Arizona, Nevada, Utah, and part of Colorado; and the **Mexican Revolution.**

The emerging Chicano consciousness reflected a growing awareness of the situation of Mexican Americans as outsiders; Chicano writers attempted directly to confront oppression, generally in two ways. The first was an effort involving most Chicano writers to create their own history and culture by denying that of the dominant society, choosing to resist a subservient integration by Chicanos into U.S. society. The second was a more integrative approach that involved a recognition that their history of oppression was part of the history of the United States. This second approach led Chicanos to make connections with other marginalized ethnic groups in the United States. Although the mode of expression of Chicano writers is mostly English, code-switching between English and Spanish is frequent, and at times there is a sprinkling of Nahuatl and "Tex-Mex"; this language, formerly regarded as substandard, became increasingly recognized as a means of expression of a unique culture.

Many Chicano writers have published works since the 1970s. Some of the texts and authors who have received widest recognition are *Heart of Aztlán* (1976) by Rudolfo Anaya (1937–), *El sueño de Santa María de las Piedras* (1986; The Dream of Santa María de las Piedras) by Miguel Méndez M. (1930–), *Generaciones y semblanzas* (1976; Generations and Sketches) by Rolando Hinojosa-Smith (1924–), and *Pocho* (1959; the title refers to a blend of English and Spanish) by José Antonio Villareal (1924–). Various Chicana women writers have also emerged. They focus more on oppression related to gender, ethnicity, or race, and class. Some of the more well-known writers and works are Gloria Anzaldúa (1950?–) with *Borderlands/La Frontera: The New Mestiza* (1987), Ana Castillo (1953?–) with *My Father Was a Toltec* (1984), Lorna Dee Cervantes (1954–) with *Emplumada* (1981; The Plumed One), Helena María Viramontes (1954–) with *The Moths and Other Stories* (1985), and

Sandra Cisneros (1954–) with *The House on Mango Street* (1985).

REFERENCES:

Antonia Castañeda-Shular, Tomás Ybarra-Frausto, and Joseph Sommers, *Literatura chicana: Texto y contexto/Chicano Literature: Text and Context* (Englewood Cliffs, N.J.: Prentice-Hall, 1972);

Marta Ester Sánchez, *Contemporary Chicana Poetry: A Critical Approach to an Emerging Literature* (Los Angeles: University of California Press, 1985).

— M.E.S.

CINEMA IN CENTRAL AMERICA

Filmmakers in Central America and the Caribbean (excluding Cuba) have not been as fortunate as their counterparts in Mexico. The Central American nations, unlike Mexico, have no real, organized national film industry. During the 1930s and 1940s, for example, Central America was saturated with movies imported from Hollywood and Mexico. There have, however, been some sparks in the Central American film industry, mainly as a result of the fusion of aesthetics and revolutionary politics. During the early 1980s the Bolivian filmmaker Alfonso Gumucio Dagrón worked in Nicaragua with the Central Obrera Sandinista (Sandinista Workers' Union) on a project funded by the United Nations and the Nicaraguan Ministry of Planning. In 1980 he offered a six-month crash course in filmmaking to students from the Sandinista Workers' Union, the Association of Agricultural Workers, the Sandinista Youth Organization, the Ministries of Planning and the Interior, and various women's organizations. The expenses for his Taller de Cine Super-8 (Super-8 Film Workshop) — including equipment, film stock, office renovations, and Dagrón's salary — were less than $30,000. This course proved fruitful for the art of film in Central America. The class produced a collective feature film, *Cooperativa Sandino* (Sandino Cooperative), which, as Dagrón recalls, has a "lot of humor and creative intelligence." He wrote a manual based on his experience, *El cine de los trabajadores* (1981; Workers' Cinema).

As in Nicaragua, filmmaking in El Salvador has been linked with the fortunes of political parties. In May 1980 the Revolutionary El Salvador Film Institute was set up by the Frente Democrático Revolucionario (Democratic Revolutionary Front), or FDR, mainly to promote the cause of the opposition in the international arena. Several Latin American filmmakers offered their resources. The Puerto Rican Diego de la Texera directed *El Salvador, el pueblo vencerá* (1981; El Salvador, The People Shall Overcome), coproduced by the Costa Rican Istmofilm, with postproduction work done in Cuba. During this same period Radio Venceremos (Radio We Shall Overcome), the communications organization of the FMLN (Farabundo Martí National Liberation Front), also produced some films to bolster its political cause, including *Carta de Mozarán* (1982; Letter from Morazán), *Tiempo de audacia* (1983; Time of Daring), and *Tiempo de victoria* (1988; Time of Victory).

In other Central American countries the history of cinematic culture has been checkered. In Guatemala during the 1980s a small group of filmmakers called Cinematografía de Guatemala produced a short documentary, *Vamos patria a caminar* (1983; Let's Go Forward, My Country), and an eight-minute short, *El gobierno civil, un engaño* (1985; Civil Government, a Fraud). The first Guatemalan full-length feature, *El silencio de Neto,* directed by Luis Argueta, was released in 1994. The first feature film directed by a Central American was *La Xegua* (1984), made by Costa Rican Oscar Castillo. The movie is the story of a beautiful female spirit who accosted men by the roadside in eighteenth-century Costa Rica and drove them mad. In Panama the Grupo Experimental de Cine Universitario (Experimental University Cinema Group), or GECU, was founded in 1972; their first short, *Canto a la patria que ahora nace* (1972; Song to a Homeland That Is Now Being Born), is based on a bloody incident in 1964, when students attempted to fly the Panamanian flag next to the U.S. flag in a school in the Canal Zone. After the U.S. Army intervened, twenty-one people were killed and five hundred were wounded.

REFERENCES:

Julianne Burton, *Cinema and Social Change in Latin America: Conversations with Filmmakers* (Austin: University of Texas Press, 1986);

John King, *Magical Reels: A History of Cinema in Latin America* (London: Verso, 1990);

Jorge A. Schnitman, *Film Industries in Latin America* (Norwood, N.J.: ABLEX, 1984).

— S.M.H.

CINEMA IN MEXICO

The film industry in Mexico has a more intriguing history than in any other Spanish American republic. Movies came early to Mexico. The first motion picture exhibited in Spanish America was shown in Mexico City in August 1896, about the same time as the medium was introduced elsewhere in the world (December 1895 in France, April 1896 in the United States). Early Mexican productions were travelogues or documentaries. In fact, Mexican engineer Salvador Toscano

managed to capture a good deal of the **Mexican Revolution** (1911–1917) on film. One of the leaders of the revolution, Pancho Villa, was conscious of the power of spectacle, and he practically became a movie star during the revolution. Signing an exclusive contract with the Mutual Film Corporation, he agreed to have battles filmed, to reenact them if filming did not go well, and even to change the time of execution of prisoners of war from 4:00 A.M. to 6:00 A.M. to give the cameramen better lighting.

Sound motion pictures came to Spanish America at roughly the same time as the rest of the world. Mexico was producing talkies by 1930. The first picture filmed in Mexico with direct sound was *Santa* (1931), based on the novel of the same title by Federico Gamboa, and the first genuine Mexican talkie was *Más fuerte que el deber* (1932; Stronger than Duty).

In the formative years of Mexican cinema, Mexican actors did apprenticeships in Hollywood. Actors such as Dolores del Río, Pedro Armendáriz, Arturo de Córdova, Jorge Negrete, Andrea Palma, Delia Magana, and Lupe Vélez, directors Emilio Fernández, Ismael Rodríguez, and Roberto Gavadón — as well as cameramen Gabriel Figueroa and Agustín Jiménez — learned their crafts in Hollywood. The Golden Age of Mexican cinema occurred between 1935 and 1955. According to the Mexican cultural critic **Carlos Monsiváis,** nationalism and the Mexican experience were turned into a great show during these years. Typical motifs in movies of the period were the Mexican fiesta, the cabaret, the dance hall, the red-light district, and the confessional. The first-prize winner at the first Cannes Film Festival (1947), for example, was *María Candelaria* (1943), directed by Emilio "El Indio" Fernández. The lead was played by Dolores del Río, who began her career in Hollywood in the 1920s and did not return to Mexico until 1942. Her performance in this movie is impressive and suggests why she eventually became the grande dame of the Mexican cinema. From the 1940s through the 1960s the Mexican film industry produced a string of popular movies, creating what was almost a new genre, the **Mexican melodrama.**

As elsewhere in Latin America, several cine clubs sprang up in Mexico in the 1950s; particularly important was the Cine Club de la Universidad. In the 1950s and 1960s the iconoclastic Luis Buñuel, exiled from his native Spain and becoming a Mexican citizen, made some of his most controversial movies in Mexico, including **Los olvidados** (1950; *The Young and the Damned*), *Viridiana* (1961), and *El ángel exterminador (1964; The Exterminating Angel)*. After World War II, Mexican cinema became heavily dependent on state investment. This reliance on public funding stifled private investment in the industry and was not wholly

Dolores del Río in *María Candelaria* (1943)

beneficial, but Mexico produced several noteworthy movies in the 1960s, including *En el balcón vacío* (1961; On the Empty Balcony), directed by Jomi García Ascot; *En este pueblo no hay ladrones* (1965; There are No Thieves In This Town), directed by Arturo Ripstein and based on a short story by Gabriel García Márquez; *Tiempo de morir* (1965; A Time to Die), also directed by Ripstein and with a script by García Márquez and **Carlos Fuentes;** and *Fando y Lis* (1967), filmed in Mexico by the Chilean Alejandro Jodorowsky. By the 1970s younger artists, including Jorge Fons, Jaime Hermosillo, Felipe Cazals, Servando González, Alberto Isaac, Arturo Ripstein, Raúl Araiza, and **Marcela Fernández Violante,** were beginning to make ripples abroad. Important Mexican movies of this decade include *Canoa* (1975), directed by Cazals; *Los albañiles* (1976; The Building Workers), directed by Fons; *Cascabel* (1976; Rattlesnake), directed by Araiza; *La pasión según Berenice* (1976; The Passion According to Berenice), directed by Hermosillo; and *María de mi corazón,* (1979; Darling Maria), also directed by Hermosillo and based on a filmscript by García Márquez. Although the majority of these artists aimed at producing movies that were commercially successful in their own country, their early successes were with audiences of intellectuals, who were mainly foreigners.

Closely responsive to the ebb and flow of Mexican politics, the film industry in Mexico has suffered in recent years. The National Cinémathèque was founded in 1979 to house the national film archives, but it was destroyed by a fire in the mid 1980s. In the 1980s many Mexican film studios were bought out by foreign, mainly U.S., capital. For two years in the early 1980s Dino De Laurentis leased the whole of Churubusco Studios, the major national movie studio, to produce *Dune* (1985); Walt Disney Studios also rented the studio for two years. Michael Douglas bought the Alatriste Studios outright. With the debt crisis of the early 1980s the Mexican government was not in a position to finance the film industry and therefore brought in foreign productions. Margarita López Portillo was in control of the Mexican movie industry during the presidency of her brother José López Portillo (1976–1982), a period in which the industry suffered. During this time the Mexican government coproduced *Campanas rojas* (1981; Red Bells), directed by the Soviet director Sergei Bondarchuk, and also financed Spanish director Carlos Saura's *Antonieta*. During the presidency of Miguel de la Madrid (1982–1988), Alberto Isaac, a highly regarded filmmaker, was named director of the newly created Instituto Mexicano de Cine (Mexican Film Institute), or IMCINE, a state corporation intended to encompass production, distribution, and exhibition. Isaac attempted to revive the fortunes of the Mexican movie industry, but with limited success, and he resigned from his post in 1984.

María Rojo and Héctor Bonilla in *María de mi corazón* (1979; Darling Maria)

During this period, as the movie industry waned, the enormous success of Mexican television provided a cushion for actors and actresses. (Some Mexican movie critics, such as Emilio García Riera, review only televised films.) Carlos Salinas de Gortari's presidency (1988–1994) ushered in an era of privatization: state enterprises such as Compañía Nacional de Cine (National Film Production Company; CONACINE), Azteca Films (which handled distribution), and Compañía Operadora de Teatros y Películas Mexicanas, S.A. (Theater and Mexican Film Operating Company, COTSA), in charge of exhibition, were sold and privatized. During this period Ignacio Durán, a film man rather than a bureaucrat, held the all-important position of head of IMCINE. As a result of privatization, some directors have become their own producers; the actor Héctor Bonilla invested his own money in Jorge Fons's controversial *Rojo amanecer* (1989; Red Dawn), based on the **Tlatelolco** massacre of students in 1968. *Cabeza de Vaca* (1990), directed by Nicolás Echeverría and Juan Mora Cattlet, explores the clash of cultures when the Spaniards first arrived in the New World through the story of Núñez Cabeza de Vaca, the first European ever to traverse the American continent; the movie makes much use of psychedelic camera shots. One important, though perhaps overrated, film of this period is *Danzón* (1991), directed by María Novaro. This movie uses a fairy-tale format to focus on a telephonist and single mother (played by Mexico's favorite film star, María Rojo) whose beloved is an old man and who has no private means but is an excellent dancer of the **danzón,** a popular Caribbean music-and-dance genre. Two of Jaime Humberto Hermosillo's features of this period were successful. His *La tarea* (1989; Homework) and *Intimidades en un cuarto de baño* (1989; Bathroom Intimacies) unmask social hypocrisy, especially in the area of sexual repression. In *La tarea,* for example, María Rojo plays a mature film-school student shooting her graduation movie as a soft-core exercise. In *Intimidades en un cuarto de baño,* where the camera is hidden behind the bathroom mirror, Hermosillo focuses on the impotence of the male and the predatory nature of the female in the Mexican middle class, a role-gender division that has become familiar in Hermosillo's cinematic world. Other Mexican features of the 1990s include Alfonso Cuarón's *Sólo con tu pareja* (1992; Only with Your Partner), a modern bedroom farce about a promiscuous male advertising executive who is the butt of a discarded lover's sinister joke (a nurse, she takes her revenge by faking a positive reading of his HIV test), and Carlos Carrera's *La mujer de Benjamín* (1991; Benjamin's Woman), a devastating portrayal of the boredom of life in a small rural village. The hit of the decade was *Como agua para chocolate* (1993; Like Water for Chocolate), Alfonso Arau's movie based on Laura Esquivel's novel of the same title. A wonderfully seasoned re-creation of the **magical realism** of Esquivel's novel, the movie played to packed audiences in Latin America and the United States, and it testifies to the continued vitality of Mexican cinema.

In October 1987 Mexico City hosted Cocina de Imágenes, the first festival of films and videos made by Latin American and Caribbean women. Organized by Angeles Necoechea and Julia Barco, it was attended by some one hundred female producers, distributors, programmers, critics, and scholars from Latin America, North America, and Europe.

REFERENCES:

Julianne Burton, *Cinema and Social Change in Latin America: Conversations with Latin American Filmmakers* (Austin: University of Texas Press, 1986);

John King, *Magical Reels: A History of Cinema in Latin America* (London: Verso, 1990);

Carl J. Mora, *Mexican Cinema: Reflections of a Society 1896–1980* (Berkeley: University of California Press, 1982);

Zuzana M. Pick, *The New Latin American Cinema* (Austin: University of Texas Press, 1993).

— S.M.H.

CINEMA IN THE CARIBBEAN

The cinema came early to Cuba, where movies were being made as early as 1896, but until the 1950s Cuban cinema followed the same predictable, Hollywood-led path as did the other Spanish American nations. Before the late 1950s more than 70 percent of the foreign films exhibited in Cuba came from the United States. Little commercial Cuban cinema existed; some eighty features were filmed there between 1930 and 1958, mostly melodramas or musical comedies made rapidly by adventurers such as Ramón Peón. The Cuban Revolution of 1959, in which forces loyal to **Fidel Castro** overthrew the government of Fulgencio Batista, brought sweeping changes in the Cuban movie industry. Like Russia after its revolution in 1917, Cuba established a government agency to organize and regulate the production, distribution, and exhibition of movies. Called the Instituto Cubano del Arte e Industria Cinematográficas (**Cuban Film Institute**), or ICAIC, it created first-rate production facilities and invited filmmakers from far afield — France, Holland, and Czechoslovakia, for example — to train Cuban personnel. Two of the founders of the ICAIC were **Tomás Gutiérrez Alea** and **Julio García Espinosa,** both of whom had studied in Italy and were therefore heavily influenced by Italian **neo-realism.**

After the United States imposed a trade embargo on Cuba in late 1960, no Hollywood movies were allowed in, and the ICAIC was forced to look elsewhere for films. As a result a great deal of European material was brought to Cuba. Later, cinematic movements such as the French New Wave (especially Jean Luc Godard's work) and Brazilian Cinema Nôvo exerted an influence on Cuban film — leading to a boom in the Cuban movie industry. Between 1959 and 1987 Cuba made 164 feature-length films. In 1987 Cubans went to the movies more than sixty-one million times. Because of this extremely high attendance, Cuban filmmakers, unlike other Latin American filmmakers, can invariably cover their production costs in their home market, despite low admission fees. Two movies, *Guardafronteras* (1981; Frontier Guard), directed by Octavio Cortázar, and *Aventuras de Juan Quin Quin* (1967; The Adventures of Juan Quin Quin), directed by García Espinosa, had audiences of more than two million. The ICAIC clearly does a good job on its annual budget of

A scene from *Lucía* (1968), directed by Humberto Solás

about $7 million, or roughly one-third the cost of one average U.S. feature film.

Historical features were among the earliest ICAIC productions, and at most times such movies have formed the bulk of Cuban film production. In the early 1960s Cuban movies focused on the recent past, the years of revolutionary struggle. The 1968–1976 period, however, when Cuban filmmakers produced their greatest works, was dominated by historical narratives that reached further back into history, from the 1930s to earliest colonial times. Manuel Octavio Gómez's *La primera carga del machete* (1969; The First Charge of the Machete) is based on the war of 1868, during which poor sugar workers, led by Máximo Gómez and armed only with their cane-cutting machetes, fought the Spaniards. According to director Gómez, "We set about trying to give the idea that we were developing the story as if it were being filmed at that very moment, as if it had been possible at the time to use a camera and recorder to collect the facts." Gómez's later feature *Ustedes tienen la palabra* (1973; Now It's Up to You) is a tale of corruption and opportunism in which the story unfolds through a series of flashbacks. The movie explores conflicts and contradictions of the past and contrasts them with the present day in sequences that show how they have been resolved in a display of popular revolutionary unity and resolve. Manuel Herrera's *Girón* (1972) is a docudrama based on the Bay of Pigs invasion of 1961. Later features — such as **Humberto Solás**'s *Lucía* (1968) and Sergio Giral's trilogy, *El otro Francisco* (1973; The Other Francisco), *Rancheador* (1975; Slave Hunter), and *Maluala* (1979) — delve further into the past. In *Maluala* the historical framework is the period of slavery in Cuba during the nineteenth century.

A new generation of cineasts emerged in Cuba during the 1980s and released notable movies such as

A scene from *El mégano* (1955; The Charcoal Worker), directed by Tomás Gutiérrez Alea and Julio García Espinosa

Se permuta (1984; House Swap), directed by Juan Carlos Tabío; *Una novia para David* (1985; A Girlfriend for David); *Lejanía* (1985; Parting of the Ways), directed by Jesús Díaz; and *Vampiros en la Habana* (1985; Vampires in Havana), directed by Juan Padrón. Not everything was good; Fernando Birri's *Un señor muy viejo con unas alas enormes* (1988; A Very Old Man with Enormous Wings), made while he was head of the Escuela de Cine y Televisón (Film and Television School) and based on a story by Colombian writer Gabriel García Márquez, is self-indulgent.

In the aftermath of the **Padilla Affair** of 1971, in which a prominent poet was forced to recant his views publicly, some Cuban intellectuals retreated into exile. Among them are the filmmakers Néstor Almendros and Orlando Jiménez Leal, who made an international impact with *L'altra Cuba* (1983; The Other Cuba) and *Mauvaise Conduite* (1984; Improper Conduct), their documentaries about the repression of homosexuality in Castro's Cuba. Gutiérrez Alea's highly successful *Fresa y chocolate* (1993; Strawberry and Chocolate) explores similar concerns.

Throughout the 1980s roughly 50 percent of movies shown in Cuba came from the Soviet Union and the Eastern bloc, and the remainder from the West. Cuban cinema has its own character. Since Cuban filmmakers do not have the means to make superproductions, they have created what Gutiérrez Alea has called "a light,

agile cinema, one that is very directly rooted in our own reality." In the 1990s Cuba has a massive and loyal filmgoing public.

On the other Caribbean islands the filmmaking situation is similar to that of Central America; while their efforts are not sustained, these movie industries have produced some significant works. In the Dominican Republic moviemaking began after the overthrow of Rafael Trujillo in 1961. Several university-based cine clubs were formed. One of the most interesting documentaries to come out of such organizations was Jimmy Sierra's *Siete días con el pueblo* (1978; Seven Days with the People). One fictional feature, *Un pasaje de ida* (1988; One-Way Ticket), was made in the 1980s. Directed by Agilberto Meléndez, the movie is based on a real event in which some Dominicans stowed away on a boat to the United States and were drowned during the journey. Though Dominican cinema is a success at home, the market there is so small that it has not yet met costs. During the 1970s a critical, national, documentary-film movement emerged in Puerto Rico and released Jacobo Morales's *Dios los cría* (1980; God Molds Them, 1980). Two other important Puerto Rican movies of the 1980s were Ana María García's *La operación* (1981; The Operation), which denounces U.S. sterilization programs, and Marcos Zurinaga's *La gran fiesta* (1986; The Gala Ball), which reconstructs the last grand gala ball at the San Juan casino, an event that took place in 1942.

REFERENCES:

Julianne Burton, ed., *Cinema and Social Change in Latin America: Conversations with Filmmakers* (Austin: University of Texas Press, 1986);

John King, *Magical Reels: A History of Cinema in Latin America* (London: Verso, 1990);

Jorge A. Schnitman, *Film Industries in Latin America* (Norwood, N.J.: ABLEX, 1984).

— S.M.H.

CLASSICAL BALLET

European classical ballet reached the Americas through the mutual efforts of European artists eager to see the new world and local enthusiasts eager to bring European culture to their developing lands. The introduction of European classical ballet into Mesoamerica and the Caribbean is typified by the case of Cuba prior to the Cuban Revolution, in terms of visiting troupes and the impetus they gave to the development of local ballet groups. Ballet was introduced on the island by the New Orleans French Opera in the early nineteenth century. The Ravels, a French pantomime-ballet troupe, appeared frequently beginning in 1836, and the Austrian dancer Fanny Eissler, one of the leading ballerinas of the Romantic era and important in bringing the aesthetic to the new world, appeared in 1841 and 1842. Anna Pavlova appeared in various Cuban cities in 1915, 1917, and 1918; Cuban dancers, either wholly untrained or partially trained at the Escuela de Ballet, were always included in her dramatic ballets. The Escuela de Ballet was created in 1931 by the Sociedad Pro Arte Musical de La Habana, a local society created by the upper classes to support the fine arts of Europe in Cuba. After Pavlova's departure, dancers copied her choreography and performed the same dances under their own names as artistic directors. The **Ballet Nacional de Cuba** was created by **Alberto, Alicia, and Fernando Alonso** in 1948 as an entity independent of the Pro-Arte Music Society, where it had been nurtured until that time. By a special decree of the revolutionary government of Fidel Castro in 1959, the company became an official entity, supported by the Cuban government. In 1967 the government created a second ballet company, the Ballet de Camagüey; a third, the Ballet Santiago de Cuba, was formed in 1990. The worldwide renown of Cuba's national ballet company is a result of its tours and successes in international ballet competitions.

In Costa Rica, Margarita Esquivel, a young and ambitious choreographer and teacher, founded the Ballet Tico in the 1940s. Previously classical ballet was used only as a tool for teaching deportment to young girls, or as a basis for other dance forms. Eventually, however, a growing number of ballet-school graduates demanded performing opportunities, leading to the creation of the Compañía Nacional de Danza, the strongest ballet institution in the country. Much as in the United States, where classical ballet companies earn the greater part of their income from Christmastime performances of Pyotr Ilich Tchaikovsky's *The Nutcracker* (1892), the Compañía Nacional de Danza maintains itself by annual performances of Sergey Sergeyevich Prokofiev's *Peter and the Wolf* (1936), performed with the National Orchestra.

Ballet was introduced into Puerto Rico in the early 1940s. In the 1950s Ana García, who had studied at the School of American Ballet in New York and danced with George Balanchine's Ballet Society and with Alicia Alonso in Cuba, returned to her native Puerto Rico. Together with her sister, Gilda Navarra, she founded Ballets de San Juan, a ballet and Spanish dance company. Since then Puerto Rico has schooled some first-rate ballerinas who have found careers with the Ballet Nacional de Cuba, the Pennsylvania Ballet, the American Ballet Theatre, the Ballet del Nuevo Mundo (Venezuela), the Pittsburgh Ballet, Ballet Concierto de San Juan, and Ballets de San Juan.

During tours in Mexico in 1919 and 1924 Pavlova put on a balletic version of Mexico's signature folk dance, the **jarabe** tapatío, delighting audiences. Ballet Theatre of New York, after touring Mexico, premiered a work by Léonide Massine in 1942, *Don Domingo de Blas,* which included music by the Mexican composer **Silvestre Revueltas** and attempted to fuse classical ballet, Spanish dance, and various Mexican indigenous dances. Between appearances in Mexico by visiting ballet companies, Gloria and **Nellie Campobello** of the Escuela Nacional de Danza (founded in 1932) and the Ballet de la Ciudad de México presented European classical works, as well as Mexican folk-dance themes adapted to classical ballet vocabulary. Classical ballet in Mexico spread more slowly than modern dance, however, primarily because of the difficulties in attaching specifically Mexican themes to a codified system with elitist European implications. More mundane, the cost of ballet shoes and costumes was prohibitive. Nonetheless, Nellie Happee (1930–) and Gloria Contreras (1934–) established themselves as prolific choreographers working in the classical ballet idiom.

In the Dominican Republic classical ballet was given its strongest impetus in the early 1950s by Magda Corbett, who directed a private studio into the 1990s. There exists a National Dance School and the National Classical Ballet company, both state institutions, as well as at least eight private ballet academies and three private companies, including the Ballet Clásico Infantil.

In El Salvador classical ballet is taught primarily at the National Dance School and at the studio of Ballet El Salvador, directed by Argentine-born teacher Alcira Alonso. At the latter the British Royal Academy of Dancing syllabus is taught and judges are brought either to El Salvador or to a regional testing site in Central America so that students and teachers may be certified and passed on to the next level, a requirement for certification that is essential to the Royal Academy of Dancing method.

— J.M.H.

COFRADÍAS

Originally founded as mutual-aid societies, cofradías are associations affiliated with local churches, whose patron saints give each association its name. The cofradía has evolved over the years, becoming chiefly the organizer of pageants for saints' days and other religious holidays. In so doing it preserves local folkloric — especially dance — traditions, which are often amalgams of European and indigenous themes and styles.

— J.M.H.

Coleccion Archivos

In 1984, with sponsorship from UNESCO, the Colección Archivos was begun under the direction of Amos Segala of the University of Paris. The Colección Archivos is an ambitious series of publications whose aim is to produce definitive editions of key literary texts of twentieth-century Latin America. The first published titles include works in both Spanish and Portuguese by **Miguel Angel Asturias,** Clarice Lispector, José María Arguedas, **José Lezama Lima,** Julio Cortázar, Mário de Andrade, and others. Each volume entails rigorous critical analysis, the compilation of exhaustive information on the author and his or her works, and the gathering of a cluster of major critical studies on the work being edited. The wish to foster knowledge of these works in the wider ambit of North-South relations led the University of Pittsburgh Press to announce in 1991 that it would undertake the translation and distribution of selected titles from the collection.

— P.S.

Enrique Colina

Enrique Colina (circa 1940–) is a Cuban film critic who frequently writes for *Cine Cubano*. He is also the host of *Veinticuatro veces por segundo* (Twenty-Four Times a Second), a popular prime-time show about movies that has appeared on national television every Saturday night since the 1970s. Closely identified with the **Cuban Film Institute,** Colina sees his role as performing a sort of aesthetic and ideological "de-montage" of what the filmmaker has assembled, thereby taking apart a movie to reveal its inner workings. One of his aims is to demonstrate how some Hollywood movies have an ideological backdrop that is clearly symptomatic of the whole capitalist social structure; entertainment, according to Colina, is not an "innocent" activity.

REFERENCE:
Julianne Burton, *Cinema and Social Change in Latin America: Conversations with Filmmakers* (Austin: University of Texas Press, 1986).

— S.M.H.

Comic Strips and Books

Comics began to appear in Mexico around the turn of the twentieth century. North American comic strips were published there as early as 1902, and within a year they were followed by the first Mexican strip, the hu-

morous *Don Lupito,* by Andrés Audiffred. For the next three decades Mexican comic strips roughly followed U.S. trends and were often simply translations of American originals. The period from the late 1930s through the 1940s is referred to as the "Golden Age" of Mexico. During that time all sorts of Mexican artists, including comics writers, took a well-tried formula from the United States, Mexicanized it, and watched it take off. Two successful humorous strips that began appearing in this period are Germán Oliver's *Los Supersabios* (1936; The Superbrains) and Gabriel Vargas's *La familia burrón* (1937; The Donkeyson Family). From the 1920s through the 1940s, adventure strips surpassed humorous strips in popularity. Since 1950, political satire, underground, and Marvel superhero comics have flourished in all of Spanish America. The most important innovation of the 1950s was Manuel de Landa's creation of "mini" comic books, pocket-size comics that sell at low prices. The best known of these are published by Guillermo de la Parra and Yolanda Vargas's Editorial Argumentos, including the best-selling romance comic in Mexico, *Lágrimas, risas y amor* (Tears, Laughter, and Love). Even in the 1990s the comic strip is the most popular reading material in Mexico. Visitors to Mexico are frequently surprised by how many comic-strip magazines (some with racy narratives) are bought, read, and exchanged by travelers on buses and trains.

Other Latin American comics that are popular throughout the Spanish-speaking world include *Mafalda,* by the Argentinean Joaquín Salvador Lavado; *Cuy* (an indigenous rodent), by the Peruvian Juan Acevedo; *Copetín* (Half-pint), by the Colombian Ernesto Franco; and the Cuban Hernán H.'s *Gugulandia,* which occupies the back page of the magazine *Dedeté* (DDT).

REFERENCE:
Harold E. Hinds Jr., "Comics," in *Handbook of Latin American Popular Culture,* edited by Hinds and Charles M. Tatum (Westport, Conn.: Greenwood Press, 1985), pp. 81–110.

— S.M.H.

Compañía Nacional de Danza

The Compañía Nacional de Danza, a Mexican classical ballet company, absorbs the largest part of the Instituto Nacional de Bellas Artes' (National Institute for the Fine Arts) budget for dance. The company is an outgrowth of earlier classical ballet companies in Mexico that were formed in the late 1940s when the French ballerina Nelsy Dambre began to professionalize her performances, originally designed for presentation in schools. The Ballet de Nelsy Dambre evolved into Bal-

Photo etching of the Taíno deities Guanbancex (Goddess of the Wind) and Guanaroca (First Woman) in Ana Medieta's *Rupestrian Sculptures* (1981), a series of female figures she carved in remote caves at Jaruco State Park, near Havana, Cuba

let Concierto; it was reorganized by Serge Unger and Felipe Segura and toured Mexico extensively from 1952 to 1969. In 1963 Ballet Concierto became officially linked to the Instituto Nacional de Bellas Artes and was renamed Ballet Clásico de México. Ballet de Cámara, founded in 1958 by Nellie Happee and Tulio de la Rosa, merged in 1973 with the Ballet Clásico de México, forming the Compañía Nacional de Danza.

— J.M.H.

CONCEPTUAL ART, INSTALLATION ART, AND PERFORMANCE ART

Conceptual Art and Installation Art are closely related art forms; in fact, it could be argued that Installation Art is an environmental expression of Conceptual Art. Also called Idea Art, Conceptual Art emerged in Latin America during the 1960s and continues to be a dominant art form. This radical artistic expression defines the work of art as an idea or concept rather than by its material quality, which could be temporary or dispos-

able. In order to convey the information that makes up the artwork, artists rely on a variety of media and visual elements, such as texts, photographs, ordinary objects, electronic media, and multimedia installations. Conceptual Art has several antecedents, which include the radical innovations introduced by Marcel Duchamp and the experiments with everyday objects, unorthodox materials, and artist/public participation that characterized Pop Art and Happenings.

In Latin America Conceptual Art did not emphasize the self-referential or tautological approach favored in this type of art in Europe and the United States, but instead developed a markedly ideological bent. Latin American artists also emphasize the appearance of the work of art, whose formal attributes and visual appeal are as carefully considered as in other, more traditional media. The most important developments in Conceptual Art, Installation Art, and Performance Art in Mexico, Central America, and the Caribbean have resulted from the work of Cubans such as **José Bedia,** Ricardo Rodríguez Brey, Flavio Garciandía, Rubén Torres Llorca, and Juan Francisco

Conga dancers at a festival in Panama (Lila R. Cheville and Richard A. Cheville)

Elso Padilla — all of whom were leading members of Volume I, a controversial group of young avant-garde artists who during the early 1980s broke with the art of the past and paved the way for radical art modes involving popular art, kitsch, ethnic identity, and other cultural issues.

Performance Art consists of personal, private, or public performances by an artist, usually done a limited number of times and often recorded in photographs or on film. **Ana Mendieta,** a Cuban artist who worked independently in the United States, produced several important performances and ephemeral pieces dealing with feminist issues and anticolonialist politics. In 1980, when she returned to Cuba for the first time, she acted as a contact between the international art scene and the new generation of Cuban artists who emerged in the 1980s and, like Mendieta, favored radical new approaches to art and the exploration of ideological and cultural issues. Outside Cuba, in Mexico, Central America, and the Caribbean, radical modes of art were practiced by a few artists working independently, such as the Puerto Rican **Rafael Ferrer,** who created several groundbreaking installations in New York in the late 1960s and early 1970s, and the Mexicans Felipe Ehrenberg, who has worked with conceptual installations since the 1970s, and Guillermo Gómez Peña, whose per-

formances have addressed issues related to the U.S.–Mexican border and to anticolonialism.

REFERENCE:

Luis Camnitzer, *New Art of Cuba* (Austin: University of Texas Press, 1994).

— F.B.N.

CONGA

Musically speaking, *conga* refers to three separate but related entities: 1) a drum of African origin, 2) the music for the carnival street dance known as *La conga*, and 3) an ensemble of primarily percussive instruments that accompany *comparsas carnavalescas* (a costumed carnival street-dance team).

La conga as both a musical and a dance genre is featured in the comparsas carnavalescas, a Cuban street festival that dates back to colonial times. The music reiterates the processional dance choreography with the typical conga rhythm (one-two-three-kick).

The conga ensemble accompanying the comparsas carnavalescas features a variety of percussion instruments, including drums of varying size and timbre, especially conga drums and the smaller and higher pitched conga-style drum, the *quinto*. To the conga drums are added the bass drum, *cencerros* (cowbells), *sartenes* (small frying pans), and trumpets.

A conga-dance craze in the United States was propelled by Desi Arnaz, the Cuban musician who costarred on the *I Love Lucy* television show.

REFERENCES:
Cristobal Díaz Ayala, *Música cubana del Areyto a la Nueva Trova* (San Juan: Editorial Cubanacán, 1981);
Natalio Galán, *Cuba y sus sones* (Valencia: Pre-Textos/Música, 1983).
— R.L.S.

Los Contemporáneos

In the 1920s, in the wake of the **Mexican Revolution,** several young Mexican writers joined to form a loosely knit literary group; one of the most notable literary groups of the time in Latin America, it was named after one of the most important journals in Mexico, *Contemporáneos* (The Contemporary Ones), founded by Bernardo Ortiz de Montellano. Members included Jaime Torres Bodet, Octavio G. Barreda, José and Celestino Gorostiza, Enrique González Rojo, Gilberto Owen, **Salvador Novo, Xavier Villaurrutia,** Jorge Cuesta, and later **Carlos Pellicer** and Elías Nandino. Their emphasis on independent, individual styles following no set of rules and proclaiming no poetic manifestos is reflected in the various names by which several members of the group referred to it: "el archipiélago de soledades" (the archipelago of solitariness), "el grupo sin grupo" (the group less group), and "el grupo de forajidos" (the group of outlaws). Each member had a particular style and cultivated various genres besides poetry, which they had in common; they also shared common ground in terms of their similar ages, backgrounds, tastes, and critical attitudes toward a national culture. All the members came from the educated middle to upper classes that had been deeply affected by the revolution and had lost much of their material wealth and land. They had grown up witnessing the violence and chaos during the revolution along with the disillusion that followed it as revolutionary leaders became corrupt politicians. For this reason most of these writers had a skeptical or cynical attitude toward social reforms, preferring to isolate themselves in their individual, private worlds and concentrate on themes of death, solitude, dreams, and eroticism. Their aesthetic, universal, and sophisticated leanings put them at odds with the other nationalist trends of the time that emphasized social messages. Although some

of the group's literary techniques derived from the vanguardists, their insistence on artistic liberty and a rigorous critical attitude, apparent in the various journals in which they participated and the cultural enterprises they helped found, had a tremendous impact on the literary schools that followed after the journal *Contemporáneos* ceased publication in 1931, largely because of internal squabbles and external criticism by the literary nationalists.

REFERENCES:
David William Foster, *Mexican Literature: A History* (Austin: University of Texas Press, 1994);
Rafael Olea Franco and Anthony Stanton, *Los contemporáneos en el laberinto de la crítica* (México: El Colegio de México, 1994);
Guillermo Sheridan, *Los contemporáneos ayer* (México: Fondo de Cultura Económica, 1985).
— M.E.S.

Roque Cordero

Roque Cordero (1917–) of Panama became the first of his family to distinguish himself as a composer, conductor, and teacher. His musical ability was demonstrated early in life through compositions as a teenager for band and popular music. Early studies in Panama were followed in 1943 by a scholarship to study music education at the University of Minnesota in Minneapolis. In 1937 Cordero won the National Prize in Panama for his carnival march, *Reina de amor*, a work that enjoyed popularity in the United States under the title *Spirit of Panamá*. A subsequent performance of the work with the University of Minnesota Concert Band brought him an influential admirer in John K. Sherman, music critic of the *Minneapolis Star-Journal*. With help from Sherman, Cordero met and showed his work to the distinguished conductor of the Minneapolis Symphony Orchestra, Dimitri Mitropoulos, who, in turn, arranged for him to study counterpoint and composition nearby with the well-known Viennese composer Ernst Krenek. In the Reichold music contest for composers of the Americas (1945) Cordero's First Symphony earned an honorable mention. The following year Mitropoulos conducted the premiere of Cordero's *Panamanian Overture No. 2.*

Cordero's own interest in conducting began while he was still in Panama. In 1939, as conductor of the Musical Union Orchestra (later the National Symphony Orchestra of Panama), he had premiered his first orchestral composition to win recognition, *Capricho interiorano* (1939), based on Panamanian traditional music. Beginning in the summer of 1946 he received a scholarship from Serge Koussevitzky, conductor of the Boston Symphony Orchestra, to study conducting at the Berkshire Music Center in Massachusetts. He received further support from the government of Panama and a Guggenheim Fellowship, permitting him to expand his catalogue of compositions.

Cordero returned to Panama in 1950 to teach at the National Institute of Music. Within three years he was appointed executive director and began an important reform of music education in Panama. In spite of his administrative and teaching duties, he continued to compose and gain an ever-widening audience for his works. Among the prizes and commissions he received were first prize for the *Rapsodia campesina* in the Ricardo Miró contest in Panama in 1953, the Caro de Boesi Award for the Second Symphony at the second Latin American Music Festival in Caracas in 1958, a commission for the Quartet No. 1 from the Elizabeth Sprague Coolidge Foundation of the Library of Congress in 1961, and a commission from the Koussevitzky Foundation for the Violin Concerto in the Third Inter American Music Festival in Washington (1962).

In his early years as a composer, Cordero's attention focused on traditional Panamanian musical sources, especially the rhythmic elements of song/dances such as the **mejorana** (of Spanish origin) and the **tamborito** (of African origin), set in traditional formal designs. Although nationalistic tendencies have been typical of the early works of many twentieth-century Latin American composers (see **nationalism in music**), those who have achieved international recognition have generally transcended the narrow parameters of nationalism to arrive at more-universal musical values without denying their own musical heritage. Such has been the case with Roque Cordero, one of the first Latin American composers to use twelve-tone techniques.

In addition to the works cited above, Cordero's catalogue includes Sonatina for Violin and Piano (1946), Sonata for Cello and Piano (1963), the Third Symphony (1965), String Quartet No. 3 (1973), Concertino for Viola and String Orchestra (1968), *Permutaciones* (1974), and *Variations and Theme for Five* (1975).

REFERENCES:

Gerard Béhague, *Music in Latin America: An Introduction* (Englewood Cliffs, N.J.: Prentice-Hall, 1979);

Gilbert Chase, "Composed by Cordero," *Inter American Music Bulletin,* no. 7 (September 1958);

Ronald R. Sider, "Roque Cordero: The Composer and His Style Seen in Three Representative Works," *Inter American Music Bulletin,* no. 61 (September 1967).

— R.L.S.

JOSÉ CORONEL URTECHO

The founder of the vanguardist poetry movement in Nicaragua in the 1920s, José Coronel Urtecho (born in Granada in 1906) inspired a whole generation of poets whose members included **Pablo Antonio Cuadra** and Joaquín Pasos. The vanguardia became most active in 1931, when its members began to publish a great amount of poetry. Prior to the years of the vanguardia, Coronel had studied literature in San Francisco, California, and had become interested in what he called poetry as a reflection of the personal and popular life of Americans. While he published translations of many U.S. poets, including his personal favorite, Ezra Pound, Coronel was reluctant to publish a compilation of his own poetry. *Pol-la d'ananata katanta paranta* (1970; And Through Many Ups and Downs, Comings and Goings), his first published poetry collection (whose Greek title is taken from Homer), was organized by Ernesto Gutiérrez, another Nicaraguan poet. This book, subtitled "imitaciones y traducciones" (Imitations and Translations), contains his most complicated piece, "Retrato de la mujer de tu prójimo" ("Portrait of Thy Neighbor's Wife"), an oneiric poem much in the style of James Joyce. Coronel himself relates writing this poem to being awake yet in a dreamlike trance. In his poetry Coronel's language is best described as conversational, informal, and nonacademic.

In addition to his poetry, as well as his translations, Coronel has written essays on Nicaragua and its history and on North American culture and poetry. Coronel lives in rustic solitude on his farm at Las Brisas, on the San Juan River, a place of pilgrimage for his many younger admirers.

REFERENCE:

Steven White, *Culture and Politics in Nicaragua: Testimonies of Poets and Writers* (New York: Lumen Books, 1986).

— M. T.

CORRIDO

Historically derived from the Spanish **romance,** the *corrido* is one of the most popular and best-known genres of Mexican music. Corridos and other song forms of the early nineteenth century related stories of special events in the lives of settlers in northern Mexico, which, until 1848, included much of today's American Southwest. The violence, survival, and tragedies of frontier life were related in narrative ballads.

The establishment of the Republic of Texas in 1836 and its admission as the twenty-eighth state in 1845 encouraged an influx into the border area of Germans, Czechs, and North Americans who brought their own musical traditions as well as cultural attitudes that produced social conflict with the native Mexican population. Toward the end of the century the corrido, more than any other song genre, focused on real and folk histories of the struggles resulting from racial and class oppression. Resistance, symbolized by the individual with his pistol defending his rights, became the heroic topic of the genre and further distanced it from its origins in the Spanish **romance.**

The **Mexican Revolution** of 1910 drew the corrido from Texas and the northern border deep into Mexico proper, where it recounted the adventures of countless bandoleros (highwaymen). After the upheavals of the revolution, the topics of the corrido were broadened to include other events: natural disasters, passionate love affairs, and even happy occasions. Its eventual function became one of informing, relating, and remembering.

Corridos are performed by one or more singers with a variety of instrumental accompaniment. Solo singers may accompany themselves on guitar or be accompanied by other instrumentalists, but the most prominent association is with the **mariachi.** Typically, octosyllabic lyrics are rhymed in quatrains, set in rather simple musical phrases that facilitate communication with interludes, especially when the corrido is performed by an ensemble rather than a solo performer. The predominant metrical organizations of corridos are 3/4, 6/8, and 9/8. Approximately ten different types of corridos are recognized by experts. The characteristics that distinguish each type are neither musical nor literary but rather focus on the subject matter or the intention of the text: the romance or balada romántica resembles the universally popular sentimental ballad; the historia relates a criminal, disastrous, or sensational event; the narración is a dramatic narration; the relato is a statement or narration; the ejemplo is a lesson in morality; the tragedia relates an accident or violent death; mañanitas may range from rude language to humor; recuerdos remember events, people, or times past; and versos and coplas are vehicles for venting one's anger or frustration or simply for setting things straight.

REFERENCES:

Celestino Fernández, "The Mexican Immigration Experience and the Corrido mexicano," *Studies in Latin American Popular Culture*, 2 (1983): 115;

Vicente T. Mendoza, *Lírica narrativa de México: El corrido* (Mexico City: Instituto de Investigaciones Estéticas Universidad Nacional Autónoma de México, 1964).

         — R.L.S.

CRIOLLISMO AND COSTUMBRISMO

The term *criollo* (from which the English word *Creole* is derived) has changed meaning slightly over the years. In colonial Spanish America, it referred to any person of European stock who had been born in America. Later it came to refer to anyone born in America. In the arts, for example painting and literature, *criollismo* has been used to refer to works that, in response to the nationalistic impulse that followed independence, emphasized typical landscapes and character types. As paradoxical as it may seem, local color came to stand for national values. In literature, criollismo is a form of realism and is closely associated with the novel. Well-known criollista writers include the Costa Rican Ricardo Fernández Guardia and the Cuban Carlos Loveira. Most criollista novels have a rural setting and emphasize descriptions of folk customs and other "typical" regional features, a fact that links criollismo to costumbrismo, a genre that flourished in literature, art, and journalism toward the middle of the nineteenth century in Latin America. Its practitioners were inspired by emergent nationalism and by the folk leanings of Romanticism to describe local customs (*costumbres* in Spanish) and human types, either with a moral intention or with the purpose of emphasizing particular national traits or tendencies. The Spanish costumbristas Mariano José de Larra and Ramón de Mesonero Romanos heavily influenced their Latin American counterparts. Two of the more noted American costumbristas were Guillermo Prieto (Mexico) and Ricardo Palma (Peru). The costumbrista "sketch of manners" was integrated with greater or lesser skill into the plots of romantic or realist novels. Representative of costumbrismo is *Cecilia Valdés,* by the Cuban Cirilo Villaverde. It is not always easy to distinguish between costumbrismo and criollismo, but criollismo, if it has any intention beyond the picturesque, tends toward the satirical or moral; costumbrismo is more explicitly concerned with portraying a national essence. Also related to criollismo and costumbrismo is the "regional novel," sometimes called the *novela de la tierra* (novel of the land), a thematic genre whose prime examples are South American.

REFERENCES:

Carlos J. Alonso, *The Spanish American Regional Novel* (Cambridge: Cambridge University Press, 1990);

Ricardo Latcham, *El criollismo* (Santiago: Editorial Universitaria, 1956);

S. Zanetti, *Costumbristas de América Latina* (Buenos Aires: Centro Editor de América Latina, 1973).

         — R.G.M. & P.S.

Cristeros attending an outdoor mass

THE CRISTERO WAR

In the wake of the **Mexican Revolution,** in 1926 a petition was drawn up by the hierarchy of the Catholic Church in Mexico protesting various anticlerical articles in the Constitution of 1917, including ones providing for the nationalization of Church properties and the prohibition of religious instruction. The petition was signed by all the archbishops and bishops of Mexico. The then-president, Plutarco Elías Calles, reacted angrily, accusing the Church of treason, and effectively enforcing the Constitution by ordering the closure of Catholic schools and convents, the deportation of foreign priests, and mandatory registration of all clerics. This response, in turn, provoked an angry reaction from the Catholic hierarchy. On 31 July 1926 the priests went on strike and refused to say mass. Outraged Catholic supporters calling themselves "cristeros" (followers of Christ the King) effectively declared war on the government, burning non-Catholic schools and killing government teachers and officials. Calles retaliated by exiling several bishops and priests, while army officers took advantage of the conflict and confiscated the property of affluent Catholic families. During this period the cristeros took it upon themselves to guard the churches and keep them open, while priests said mass clandestinely in private homes. The conflict lasted three years, until Calles's successor, Emilio Portes Gil, negotiated a compromise by agreeing to recognize the importance of the Church in directing spiritual matters and the right to practice religious instruction within Church properties.

REFERENCES:

David C. Bailey, *¡Viva Cristo Rey!* (Austin: University of Texas Press, 1974);

Peter Calvert, *The Mexican Revolution* (Cambridge: Cambridge University Press, 1968);

Robert E. Quirk, *The Mexican Revolution and the Catholic Church* (Bloomington: Indiana University Press, 1973);

John Rutherford, *Mexican Society during the Revolution: A Literary Approach* (Oxford: Clarendon Press, 1971);

Jim Tuck, *The Holy War in Los Altos* (Tucson: University of Arizona Press, 1982).

—M.E.S.

CELIA CRUZ

Celia Cruz, born in Havana in 1924, is affectionately known in much of the world as the "Queen of **Salsa**." Combining studies at the Havana Municipal Conservatory with an early singing career, she began appearing on Cuban radio programs such as *La Corte Suprema del Arte* (The Supreme Court of Art), but it was with the famous orchestra Sonora Matancera that she gained popularity among Cuban audiences. Her enduring association with Sonora Matancera produced her first recordings (1950) and was cemented by her marriage to the first trumpet player, Pedro Knight, who later became the conductor for her personal appearances. In addition to frequent appearances at the popular cabarets of Havana (Sans Souci, Tropicana, Montmartre) her distinctive voice was heard often on radio, in theaters and films, and eventually on television.

In 1960 Celia Cruz joined the thousands of Cubans who felt it necessary to leave their homeland. Most of the many artists who left were forced to adjust to a new lifestyle and were unable to recuperate their former celebrity status in exile. Others saw their careers as performers temporarily suspended. Among those who developed impressive new careers in the wider Caribbean Basin were Celia Cruz, **Olga Guillot**, Xiomara Alfaro, Bobby Collazo, Osvaldo Farrés, Blanca Rosa Gil, Luisa María Güell, "Cachao" López, La Lupe, and Paquito Rivera.

Celia Cruz ensured her continued popularity through an impressive number of successful recordings, many of which were shared with other outstanding artists and ensembles, such as Johnny Pacheco, So-nora Matancera, Sonora Ponceña, **Tito Puente,** and Willie Colón. It is estimated that the Queen of Salsa produced more than a hundred recordings.

REFERENCES:

Cristóbal Díaz Ayala, *Música cubana del Areyto a la Nueva Trova,* second edition (San Juan: Editorial Cubanacán, 1981);

Jeremy Marre and Hannah Charlton, *Beats of the Heart: Popular Music of the World* (New York: Pantheon Books, 1985);

Rebeca Mauleón, *Salsa Guidebook for Piano and Ensemble* (Petaluma, Cal.: Sher Music, 1993).

— R.L.S.

Luis Cruz Azaceta

The Cuban American Luis Salvador de Jesús Cruz Azaceta (1942–), an important Latin American painter, belongs to a group of artists who adopted Neo-Expressionist modes during the 1980s, artists such as the Puerto Rican **Arnaldo Roche Rabell** and the Mexican **Rocío Maldonado.** Born in Havana, Azaceta left for New York in 1960, where he considers himself to be in exile. There he attended the School of Visual Arts and studied with the painter Leon Golub. Impressed by the expressionistic art of Hieronymus Bosch, Francisco de Goya, and Francis Bacon, which he saw when he visited Europe in 1969, Azaceta abandoned his early geometric abstract style and formulated an expressive figurative mode characterized by strong colors, car-toonlike forms, and Pop Art elements. Many of his works during the 1970s comment on violence, which the artist first encountered in Cuba during the revolution that brought **Fidel Castro** to power. In paintings such as *Do Not Die Here From 8 am to 6 pm* (1978), Azaceta shows with sardonic humor the random cruelty and violence of New York City streets, through a series of visual fragments that include rats, parking signs, weapons, and torn body parts, while in the more hopeful *The Urban Painter of Hearts* (1981) he represents himself painting a heart on his easel in front of a burning city, indicating his determination to purge evil through art.

During the 1980s Azaceta joined the Neo-Expressionist tendencies emerging in New York as he formulated a bold figurative style with bright colors and a loose, strong brushwork that emphasizes a sense of texture. He also developed a lasting interest in self-portraiture, which he shares with other Latin American painters such as **Frida Kahlo,** Roche Rabell, and **Nahum Zenil.** Through self-representation he contin-ued to explore the subject of violence, especially in Latin America, where individuals have often been threatened by poverty and state terrorism. In works such as *Homo-Fragile* (1983) and *Latin American Vic-*

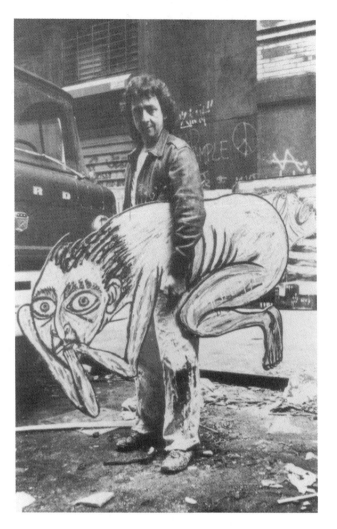

Luis Cruz Azaceta holding a self-portrait, New York City, 1987 (photograph by Eeva Inkeri)

tims of Dictators, Oppression, Torture, and Assassina-tion (1987), Azaceta represents himself as a fetishlike figure, subjected to a nightmarish torture.

The monumental quality of his figures, for whom he seeks compassion, transforms them into universal symbols of human tragedy, as in *The Journey* (1986), where a lonely figure, also a self-portrait, stands for an anonymous refugee undertaking the dangerous voyage into exile, as well as a poignant symbol for the journey of life. Since the late 1980s Azaceta has produced a series of paintings dealing with AIDS, such as *AIDS Count III* (1988), that reflect the hopelessness of those dying in the midst of general indifference.

REFERENCE:

Susana Torruella Leval, "Luis Cruz Azaceta: Arte y conciencia," translated by Brian J. Mallet, *Arte en Colombia,* no. 43 (Feb-ruary 1990): 40–43, 130–131.

— F.B.N.

MANUEL DE LA CRUZ GONZÁLEZ

Manuel de la Cruz González (1909–   ), one of the most important Costa Rican painters, worked with different types of figuration and **abstract art.** During the 1930s and 1940s the self-taught Cruz González belonged to a generation of Costa Rican artists, including **Francisco Zúñiga,** who were interested in modern art and opposed to the conservative tendencies of the public. Like the other members of the group, Cruz González used a modernized, stylized realism while concentrating on national or **costumbrista** themes, including local landscapes, typical adobe houses, and the people of Costa Rica. At the end of the 1940s he went to Cuba, where his art became more expressionistic, and later to Venezuela, where he came into contact with vanguardist artists such as Alejandro Otero and Jesús Rafael Soto. During this period Cruz González produced a series of paintings about peasant figures, including Goajira women, in which he transforms his models into a series of brightly colored geometric planes typical of Geometric Abstraction, and thick textures characteristic of Informal Abstraction. Such a combination of abstraction and figuration links his work with Neofiguration.

By the time Cruz González went back to Costa Rica in 1959, his art had turned completely toward Geometric Abstraction, and he was producing lacquer paintings on wood, featuring hard-edge flat areas of color, as in *Espacio color* (late 1960s; Space Color). Back in the Costa Rican context, he returned to his earlier neofigurative and costumbrista styles. During the 1960s Cruz González's art influenced the artists of the Grupo Ocho (1960–1963), who wanted to modernize Costa Rican art. He was also the leader of the Grupo Taller (1961–1970), which had a similar objective. To that end the group organized numerous lectures and exhibitions that included artists from abroad. Many of these Costa Rican artists worked with Informal Abstraction and Neofiguration but had no interest in local themes. Cruz González also organized his own art school and during the 1970s taught at the Universidad de Costa Rica.

REFERENCE:

Carlos Francisco Echeverría, *Historia crítica del arte costarricense* (San José, Costa Rica: Editorial Universidad Estatal a Distancia, 1986).

—F.B.N.

PABLO ANTONIO CUADRA

Although born in Managua (1912), the Nicaraguan poet Pablo Antonio Cuadra has always considered Granada his home. Because of his editorial position on the Managua newspaper *La Prensa,* he has had to spend most of his time in the capital. As a young man Cuadra traveled extensively throughout Spanish America, where he met several important writers, including the celebrated Spanish poet and dramatist Federico García Lorca. At age eighteen Cuadra joined the *vanguardia* movement in Nicaragua, headed by **José Coronel Urtecho;** Cuadra was one of the movement's youngest members. *Poemas nicaragüenses* (1934; Nicaraguan Poems) was Cuadra's first published book of poetry. It included his anti–United States poem "Poema del momento extranjero en la selva" ("Poem of an Alien Moment in the Jungle"), which condemned U.S. Marine interference in Nicaragua. His later poetry, best understood as a response to the continual cultural and political repression in Latin America, is characterized by a focus on indigenous themes and history. In addition to Nahua (Aztec) mythology, Cuadra's works reflect thematic and stylistic influences from the Greco-Roman tradition as can be seen in his book of poetry *El jaguar y la luna* (1959; The Jaguar and the Moon). *Cantos de Cifar y de la mar dulce* (1971; Songs of Cifar and the Gentle Sea) is Homeric in style, assimilating indigenous myths of Nicaragua.

Cuadra's life was marked by his opposition to the regime of Anastasio Somoza Dabayle, which imprisoned him twice. Cuadra's opposition to the Somoza regime intensified in the 1970s following the assassination in 1978 of his friend, the former editor of *La Prensa,* Pedro Joaquín Chamorro, and the subsequent destruction of the newspaper by Somoza's forces in 1979.

Although always affirming his Nicaraguan cultural identity, Cuadra's poetry has maintained a wide appeal by combining indigenous mythology and Christian values. *Siete árboles contra el atardecer* (1980; Seven Trees Against the Dying Light) confirms his universal stance, transcending ideology with humanistic values. Cuadra is considered by his fellow Nicaraguan poet Ernesto Cardenal to be "the most Nicaraguan of all our poets." Although known for his poetry, Cuadra has produced short stories, theater, essays, and literary criticism.

REFERENCE:

Steven White, *Culture and Politics in Nicaragua: Testimonies of Poets and Writers* (New York: Lumen Books, 1986).

—M.T.

CUATRO

The *cuatro* is a stringed instrument derived from the Spanish guitar. Two quite different versions are popular folk instruments in the Caribbean basin: the Puerto Rican cuatro and the Venezuelan cuatro.

The Puerto Rican cuatro, as constructed by local artisans, is visually recognizable as a descendant of the guitar but with variations of shape and size. It may have four courses of double strings, but the most common type has five courses. The typical tuning of the strings of the cuatro is as follows: the lowest pair of strings is tuned to b (below middle C) with each successive ascending pair of strings tuned a perfect fourth higher (b–e^1–a^1–d^2–g^2). The individual pairs of strings may be tuned in unison or octaves. The Puerto Rican cuatro is played with a plectrum and normally fulfills a melodic role in the manner of a mandolin. Chords may be played on the instrument, but chordal playing is usually reserved for passages in which the cuatro is accompanying the voice or another instrument that has assumed responsibility for the melody.

The Venezuelan cuatro resembles the ukelele in structure, with four single strings tuned in ascending order: a–d^1–$f\#^1$–b. The Venezuelan instrument commonly functions as an accompaniment, the musician providing a variety of complex rhythms by strumming the strings.

REFERENCE:

Francisco Lopez Cruz, *Método para la enseñanza del cuatro puertorriqueño* (San Juan: Instituto de Cultura Puertorriqueña, 1967).

— R.L.S.

The Cuban Film Institute

In 1959 one of the first official acts of **Fidel Castro**'s new government was to establish the Instituto Cubano del Arte e Industria Cinematográficas (Cuban Film Institute), which is commonly known as ICAIC. Twenty years later the Festival Internacional de Nuevo Cine Latinoamericano (International Festival of New Latin American Cinema) was begun under the auspices of ICAIC and became the major world showcase for Latin American cinema. Each year the festival, which is attended by filmmakers, film distributors, and critics, attracts large numbers of the Cuban public to its screenings of hundreds of motion pictures. In December 1988 the police had to control the crowds with tear gas and batons, such was their eagerness to view a particular film from Venezuela. This concentration of filmic activities in Cuba has led to other initiatives. Most important, the festival allows Latin American filmmakers to meet and discuss strategies of cooperation and marketing, reviving an initiative taken at the film festival held in Viña del Mar, Chile, in 1967. Fur-

thermore, the Latin American Film Market (MECLA) has been established, creating a marketplace for the distribution of Latin American films. The parallel Federación de Distribuidoras Alternativas de América Latina y el Caribe (Federation of Alternative Distributors of Latin America and the Caribbean), or FEDALC, was set up during a distributors' meeting in Havana in 1985 — offering Latin American filmmakers the opportunity to achieve some measure of success in competition with U.S. movies, which are widely distributed and heavily publicized all over the region. The movie houses in the main square (zócalo) in downtown Mexico City, as much as in downtown San Juan in Puerto Rico, carry the latest U.S. blockbusters rather than Latin American films. The Argentine filmmaker Octavio Getino estimates that Latin America represents some 11 percent of Hollywood's total income. Using techniques of "block booking" — a practice prohibited in the United States — U.S. cinema accounts for nearly half of all films distributed throughout Latin America and a similar proportion of all screen time in every Latin American country except Mexico and Cuba. This market penetration remained at about a constant level for the thirty years preceding 1990, and there are no signs that this situation will change as the century nears its end.

Other important initiatives were the establishment of the **Fundación de Nuevo Cine Latinoamericano** (Foundation for New Latin American Cinema), under the leadership of the celebrated Colombian author and scriptwriter Gabriel García Márquez, and the Escuela de Cine y Televisión (School of Cinema and Television) for Latin American, African, and Asian filmmakers in San Antonio de los Baños, near Havana. The school has been directed by Fernando Birri since 1986. There have also been joint projects with Televisión Española, including the *Amores difíciles* (Difficulty Loves) series, under the direction of García Márquez. Finally, the international symposium Women and the Audiovisual World, held during the 1986 festival, was a first attempt to integrate women directors into the Latin American movie industry. The following year an important retrospective of work by Latin American women was a special part of the festival. The uncertain economic and political future of Cuba does not guarantee that such activities will endure.

REFERENCE:

John King, Ana M. López, and Manuel Alvarado, eds., *Mediating Two Worlds: Cinematic Encounters in the Americas* (London: BFI, 1993).

— S.M.H.

Autorretrato con las señoritas de Aviñón (1973; Self-Portrait with the Young Ladies of Avignon) by José Luis Cuevas, part of his *Homenaje a Picasso* (Tribute to Picasso) series (Art Museum of the Americas, Organization of American States, Washington, D.C.)

José Luis Cuevas

The Mexican artist José Luis Cuevas (1934–) was an important force in **La Ruptura Generation** (the break generation), which during the 1950s denounced the didactic, ideological, and stylistic limitations of **Muralism.** Although he was not a member of the **Nueva Presencia** group, he was influential in the group's re-

jection of the Mexican School. By 1953 the self-taught Cuevas had already had an important exhibition at the avant-garde Galería Prisse in Mexico City. He rapidly rose to national prominence not only through his considerable talent but also because of his public attacks on well-established artists of the Mexican School, such as **Diego Rivera** and **David Alfaro Siqueiros,** and his demands for greater artistic freedom. The young Cuevas achieved international fame in the late 1950s through the support of José Gómez Sicre, director of the Division of Visual Arts at the Pan-American Union in Washington, D.C.

The expressionist and subjective representation of the human figure in Cuevas's art, consisting mainly of drawings and prints, is comparable in its existentialist emphasis to the work of neofigurative artists active during the 1950s and 1960s such as the Irishman Francis Bacon, the members of the Argentinean group Otra Figuración, the Venezuelan Jacobo Borges, and the Mexican **Alberto Gironella,** another member of La Ruptura Generation. *Loco* (1954; Madman), *Estudios de Kafka y su padre* (1957; Studies of Kafka and His Father), and *Autoretrato en la noche* (1978; Self-Portrait at Night) are drawings in which Cuevas identifies with the dark vision of human nature found not only in the graphic art of Francisco de Goya and **José Clemente Orozco** but also in the writings of Fyodor Dostoyevsky and Franz Kafka. Cuevas formulated a subjective, nightmarish universe populated by alienated and marginal figures: criminals and prostitutes, the insane and the grotesque.

REFERENCES:

Shifra M. Goldman, *Contemporary Mexican Painting in a Time of Change* (Albuquerque: University of New Mexico Press, 1995);

Marta Traba, *Los cuatro monstruos cardinales* (Mexico City: Ediciones Era, 1965).

— F.B.N.

D

THE DAILY PRESS IN CENTRAL AMERICA

The leading newspapers in late-twentieth-century Central America cannot compare with their counterparts in Mexico City or other large Spanish American cities. In Costa Rica (population 2.8 million) the leading newspaper, *La Nación,* established in 1946, publishes 135,000 copies on weekday mornings and 150,000 copies on Sundays in a metropolitan area that has just 278,000 residents. It came close to declaring bankruptcy in 1982, when the country devalued its currency. *La Nación* is the first Spanish-language Central American newspaper to be available on the World Wide Web. In El Salvador the two largest newspapers are *La Prensa Gráfica* and *El Diario de Hoy.* In Guatemala, with a rural and mostly Indian population of 8 million, newspapers have a weak market compared to those in other Latin American countries. The two main newspapers are *Prensa Libre* (circulation 68,000) and *El Gráfico* (circulation 60,000). When the total readership of the these papers is combined with that of the two other main Guatemalan newspapers — *La Hora* (20,000) and *Diario de Centroamérica* (15,000) — the result is a rough figure of one newspaper per fifty Guatemalans, one of the lowest ratios in Latin America. Honduras, with a heavily rural population of slightly more than 4 million, faces similar problems; the two main newspapers are *La Prensa* (circulation 50,000) and *El Tiempo* (circulation 35,000), both of which are published in San Pedro Sula. Newspapers in Honduras are read by government workers and the educated upper class.

The press in Nicaragua is deeply divided and closely linked to government circles. *La Prensa* has been connected since the 1920s with the powerful Chamorro family, which has contributed five presidents to the nation, including the one who followed the rule of the Sandinistas: Violeta Chamorro, wife of Pedro Joaquín Chamorro, who was murdered in 1978. In 1979, when the left-wing Sandinista government came to power, all news media were censored by the government, and only one newspaper, the Sandinista organ *Barricada,* and Sandinista radio stations were permitted to operate freely. When Violeta Chamorro came to power in 1990, all pressure on *La Prensa,* as might be expected, was lifted. In Panama during the regime of Gen. Manuel Antonio Noriega the press was regularly muzzled, but following the U.S. invasion of Panama in December 1989, many newspapers sprang back into life. Below are the circulation figures of the main Central American newspapers in 1990:

Costa Rica
La Nación (San José): 135,000
El Salvador
El Diario de Hoy (San Salvador): 88,000
La Prensa Gráfica (San Salvador): 106,000
Guatemala
Prensa Libre (Guatemala City): 68,000
El Gráfico (Guatemala City): 60,000
Honduras
El Tiempo (San Pedro Sula): 35,000
La Prensa (San Pedro Sula): 50,000
Nicaragua
La Prensa (Managua): 74,000
Barricada (Managua): 6,000
Panama
La Prensa (Panama City): 35,000
La Estrella de Panamá (Panama City): 40,000

Another indicator of the relative strength of the news industry in the various Central American countries is the number of newspapers published. For the period 1965–1984 the available statistics are as follows:

	1965	1975	1978	1979	1982	1984
Costa Rica		6	4	4	4	5
El Salvador		12	12	12	6	6
Guatemala		10	9	9	9	5
Honduras		8	7	7	6	6
Nicaragua	6	7	6	8	3	3
Panama	10	6	6	6	5	6

REFERENCES:

Marvin Alisky, "Latin America," in *Global Journalism*, edited by John C. Merrill (New York: Longman, 1983), pp. 249–301;

Jesús Timoteo Alvarez and Ascensión Martínez Riaza, *Historia de la prensa hispanoamerica* (Madrid: Editorial MAPFRE, 1992);

Michael B. Salwen and Bruce Garrison, *Latin American Journalism* (Hillsdale, N.J.: Lawrence Erlbaum, 1991).

— S.M.H.

/

THE DAILY PRESS IN MEXICO

Throughout its history in Mexico, the newspaper press has been both a vehicle for and evidence of the links of Mexico to Europe and the United States. Various nuclei of Mexican literati were aware of western journalistic standards and demanded newspapers and magazines roughly resembling those of Paris, Madrid, New York, and London. Before 1900 the Mexican press was primarily an instrument by which other institutions achieved their ends. In the twentieth century, however, it began to develop an identity of its own, separate from political, religious, and economic institutions.

The first Mexican periodical publication, or gazette, was *La gaceta de México,* founded in 1722 by Juan Ignacio de Castoreña. Seven years later Guatemala, the most important colonial offshoot of Mexico, started its own gazette, *La gaceta de Guatemala.* These publications were court gazettes licensed and in some cases published by the local governors and, by extension, the Spanish Crown. Typically they included official announcements about Spain and the colonies, as well as information about religious festivals. Sparks from the American and French Revolutions ignited the first journalistic tinder in Spanish America. In the three decades following 1790, when the journalistic phase proper began, all the larger countries saw the birth of newspapers.

Unlike other Spanish American countries, where one premium newspaper often dominates, Mexico has several major newspapers. Given that roughly one-third of Mexico's entire population is concentrated in Mexico City, it is not surprising that the main national newspapers are based there. Among the prominent papers of that capital city are *La Prensa* (established in 1928), *Excelsior* (1916), *El Nacional* (1928), *El Universal* (1916), *El Sol de México* (1965), and *El Heraldo de México* (1965). Of these, *La Prensa* appears to have the largest circulation; it is a nonbulky, informative newspaper with a popular edge, concentrating on national politics, some international news, editorials on current events, sports, the economy and finance, and national news of a more sensational character. *El Nacional* is more serious-minded and treats local news in greater depth, with separate sections on culture, sports, the economy, and international events. *El Universal* is a bulky, highbrow newspaper with in-depth coverage of international as well as national events. *Excelsior,* another highbrow, quality newspaper, has a special cultural section. *El Sol de México* combines serious reporting in a section on international news, national news, and finance with more-colorful coverage of entertainment, sports, and society. *El Heraldo de México* covers political events on the national and international scenes, as well as national events of a sensational nature, and has separate sections on finance and local news. One of the best of the Mexico City newspapers is *La Jornada,* which offers good, independent coverage. In summer 1995 it became the first Mexican newspaper to offer its news over the World Wide Web. (Other Latin American newspapers on the Internet are *El Norte* of Monterrey and *La Nación* of Costa Rica.)

Despite the national dominance of newspapers based in Mexico City, the various states of Mexico have their own local papers, an example of which is *Diario de Yucatán* (Mérida), which focuses almost exclusively on regional matters. Between 1965 and 1984 the number of newspapers published in Mexico rose from 220 to 312. The 1990 circulation figures for the top eleven newspapers in Mexico were as follows:

Excelsior (Mexico City): 175,000
El Heraldo de México (Mexico City): 300,000
El Nacional (Mexico City): 120,000
Novedades (Mexico City): 190,000
Novedades de la tarde (Mexico City): 111,000
La Prensa (Mexico City) 300,000
El Sol de México (Mexico City): 120,000
Ultimas Noticias de Excelsior (Mexico City): 108,000
El Universal (Mexico City): 185,000
Uno Más Uno (Mexico City): 70,000
El Norte (Monterrey): 100,000

REFERENCES:

Marvin Alisky, "Latin America," in *Global Journalism,* edited by John C. Merrill (New York: Longman, 1983), pp. 249–301;

Robert N. Pierce and Kurt Kent, "Newspapers," in *Handbook of Latin American Popular Culture,* edited by Harold E. Hinds

Jr. and Charles M. Tatum (Westport, Conn.: Greenwood Press, 1985), pp. 229–250;

Michael B. Salwen and Bruce Garrison, *Latin American Journalism* (Hillsdale, N.J.: Lawrence Erlbaum, 1991).

— S.M.H.

THE DAILY PRESS IN THE CARIBBEAN

While there has been no region-wide newspaper for the Hispanic Caribbean, by the late twentieth century most of the news coverage for the Spanish-speaking nations of the region, except for Cuba, was coming from **CANA,** the Caribbean News Agency. Despite their geographical proximity and similar histories, newspapers in Cuba, Santo Domingo, and Puerto Rico demonstrate surprisingly different patterns of development.

Cuba no longer has any privately owned press: its official newspapers and magazines are owned and operated by the government. *Granma,* named after the boat that brought **Fidel Castro** and his eighty-one rebels from Mexico to launch the revolution in Cuba in 1956, was established in 1965 as a morning daily. *Granma* has a political focus. Like some of the dailies set up soon after the revolution, such as *Revolución* (1959–1960), *Granma* strives to speak on behalf of Latin America and to expose the injustices of the capitalist system in the United States. It is the most widely read newspaper in the Caribbean, with an estimated circulation of 700,000 in the early 1990s. The largest afternoon newspaper in Cuba is *Juventud Rebelde* (Rebellious Youth), which models itself after Soviet youth publications and seeks to instill communist virtues in the youth of Cuba.

The press in the Dominican Republic is more varied; there are ten newspapers, each with a circulation between 15,000 and 50,000. Of these papers the most prestigious is *El Listín Diario,* a staid, highbrow, and informative newspaper with high journalistic standards and a circulation of 50,000. It is the oldest Spanish-language newspaper in the Caribbean, having been founded in 1889. (The oldest newspaper in the Caribbean at large is the English-language *The Daily Gleaner,* published in Kingston, Jamaica, and founded in 1834.)

The press in Puerto Rico is different from that in either the Dominican Republic or Cuba. A U.S. commonwealth since 1952, Puerto Rico has several English-language newspapers, which are read mainly by the tourists who flood into Puerto Rico every year and by the U.S. citizens who work there. The two major Spanish-language newspapers, *El Nuevo Día* and *El Vocero de Puerto Rico,* both based in San Juan, dominate daily circulation in Puerto Rico. *El Nuevo Día* is the larger (with a circulation of 70,000) and is regarded as the better of the two newspapers. Unlike the rest of Latin America, where newspapers are sold in kiosks (newsstands), *El Nuevo Día* is normally sold, like newspapers in the United States, via street vending machines or by subscription.

Below are the 1990 circulation figures for the major Spanish-language newspapers in Cuba, the Dominican Republic, and Puerto Rico.

Cuba

Granma (Havana): 700,000
Tribuna de la Habana (Havana): 33,000
Guerrillero (Pinar del Río): 33,000
Adelante (Camagüey): 32,000
Girón (Matanzas): 25,000
Sierra Maestra (Santiago): 25,000

Dominican Republic

El Listín Diario (Santo Domingo): 50,000
Ultima hora (Santo Domingo): 40,000
El Nacional (Santo Domingo): 40,000
El Caribe (Santo Domingo): 37,000
El Siglo (Santo Domingo): 35,000
Hoy (Santo Domingo): 30,000
El Nuevo Diario (Santo Domingo): 20,000
El Sol (Santo Domingo): 19,000
La Noticia (Santo Domingo): 15,000
La Información (Santiago de los Caballeros): 15,000

Puerto Rico

El Nuevo Día (San Juan): 70,000
El Vocero de Puerto Rico (San Juan): [not available]

REFERENCES:

Marvin Alisky, "Latin America," in *Global Journalism,* edited by John C. Merrill (New York: Longman, 1983), pp. 249–301;

Jesús Timoteo Alvarez and Ascensión Martínez Riaza, *Historia de la prensa hispanoamerica* (Madrid: Editorial MAPFRE, 1992);

Michael B. Salwen and Bruce Garrison, *Latin American Journalism* (Hillsdale, N.J.: Lawrence Erlbaum, 1991).

— S.M.H.

ROQUE DALTON

An important poet, novelist, and journalist, Roque Dalton (1935–1975) was born in El Salvador of a Salvadoran mother and a father from the United States. He studied in El Salvador with the Jesuits and continued his learning in Costa Rica and later in Chile, where he came into contact with the Marxist ideas that would so profoundly influence his life and works. Upon returning to El Salvador he was persecuted, jailed, and exiled for his revolutionary ideals, after which he spent time in Cuba and Mexico. He won the Central American Prize for Poetry three times (1956, 1958, and 1959); his book of poetry *Taberna y otros lugares* (1969; Tavern and Other Places) won him a prestigious **Casa de las Américas Prize** in 1969. Dalton's poetry and other writings are marked by strong social protest, condemning the injustices apparent in his society and emphasizing the political function of literature as an instrument to influence and transform society; in this sense he was much influenced by the writings of Chilean Nobel laureate Pablo Neruda. His style is vibrant, colorful, and visual, with ample use of popular language, wordplay, and humorous twists. His other works include a biography of Miguel Mármol (1972), essays on the Peruvian poet César Vallejo (1963), *¿Revolución en la revolución? y la crítica de derecha* (1970; Revolution within the Revolution? And a Critique of the Right), and various books of poetry, including *Los testimonios* (1964; Testimonies), *Los pequeños infiernos* (1970; Small Hells), and *Poemas clandestinos* (1981; Clandestine Poems). The circumstances of his death are tragic: unjustly condemned by his own comrades as a spy, he was executed.

REFERENCES:

John Beverley and Marc Zimmerman, *Literature and Politics in the Central American Revolutions* (Austin: University of Texas Press, 1990);

Mario Noel Rodríguez, *Nombre de guerra y otros ensayos* (San Salvador: Ediciones Certamen, 1988).

— M.E.S.

DANCE

Dance has always flourished as an integral component of religious, social, and cultural life in Mexico, Central America, and the Hispanic Caribbean. In the twentieth century, pre- and postconquest indigenous traditions survive in the religious and secular practices of many local communities, while international styles and genres have contributed to urban social dance and professional theater dance. Several countries in the Caribbean and Central America have devoted government and other institutional resources to the practice and study of the arts. Mexico, for example, has published books and articles on aspects of its dance culture from the pre-Hispanic era to the present, and writings about dance in Cuba have proliferated since 1959, when **Fidel Castro** initiated an aggressive policy of sup-

port and promotion. Coverage also exists for Puerto Rico, but information is more sparse for other countries. Nevertheless, the available data suggest a continuing richness of dance activity in all spheres, throughout the century.

The Spanish language has two terms for dance: *danza* and *baile*. In some countries of the Caribbean and Central America they are interchangeable. In others, such as Mexico, *danza* usually refers to dance forms with indigenous content and *baile* to European-based forms, specifically to partner dances. Somewhat confusingly, however, the term *danza* is also applied to modern theater dance.

In the ritual context the term *danza* (or *danza indígena*) refers to traditional religious or secular dances or dance dramas in indigenous communities throughout Mexico and much of Central America. Such performances developed after the arrival of the Spaniards and the imposition of Catholicism and often included both preconquest and Spanish cultural elements. The dancers (*danzantes*) are usually men and participate as a form of religious obligation. Danzante groups are hierarchical organizations, each committed to the performance of one type of danza that is its charge. Each local area has specific danzas that are performed for church holidays or other commemorations.

In twentieth-century Spanish America the term *baile* is roughly equivalent to the English "folk dance" or "social dance." In Mexico hybrid folk dances derived from a variety of European prototypes are termed *bailes populares* or *bailes regionales* and are an important part of community festivities and courtship practices. In urban social contexts throughout the area, *bailes de salón* include national and internationally popular dances such as the **danzón, rumba,** tango, **mambo,** fox trot, waltz, and disco dances.

As they developed historically, the area's dance cultures incorporated and retained differing proportions of indigenous, European, and African elements. While indigenous dance traditions long ago disappeared in the Caribbean and are minimal in much of Central America, they remain strong in Mexico and Guatemala and are also present to a lesser extent in Honduras, El Salvador, and Nicaragua. Indigenous dance vocabulary includes movements such as walking steps, stamps, skips, slides, jumps on two feet, turns, squats, and leg lifts, usually in duple rhythmic patterns. The musical accompaniment for dances — sometimes provided by the dancers themselves — might be solely from traditional indigenous percussion and wind instruments or include songs, stringed instrumental music, and musical styles from the Spanish tradition.

The European components in the dance of this region come predominantly from Spain. There are exceptions, including central European forms such as the polka, schottische, redowa, and mazurka, introduced into northern Mexico by German and Czech immigrant ranchers in the nineteenth century. Such dances continued as staples of the **norteño** dance repertoire through the twentieth century. A highly significant European dance element in the above-mentioned dances, as well as in the waltz and *paso doble,* is the ubiquitous male-female couple formation that often includes physical contact and serves as an important part of courtship practice. Close physical contact between the sexes is absent in both indigenous and African dance traditions. Also important as part of the pan-European heritage are figure dances such as the *cuadrilla* (quadrille, danced by four couples in a square) and the *contradanza* (with couples in facing lines). Of Spanish heritage, deriving particularly from the tradition of flamenco, are **zapateo** (staccato footwork) and the woman's skirt manipulation. Also from Spain came string and wind instrumental (and often sung) accompaniment in triple meter, a frequent dance and musical structure alternating chorus and verse, and various other dance forms.

African-related dance practices have been particularly important in Cuba, Puerto Rico, and the Dominican Republic, but there was also African influence in parts of Mexico and Central America. African slaves imported into the Americas in early colonial times represented various ethnic groups, but the strong Yoruba tradition of West Africa and the Congolese influence from Central Africa have been especially significant in the music and dance of Cuba. The African elements prominent in the Caribbean include religious and secular dance content; the religious and social uses made of the dance; an improvisational format involving individuals, couples, or groups; accompaniment featuring drums and sometimes songs or chants; polyrhythms and syncopation in both the drum patterns and the dancers' bodies; and emphasis on torso, hip, and pelvic movement. The rich African-derived dance culture of the area manifests itself in the practices of religious cults and in carnival processions; it also figures prominently in secular entertainments.

In addition to the manifestations of nonprofessional dance, theatrical and concert dance has been an increasingly important cultural element in the twentieth century. Together with popular theatrical forms, the major professional dance genres have been ballet; modern dance; and theatricalized folk, social, and ritual dance (*ballet folklórico*). The terminology used to describe these genres can also be confusing, since modern or folkloric dance groups often include "ballet" in

Alicia Alonso of the Ballet Nacional de Cuba (courtesy of the Organization of American States)

their names, while classical ballet companies may use "danza." Theatrical and concert dancers are generally referred to as *bailarines*. Ballet, which had been developing in Europe since the Renaissance, was first introduced into the Latin American context in the late eighteenth century. Initially stimulated by the visits of European companies and ballet masters, this theatrical genre, with its codified movement vocabulary and its formal structures, developed under the direction of native artists particularly in Cuba and also in Puerto Rico and Mexico.

Modern dance (danza moderna or danza contemporánea) is a concert art that first emerged in the United States and Germany in the early twentieth century. The most fundamental characteristic of this genre is that it is not bound to any one canonical movement vocabulary or choreographic approach. Rather, the content and intent of a work determines the movement and formations of the dancers. The early pioneers of this approach explored contemporary social, cultural, and political themes, as well as various formal structures such as ABA, rondo, and organic form. Dancers in the United States first presented modern dance in Mexico in the 1930s, and Mexican dancers soon appropriated the approach to explore their own cultural roots, political concerns, and social aspirations.

Modern dance was committed to the use of a developed theatrical dance vocabulary and well-known Western formal structures. In contrast, postmodern dance has featured elements borrowed from everyday movement, nontheatrical performance venues, random juxtapositions, improvisation, choreography by chance methods, and the German Tanztheater (which combines all elements of theater in often outrageous ways, to make potent but nonliteral political and social statements). By the late twentieth century, contemporary dance in all these guises had entered the mainstream of Mexican dance art, and various manifestations had also become important elsewhere.

While adapted folk dances or dances with folk motifs have been presented in European theatrical contexts since at least the Renaissance, it was only in the twentieth century that the "folk ballet" appeared. Stimulated by the work of the Soviet choreographer Igor Moiseyev, who founded the first such company in the late 1930s, Mexico, followed by other countries in Latin America, developed its own ballet folklórico. (See **National Folkloric Dance Companies.**) Such companies feature theatricalized and romanticized versions of traditional dances and dance contexts, and their members train in ballet or modern dance as well as in the techniques specific to the adapted folk, social, and ritual dances performed. In addition to the professional ballets folklóricos, Mexico and some of the other countries in the region also have many amateur companies that model their productions on those of the professionals.

Professional and amateur dance training, university dance education, and dance research have become increasingly important in the last decades of the twentieth century. Predictably, such activities in Mexico and Cuba have been more developed — because of relatively substantial government sponsorship — and more visible because more has been published about them, although economic pressures as the century closes have taken their toll on governmental support. The late twentieth century has also seen an increasing number of international Latin American dance conferences and festivals, and increasing exchanges between teachers, scholars, dancers, and choreographers. Thus a network that contributes significantly to training and research is being developed.

International awareness of the Latin American dance scene has been fragmentary. Audiences outside of Latin America have become familiar with companies such as Mexico's Ballet Folklórico de Amalia

Hernández and Cuba's **Ballet Nacional,** with its superstar **Alicia Alonso,** and social dance enthusiasts all over the world have become addicted to the sensual delights of each successive Latino dance fashion. However, few people have experienced the variety and beauty of dances that have been integral elements in the cultural, social, and ritual life of indigenous and mestizo communities; the excitement of Afro-Caribbean ritual and secular dancing; or the profundity, daring, and whimsy of the area's innovative modern dance choreographers.

REFERENCES:

Susan Cashion, "Educating the Dancer in Cuba," in *Dance: Current Selected Research*, volume 1, edited by Lynette Y. Overby and James H. Humphrey (New York: AMS Press, 1989), pp. 165–197;

Lisa Lekis, *Folk Dances of Latin America* (New York: Scarecrow Press, 1958);

Paulina Ossona, Cassia Navas, Víctor Hugo Fernández, Miguel Cabrera, Alberto Dallal, and Carlos Paolillo, *Itinerario por la danza escénica de América Latina* (Caracas: Consejo Nacional de la Cultura, 1994);

Olga Nájera Ramírez, "Social and Political Dimensions of Folklórico Dance," *Western Folklore*, 48 (January 1989): 15–32;

Susanna Rostas, "The Concheros of Mexico: A Search for Ethnic Identity," *Dance Research*, 9 (Autumn 1991): 3–17;

Nancy Lee Ruyter, "Resources for the Study of Dance in Hispanic Cultures," *Choreography and Dance*, 3, part 4 (1994): 109–123.

— N.L.R.

DANCE FESTIVALS

Dance is celebrated in festivals throughout Mexico, Central America, and the Hispanic Caribbean. One of the world's richest systems of arts festivals is supported by Mexico's Instituto Nacional de Bellas Artes (National Institute of Fine Arts). Festivals that exclusively or predominantly feature dance include the Festival José Limón in Culiacán (founded in 1986), the Festival Cervantino in Guanajuato, the Festival Nacional e Internacional de Danza Contemporánea de San Luis Potosí (founded in 1981), the defunct Gran Festival de la Ciudad de México, the Encuentro Callejero de Danza Contemporánea (Modern Dance Street Meeting) in Mexico City (founded in 1986), the Festival Metropolitano de Monterrey, the Encuentro Binacional de Danza Contemporánea (the Binational Modern Dance Meeting, founded in 1993), the Festival of Oaxaca, the Oc Ohtic Festival of Yucatán, and the Festival del Golfo in Veracruz.

In Guatemala the Programa Permanente de Cultura of the Fundación Paiz, supported by Paiz department stores and directed by Jacqueline Riera de Paiz, holds a biennial festival in the city of Antigua; it has featured the Miami City Ballet. Costa Rica held an annual festival of young choreographers throughout the 1980s, and two other Costa Rican festivals are the Festivales de los Santos and the Diablitos (Little Devils) Festival. The Festival Permanente de Arte y Cultura of Suchitoto, El Salvador, has hosted the José Limón Dance Company, Country Dancers from Utah, performances of original choreography by local adolescents, and a yearlong series of modern-dance workshops supported by the Fulbright program. Nicaragua has organized various national festivals representing all forms of dance in that country.

The Festival Internacional de Ballet de la Habana, Cuba, was founded in 1960 with primary support from the Instituto Nacional de la Industria Turística (National Tourism Institute) and additional support from other governmental cultural agencies. It was designed to present dance from around the world to Cuban audiences and to publicize the high quality of Cuban dance to foreign visitors. Different focuses have been chosen for different years. In 1978 the aim was to feature as many world premieres as possible. In 1980 the focus was the relationship between dance and other artistic forms, including the visual arts, folklore, and film. In 1982 the focus was Latin America, with companies invited from Mexico, Chile, and Brazil. There are no competitive aspects to this festival.

REFERENCES:

Miguel Cabrera, "Festival Internacional de Ballet de La Habana," *Boletín Informativo 3 del CID-Danza* (Mexico City, 1985);

Rulio de la Rosa, "Impresiones sobre el Festival Internacional de Ballet," *Boletín Informativo 3 del CID-Danza* (Mexico City, 1985).

— J.M.H.

DANZÓN

It is thought by musicologists that the earliest examples of danzón were composed in Cuba by Miguel Failde in 1879. A musical descendant of the contradanza, the danzón eventually became more popular than the **habanera** in twentieth-century urban contexts, although both exerted considerable influence throughout Latin America, especially in the Caribbean basin. The European roots of danzón were combined with Creole innovations and Afro-Caribbean rhythms, representing a true cultural syncretism. The danzón is considered by many people to be the national dance of Cuba.

The structure of the danzón is derived from the European rondo form, that is, ABACADA (letter A represents a repeated section alternating with changing melodic/harmonic material). The sections B, C, and D not only feature new music, but also distinctive instrumentations, such as: B (clarinet trio) and C (brass trio). The early danzón ensembles depended largely on the percussion and wind instruments of the military band and were typically played out of doors. When the same danzones were played indoors, the ensembles employed violins and flutes and the timpani were replaced with the smaller timbales. The indoor ensembles were called charangas francesas (French orchestras) or charangas for short.

REFERENCES:

Peter Manuel, *Popular Musics of the Non-Western World* (New York: Oxford University Press, 1988);

John Storm Roberts, "The Latin Dimension," in *The Many Worlds of Music* (New York: Broadcast Music, 1976);

Roberts, "The Roots," in *Salsiology*, edited by Vernon W. Boggs (New York: Excelsior Music Publishing, 1992);

Olavo Alén Rodríguez, *Géneros musicales de Cuba: De lo afrocubano a la salsa* (San Juan: Editorial Cubanacán, 1992).

— R.L.S.

RUBÉN DARÍO

Considered the leader of **Modernismo** in Latin America, Rubén Darío (1867–1916) was born in Metapa, Nicaragua (subsequently renamed Ciudad Darío in his honor), and grew up with an aunt in León. He studied with the Jesuits and then at the National Institute, establishing a reputation as a poet at a very young age and acquiring an admiration for Spanish and French classical culture and literature. Throughout his lifetime Darío traveled extensively, frequently at the invitation of influential national leaders, and he served in various diplomatic capacities, which allowed him to meet important literary and political figures. In Valparaíso, Chile, in 1886 he met Pedro Balmaceda Toro, the son of the Chilean president, and through this friend's extensive library became acquainted with the work of the French Symbolist and Parnassian poets. The French influence was central to Darío's famous book of prose and verse, *Azul* (1888; Blue), which some consider the initiator of Modernismo. With the publication of *Azul* Darío earned the reproach of the well-known Spanish writer and critic Juan Valera, who accused Darío of a "mental gallicism," that is, of being too influenced by the French and forgetting other European and especially Hispanic cultures.

In the next few years Darío traveled to Central America, Spain, Cuba, Colombia, the United States, and France, establishing important friends and contacts everywhere he went. In Buenos Aires, where he was acting as consul for Colombia, he wrote and published *Los raros* (1893; The Rare Ones), a collection of essays about literary figures he most admired. He also published his famous book of poems, *Prosas profanas* (1896; Profane Prose), which cemented Darío's reputation as a formal innovator and cultivator of elegant language. The book is heavily influenced by the French Parnassians and Symbolists and reflects tendencies that were in vogue among young Latin American writers who were attempting to escape the remnants of a lackluster and fading Romanticism. These tendencies involved an aesthetic revival, including a renewal of metrical forms, a cultivation of sonorous language, plastic imagery, cosmopolitanism, and an admiration for the foreign, exotic, extravagant, and aristocratic. Although *Prosas profanas* was criticized for its lack of representation of American realities (most notably by the famous Uruguayan intellectual José Enrique Rodó), it also revealed profound themes that would later be cultivated more deeply by Darío, namely the existential anguish of human life and death and the conflict between physical and spiritual passions. In 1901, while he was in Spain, *España contemporánea* (Contemporary Spain) was published, reflecting his views on the then current artistic trends among Spanish artists. In 1905 he published *Cantos de vida y esperanza* (Songs of Life and Hope), considered by many the culmination of his previous works. *Cantos de vida y esperanza* continues to explore the rhythmic and musical dimensions of a language laden with elegant metaphors, while its themes reflect deeper, philosophical meditations on what it means to be mortal. Darío's poems on the passing of time and the loss of youth, existential anguish when confronted by death and the unknown, doubts, remorse, and passion achieve universal dimensions. Also included in *Cantos de vida y esperanza* are political themes involving Latin America's relationship with the United States. Darío later published *El canto errante* (1907; The Errant Canto), *El viaje a Nicaragua* (1909; The Trip to Nicaragua), and *Poema del otoño* (1910; Autumn Poem). Although well-received for their simpler, purer language, they did not achieve the level of popularity of *Cantos de vida y esperanza.* Toward the end of his life, struggling to make ends meet while working for the journal *Mundial,* he continued traveling extensively and published *Vida de Rubén Darío, escrita por él mismo* (1915; The Life of Rubén Darío, Written by Him) and *Historia de mis libros* (1915; A History of My Books). He died in León on 6 February 1916, of health problems apparently caused by his bohemian lifestyle.

Darío was able to assimilate foreign influences, especially the Spanish and French, and transform them into his own elegant style, with masterly formal linguistic innovations in the use of meter, imagery, and rhythm, matched by a rich content reflecting a wide range of human emotions. His earlier works escape the sordidness of his immediate surroundings by portraying fantastic and exotic worlds, reflecting a certain evasive and frivolous nature that has led him to be characterized by some critics as a poet of the "ivory tower." However, many of his poems, which strongly appeal to the physical senses, also approach the deeper, spiritual perceptions of humankind, reflecting a disenchantment with the realities of everyday existence. In his later works, especially in *Cantos de vida y esperanza,* the exotic nature of his poetry diminishes as he concentrates more on existential dilemmas arising from immediate realities, with their complex social, historic, political, and human dimensions. Darío has been viewed as one of the writers who best represents the changing times at the turn of the century. His work had a tremendous impact on the artists of his time as well as those who came after him, and it served as an inspiration for the postmodernists and vanguardists early in the twentieth century. His influence on Spanish American writers and artists is immeasurable. Today Rubén Darío is considered one of the greatest Hispanic poets of all time.

REFERENCES:

Keith Ellis, *Critical Approaches to Rubén Darío* (Toronto: University of Toronto Press, 1974);

Manuel Pedro González and Ivan A. Schulman, *José Martí, Rubén Darío y el modernismo* (Madrid: Gredos, 1969).

—M.E.S.

DE CIERTA MANERA

Directed by black Cuban director Sara Gómez, *De cierta manera* (One Way or Another) is a fictional movie made in the style of a documentary. Concentrating on social problems facing blacks and women, the movie follows a middle-class teacher called Yolanda (played by the actress Yolanda Cuéllar) and tells the story of her love for a bus-factory worker called Mario (played by the actor Mario Balmaceda). Their relationship is affected by tensions that each needs to resolve at work, while the demands of the group are shown in conflict with the aspirations of the individual. At the time when *De cierta manera* was filmed (1974–1978) Gómez was the only woman director working at the **Cuban Film Institute.** She died during the postproduction phase, and the movie was completed by **Tomás Gutiérrez Alea,** who had been serving as a consultant. According to Gutiérrez Alea, *De cierta manera* is successful because it offers open-minded solutions to social conflicts, documenting a situation in which the contradictions are manifest and in the process of being resolved. Although filming in color had become prevalent in Cuban cinema by the time this movie was made, *De cierta manera* was shot in black and white.

REFERENCES:

Julianne Burton, *Cinema and Social Change in Latin America: Conversations with Filmmakers* (Austin: University of Texas Press, 1986);

John King, *Magical Reels: A History of Cinema in Latin America* (London: Verso, 1990).

— S.M.H.

Décima

The décima became an important format for the structural organization of lyrics in many Creole folk genres of Caribbean and Latin American song. Often improvised, especially in competitions, it consists of ten octosyllabic lines of text with the rhyme scheme ABBAACCDDC.

Although the décima in the Americas dates from the colonial era, its prominence continues, for example, in the Cuban punto guajira (rural folksong), the **son,** and various **rumbas**; in the Dominican mangulina (a moderate couple dance with song), and the media tuna (improvised singing at folk celebrations known as bachatas); and especially in Puerto Rico, where the décima has been said to be an essential part of the definition of criollo music, while the **seis**, a dance with song set in décimas and originally danced by six couples, is the backbone of Puerto Rican folk music. Although currently diminished in popular status, the **romance** set in décimas continues as a viable genre in many parts of Latin America.

The instrumental accompaniment of décimas varies from country to country but generally features typical folk ensembles including minor percussion instruments such as the **güiro** and **maracas**, and the guitar and various versions of it, such as the **tres, cuatro,** and bandurria. Décimas are sung by a soloist or two singers in a controversia (literally a "controversy," between two singers in amusing competition).

REFERENCES:

Marcelino Canino Salgado, *El cantar folklórico de Puerto Rico: Mente y palabra* (Río Piedras: Editorial de la Universidad de Puerto Rico, 1986);

Bernarda Jorge, *La música dominicana: Siglos XIX-XX* (Santo Domingo: Universidad Autónoma de Santo Domingo, 1982);

Francisco López Cruz, *La música folklórica de Puerto Rico* (Sharon, Conn.: Troutman Press, 1967);

Peter Manuel, *Popular Musics of the Non-Western World: An Introductory Survey* (New York: Oxford University Press, 1988).

— R.L.S.

Décima performers in Panama (Lila R. Cheville and Richard A. Cheville)

Detective Fiction

Detective fiction in Spanish America before the 1950s was largely derivative; it consisted mostly of second-rate imitations of British and U.S. works. A national detective-fiction tradition stressing local themes and issues emerged, however, in the 1960s, particularly in Mexico, Cuba, and Argentina. While many Latin American detective tales are of the "closed-room" variety, inspired by writers such as G. K. Chesterton and Edgar Allan Poe, there is also a variety called "literatura negra" (black literature), hard-boiled fiction in the tradition of writers such as Dashiell Hammett and Raymond Chandler. The name is probably borrowed from *La série noire,* a paperback series of hard-boiled detective fiction published in France by Gallimard.

By the 1930s and 1940s Mexico had a solid detective short-story tradition associated with writers such as Antonio Helú, Pepe Martínez de la Vega, and María Elvira Bermúdez, but the detective novel never became an important genre there. As in Argentina, elite writers experimented with detective fiction but did not devote themselves to it exclusively. The best-known Mexican detective novels are **Rodolfo Usigli**'s *Ensayo de un crimen* (1944; Rehearsal of a Crime), Paco Ignacio Taibo's *Días de combate* (1976; Battle Days), **José Emilio Pacheco**'s *Morirás lejos* (1967; You Will Die Far Away), **Carlos Fuentes**'s *La cabeza de la hidra* (1978; translated as *The Hydra Head*), and **Vicente Leñero**'s *Asesinato: El doble crimen de los Flores Muñoz* (1985; The Double Crime of the Flores Muñozes). Until the Cuban Revolution detective fiction was virtually nonexistent in Cuba, but by the 1990s it had become extremely popular. As part of the Concurso Aniversario del Triunfo de la Revolución (Contest Celebrating the Triumph of the Revolution), a state-sponsored prize for the best detective story has been awarded since 1972, ensuring the continued existence of the genre in Cuba. Cuban detective novels reflect the ideology of the revolution. Typically the protagonist, rather than being an independent detective, is a police officer investigating crimes against the state and tracking down the perpetrator of these heinous deeds with the help of the common people. Two of the best examples of Cuban detective fiction are Juan Angel Cardi's *El American Way of Death* (1980) and Arnaldo Correa's *El terror* (1982), a collection of detective stories.

REFERENCE:

Amelia Simpson, *Detective Fiction from Latin America* (Rutherford, N.J.: Fairleigh Dickinson University Press, 1990).

–S.M.H.

DICTATORSHIP NOVEL

During the 1970s several important novels dealing with dictatorship were published in Latin America, novels that revived a thematic genre dating from the middle of the nineteenth century. It can be argued that Domingo Faustino Sarmiento's *Facundo* (1845) inaugurated the dictatorship genre in Latin American narrative. *Facundo* is a hybrid work that ostensibly centers on the life and death of the regional Argentinean caudillo Facundo Quiroga (1793–1835), but it is ultimately a liberal diatribe against the dictatorship of Juan Manuel de Rosas (in power 1829–1852), a magnified version of the book's eponymous protagonist. Sarmiento, who was exiled in Chile when he wrote *Facundo*, explains Rosas's power in terms of the ascendancy of the archaic interior over the progressive ideals of his own coreligionaries in the port city of Buenos Aires. Toward the end of the century Sarmiento's thesis concerning dictatorship was overturned by the Cuban intellectual **José Martí**, who argued that the enabling cause of de facto governments in Latin America was the liberal intelligentsia's failure to understand the cultural soil from which tyranny sprouted. Martí called for a new generation of political leaders that would be more responsive to local realities and less concerned with imposing extraneous models on the emerging Latin American nations.

The interpretation of dictatorship as a cultural and political phenomenon is one aspect of the modern novel of dictatorship. Another one has to do with the evolution of dictatorship over the course of Latin American history. Sarmiento's barbarian caudillo was replaced by the enlightened dictator and later by the military dictator who functions within a bureaucratic institutional framework.

The first modern dictatorship novel was Ramón del Valle-Inclán's *Tirano Banderas* (1926), written by a Spaniard but set in an unspecified Latin American location. (The novel was subtitled *Novela de tierra caliente* [Novel of the Tropics].) Valle-Inclán's dictator is a syncretic figure, departing from the tradition of such novels — which, since Sarmiento, had tended to focus on specific historical figures — and anticipating later works by Gabriel García Márquez and **Alejo Carpentier.**

The first notable Latin American novel of dictatorship was *El Señor Presidente* (1946; translated) by **Miguel Angel Asturias,** a novel that focuses on the historical figure Manuel Estrada Cabrera (in power 1898–1920). Cabrera was a corrupt Guatemalan dictator who assumed office after the president in power was assassinated. His rule coincided with the heyday of the United Fruit Company in Central America. The situation of the Maya Indians deteriorated rapidly in this period, and he was driven out by a revolution. Asturias, who had made Valle-Inclán's acquaintance in Mexico, describes Cabrera as a mythical and satanic character whose lust for power corrupts an entire society. Asturias, who began to write *El Señor Presidente* in Paris during the heyday of Surrealism, developed an incantatory and hallucinatory style indebted as much to the surrealists' experiments with free association as to his discovery of Mayan mythology and literature. The novel is in the mode of the grotesque. Farcical and melodramatic elements abound, and exaggeration and deformation characterize Asturias's presentation of events and people. Asturias, though, is unequivocal in his interpretation of dictatorship; he shows all the horrors that unbridled power brings upon an impotent population.

In the 1970s the dictatorship genre boomed, beginning in 1974 with the twin publication of *El recurso del método* (translated as *Reasons of State*) by Carpentier and Augusto Roa Bastos's *Yo el Supremo* (translated as *I, the Supreme*). The dictator portrayed by Carpentier is a generic and allegorical figure constructed from bits and pieces of several historical tyrants (chiefly Gerardo Machado of Cuba and Rafael Leonidas Trujillo of the Dominican Republic), and he is meant to be an ironic representation of the enlightened despot. He divides his time between Paris and his unnamed and turbulent native land, that is, between civilization and barbarism, between the refinements of culture and the cycles of revolutionary upheaval that he must put down if he is to hold on to power and finance his Parisian sojourns. Carpentier, however, dismantles the civilization/barbarism antithesis, showing how French history has been riddled with the same kind of violence as afflicts the less fortunate lands of the tropics.

Roa Bastos's version of the dictatorship novel is based on the man who dominated the first decades of Paraguayan independence, José Gaspar Rodríguez de Francia (in power 1814–1840). Dr. Francia, as he was known, declared himself dictator for life and shut Paraguay off from international commerce and diplomacy, in an effort to make the nation self-sufficient and to avoid the political strife that characterized Latin America in the first half of the nineteenth century. He antagonized and terrorized the Creole class and the church and kept a large army recruited from among his faithful Indian supporters. Yet Francia was no petty tyrant but rather an intellectual who was fully conversant with the French Enlightenment and deserving of a chapter in Thomas Carlyle's *On Heroes, Hero-Worship, and the Heroic in History* (1849). Roa Bastos's novel, however, is not historical in any conventional sense, for historical verisimilitude is not strictly adhered to, and the very notion of history is suspect. It is difficult, for example, to identify a main narrator. Dr. Francia plays his role as dictator literally by dictating the text to his secretary Patiño, who in turn transcribes it and alters it at will, a process meant to underscore the point that history is difficult to record and even more difficult to represent in terms of the truth. There are also several other "voices" in the novel (often belonging to recognizable historical characters) that put forth their own claims to truth. Finally, there is a compiler who filters the vast archival material pertaining to Dr. Francia and Paraguayan history, in what at times is a particularly idiosyncratic way. Much of the book is made up of free linkages among episodes and among history, myth, and literature, made possible by textual affinities of one kind or another. *Yo el Supremo* is one of the landmarks of modern Latin American literature.

A year later García Márquez brought out *El otoño del patriarca* (1975; translated as *The Autumn of the Patriarch*). The patriarch, like Carpentier's protagonist, is a composite of various historical figures and the embodiment of the barbarian chieftain. The language of García Márquez's novel, however, differs greatly from Carpentier's erudite style: one constantly hears the voice of the people, the orality of an illiterate culture that construes the dictator's power as mythical. This pervasive popular note and García Márquez's attempt to demystify the dictator are closely linked to the carnivalesque mode that characterizes the novel. Both Carpentier and García Márquez display an ambiguous attitude toward dictatorship. By the mid 1970s their protagonists are anachronistic, folkloric figures, and this distance from immediate political reality allows the characters to be portrayed at one and the same time as charismatic cultural symbols and abhorrent, depraved tyrants.

Miguel Angel Asturias with a French translation of his *El Señor Presidente* (1946)

Other dictatorship novels of the 1970s include *El gran solitario de palacio* (1971, 1976; The Great Recluse of Government House) by the Mexican René Avilés Fábila, *El secuestro del general* (1973; The General's Kidnapping) by the Ecuadoran Demetrio Aguilera Malta, and *Oficio de difuntos* (1976; Mass for the Dead) by the Venezuelan Arturo Uslar Pietri.

In addition to Cabrera (described above), the following Caribbean and Central American dictators have often been alluded to in fiction. (For further information on South American dictatorship novels see *Dictionary of Twentieth Century Culture: Hispanic Culture of South America.*)

One of the models for the dictator in Carpentier's *El recurso del método*, Gerardo Machado (in power 1925–1933), was head of the Cuban Liberal Party and began as constitutional president. Yet he progressively hardened his rule, suppressing civil liberties on several occasions and having the Constitution amended in order to extend his term of office. He imprisoned and deported many opponents and closed the national university. He was forced to resign and went into exile in the United States.

Anastasio Somoza Debayle (1967–1979) was the third and last member of the dynasty that ruled Nicaragua from 1933 until the triumph of the Sandinistas. Somoza was a graduate of West Point and head of the National Guard, through which he terrorized enemies. Self-seeking and corrupt, Somoza is said to have profiteered from the international aid that poured into the country after a devastating earthquake that leveled Managua in 1972. He controlled or had a stake in every profitable business in the country. His excesses promoted armed resistance. He was deposed by Sandinista guerrillas in 1979 and later assassinated in exile in Paraguay. He is the model for the dictator in *La insurrección* (1982; translated as *The Insurrection*) by Chilean Antonio Skármeta. (See **Nicaraguan Revolution**.)

Rafael Leonidas Trujillo (1930–1961) was a Dominican dictator who used the army to assume power in a coup, reformed the Constitution to perpetuate his regime, and was reelected several times, alternating with friends and relatives whom he allowed to be president for a period. He was a megalomaniac who renamed the capital city after himself and gave himself extravagant titles. He controlled every monopoly in the country, as well as the press, and employed repressive methods as a matter of course, once massacring seven thousand Haitians who had entered the country to cut sugarcane. He tried to assassinate the president of Venezuela in 1960 and was himself assassinated a year later. His figure is behind Alejo Carpentier's *El recurso del método*, Gabriel García Márquez's *El otoño del patriarca,* and Enrique Lafourcade's *La fiesta del rey Acab* (1959; King Acab's Party).

REFERENCE:

Carlos Pacheco, *Narrativa de la dictadura y crítica literaria* (Caracas: Fundación Centro de Estudios Latinoamericanos Rómulo Gallegos, 1987).

— R.G.M. & P.S.

Plácido Domingo

Born in Madrid in 1941, Plácido Domingo immigrated to Mexico with his family in 1950. His parents were singers in a touring **zarzuela** company, continuing a tradition that has enjoyed great popularity throughout Latin America since colonial times. Exposed throughout his childhood to this genre of lyrical, musical theater and endowed with an extraordinary musical talent, Plácido Domingo followed in his family's steps. Early studies in Mexico began with piano and continued at the conservatory in conducting and singing. His debut at sixteen in Fernández Caballero's zarzuela, *Gigantes y cabezudos* (Giants and Bigheads), was made as a baritone, but within a few years he began to sing tenor roles with the Mexican National Opera. For his debut in the United States he sang Arturo in *Lucia di Lammermoor* with the Dallas Civic Opera (1961). From 1962–1965 he sang hundreds of performances, many in Hebrew, with the Israeli National Opera. Domingo's performances with the New York City Opera began in 1965 with the role of Pinkerton in *Madame Butterfly,* and later he took the title role in the United States premiere of Alberto Ginastera's *Don Rodrigo* (1966). Major roles soon followed in Vienna (*Don Carlos*), Hamburg (*Tosca, Lohengrin*), and Berlin (*Un Ballo in Maschera*). Only eleven years after his zarzuela debut in Mexico City, he sang the role of Maurizio in Francesco Cilea's *Adriana Lecouvreur* at New York's Metropolitan Opera.

Plácido Domingo's many operatic performances throughout the world, on stage and on television, won unequaled praise, and he has come to be regarded as the leading dramatic-lyric tenor of the late twentieth century. In addition, he is one of the most electronically recorded artists the opera world has ever known. He has recorded not only the standard repertoire for operatic tenor but also works that are now rarely performed on stage. Plácido Domingo's operatic interests, however, have never deprived the wider public, those beyond the opera audience, of his outstanding talent. In numerous concerts and recordings, not to mention advertisements, he has "crossed over," as have many twentieth-century musicians, and has performed lighter and more popular music in a variety of languages. In addition to his recordings of many songs from the Hispanic repertoire, traditional and modern (for example, his recording of *Siempre en mi corazón* and the popular songs of the Cuban composer **Ernesto Lecuona**), he took part in a Spanish production in the 1990s, *Antología de la zarzuela*, broadcast on television throughout the Americas and combined with an extensive tour.

Plácido Domingo has also pursued his interest in conducting music, both orchestral and operatic, of which he has made several recordings. Quite apart from his vocal prowess, he is distinguished by an irrepressible and wide-ranging enthusiasm for music, boundless energy to perform, and an enviable musicality.

REFERENCES:

Plácido Domingo, *My First Forty Years* (New York & London: Knopf, 1983);

David Hamilton, "Plácido Domingo," in *Metropolitan Opera Encyclopedia* (New York: Simon & Schuster, 1987);

Daniel Snowman, "Plácido Domingo," in *International Dictionary of Opera*, volume 1, C, edited by Steven Larue (Detroit: St. James Press, 1993).

— R.L.S.

E

EDITORIAL CARTOONS

During the nineteenth century the publication of editorial cartoons became widespread throughout Spanish America, as independence and liberal-reform movements created a new awareness of the importance of justice and lawful government. Cartoons published during the years 1870–1910 often named the individuals and politicians they satirized. They sometimes depended on classical mythology for a type of humor and a context that were accessible mainly to an elite readership.

Buenos Aires and Mexico City dominated Latin American cartoon publishing until the late twentieth century, often attracting talent from other countries. There is a rich tradition of the single-panel cartoon in Mexico, dating from the beginning of the twentieth century, when cartoonists turned their focus to the vicissitudes of everyday life. The best-known Mexican cartoonist was **José Guadalupe Posada,** who in the early decades of the twentieth century reached a mass audience with etchings that used skeleton motifs to satirize elements of the establishment such as the church and the landowning elite. Posada influenced artists and cartoonists such as **José Clemente Orozco** and Miguel Covarrubias. The exaggerated conventions for portraying emotions that became common in the 1940s under the influence of Walt Disney can be seen in the magazine *Siempre* of Mexico City, which published Rius (Eduardo del Río) cartoons that typically mocked superpower politics. Mexico City magazines, especially the independents, are great masters at using cartoons to satirize the political establishment. After the heated, and sometimes disrespectful, televised Mexican presidential debate of May 1994, *Proceso* ran a half-page cartoon of Diego de Cevallos, the leader of the PAN Party, standing on a television set with his tongue sticking out.

Following the 1959 revolution in Cuba, cartoons there were used for political ends. For example, those in the state-supported magazine *Granma* satirize Uncle Sam, the CIA, and international capitalism.

REFERENCE:

Naomi Lindstrom, "The Single-Panel Cartoon," in *Handbook of Latin American Popular Culture,* edited by Harold E. Hinds Jr. and Charles M. Tatum (Westport, Conn.: Greenwood Press, 1985), pp. 207–227.

— S.M.H.

SANDRA ELETA

Sandra Eleta, one of the first female professional photographers in Panama, studied **photography** in Panama City as an apprentice of Carlos Monfour and in New York at Finch College, the New School for Social Research, and the International Center of Photography. Eleta reacted against the picturesque regionalism that was dominant in Panamanian photography and opted for a more subjective approach, focusing on black-and-white photographs of people. Although her work reveals a strong concern for formal issues, Eleta tries to show her subjects as directly as possible, without interpretative intentions. She considers the camera an extension of herself and the final result to come from a collaboration between herself and those she portrays. Eleta has worked as a photojournalist for several magazines, including *Camera* and *Zoom,* on projects such as her photographs of the Nicaraguan poet and priest **Ernesto Cardenal.** Nevertheless, she prefers to connect with her subjects on a more familiar, everyday level.

According to Eleta, her most important photographic series is about the people of Portobelo. This fishing port on the eastern coast of Panama was the site of a free republic founded in the eighteenth century by runaway slaves. Many of their descendants still reside there and have kept alive some of the West African

The first Estridentista manifesto (1921)

traditions of their ancestors, traditions that inspire their carnivals and other ritual celebrations. Eleta settled in Portobelo in 1973 and eventually became a member of the community. She worked for the women's textile cooperative while also producing well-known photographs such as *Putulungo, El hombre pulpo* (1973; Putulungo, The Octopus Man) and *Catalina, Reina de los Congos* (1980; Catalina, Queen of the Congos).

REFERENCE:

Sandra Eleta, "Portobelo, Panama," in *Desires and Disguises: Five Latin American Photographers,* translated and edited by Amanda Hopkinson (London & New York: Serpent's Tail, 1992), pp. 17–28.

— F.B.N.

ESTRIDENTISMO

Estridentismo is related to other Latin American vanguardist groups, such as Klaxon (São Paulo), Argentin-

ean Ultraismo and Martínfierrismo (Buenos Aires), the Generation of 1927 (Havana), and **Muralism** (Mexico City). These groups were primarily formed by Latin American artists and writers who had actively participated in European avant-garde movements and returned home in the 1920s. Back in their native or adopted countries, artists such as **Diego Rivera** and **Jean Charlot** (Mexico) helped organize movements that introduced the radical strategies of modern art to replace the dominant but exhausted aesthetics of academic art and **Impressionism.** These first modern movements developed artistic languages that became independent from European art because they were expressions of specific national cultures.

Estridentismo has often been overshadowed by Muralism, the best-known Mexican artistic movement during the 1920s. Estridentismo began in Mexico City in 1921 under the leadership of Mexican poet Manuel Maples Arce. It included the writers Arqueles Vega, Germán List Arzubide, and Salvador Gallardo, as well as the artists Ramón Alva de la Canal, Jean Charlot, Fermín Revueltas, Leopoldo Méndez, and Germán Cueto. They worked together to produce an art that was revolutionary both in form and content, a feat achieved in the twentieth century by only a few movements such as Dada, German Expressionism, **Surrealism,** and early Mexican Muralism. The Estridentista project, presented in a series of scandalous posterlike manifestos, was utopian, aimed at improving society through science and technology. While Muralism emphasized national themes, the Estridentistas sought to create an urban international art related to the European and Latin American avant-gardes.

Estridentista artists collaborated with writers on many projects, which included avant-garde illustrations and designs for magazines, such as *Irradiador* and *Horizonte,* and books, such as Maples Arce's *Urbe: Poema bolchevique en 5 cantos* (1924; translated as *Metropolis*), illustrated by Charlot. They also organized avant-garde activities, including art exhibitions and poetry readings held in their favorite meeting place in Mexico City, the Café de Nadie, a cosmopolitan venue that became an important Estridentista theme. In 1925 the group moved their activities to Jalapa, where they received official support until 1927, when the group disbanded.

REFERENCES:

Modernidad y modernización en el arte mexicano: 1920–1960 (Mexico City: Instituto Nacional de Bellas Artes, Museo Nacional de Arte, 1991);

Luis Mario Schneider, *El estridentismo: Mexico 1921–1927* (Mexico City: Universidad Autónoma de México, Instituto de Investigaciones Estéticas, 1985).

— F.B.N.

F

CARLOS LUIS FALLAS

The writer Carlos Luis Fallas (1912–1966) was born in San José, Costa Rica. His parents were quite poor, and Fallas was unable to study beyond primary school because of economic pressures. At a young age he became a worker on the banana plantations of the United Fruit Company; his six years working under conditions of extreme hardship on the Atlantic coast made him aware of the unjust conditions of most laborers, and he became a union leader and political activist.

His most important novel was his first, *Mamita Yunai* (1941; the title is a reference to the area dominated by the United Fruit Company), in which he describes and condemns the exploitation of workers by the United Fruit Company. Fallas's style is plain and direct; his experiences and those of others are described in a realistic manner, incorporating the language of the "conchos" (Indians and blacks). In his other works he adopts the same anti-imperialist stance, condemning the oppressed conditions of the underprivileged in his country. They are the novels *Gentes y gentecillas* (1947; Big Shots and Small Guys) and *Marcos Ramírez* (1952). He has also published short stories in *Tres cuentos* (1967; Three Stories).

REFERENCE:
Marielos Aguilar, *Carlos Luis Fallas: Su época y sus luchas* (San José, Costa Rica: Editorial Porvenir, 1983).
— M.E.S.

MARCELA FERNÁNDEZ VIOLANTE

Born in the 1940s, Marcela Fernández Violante is the only female movie director working within the notoriously closed ranks of the official Mexican film industry. Fernández Violante entered the Universidad Nacional Autónoma de México (UNAM; National Autonomous University of Mexico) in Mexico City in 1964, the same year in which the Centro Universitario de Educación Cinematográfica (CUEC; University Center for Film Education) was opened. She began studying the humanities but was soon taking film courses as well. Her first screenplay was for a small-scale experimental movie called *Azul* (Blue), which was awarded a Diosa de Plata (Silver Goddess) critics' award in 1967. She subsequently directed the first feature-length CUEC film, *Gayoso da descuentos* (Gayoso Gives Discounts; Gayoso is a major chain of funeral homes in Mexico City). Shooting started in 1968 but was interrupted by the **Tlatelolco** massacre of student demonstrators in Mexico City just before the Olympic Games were about to start.

Fernández Violante's first completed movie is *Frida Kahlo* (1971), based on the life and work of Mexico's best-known female artist. This documentary was a great success and was shown at the Museum of Modern Art in New York as well as in Moscow and London. It received another Diosa de Plata award and an Ariel, the Mexican equivalent of an Oscar. Fernández Violante's *De todos modos Juan te llamas* (1975; Whatever You Do, It's No Good) focuses on the phase of the **Mexican Revolution** known as the **Cristero War** (1926–1927), a counterrevolution led by the clergy and supported by the rural landowners. The rebellion is viewed through the eyes of a young girl. The film critically examines two of the most powerful institutions in Mexico, the military and the clergy, and attempts to demystify the revolution. The movie cost about $50,000 and was nominated for almost all categories of the Ariel awards, winning two for best acting, as well as Diosa de Plata awards for acting and directing. Fernández Violante next directed *Cananea* (1977), which is set in the period before the Mexican Revolu-

Marcela Fernández Violante and cameraman Danny López on the set of *Misterio* (1980; Mystery)

tion. In this motion picture, about a North American mine owner in northern Mexico who violently suppresses a strike by calling in the Texas Rangers from across the border, Violante strove to demonstrate the conflict between two different ideologies: Protestantism, which teaches that the rich get richer through God's help, and Catholicism, which teaches that the rich do not go to heaven. Her next project was *Misterio* (1980; Mystery), based on an old script by the Mexican writer **Vicente Leñero;** it is a critique of **Televisa,** the privately owned Mexican television production monopoly. Though it did badly at the box office in Mexico (it was withdrawn after one week), the movie swept the Ariel awards, winning eight out of twelve that year, and it was shown at the **Biarritz Festival.** *En el país de los pies ligeros* (1981; In the Land of Light Feet) centers on two young boys — one from Mexico City and the other a Tarahumara Indian — and reverses the customary situation by showing the city boy trying to adapt to life among the Indians. Fernández Violante was appointed director of CUEC in 1985.

REFERENCE:

Julianne Burton, *Cinema and Social Change in Latin America: Conversations with Filmmakers* (Austin: University of Texas Press, 1986).

— S.M.H.

ROSARIO FERRÉ

One of Puerto Rico's most recognized writers in the last third of the twentieth century, Rosario Ferré (1942–) gained fame as a short-story writer, essayist, novelist, and poet whose principal themes concentrate on the demythification of woman's role and status in most societies along with the subservient condition of Puerto Rican people in a neocolonial society dominated by the United States. Her sharply satirical wit is prevalent throughout her writings, including her first book of short stories, *Papeles de Pandora* (1976; Pandora's Papers/Roles), in which she ridicules a patriarchal society that relegates women to fulfilling only the roles dictated by it: those of virgin, bride, wife, and mother. In many of her pieces she also connects gender oppression with racial, ethnic, and class oppression. One of her best-known short stories, "Cuando las mujeres quieren a los hombres" ("When Women Love Men"), shows how domination by a white, male society relegates all women to a dependent, subordinate position, especially when dealing with sexuality; white or black, rich or poor, aware or not, most women are obliged to grant sexual favors as a means of survival.

Influenced by the Puerto Rican poet **Julia de Burgos,** Ferré's controversial themes are frequently developed through explicit erotic and sexual language, which has called attention to her writings while leaving

Rosario Ferré, 1976

an imprint on other writers of her generation. The erotic dimensions of women's sexuality are repeated in various ways in many of her stories. They tend to demythify the virginal stereotype while underscoring the importance of women's writing as a means of making others aware of the hidden manipulations intended to keep women in their subordinate position. In her well-received book of essays, *Sitio a Eros: Siete ensayos literarios* (1986; Besieging Eros: Seven Literary Essays), Ferré insists on woman's responsibility to discover her authentic self, a self that is different from the subservient identity imposed on her from birth. For Ferré the ideal means of self-discovery is through writing. Criticism of machismo in Puerto Rico, and of what she sees as being one of the faces of machismo, the imperialist U.S. domination of the island, is also found in her novella *Maldito amor* (1986; translated as *Sweet Diamond Dust*), which includes several other narratives in addition. One of her most celebrated essays, "La cocina de la escritura" (1984; translated as "The Writing Kitchen"), describes her own process as a woman writer searching for an authentic voice. Ferré's entertaining but highly sarcastic sense of humor is especially apparent in her 1992 book of essays on women's writing, *El coloquio de las perras* (Bitches' Dialogue), whose title is a parody of the title of a well-known novella by Miguel de Cervantes, *El coloquio de los perros* (1613; translated as *Dialogue of the Dogs*). In it she uncovers various sexual stereotypes, especially those involving the obstacles a woman writer must confront in a male-dominated society that has profound influences on her family, her lovers, the pub-

lishing world, the critics, society at large, and herself. This work, among others, has earned Ferré a reputation as a sharp and lucid critic of a system she regards as oppressive and hierarchical, one that privileges the abusers while dismissing the marginalized. For many critics she raises awareness of issues that have been ignored in Puerto Rico and elsewhere. Her other works include several collections of short stories for children, *El medio pollito* (1976; Half a Little Chicken), *La mona que le pisaron la cola* (1980; The Monkey Whose Tail Was Stepped On), and *Los cuentos de Juan Bobo* (1981; Tales of Juan Bobo), as well as a short novel, *La caja de cristal* (1978; translated as *The Glass Box*); a book of poems, *Fábulas de la garza desangrada* (1982; Fables of the Bled Heron); and a book of essays on the Uruguayan writer Felisberto Hernández titled *El acomodador: Una lectura fantástica de Felisberto Hernández* (1986; The Usher: A Fantastic Reading of Felisberto Hernández).

REFERENCES:

Margarite Fernández-Olmos, "From a Woman's Perspective: The Short Stories of Rosario Ferré and Ana Lydia Vega," in *Contemporary Women Authors of Latin America*, edited by Doris Meyer and Fernández-Olmos (New York: Brooklyn College Press, 1983), pp. 78–90;

Fernández-Olmos, "Survival, Growth and Change in the Prose Fiction of Contemporary Puerto Rican Women Writers," in *Images and Identities: The Puerto Rican in Two World Contexts*, edited by Asela Rodríguez de Laguna (New Brunswick, N.J.: Transaction Press, 1987), pp. 76–88.

           — M.E.S.

RAFAEL FERRER

Rafael Ferrer (1933–) is one of the most controversial Puerto Rican artists because of his involvement with avant-garde movements such as **Conceptual Art, Installation Art, and Performance Art.** In the late 1940s Rafael Ferrer, brother of the movie star José Ferrer, went to military school in the United States, where he learned to play the drums. He also studied art in the United States and at the Universidad de Puerto Rico, with the Spanish surrealist painter Eugenio F. Granell. Granell encouraged his interest in **Surrealism**'s emphasis on fantasy and in Dada's anti-art statements. In the 1950s Ferrer moved to New York and played the drums in a Latin American band. Meanwhile, he continued to paint. At the end of the decade he returned to the island, where his exhibit at the Universidad de Puerto Rico in 1960 caused a scandal because his works transgressed the rules of careful execution and elegant treatment of the surface that were traditional in Puerto Rican art. By contrast, his art was aggressive, spontaneous, and sexually explicit.

Tableau (1964), installation by Rafael Ferrer (Museo de Arte y Antropología, Universidad de Puerto Rico, San Juan)

Ferrer's early figurative paintings soon gave way to informal abstract works and then to collages, which became increasingly avant-garde and three-dimensional. He began to produce sculptures such as *La herencia* (1950s; The Inheritance) and *Buenas costumbres (y de buena familia)* (1950s; Good Manners [and from a Good Family]), which were provocative. They not only included discarded metal objects welded together but also made references to the racially mixed character of Puerto Rican society, a subject that was considered taboo at the time. These works were included in Ferrer's second show at the Universidad de Puerto Rico, a show that once more resulted in a negative public reaction. The exhibition also featured neo-Dadaist sculptures (made with old shoes, car parts, and discarded objects) and included his well-known installation *Tableau* (1964), which consisted of hybrid assemblages of cast-off materials staged within rough wood walls.

Ferrer returned to the United States in 1967, weary of the general hostility toward his art in Puerto Rico. He soon became one of the most provocative artists in New York, and his work was recognized in international art centers. During this period Ferrer worked on avant-garde performances and installations that contested the role of museums as arbiters of art. In his three *Leaf Pieces* (1968) Ferrer had dry leaves delivered to three art galleries in order to condemn the banality of the abstract art they exhibited. The *Hay and Grease* and *Ice* installations (1969) at the Whitney Museum of American Art used ephemeral and unorthodox materials that challenged the view of art as permanent and static. During the 1970s Ferrer became concerned with the notion of geography and imaginary travel. For instance, in his installation *Tierra del Fuego* (1972) at the Chicago Museum of Contemporary Art, Ferrer included names of places in neon lights, paper masks, and overpainted maps, as well as worn-out kayaks suspended from the ceiling.

REFERENCE:

Rafael Ferrer, *Deseo: An Adventure, Rafael Ferrer* (Cincinnati: Contemporary Arts Center, 1973).

— F.B.N.

FICTION

As the new republics of the nineteenth century began to forge their separate identities, their writers tended to remain formally imitative of the styles of the old continent, while in their themes they increasingly sought to be different by highlighting local color. It was well into the twentieth century before the novel achieved universal importance, but important developments in **poetry** were taking place as the century began.

The modern Spanish American novel was the result of a process that bore its earliest fruits in the 1940s and culminated two decades later with the **Boom.** Prior to that time the novel was marked by regionalism and **Indigenism,** grounded in the documentation of the distinctive social and natural traits that made up the author's national territory. From these tendencies the modern novel effected a self-conscious break. Against the regionalist paradigm the modern novel showed a propensity for the universal and the cosmopolitan. Against the social and utilitarian imperatives of the Indigenist novel, modern fiction claimed a fundamentally aesthetic raison d'être. Thus, the modern novel may be said to have more significant affinities with the short story genre (particularly in the form that short fiction took in the Río de la Plata area in the early decades of the century) and with avant-garde poetry than with the regionalist and Indigenist fiction that preceded it.

The beginnings of the modern novel coincided with the rise of anthropology as a discipline and with the predominance of Surrealism in the field of artistic ideas; the Surrealists themselves were deeply interested in the objects, discourses, and cultural practices studied by ethnographers. One of the early modern novelists was the Guatemalan **Miguel Angel Asturias,** the Nobel Prize laureate who was inspired by his anthropological studies at the Sorbonne to translate the sacred book of the Mayas, the *Popol Vuh,* into Spanish. His own work (his best-known novel is *El señor presidente*) blends an interest in the indigenous culture of Guatemala with Surrealist images and language. Another of the early modern novelists was the Cuban **Alejo Carpentier,** whose ethnographic interests and firsthand contact with the Surrealists in Paris ultimately led him to formulate the theory of **magical realism,** or what he called "lo real maravilloso" (the marvelous real). The gist of Carpentier's theory was that the distinctiveness of Latin American and Caribbean identity was to be found in the survival of archaic beliefs and cultural forms (derived from indigenous and African cultures) that incarnate the Surrealist vision in terms more authentic and significant than those put forth in Surrealist experiments, for which Carpentier expressed nothing but disdain. Carpentier's influential third novel, *Los pasos perdidos* (1953; translated as *The Lost Steps*), may be read as an exploration of the

Dust jacket for Alejo Carpentier's influential 1953 novel

contradictions inherent in the concept of magical realism, despite which the term has since gained considerable currency.

In South America the influence of anthropology arrived in a more indirect fashion (through Sir James George Frazer's *The Golden Bough*) but made a deep imprint upon Jorge Luis Borges's theory of narrative, formulated in the essay "Narrative Art and Magic" (1932) and rehearsed in stories that had a profound effect on the subsequent development of Latin American fiction as a whole. Borges held that stories were autonomous structures ruled by magic causality and analogy. His emphasis on the formal autonomy of narrative texts, and the brilliant experimentation that went along with it, incarnated one of the key demands of literary modernity. Another was the claim to universality. Borges was the most influential of a group of short story writers who foreshadowed the advent of the modern Latin American novel. Detective, fantastic, and science-fiction stories broadened the scope of literary representation and showed that Latin American writers belonged in a cosmopolitan setting. In the 1950s and 1960s the Latin American short story continued its impressive evolution side by side with the development of the modern novel. In fact, many major novelists also made significant contributions to the short-story genre: examples from the areas covered in the present volume are **Juan Rulfo,** Carpentier, and **Carlos Fuentes,** not to mention their peers in Hispanic countries to the south. Other writers have made the short story their preferred genre; it is a genre that has never been a mere by-product of more elaborate novelistic projects.

Many Spanish American writers who had been active in the 1950s and earlier but who had worked in isolation from one another later discovered that they had all been influenced by reading the same "high-modernist" authors of European and U.S. fiction: James Joyce, Franz Kafka, Marcel Proust, Virginia Woolf, Ernest Hemingway, Malcolm Lowry, F. Scott Fitzgerald, John Dos Passos, and especially William Faulkner. Two of the most notable works of the 1950s were Rulfo's *Pedro Páramo* (1955) and Juan Carlos Onetti's *La vida breve* (1950), groundbreaking and influential novels that "translated" the literary idiom of high modernism into the cultural vernacular of Mexico and Uruguay respectively. It is impossible to overstate the importance of international modernism in the evolution of modern Latin American fiction, but even older authors such as Honoré de Balzac, Gustave Flaubert, and Henry James played a major role in the formulation of a modern Latin American narrative style. Varied as the different regions and national traditions are, they are now more similar to each other and to their foreign models than to anything that might be described as a previous Latin American narrative tradition.

The 1950s also marked the decade of existentialism in Latin America, and many novelists, particularly in the Southern Cone, paid homage to the themes of alienation and moral degradation in their work. Because of the crucial role played by outside influences in the development of Latin American fiction, many writers have been vulnerable to the charge of "extraterritoriality" (if not vulgar imitation) made by Marxist and nationalist intellectuals. As their influence wanes, however, a debate that once seemed heated either simmers today or has fully evaporated. The very fact that Spanish American fiction has found widespread acceptance in the continent itself is sufficient proof that even the most "exotic" authors (such as Borges and Fuentes) are culturally rooted in the realities of Spanish America, however varied and foreign their sources are.

In the 1970s and 1980s it became customary to speak of postmodern or **postboom** fiction, terms that tend to be used in a chronological rather than in a properly categorical sense. Late-twentieth-century fiction in Spanish America is less hermetic, less aesthetically ambitious, and more socially and politically rooted than the fiction of the 1960s. Women writers are more visible than before, and **testimonial narratives** have been in vogue for two decades. Testimonials have made a strong showing in Mexico, Central America, and the Caribbean and were given official recognition as a genre by the government of **Fidel Castro.** In Mexico two political turning points in particular, the **Mexican Revolution** and the **Tlatelolco** massacre, have acted as stimuli to writers, while similar claims can be made for certain political events and socio-economic conditions in the countries of the isthmus. The grand aesthetic syntheses of the 1960s have long been replaced by minimalism and by writing steeped in the various genres of mass or popular culture. Carlos Fuentes once defined the modern novel in Latin America as the "critical synthesis of society." Postboom novels remain to a large extent critical but have given up the synthetic structuring principle.

REFERENCES:

David William Foster, *Handbook of Latin American Literature,* second edition (New York & London: Garland, 1992);

Gerald Martin, *Journeys Through the Labyrinth: Latin American Fiction in the Twentieth Century* (London: Verso, 1989);

Donald L. Shaw, *Nueva narrativa hispanoamericana* (Madrid: Cátedra, 1980);

Doris Sommer, *Foundational Fictions: The National Romances of Latin America* (Berkeley: University of California Press, 1991);

Philip Swanson, *Landmarks in Modern Latin American Fiction* (London & New York: Routledge, 1990).

—R.G.M. & P.S.

BERNAL FLORES

Bernal Flores (1937–) received his early musical training in his native Costa Rica. Following his graduation from high school he entered the Eastman School of Music, where he completed a B.M. (1961), an M.M. (1962), and a Ph.D. (1964). His studies in the United States were partially supported by a scholarship from the **Organization of American States.** Upon his return to Costa Rica in 1964 he was appointed to the staff of the National Conservatory of Music (now the School of Music of the University of Costa Rica) and the Castella Conservatory. He returned to the Eastman School of Music for the period 1966–1969 to teach theory and counterpoint.

For his doctoral dissertation Flores composed the opera *La tierra de los deseos del corazón* (1964; The Land of Heart's Desire) to a text by William Butler Yeats; the work is atonal and uses six different musical intervals to identify the six personages of the opera. He has composed two symphonies and several tone poems, including *El espejo* (1962; The Mirror) and *Soledad de ausencia* (1964; Loneliness of Absence). Symphony No. 1 for string orchestra (1965) was premiered at the Third Inter American Festival in Washington. His first concerto, *William concierto* (1963), for piano, percussion, and orchestra, had its premiere in Rochester, New York; the second, Concierto pentatónico para clarinete y orquesta (1968; Pentatonic Concerto for Clarinet and Orchestra), was first performed by the Costa Rica Symphony Orchestra and won the Costa Rica National Prize for Music. Flores has also composed songs with orchestral accompaniment and songs for voice and piano.

REFERENCES:

"Bernal Flores," in *Composers of the Americas: Biographical Data and Catalogs of Their Works*, volume 15 (Washington, D.C.: Pan American Union, General Secretariat, Organization of American States, 1969);

Ronald R. Sider, "Central America and its Composers," in *Inter American Music Bulletin*, no. 77 (1970).

— R.L.S.

Pedro Flores

Pedro Flores (1894–1979), one of Puerto Rico's most admired composers of popular songs, began his musical career in his midthirties, armed with only mediocre talent as a guitarist and no musical training. His father died when Pedro was nine years old, leaving his mother and eleven children destitute. Pedro Flores played baseball to pay for his university tuition fees and upon graduation became a rural teacher of English, a job that lasted for five years. An unstable period followed his teaching career, including employment as a supervisor in a sugar mill, a job with a railroad company, a position with the U.S. Postal Service, and a tour of duty in the U.S. Army during World War I. In his early thirties he went to New York in search of better opportunities. He was not immediately successful: his first job there was digging the Eighth Avenue subway tunnel; the next was painting buildings.

In New York he became friends with **Rafael Hernández,** Luis Muñoz Marín (later to become the first native governor of Puerto Rico), **Luis Palés Matos** (later to become a celebrated author of Afro-Antillean poetry), and others of the destitute Hispanic community of artists and literati. Encouraged by the

musical successes of Hernández's *Trio Borinquen* in New York (*Borinquen* was the Taino Indian name for Puerto Rico), Flores began to compose and formed a similar ensemble, the *Trío Galón* (The Insignia Trio). His lack of musical training was compensated for by an inherent ability to conceive songs that attracted the admiration of talented performers and an adoring public. In 1930 he began an active period of commercial recordings with ensembles of various names: the Flores Quartet, the Flores Sextet, and Pedro Flores and His Orchestra. He recorded for the Brunswick company, RCA Victor, Decca, and Columbia. This productive period lasted until many of the numerous musicians associated with him were drafted for service in World War II.

After the war Flores tried to reorganize a performing group, but the attempt failed. Living for periods in Mexico and Cuba, he continued to compose **sones, danzas,** and **boleros** that were performed and recorded by international artists. Among his most popular songs are *Amor perdido* (Lost Love), *Contigo* (With You), *Despedida* (Farewell), *Irresistible,* and *Perdón* (Pardon).

REFERENCES:

Hernán Restrepo Duque, *Lo que cuentan los boleros* (Bogotá: Centro Editorial de Estudios Musicales, 1992);

Jaime Rico Salazar, *Cien años de boleros* (Bogotá: Academia de Guitarra Latinoamericana, 1987);

Alfredo Romero Bravo and Modesto Neco Quiñones, *Notas biográficas, citas y pensamientos de puertorriqueños distinguidos* (Gurabo, Puerto Rico: Editorial Jaquemate, 1992).

— R.L.S.

Folletines

Folletines are serial novels, which enjoy immense popularity in Latin America. When they first appeared as a popular art form, they met with the disapproval of the literary establishment; yet they flourished in large urban areas such as Lima and Mexico City. The popularity of folletines may be gauged by the fact that they have had far larger print runs than editions of more lofty literary works. Tens of thousands of copies of popular literature in the folletín format are often sold. Particularly popular are cliff-hangers and melodrama. The folletines also include specialized women's serials, some of which have reached a circulation of two hundred thousand copies. They are available not only in bookshops but also may be bought from kiosks or traveling salesmen. Folletines, which often deal with criollista themes (see **criollismo**), have provided an important stage in the acquisition of literacy. The time structure of the serial, continually interrupted by the

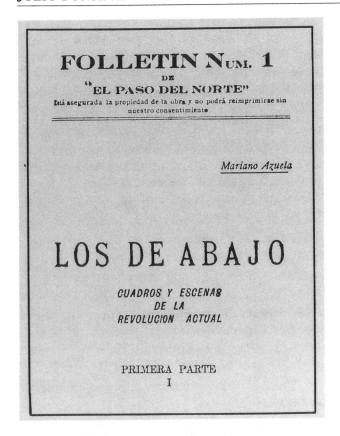

FOLLETIN Num. 1
DE
"EL PASO DEL NORTE"
Está asegurada la propiedad de la obra y no podrá reimprimirse sin
nuestro consentimiento

Mariano Azuela

LOS DE ABAJO

CUADROS Y ESCENAS
DE LA
REVOLUCION ACTUAL

PRIMERA PARTE
I

Cover for the first installment of Mariano Azuela's *Los de abajo* (translated as *The Underdogs*), 27 October 1915.

wait for the next installment, makes for a fragmented manner of reading, interrupted by everyday life and thus porous to its experiences.

REFERENCE:

William Rowe and Vivian Schelling, *Memory and Modernity: Popular Culture in Latin America* (London: Verso, 1991).
— S.M.H. & P.S.

JULIO FONSECA

The son of a military bandmaster, Julio Fonseca (1885–1950) began his musical studies at the National School of Music in his native San'José, Costa Rica. In 1902 he received a government scholarship for further studies in Italy, first at the Milan Lyceum of the Arts and subsequently at the Royal Conservatory in the same city. Discontented with the instruction he received in Italy, he transferred to the Brussels Conservatory. He returned to Costa Rica in 1906 and taught piano there for six years before leaving for the United States to promote his works and to find a publisher. Failing to achieve either, he returned to Costa Rica. In San José he taught music at the Colegio Superior de Señoritas

and became director of the Santa Cecilia School of Music. In 1942 he was named professor of theory and harmony at the National Conservatory of Music.

Fonseca's early works for piano were followed by a tone poem, *El cenáculo y el Gólgota* (1904; The Hall of the Last Supper and Golgotha), for piano and string orchestra, which was performed by the Brussels Conservatory Orchestra. His other works include several chamber compositions for strings and piano, nationalistic works for orchestra, sacred choral pieces including several masses, character pieces for piano, art songs, and popular pieces. In the nationalistic orchestral works such as *Gran fantasía sinfónica* (1937; Great Symphonic Fantasy) he combines tunes from the vernacular repertoire with fragments from the Costa Rican national anthem. Additional orchestral titles include *¡O, Costa Rica!* (1928; Oh, Costa Rica!), *Selección de música criolla* (1932; Creole Music Selection), and *Suite tropical sobre temas costarricenses* (1934; Tropical Suite on Costa Rican Themes).

REFERENCE:

"Julio Fonseca," in *Composers of the Americas: Biographical Data and Catalogs of Their Works*, volume 2 (Washington, D.C.: Pan American Union, General Secretariat, Organization of American States, 1956).
— R.L.S.

FOTONOVELAS

A popular printed format for romantic fiction, which is widely distributed in Latin America, the fotonovela (photonovel) tells a story in pictures with captions, like **comic books.** Photonovels came to Latin America from Spain (or Italy, in the case of the Southern Cone). During the improved economic conditions of the 1950s and early 1960s, fotonovelas prospered in places such as Argentina and Mexico. As television became more popular, dual productions of fotonovelas and **telenovelas** emerged; in the late 1960s and early 1970s in Peru, for example, the most popular television soap opera on the whole continent, *Simplemente María* (Simply Mary), gave rise to a companion photonovel.

Among the different types of photonovels is the *fotonovela rosa* (pink photonovel), which shares some characteristics with the **novela rosa.** For example, stereotypical poor, virtuous women must compete with rich, conniving women for the love of aristocratic men. The men must choose between their lowest instincts, symbolized by the evil woman, and their higher consciousness of duty and moral obligation, symbolized by marriage to the poor but virtuous heroine. The titles are indicative of their subject matter: for example,

Novelas de amor (Novels of Love) and *Secretos de corazón* (Secrets of the Heart).

In the 1960s and 1970s a new version of the photonovel, the *fotonovela suave* (soft photonovel), appeared. Typically the plot — based on the same tensions as in the pink photonovel (the relative importance of money and romance) — adopted a more middle-class position with the assumption that these two seemingly opposite goals are not necessarily mutually exclusive.

A third version of the photonovel is the *fotonovela roja* (red photonovel), which finds its subject matter in baser stories, as the following titles suggest: *Casos de la vida* (Real Life Stories) and *Pecado mortal* (Mortal Sin). Characters in red photonovels are physically darker (as opposed to white middle- and upper-class characters), generally out of work, and flashy in their tastes and attire; action is set in the poorer parts of town.

The covers of the *fotonovela rosa* and the *fotonovela suave* appeal to women's tenderness and desire for romance, whereas the covers of red photonovels, with their full-body shots of scantily clad women, emphasize female sexuality, portrayed as that irresistible temptation leading men to ruin. The *roja* genre is an amalgam of moral preaching and explicit photographs that approach soft-core pornography, with plots that revolve around violence, family disintegration, and sex, generally rape and incest. Among the poor of Lima, Bogotá, and Mexico City the red photonovels far outsell the other two types.

Finally, a fourth type of photonovel is the *fotonovela picaresca* (picaresque photonovel), which focuses specifically on sex. The picaresque version employs explicitly sexual photographs, using lower-class models and settings, and totally separates sex from love. The plots revolve around young, virile men whose sexual prowess women find irresistible. The women — almost always full-figured, bleached blonds wearing revealing clothes and married to impotent older men — compete with each other for the opportunity to make love to the hero. Again the titles are revealing: *Sexy risas* (Sexy Laughs) and *Fiebre de pasiones* (Fever of Passions).

Mexican publishers control much of the market in both Central America and the Caribbean and distribute issues via a tier system, first to major cities.

REFERENCE:

Cornelia Butler Flora, "Photonovels," in *Handbook of Latin American Popular Culture*, edited by Harold E. Hinds Jr. and Charles M. Tatum (Westport, Conn.: Greenwood Press, 1985), pp. 151–171.

— S.M.H. & P.S.

RAMÓN FRADE

Ramón Frade (1875–1954) is one of the most important Puerto Rican painters. Like most of his contemporaries, Frade was forced to go abroad in order to study art. He received formal training in the Dominican Republic and also traveled throughout Central and South America. Frade's realist figuration can be thought of as a link to the art of the nineteenth-century Puerto Rican painter Francisco Oller. Both Oller and Frade were important influences on other artists, such as **Miguel Pou** and **Lorenzo Homar,** two men whose objective was to affirm and safeguard the heritage of the island and prevent its replacement by that of the United States, which had direct control of Puerto Rico from the end of Spanish colonial rule until the 1950s.

In paintings such as *El pan nuestro* (circa 1905; Our Daily Bread), his best-known composition, Frade both affirms part of Puerto Rican culture and expresses a social critique: he depicts a *jíbaro,* a poor white peasant many considered a nostalgic symbol for Puerto Rico and its resistance to North American culture. The peasant stands, a dignified and monumental figure, wearing his typical working clothes, in front of a Puerto Rican landscape; in his hands he holds his meager daily food, a bunch of plantains.

In 1907 Frade went to Europe and studied in Madrid and Paris, but after his return to the island he became isolated and painted only a few works giving nostalgic views of peasant life.

REFERENCE:

Marimar Benítez, "The Special Case of Puerto Rico," in *The Latin American Spirit: Art and Artists in the United States, 1920–70* (New York: Bronx Museum of the Arts/Abrams, 1988), pp. 72–105.

— F.B.N.

FRIDA, NATURALEZA VIVA

A formally innovative motion picture directed by Paul Leduc, *Frida, Naturaleza viva* (1984) is about the Mexican painter **Frida Kahlo,** wife of the artist **Diego Rivera.** The movie was much more successful than Leduc's earlier *Reed: México insurgente* (1971; Reed: Insurgent Mexico), about American journalist John Reed, who wrote about his experiences covering the **Mexican Revolution** in *Insurgent Mexico* (1914). *Frida, Naturaleza viva* was produced independently by Manuel Barbachano Ponce and shot by Angel Godad. The title alludes to the Spanish phrase *naturaleza muerta,* meaning "still life" in painting; *viva* means "alive." Set in Kahlo's house in Coyoacán, on the outskirts of Mexico City (a house that is now a museum

Ofelia Medina as Frida Kahlo in *Frida, Naturaleza viva* (1983; Frida, Un–Still Life)

open to the public), the movie is characterized by a highly decorative mise-en-scène, a camera that glides through elaborate sets, a preference for sparse dialogue, and a skillful use of period music. Structured around the recurring image of Kahlo lying on her deathbed, the movie is divided into eight segments, each focusing on memories evolving from a thematic axis. This film effectively illustrates Leduc's view that cinematic culture must derive from "collective action and solidarity" and that filmmakers must strive to be "exemplars of national dignity."

REFERENCE:

John King, Ana M. López, and Manuel Alvarado, eds., *Mediating Two Worlds: Cinematic Encounters in the Americas* (London: BFI, 1993).

— S.M.H.

CARLOS FUENTES

The single most important novelist of the century in Mexico and one of the four major figures of the Latin American **Boom** in fiction, Carlos Fuentes was born in 1928 into a Mexican diplomat's family. He began his primary-school education in Washington, D.C., where he became fluent in English and later studied in Chile and Switzerland. He returned to Mexico to complete a law degree at the Universidad Nacional Autónoma (the National Autonomous University) in 1955. Fuentes has held important university posts in Mexico and the United States and has served as a diplomat in Switzerland and France. Although he is known principally for his narrative writing, he has also received widespread attention thanks to the many articles he has published in international journals and the lectures he has delivered abroad. His fascination with the cin-

ema has led him to experiment with movie scripts, and he has been involved in various movie productions, including the one of **Old Gringo,** based on his novel *Gringo viejo* of 1985.

Fuentes's short stories and novels draw on a rich mythological tradition in an attempt to reinterpret historical events and offer an original vision of past and contemporary societies. His first book of short stories, *Los días enmascarados* (1954; The Masked Days), already includes elements of Aztec mythology, especially evident in the story "Chac Mool," the name of an Aztec rain god who in the story comes to life in contemporary Mexican society. The blend of historical and mythical time is represented in the juxtaposition of the two cultures.

In his first major work, *La región más transparente* (1958; translated as *Where the Air is Clear*), Fuentes draws on elements of Mexico's mythical past to reinterpret present historical realities of the four million inhabitants of Mexico City (in 1958). Characters who represent disillusionment with the **Mexican Revolution** intermingle with others who enact an Aztec ritual past, with its concentration on human sacrifices in order to ensure the survival of the human race. In this novel Fuentes establishes his skill with a variety of novelistic techniques: allegory, symbolism, juxtaposition, interior monologues, fragmented time, rich metaphors, and vivid, cinematic imagery. His next novel, *Las buenas conciencias* (1959; translated as *The Good Consciences*), follows a more traditional realist mode and criticizes the hypocrisy and vacuity of the aristocratic, Catholic elite of the city of Guanajuato.

The novel most associated with the early years of the Boom is *La muerte de Artemio Cruz* (1962; translated as *The Death of Artemio Cruz*), which traces the history of Mexico from the latter part of the nineteenth century to the middle of the twentieth century, concentrating especially on the period of the Mexican Revolution. The techniques and structure employed by Fuentes, however, differentiate this novel from others of the Mexican Revolution and to a large extent from his own previous work. During the twelve hours before the death of Artemio Cruz, the twelve most important moments of the protagonist's life are reviewed. On one level these moments represent the triumphs and failures of the revolution and reflect the gradual disillusionment of the idealists who had thought that it would transform their society into a more equitable one. The originality of the novel, however, really lies in its narrative strategies, which have attracted considerable critical attention. In passages related in first, second, or third person the inner musings of the narrator in the present, future, and past are respectively explored. This change in narrative perspective tends to blend historical and mythical time in the consciousness of the narrator as he reviews his life.

A somewhat similar narrative technique is employed in *Aura,* also published in 1962. Here Fuentes uses the second person as an elusive narrative voice to tell the story of Felipe, a young Mexican historian who enters a magical world representing Mexico's past; as he transcribes the memoirs of a general from the time of the Emperor Maximilian, he is transformed into the general's double. There are also two female archetypes: Consuelo, the general's wife, is an enchantress who relives her youth through Aura, the embodiment of youth and beauty. As these personalities blend into each other, it seems that the narrator's *you* may be referring to himself, to his double, to Consuelo, or to her double (Aura), or even to the reader. The narration, largely told in future tense, unfolds in a dreamlike sequence that blends past, present, and future. Most of the action takes place in an archaic mansion built in the center of Mexico City on the ruins of what used to be the heart of the Aztec capital, Tenochtitlán.

This idea of a sacred space is found in Fuentes's next novel, *Zona sagrada* (1967; translated as *Sacred Zone*), which places various manifestations of mythological characters in a contemporary Mexican football field, where ritual transformations occur. *Cambio de piel* (translated as *A Change of Skin*) was also published in 1967 and reflects Fuentes's ability to manipulate experimental stratagems. It is an extremely complex novel in which Fuentes looks for the roots of contemporary Mexico in its mythical past, paralleling a current reality lived by the main characters with scenes from other times and places, including the encounter between the Spaniards and the Aztecs in 1519. Time fluctuates with no transitions; the points of view vary deliberately, confusing the plot; and language is masterfully manipulated to reflect linguistic possibilities that range from vulgar speech to lyrical passages. The structure of the novel in itself reflects the existentialist struggle to assert oneself in the face of an absurd and tragic human condition. *Cambio de piel* appeared at about the same time as Chilean author José Donoso's *El obsceno pájaro de la noche* (1970; translated as *The Obscene Bird of Night*), and together they perhaps mark the Boom at its loudest, most experimental extreme. *Cumpleaños* (1969; Birthday) differs from Fuentes's previous novels in that it focuses on European rather than Mexican myth and history and combines current everyday life in London with the life of a French philosopher in the thirteenth century.

Terra Nostra (1975), which many regard as the culminating point of Fuentes's fiction, links European and Mexican history and myth with little respect, as Fuentes himself has confessed, for rigorous historical

Carlos Fuentes (photograph by Carlos Fuentes Jr.)

chronology. The author compresses significant events that occurred during colonial Spanish rule of the sixteenth and seventeenth centuries, starting with 1492, the time of the expulsion of Jews from Spain and the arrival of Columbus in the New World. In the protagonist, Señor Don Felipe, who is supervising the construction of the palace-cum-mausoleum of El Escorial near Madrid, Fuentes fuses the characteristics of various Spanish rulers (notably the Catholic monarchs, Charles V, and Philip II). Don Felipe epitomizes the rigid, intolerant absolutism of the Spanish monarchy, and his mausoleum marks its mummification. Particularly successful (and ambitious) is the use of mythical and historical elements to forge an understanding of Hispanic culture on both sides of the ocean.

In *La cabeza de la hidra* (1978; translated as *The Hydra Head*) and *Una familia lejana* (1980; A Faraway Family) history and myth again interact to produce an understanding of Mexican cultural identity; the first is parodic and accessible, the second more hermetic. Fuentes has also published several plays that deal with the same preoccupations; the best known is *Todos los gatos son pardos* (1970; All Cats Are Grey), which concentrates on the encounter of the Spanish conquistador Hernán Cortés and the Aztec monarch Montezuma II, mediated by **Malinche.**

Always a person much in evidence in the United States, in recent years Fuentes has turned his attention to the relationship between his country and its neighbor to the north, as in *Gringo viejo* and *Cristóbal Nonato* (1987; translated as *Christopher Unborn*). Fuentes is also the author of the short-story collections *Agua quemada* (1981; Burnt Water) and *Constancia y otros cuentos para vírgenes* (1989; translated as *Constancia and Other Stories for Virgins*). *La campaña* (1990; translated as *The Campaign*) is a novel about a period in the Spanish American struggle for independence in which the fervor of revolution is matched by the ardor of love. In 1995, shortly after the publication of *Diana o la cazadora solitaria* (1994; translated as *Diana, The Goddess Who Hunts Alone*), Fuentes explained that the figure of Diana had been based on the U.S. actress Jean Seberg, with whom he had had a passionate affair in the late 1960s. That novel, he said, was the first of a trilogy with erotic and political themes, to be followed by the other two projected volumes, *Aquiles el guerrillero* (Aquilles the Warrior) and *Prometeo, el precio de la libertad* (Prometheus, the Price of Liberty). Prolific though he has been as an author of fiction, Fuentes has also produced various works of criticism, including *La nueva novela hispanoamericana* (1969; translated as *The New Spanish American Novel*).

REFERENCES:

Aziza Bennani, *Monde Mental et Monde Romanesque de Carlos Fuentes* (Rabat: Publications de la Faculté des Lettres et des Sciences Humaines, 1985);

Robert Brody and Charles Rossman, *Carlos Fuentes* (Austin: University of Texas Press, 1982);

Daniel de Guzmán, *Carlos Fuentes* (New York: Twayne, 1972);

World Literature Today, special Fuentes issue, 57 (Autumn 1983).

             — M.E.S. & P.S.

FUNDACIÓN DE NUEVO CINE LATINOAMERICANO

The Fundación de Nuevo Cine Latinoamericano (Foundation for New Latin American Cinema), or FNCL, was established in 1985 in Havana. Part of the outreach of the Committee of Latin American filmmakers, the FNCL is presided over by the distinguished Colombian writer Gabriel García Márquez. One of the first activities of this foundation was the publication of *Hojas del Cine* (1986–1988; Cinema Documents), a three-part collection of documents and manifestos. In 1987 it provided screenplays for *Amores difíciles* (Difficult Loves), a series of six teleplays — all of which were based on stories or scripts by García Márquez — jointly produced by Latin American and Spanish filmmakers for Spanish television. This series, jokingly referred to as "the return of the conquistadors," achieved good ratings when broadcast in Spain. The most ambitious undertaking of the foundation was the establishment of the Escuela de Cine y Televisión (School of Film and Television) at San Antonio de los Baños, near Havana, in 1986. Originally headed by the Argentinean Fernando Birri and later by the Brazilian Orlando Senna, this school was set up as a training place for young filmmakers from Asia, Africa, and Latin America. The school has been involved in coproductions with Televisión Española, including *Barroco* (1989; Baroque), directed by Paul Leduc of Mexico and based on **Alejo Carpentier**'s *Concierto barroco* (Baroque Concert), a novella in which the Cuban writer pays tribute to his lifelong passion for music and celebrates the syncretic cross-fertilization of Old World and New World cultures.

REFERENCE:

John King, Ana M. López, and Manuel Alvarado, eds., *Mediating Two Worlds: Cinematic Encounters in the Americas* (London: BFI, 1993).
             — S.M.H.

G

Lucila Gamero Moncada de Medina

Honduran writer, physician, and women's rights advocate Lucila Gamero Moncada de Medina (1873–1964) was born in Danlí in the department of El Paraíso. She traveled to Mexico and Guatemala as a delegate to women's congresses and was a member of the International Women's League for Peace and Freedom. She published various novels, among them *Páginas del corazón* (1897; Pages from the Heart), *Adriana y Margarita* (1897), *Blanca Olmedo* (1900), *Amor exótico* (1954; Exotic Love), and *El dolor de amar* (1955; The Pain of Loving). Her most recognized work is *Blanca Olmedo,* a novel that reflects the lingerings of Romanticism along with positivist influences; Arthur Schopenhauer is frequently the topic of conversation among the characters. The novel focuses on the experiences of the young, beautiful, and idealized protagonist. Nevertheless, it differs from other Romantic novels, such as the Colombian Jorge Isaac's *María* (1867), in that Blanca Olmedo is an intelligent, strong, and resourceful woman who is quite aware of her precarious existence in a society that is based on a double standard. She does what she can to combat gender, class, and racial stereotyping, reflecting a new turn-of-the-century awareness. Gamero de Medina's narrative style is clear and flows smoothly; her use of interior monologue and especially of dialogue is one of the strong points of the novel. In Honduras she is recognized as one of the most important writers of the early part of the century.

REFERENCE:

Diane Marting, ed., *Women Writers of Spanish America: An Annotated Bio-Bibliographical Guide* (Westport, Conn.: Greenwood Press, 1987).

— M.E.S.

Alejandro García Caturla

Alejandro García Caturla (1906–1940) was born in Remedios, a city on the Atlantic coast of Cuba. In his childhood he studied violin and began to compose music in popular and Creole folk styles. At the age of sixteen he pursued studies in composition with the Spanish-born composer Pedro San Juan while completing a degree in law at the University of Havana. On the first of many visits to Paris he studied briefly with Nadia Boulanger and was exposed to the works of Darius Milhaud, Erik Satie, and Igor Stravinsky, composers whose musical aesthetics were not restrained by convention and whose audacity exercised considerable influence on his development.

On his return to Cuba, García Caturla maintained his law practice but also continued his activities as a composer. In recognition of his musical contributions, the municipal government of Remedios named him "Eminent and Distinguished Son" and gave his name to the concert hall of the local museum. The following year (1929) he returned to Europe for the Ibero-American Symphonic Festival, held in conjunction with the International Exhibition in Barcelona, for a performance of the symphonic work *Tres danzas cubanas* (1927; Three Cuban Dances). From Barcelona he proceeded to Paris for the premiere of *Dos poemas para voz y piano* (Two Poems for Voice and Piano). *Bembé*, a work for brass and woodwind instruments, piano, and percussion, also had its premiere in Paris. *Bembé* is an Afro-Cuban ritual of Santería, normally celebrated with three drums; a second version for percussion instruments only was written in 1930.

García Caturla's last ten years were filled with activity. In addition to writing many compositions, he founded the Sociedad de Conciertos de Caibarién (the Caibarién Concert Society) and conducted a wide variety of works by famous composers. He also played violin and viola in the Havana Symphony Orchestra and occasionally played the piano for special presentations. In the Cuban National Music Contest of 1937 his *Obertura cubana* was awarded first prize and the *Suite para orquesta* received an honorable mention. Among his other compositions of the period were the symphonic movements *Yamba-O* (1928–1931) and *La rumba* (1933); the first is for male chorus and orchestra, and the second is for solo voice and orchestra, (though a revised version eliminated the vocal part).

Following the long struggle for independence from Spain, the unstable political ambience in Cuba at the turn of the century led to a revaluation of the island's artistic direction by young musicians, poets, and artists. Inspired by nationalistic movements in the South American republics and by the artistic successes stemming from the **Mexican Revolution,** young revolutionaries known as the Grupo Minorista established a new cultural identity, Afro-Cubanism. Outstanding among its many advocates in the arts were **Amadeo Roldán** and Alejandro García Caturla.

Over time, and in spite of the disdain with which the Cuban upper classes viewed such developments, African musical elements had gradually and almost surreptitiously invaded the popular and folk genres of Cuba (see **Afro-Caribbean Music**). García Caturla was born into this pervasive musical environment, which surfaced in his pubescent music and dominated his mature compositions. García Caturla clarified the definition of Afro-Cubanism in concert music by effecting a creative synthesis of Creole and African musical ingredients. Rather than simply restating typical passages from African and Creole musics, as others had done, he sought to express the syncretized essence of both traditions. The collective heritage of Creole melody and African rhythm, accompanied by adventurous harmonies, was conveyed through an ingenious approach to orchestration, with expressive results that are sometimes brutal. According to **Alejo Carpentier,** here was "a barbaric, primitive force ... taken to the field of civilized instruments with all of the luxury that one who knows about the modern schools [of composition] can allow himself."

García Caturla's works have been performed widely throughout the world by distinguished conductors, including Nicolas Slonimsky, **Carlos Chávez, Silvestre Revueltas,** and Leopold Stokowski. García Caturla's life ended prematurely in 1940, when he was shot at point-blank range by a convicted criminal he was to sentence the next day.

REFERENCES:

Gerard Béhague, *Music in Latin America: An Introduction* (Englewood Cliffs, N.J.: Prentice-Hall, 1979);

Alejo Carpentier, *La música en Cuba,* second edition (Mexico City: Fondo Cultura Económica, 1972);

Argeliers León, "Of the Axle and the Hinge: Nationalism, Afro-Cubanism, and Music in Pre-Revolutionary Cuba," translated by Terence Sweeny, in *Essays on Cuban Music: North American and Cuban Perspectives*, edited by Peter Manuel (Lanham, Md.: University Press of America, 1991).

          — R.L.S.

JULIO GARCÍA ESPINOSA

Julio García Espinosa is a Cuban movie director who started out working in radio and theater before going abroad in 1952 to study filmmaking at the legendary Centro Sperimentale di Cinematografia (Center for Experimental Cinematography) at the University of Rome. In 1954, after they returned to Cuba, García Espinosa and **Tomás Gutiérrez Alea,** a fellow student at the Centro Sperimentale, collaborated on a medium-length, neorealist feature, *El mégano* (1955; The Charcoal Worker), which was banned by President Fulgencio Batista. (See **Neorealism in Motion Pictures.**) During **Fidel Castro**'s guerrilla war against the Batista government, García Espinosa headed the insurgent film unit Cine Rebelde, set up to document the activities of the rebels. After Castro took control of the Cuban government in 1959, García Espinosa and Gutiérrez Alea were associated for many years with the Instituto Cubano de Arte e Industria Cinematográficas (**Cuban Film Institute**), or ICAIC, and García Espinosa had a crucial role in the creation of the new aesthetic that eventually coalesced as the **New Latin American Cinema.**

During its early years the New Latin American Cinema was characterized by a neorealist style adapted to portray a politicized Latin American reality. Objecting to the long-dominant Hollywood style of studio shooting and seamlessly composed narratives, the artists of the New Latin American Cinema freed the camera from isolation in the studio and roamed the streets with it. Using nonprofessional actors instead of Hollywood stars, they presented vivid depictions of a forgotten class that had never before seen its own image on the big screen. The New Latin American Cinema was an oppositional cinema at every level, self-consciously searching out new ways of expressing the new sentiments of a newly recovered Latin American reality.

García Espinosa's first feature-length project was *Cuba baila* (1960; Cuba Dances), which depicts class and generational conflict in prerevolutionary Havana. His first major success was *Las aventuras de Juan Quin Quin* (1967; The Adventures of Juan Quin Quin), an effective example of the new politicized aesthetic, and one that drew an audience of more than two million

Julio García Espinosa (third from left) in Vietnam, where he filmed *Tercer mundo, tercera guerra mundial* (1970; Third World, Third World War)

people in Cuba. Following the picaresque adventures of the hero before he becomes a guerrilla fighter, the movie subverts some of the conventional stereotypes of Hollywood cinema, such as strong heroes and ravishing heroines.

During this period García Espinosa wrote a provocative theoretical essay, "Por une cine imperfecto" (1969; For an Imperfect Cinema), which rejects the pursuit of formal perfection, or technique for technique's sake, in favor of true-to-life authenticity. He argues that "a new aesthetic cannot emerge if we do not contribute to the development of a new culture." Encouraging cooperative creative projects instead of individual authorship, he calls for a new, "imperfect cinema" and argues that "popular art has always been created by the least learned sector of society, yet this 'uncultured' sector has managed to conserve profoundly cultured artistic features. One of the most important of these is the fact that the creators are the spectators and vice versa." He therefore calls for a new "spectator-creator," rendering film criticism obsolete. Above all, García Espinosa's essay identifies the need to enable spectators to become genuine cocreators of revolutionary culture.

In 1977, after many years of association with the ICAIC, García Espinosa was elected to the position of deputy minister for music and spectacles in the newly founded Ministry of Culture, and he was given responsibility for state-funded festivities, regional fairs, variety shows, nightclub acts, and circuses. The minister of culture, Armando Hart, was seeking to "elevate" the expression of mass culture to a higher art form by providing it with more institutional support. In 1980 García Espinosa relinquished his post to succeed **Alfredo Guevara** as the head of the ICAIC. In the same year he released *Son o no son* (Sound or Not), which focuses on the various forms that musical comedy takes in Cuba. Even more important than the documentaries and feature-length movies he directed while at the ICAIC were his collaboration and consultation on many of the major ICAIC projects, including **Humberto Solás**'s *Lucía* (1968) and the Chilean Patricio Guzmán's *La batalla de Chile* (1975–1979).

REFERENCE:

Julianne Burton, *Cinema and Social Change in Latin America: Conversations with Filmmakers* (Austin: University of Texas Press, 1986).

— S.M.H.

FLOR GARDUÑO

The work of the Mexican photographer Flor Garduño (1957–) suggests both the present and the eternal by portraying indigenous people in daily activities that perpetuate traditions (see **photography**). Garduño studied in Mexico City at the Instituto Nacional de Bellas Artes (National Institute of Fine Arts) and the Universidad Nacional Autónoma de México (National Autonomous University of Mexico) and also worked as a studio assistant to photographer **Manuel Alvarez Bravo** in the late 1970s. She continued Alvarez Bravo's tradition of lyricism in black-and-white photography as well as his synthesis of formal concerns with a strong interest in the culture of Mexico. However, her first internationally acclaimed photographic series, *Bestiario* (1987; Bestiarium), presents a renewed vision of **Indigenism,** one that makes no political assumptions. In this series, which features indigenous peoples dressed in zoomorphic costumes from pre-Columbian rituals, indigenous traditions are often integrated with the Catholic faith and modern trends. Perhaps in an idealized way, Garduño makes evident the closely intertwined lives of humans, animals, and nature in traditional Mexican culture.

Garduño allows light and shadow to sculpt space. While most figures appear carefully framed, though not necessarily posed, the subjects evoke a sense of chronological continuation beyond the constraints of the photographs. Garduño also worked and traveled in Central America and the Andes, continuing the photographic survey of native lives and traditions that she had begun in Mexico. Her photographs capture moments of spirituality and death. *Huilancha-Sacrificio* (1990; Huilancha Sacrifice) offers the viewer a ceremonially sacrificed llama. From its slit throat blood has poured over the bouquet of flowers beneath its head and soaked into the fissures of the earth. The photograph's closely cropped quality frames a traditional subject that embodies the pains of daily life. Such pains are clearly stated in *Camino al cementerio* (1988; Way to the Cemetery), a four-person burial procession in which a child's coffin is tied to the back of the central figure while a figure on the right carries a shovel. The figures, whose backs are turned to the camera, lead the viewer into their world but remain anonymous and therefore universal. Throughout her work Garduño uses this anonymity at intimate moments to evoke in the viewer an affinity with indigenous lives and rituals.

REFERENCES:

Elizabeth Ferrer, "Flor Garduño," *Review: Latin American Literature and Arts,* no. 41 (July–December 1989): 14–21;

Flor Garduño, *Witness of Time* (New York: Thames & Hudson, 1992).

— C.M.

ELENA GARRO

Playwright, essayist, novelist, and short-story writer, Elena Garro (1920–) was born in Puebla, Mexico, of a Spanish father and a Mexican mother. Her father acted

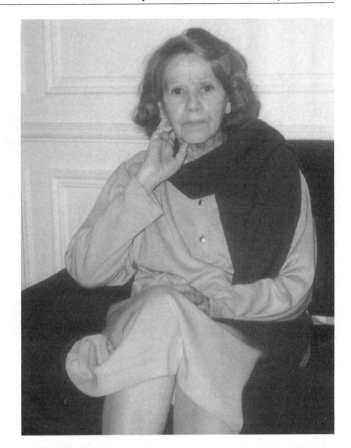

Elena Garro, 1986

as tutor to all his children in their early years, and Garro later continued her education at the Universidad Autónoma de México (Autonomous University of Mexico) in Mexico City. There she studied dance and became an actress and choreographer. In 1937 she married **Octavio Paz** and, because of the traveling that resulted from his diplomatic postings, met many writers abroad, including the Surrealists in Paris, who had a marked influence on her writing. Her marriage to Paz dissolved in 1959. Her reputation as a playwright began with the 1958 publication of *Andarse por las ramas* (Wandering Astray) and *Los pilares de Doña Blanca, y un hogar sólido* (The Pillars of Doña Blanca and a Solid Home). One year later she published *La mudanza* (The Move) and in 1960 *La señora en su balcón* (The Woman On Her Balcony), a play about a middle-aged woman who rejects the reality of her routine life of poverty and exploitation by the macho society in which she lives. At the same time her play *El rey mago* (The Wise Man) was televised. In 1963–1964 several of her works were published, including *El árbol* (The Tree) and *La dama boba* (The Foolish Lady), the latter a three-act play that combines indigenous beliefs with the traditions of Greek theater. That play also demonstrates the influence of the Spanish classics: its title is taken from a play by Lope de Vega, while its subject matter reflects his interest in the confusion of reality and appearance. *La muerte de Felipe Angeles* (The Death of Felipe Angeles), a critique of false revolutions, appeared in the journal *Coatl* in 1967.

Garro wrote essays such as "La cultura en Mexico" (Culture in Mexico) and a film script, *¿Qué pasa con los tlaxcaltecas?* (1964; What's Happening with the Tlaxcaltecas?). Her narrative writing includes a collection of short stories, *La semana de colores* (1964; The Week of Colors), which contains a mixture of fantasy and reality, with ironic, folkloric, and fantastic characters who move between past, present, and future. One of Garro's most famous short stories, "La culpa es de los tlaxcaltecas" (The Fault Lies with the Tlaxcaltecas), is her interpretation of the archetypal figure of Doña Marina, better known in Mexico as **Malinche.** Another collection of short stories, *Andamos huyendo Lola* (1980; We're Running Away, Lola), uses the technique of **magical realism** to portray the anguish of characters lost in a world of violence and persecution, while in the consciousness of those characters, time and memory blend to create an alternative reality.

Garro's most famous work is her novel *Los recuerdos del porvenir* (1963; translated as *Recollections of Things to Come*), which won the Villaurrutia Prize. The novel presents a series of conflicts involving the town of Ixtepec, an imaginary Mexican community embroiled in political, religious, and family problems. The collective narrator is the town itself, which describes a rigidly stratified society living two realities, that of the **Cristero War** (1926–1928), a reaction against the anticlerical reforms of the **Mexican Revolution,** and another composed of myths and fantasies that represent the memory of the town. Mythical time clashes with historical time, and magical realist scenes are presented along with historical ones. The famous Colombian writer Gabriel García Márquez has stated that he was very much influenced by the magical realist elements of Garro's works. *Testimonios sobre Mariana* (1981; Testimonies of Mariana) portrays the protagonist Mariana through three different narrators, again combining real and magical elements. Garro's other works include *Reencuentro de personajes* (1982; Reencounter of Characters), *La casa junto al río* (1983; The House by the River), and *Y Matarazo no llamó* (1989; And Matarazo Did Not Call). Garro's works were influenced by her childhood among the peasants of Mexico, where myths, legends, and fantastic beliefs were part of the daily fare. Her preoccupation with women's limited situation in a macho society is combined with a vivid imagination, making her one of Latin America's outstanding writers.

La reina de los yugos (1975–1978; The Queen of the Yokes) by Alberto Gironella (Collection of Luis Felipe del Valle)

REFERENCE:

Anita K. Stoll, *A Different Reality: Studies on the Work of Elena Garro* (London: Associated University Presses, 1990).

— J.P. & M.E.S.

ALBERTO GIRONELLA

The Mexican painter Alberto Gironella (1929–) is an important member of **La Ruptura Generation.** Influenced by his Catalan father, Gironella became interested in the culture of Spain, especially the writings of Ramón Goméz de la Serna and Ramón del Valle-Inclán. He studied Spanish at the Universidad Nacional Autónoma de México (National Autonomous University of Mexico), and later his studio became a meeting place for Spanish and Mexican writers and artists. In the early 1950s Gironella turned to painting and founded the Galería Prisse with fellow artist Vlady (Vladimir Kibalchich Rusakov). As members of La Ruptura Generation, Gironella and Vlady rejected the emphasis on the **Muralism** and **Indigenism** of the Mexican

Tata Jesucristo (1926; Father Jesus Christ) by Francisco Goitia (CNCA-INBA, Museo Nacional de Arte, Mexico City)

School. Their gallery supported **José Luis Cuevas,** José Bartolí, and Héctor Xavier, artists who broke away from the dominant art in spite of intense opposition by well-established artists such as **Diego Rivera** and **David Alfaro Siqueiros.**

After the demise of the Galería Prisse, in 1954 Gironella opened the Galería Proteo, which continued to support the aims of La Ruptura Generation. In the late 1950s Gironella reached artistic maturity, although his style involved appropriating the work of the Spanish painters El Greco, Diego Velázquez, and Francisco de Goya. Gironella was fascinated by the most sinister aspects of Spanish culture and sometimes used such aspects to comment on Mexico. In his painting *Entierro de Zapata* (1957; Burial of Zapata) he took as his source of inspiration El Greco's *Entierro del Conde de Orgaz* (Burial of the Count of Orgaz). In order to decry the betrayal of the ideals of the **Mexican Revolution** by later governments Gironella returned to the theme of Emiliano Zapata in the 1970s.

Gironella's most important works belong to the *Series de las reinas* (1960s–1970s; Series of the

Queens), in which he appropriates and deconstructs images of Queen Mariana of Austria painted by Velázquez. Gironella's sinister vision of Mariana was influenced by Valle-Inclán's writings about the decadence of the Spanish monarchy. At the beginning of the series Gironella reinterpreted Velázquez's portraits in an expressionist style influenced by Informal Abstraction (see **Abstract Art**), which gives the figure of the queen the near abstract quality characteristic of Neofiguration. Soon Gironella began to introduce found objects into his works, which eventually became complex collages. The metamorphosis of Mariana reached an important stage in collages such as *Gran obrador* (1964; Great Maker), in which he represented her as a dog. In *La reina de los yugos* (1975–1978; The Queen of the Yokes) the figure of the queen, constructed with found objects, becomes a deconstructive statement connoting both power and defeat, Spanish domination and colonial subjection. This paradoxical identification of Mexico with Spain also appears in Gironella's painting *El sueño de Doña Marina 2* (1977; The Dream of Doña Marina 2), where Mariana becomes Doña Marina, or **Malinche,** Hernán Cortés's

126

translator and concubine, considered both a traitor to and a symbol of Mexico. During the 1970s Gironella returned to the theme of Zapata in a series of performances representing the burial of the revolutionary leader.

REFERENCE:

Rita Eder, *Gironella* (Mexico City: Universidad Autónoma de México, Instituto de Investigaciones Estéticas, 1981).

— F.B.N.

Francisco Goitia

The Mexican artist Francisco Goitia (1882–1960) is best known for his bleak images of the **Mexican Revolution** and his **Indigenist** paintings. He studied at the Academia de San Carlos with some of the most important painters of the nineteenth century: Santiago Rebull, José María Velasco, and Félix Parra. In 1904 Goitia left for Spain, where he became familiar with the art of Diego Velázquez, El Greco, and Francisco de Goya, whose oeuvres influenced his own. Goitia exhibited his work with such success that the Mexican government gave him a scholarship to travel in Spain, France, and Italy. At the beginning of the Mexican Revolution his grant was suspended, and Goitia returned to Mexico in 1912. He joined the forces of Francisco "Pancho" Villa and recorded the desolation of the war by creating some of the most somber images of the revolution, comparable to those produced by **José Guadalupe Posada** and the anonymous photographers whose works are included in the Archivo Casasola. In *El ahorcado* (1917; The Hanged Man) Goitia represents, with expressionistic realism, the tragic figure of a skeleton, still dressed in rags, sadly swaying under a tree.

After the revolution, while working for the anthropologist Manuel Gamio, one of the main proponents of Indigenism, Goitia traveled through Mexico and took part in several archaeological and ethnological research projects. In his works Goitia recorded not only indigenous peoples and their traditions, but also different psychological states. In *Las danzas indígenas* (1921; Indigenous Dances) Goitia reflects a festive environment, while *Tata Jesucristo* (1926; Father Jesus Christ), one of his best-known works, shows a moment of deep despair and *Viejo en el muladar* (1926; Old Man on the Dung Hill) one of solitude and introspection. In the 1930s he began teaching in the elementary schools of Xochimilco, where he had settled in a humble home; later he taught at the Universidad Nacional Autónoma de México (National Autonomous University of Mexico). Goitia had his first individual exhibition in 1946 and later participated in exhibitions trav-

eling abroad that helped him achieve national and international recognition. During his last years Goitia worked on a series of paintings, such as *Paisaje de Zacatecas con ahorcados* (1959; Zacatecas Landscape with Hanged Men), inspired by his experiences in the revolution.

REFERENCE:

Alfonso de Neuvillate, *Francisco Goitia: Precursor de la escuela mexicana* (Mexico City: Universidad Nacional Autónoma de México, Dirección General de Publicaciones, 1964).

— F.B.N.

Enrique Gómez Carrillo

Like many writers of his generation, the Guatemalan Enrique Gómez Carrillo (1873–1927) lived in Europe, where he wrote articles for Spanish and Spanish American periodicals, served as consul for Argentina, and was an active participant in the intellectual life of Paris. Central to his literary life is his relationship with the **Modernista** movement. Gómez Carrillo's active involvement with French intellectuals and his friendship with other Spanish American writers living in Paris, such as **Rubén Darío,** Rufino Blanco Fombona, and José María Vargas Vila, made him an intermediary between Spanish American and French cultural and literary production. Gómez Carrillo was often referred to by Spanish American writers and intellectuals as "our agent in Paris." In contrast to other modernistas such as Darío, translations of his works into French were sympathetically received by European readers. Gómez Carrillo's chronicles of his travels and life in Paris are good examples of the "light" style of prose writing the author cultivated. Such a style was recognized by other writers and critics of the period as a major development, one that stood in contrast to the heavier, more pompous and solemn style of previous prose writing.

Among his texts, *De Marsella a Tokio* (1906; From Marseille to Tokyo) is a collection of chronicles written for the Buenos Aires newspaper *La Nación*. These chronicles can be read as instances of reading and reinterpreting issues of orientalism and colonialism from the standpoint of an author who seeks a third space, that of the informer, for a third readership, the Spanish American audience. Many of Gómez Carrillo's works are collections of his articles and chronicles that were edited and republished by the author in successive volumes. Among them it is worth noting his biography, written in three parts and collected as *Treinta años de mi vida* (1920–1923; Thirty Years of My Life), and the twenty-seven volumes of his *Obras completas* (1919–1923).

REFERENCE:

Alfonso E. Barrientos, *Enrique Gómez Carrillo* (Guatemala: Editorial José Piñeda Ibarra, 1973).

— J.F.

JOSÉ LUIS GONZÁLEZ

Born in Puerto Rico, José Luis González (1926–) earned a degree in political science and a doctorate in literary studies at the National Autonomous University of Mexico. He has published several books of fiction and many uncollected short stories. Several of his books were published between 1943 and 1954, among them *En la sombra* (1943; In the Shade), *Cinco cuentos de sangre* (1945; Five Tales of Blood), *Paisa* (1950), and *En este lado* (1954; On This Side). Many of González's stories of this period center on the realities of rural life in Puerto Rico, a fact that caused González to be classified as a regional writer. A long silence followed until 1972 when González published several other books containing new stories as well as revisions of earlier ones, offering sharp criticism of Puerto Rican society. In addition to depicting the marginalization of the rural peasant, numerous tales take place in urban settings in Puerto Rico and New York and reflect the exodus of peasants from the countryside to San Juan, and finally to New York, depicted as a hostile giant that swallows up immigrants. Other settings include Mexico, Europe, and the battlefields of Korea and Vietnam — evidence of a more universal trend in González's prose, also reflected in his condemnation of racism, U.S. imperialism, and warfare. González's style is carefully constructed, effectively presenting his characters through a skillful use of dialogue with a mixture of sarcasm, irony, pity, and sympathy. His vivid imagination is matched by an ability to evoke anger, frustration, hope, and love, among other emotions that cause the reader to reflect on disturbing realities. Several of his books were published in the early 1970s: *La galería* (1972; The Gallery), *Mambrú se fue a la guerra* (1972; Mambrú Has Gone to War), and *En Nueva York y otras desgracias* (1973; In New York Among Other Misfortunes). His novel *Balada de otro tiempo* (1978; Ballad of Another Time) won the Xavier Villaurrutia Prize. He has also published *La llegada* (1980; The Arrival) and *Las caricias del tigre* (1984; The Caresses of the Tiger).

REFERENCE:

Andrés O. Avellaneda, "Para leer a José Luis González," in *En Nueva York y otras desgracias*, by José Luis González (Río Piedras, Puerto Rico: Edición Huracán, 1973), pp. 9–28.

— M.E.S.

GOVERNMENT SUPPORT FOR THE ARTS

Cultural and artistic activities in Latin America, as in many parts of the world, are often supported by government agencies, but such support can be double-edged, since established authority usually has a political agenda and often views artists as subversive. The administration of arts and culture programs often begins with the ministry of education, within which is an office or directorate of culture, under which are national schools of dance, music, theater, and the visual arts. In the latter part of the twentieth century, however, other methods of organizing and financing the arts have come into being. Foundations or councils for culture, which are semi-autonomous and are able to raise and spend their funds independently and to make independent contractual arrangements, now exist in Guatemala and El Salvador, among other countries.

Governmental support for the arts is nowhere as strong as it is in Mexico. Early in the century the search for a national identity, which acquired renewed importance following the **Mexican Revolution,** led to the creation of national schools of the arts in 1920. One effect of this movement was the "rescue" by government-assigned researchers of indigenous cultural traditions, which were in danger of being lost in a rapidly urbanizing country. A somewhat contradictory effect was the standardization of regional forms as they were passed on in the schools, so that Mexico's ethnic complexity was minimized to form a "new," cohesive Mexican cultural identity. In this entry government support for dance is discussed as an example of the range of government backing for all artistic activities.

The Instituto Nacional de Bellas Artes (INBA; the National Fine Arts Institute) of Mexico was created in 1946–1947, early in the presidency of Miguel Alemán, and has had a crucial role in supporting the arts in Mexico; its first director was the world-renowned composer **Carlos Chávez.** While an Escuela Nacional de Danza (National Dance School) existed primarily to train interpreters of classical ballet, in 1947 Chávez created the Academia de la Danza Mexicana with the goals of preserving and promoting the rich Mexican traditions of popular and ritual dance and forming a nucleus of dancers, researchers, and creators of a new Mexican choreography. In 1955 the academia was reorganized as the Ballet de Bellas Artes.

The INBA has made available enormous resources for the development of dance in Mexico, making dance a powerful and visible part of the country's arts panorama. Dancers, teachers, and choreographers from surrounding countries come to Mexico to study, and Mexico exports dancers and teachers to perform and teach. One of the INBA's means of supporting dance is the Sistema Nacional de Creadores de Arte (National System for Creators of Art), which finances artists' living expenses so that they may devote themselves to creative activity. Also important is the Programa de Apoyo a Proyectos y Coinversiones Culturales (Program of Support for Cultural Projects and Coinvestments) of the National Council for Culture and the Arts. The INBA has long supported an impressive budget to bring specialists from abroad to teach modern-dance techniques, improvisation, administration of dance companies, massage, anatomy, and injury prevention. Yet another means of support is the network of Mexican festivals devoted exclusively or largely to dance. The INBA also fosters a series of competitions to promote and support dance, including the First National Ballet Competition in 1994, the National Dance Prize, and the National Prize for Dance for Children.

State-funded university support is also strong: nearly all of the major national university centers, including Mexico City, Mérida, Guadalajara, Xalapa (Veracruz), and Monterrey, sponsor dance training programs and professional dance companies. The Universidad Nacional Autónoma de México has supported the Ballet de la UNAM since the early 1950s and later the choreographer Gloria Contreras and her Taller Coreográfico de la UNAM, a proving ground for many emerging choreographers. In 1969 the Dirección General de Difusión Cultural of the Universidad Nacional Autónoma collaborated with the Ballet Nacional in the creation of intensive modern-dance courses, the objective being to educate young college students about modern dance, challenging the frequently held belief that dance was most valuable as a weight-loss program. From 1970 to 1979 the Seminario de Danza Moderna y Experimentación Coreográfica (Seminar on Modern Dance and Experimental Choreography) was held at the UNAM, under the direction of Lin Durán, later the director of the Centro Nacional de Investigación, Documentación e Información de la Danza "José Limón" (**CENIDI-Danza**) and **Guillermina Bravo.** In 1991 the Colegio Nacional de Danza Contemporánea was established by Guillermina Bravo in Querétaro, Mexico.

Another case of government intervention in the arts to create a national identity is that of El Salvador, which adapted Mexican folkloric dance to "create" a Salvadoran folk dance, institutionalized as the Ballet del Instituto Salvadoreño de Turismo, or Ballet del ISTU. After the near extermination of El Salvador's indigenous population in the 1930s, the remaining natives dispersed or went underground. In the 1950s the Salvadoran dancer and teacher Morena Celarié studied

folkloric dance in Mexico, brought it back to El Salvador, and created Salvadoran folkloric dance to be performed theatrically at government-sponsored events. The National Dance School of El Salvador, a training academy for ballet, modern, and folk dance, is named after her, reflecting the government's approval of this forged indigenous dance.

Prior to the Cuban Revolution dance in that country was sustained and promoted by the Ballet School of the Pro-Arte Music Society, a private group of upper-class Havana citizens who wished to train young girls in the best of European classical ballet traditions. After the revolution, with the full support of the Cuban government, national contemporary, folkloric, and ballet companies and schools were opened. A specific purpose of these organizations was to include the poor and the Afro-Cuban population in training and in performances. Frequent exchanges of teachers between Cuba and Mexico and between Cuba and the former Iron Curtain countries characterized dance training in this era (See also **National Folkloric Dance Companies**).

— J.M.H.

GRAPHIC ART

Some of the best graphic art in the twentieth century has been produced in Mexico, Puerto Rico, and Cuba. As in the case of important art movements that emphasized printmaking, such as European Post-Impressionism and German Expressionism, graphic art in Latin America was often a vehicle for political and social commentary. In Mexico the main precursor of graphic art was the work of the famous nineteenth-century printmaker **José Guadalupe Posada,** who in thousands of inexpensive broadsides conveyed political messages and images of popular customs, often using a cast of skeletal characters (*calaveras*). Posada's work was revalued and continued through the efforts of **José Clemente Orozco,** one of the leaders of the Muralist movement, and **Jean Charlot,** who participated in both Mexican **Muralism** and **Estridentismo.** Orozco's most important graphic works, completed at the beginning of his artistic career, were inspired in the expressionistic style of Posada and Goya. While Orozco's early prints focused on images of schoolgirls and prostitutes, he later produced more-politicized cartoons and compositions for the pro-Carranza newspaper *La Vanguardia,* directed by **Dr. Atl** during the **Mexican Revolution.** Orozco's prints emphasized the stupidity of violence and his undying sympathy for the underdog; the expressionist, cartoonlike style of the prints later influenced many of his mural paintings.

Rich People in Hell (1924), woodcut by Jean Charlot

Charlot, a printmaker and teacher of graphic art, helped revalue the art of Posada and revive woodcut technique as a vehicle to represent social themes. In 1922 he ran a print workshop with Fernando Leal in the open-air school in Coyoacán (see **Impressionism**), teaching woodcut and lithography to Francisco Díaz de León, Gabriel Fernández Ledesma, and Emilio Ameto, who became important contributors to the graphic revival of the 1930s and 1940s. Most of Charlot's works for Estridentismo, avant-garde woodcuts published in the group's magazines and books, reflected the estridentistas' utopian interest in technology and revolutionary politics. After the estridentista group disbanded in 1927, Charlot turned to **Indigenism,** while some of its other members, such as Leal and Ramón Alva de la Canal, joined the "30–30" group of artists, which focused on printmaking.

In 1930 an important graphic arts workshop was established at the Instituto Nacional de Bellas Artes (National Institute of Fine Arts). It soon become the main training center for printmaking in Mexico. The interest in graphic arts was continued by LEAR (Liga de Escritores y Artistas Revolucionarios; League of Revolutionary Writers and Artists). From 1935 to 1938 LEAR supported a collective graphic art studio, fur-

ther affirming the connection between leftist politics, mural painting, and printmaking. After the LEAR workshop dissolved, Leopoldo Méndez, Pablo O'Higgins, and Luis Arenal founded the Taller de Gráfica Popular (Popular Graphic Workshop), which also included important graphic artists such as Alberto Beltrán, Angel Bracho, Charlot, Fernández Ledesma, Méndez, José Chávez Morado, Orozco, **David Alfaro Siqueiros,** and Alfredo Zalce. During the 1930s and 1940s the workshop members used a variety of techniques, such as woodcut, linocut, and lithography, and represented themes dealing with **Indigenism,** the Spanish Civil War, the threat of Nazism, Mexican history, and the Mexican Revolution. Various figurative styles were used. The activities of the Taller de Gráfica Popular generated a printmaking revival in Mexico, which eventually had an important influence on the graphic arts in Puerto Rico and the United States.

In Puerto Rico the development of graphic art was tied to a series of social and political measures implemented by Gov. Luis Muñoz Marín. In the late 1940s the Commission for Public Parks and Recreation — through its motion-picture and graphic arts workshop, founded and directed by Jack and Irene Delano — used graphic design for public campaigns dealing with issues of health, politics, and education. Later, when the Delanos' workshop became the Taller de Artes Gráficas (Graphic Arts Workshop) of the Division of Community Education under the Department of Public Education, the focus on education became more important. The workshop hired artists such as **Lorenzo Homar** and Juan Díaz on a full-time basis to illustrate books and produce silk-screen posters in order to convey information about education and about cultural events. Poster art became an important art form in Puerto Rico, especially for the Generation of 1950, whose members, including Homar, José Antonio Torres Martinó, Félix Rodríguez Báez, Rafael Tufiño, and **Carlos Raquel Rivera,** joined the Centro de Arte Puertorriqueño (Puerto Rican Art Center) and its printmaking studio under the direction of Homar.

Inspired by the Mexican Taller de Gráfica Popular, the center's graphic art workshop encouraged collective work, figurative styles, national and political themes, and experimentation with different printing techniques, such as silk screen, xylography, linocut, typography, and calligraphy. After Puerto Rico achieved commonwealth status in 1952, the proindependence members of the center emphasized their rejection of avant-garde styles as a way of opposing United States cultural colonialism while reaching a broad popular audience. Such an approach links the **costumbrismo** and nationalism of the center members to that of earlier Puerto Rican artists such as Francisco Oller,

Ramón Frade, and **Miguel Pou.** When the center closed in 1954, the Instituto de Cultura Puertorriqueña (Institute of Puerto Rican Culture) took its place, encouraging a more international approach to art. During the 1960s the graphic art of Homar and other members of the Generation of 1950 reached its creative peak as a new generation of artists came of age. Younger artists such as **Myrna Báez** adopted more avant-garde styles while continuing to work with national themes. In the following decade active support of printmaking continued through the organization of biennial exhibitions, such as the successful Bienal de San Juan del Grabado Latinoamericano y del Caribe (San Juan Biennial of Latin American and Caribbean Engraving).

Although state-supported poster art in Cuba did not respond to specific stylistic and thematic guidelines, after the Cuban Revolution, **Fidel Castro**'s administration encouraged the development of poster making rather than mural painting, unlike the postrevolutionary governments in Mexico during the 1920s and Nicaragua in the 1980s. Millions of posters were designed between 1964 and the early 1970s in a rich variety of traditional and avant-garde styles. Important Cuban printmakers, such as Raúl Martínez, René Azcuy, and Alfredo J. González Rostgaard, synthesized eclectic international influences, including U.S. Pop Art and French and Polish poster designs, with traditional fine-art techniques, finding new ways of expressing cultural, social, and political content. Their silk-screen posters achieved a high degree of visual sophistication that has won international acclaim. The earlier posters were produced for the ICAIC (Instituto Cubano de Arte e Industria Cinematográficas; Cuban Institute of Cinematographic Art and Industry), which replaced the movie advertisements sent from abroad — considered too capitalistic — with more artistic and interpretative designs. The ICAIC posters had a great influence over later graphic art, such as the posters produced for **Casa de las Américas** and the OSPAAAL (Organization of Solidarity with the Peoples of Asia, Africa, and Latin America). The OSPAAAL posters circulated widely in the multilingual Cuban magazine *Tricontinental,* disseminating their antiimperialist messages throughout the Third World. Also, the Departamento de Orientación Revolucionaria (Department of Revolutionary Orientation) produced posters for educational and political campaigns during periods of crisis.

Until the late 1970s *vallas* (billboards) were another important form of graphic art. These mural-sized posters, created by artists such as René Mederos, were sometimes designed in series to be seen in sequence along a street or avenue, such as those on the Avenida de la Revolución, where Castro gave some of his public speeches. Serial vallas posters involved simplified images and text, often expressing revolutionary concepts. Although in the 1980s the revolutionary graphic art developed in Mexico, Puerto Rico, and Cuba saw a decline in quality, the tradition of printmaking with social and political content has received a remarkable infusion since the early 1970s through the work of important Chicano artists such as Carlos Cortéz Koyokikatl, Rupert García, Ester Hernández, and Malaquías Montoya.

REFERENCES:

Luis Camnitzer, *New Art of Cuba* (Austin: University of Texas Press, 1994);

Luis R. Cancel and others, *The Latin American Spirit: Art and Artists in the United States, 1920–1970* (New York: Bronx Museum of the Art/Abrams, 1988);

Judith Keller, *El Taller de Gráfica Popular: Block Prints and Lithographs by Artists of the TGP from the Archer M. Huntington Art Gallery* (Austin: Archer M. Huntington Art Gallery/University of Texas Press, 1985).

— F.B.N.

MARÍA GREVER

María Grever, née María Joaquina de la Portilla (1884?–1951) was born in León, Guanajuato, Mexico, but spent much of her youth in Spain, where her parents maintained a residence. Recognizing an unusual talent in their daughter, her parents arranged for her to study in Paris with the renowned composer Claude Debussy. On the death of her father, María returned with her mother to live in Mexico, fell in love, and married Leon Grever, a North American. The young couple left Mexico to live in New York City in 1922.

María Grever became a prominent composer of the early, romantic **canción mexicana**. By her own accounts, she began writing songs in her midteens, but the first recorded song, *Bésame* (Kiss Me), did not appear until 1924 — on the Victor label, sung by the tenor José Moriche. Two years later **José Mojica** inscribed María Grever's name in the history of Latin American song with his recording of the popular *Júrame* (Promise Me), a song he discovered in a warehouse. Other memorable songs by Grever, also recorded by Mojica, include *Cuando me vaya* (When I Leave), *Alma mía* (My Soul), and one of her most popular songs, *Cuando vuelva a tu lado* (When I Return to Your Side). Many other artists enhanced their popularity through recordings of subsequent Grever songs, such as *Tú, tú, y tú* (You, You, and You), *Brisas* (Breezes), *El gavilán* (The Sparrow Hawk), *Te quiero, dijiste* (I Love You, You Said), *Cobarde* (Coward), *Así* (Like This), *Despedida* (Dismissed), and many more.

Frank "Machito" Grillo, singer Graciela, and musical director Mario Bauzá, mid 1940s

Libertad Lamarque also recorded many of Grever's songs and played Grever's character in a movie about her life called *Cuando me vaya* (When I Leave). Two of Grever's most popular songs, *Tipitín* and *Alma mía*, were included in that film.

Following a paralyzing stroke in 1948, María Grever returned to Mexico to receive numerous medals and awards and to be honored in various festivities. In 1951 she returned to New York, only to die a few days later.

REFERENCES:

Cristóbal Díaz Ayala, *Música cubana del Areyto a la Nueva Trova*, second edition (San Juan: Editorial Cubanacán, 1981);

Hernán Restrepo Duque, *Lo que cuentan los boleros* (Bogotá: Centro Editorial de Estudios Musicales, 1992);

Jaime Rico Salazar, *Cien años de boleros* (Bogotá: Centro Editorial de Estudios Musicales, 1987).

— R.L.S.

FRANK "MACHITO" GRILLO

The surge of interest in **Afro-Caribbean music** in the United States during the 1940s was partially because of the immigration of many talented Latin American musicians. "Downtown" New York society bands typically included some Latino musicians to add authenticity to specialty numbers, in recognition of the public's growing interest in Latin music and dance. Uptown, in the Hispanic neighborhoods, small groups satisfied the de-

mands for authentic Afro-Caribbean music among the immigrant Hispanics.

In 1947 Frank Grillo (1908–1984) was the singer/**maracas** player of the most prominent Latin orchestra in New York City, an orchestra that had crossed ethnic lines and built a popular following among Latinos as well as the Anglo and Jewish populations. Known as "Machito and his Afrocubans," the band specialized in a hybrid music that combined elements of jazz with Afro-Cuban rhythms, a "fusion" style of music created largely by the band's musical director, Mario Bauzá, Grillo's brother-in-law. Bauzá had been in New York City since 1930, playing jazz with black swing groups such as Cab Calloway's band. Bauzá and Grillo agreed that they needed a permanent venue in which regularly scheduled Latino dances could be provided for the general public. They gained access to the Palladium on Broadway and Fifty-third Street, a large, formerly popular dance hall that no longer attracted audiences for the tango, fox-trot, and swing. They named their club the Blen Blen Club, envisaging a regular Sunday afternoon dance club that would exploit the name of a hit Latin/jazz composition (*Blen Blen*) by Chano Pozo, a Cuban musician in Dizzy Gillespie's orchestra. The first dance session drew an overflow crowd, and within a few weeks they were forced to schedule dances on Wednesday nights as well. Before the end of the first year the Palladium became exclusively dedicated for several nights a week to Afro-Caribbean musics from Cuba, Puerto Rico, and the Dominican Republic: **mambo, cha-cha-cha, bomba, plena,, merengue,** and the ever popular **bolero**. Two young Puerto Ricans had joined Machito and his Afrocubans earlier, to form the nucleus of the Blen Blen Club: **Tito Puente** (and The Picadilly Boys) and **Tito Rodríguez** and His Orchestra. The boom in Latin music at the Palladium lasted until the mid 1960s when the old ballroom was closed. Many of the big bands that had played there split into smaller ensembles that could be accommodated in the smaller clubs of the city, dance clubs that had been spawned by the success of the Palladium. Such was the destiny of Machito and his Afrocubans, the group that had served as the primary force in establishing a lasting presence of Latin music in New York. By then "Machito" had come to symbolize the 1940s revolution in U.S. Latin music.

REFERENCES:

Vernon W. Boggs, *Salsiology: Afro-Cuban Music and the Evolution of Salsa in New York City* (New York: Excelsior Music, 1992);

John Storm Roberts, *The Many Worlds of Music*, no. 3 (New York: Broadcast Music, 1976);

César Miguel Rondón, *El libro de la salsa: Crónica de la música del caribe urbano* (Caracas: Editorial Arte, 1980).

— R.L.S.

GRUPO RENOVACIÓN MUSICAL

The premature deaths of **Amadeo Roldán** in 1939 and **Alejandro García Caturla** in 1940 left a vacuum in the leadership of Cuban art music. **José Ardévol,** a close friend of Roldán and professor at the Conservatorio Municipal de la Habana, became the leader of a group of young composers known as the Grupo Renovación Musical (Group for Renovation in Music). Their work together began in 1942 as a series of seminars, in which great works of the past were studied, analyzed, discussed, and approached with rigorous discipline. Their efforts produced the new leaders of Cuban art music at midcentury, a group of composers who aspired to creating music capable of expressing universal values. Julián Orbón, Hilario González, Harold Gramatges, **Argeliers León**, Edgardo Martín, Serafín Pro, and Gisela Hernández formed the nucleus of what became a rather large group. All were, to some extent, influenced by the neoclassical orientation of their leader, José Ardévol; yet each one eventually developed his or her own path. The variety of directions taken individually may be seen in the examples of Orbón, González, and Gramatges.

Julián Orbón (1925–1991) immigrated to Cuba from his native Spain in 1940 following early studies with his father and at the Oviedo Conservatory. Honoring the Spanish classical tradition, he generally avoided the interest in and influence of the Afro-

Cubanism that had consumed the creative talents of many of his new compatriots. His progressive, neoclassical approach was expressed in multimovement orchestral works, piano sonatas, toccatas and preludes, chamber works, and choral pieces. Orbón moved to the United States in the 1960s.

Hilario González (1920–) responded to the surge of interest in Afro-Cuban resources in a distinctively individual manner. Avoiding the direct quotations of folk and popular genres that had become common in his time, he recognized the potential of musics on a higher level. He was capable of lyricism; yet, his harmonies tended to be dissonant. González spent several years in Venezuela teaching piano. He was also in charge of production at the Teatro Nacional Popular (National Popular Theater) in Caracas. Upon his return to Cuba in 1960 he taught piano at the Amadeo Roldán Conservatory and at the Seminary of Popular Music. Subsequently he worked on research at the National Museum of Music. In addition to publishing many works about music, his own compositions include genres such as the symphony, the concerto, ballet, piano works, songs for voice and piano, and symphonic songs.

Harold Gramatges (1918–) studied harmony, composition, aesthetics, and music history in the Municipal Conservatory of Havana with Amadeo Roldán, before joining Ardévol's Grupo Renovación Musical. In 1942 he attended the Berkshire Music Center in the United States, where he studied with Aaron Copland and Serge Koussevitzky. In 1945 he founded and conducted the Orchestra of the Municipal Conservatory of Havana. In 1958 he won the Reichold Prize, awarded by the Detroit Symphony Orchestra, for *Sinfonía en mi* (Symphony in E). During the decade of the 1950s he directed his principal attention to the foundation and direction of the Sociedad Cultural Nuestro Tiempo (Society for the Culture of Our Time), an organization that resisted the repressive policies of the Fulgencio Batista regime. After the success of the Cuban Revolution, he played a major role in reforming music education in Cuba and creating the National Symphony Orchestra. His early orientation as a composer was neoclassical, but after the revolution he incorporated elements of nationalism (see **nationalism in music**). His mature style has been eclectic, experimenting with an independent approach to serialism, microtonalism, and aleatory music. The genres encompassed by his works include the symphony, the concerto, chamber music, ballet, solo vocal, and choral music.

REFERENCES:

Leonardo Acosta, "Harold Gramatges y sus 'Móviles,'" in *Boletín de Música*, no. 106 (Havana: Casa de las Américas, 1985);

Gerard Béhague, *Music in Latin America: An Introduction* (Englewood Cliffs, N.J.: Prentice-Hall, 1979);

Juan Orrego Salas, "The Young Generation of Latin American Composers: Backgrounds and Perspectives," *Inter American Music Bulletin,* no. 38 (1963).

— R.L.S.

Crook, "A Musical Analysis of the Cuban Rumba," *Latin American Music Review*, 3 (Spring/Summer 1982): 92-123;

Helio Orovio, *Diccionario de la música cubana: Biográfico y técnico* (Havana: Editorial Letras Cubanas, 1992).

— R.L.S.

GUAGUANCÓ

In its late-nineteenth-century developmental stage, the **rumba** pertained exclusively to black populations of emerging urban neighborhoods. As such, the genre was viewed with scorn and disdain by upper-class whites. During the 1920s and 1930s, however, various types of rumba were extracted from their urban folk settings for stylized performances in clubs and second-class theaters. The guaguancó became the best-known and most popular, due in part to its lively, syncopated rhythmic structure, its textual relevance as a commentary on contemporary life, and the expansion of the musical resources employed in its instrumental accompaniment. No longer confined to accompaniments by **conga** drums and minor percussion instruments, the stylized guaguancó became the province of popular dance bands that catered to the growing tourism industry in Cuba. The coincidental development of the guaguancó with Cuban tourism and its assimilation of elements of the Cuban **son** into the genre led to its commercial development and exportation to Europe and the United States, and finally to its current prominent position in the repertoire of international orchestras and ensembles specializing in **salsa**.

Song texts of the guaguancó may be of serious or humorous tone and may narrate events of local interest, including romantic adventures. The formal structure of the guaguancó includes a brief introduction in which the principal melodic materials may be introduced. Following the introduction, the main body of solo song (canto) is presented. The song may be organized in modified strophic or nonstrophic verses, in rhymed couplets, prose, or in **décimas**. It may also include a choral refrain. The concluding call-and-response section features improvisation by the solo singer, punctuated by a choral refrain. The true art of the *rumbero* (solo singer) is revealed through his subtle expansion of melodic and rhythmic material presented in the canto.

REFERENCES:

Larry Crook, "The Form and Formation of the Rumba in Cuba," in *Salsiology: Afro-Cuban Music and the Evolution of Salsa in New York City,* by Vernon W. Boggs (New York: Excelsior Music, 1992);

GUAJIRA

The guajira is a picturesque Cuban folk-song genre that portrays idyllic values of rural life. Accompanied by guitar, **tres, güiro**, and claves (rhythm sticks), a solo singer improvises verses modeled after the **décima** (ten lines of octosyllabic verse), a poetic form that is also popular in folk music of the Dominican Republic and Puerto Rico. The solo verses may alternate with a communal refrain. In a modified form, guajiras may be performed by two singers in a simulated argument or humorous controversy (controversia). The rhythm of the guajira alternates between 3/4 and 6/8, while the harmonic/melodic mode changes from minor in the opening section to major in the second section. Although much music of the Hispanic Caribbean reveals the strong influence of African culture, the guajira and other similar genres closely follow the Spanish tradition.

REFERENCES:

Gerard Béhague, "Latin American Folk Music," in *Folk and Traditional Music of the Western Continents,* edited by Bruno Nettl (Englewood Cliffs, N.J.: Prentice Hall, 1990);

Argeliers León, "Notes toward a Panorama of Popular and Folk Musics," in *Essays on Cuban Music*, edited by Peter Manuel (Lanham, Md.: University Press of America, 1991).

— R.L.S.

GUARACHA

The guaracha is a song/dance genre of mixed Hispanic and African origin that developed in rural Cuba in the nineteenth century and later became popular in Cuban comic operas. Emerging from the theaters, guarachas became popular entertainments in urban street music. Originally consisting of a verse and refrain, the guaracha developed into the call-and-response format, featuring satirical lyrics. Syncopated rhythms in combined 2/4 and 6/8 meters and lively tempos are characteristic. The guaracha became a favorite genre among **salsa** bands in the mid twentieth century.

REFERENCES:

Alejo Carpentier, *La música en Cuba*, second edition (Mexico City: Fondo de Cultura Económica, 1972);

Argeliers León, "Notes toward a Panorama of Popular and Folk Musics," in *Essays on Cuban Music*, edited by Peter Manuel (Lanham, Md.: University Press of America, 1991).

— R.L.S.

GUATEMALAN WOMEN POETS

Ana María Rodas (1937–   ) represents a group of Guatemalan women poets of the 1970s who wrote resistance poetry condemning the oppression of military regimes as well as the machismo apparent not only in right-wing but also leftist political groups. Her books of poetry are *Poemas de la izquierda erótica* (1973; Poems of an Erotic Left), *Cuatro esquinas del juego de una muñeca* (1980; Four Corners in the Doll Set), and *El fin de los mitos y los sueños* (1984; The End of Myths and Dreams). For this last she won the Guatemalan National Poetry Prize. She belongs to the same generation as Alaída Foppa and Luz Méndez de la Vega.

Foppa, married to a Guatemalan politician, spent many years in exile with him in Mexico after the 1954 coup. There she became involved in feminist activities, especially the Guatemalan women's movement. Her poetry collections are *Elogio de mi cuerpo* (1970; Eulogy to My Body) and *Las palabras y el tiempo* (1979; Words and Time). After returning to Guatemala she was kidnapped and murdered by the Guatemalan death squads, becoming a martyr and a symbol of Guatemalan women's resistance.

Luz Méndez de la Vega is a journalist and director of the cultural supplement of *La Hora* (The Hour). Her poetry reflects cultural realities of different sectors of Guatemalan society and is also marked by a feminist perspective and a resistance to oppressive regimes. She has won six poetry prizes and has published nine collections of poetry. Among them are *Flor de varia poesía* (1978; A Flowering of Poetry), *Eva sin Dios* (1979; Eve without God), *De las palabras y la sombra* (1984; Of Words and Shadows), and *Las voces silenciadas* (1985; The Silenced Voices).

REFERENCES:

Zoe Anglesey, ed., *Ixoc Amar Go: Central American Women's Poetry for Peace* (Penobscot, Maine: Granite Press, 1987);

John Beverley and Marc Zimmerman, *Literature and Politics in the Central American Revolutions* (Austin: University of Texas Press, 1990).

— M.E.S.

ERNESTO "CHE" GUEVARA

Ernesto "Che" Guevara (1927–1967), born in Argentina and trained as a doctor, was closely identified with

Che Guevara and Fidel Castro, Havana, 1961 (photograph by Osvaldo Salas)

the Cuban Revolution and became internationally known in the 1960s. Guevara was traveling through Guatemala in 1954 when a right-wing military coup plotted by the CIA overthrew the nationalist government of Jacobo Arbenz, and the experience radicalized the young bourgeois physician. Guevara met **Fidel Castro** two years later in Mexico and helped him organize the Cuban Revolution.

In the early years of the Castro government Guevara was involved in economic planning. First he pushed for diversification to counter reliance on sugar exports. When this initiative failed, he proposed a strategy of moral incentives aimed at eradicating all vestiges of capitalism from the Cuban economy, doing away with material incentives for work and production. Guevara called for a "New Man," a socially conscious and self-sacrificing subject he described in a 1965 essay, "Socialism and Man in Cuba," originally published in *Granma*, the official organ of Castro's government. The New Man was to break with the capitalist conception of work by viewing labor as a social duty. Work would thus reflect the individual's humanity, and

135

Langston Hughes, Mikhail Koltzov, Ernest Hemingway, and Nicolás Guillén in Madrid, 1937

it would no longer be performed out of need. Volunteerism was an integral part of Guevara's vision, and after 1966, when Castro endorsed the moral-incentive approach to economic production, Cubans were mobilized on a massive scale to undertake various projects — especially Castro's goal of harvesting ten million tons of sugar by 1970.

Another aspect of Guevara's thought that characterized the Cuban Revolution was "Proletarian Internationalism," which insisted that the true revolutionary could not rest after local affairs were improved; rather he must strive on a global scale to thwart the enemies of revolution. In the 1960s revolutionaries from all over the world came to Cuba for training in guerrilla warfare, and Guevara took the revolutionary torch abroad. In October 1967 he was captured in Bolivia by counterinsurgency troops and executed. Guevara's revolutionary idealism defined a decade in the West, and the handsome face of the martyred *guerrillero* appeared on thousands of posters, placards, and T-shirts in the massive student demonstrations of 1968 in Paris, Mexico City, and the United States.

REFERENCE:

Andrew Sinclair, *Guevara* (London: Fontana, 1970).

— R.G.M.

NICOLÁS GUILLÉN

Nicolás Guillén was born in Camagüey, Cuba, in 1902. A mulatto raised within the society of the black middle class in Cuba, Guillén embodied the cultural blend of African and Spanish elements that characterizes his poetry. In his early years as a writer, Guillén showed a preference for the **Modernista** literary style that **José Martí,** the nineteenth-century Cuban nationalist and intellectual, had first popularized. Much like Martí's, Guillén's first poems focused on historical and social issues of his country. He was concerned with exploring the possibility of writing a uniquely Cuban poetry, one that would necessarily incorporate both the Spanish and the African cultures that flourished on the island. His idea of a national literature that would transcend race and class was a foretaste of the Marxist ideal adopted by **Fidel Castro** in his plan to lead a country that was not divided by race or social standing. In 1930 Guillén met the Spanish playwright Federico García Lorca, who was a decisive influence on his poetry. Later Guillén traveled to Europe, and, like his fellow Spanish American poets César Vallejo and Pablo Neruda, he espoused the Republican cause in the Spanish Civil War. Both Lorca and the Spanish Civil War inspired one of his books of poetry, *España*

(Spain), published in 1937, the year in which Guillén joined the Communist Party. Guillén became actively involved in Cuban politics, both before and after Castro's rise to power. During the 1950s he was a participant in activities against the Fulgencio Batista government, which led to his exile from Cuba. Guillén spent six years outside Cuba in Chile, France, and Argentina. When he returned in 1961 after the revolution, he was named poet laureate. He also helped form the National Union of Cuban Writers and Artists.

The greater part of Guillén's poetry expresses his political concerns while also revealing the mixture of African and Spanish cultures in Cuba. This synthesis of such diverse elements came to be known as Afro-Cuban literature. The most original element found in Guillén's collections of poems is the **son,** based on African music. Another musical element is insistent rhythm with strong, repetitive accents that create a drumlike beat. In addition to the African musicality of the poems, Guillén's poetry features peculiarities of the Afro-Cuban dialect. Nicolás Guillén addressed racial issues on a thematic level in his poetry, reinforcing his message of hope for a truly integrated Cuban culture by employing musical and literary elements from his Spanish and African heritage. His poetry collections are: *Motivos de son* (1930; translated as *Son Motifs*), *Sóngoro Cosongo: Poemas mulatos* (1931; Sóngoro Cosongo: Mulatto Poems), *West Indies, Ltd.: Poemas* (1934), *Cantos para soldados y sones para turistas* (1937; Songs for Soldiers and Sones for Tourists), *España: Poema en cuatro angustias y una esperanza* (1937; Spain: A Poem in Four Anguishes and One Hope), *Cuba Libre: Poems by Nicolás Guillén* (1948), *La paloma de vuelo popular: Elegías* (1948; The Dove of Popular Flight: Elegies), *Elegía a Jesús Menéndez* (1951; Elegy for Jesús Menéndez), *Elegía cubana* (1952; Cuban Elegy), *Buenos días, Fidel* (1959; Good Morning, Fidel), *Poemas de amor* (1964; Love Poems), *Tengo* (1964; translated as *I Have*), *Che Comandante* (1967), *Cuatro canciones para el Che* (1969; Four Songs for Che), *El gran zoo* (1967; The Great Zoo), *El diario que a diario* (1972; translated as *The Daily Daily*), *La rueda dentada* (1972; The Spiked Wheel), *El corazón con que vivo* (1975; The Heart with Which I Live), *Poemas manuables* (1975; Handy Poems), *Por el mar de las Antillas anda un barco de papel* (1977; A Paper Boat Floats Across the Antillean Sea), and *Sol de domingo* (1982; Sunday Sun). Some of his work was published in English translation in *Man-making Words: Selected Poems of Nicolás Guillén* (1972) and *¡Patria o muerte! The Great Zoo and Other Poems by Nicolás Guillén* (1972). (See also **Négritude**.)

REFERENCES:

Keith Ellis, *Cuba's Nicolás Guillén: Poetry and Ideology* (Buffalo: University of Toronto Press, 1983);

Ian Isidore Smart, *Nicolás Guillén: Popular Poet of the Caribbean* (Columbia: The Curators of the University of Missouri, 1990);

Lorna V. Williams, *Self and Society in the Poetry of Nicolás Guillén* (Baltimore: Johns Hopkins University Press, 1982).

— D.H.& P.S.

OLGA GUILLOT

Olga Guillot (1922–), one of the most popular Latin American singers, was born in Santiago, Cuba, but moved to Havana at an early age. As children she and her sister appeared on radio programs as a popular duo. Later she performed in Isolina Carrillo's quartet, Siboney, with another future Cuban star, **Celia Cruz,** the "Queen of Salsa." Guillot's recording career began with the first Cuban recording company, Ramón Sabat's Panart label. Her first recording was "Melodía gris" (the U.S. song known as "Stormy Weather"; in other contexts its title is given as "Lluvia gris"), and there followed contracts with the famous Zombie Club and other upscale theaters in Havana. In 1946 she proceeded to New York, to record for Decca. Two years later she made her first film in Mexico, *La Venus de fuego*. Following concert tours to Puerto Rico and the Dominican Republic in 1951, she was voted "Queen of the Radio." The following year she embarked on a South American tour to Colombia, Chile, Argentina, Brazil, Peru, and Venezuela.

In 1952, with 78 rpm recordings becoming obsolete, Panart Records decided to produce a recording of Guillot with a full orchestra, Los Hermanos Castro. The first release was a 45 rpm with "Miénteme" on side A and "Estamos en paz" on side B. The success was far greater than anyone could have imagined; the recording industry in Cuba had been revolutionized. In 1954 she recorded "Palabras calladas" and "Vivir de los recuerdos"—both became huge hits. Guillot had become the "Queen of Popular Song"; in 1954, 1955, and 1956 she was acclaimed the best popular singer in Cuba.

As a result of rumors regarding comments she had made while outside Cuba about **Fidel Castro,** her home was invaded and all of her recordings were burned. In 1961 she established her home in Caracas and distanced herself from her professional career for a time. An invitation from Mexico to renew her career drew her back into the limelight, and tours abroad followed. In 1963 she was awarded the Golden Palm by the John F. Kennedy Academy of Arts, and the following year she sold out Carnegie Hall in New York. In the mid 1960s she had spectacular successes in Spain. In 1988 she performed in the Dominican Republic in the celebration of one hundred years of the **bolero** and also celebrated her own fifty years of performing boleros.

During her career Guillot acted in sixteen films and as a principal in the soap opera *Un color para esta piel,* but her crowning achievement remains the more than fifty LP albums that preserve her inimitable style.

REFERENCES:

Cristóbal Díaz Ayala, *Música cubana del Areyto a la Nueva Trova,* second edition (San Juan: Editorial Cubanacán, 1981);

Hernán Restrepo Duque, *Lo que cuentan los boleros* (Santafé de Bogotá: Centro Editorial de Estudios Musicales, 1992);

Jaime Rico Salazar, *Cien años de boleros* (Bogotá: Centro Editorial de Estudios Musicales, 1987).

— R.L.S.

GÜIRO

The güiro is one of few pre-Columbian instruments that remain in use in folk, popular, and commercial Latin American musics, especially in the Caribbean. It is a gourd with parallel grooves cut horizontally on one side, and it is employed as a scraper instrument. Its function is to provide a distinctive rhythmic pattern with an individual timbre. To construct a güiro, the seeds and fiber inside the gourd must be removed and the lines cut when the gourd is still fresh and green. Once dried, the shell is hard and brittle, producing a resonant sound that fits well with the sonority of the guitar and other string instruments.

The gourd güiro does not project well within large ensembles that include brass and electric instruments. The güira is a variant developed in the Dominican Republic to project a more formidable sound in larger ensembles. The güira is made of a small sheet of tin with many holes punched in it. The tin sheet is then shaped into a cylinder and soldered closed with the flared side of the holes on the outside. The Dominican güira and the **tambora** are among the principal instruments that provide the distinctive rhythm of the **merengue**.

Both the güiro and the güira are scraped with an accessory consisting of a wooden handle with six or more metal tines embedded in one end. Thin bicycle spokes are commonly used for the tines.

— R.L.S.

GUITARRA DE GOLPE

A principal instrument of the **mariachi** ensemble, this five-string member of the guitar family fulfills a rhyth-

mic and harmonic function similar to that of the **vihuela**. Both instruments provide chordal accompaniments that accentuate underlying rhythmic patterns — hence the loosely translated name, "strummed guitar." Smaller than the acoustic guitar and pitched higher, the open strings of the guitarra de golpe are tuned in descending order from the first: D–A–E–C–G.

— R.L.S.

GUITARRÓN

The large bass guitar of the **mariachi** ensemble, the guitarrón, came into existence in Mexico to accommodate the ambulatory nature of mariachi performance practice: its predecessor in the ensemble, the harp, was awkward as a portable instrument, requiring one person to carry it while another played it.

The oversized body of the guitarrón, deepened by a convex back, projects a clear and authoritative bass sound that provides a foundation for the harmony and an active rhythmic role. The modern guitarrón has six strings that permit the bass line to be played in octaves, rather than in single notes as in the European double bass instrument. Playing in octaves considerably increases the dynamic level of the instrument. Whereas the **vihuela** and the **guitarra de golpe** are played in a vigorous strumming fashion, the guitarrón strings are plucked, adding a sharp, percussive dimension to its sound. The three highest strings are made of nylon, but the three lower bass strings are made of metal wound around a core string. The high tension of the strings requires considerable strength in the fingers of the left hand. The short neck of the instrument provides a range of only two octaves, which is adequate for the requirements of the bass part.

REFERENCE:

David Kilpatrick, *El Mariachi: Traditional Music of Mexico,* volume 1 (Pico Rivera, Cal.: Fiesta Publications, 1988).

— R.L.S.

TOMÁS GUTIÉRREZ ALEA

Born in the late 1930s, Tomás Gutiérrez Alea is the best-known Cuban director. On their return from film study at the Centro Sperimentale di Cinematografia (Center for Experimental Cinematography) at the University of Rome, Titón, as he is familiarly called, and fellow student **Julio García Espinosa** collaborated on a medium-length, documentary-style feature called *El mégano* (1955; The Charcoal Worker), a brutally honest view of the exploitation of the working classes, which was seen as subversive and therefore suppressed by the Batista regime. (See also **Neorealism in Motion Pictures.**) Since Fulgencio Batista's overthrow and the founding of the Instituto Cubano de Arte e Industria Cinematográficas (**Cuban Film Institute**), or ICAIC, in 1959, Gutiérrez Alea has made many documentaries and ten feature films.

His most acclaimed movie is *Memorias del subdesarrollo* (1968; Memories of Underdevelopment), in which the first-rate actor Sergio Corrieri plays a starring role. *Memorias del subdesarrollo* focuses on the life of Sergio, who is rich, good-looking, and intelligent and has access to the upper social strata and to beautiful women who are willing to go to bed with him. The movie is critical of the bourgeois mentality that continues to exist in Cuba despite the many changes that occurred as a result of the revolution. According to Gutiérrez Alea the movie is revolutionary because it forces the audience dialectically to reassess their assumptions. Far from serving any obvious agitprop function, *Memorias del subdesarrollo* chronicles the spiritual displacement of a bourgeois intellectual within the postrevolutionary Cuban culture, doing so with a cinematic sophistication and emotional detachment that place it within the mainstream of modern world cinema. Gutiérrez Alea puts himself in the film, as well as some important revolutionary intellectuals, including Edmundo Desnoes, whose novel of the same title (1965; translated as *Inconsolable Memories*) served as a basis for the screenplay. The movie was extremely popular in Cuba and abroad; some Cubans went to see it as many as five times.

In 1971 Gutiérrez Alea filmed *Una pelea contra los demonios* (A Cuban Struggle Against the Demons), one of his least seen and most experimental works. Based on **Fernando Ortiz Fernández**'s account of a case of religious fanaticism in 1672, *Una pelea contra los demonios* reaches further back in history than any other Cuban film. Shuttling between the past and the present, it includes juxtapositions such as historical scenes of a shaman speaking in a trance off screen while the viewer sees black-and-white photographs of **José Martí**, **Che Guevara,** and **Fidel Castro.**

Gutiérrez Alea's *La muerte de un burócrata* (1966; The Death of a Bureaucrat) addresses in a playful and comic way the risks of bureaucratization in the socialist society of Cuba. *La última cena* (1977; The Last Supper), with a linear plot based on a simple anecdote from the Cuban slave era, was the first feature film for which Gutiérrez Alea used color. The director of photography, Mario García Joya, had a major part in determining how color would be used and drew much praise for the atmospheric supper sequence. Gutiérrez Alea's *Cartas del parque* (1988; Letters from

Sergio Corrieri in Tomás Gutiérrez Alea's *Memorias del subdesarrollo* (1968; Memories of Underdevelopment)

the Park), based on Gabriel García Márquez's *El amor en los tiempos del cólera* (1985; translated as *Love in the Time of Cholera*) is delicately sensual. His *Fresa y chocolate* (1993; Strawberry and Chocolate) focuses on homosexuality in modern-day Cuba. It received excellent reviews in Cuba, the United States, and Europe. In 1982 Gutiérrez Alea published *Dialéctica del espectador* (The Dialectics of Spectatorship), a collection of theoretical essays reflecting on his experience in and approach to filmmaking.

REFERENCES:

Julianne Burton, *Cinema and Social Change in Latin America: Conversations with Filmmakers* (Austin: University of Texas Press, 1986);

John King, *Magical Reels: A History of Cinema in Latin America* (London: Verso, 1990).

— S.M.H.

MARTÍN LUIS GUZMÁN

One of the most important writers of the **Mexican Revolution,** Martín Luis Guzmán (1887–1976) was born in Chihuahua and later moved to Mexico City to study law. He became a member of the "Generation of the Athenaeum of Youth," a group of young writers who were reacting against the positivist way of thinking that was dominant in Mexico at the beginning of the twentieth century. Guzmán abandoned his university studies to fight in the Mexican Revolution. He served as a journalist for various generals; the final and most famous was Francisco "Pancho" Villa, under whom he became a colonel. He fled into exile in 1914 and remained abroad for twenty years in Havana, New York, and Madrid, during which time he directed and wrote for various newspapers. Besides his career as a journalist, Guzmán wrote numerous essays, chronicles, novels, and memoirs.

His reputation as a novelist became established with the publication of his most popular work, *El águila y la serpiente* (1928; translated as *The Eagle and the Serpent*). The title alludes to the national emblem, and the novel describes the chaotic years of the Mexican Revolution. Written in first person, it narrates his adventures as a participant in the revolution and describes his meetings and interactions with famous leaders. Guzmán's journalistic style is evident in his prose, which is concise and vivid, and in his accomplished use of dialogue. Through his descriptions and psychological portrayals of various historical figures, Guzmán captures the drama of the Mexican Revolution.

His second most important novel is *La sombra del caudillo* (1929; The Shadow of the Caudillo), a pessimistic work representing the aftermath of the Mexican Revolution, when a popular leader assumes the presidency. This period is depicted as full of corruption and abuses by the authorities who come to power. *La sombra del caudillo* is considered one of the best Latin American political novels. Guzmán's novels are laden with historical characters, the most noteworthy being Pancho Villa. Guzmán dedicates four volumes of fictitious memoirs to him in *Memorias de Pancho Villa* (1938–1940; Memoirs of Pancho Villa), and in them he uses a first-person narrator who pretends to be Villa recounting his life. Although contrived, these "memoirs" were quite well-received in Mexico.

REFERENCE:

Larry M. Grimes, *The Revolutionary Cycle in the Literary Production of Martín Luis Guzmán* (Cuernavaca: Centro Intercultural de Documentación, 1969).

— M.E.S.

H

HABANERA

Although infrequently performed these days, the habanera occupies an important historical position in Latin American music. It was a precursor of the Argentinean tango and the Cuban **danzón,** from which the **mambo** and the **cha-cha-cha** were derived. The habanera was itself derived from Cuban Creole dances. It has survived in Caribbean musical cultures more as a song form than as a dance. Its distinguishing features include a lyrical melody in 2/4 meter, accompanied by a relaxed dotted rhythmic figure. The habanera rhythm probably originated in Spain and has been attractive to European composers such as Isaac Albéniz, Esprit Auber, Emmanuel Chabrier, Manuel de Falla, and Maurice Ravel.

REFERENCE:

John Storm Roberts, "The Latin Dimension," in *The Many Worlds of Music* (New York: Broadcast Music, 1976).

— R.L.S.

RODOLFO HALFFTER

Both Rodolfo Halffter and his brother Ernesto are noted musical figures who were born in Spain (in 1900 and 1905, respectively). Both escaped from Spain toward the end of the Spanish Civil War. Ernesto left Spain for Portugal, later to return and establish and conduct a chamber orchestra in Seville. His compositional influence was eventually felt in the Americas, in the music of Cuba's Julián Orbón. Rodolfo, however, fled on foot to France and continued on to Mexico. As a composer, Rodolfo Halffter was basically self-taught, though he benefited from advice and informal training from one of Spain's foremost twentieth-century composers, Manuel de Falla (1876–1946). He also worked as a journalist with two of Madrid's daily newspapers, *El Sol* and *La Voz.*

Rodolfo Halffter's early works, premiered in Spain, reflect the neoclassical influence of de Falla and mark the first of two phases in his compositional career. Among those early works are the *Suite para orquesta* (which had its premiere in 1930 by the Orquesta Clásica de Madrid); *Impromptu para orquesta* (1932, by the Orquesta Sinfónica de Madrid); the suite from the ballet *Don Lindo de Almería* (1936, Festival of Barcelona); and *Obertura concertante para piano y orquesta* (1937, by the Orquesta Sinfónica de Valencia; later [1941] performed at the International Society of Contemporary Music in New York).

After establishing his residence in Mexico in 1939 (a year later he took Mexican citizenship), Rodolfo Halffter was named professor of composition at the National Conservatory of Music. In addition to founding the Mexican ballet group La Paloma Azul, he became editor of the journal *Nuestra Música,* a contributor to the newspaper *El Universal Gráfico,* and manager of Ediciones Mexicanas de Música (a music publisher).

Musical works of his Mexican period include the choreographed premieres of the ballets *Don Lindo de Almería* (at the Teatro Fábrigas in Mexico City, 1940), *La madrugada del panadero* (1940), and *Elena la traicionera* (1945). Orchestral works of the period include the suite from the ballet *La madrugada del panadero* (1948), the *Obertura festiva* (1953), and *Tres piezas para orquesta de cuerda* (Three Pieces for String Orchestra, 1955). His outstanding *Concerto para violín y orquesta* was given its premiere by the Symphony Orchestra of Mexico, with Samuel Dushkin as soloist, in 1942. He also composed various works for chamber ensembles, chorus, and piano. In later works, such as the Three Pieces for String Orchestra and the Third Piano Sonata, Halffter approaches the twelve-tone method of composition, but he does not strictly observe the basic processes of that method.

Juan Carlos Tablo and Serafín Quiñones in Tomás Gutiérrez Alea's *Hasta cierto punto* (1983; Up to a Point)

Rodolfo Halffter was an active leader as general secretary of the Mexican section of the International Society for Contemporary Music, as president of the **Manuel Ponce** Musical Association, and in directing the concert program of the Instituto Nacional de Bellas Artes (National Institute for Fine Arts).

REFERENCES:

Gerard Béhague, *Music in Latin America: An Introduction* (Englewood Cliffs, N.J.: Prentice-Hall, 1979);

"Rodolfo Halffter," in *Composers of the Americas: Biographical Data and Catalogs of their Works*, volume 2 (Washington, D.C.: Music Section, Department of Cultural Affairs, Pan American Union, 1956).

— R.L.S.

HASTA CIERTO PUNTO

Hasta cierto punto (1983; Up to a Point), directed by **Tomás Gutiérrez Alea,** is a Cuban film that deals with the filming of a script about machismo in the Havana dockyards. Shooting of the actual movie began with a provisional script, a blueprint. The film opens with videotapes of dockworkers discussing machismo while the movie director Arturo (Omar Valdés) tells Oscar (Oscar Alvarez), a playwright, how the script should be written. Arturo's artistic aims are pushed aside after Oscar becomes infatuated with Lina (Mirta Ibarra), an angry female worker, and asks her to be the model for his female protagonist. The project falls through after Arturo and Oscar become incapable of facing the discrepancies between reality and their preconceived notions. After the movie was released there was a structural reorganization within the **Cuban Film Institute,** which took the emphasis away from the individual director and moved it toward greater participation in authorship by the cast.

REFERENCES:

Latin American Cinema: Le Cinéma Latino-Américain, special issue of *Iris: Revue de Théorie de l'Image et du Son. A Journal of Theory on Image and Sound,* no. 13 (Summer 1991);

Zuzana M. Pick, *The New Latin American Cinema: A Continental Project* (Austin: University of Texas Press, 1993).

— S.M.H.

LUISA JOSEFINA HERNÁNDEZ

Born in Mexico City, Luisa Josefina Hernández (1928–) demonstrated a dedication to learning at an early age. She read the works in her father's library and became interested in literature and the arts. At the National Autonomous University of Mexico (UNAM) she enrolled in the faculty of philosophy and letters to study literature and theater. She studied under **Rodolfo Usigli** and later became a faculty member at the

UNAM, where she taught for more than thirty years. Considered one of Mexico's most important women writers, she has been quite firm in correcting the assumption that she is a feminist. She believes that success has to do with individual effort regardless of gender and that both men and women suffer from the effects of machismo. Although she wrote thirteen novels, she is best known for her dramas, which number more than thirty. Her first play, which she wrote and published at age twenty-two, is *El ambiente jurídico* (1950; Judicial Surroundings), a one-act drama about two female law students and their attempts to enter the male-dominated field. Many of Hernández's plays are about women struggling to understand their sexuality and relationships, primarily with men, and about their will or lack of will to overcome obstacles. Other plays that deal with these themes in some form were given their premieres one after another: *Aguardiente de caña* (1950; Sugar-Cane Liquor), *Los sordomudos* (1953; The Deaf-Mutes), *Botica modelo* (1954; A Model Pharmacy), *Los frutos caídos* (1957; The Fallen Fruit), *La hija del rey* (1959; The King's Daughter), and *Los huéspedes reales* (1959; The Real — or Royal — Guests). Among the plays focusing on the theme of social justice are *La paz ficticia* (1960; The Fictitious Peace), which describes the brutal massacres of the Yaqui people during the regime of Porfirio Díaz, *Historia de un anillo* (1961; The History of a Ring), and *La fiesta del mulato* (1966; translated as *The Mulatto's Orgy*). Her novel *La primera batalla* (1965; The First Battle) describes the betrayal of the ideals of the **Mexican Revolution,** which is compared unfavorably to the Cuban Revolution. The theme of mysticism is found in the farcical drama *Los duendes* (1960; The Elves) and in her novels *Los trovadores* (1973; The Troubadours), *Apostasía* (1978; Apostasy), *Las fuentes ocultas* (1980; The Hidden Fountains), and *Apocalipsis cum figuris* (1982; Apocalypse *cum figuris*). Hernández's literature has been described as one of anger in which the characters are motivated by moral indignation. In her plays, the ability to present ideological constructs of Mexican history through dramatization masks complex psychological underpinnings and avoids making direct statements. While her plays have been well received in Mexico, her novels for the most part have not been favorably reviewed.

REFERENCE:

María Elena Valdés, "Luisa Josefina Hernández," in *Spanish American Women Writers,* edited by Diane E. Marting (Westport, Conn.: Greenwood Press, 1990).

            — M.E.S.

Rafael Hernández

Puerto Rico's most celebrated twentieth-century composer and preeminent musical figure, Rafael Hernández, was born to a humble black family in Aguadilla at the end of the nineteenth century (the year of his birth is uncertain for he did not wish to disclose it; the years 1889, 1890, 1891, and 1896 have all been given). His death from cancer in 1965 was mourned by millions throughout the Caribbean basin, Mexico, and the United States.

Affectionately known as "El Jibarito" (a reference to his rural beginnings), Hernández began to play the trombone at an early age, eventually progressing to the violin, guitar, banjo, and cornet. His first composition, the waltz *Miprovisa*, earned him $1.25 and popularity while still a teenager, but his mature career, beginning in the 1920s, made him one of Latin America's most admired composers. He played the trombone and the baritone horn in the municipal band and at the elegant Tapai Theatre in San Juan until he went to New York, just prior to the outbreak of World War I. As a member of the U.S. Expeditionary Forces, he was sent to France and Germany as a military bandsman.

After the war Hernández joined a band that played in the southern United States, but he soon returned to New York, where in 1920 he accepted an invitation to go to Havana as director of the Teatro Fausto Orchestra. After five years in Cuba, Hernández returned to New York, where he organized the Trío Borinquen (*Borinquen* was the Taino Indian name for Puerto Rico). He played guitar in the trio and composed most of their repertoire. Experts identify this ensemble as one of the earliest examples of the trios of voices and guitars that eventually dominated the recording market in Latin America. Later, at the request of the Columbia recording company, the Trío Borinquen became known as the Trío Quisqueya in order to exploit the market in the Dominican Republic (*Quisqueya* was the Taino name for the island of Hispaniola). Hernández's successes with recordings and personal appearances with the trio led him to begin a new recording label with his sister Victoria. The failure of their bank in New York during the Great Depression ended this entrepreneurial venture in 1931.

Hernández's popularity was in part because of his recordings, but he also traveled often to make personal appearances in New York, Puerto Rico, Cuba, the Dominican Republic, and Mexico, where he married María Pérez, a Mexican citizen, and established his residence for approximately twelve years. In Mexico, although he was already an international musical celebrity, he studied at the National Conservatory with **Julián Carrillo,** among others. Leaving Mexico in 1947, Hernández returned to Puerto Rico and founded an orchestra that specialized in light and semiclassical music. When the orchestra eventually disbanded, Hernández was appointed music adviser to the

Puerto Rican government's radio station. During the last years of his life, he was honored on numerous occasions for his contributions to Latin American music. In 1961 he was invited to the **Pablo Casals** concert at the White House, along with Gov. Luis Muñoz Marín of Puerto Rico and Jesús María Sanromá, a concert pianist and former staff pianist of the Boston Symphony. (President John F. Kennedy greeted Hernández with a reference to one of his most popular works: "Hello, Mr. Cumbanchero!") In 1963 Hernández appeared at the Teatro Puerto Rico in the Bronx with Libertad Lamarque, the great Argentinean singer and movie star. He was subsequently honored by the Legislative Assembly of Puerto Rico; special television programs were dedicated to his music; and recorded albums of his music were produced, featuring Puerto Rico's most outstanding performers. A Rafael Hernández Festival instituted in 1967 is held annually in New York.

Hernández composed more than a thousand, some say closer to two thousand, works. Many of them are still favorites throughout Latin America. Among the best-known popular songs are *Preciosa*, *Lamento borincano*, *Capullito de alelí*, *El cumbanchero*, *Silencio*, *Los carreteros*, *Campanitas de cristal*, and *Perfume de gardenia*. Hernández was also active in the composition of theatrical and concert music: the musical play *Día de Reyes* (Feast of the Magi), *Amarga Navidad* (Bitter Christmas), *Cofresí* (the nineteenth-century pirate), and lesser-known piano, chamber, and orchestral works.

REFERENCES:

Peter Block, *LA-LE-LO-LAI: Puerto Rican Music and Its Performers* (New York: Plus Ultra Educational Publishers, 1973);

Pablo Marcial Ortíz Ramos, *A tres voces y guitarras: Los tríos en Puerto Rico* (Santo Domingo: Editora Corripio, 1991);

Jaime Rico Salazar, *Cien años de boleros* (Bogotá: Centro Editorial de Estudios Musicales, 1987).

—R.L.S.

LUIS HERNÁNDEZ CRUZ

The painter and sculptor Luis Hernández Cruz (1936–) is one of the earliest and most influential abstract artists in Puerto Rico (see **Abstract Art**). He studied art both on the island and in the United States and was later director of the fine arts section at the Ateneo Puertorriqueño and a professor of art at the Universidad de Puerto Rico. Hernández Cruz's early works, produced during the late 1950s, consisted of postcubist representations of figures involved in everyday activities. He later concentrated on urban landscapes, in which he progressively eliminated details as he simplified forms. Some of these works emphasize the use of expressive brush strokes and heavy impastos, while others transform elements of nature into

simplified geometric shapes that eventually give way to completely abstract works. In 1961 he exhibited abstract pieces in the Sala de Exposiciones at the Instituto de Cultura Puertorriqueña, drawing strong criticism from those who equated abstraction with United States cultural colonialism; but like other Puerto Rican artists who came of age during the 1960s, Hernández Cruz strove to expand the nature of politically engaged art beyond the confines of figuration.

In the mid 1960s Hernández Cruz's work became closer to Geometric Abstraction and Minimalism. He experimented with two-dimensional and three-dimensional geometric modules installed in an environment, an approach that in Puerto Rico was called Arte Estructural (Structural Art). In pieces such as *Cámara de tortura* (1967; Torture Chamber), Hernández Cruz's geometric modules alluded to political issues through the symbolic use of dark funereal colors and surfaces with large nails pointing toward the viewer. Soon his art began to approximate Op Art and Kinetic Art, as he included superimposed metal lattices that produced color interactions and moiré effects.

By the end of the 1960s Hernández Cruz's painting turned toward Informal Abstraction, working with lightly textured areas of color and subtle allusions to the landscape, as can be seen in *Paisaje marino* (1970; Seascape). Hernández Cruz also reintroduced the human figure into his art, combining an abstract conception of the figure with a textural treatment of the surface, something that connects his work to neofiguration. In *Figura mecanizada* (1982; Mechanized Figure) the human figure becomes simply a silhouette immersed in a series of abstract shapes with similar earth tones and uneven textures. During this period Hernández Cruz further developed his work with sculpture, creating forms that resemble his informal abstract paintings. For instance, in his wood relief *El navegante I* (1982; The Navigator I) he fragments a square block into a variety of geometric and organic shapes that are later reassembled like the pieces of a puzzle. This interlocking of abstract forms can also be seen in many of Hernández Cruz's paintings, such as *Sombra arqueológica VII* (1982; Archaeological Shadow VII).

REFERENCE:

Manuel Pérez-Lizano, *Arte contemporáneo de Puerto Rico 1950–1983: Cerámica, escultura, pintura* (Puerto Rico: Universidad Central de Bayamón, Ediciones Cruz Ansata, 1985).

—F.B.N.

SATURNINO HERRÁN

Mexican painter and draftsman Saturnino Herrán (1887–1931) was one of the first artists to embrace

Indigenism and portray indigenous themes in the style of **Symbolist art.** His paintings espoused neither the radicalism nor the didacticism of the mature works of **Diego Rivera.** Herrán studied art at the Academia de San Carlos and was inspired by the indigenist interests of one of his teachers. He undertook the difficult task of visually portraying the native heritage of his country during the dictatorship of Porfirio Díaz, but he was also influenced by Díaz's attempt to Europeanize the culture of Mexico. Better known as a printer, draftsman, and illustrator during his lifetime, Herrán produced cover illustrations intermittently throughout his career for publications such as *El Universal Ilustrado* (The Illustrated Universal). He was first employed as a draftsman in 1907 by the government's Inspección de Monumentos Arqueológicos (Archaeological Monuments Inspection Service). In that same year he was commissioned by the Museo Nacional to copy Teotihuacán frescoes, a commission that enhanced his interest in pre-Columbian cultures.

In 1910 Herrán was hired to teach drawing at the Escuela Normal de Maestros (Teacher Training School), where the celebrations, dramas, and ways of life unique to Mexico were his primary themes. To indigenous subjects and popular genre scenes Herrán brought the stylized realism, lyricism, and classically structured compositions typical of Symbolist Art. His treatment of form, his delicate brushwork, and his romantic sense of color are comparable to those of the Ecuadoran painter Camilo Egas, who, like Herrán, was influenced by the figural style of the Spanish painter Ignacio Zuloaga. *Nuestros dioses* (1918; Our Gods), conceived as part of a decorative frieze for the new Teatro Nacional building, depicts an Aztec ritual of reverence and sacrifice. Herrán's work is not documentary but rather a Europeanized representation of Aztec life as the golden age of Mexico. The languidness of the Indians made them palatable to the French-oriented public of Porfirio Díaz's day. Herrán was acquainted with the great poets of his era, who provided another source of symbolist and indigenist ideals; his work often paralleled that of a close friend, the poet **Ramón López Velarde.** *Nuestros dioses* and *La viejecita* (1917; The Little Old Woman), for example, have thematic counterparts in López Velarde's poetry. The symbolist style of Herrán's paintings has also been viewed in terms of traditional gender role reversal. Male figures were often sensuously rendered, while female figures often embodied intellectual and psychological strength.

REFERENCE:

José Fuentes Salinas, "Saturnino Herrán: The Ephemeral and the Grandiose," *Voices of Mexico,* 6 (December 1987–February 1988): 58–59.

— C.M.

Lorenzo Homar

Lorenzo Homar (1913–), a member of the Generation of 1950, was instrumental in the development of **graphic art** in his native Puerto Rico. After his family moved to New York in 1928, Homar worked as an acrobat and studied at the Art Students' League and at the Pratt Graphic Art Center. He also learned jewelry design at Cartier, where he returned to work after fighting in World War II. In 1950 Homar settled in Puerto Rico and participated in a graphic-art workshop called Estudio 17. With José Antonio Torres Martinó, Félix Rodríguez Báez, and Rafael Tufiño, Homar cofounded the Centro de Arte Puertorriqueño. Their objective was to support graphic art, to work collectively, and to reach a broad popular audience through their print portfolios and posters advertising cultural events and giving artistic information. Homar and other members of the Generation of 1950 rejected avant-garde styles, worked with figuration, and depicted national themes as a way of opposing United States cultural colonialism, an approach that links their **Costumbrismo** to that of earlier Puerto Rican artists such as **Miguel Pou.** In Homar's linoleum *La guagua* (The Bus), part of his and Tufiño's *Portafolio de plenas* (1953–1954; Portfolio of Plenas), he includes the music and lyrics of the **plena,** a humorous folk song that describes local events, depicted with expressive realism.

Homar was later appointed director of the Department of Education's Taller de Artes Gráficas (Graphic Arts Workshop), which hired artists full-time to produce book illustrations and posters conveying information about health, educational, and political issues. In 1957 Homar also became the director of the Taller de Artes Gráficas of the Instituto de Cultura Puertorriqueña, where he continued experimenting with different printing techniques, such as silk-screening, xylography, linoleum, typography, and calligraphy. In his remarkable xylograph *Unicornio en la isla* (1965; Unicorn on the Island), Homar juxtaposes the text of Tomás Blanco's poem of the same title over a landscape of Puerto Rico. During the 1970s Homar actively continued to support graphic art through the organization of biennial exhibitions and his own graphic-art workshop.

REFERENCE:

Juan David Cupeles, *Lorenzo Homar: Artista ejemplar de la gráfica contemporánea de Puerto Rico,* third edition (Mexico City: Juan David Cupeles, 1992).

— F.B.N.

Huapango

Huapango is a generic name derived from *cuauhpanco* (whose literal meaning is "over the stage"), and it des-

Unicornio en la isla (1965; Unicorn on the Island), woodcut by Lorenzo Homar

ignates typical rhythmic styles of songs and dances from the Mexican state of Veracruz and along the coast of the Gulf of Mexico. As a musical term, huapango refers to the simultaneous and alternating use of 6/8 and 3/4 metrical organizations that produce intricate cross rhythms in fast tempi. Instrumentation may range from a typical trio of violin, **jarana,** and a high-pitched guitar (*quinta*), to a harp and guitar duo, or even a **mariachi** ensemble. As the popularity of the huapango increased, an urban, commercial type developed that was more stylized, in the manner of the **canción mexicana**.

REFERENCE:

Gerard Béhague, "Popular Music in Latin America," *Studies in Latin American Culture*, 5 (1986):41–67.

— R.L.S.

Huelva Film Festival

With Hollywood at the forefront of the movie business, other countries often find the distribution of nationally made movies difficult, even at home. **Censorship,** particularly in Latin American countries with oppressive regimes, also limits the showing of nationally produced movies. The Huelva festival, like the **Biarritz Festival,** has become a major outlet for Latin American directors, allowing them to draw attention to their work even in their home countries. The Huelva Film Festival or Festival de Cine Iberoamericano, to give it its full title, held annually in southern Spain, was founded in 1974, primarily to increase awareness of Latin American cinema. The festival has had significant Spanish government funding but is increasingly under pressure to seek commercial sponsors.

Most movies shown at the festival are feature films produced by Latin Americans and made in Latin America, but films about Latin America can also be included, even if produced elsewhere. In addition to an official film season, the festival has a competition, with several categories and prizes. The most coveted prizes are the "colones de oro" (Golden Columbuses), each worth about $25,000. One such prize for full-length movies is awarded by an international professional jury, and a second is awarded following a vote by the audience. There are also prizes for shorts. Among the Spanish American films that have won a Colón de Oro are *Un pasaje de ida* (directed by Agilberto Meléndez, Dominican Republic, 1988; One-Way Ticket); *Juliana* (by Fernando Espinosa and Alejandro Legaspi, Peru, which received both "colones" in 1989); *Yo, la peor de todas* (María Luisa Bemberg, Argentina, 1990; I, the Worst of All); *Después de la tormenta* (Tristán Bauer, Argentina, 1990; After the Storm); *Disparen a matar* (Carlos Azpurúa, Venezuela, 1991; Shoot to Kill); *Las tumbas* (Javier Torre, Argentina, 1991; The Tombs); *Como agua para chocolate* (Alfonso Arau, Mexico, 1993; Like Water for Chocolate); *La estrategia del caracol* (The Snail's Stratagem) and *Aguilas no cazan moscas* (Eagles Don't Hunt Flies) — both by the Colombian Sergio Cabrera and receiving prizes in 1993 and 1994, respectively; and *Reina y rey* (**Julio García Espinosa,** Cuba, 1994; Queen and King).

— P.S.

I

IMPRESSIONISM AND POST-IMPRESSIONISM IN ART

Impressionism and Post-Impressionism were introduced into Latin America by artists such as Alfredo Ramos Martínez, Joaquín Clausell, Francisco Oller, **Miguel Pou,** Víctor Manuel, and Antonio Gattorno, who at the turn of the century had studied art abroad, for the most part in Paris. Although there were few contacts among them, upon their return home they followed a pattern of rejection of the dominant academic schools and the Spanish modernist style popularized by Ignacio Zuloaga. Most of them concentrated on regional and nationalist themes, especially landscapes. At the same time, many impressionists were encouraged by collectors, who often bought the works of the Spanish open-air painter Joaquín Sorolla.

In Mexico the reaction against academic art began in 1911 with a student strike at the Instituto Nacional de Bellas Artes (National Institute of Fine Arts) against the director, Antonio Rivas Mercado, and Antonio Fabrés, a Spanish painter who was using outdated teaching methods to impose the Spanish Modernism of Zuloaga as the official style of the school. The strike eventually resulted in the appointment of the impressionist painter Ramos Martínez, who had just returned from Paris in 1913, as director of the Escuela Nacional de Bellas Artes. In that capacity Ramos Martínez founded in Santa Anita the first Escuela de Pintura al Aire Libre (Open-Air School of Painting), calling it Escuela Barbizón, after the French school in Barbizon. At Santa Anita, students produced art that focused on Mexican themes and was based on the direct observation of nature.

Although experimentation with impressionist techniques helped students such as **David Alfaro Siqueiros** and Fernando Leal free themselves from the academic tradition, Ramos Martínez's project was limited by the fact that Impressionism was out of touch, not only with the political reality of the **Mexican Revolution** but also with more recent developments in modern art. Furthermore, the impressionist-like figuration achieved by Ramos Martínez and his students only produced picturesque representations of the Mexican people influenced by the **Indigenism** of scholars such as Manuel Gamio, as in Ramos Martínez's *Mujer vestida de China Poblana* (late nineteenth century; Woman Wearing China Poblana Costume), in Francisco Díaz de León's *Vendedor de vasijas* (1922; Pottery Vendor), and in Fernando Leal's *Indio con sarape rojo* (1920; Indian with Red Sarape). Although the Escuela Barbizón was closed in 1914, after the end of the revolution, the Mexican government opened dozens of open-air schools for children that remained in operation until 1937.

In spite of the influential activities of Ramos Martínez and the Mexican painter **Dr. Atl,** who had a brief impressionist period during the 1910s, the most important impressionist painter in Mexico was Joaquín Clausell. He studied law and around 1893 had to leave Mexico because of his anti–Porfirio Díaz political activities. He went to France, where he studied art, met the painter Camille Pissarro, and adopted Impressionism. After Clausell returned to Mexico in 1895, he became an important landscape painter in the tradition of José María Velasco. Many of Clausell's landscapes include images of water, such as *Un manantial en otoño* (early twentieth century; A Flowing Spring in Autumn). Here and elsewhere

Clausell demonstrated both his great command of impressionist techniques and the fact that his approach to that style was a personal one.

There were several painters in Central America and the Caribbean who experimented with Impressionism and Post-Impressionism applied to regional themes. Among these were the Guatemalans Carlos Valenti and Humberto Garavito, the Costa Ricans Juan Ramón Bonilla and Fausto Pacheco, and the Nicaraguan Juan Bautista Cuadra. In Puerto Rico at the turn of the century, the well-known nineteenth-century painter Francisco Oller produced several impressionist landscapes of the island, such as *Paisaje palma real* (1897; Landscape with Royal Palm Tree). Oller, who had met the French impressionists in Paris during the 1850s, had a significant influence over following generations of Puerto Rican artists. During the first half of the twentieth century these artists rejected both academic and avant-garde styles while resisting the cultural hegemony of the United States. Miguel Pou, a follower of Oller, often used impressionist techniques for landscapes of Puerto Rico, as in *Los coches de Ponce* (1926; The Coaches of Ponce).

In Cuba the avant-garde artists of the Generation of 1927 initiated the break from traditional academic art to introduce modern art trends. During the early 1920s, vanguardists such as Víctor Manuel (pseudonym of Víctor Manuel García) and Antonio Gattorno studied art in Paris; they returned to their country in 1927, contributed to the avant-garde *Revista de Avance,* and became the first artists to exhibit modern art in Cuba. In paintings such as Manuel's *Paisaje con figuras* (undated; Landscape with Figures) and Gattorno's *Mujeres junto al río* (1927; Women by the River), these artists expressed their interest in local themes or *cubanismo* (Cubanness) using styles inspired by the Post-Impressionism of Paul Gauguin and Paul Cézanne.

REFERENCES:

Marimar Benítez, "The Special Case of Puerto Rico," in *The Latin American Spirit: Art and Artists in the United States, 1920–1970,* by Luis Cancel and others (New York: Bronx Museum of the Arts/Abrams, 1988), pp. 72–105;

Juan A. Martínez, *Cuban Art and National Identity: The Vanguardia Painters, 1927–1950* (Gainesville: University Press of Florida, 1994);

Laura González Matute, *Escuelas de pintura al aire libre y centros populares de pintura* (Mexico City: INBA, Centro Nacional de Investigación, Documentación e Información de Artes Plásticas, Dirección de Investigación y Documentación de los Artes, 1987).

— F.B.N.

INCINE

The Instituto Nacional de Cine (National Film Institute), or INCINE, was sponsored by the Frente Sandinista de Liberación Nacional (Sandinista National Liberation Front), or FSLN (see **Nicaraguan Revolution**). During the Sandinistas' struggle to gain control of the Nicaraguan government, Istmo, a Costa Rican film group sympathetic to the Sandinistas, presented a proposal to the FSLN leadership to make a movie about the Sandinistas. The project found favor and led to the production of *Patria libre o morir* (A Free Homeland or Death). In April 1979 the FSLN organized the Office for Information Abroad, composed primarily of journalists, and the War Correspondents' Corps, which included photographers and filmmakers. After the FSLN came to power in July of that year, it established INCINE, taking advantage of the experience of directors, photographers, and journalists who had been in Nicaragua during the insurrectionary struggle. Among those individuals were the director Emilio Rodríguez Vázquez (1949–) of Puerto Rico and Carlos Jiménez, a young Colombian cameraman. Rodríguez Vázquez studied Latin American literature at the University of San Juan and then moved to New York City to work as a filmmaker; his inspiration at that time was **Julio García Espinosa**'s notion of "imperfect cinema." After spending time in Costa Rica, Rodríguez Vázquez went to Nicaragua in spring 1979 to join the FSLN War Correspondents' Corps, filming combat on the southern front bordering Costa Rica from April until the Sandinistas came to power that July. Rodríguez Vázquez then stayed on to work at INCINE.

Under the auspices of the Ministry of Culture, the three leaders of INCINE — Carlos Vicente Ibarra, Franklin Caldera, and Ramiro Lacayo — set up operations at Anastasio Somoza's film-production company, Producine. (Ibarra, a Nicaraguan, had been a member of GECU, a university-based experimental film group, and like Rodríguez Vázquez, he had filmed some of the action on the southern front.) Some 750,000 feet of newsreel footage shot during the Somoza regime were retrieved. Over the years INCINE produced about 60,000 feet of 16mm color film for distribution to newspapers throughout Latin America and the Caribbean. In the 1980s it had a production department of about twenty-five people and a distribution department with another twenty. One important goal was to set up a mobile-cinema program and to take movies to rural areas of Nicaragua where people were unfamiliar with the film medium. The first INCINE newsreel, which covered the nationalization of the Nicaraguan gold mines, had its international premiere on the opening night of the first International Festival of the New Latin American Cinema in Havana in December 1979. After beginning with news-

Carlos Vicente Ibarra, one of the founders of INCINE, 1979 (photograph by Julianne Burton)

reels INCINE started to make documentaries and eventually full-length features.

All INCINE movies focus on the realities of everyday struggle against imperialist aggression. Two of the best fictional INCINE films are *Mujeres de la frontera* (1986; Frontier Women), directed by Iván Argüello and dealing with the changes in male-female relationships brought on by warfare, and Mariano Marín's *Esbozo de Daniel* (1984; A Sketch of Daniel), in which the relationship between a teacher and a child is brutally ended when the teacher is murdered by Contra troops opposing the Sandinista government.

REFERENCES:

Julianne Burton, *Cinema and Social Change in Latin America: Conversations with Filmmakers* (Austin: University of Texas Press, 1986);

John King, *Magical Reels: A History of Cinema in Latin America* (London: Verso, 1990).

— S.M.H.

INDIGENISM IN ART

The representation of indigenous themes and appreciation of indigenous cultures have been important issues in the arts in Latin America, especially in regions with large Indian populations, such as in Mexico and Guatemala. In Mexico, during the period following independence, as the Mesoamerican past became associated with the idea of Mexican nationality, many intellectuals and artists began to revaluate their unappreciative attitudes toward the local indigenous and pre-Hispanic heritages. In the latter part of the nineteenth century, while Félix Parra, José María Obregón, and other painters of historical subjects created classicized images of an idealized precolonial past, the state, under the dictatorship of Porfirio Díaz, considered contemporary Indian traditions an obstacle to modern progress.

During the early twentieth century, some of the porfirian attitudes to Mexican indigenous races were perpetuated by influential scholars such as the indigenist Manuel Gamio, who in his book *Forjando patria* (1916) defined Mexico as a mestizo nation. Gamio saw mestizos as part of the dominant white culture and considered Indians to be a separate group that needed to be assimilated and civilized through education. Although Gamio's ideas encouraged interest in indigenous arts and crafts and in ancient Mesoamerica, he saw the Indian as part of an

Mujeres de Metepec (1922; Women of Metepec) by Carlos Mérida (from Margarita Nelken, *Carlos Mérida,* 1961)

idealized past and belonging to the "primitive" realm of nature. The earliest twentieth-century visual representations of Indian peoples reflect a similar tendency to Europeanize them, for instance the classicized versions of Aztec rituals in the art of **Saturnino Herrán.** At the same time, artists such as Alfredo Ramos Martínez, Fernando Leal, Antonio Ruiz, and even **Diego Rivera** often represented Indians as immersed in and identified with nature. Although Indigenism was more a thematic approach than a specific style, in general it was characterized by an emphasis on figuration, ranging from the **Impressionism** of Ramos Martínez and the **Symbolist Art** of Herrán to the post-Cubist figuration of Rivera and **José Clemente Orozco.**

The writings of Gamio and **José Vasconcelos** found an echo in the populist rhetoric of Alvaro Obregón's administration, which provided official support for excavations of Mesoamerican sites and studies of folk and popular art, including Adolfo Best Maugard's method of art education based on indigenous and folk-art designs. Muralists, also influenced by Indigenist ideas and Obregón's populism, defined a new iconography of Mexican identity based on the concept of *el pueblo* (the people) that

included urban and rural workers as well as indigenous groups. José Clemente Orozco in general rejected Indigenist themes, but in a few murals, such as *El franciscano y el indio* (1926; The Franciscan and the Indian), he presented a rather bleak view of the unbalanced exchange between European and Indian peoples. On the other hand, Rivera focused on idyllic views of the ancient past, as in his monumental murals at Mexico City's Palacio Nacional (1929, 1942–1945; National Palace). During the 1930s and 1940s **Muralism** and Indigenism became dominant forces in art, influencing the work of numerous artists, including the members of the Taller de Gráfica Popular (see **Graphic Art**).

Although in Central America there was a pronounced emphasis on regionalist themes during the first half of the twentieth century, Indigenism was not generally as important as in Mexico. The principal exception is Guatemala, where Indigenism did become an important trend in the 1920s and 1930s, influencing the work of artists such as **Carlos Mérida,** Rafael Yela Gunther, Rodolfo Galeotti Torres, Humberto Garavito, and Alfredo Gálvez Suárez. Mérida began to depict Indigenist themes in 1914, using a highly simplified figuration with flat areas of color, as in *Mujeres de Metepec* (1922; Women of Metepec). In the 1920s Mérida settled in Mexico and participated in the mural movement. Although he later turned to **Surrealism** and abstract styles, his work always referred to indigenous traditions. Gálvez Suárez, who studied in Mexico, painted several murals at the Palacio Nacional (1944; National Palace) in Guatemala City, representing the theme of national identity, with images of Chichicasteco and Maya Indians in an idealized realist style. Gálvez Suárez's contemporaries, the sculptors Galeotti Torres and Yela Gunther, also concentrated on Indigenist themes after the mid 1930s, using realist styles.

Indigenism also had an impact in El Salvador through the activities of the Asociación de Amigos del Arte (Association of Friends of Art) during the 1930s and 1940s. Through the work of writers such as Napoleón Rodríguez Ruiz and **Salarrué** (Salvador Salazar Arrué), as well as artists such as Miguel Ortiz Villacorta, José Mejía Vides, and Luis Alfredo Cáceres Madrid, the association strongly opposed the proposal to exterminate indigenous peoples that the journalist Joaquín Méndez and Prof. Adolfo Herrera Vega, among others, had put forward in the 1930s. Many Salvadoran artists, such as Camilo Minero, Noé Canjura, and Carlos Gonzalo Cañas, continued to work with indigenous themes during the 1950s. In Costa Rica Indigenism found only one important practitioner, **Francisco Zúñiga.** Most Costa Rican artists have expressed their views about local culture through landscapes rather than in representations of indigenous traditions. During the 1930s and 1940s in Nicaragua only a few artists (most notably Roberto de la Selva and Rodrigo Peñalba) painted images inspired by indigenous peoples. (See also **Indigenism in Literature.**)

REFERENCES:

Erika Billeter, *Images of Mexico: The Contribution of Mexico to 20th Century Art* (Dallas: Dallas Museum of Art, 1987);

Gilbert Chase, *Contemporary Art in Latin America* (New York: Free Press / London: Collier-Macmillan, 1970).

—F.B.N.

INDIGENISM IN LITERATURE

As a literary genre, Indigenism has its roots in the chronicles written by Bartolomé de las Casas, a priest who championed the rights of oppressed Indians in early colonial times. In its broadest sense, *indigenismo* relates to artistic endeavors that in some way portray the social conditions or worldview of the **indigenous peoples** of Latin America. The term has particular importance in the

study of art and literature, and, naturally enough, for those countries with significant Indian populations (Guatemala, Mexico, Ecuador, Peru, Bolivia). Various ideological perspectives have been used in creating Indigenist art and literature. There is a close relationship with Indigenism in sociology and anthropology, that is, with the scientific study of the Indian, often aimed at vindicating the original inhabitants of the New World.

The term *Indigenist* is most often applied to modern novelists, most of whom in fact have little or no Indian ancestry; rather, they are mestizo or white intellectuals speaking on Indians' behalf. The first significant Indigenist novelist, the Peruvian Clorinda Matto de Turner, was the wife of a landowner. The argument of her *Aves sin nido* (1889; Birds Without Nests) in defense of the Quechua Indians is couched in the terms of nineteenth-century liberalism; the book idealizes its Indian subjects and indulges in exotic landscape descriptions. Matto de Turner's mentor was Manuel González Prada, a liberal intellectual whose spirited pronouncements against the exploitation of Indians signaled the transition from "Indianism" (the romantic idealization of the Indian) to Indigenism, although he was still prone to the former.

The transition progressed in the works of José Carlos Mariátegui and José María Arguedas. Mariátegui was the most influential Peruvian thinker of the early twentieth century and the first to make the case for the Indians in socialist terms, arguing that their exploitation was a function of landownership and that the only viable solution was a radical transformation in the system of land tenure. Arguedas (an ethnologist as well as a novelist) successfully represented the Indian world from within, having spent his early years among Indians. Among Indigenist writers he probably comes closest to identifying with his subject.

Aware of some of their limitations as outsiders, Indigenist writers used several devices drawn from indigenous cultures in their fiction: folk songs, legends, and myths; the presentation of conflict in terms of the whole collectivity; the construction of the plot by accumulation of events rather than by the conventional rules of European realism; and a different perception of time. Arguedas was also the most successful of Indigenist writers in this formal sense, since he was able to write in a syncretic, Quechua-inflected Spanish that effectively communicated the perceptions of Indian characters. The Guatemalan writer **Miguel Angel Asturias** also strove to achieve this syncretic effect by appealing to the Mayan repertory of legend and myth (though he studied them in Paris); particularly important is his *Hombres de maíz* (1949; translated as *Men of Maize*).

The term *Indigenism* is often associated with the period 1920–1940 and with the Andean highlands, but it properly covers a wider temporal and spatial range: the

Rain-dance ceremonies enacted by descendants of the Totonacs during the Vanilla Festival at Papantla, Veracruz, Mexico (courtesy of the Organization of American States)

first Indigenist novel was written in 1889, and the work of José María Arguedas belongs to the second half of the century. The genre also flourished in Mexico and Guatemala, and in Peru it has continued to evolve in the works of Manuel Scorza. The best-known Indigenist novels include *Raza de bronce* (1919; Bronze Race), by the Bolivian Alcides Arguedas; *Huasipungo* (1934), by the Ecuadoran Jorge Icaza; *El indio* (1935; The Indian), by the Mexican **Gregorio López y Fuentes**; *El mundo es ancho y ajeno* (1940; translated as *Broad and Alien Is the*

World), by the Peruvian Ciro Alegría; *Los ríos profundos* (1958; translated as *Deep Rivers*), by José María Arguedas; and *Balún-Canán* (1957) and *Oficio de Tinieblas* (1960; Rites of Darkness), by the Mexican **Rosario Castellanos.**

An important development in the Indigenist genre is the late appearance of ethnographic narratives and **testimonial narratives,** which cut across the cultural and ethnic divide and try to allow the Indians to speak for themselves. The first of these works was the Mexican

Ricardo Pozas's *Juan Pérez Jolote* (1948), a first-person account of the life of a Chamula Indian that had originally appeared in an anthropological journal. The best known of these ethnographic "autobiographies" is Elisabeth Burgos's *Me llamo Rigoberta Menchú y así me nació la conciencia* (1985; translated as *I, Rigoberta Menchú*), based on the account of **Rigoberta Menchú,** a Mayan woman who went on to win the Nobel Peace Prize.

REFERENCES:

René Prieto, *Miguel Angel Asturias' Archaeology of Return* (Cambridge: Cambridge University Press, 1993);

Angel Rama, *Transculturación narrativa en América Latina* (Mexico City: Siglo XXI, 1982);

Julio Rodríguez-Luis, *Hermenéutica y praxis del indigenismo* (Mexico City: Fondo de Cultura Económica, 1980).

— R.G.M. & P.S.

INDIGENOUS CULTURES

When Europeans first set foot in the New World, the population of indigenous peoples is estimated to have been twenty-two million in Mexico, eight million in Central America, and eight million in the Caribbean. Yet during the first century of Spanish occupation, fighting and the Indians' lack of resistance to new diseases brought from Europe contributed heavily to a demographic collapse of native populations that in some areas, notably the Antilles, resulted in near extinction. The native peoples who survived quickly discovered the expediency of assimilating to the European way of life, converting to Catholicism and accepting the authority of colonial governments, which rewarded loyal subjects with land for farming or mining. Many areas of Latin America that once had significant indigenous populations are now largely Hispanic; yet indigenous peoples continue to constitute substantial segments of the population in some countries and to constitute a major cultural force. In the Antilles the African cultures brought in by the slave trade have mixed with the Hispanic culture to form a distinctive blend.

With some exceptions — including indigenous peoples living in relatively isolated areas, such as the Mísquito (or Mósquito) of Nicaragua, and those in areas where they still constitute the majority of a population, as is the case with the Mayans in Guatemala — most of the peoples of Latin America are mestizo (of mixed Indian and European descent). The degree of racial intermingling varies from country to country, but in countries such as Guatemala, for instance, racial and ethnic blending has occurred to such a degree that it makes it difficult to label individuals as Indian or non-Indian on the basis of racial origin. In general, individuals or groups may be identified as Indians by where they live and how they relate to the land, by the language or languages they speak, by the food they eat, by their principal sources of income, by their dress and crafts, and by their religious practices; one individual may be identified as an Indian while another with the same racial heritage may not. Because class is inextricably linked to race and ethnicity, an impoverished person with Indian blood is more likely to be labeled an Indian than a member of the middle class with the same racial background.

It is difficult to estimate accurately the numbers of the indigenous populations in Latin America. Some such groups live in isolated, inaccessible regions, and in general indigenous peoples tend to view census takers as collectors of information that will be used as the basis for taxation, military conscription, and official discrimination or abuse. These suspicions are especially prevalent in Guatemala, where tens of thousands of Mayans were massacred by the military, which boasted of annihilating 440 Indian villages during the late 1970s and early 1980s. The Mayans, however, still form at least 54 percent of the Guatemalan population, followed by 42 percent mestizo (or *ladino,* the term used in Guatemala). Other countries in North and Central America have significant numbers of Indians: Mexico (10 percent Indian, 15 percent European, and 75 percent mestizo) and El Salvador (10 percent Indian, 1 percent European, and 89 percent mestizo). The population of Honduras is estimated to be 5 percent Indian, 1 percent European, 2 percent African, and 92 percent mestizo; while that of Nicaragua is 3 percent Indian, 10 percent European, 11 percent African, and 76 percent mestizo. The population of Panama is 3 percent Indian, 20 percent European, 1 percent African, and 76 percent mestizo. In Belize, formerly British Honduras, where English and Spanish are spoken, there are also Mayan and black Carib groups that have their own separate languages. Indigenous languages are the major cultural survivors and serve as bridges to the future for the indigenous peoples of Latin America.

Before the advent of colonialism the Indians of this region lived in highly developed, largely agricultural societies that supplemented their way of life through hunting, fishing, and gathering. The legacy of these cultures may be found in the preference of indigenous peoples for living in "undeveloped" natural surroundings and in their sense of intimate connection to the land. European colonists, who brought with them the concept of private property, radically transformed the Indians' way of life. In the Caribbean those native peoples who survived were forced into slavery on land claimed by their conquerors. In Mexico the Aztec civilization was the dominant one when the Spaniards arrived in 1519. Within two years the Spaniards had conquered the Aztec capital of Tenochtitlán, the site of what is now Mexico City. At the time of the Spaniards' arrival in southern Mexico and parts of Guatemala, the Mayan empire was already in decline, owing in part to internal warring factions. It is thought that the more than five million Mayans still living in Guatemala survived as a cultural group because they retreated into their own communities, living on a maize-based subsistence economy and seldom venturing out into European settlements. Spectacular archaeological sites attest to the sophistication of these civilizations at their heights, before or at the time of the Europeans' arrival. The most impressive Mayan ruins in the Yucatán peninsula (Mexico), Guatemala, and Honduras are Copán, Quiriguá, Palenque, Uxmal, Tikal, and Chichén Itzá. Outside Mexico City are the famous pyramids of Teotihuacán, structures from a civilization that antedates the Aztecs. While indigenous peoples feel a deep connection to what such ruins represent, they also insist on the importance and value of their cultural survival in the present, despite frequent denigration of their ways by non-Indians.

All the indigenous communities of Latin America celebrate their connection to nature through a syncretic combination of Catholic and Indian rituals and festivals, especially the various carnival celebrations that signal the beginning of Lent and take place throughout Central America, Mexico, and the Caribbean. Holy Week rituals are particularly dramatic in Guatemala, and a popular celebration of the tree of life takes place in various areas of Mexico. Men known as *voladores* (flyers), wearing colorful feathered attire, hang suspended by their heels from the top of a tall, sturdy tree and simulate the act of flying as they are rotated around the tree, gradually descending while another volador dances on a minuscule platform at the top. Among the Mayans of Guatemala the popular, hard-drinking, cigar-smoking male deity Maximón receives offerings of guaro (the local moonshine), smoking materials, and money in return for granting personal requests such as wishes regarding crops, fishing, health, love, sex, or revenge.

Textiles have always been important among the tribes of Mexico and Central America, thread being spun from cotton, agave, and palm fibers in various areas. While in many areas everyday clothing made from homespun fabrics has been replaced by cheaper, machine-made substitutes, traditional textiles and clothing retain their value in others. In Guatemala making clothing has become a major source of economic survival for the Mayans. Weaving has become so lucrative that in some cases women weavers contribute more to their household finances than their landless husbands do. Mayan women use easily transport-

able backstrap looms, which may be attached to trees, rafters, or any other accessible structures. They have become renowned internationally for their huipiles, women's woven blouses whose intricate designs are specific to their areas of origin. Some Mayan men also weave, using larger and more unwieldy footlooms and generally producing colorful but less elaborate clothes than the women, including cortes, wraparound skirts worn by Mayan women. Textiles woven by other indigenous women in Central America are largely being supplanted by imported cloth; yet the textiles still produced by the Cuna of Panama are widely admired for their bright colors and original designs.

Indigenous peoples also practice basketry, especially in areas where there are abundant leaf and grass fibers. Petate making, the weaving together of reeds to form a kind of mattress, is common in several regions. Indians of Mexico and Central America have traditionally produced a wide variety of ceramics for everyday and ceremonial occasions, including burials. The designs of these objects range from simple to intricate and vary in color from dull to bright. After the arrival of the Europeans the art of pottery as an outlet for artistic or cosmological expression declined, reflecting a diminishing of native cultural identity and pride. Somewhat ironically the making of ornate pottery has been revived in certain areas, partly in response to the demands of the European trade. (See also **Peoples and Races** and **Languages**.)

REFERENCES:

Sheldon Annis, *God and Production in a Guatemalan Town* (Austin: University of Texas Press, 1987);

William H. Beezley, Cheryl English Martin, and William F. French, *Rituals of Rule, Rituals of Resistance: Public Celebrations and Popular Culture in Mexico* (Wilmington, Del.: Scholarly Resources, 1994);

John E. Kicza, ed., *The Indian in Latin American History* (Wilmington, Del.: Scholarly Resources, 1993);

Rigoberta Menchú and Elisabeth Burgos, *I . . . Rigoberta Menchú: An Indian Woman in Guatemala,* translated by Ann Wright (London: Verso, 1984);

Carol Smith, *Guatemalan Indians and the State, 1540 to 1988* (Austin: University of Texas Press, 1990).

— M.E.S.

GRACIELA ITURBIDE

Graciela Iturbide (1942–) is an important Mexican photographer who has been professionally active since the 1970s (see **Photography**). The daughter of a photographer, Iturbide has used a camera since she was a teenager taking photos of her many siblings. From 1969 to 1972 she studied at the Centro Universitario de Estudios Cinematográficos (University Center for

Cinematic Studies) of the Universidad Nacional Autónoma de México (National Autonomous University of Mexico) and was later an assistant to the Mexican photographer **Manuel Alvarez Bravo.** In 1974 she became a full-time professional, but instead of focusing on advertisements or photojournalism, she has supported her documentary black-and-white photography mostly through grants and commissions from the United States and Europe.

The main themes of Iturbide's oeuvre are the dignity of human life and the efforts of different groups and individuals to maintain a sense of identity. She tends to work in series of images rich in meaning, reflecting the lives of marginal groups and often concentrating on women. While in Spain and Portugal she produced a series about Gypsies, and in Newcastle, England, she photographed a group of unemployed women. She also has a strong interest in mysticism as experienced by different groups. In Cuba she took photographs of Santería celebrations, which were later included in her book *Sueños de papel* (1985; Paper Dreams), and in Mexico she explored the theme of death in photographs relating people to animals that are dead or about to be killed or sacrificed, such as *Los pollos* (1980; The Chickens) and *Gansos* (1980; Geese).

Iturbide's Mexican work often explores the traditional ways of life of indigenous groups. Perhaps the most important of these suggestive but ultimately ambiguous and nonnarrative images are her photographs of Juchitán women, later published in her book *Juchitán de las mujeres* (1989; Women's Juchitán). Of Zapotec ancestry, these women live in the matriarchal town of Juchitán, in the Isthmus of Tehuantepec, where Iturbide spent long periods developing a personal relationship with the community, something that has given her photographs great poetic and psychological insight. This series includes her well-known photograph *Nuestra Señora de las Iguanas* (1979; Our Lady of the Iguanas), also called "The Juchitán Medusa" because of the startling crownlike arrangement of live iguanas the portrayed woman is carrying on her head to market. In the late 1980s Iturbide traveled to East Los Angeles, where she produced powerful images based on her exploration of the private and collective activities of members of Mexican American street gangs.

REFERENCES:

Elizabeth Ferrer, "Manos poderosas: The Photography of Graciela Iturbide," *Review: Latin American Literature and Arts,* no. 47 (Fall 1993): 69–78;

Graciela Iturbide, "Mexican Street Gangs of Los Angeles and Tijuana," in *Desires and Disguises: Five Latin American Pho-*

Mi tía, un amiguito y yo (1942; My Aunt, a Little Friend, and I) by María Izquierdo (private collection)

tographers, translated and edited by Amanda Hopkinson (London & New York: Serpent's Tail, 1992), pp. 65–77.

— F.B.N.

MARÍA IZQUIERDO

Like contemporaries such as **Frida Kahlo** and **Rufino Tamayo,** Mexican painter María Cenobia Izquierdo (1902–1955) was concerned with the issue of *Mexicanidad* (Mexicanness). Izquierdo made full use of motifs that are readily recognizable as Mexican, including Catholic and native religious images. *Altar de los dolores* (1943; Altar of Sorrows) and *La Virgen de los dolores* (1947; The Virgin of Sorrows) both reveal Izquierdo's familiarity with retablos and home altars;

both involve folk renditions of the Virgin with offerings of food placed before her. The emphasis in both paintings is on the Mexicanness of the altar and the surrounding items rather than the person of the Virgin.

Although Izquierdo attended the Instituto Nacional de Bellas Artes in Mexico City in 1928, she is considered a self-taught artist. She had her first major exhibition in 1929. During the early 1930s Izquierdo worked and lived with Tamayo. Later Izquierdo's house became a popular meeting place for intellectuals, in part because of its close proximity to the university and the Instituto Nacional de Bellas Artes. She was well acquainted with the **Muralists,** but she shared Tamayo's rejection of their didacticism and political posturing. In 1931 Izquierdo was hired by the Secretaría de Educación Pública (Ministry of Public Education) to teach painting in its fine-arts department. There she continued to paint a variety of subjects, including portraits, landscapes, still lifes, and images of the circus. Many of these paintings included elements from her imagination, which had been fertilized by the traditional folk crafts of Jalisco and Coahuila, where she spent the first seventeen years of her life. She did not, however, reject European traditions, as several of her portraits show. *Mi tía, un amiguito y yo* (1942; My Aunt, a Playmate, and Me), for instance, captures Mexican dress at its most Victorian.

The French Surrealist poet Antonin Artaud, who claimed Izquierdo's works were Surrealist, wrote a critique of her paintings, published in Mexico City's newspaper *Excelsior* in 1936. His essay enhanced the appeal of her works both nationally and internationally, but its European perspective led to a similar bias in much of the later criticism of Izquierdo's art. Izquierdo was not strictly a surrealist, but the dreamlike landscapes and odd juxtaposition of images in paintings such as *Sueño y presentimiento* (1947; Dream and Presentiment) do connect her work with **Surrealism.**

In 1945 Izquierdo was commissioned to paint a large mural at the Palacio de Gobierno in Mexico City. Nevertheless, she was prevented from carrying out this work, in part by **Diego Rivera** and **David Alfaro Siqueiros,** who claimed that Izquierdo was an excellent painter but unqualified as a muralist.

Among Izquierdo's most unusual works were those of the 1950s, such as *La alacena* (1952; The Cupboard), depicting the interiors of cupboards containing a variety of fruits, toys, statuettes, and candles. These common items were too carefully arranged to have been a part of daily life. Their surreal quality comes from the sense that these tiny cupboard-dwelling objects are usually animated but suspend their actions only in the presence of human eyes.

REFERENCE:

Elizabeth Ferrer, "María Izquierdo," *Latin American Artists of the Twentieth Century* (New York: Museum of Modern Art, 1993), pp. 116–121.

                                                           — C.M.

J-K

JARABE

The jarabe *tapatío* (jarabe from Jalisco) is popularly known as the national dance of Mexico and is widely recognized in the English-speaking world as the Mexican Hat Dance. Although the dance can be traced to the fifteenth century, the name *jarabe* appeared in the eighteenth in jarabe gitano (gypsy jarabe) to identify the licentious lyrics applied to the Spanish seguidilla manchega (seguidilla from La Mancha). Despite various attempts by church and state authorities to suppress the jarabe in Mexico during the colonial period, its popularity grew, as did its repertoire, especially following independence from Spain. In the process of acculturation, regional characteristics and dance gestures from indigenous groups were added, such as the pantomimes of Huichol Indians in the Jalisco area. The original six different melodies of the jarabe were eventually expanded to nine. The different melodies are often presented in the form of a medley. They are commonly harmonized in parallel thirds and sixths, range from adagio to prestissimo, and vary according to regional tastes, but preference for the faster tempos is apparent. The typical metrical organizations are 6/8 and 3/4, which often appear in alternation within the same piece. Simple accompaniments for jarabes are provided by **mariachi** ensembles as well as other instrumental combinations, according to regional tastes.

REFERENCES:

Gerard Béhague, "Popular Music in Latin America," *Studies in Latin American Popular Culture*, 5 (1986), pp. 41–67;

Gabriel Saldivar, *Historia de la música en México: Epocas precortesiana y colonial* (Mexico: Editorial "Cultura," 1934).

— R.L.S.

JARANA

Jarana is the name of an instrument as well as a dance. The instrument evolved in Mexico during the colonial period as one of many adaptations of the guitar in the Americas. At first known as the *jaranita* (little jarana), the instrument is smaller than the guitar and has a slightly different shape. Certain technical features may vary according to regional usage. For example, the number of gut strings may vary from four to twelve. As a strummed instrument, the jarana provides a penetrating, percussive harmonic and rhythmic accompaniment to folk songs and dances.

The music for the jarana dance proceeds in a lively and boisterous fashion. Regionally associated with the state of Yucatán, it has varied rhythms, often featuring 3/4 and 6/8 meters in alternation. The quick movements of the dance, the occasionally lewd texts, and the references to drunken behavior earned the disdain of church authorities. Nevertheless, in the Hispanic Antilles (for example Puerto Rico) *jarana* denotes a rather innocent gathering of young people for social dancing, usually with recorded music.

REFERENCE:

Otto Mayer-Serra, *Panorama de la música mexicana desde la independencia hasta la actualidad* (Mexico City: Fondo de Cultura Económica, 1941).

— R.L.S.

FRIDA KAHLO

Mexican painter Magdalena Carmen Frida Kahlo y Calderón (1907–1954) has become one of the best-known Latin American artists. Daughter of photographer

Frida Kahlo painting *La mesa herida* (1940; The Wounded Table)

Guillermo Kahlo, a Hungarian Jewish immigrant from Germany, and Matilde Calderón, of Spanish and indigenous ancestry, Kahlo studied art at the Escuela Nacional Preparatoria (National Preparatory School) and at the studio of printmaker Fernando Fernández. Kahlo's most frequent subject was herself, in part as a result of periods of illness caused by polio and a serious traffic accident in 1926. Kahlo first began to paint in 1926 during convalescence and continued to paint steadily throughout her life, developing a personal style that contrasted with the institutional emphasis in the work of muralist **Diego Rivera,** whom she married in 1929. Stoic facial expressions amid graphic portrayals of physical and emotional pain can be found in many of Kahlo's self-portraits. *El Hospital Henry Ford* (1932; Henry Ford Hospital), *Las dos Fridas* (1939; The Two Fridas), and *La columna rota* (1944; The Broken Column) record the sufferings that resulted from her physical distress, marital unhappiness, and her inability to bear children.

Although André Breton, the leader of **Surrealism,** claimed Kahlo's work was surreal, she stated that she painted her personal reality rather than dream imagery. Nevertheless, many critics believe that Kahlo's art lends itself to a Surrealist interpretation because she included dreamlike combinations in several of her paintings, for instance *Lo que me dio el agua* (1938; What Water Gave Me), and exhibited her work in the Exposición Internacional del Surrealismo, which took place in Mexico City in 1940. On the other hand, Kahlo did not share the Surrealists' disenchantment with Western culture nor their belief in its decline; her works, often strikingly candid, were records of lived events and their accompanying psychological and emotional states.

Although Kahlo had rejected religion at an early age, she was greatly interested in the Mexican cultural heritage embedded in the Catholic folk-art tradition of ex-votos. Kahlo and her husband owned a sizable collection of ex-voto paintings on tin or copper plates, featuring painted prayers and images of thanksgiving. A naive style, a narrative approach to the subject matter, an area reserved for explanatory captions, and a supernaturally charged space associated with ex-votos appear in many of Kahlo's paintings. The primitivizing style that pervades her votivelike paintings balances a retreat from realistic representation and the resulting psychological distance from dramatic subjects with a graphic attention to scien-

Frida Kahlo, 1939

tific detail. Unlike true naive artists, Kahlo achieved a sophisticated yet subtle balance between a primitivizing style and types of subject matter not previously represented, a balance from which dramas of both personal and mythic proportions emerge.

Like many of her contemporaries, Kahlo was obsessed with the concept of *Mexicanidad* (Mexicanness). She had been involved in leftist social and political causes since joining the Communist Party in 1928; yet paintings bearing related themes are not numerous in Kahlo's body of work. Instead, her paintings are full of references to the pre-Columbian past and indigenous folk traditions. In *Mi nana y yo* (1937; My Nanny and I) Kahlo is suckled by a dark-skinned woman wearing an Aztec mask who thus becomes an allegory of Mexico herself giving sustenance to her people. This theme is further developed in *El abrazo amoroso del Universo, la Tierra (México), Diego, Yo, y el Señor Xolotl* (1949; The Love Embrace of the Universe, the Earth [Mexico], Diego, Me, and Señor Xolotl), in which the

image of the indigenous woman takes on the role of universal mother-creator. Kahlo's numerous self-portraits are personalized statements of Mexicanness as much as they are expressions of her pain and experiments in catharsis. In her self-portraits, as in real life, the artist adorned herself with costumes native to Mexico.

Kahlo was a respected teacher who was hired as a professor of painting at Mexico City's Escuela de Pintura y Escultura "La Esmeralda" in 1943. She eventually achieved financial success as an artist and won international acclaim, but it was not until 1953 that she was honored with her first individual exhibition in Mexico. Kahlo's art won widespread international acclaim during the 1970s and 1980s. It became not only an important influence in contemporary Mexican art and Chicano art but also the source of a posthumous cult of personality that transformed Kahlo's image into a popular icon. Kahlo and Rivera achieved the status of national treasures in the popular press; their relationship is explored in Paul Leduc's movie *Frida: Naturaleza viva* (1984).

REFERENCE:

Hayden Herrera, *Frida Kahlo: The Paintings* (New York: HarperCollins, 1991).

— C.M.

MARIO KURI-ALDANA

Born in Tampico, Mexico, in 1931, Mario Kuri-Aldana was a student of piano at the Academia Juan Sebastián Bach. He entered the National School of Music at the Universidad Nacional Autónoma de México in 1952 and earned a degree in composition in 1960. Subsequent work with Luis Herrera de la Fuente and **Rodolfo Halffter** was followed by studies with distinguished contemporary composers and musicians at the famous Centro Latinoamericano de Altos Estudios Musicales (Latin American Center for Advanced Musical Studies) at the Torcuato Di Tella Institute in Buenos Aires; they included Alberto Ginastera, Riccardo Malipiero, Olivier Messiaen, Bruno Maderna, Luigi Dallapiccola, Aaron Copland, and Gilbert Chase. In addition, he studied orchestral conducting at the Mexican Instituto Nacional de Bellas Artes (National Institute of Fine Arts; 1957–1958) and worked with Karlheinz Stockhausen at the Mexican National Conservatory (1968). Kuri-Aldana's research into folk music, together with the influence of **Silvestre Revueltas** and **Carlos Chávez** on his early works, gave rise to a neonationalistic tendency in his music.

Kuri-Aldana has produced a large number of works in manuscript. Although relatively few of them have been published, his works have been widely performed in Mexico, especially by the National Symphony Orchestra and other regional orchestras. His works have occasionally been performed in the United States and South America. Among the orchestral compositions are *Sacrificio* (First Symphony, 1959), Second Symphony (1967), *Los Bacabs* (1969), and *Ce Acatl-1521* (Third Symphony, 1976). He has also written works for soloist and orchestra, featuring the oboe, **marimba**, piano, and violin.

Kuri-Aldana has been active as a music educator and conductor. He has served as director of symphonic bands of the Department of Public Education, lecturer in music and folklore at the Academy of Mexican Dance of the Instituto Nacional de Bellas Artes, teacher of composition at the Escuela Superior de Música, conductor of the Lebanese Center Chamber Orchestra, coordinator of

research for the National Fund for the Development of Popular Mexican Dance, and president of the League of Composers of Concert Music in Mexico. He has received many honors and awards for his compositions and for his services to music.

REFERENCES:

Gerard Béhague, *Music in Latin America: An Introduction* (Englewood Cliffs, N.J.: Prentice-Hall, 1979);

"Mario Kuri-Aldana," in *Composers of the Americas: Biographical Data and Catalogs of their Works*, volume 19 (Washington, D.C.: Music Section, Department of Cultural Affairs, Pan American Union, 1979).

— R.L.S.

L

WIFREDO LAM

The Cuban Wifredo Oscar de la Concepción Lam y Castilla (1902–1982) is one of the most important and internationally acclaimed of all Latin American artists. Lam's varied cultural and racial background had a strong impact on his life and art. Born of a Chinese father and an African European mother, Lam grew up in contact with both African and Chinese communities. At the same time, he learned about the cult of Santería from his godmother, who was a priestess in this syncretic religion combining Yoruba and Catholic beliefs. In 1916 Lam moved to Havana and studied art at the Academia San Alejandro; he later continued his art training in Madrid, where he settled in 1923. There Lam often visited the Museo del Prado, where he admired the art of El Greco and especially that of Hieronymus Bosch, whose paintings inspired Lam's interest in alchemy. In Madrid he also saw an exhibition of the work of Pablo Picasso, who would eventually become his friend and mentor. During this period Lam abandoned the realism of his early works and began to adopt more-modern styles. Paintings such as *La guerra civil española* (1936; The Spanish Civil War) reveal Lam's incipient interest in Cubism and Expressionism, as well as his support for the Spanish Loyalist cause. Lam left Spain for France in 1938.

In Paris Lam became Picasso's protégé and was introduced by him to African art and to the Parisian avant-garde. Lam continued to develop his own style in works such as *Mujer en violeta* (1938; Woman in Violet), which synthesizes Cubist and African sources. In 1940 Lam left Paris for Marseille, where he befriended several Surrealists, including André Breton and Max Ernst. Lam's 1940 illustrations for Breton's *Fata Morgana* include fantastic horned and masked beings, which reveal his interest in **Surrealism**'s use of automatist drawing, dreamlike configurations, archetypal symbols, and metamorphic imagery. In the company of Breton and the anthropologist Claude Lévi-Strauss, Lam traveled to Martinique, where he met Aimé Césaire, one of the leaders of the **Négritude** movement.

Lam returned to Havana in 1941. Renewed direct experience of African Cuban culture and his friendship with the principal supporters of the African Cuban movement, such as **Fernando Ortiz, Lydia Cabrera,** and **Alejo Carpentier,** had a decisive influence on the orientation of his art. During the 1940s Lam formulated a masterly and personal synthesis of African and Cuban elements with modern styles, including Cubism and Surrealism. In masterpieces such as *La jungla* (1943; The Jungle) and *Le Présent éternel (Hommage à Alejandro García Caturla)* (1944; Eternal Present [Homage to Alejandro García Caturla]), Lam used fragmented shapes and shallow space inspired by Cubism and organic metamorphic forms borrowed from Surrealism to suggest Santería symbols and the tropical flora of Cuba. Lam subtly evokes ritual offerings in honor of the Yoruba Orishas (divine spirits) Ogún, Eleguá, and Changó and through horselike motifs also suggests the possesion by an Orisha of a devotee, who is "ridden" by the god during a Santería ritual. Although in works such as *Le Présent éternel* Lam criticizes the sexual exploitation of African Cuban women and the lack of social identity of African Cuban men, in most of his paintings his approach is more poetic than political, seeking to elicit a psychic response through the use of archetypal images.

After a visit to Haiti with Breton in 1945, where he attended voodoo rituals, Lam introduced more-violent and threatening symbols in his art. In 1946 Lam began to share his time between Havana and Paris, and although in 1952 Paris became his primary place of residence he visited Cuba often, both before and after the Cuban Revolution, which he supported. After the

Wifredo Lam in his studio with *Le Présent éternel* (1944; Eternal Present) and *Figure* (1947), Havana, 1947

late 1940s Lam continued to work with similar themes, but his style became more simplified, and he eventually abandoned the impressionistic treatment of color and brushstroke of the early 1940s for the use of flat areas of darker colors, as in *Luz de arcilla* (1950; Light of Clay). During the 1950s Lam achieved international acclaim.

REFERENCES:

Valerie Fletcher, ed., *Crosscurrents of Modernism: Four Latin American Pioneers: Diego Rivera, Joaquín Torres-García, Wifredo Lam, Matta* (Washington, D.C.: Hirshhorn Museum and Sculpture Garden, 1992);

Juan A. Martínez, *Cuban Art and National Identity: The Vanguardia Painters, 1927–1950* (Gainesville: University Press of Florida, 1994).

—F.B.N.

LANGUAGES

Spanish is the language spoken by the majority of the populations in most of the countries covered in the present volume; however, there is also a save the con-

siderable presence of Indian languages in southern Mexico and the northern part of Central America and pockets of English and African dialects spoken along the Atlantic coast of Central America. (Spanish is also a major language in Belize, formerly known as British Honduras.)

Several varieties of Spanish were spoken by the colonists and explorers of the new American territories. The language of the newcomers, who came from different parts of Spain, varied according to their home regions. (In the late fifteenth century Spain was just becoming unified.) When these people were poorly educated, as was often the case, those linguistic variations tended to be accentuated.

Although some features of modern American Spanish are often thought to be distinctively American, in fact, few such features cannot be found in one or another of the dialects of Spanish spoken in the Iberian Peninsula. Some American habits have become antiquated in the peninsula; others can be accounted for by the different evolutionary path American varieties have taken, sometimes as a result of contact with other languages. Some words that were first assimilated into American Spanish from Indian languages subsequently made their way back to Europe (and via Spain to other countries).

Spanish American countries charge their official national academies of the Spanish language, modeled on Spain's Real Academia de la Lengua, with respecting national differences while preserving linguistic unity throughout the Hispanic world. Through their work these national entities give formal acceptance (often with great reluctance) to changes in the language. The achievements of Spanish American writers in the second half of this century have greatly enhanced the prestige of American varieties of Spanish.

The number of varieties of American Spanish depends on the classification system used to draw distinctions. According to the system used by Pedro Henríquez Ureña, a well-known researcher from the Dominican Republic, there are half a dozen principal varieties of American Spanish; a later classification by a South American linguist, José Pedro Rona, proposes four times that number. As far as the particular areas covered in the present volume are concerned, a rather crude dialectal division (after Henríquez Ureña) identifies the following varieties of Spanish: Northern and Central Mexican, Southern Mexican and Central American, and the Caribbean (including Panama and the Caribbean coastal areas of Colombia and Venezuela). While it is quite possible to tell a Puerto Rican from a Cuban or a Costa Rican from a Mexican, the level of mutual intelligibility is extremely high, especially among educated people. Among the many dialectal differences, a large number derive from vocabulary and pronunciation, particularly the pronunciation of consonants. Vowels tend to disappear and consonants to be more precise in much of Mexico (a phenomenon that has been attributed variously to indigenous influences and even to altitude). In lowland areas, especially around the Caribbean, the opposite is often the case. Certain parts of Central America use antiquated and much-modified pronoun and verb forms, a phenomenon known as *voseo* (also found in areas of Uruguay and Argentina).

Many indigenous languages are spoken in parts of Mexico and Central America. The language of the Aztecs, Nahuatl, is spoken mostly in the central plateau of Mexico by about one million speakers; about one fourth are monolingual. In the southernmost area of Mexico several Mayan languages are spoken, especially Yucatecan Mayan. Huastec is spoken in Veracruz, and in the southeast Mixtec, Zapotec, Otomi, and Totonac are spoken by about one hundred thousand Indians each. Altogether it is estimated that Mexico has some two million to three million speakers of in-

digenous languages. In El Salvador and northern Honduras, Mísquito and Lenca are spoken by a few hundred. (Honduras in the mid twentieth century had 80,550 speakers of indigenous languages; at that same time it was estimated that there were 21,500 indigenous-language speakers in Nicaragua, with Mísquito dominating). In Costa Rica about twenty thousand indigenes speak a variety of native languages, and in Panama the indigenous speakers are the Cuna of the Saint Blas islands and the Darien mainland and the Choc.

A large number of Indian languages are still spoken in the highlands of Guatemala. There are twenty-two recognized Mayan languages, and it is estimated that if one includes the more-remote areas the number would be closer to thirty-five. The major languages are Quiché (spoken by approximately 618,000 speakers in sixty-six different villages), Mam (with 378,000 speakers in fifty-three villages), Kaqchikel (with 337,200 in forty-eight villages), and Kekchi (spoken by 250,800 Mayas in twelve villages). Many of the major languages also include a variety of dialects that are different enough from each other to make it difficult for communication even among speakers of languages in the same linguistic group. Also, in order to survive economically and reduce discriminatory practices by the dominant non-Indian sectors, the indigenous peoples generally have recognized the necessity of learning Spanish. Therefore, many of them are bilingual, and the growing tendency to concentrate only on Spanish may point to a major cultural loss in future decades. Nevertheless, Mayan intellectuals were able to win a significant victory in 1992, when Mayan languages were at last recognized as official languages by the Guatemalan government, which had previously dismissed them as inferior, favoring their replacement by Spanish. What has been termed the Mayan "revitalization movement" has made progress in establishing the importance and value of Mayan languages and culture in a ladino-dominated environment. (See also **Indigenous Peoples**.)

REFERENCES:

Simon Collier and others, eds. *Cambridge Encyclopaedia of Latin America and the Caribbean* (Cambridge: Cambridge University Press, 1985);

Alonso Zamora Vicente, *Dialectología Española* (Madrid: Editorial Gredos, 1974).

— P.S. & M.E.S.

AGUSTÍN LARA

Agustín Lara (1897–1970) was born in Mexico City into what today would be labeled a dysfunctional family.

His father, a doctor in the military service of the government of Porfirio Díaz, maintained a confrontational relationship with the rebellious Agustín. The fact that the latter played the piano by ear at the age of seven (he refused to learn to read music) failed to attract the support of his father, who wanted him to pursue the medical profession. He ran away from home for a year at the age of twelve, returning only when he learned that his father had been sent to Europe. During his father's absence Agustín played piano in a local brothel. However, he was surprised there by his father and sent first to a military school and subsequently to work in a railroad station in Durango as punishment. During the **Mexican Revolution** he enlisted with the *villistas*, the revolutionary group of Pancho Villa, but was dismissed because of his fragile physical condition. Relying once again on his musical talent, he began playing in cabarets, in one of which, in a fit of jealousy, a woman severely disfigured his face with a broken bottle. Bitter and ashamed of his appearance, Lara spent the next few years playing in seedy bars.

In 1929, having begun to compose popular songs, Lara returned to Mexico City to find work. Later in life he was unable to remember clearly this period of composition; he could not even remember the title of his first **bolero**. It is known, however, that "Imposible" was among his first and that, desperate for money, he sold the rights to this popular work for a mere forty pesos. It would not be the last ill-advised business deal to which he would agree.

Lara's life changed drastically when he became the accompanist for the popular singer Juan Arvizu. Concert tours, appearances in elegant clubs and theaters, and Arvizu's performances of his songs brought Lara fame, wealth, and the admiration of an adoring public. In 1930 the radio station XEW La Voz de América Latina (The Voice of Latin America) began broadcasting, and many of Lara's new songs were presented on his program called *La hora íntima de Augustín Lara* (An Intimate Hour with Augustín Lara): *Reliquia* (Relic), *Nunca te ovidaré* (I'll Never Forget You), *Boca chiquita* (Tiny Mouth), and *Serenata* (Serenade).

Lara's propensity for the company of beautiful women led him through a series of unsuccessful marriages, several of which were immortalized in hit songs: *Mujer* for Angelina Bruschetta, *Cuando vuelvas* for Carmen Zozaya, *María bonita* and *Aquel amor* for María Félix. His prodigious production of songs between 1930 and 1968 was unmatched by any other composer of his time.

Despite his disfigured face, Lara enjoyed considerable popularity in the Mexican film industry. In the 1940s and 1950s he appeared in *Novillero*, *Perdida*, *Coqueta*, *La mujer que yo amé*, and *Mujeres en mi vida.*

Among the many honors and tributes that were extended to Lara toward the end of his life was a home in Granada, Spain, presented by Spain's dictator Francisco Franco in gratitude for the songs that honored Spanish cities: *Granada*, *Sevilla*, *Murcia*, *Toledo*, and *Madrid*. Lara retired from his active professional life in 1968 and spent his last years as a recluse. He died on 6 November 1970 at the age of seventy-three. His body lay in state at the Society of Authors and Composers and later at the Palace of Fine Arts; finally, on the order of the then-president of Mexico Gustavo Díaz Ordaz, his remains were placed in the Rotunda de los Hombres Ilustres del Panteón de Dolores (The Pantheon of Suffering Rotunda of Illustrious Men).

REFERENCES:

Hernán Restrepo Duque, *Lo que cuentan los boleros* (Santafé de Bogotá: Centro Editorial de Estudios Musicales, 1992);

Jaime Rico Salazar, *Cien años de boleros* (Santafé de Bogotá: Centro Editorial de Estudios Musicales, 1987).

            — R.L.S.

CLAUDIA LARS

Claudia Lars is the pen name of Carmen Brannon (1899–1974), a Salvadoran poet born in Armenia to a U.S./Irish father and a Salvadoran mother whose own father was of Indian origin. Lars's eclectic ancestry contributed to her unique approach to poetry. Although the publication of many of her collections of poems coincides with the time of the avant-garde movement in Latin American literature, Claudia Lars was not part of it. She chose to place her very personal themes within more traditional forms of poetry, such as the sonnet and the **romance.** It is not difficult to recognize her affinity with certain great poets of Ireland, England, and Spain.

Although Lars's paternal background explains a natural inclination to study European classics of poetry, her relationship with the young Nicaraguan writer Salomón de la Selva, author of *El soldado desconocido* (1922; The Unknown Soldier), influenced her choice of poetic models. With Salomón de la Selva, Lars studied the works of earlier Spanish, English, and American poets and then transformed the models they provided her into a highly personal mode of expression. The relationship between the two writers ended abruptly when Lars's father opposed their marriage and sent his daughter to live with relatives in the United States.

After returning to El Salvador, Lars published her first book of poetry, *Estrellas en el pozo* (1934;

Stars in the Well), when she was thirty-five years old. The collections of poems that followed were *Canción redonda* (1937; Round Song), *Casa de vidrio* (1942; House of Glass), which was a book for and about children and was dedicated to her newly born son, and *Sonetos* (1946; Sonnets). The poetry of Lars consistently projects a tone of familiarity and domesticity, all contained within traditional structures. The recurring themes of her work often involve seemingly disparate elements, such as a comparison of divine and human love, an accentuation of the beauty of the Salvadoran landscape, a questioning of the unhappy fate of its people living in political turmoil, and the reconciliation of the two different traditions, Irish and Spanish, that comprised her genealogical background. In her final years Lars took to writing poetry in prose published in the collections *Sobre el ángel y el hombre* (1962; Of Angels and Men) and *Tierra de infancia* (1958; Land of Childhood), which contains references to Lars's Indian ancestry and reflects a preoccupation with equitable treatment for the Indians of El Salvador.

REFERENCE:

Claudia Lars, *Sus mejores poemas* (San Salvador: Ministerio de Educacion, 1976).

— D.H., M.E.S., & P.S.

ERNESTO LECUONA

Ernesto Lecuona (1895–1963), born in Guanabacoa, Cuba, began early studies in piano with his sister, Ernestina, who also became a popular composer. At the age of five he gave his first public recital, and at eleven, following his father's death, he began playing piano for silent films at various theaters, among them the Teatro Fedora de la Habana. He wrote his first compositions at age twelve, including the *danza* "La comparsa," and began playing them in public recitals. In 1908, during the second occupation of Cuba by American forces, he published his first piece, the two-step *Cuba y América*, and produced various short musical comedies in the Teatro Martí to librettos by his brother, Fernando. Despite his active life in popular theaters, Lecuona continued serious studies of music at the National Conservatory and won its Gold Medal in 1913.

In 1917 Lecuona's debut at the Aeolian Hall in New York was well received, and he began a period of more than two decades on the international concert stage, performing both his own works and those of classical composers. Ignacy Paderewsky, the Polish composer/virtuoso pianist, and Maurice Ravel were said to be amazed at his talent. Another world-class pianist, Artur Rubinstein, upon hearing Lecuona play

"Malagueña," said that he was not sure whether he admired him more for his genius as a pianist or as a composer.

Lecuona always returned to Cuba between his international commitments. In 1922 Lecuona and Gonzalo Roig, the Cuban violinist/conductor and composer of numerous **zarzuelas** and romantic songs, founded Cuba's first orchestra, the Orquesta Sinfónica de la Habana. Lecuona later played the Cuban premiere of George Gershwin's *Rhapsody in Blue* (1931), with Roig conducting. In the late 1920s Lecuona began to compose a series of successful zarzuelas: *Niña Rita* and *La Habana en 1830* (1927); *El cafetal*, *El Batey*, and *El maizal* (1928); and *María la O* (1930). The star of many of Lecuona's works for the stage was Rita Montaner, a singer from his hometown who had gained her theatrical experience in the United States, touring with the Schubert Follies.

Among Lecuona's numerous salon works for piano that have continued to be popular are the suite *Andalucía*, the *Danzas Afro-Cubanas*, and more than seventy others, including "Allí viene el chino," "Danza negra," "La comparsa," and "Danza lucumí." His romantic songs, some originating in the zarzuelas, became standards throughout Latin America, and many became popular in North America as well. Among them are "Siboney," "Tengo un nuevo amor," "Aquella tarde," "Como arrullo de palmas," and "Siempre en mi corazón." In 1931 he formed a touring **rumba/bolero** group, the Lecuona Cuban Boys, which became very popular. Lecuona returned to Cuba during the first year of the European tour because of illness, but the ensemble, under the direction of Armando Oráfiche, stayed on until the beginning of World War I, when they returned to the Americas. They continued under Lecuona's name until 1946, when their name changed to the Habana Cuban Boys.

Lecuona was criticized and neglected by some serious musicians and writers for devoting his talent and energy to popular and commercial music rather than to classical genres. For enthusiasts of popular music, however, he made a significant contribution to the quality of radio and television broadcasts and to the history of Cuban music, through the numerous recordings of his works. In early January 1960, shortly after the successful revolution led by **Fidel Castro**, Lecuona arrived in Tampa, Florida, where he remained until he moved to Spain in 1963 in search of relief from asthma. Following his death later the same year, his body was returned for burial in Westchester, New York.

REFERENCES:

Cristóbal Díaz Ayala, *Música cubana del Areyto a la Nueva Trova* (San Juan: Editorial Cubanacán, 1981);

Hernán Resprepo Duque, *Lo que cuentan los boleros* (Santafé de Bogotá: Centro Editorial de Estudios Musicales, 1922);

Jaime Rico Salazar, *Cien años de boleros* (Santafé de Bogotá: Centro Editorial de Estudios Musicales, 1987).

— R.L.S.

VICENTE LEÑERO

Born in Guadalajara, Jalisco, in 1933, Vicente Leñero is one of the most influential Mexican dramatists of the 1960s and 1970s. A civil engineer, he became an active journalist in 1959. In addition Leñero has been professionally involved with television as a screenwriter of several soap operas. His first literary production was a collection of short stories, *La polvareda y otros cuentos* (1958, The Dust Cloud and Other Stories), followed by four novels: *La voz adolorida* (1961; The Pained Voice), *Los albañiles* (1963; The Stonemasons), *Estudio Q* (1965; Study Q), and *El garabato* (1967; The Scribble). Leñero uses vanguardist techniques associated with documentary theater to reveal social messages. The prime example is *Pueblo rechazado* (1968; The Rejects). This drama blends reality and fiction to reproduce the true story of a Mexican monk, Father Gregorio Lemercier, and his struggles with church authorities. Leñero's play *El juicio* (1972; The Judgment), the story of a high-profile murder trial in Mexico, combines personal conjecture with trial facts as recorded by the clerk of the court. This combination of history and drama functions as a creative device to provoke cultural introspection.

The only Mexican writer of his generation to win a major international literary award, Leñero received the Biblioteca Breve prize for his novel *Los albañiles,* which examines social guilt in postrevolutionary Mexico. A detective fails to solve a murder case that took place on the construction site of a high-rise apartment complex in Mexico City. The workers, unskilled laborers who have migrated from provincial areas, form the suspected group; however, the detective is unable to name a murderer from among the suspects. *Los albañiles* is really concerned with understanding the results of the historical process of urbanization in Mexico. No individual is condemned for the crime; instead, society as a collective body is found guilty. Leñero completely rewrote *Los albañiles* for the theater and won the Ruíz de Alarcón prize in 1969 for the best play of the year in Mexico. It was later made into a film.

REFERENCE:

Vicente Leñero, *Vivir del teatro* (Mexico: Empresas Editoriales, 1967).

— M.T.

ARGELIERS LEÓN

Argeliers León (1918–), a prolific ethnomusicologist, professor, composer, and staunch defender of the socialist principles of the Cuban Revolution, is the most important of the musicians who followed in the footsteps of **Amadeo Roldán**, pursuing an Afro-Cuban nationalism (see **Afro-Caribbean music**). León's early composition studies in Cuba with the Spanish-born **José Ardévol** were followed by a residency in Paris with the mentor of many contemporary composers, Nadia Boulanger. León was awarded an additional residency to study folklore and teaching methods at the University of Chile. His musical works reflect a vibrant disdain for what he saw as Yankee cultural domination and for the socio-economic class structure of capitalism. Works such as *Yambú, Bolero y guaguancó*, and *Akorín* (adaptations for piano of Afro-Cuban ritual songs) echo the culture of common people, of the Afro-Cuban collective.

REFERENCES:

Alejo Carpentier, *La música en Cuba*, second edition (Mexico City: Fondo de Cultura Económica, 1972);

Cristóbal Díaz Ayala, *Música cubana del Areyto a la Nueva Trova*, second edition (San Juan: Editorial Cubanacán, 1981);

Argeliers León, "Of the Axle and the Hinge: Nationalism, Afro-Cubanism, and Music in Pre-Revolutionary Cuba," translated by Terence Sweeny in *Essays on Cuban Music: North American and Cuban Perspectives*, edited by Peter Manuel (Lanham, Md.: University Press of America, 1991).

— R.L.S.

MIGUEL LEÓN-PORTILLA

A prominent Mexican scholar and educator, Miguel León-Portilla has been at the forefront of the study of indigenous cultures, especially those involving the Aztecs. León-Portilla spent decades researching, organizing, and translating documents from Nahuatl, documents that offer a fresh outlook on the encounter between the Spaniards and the Aztecs in 1521, on the aftermath in colonial Mexico, and the repercussions of it all in modern Mexican society. Although numerous accounts of the encounter exist, the vast majority have been written by the victors, whether conquistadors or missionaries. León-Portilla's efforts at presenting the Aztec version met with tremendous success: hundreds of thousands of copies of his book, *Visión de los vencidos* (1959; translated as *Broken Spears: The Aztec Account of the Conquest of Mexico*), were sold; it was translated into more than a dozen languages, and it has been used as a textbook in universities. Part of this success may be attributed to an increasing general interest among scholars and intellectuals in revitalizing an indigenous past, as a way of understanding national origins.

Visión de los vencidos is a result of León-Portilla's painstaking research into documents dating back to a few years after the defeat of the Aztec capital, Tenochtitlán, in 1521. The documents themselves were accounts by Nahua eyewitnesses and survivors who had been trained by Spanish priests and missionaries, especially by the famous Dominican friar Bernardino de Sahagún, to write down their stories in Nahuatl. They recorded accounts passed down by oral tradition and interpreted pictoglyphs. With his anthropological studies León-Portilla influenced many other scholars to learn Nahuatl and to contribute to ongoing research into Nahua history and culture.

REFERENCE:

Miguel León-Portilla, ed., *Broken Spears: The Aztec Account of the Conquest of Mexico,* foreword by J. Jorge Klor de Alva (Boston: Beacon, 1992).

—M.E.S.

José Lezama Lima

José Lezama Lima (1910–1976), a major Cuban author, was born near Havana. He was an asthmatic child who grew up haunted by the absence of his father, a soldier who had died in 1919, not in battle but of influenza while in Pensacola, Florida. After his two sisters married, Lezama lived with his mother until her death in 1964. During the course of their many years together he became so closely identified with his mother that he acquired her speech patterns. Only after her death did he marry (as she had urged him to do), and with his wife he continued to live in his mother's house until his death.

The asthma that had limited Lezama's childhood activities and helped foster his wide reading did not prevent him altogether from becoming a participant in student political actions. Following his mother's wishes, he studied law, but he was fundamentally a reader, writer, and conversationalist. Lezama was also a Catholic, though a Catholic of a very unusual kind, drawn to oriental mysticism and capable of reconciling his lifestyle with his religion and his religion with the tenets of the Cuban Revolution. Lezama became a close friend of a Spanish priest, whom he would visit in the company of other intellectuals who eventually came to be associated with a journal called *Orígenes* (Origins); the journal was named after the priest's church, which was also the recipient of some of the

group's artistic works. Lezama was also a close friend of **Virgilio Piñera.**

In 1937 Lezama caused a stir in Cuban artistic circles with the daring metaphorical language he used in an address to a cultural association. The address, called "Garcilaso's Secret," reflected his interest in the Spanish classics and was probably influenced by his recent acquaintance with the Spanish poet Juan Ramón Jiménez, an advocate of pure poetry. By that time, however, Lezama was already a respected poet; 1937 was also the year that saw the publication of his key poetic work, *Muerte de Narciso* (The Death of Narcissus). *Orígenes,* became the most important literary and artistic journal of its time and published the work of many of the most important Spanish and Spanish American poets of the day. (Much later it inspired the establishment of a publishing house in Spain under the same name.) The journal gives many clues to an understanding of Lezama's poetics. In it Lezama also published some of his stories and a few chapters of his novel *Paradiso* (1966; translated in 1974). The journal *Orígenes* began to appear in 1944 and continued until the mid 1950s, when an editorial disagreement led first to the publication of rival issues and ultimately to the journal's demise. Some of those writers who parted company with Lezama used a new journal, *Ciclón,* to advocate a more accessible poetry that they thought would be more relevant to Cuba.

If the revolution of 1959 seemed to bring about some of the changes for which Lezama had hoped, his relationship with it was uneven. He was attacked as an influential figure of the past and yet was appointed director of publications for the Consejo Nacional de Cultura (National Cultural Council). In 1961 he became president of the Unión de Escritores y Artistas de Cuba (UNEAC—the writers' and artists' union), and a year later he began work as an advisor to the Centro Cubano de Investigaciones Literarias (Cuban Center for Literary Research). When his novel *Paradiso* first appeared in an edition prepared by CEAC, an attempt was made by government officials to withdraw it from circulation. In 1971 he became implicated in the **Padilla Affair** and was accused of antirevolutionary behavior. By this time his overindulgent lifestyle and his obesity were taking their toll, and he was already reclusive. Lezama died in 1976; in the 1980s the Cuban government made efforts to rehabilitate his image.

Lezama Lima's poetry and prose are characterized by a neobaroque style, with complex, hermetic language, fragmented imagery, and enigmatic metaphors. His work has been compared to that of James Joyce. Lezama is best known for his poetry and for *Paradiso. Paradiso* met with an immediate reaction

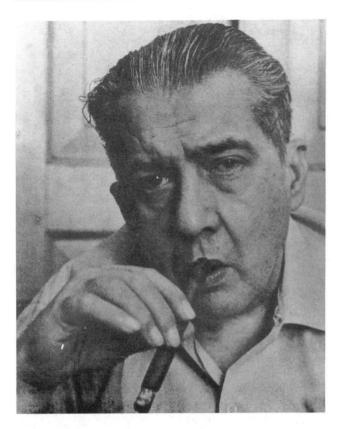

José Lezama Lima

when it became known outside Cuba, thanks to a Mexican edition published in 1968, with illustrations by fellow Cuban **René Portocarrero,** an artist who had been associated with the *Orígenes* group. Among the prominent writers who lauded *Paradiso* were two of the major figures of the **Boom,** Julio Cortázar and Mario Vargas Llosa. Others (including the Cuban government) were troubled by the novel's homosexual elements or by its apparent incoherence. *Paradiso,* like most of Lezama's works, has taxed critics. It is not structured on the basis of cause and effect, nor does it have a single, clear theme. Its characters launch into discourses on the nature of poetry, the unknown, and the possibilities of redemption through the power of the image. There is a clear preoccupation with death and a return to origins (for which the image of the genealogical tree provides a structural focus). Also evoked is a world of phallic images and detailed sexual practices. Many elements in the novel parallel Lezama's own experiences: for example, the protagonist's asthma, his mystical experiences, his chosen profession, and his introspection. (The protagonist retreats, as did Lezama, from society in order to focus on the purity of poetic expression.) *Paradiso* contains a character whose name became the title of an unfin-

ished sequel, *Oppiano Licario,* published posthumously (1977).

Important sources for an understanding of Lezama's literature are his *Introducción a los vasos órficos* (1971; Introduction to the Orphic vessels) and *La expresión americana* (1957; American Expression). Other poetry collections are *Enemigo rumor* (1941; Enemy rumor), *Aventuras sigilosas* (1945; Secret Adventures), *La fijeza* (1945; Persistence), and *Dador* (1960).

REFERENCES:

Emilio Bejel, *José Lezama Lima: Poet of the Image* (Gainesville: University of Florida Press, 1990);

Raymond D. Souza, *Major Cuban Novelists: Innovation and Tradition* (Columbia: University of Missouri Press, 1976);

Justo C. Ulloa, ed., *José Lezama Lima: Textos críticos* (Miami & Madrid: Universal, 1979).

— P.S.

HUGO LINDO

Unlike fellow poets in his native El Salvador, Hugo Lindo (1917–1985) achieved both critical acclaim and public acknowledgment of his abilities during his lifetime. By the time of his death Lindo had received several literary awards, mostly for his poetry; he had also served as ambassador to three different countries: Chile, Colombia, and Spain.

His poetry differs from the standard in El Salvador; Lindo chose to universalize personal issues rather than focus on social protest based on his country's situation. The recurrent themes in Lindo's poetry include the Catholic religion, the paradox of life and death, the role of the poet in relation to his world, and the nature of the limits of time and space. His best-known poetic works are *Poema eucarístico y otros* (1943; A Eucharist Poem and Others), *Libro de horas* (1947; Book of Hours), *Sinfonía del límite* (1953; Symphony of Limits), *Sangre de Hispania fecunda* (1972; Blood of Fertile Hispania), *Sólo la voz* (1967; translated as *Only the Voice,* 1984), *Maneras de llover* (1968; translated as *Ways to Rain,* 1986), and *Este pequeño siempre* (1971; This Little Always). Lindo handles complex human issues in his poems and strives for perfection of form. His careful use of stress creates a subtle internal rhythm that lends a lyrical quality to the majority of his typically lengthy poetic compositions. Another distinctive element in Lindo's poetry is the careful selection of vocabulary to create a harmonious overall sound when read aloud. Both the sonorous qualities of the words and the musicality of the verse serve as testimony to the strong influence of **Rubén Darío,** the Nicaraguan **Modernista** poet. Maintaining the same themes he explored in his poetry, Lindo expanded his literary achievements with his novels: *El anzuelo de Dios* (1956; The Pull of God), *Cada día tiene su afán* (1965; Each Day Has Its Enthusiasm), *Yo soy la memoria* (1983; I Am Memory), and *Fácil palabra* (1985; Easy Word). He also published several collections of short stories: *Guaro y champaña* (1947; Moonshine and Champagne), *Aquí se cuentan cuentos* (1960; Stories Told Here), and *Espejos paralelos* (1974; Parallel Mirrors).

REFERENCE:

Hugo Lindo, *Sólo la voz / Only the Voice,* translated by Elizabeth Gamble Miller (Richardson, Tex.: Mundus Artium Press, 1984).

— D.H.

RAMÓN LÓPEZ VELARDE

One of the initiators of contemporary poetry in Spanish America, the Mexican Ramón López Velarde (1888–1921) is a member of a generation that bridges **Modernismo** and the avant-garde spearheaded by the Chilean Vicente Huidobro. López Velarde was born in Jerez in the province of Zacatecas, studied law at the University of San Luis de Potosí, and then moved to Mexico City, where he worked for the rest of his brief life as a journalist and public servant. The sentimental and nostalgic provincial themes that predominate in the early poems in López Velarde's *La sangre devota* (1916; Devout Blood), are mixed with a certain sensual evocation of Catholic imagery, the latter reminiscent of the Spanish mystics. Later these emotive themes are found in regional descriptions focusing on everyday life that evoke a spirit of Mexican nationalism, especially notable in his poem "La suave patria" ("Sweet Land") and in *Zozobra* (1919; Anxiety), in which he uses innovative and varied rhymes, structures, and images. López Velarde is essentially a poet of feelings, who manipulates language with daring metaphors and erotic imagery that appeal to the visual, olfactory, and tactile senses. In his search for different metaphors and techniques as ways of provoking feelings, he was much influenced by the Argentinean Modernista poet Leopoldo Lugones. His principal themes include pain, love, and Catholicism, all situated in a regional and patriotic context, but with universal implications. A bilingual collection of López Velarde's poems, *Song of the Heart,* was published in 1995.

REFERENCES:

Ramón López Velarde, *Song of the Heart: Selected Poems,* translated by Margaret Sayers Peden (Austin: University of Texas Press, 1995);

Ramón López Velarde at age thirty

Judy Held Monsour, *La suave patria in the works of Ramón López Velarde* (New Orleans, 1964).

— M.E.S.

GREGORIO LÓPEZ Y FUENTES

Born on a ranch in the state of Veracruz, Mexico, Gregorio López y Fuentes (1897–1966) grew up mingling with farmhands and Indians and became familiar with the problems of the rural poor. While studying in Mexico City to become a teacher, he came into contact with various writers and realized that writing was his true vocation. After being caught up in the fighting of the **Mexican Revolution,** he dedicated himself to journalism and literature. Although he first published two books of poetry, López y Fuentes became known as a novelist of the Mexican Revolution. The masses were his protagonists.

His first important novel is *Campamento* (1931; Camp), considered quite original because of its cinematographic sketches of what occurs among different groups of revolutionary soldiers in a camp at night. His next novel, *Tierra* (1932; Earth), is a dramatic rendering of the agrarian revolution between 1910 and 1920, under the leadership of Emiliano Zapata. In *Tierra* centuries-long conflict between the landowners and the agrarian peasants is portrayed: the landowners control all resources because of the corruption of politicians and the support of the army and the Catholic Church, while the peasants struggle to survive in miserable poverty. López y Fuentes's most famous novel, however, is *El indio* (1935; The Indian), regarded as the initiator of the novel of the Indian in Mexico. It is a dramatic presentation of the misery and exploitation of the Indians in the wake of the Mexican Revolution, as well as a colorful, if stereotypical, depiction of their customs and traditions. His next most important novel is *Los peregrinos inmóviles* (1944; The Motionless Pilgrims), a novel about an Indian tribe that was freed after the Mexican Revolution and embarked on a pilgrimage to find a suitable place to settle. It is an obvious allegory of an enslaved people who gain their freedom and set out to find the promised land. Like *El indio* the end of this novel offers no solution but rather reflects a hopeless, pessimistic, yet realistic assessment of the general situation of Indians in Mexico.

López y Fuentes also published *Entresuelo* (1948; Mezzanine), which deals with migration from rural to urban areas, and *Milpa, potrero y monte* (1951; Field, Pasture, and Forest), which depicts the lives of peasants, cattlemen, and hunters. In addition, he has an excellent collection of short stories, *Cuentos campesinos de Mexico* (1940; Peasant Stories of Mexico). (See also **Indigenism in Literature.**)

REFERENCE:

John S. Brushwood, *Mexico in Its Novel: A Nation's Search for Identity* (Austin: University of Texas Press, 1966).

          —M.E.S.

DULCE MARÍA LOYNAZ

The Cuban writer Dulce María Loynaz (1902–) was catapulted into the critical limelight by the award, at the age of ninety, of the **Premio Cervantes,** one of the most coveted literary prizes open only to writers in Spanish. She had previously been best known for the poetry she had published largely in Madrid during the 1950s: for example, *Poemas sin nombre* (1953; Poems Without a Name), *Obra lírica* (1955; Lyrical Works), and *Ultimos días de una casa* (1958; The Last Days of a House). It is ironic that she should have received recognition in Spain since she was the daughter of a general who had fought in Cuba's war of independence against Spain and since love of her native country is a theme in her work, notably in "Isla mía," one of the poems in *Poemas sin nombre.* Her family background and her attachment to Cuba led her to stay on the island, although she distanced herself from the 1959 revolution. Despite her patrician roots, she was something of a feminist and an innovator. Her patriotic love poems are not cast in the bombastic style that is common in patriotic verse; hers is a poetry rich in sources and in natural imagery. Elsewhere, she writes of a sense of limitation because she is a woman. Her one novel, *Jardín* (Garden), published in 1951 though written some thirty years previously, is unconventional, a novel she herself described as "incoherent and monotonous." In 1993 Loynaz's collected poetry was published in Havana as *Poesía completa.*

REFERENCES:

Ana Rosa Núñez, ed., *Homenaje a Dulce María Loynaz, Premio Cervantes* (Miami: Universal, 1993);

Pedro Simón, *Dulce María Loynaz* (Havana: Letras Cubanas, 1991).

          —P.S.

M

MAGAZINES

As in Europe, magazines from Mexico to the Caribbean are bought from kiosks on street corners, rather than via mail order as they are in the United States. Editorial América, a major international magazine publisher of Latin America, circulates its magazines only by newsstand sales in Latin America. In the 1990s there are some five thousand periodicals in Latin America.

Mexico is the leading magazine-publishing nation in Latin America. There are approximately two thousand periodicals published there, the vast majority privately owned and distributed. *Televisión y Novelas* (a television-program guide), *Tú* (a beauty and fashion magazine), and *Almas* (a Catholic Church publication) are among the most widely circulated magazines in Mexico. Panama and Honduras are the leading periodical-publishing nations in Central America. Panama has roughly 140 periodicals. Its *Análisis* is perhaps the most highly regarded political-commentary magazine in the region. Honduras produces about forty periodicals, of which the most influential is *Revista Militar,* a magazine published by the army. In the Caribbean magazines are regularly imported from North America, South America, and Europe. The most popular magazine in Puerto Rico is *Vea Televisión Guide;* another widely read magazine in Puerto Rico is *Caribbean Business,* a regional weekly with a circulation of about fifty thousand. The oldest national magazine in Cuba is the weekly *Revista Bohemia,* founded in 1908, with a circulation of more than three hundred thousand copies. *Verde Olivo* of Cuba is another national magazine, a weekly publication of the Revolutionary Armed Forces that has a circulation of about one hundred thousand. The major sports magazines in Cuba are *Semanario Deportivo Listos Para Vencer* (Ready to Win Sports Weekly) and *El Deporte — Derecho del Pueblo* (Sport — A Right of the People).

Some of the highest-quality newsmagazines in the region are published in Mexico. *Revista de Revistas,* a weekly newsmagazine published by the daily newspaper *Excelsior,* focuses on progovernment political reporting, business, and the urban lifestyle. One of the best commentary magazines in the whole of Latin America is *Proceso,* which represents the leading voices of the political Left in Mexico. It is frank about politicians and corruption. *Siempre,* another popular weekly commentary magazine in Mexico, is produced by the Partido Socialista Popular (Popular Socialist Party). In Cuba political-commentary magazines, like all mass media, are funded by the Communist Party. More than one hundred periodicals are published by various departments of the national and regional governments. Also influential throughout Latin America is *Visión,* a Colombian newsmagazine with editorial offices in Mexico City, Bogotá, Buenos Aires, Santiago, and Washington, D.C.

Censorship can come into play in magazine production and distribution. For example, if an article in a magazine discusses sexual behavior too explicitly, the issue for that month may not be allowed through customs in some countries. Such articles must be "softened" to be acceptable in some Latin American countries. For example, to obviate censorship difficulties the editor of *Cosmopolitán en Español,* the Mexican edition of *Cosmopolitan,* sometimes clears sensitive contents with the company representative in Mexico City prior to publication. Two *Cosmopolitán en Español* advertisers from Mexico once withdrew advertising because they were offended by a fashion photograph showing a popular Brazilian singer, Xuxa, in an overtly sensual pose.

REFERENCES:

Marvin Alisky, "Latin America," in *Global Journalism*, edited by John C. Merrill (New York: Longman, 1983), pp. 249–301;

Michael B. Salwen and Bruce Garrison, *Latin American Journalism* (Hillsdale, N.J.: Lawrence Erlbaum, 1991).

—S.M.H.

MAGICAL REALISM

The international fashionability of Latin American writers ushered in by the **Boom** of the 1960s brought the term *magical realism* into widespread critical use, though its meaning is somewhat problematic and lacking in rigor. Generally speaking, magical realism does not distinguish between realistic and nonrealistic events; it is fiction in which the supernatural, the mythical, or the implausible are assimilated to the cognitive structure of reality without a perceptive break in the narrator's or characters' consciousness.

The term was apparently first used by art critic and historian Franz Roh in his book *Nach Expressionismus (Magischer Realismus)* (1925) in reference to German Postexpressionism. Roh argued that Postexpressionist painters sought to represent concrete and palpable objects so as to reveal their hidden mystery. Like later proponents of magical realism, Roh vacillates between an ontological and a phenomenological approach to the idea: that is, the question of whether objects are miraculous in themselves or whether the artist's perception endows them with a magical quality is never resolved. Another European aesthetician, Massimo Bontempelli, uses the term in his book *L'avventura novecentista* (1938). He refers to magical realism as an attempt to go beyond the aesthetic of Futurism by appealing to the fantastic dimensions of reality. The appeal to fantasy, however, is firmly grounded in the visible and concrete. Neither of these approaches to magical realism is linked to Latin American art or literature.

The first Latin American postulation of magical realism is in Arturo Uslar Pietri's *Letras y hombres de Venezuela* (1948; Literature and Folks of Venezuela). Uslar Pietri uses the concept in the context of the Venezuelan short story of the 1930s and 1940s, which he claims frequently offers a "poetic decipherment" or "poetic negation" of reality. Uslar Pietri knew Bontempelli in Europe and may have adapted his notion of magical realism to a specifically Latin American situation. Nevertheless, Uslar Pietri's version of magical realism does not readily apply to the modern Latin American novel.

In "Magical Realism in Spanish American Fiction," a 1954 lecture published the following year in the journal *Hispania,* the critic Angel Flores proposes the term *magical realism* as a solution to the problem of ordering Latin American literary movements according to European categories. He traces its genealogy to a double origin in the realism of nineteenth-century European and Latin American fiction and the fabulous chronicles of discovery and conquest sent back to Europe by the first explorers of the New World; these strands of realism and fantasy combine in contemporary magical realism. Flores's paper fails to discriminate, however, between literature inspired by French Symbolism and Parnassianism, fantastic literature, and magical realism per se; not surprisingly, his list of magical realist authors is a hodgepodge of styles and names. Flores also fails to make any reference to Uslar Pietri's use of the term, underscoring the historical discontinuity of the notion.

Another version of magical realism was proposed by the Cuban writer **Alejo Carpentier** in "De lo real maravilloso americano" (On the Marvellous Real in America), an essay published in the Venezuelan daily *El Nacional* (1948). Carpentier's concern is the originality of Latin American culture, traditionally burdened by the weight and prestige of European models. Carpentier, whose father was French and who lived for many years in Paris before discovering the Caribbean and the Venezuelan jungle, derives his notion of the marvelous from a critique of the French Surrealists. He charges that the Surrealists attempted to provoke marvelous epiphanies by devices (dreams, delirium, madness, games, trances, and so on) that ultimately seemed artificial, contrived, even "bureaucratic," while the basic experience behind the Surrealist aesthetic was available in natural form in Latin America, a continent with a history, culture, and natural environment alien to European forms of representation.

Carpentier does not reject Europe in order to invent a Latin American identity; on the contrary, without a European perspective such a cultural invention would not be possible. For Carpentier magical realism is the mixture of elements from heterogeneous cultures that forms a new historical entity in a natural environment beyond the imaginings of the European mind. In other words, Carpentier's marvelous realism is what happens to European culture when it is transplanted to the Americas in the form of European observers or of artifacts, institutions, and beliefs that either seem out of place in their new environment or undergo a startling metamorphosis. Religious syncretism and the Napoleonic court of Henri Christophe of Haiti, the first black king in the Americas, are examples of Carpentier's brand of magical realism.

Carpentier, then, legitimizes the intellectual invention of magical realism in terms of the search for cultural identity and authenticity. He also demonstrates a powerful historical consciousness that grounds the originality of Latin America in its history, while not ignoring the fact that the European presence in the New World is the equivalent of colonialism. In fact, magical realism is a cultural response to colonialism, an affirmation of identity both against and partially thanks to the colonial master.

Even Carpentier's version of magical realism has been viewed with suspicion in Latin America, however. His novels demonstrate the collapse of the concept under the weight of its own contradictions. In what aspect of the real is the marvelous located — in the objective, empirical world (the ontological approach) or in the perceiver (the phenomenological one)? If in the perceiver, then is this subject the foreigner, or is it the credulous naïf, as Carpentier suggests? If the foreigner, then the cultural authenticity of magical realism loses all credibility; if the naïf, then what role can legitimately be played by an intellectual such as Carpentier? Can such an intellectual put forth the concept in good faith? This concept of magical realism, furthermore, has been attacked by the Left as an aestheticization of poverty and of the neocolonial status of the Caribbean and Latin America in general. It has been ridiculed by other critics as an exotic label stuck by publishers on cultural artifacts from Latin America that have penetrated foreign markets but have made no dent in foreign consciousness. It has also been derided as a naive revival of the stereotype of Latin America as the site of Nature in opposition to Europe as the site of Civilization.

If magical realism has any future as a serious intellectual concept it is in the realm of literary theory. Carpentier's version was modified by Gabriel García Márquez in "Fantasía y creación artística en América Latina y el Caribe," a short article originally published in Mexico in 1979. García Márquez affirms Carpentier's emphasis on magical realism as a variation on the theme of Latin American identity and restates its link to the early chronicles of discovery, but he shifts its field of pertinence from the broadly cultural to the literary and the tone of its postulation from the transcendental to the carnivalesque. For him the problem of magical realism (which, incidentally, he never refers to as such) is a literary problem. Carpentier had placed the question of belief at the center of the "marvellous real" by saying that faith would determine the validity of the concept; García Márquez turns the issue of faith into the literary problem of verisimilitude. He intimates that Latin America is already a novel that exceeds the canon of verisimilitude established by realism. The issue raised by García Márquez involves the general problem of the relation between traditional literary forms (in this case, the novel) and the new contents that such a form — itself a product of social history — attempts to represent. Can one write about Latin America or as a Latin American in a genre developed for and by the European bourgeoisie of the last century?

Some other writers associated with magical realism are Isabel Allende, **Miguel Angel Asturias, Juan Rulfo,** Demetrio Aguilera Malta, and the Brazilian novelist Jorge Amado. A recent and popular example of a work in the magical-realist vein is Laura Esquivel's *Como agua para chocolate* (1989; translated as *Like Water for Chocolate*).

REFERENCE:

Irlemar Chiampi, *El realismo maravilloso* (Caracas: Monte Avila, 1983).

— R.G.M.

ROCÍO MALDONADO

Rocío Maldonado (1951–) is one of the most important members of neo-Mexicanism, a loosely connected group of contemporary Mexican artists which emerged in the 1980s and included **Nahum Zenil** and Julio Galán. Maldonado studied art at the Escuela Nacional de Pintura y Escultura (National School of Painting and Sculpture) during the 1970s and later at the Universidad Nacional Autónoma de México (National Autonomous University of Mexico). Maldonado's style is connected to Neo-expressionism, which emerged in Europe and the Americas during the early 1980s and is favored by other Latin American painters such as **Arnaldo Roche Rabell** and **Luis Cruz Azaceta.** On the other hand, her postmodern concern with the history of art and popular culture is a thematic approach that also characterizes the work of other members of neo-Mexicanism.

According to several critics, Maldonado exposes cultural stereotypes that present women as weak and subordinate to men. A recurrent motif in early works such as *La virgen* (1985; The Virgin) is the image of Mexican popular dolls made of painted leather or papier-mâché, often accompanied by representations of male and female reproductive systems and genitalia, which symbolize the passive role that has been traditionally expected of women. In more-recent paintings Maldonado expresses her feminist concerns through a postmodern combination of images taken from the history of art and religion. For instance, in *Extasis de Santa Teresa II* (1989; Ecstasy of Saint Teresa, II), through the appropriation of the well-known sculpture by the baroque artist Gian Lorenzo Bernini,

La virgen (1985; The Virgin) by Rocío Maldonado (Centro Cultural/Arte Contemporáneo, Mexico City)

Maldonado explores the relationship between past and present, sacred and profane, passive and active female sexuality.

REFERENCE:

Elizabeth Ferrer, *Rocío Maldonado* (Mexico City: Galería OMR, 1993).

— F.B.N.

MALINCHE

Malinche, also known as Malintzín, Malinal, or Doña Marina, was an Aztec princess sold into slavery by her own people. She was later given to the Spanish conquistador Hernán Cortés when he arrived in the Aztec empire in 1519. She apparently had a remarkable ability to learn languages and spoke various Mayan languages as well as Nahuatl, the language of the Aztecs. She learned Spanish very quickly and became Cortés's interpreter, not only of languages but also of Aztec customs and beliefs. In addition, she became his concubine, and their offspring are considered the first of the

mestizo race that now dominates Mexico; hence she is known as the mother of the Mexican people. Because Malinche aided Cortés in his conquest of the Aztec empire in 1521, she is also seen in Mexican culture as the essence of betrayal, the one who, through her words, delivered herself, her people, her culture, and an entire empire to outside hostile forces, engendering a new race that would eventually replace her own. She is represented in numerous literary and artistic works in various manners, frequently functioning as a symbol of female or national betrayal or as an archetype for the sexual appropriation of indigenous women by European invaders.

REFERENCE:

Sandra Messinger Cypess, *La Malinche in Mexican Literature* (Austin: University of Texas Press, 1991).

— M.E.S.

MAMBO

The mambo is an Afro-Cuban genre that is derived from religious cults from the Congo and that includes sung parts. Various artists have claimed or have been given credit for its development, but it appears that the mambo is the result of a collective effort by many musicians. Among the early names associated with the genre in the 1930s, 1940s, and 1950s are Orestes López, "Bebo" Valdés, René Hernández, Arsenio Rodríguez, Cachao López, and Dámaso Pérez Prado. Pérez Prado's many recordings converted the mambo into a popular music craze in the 1950s. Many of his recordings emphasized the brass in faster, simplified versions. **Tito Puente,** although Puerto Rican, tended to preserve more of the Cuban structure in his renditions.

The idea of the mambo originated in an open vamp section of the Cuban **danzón** in which instrumental improvisation was employed. The name *mambo* is also given to the section in **salsa** in which solo improvisations may be played over repeated horn lines.

REFERENCES:

Charley Gerard, *Salsa! The Rhythm of Latin Music* (Crown Point, Ind.: White Cliffs Media Company, 1989);

Rebecca Mauleón, *Salsa: Guidebook for Piano and Ensemble* (Petaluma, Cal.: Sher Music, 1993);

John Storm Roberts, "The Latin Dimension," in *The Many Worlds of Music* (New York: Broadcast Music Incorporated, 1976).

— R.L.S.

MARACAS

Maracas are made from various types of vessels containing beads, pebbles, shells, and seeds and have been prominent as shaken instruments in Latin American music. The vessels are typically made of easily accessible materials, such as gourds or clay, but may be constructed of solid wooden parts or metal. Even dried seed pods, such as the ones produced by the royal poinciana tree, can provide a natural shaker instrument. Maracas are commonly played in pairs as part of an ensemble percussion section. Among indigenous tribes a single maraca is commonly used by the shaman and may be adorned with feathers or other objects and include symbolic drawings or carvings. The maracas used by popular nightclub orchestras are typically decorated with colorful designs.

Different names identify the maraca in various parts of Latin America: *alfandoque, carángano,* and *guazá* in Colombia; *chinchín* in Guatemala; *huada* or *wada* in Chile; *maruga* in Cuba; and *sonaja* in Mexico.

— R.L.S.

MARIACHI

Perhaps the most popular of Mexico's various folk ensembles, the mariachi continues to represent the nation as a musical postcard throughout the world. The various explanations of the origin of the name are inconclusive. One widely held view refers to the time of the French occupation under Maximilian in the 1860s, when strolling musicians entertained guests at wedding receptions; in this version the French word *mariage* was corrupted, resulting in *mariachi.* A more nationalistic version has the word coming from the Coca Indian language of Jalisco, relating it to the term for the wooden platforms on which dancers performed. There appears to be little disagreement, however, that the origins of the folk music traditions of mariachi are to be found in Jalisco and its neighboring states.

The original mariachi ensemble appears to have consisted of a harp, a **guitarra de golpe,** a **vihuela,** and several violins. The difficulty of playing the harp while strolling was overcome by replacing it with a large bass guitar, the **guitarrón.** In the 1920s one trumpet was added, and a second one joined the ensemble some twenty years later, completing the basic instrumentation that is used today. A major part of the mariachi repertoire consists of songs that may be interpreted by one of the instrumentalists or by a featured vocalist, traditionally male. Variations in the ensemble may include additional violins or regional instrumentation,

A mariachi band serenading two women, Mexico, 1970
(courtesy of the Organization of American States)

such as the accordion in **norteño** style or the harp, known as jarocho, in Veracruz. Authorities on the subject recognize numerous regional styles of mariachi music, based on geographic and demographic divisions.

The typical repertoire of mariachi ensembles focuses on songs and dances from the various regions of Mexico, but performances may include music from other countries and cultures as well. Among the songs **sones, rancheras**, and **corridos** predominate. Highly descriptive of life, love, and memorable national events, the texts of the songs celebrate both the glories and the traumas of the people. Practically every city, town, and village can boast of at least one song written in its honor; villains and heroes are equally well represented in the repertoire. There are few occasions in Mexican life when the appearance of a mariachi ensemble would be inappropriate: birthdays, baptisms, weddings, funerals, and even masses are celebrated with mariachi music.

The international presence of mariachi is particularly strong in Central America and the southwestern United States; it is also prominent in South America,

Members of a Guatemalan band with a marimba con tecomates (marimba with gourd resonators) and a marimba sencilla (simple marimba), 1930 (courtesy of the Organization of American States)

Western Europe, and Japan. The first International Mariachi Festival was held in Guadalajara in 1994. Sponsored by the National Council for Culture and the Arts, the festival featured numerous musical performances as well as exhibits of instruments, traditional costumes, films, and paintings, together with masses, parades, conferences, and public addresses on mariachi music and history. In the United States, especially in the formerly Mexican territory of the Southwest, ethnomusicological interest has led to the establishment of various university-sponsored mariachi ensembles. Even in Florida, which is traditionally influenced by Caribbean cultures, Walt Disney World features regular mariachi performances by one of the finest mariachi ensembles in the hemisphere, Mariachi Cobre.

REFERENCES:

Gerard Béhague, "Latin American Folk Music," in *Folk and Traditional Music of the Western Continents,* by Bruno Nettl (Englewood Cliffs, N.J.: Prentice-Hall, 1990);

David Kilpatrick, *El Mariachi: Traditional Music of Mexico,* volume 1 (Pico Rivera, Cal.: Fiesta Publications, 1988).

— R.L.S.

MARIMBA

The marimba, the most representative instrument of Central America, is an idiophone (see **musical instruments**) that consists of tuned, wooden keys attached to resonators that amplify the sound. Although considered by some experts to be indigenous to Guatemala, its ancient origins have been traced from southeast Asia to Africa, where it was modified into various forms. The most reasonable evidence supports its introduction by African slaves into Central America, where it was soon adopted by the Mayans. While its African legacy is acknowledged, subsequent adaptations and improvements are credited to Central America.

There are three principal types of marimba common to Central America: the marimba con tecomates (with gourd resonators); the marimba doble (double), or chromatic marimba; and the marimba sencilla (simple). Of these three types, the marimba con tecomates is the most closely related to its African counterpart. Each wooden key has a hollowed gourd attached beneath it and sealed with beeswax. It is supported by a strap across the shoulders, attached to both ends of the instrument, and includes a convex wooden arc that rests on the player's stomach and that serves to separate the instrument from his body. Normally played standing, it may also be played from a sitting position by propping up the outer frame with a forked stick, to prevent the gourds from touching the ground. Marimbas are played with mallets whose tips are bound with locally produced rubber.

The marimba doble is actually two separate instruments played as one. The larger of the two is the *marimba grande* (large). The smaller one is known by several names: *cuache* (twin); *requinto* (implying a higher pitch); piccolo; and tenor. In the marimba doble the resonators are constructed of special woods rather than gourds, thus improving the acoustics of the instrument. The performance position of the two instruments may be end to end, or at an angle to each other. The marimba grande is played by four men, the cuache by three. The function of the smaller cuache is to duplicate at a higher pitch the parts played on the marimba grande. To balance the emphasis placed on the melodic part, the rhythm and bass parts are often supported by the addition of drum and string bass players.

The third type of marimba, the sencilla, is a single instrument similar in construction to the grande. It has a range of more than five octaves and features a diatonic scale. It is played by three men — one each assigned to the melody, the harmonic/rhythmic centro, and the bass. The instrument rests on a platform with removable legs and is easily transported by one person, slung over the person's back and held by straps.

Often the members of a marimba ensemble are from the same family or are related by family ties. Except in unusual circumstances, such as a marimba group from a school for girls, marimbas are traditionally played by men. Mixed-gender marimba groups are completely foreign to the tradition.

The music played by marimberos (marimba players) on the marimba grande may be of national and regional origin, but international favorites are also popular. The marimba grande ensembles are more closely associated with urban and commercial activities, while the marimba con tecomates has closer ties with rural and ceremonial events. The musical role of the marimba sencilla lies somewhere between the other two.

Marimberos of popular and vernacular musical traditions in Central America typically play by ear; reading music from scores is practically confined to academic or art-music traditions. The marimba appears to be especially popular in what was once Maya territory, especially Guatemala and its close neighbors, including the Chiapas region of southern Mexico, but the instrument is prominent throughout Central America and down the Pacific littoral into South America.

REFERENCE:

Vida Chenoweth, *The Marimbas of Guatemala* (Lexington: University of Kentucky Press, 1964).

— R.L.S.

MARÍMBOLA

The marímbola, sometimes referred to as marímbula, is a bass instrument common to rural areas of the Caribbean. A descendant of the African finger piano (mbira), the marímbola consists of a wooden box fitted with thin metal strips attached so that they form a row of projecting keys that may be plucked with the fingers. Machine bolts may be tightened or loosened for tuning. The low pitches of the keys combined with the deep resonance of the wooden box provide a percussive harmonic bass suitable for accompanying guitars and other folk instruments. The player sits on top of the instrument while playing. When located on the wooden floors typical of many rural houses, the acoustics of the instrument are considerably enhanced.

Affectionately referred to as the "poor man's bass," the marímbola became a familiar member of many Creole music ensembles. In its heyday the coil spring of the windup victrola was preferred for construction of the keys. Serious abrasions of the fingers were avoided by fitting the fingertips with short lengths of discarded garden hose. Nevertheless, once the string bass and ultimately the electric bass became generally accessible, the prominence of the marímbola in folk musics diminished considerably.

— R.L.S.

RENÉ MARQUÉS

René Marqués (1919–1979) was a Puerto Rican author of social and political protest. The many genres he mastered — theater, novels, essays, and short stories — all served as outlets to express his hopes for and frustrations with his native country. Marqués came from a wealthy family of landowners who specialized in agriculture. He continued in the family tradition by receiving a degree in agronomy and working in that field of expertise for two years. Despite his success, Marqués's inclination to write overcame years of tradition.

His first published work, the book of poetry *Peregrinación* (1944; Pilgrimage), proved his talent and was the gateway for his transition to the literary field. In 1946 Marqués traveled to Spain to study literature, and there he wrote two plays: *El hombre y sus sueños* (1946; Man and his Dreams) and *El sol y los MacDonald* (1947; The Sun and the MacDonalds).

Marqués's dramatic style is innovative and constantly changing. He creates well-developed characters who engage in complex dialogues and monologues, all of which help to elucidate the author's social or political message. The play *Palm Sunday,* written in English during Marqués's year of study in New York (1949), is highly critical of the activities of tyrannical governments. It dramatizcs the 1937 Ponce Massacre by Puerto Rican police forces of nationalists demonstrating in favor of Puerto Rico's independence from the United States.

The issue of liberation for Puerto Rico is repeated throughout the literature of Marqués. He criticizes the materialistic citizens of his country who place economic advantage over political sovereignty. In many of his ideas Marqués was greatly influenced by his mother, Doña Padrina Padilla de Sanz, who was an ardent supporter of Puerto Rican liberation. The theme of Puerto Rican identity and relations with the United States surfaces again in *La carreta* (1952; The Oxcart), one of his best-known plays and one that portrays the difficulties Puerto Rico and its people faced after the forced industrialization project Operation Bootstrap failed and sent many people into exile in the United States. That play illustrates the problems Puerto Ricans encountered when adjusting to a foreign culture and a new language. Along the same thematic lines are the short-story collections *Otro día nuestro* (1955; Another of Our Days), *En una ciudad llamada San Juan* (1960; In a City Called San Juan), and *Inmersos en el silencio* (1976; Immersed in Silence). René Marqués also wrote many essays, collected in *Ensayos 1953–1971* (1971; Essays 1953–1971), that expressed his hopes for a better Puerto Rico.

In all of his writings Marqués struggled with the existentialist idea that life is absurd and full of anguish. Like other young writers in Puerto Rico, Marqués understood the increasing industrialization of his country to be the cause of its lost values. He hoped for a return to the simplicity of rural life. In spite of his increasing feeling of futility, Marqués did provide a hopeful message with his literature, by proposing that people should remain in a constant state of doubt and never unquestioningly accept any one system of thought.

REFERENCE:

Eleanor J. Martin, *René Marqués* (Boston: Twayne, 1979).

— D.H.

José Martí (courtesy of the Organization of American States)

JOSÉ MARTÍ

Poet, essayist, novelist, orator, and revolutionary, José Martí (1853–1895) is considered Cuba's founding father and, in the wider context of Latin America, ranks as one of the leading intellectual figures of the late nineteenth century. He was born in Havana and at an early age began to wage his lifelong battle against Spanish colonial tyranny. At seventeen he was imprisoned and then banished from Cuba, in 1870. He spent the next four years in exile in Spain, where he studied law and philosophy and received a degree in 1874. He then traveled throughout Latin America, writing and speaking to various groups with the aim of winning support for the Cuban independence movement before making New York City his home base for future revolutionary activities. From there he published many articles in newspapers and journals in the United States as well as Latin America, translated several books into Spanish, and published his only novel, *Amistad funesta* (1885; Fatal Friendship), also known as *Lucía Jerez* (the name of the protagonist).

He also published two important books of poetry: *Ismaelillo* (1882), a collection of lyrical and emotive poems dedicated to his son, and *Versos sencillos* (1891; Plain Verses), a group of poems in the traditional octosyllabic style of the Spanish lyrical poets. In view of the innovative imagery, the musicality, the natural and sincere emotional expression evoked by the uncomplicated language of these books of poems, Martí has been considered the precursor, or initiator, of Latin American **Modernismo.** Two other books of poems were published posthumously: *Versos libres* (1913; Free Verses) and *Flores del destierro* (1932; Flowers of Exile), which were written during intense political moments and reflect Martí's passion for justice. In these collections, as well as his essays and speeches, Martí's preoccupations with friendship, dignity, liberty, and equality for all predominate.

In one of his best-known essays, "Our America," Martí describes his vision of the future of Latin America, which must overcome a colonial legacy by studying its native history and culture, erased by centuries of foreign domination. He insists on the importance of integrating all elements into society, including those native and African elements shunned by many of his contemporaries, underscoring his belief that there are no races, only modifications of human beings. Martí emphasizes the importance of cultivating native products rather than preferring foreign ones, in order to develop cultural and economic autonomy. Although he felt deep admiration for the United States, he foresaw and warned of the dangers of expansionism. In 1892 he founded the Cuban Revolutionary Party in Key West, Florida, and shortly afterward traveled to his homeland to join the revolutionary forces attempting to win Cuban independence from Spain. He was killed in battle in Dos Ríos three years before his country's revolutionary struggle succeeded.

REFERENCE:

José Martí, *Our America: Writings on Latin America and the Struggle for Cuban Independence,* edited by Philip S. Foner (New York: Monthly Review Press, 1977).

— M.E.S.

ANGELES MASTRETTA

An important emerging novelist, Angeles Mastretta (1949–) was born in Puebla, Mexico, studied journalism in the Universidad Nacional Autónoma de México (National Autonomous University of Mexico), and has practiced journalism for years. Her first novel, *Arráncame la vida* (1988; translated as *Mexican Bolero*), was an immediate and widespread success with the public and the Mexican literary-critical world. More than a dozen editions have appeared; it has been translated into many languages; and in 1985 it won the Mazatlán Prize for literature. For this first novel Mastretta chose the historical period of the 1940s and

1950s in Mexico, decades following the **Mexican Revolution** that were crucial in influencing future political developments. Part of the popularity of the novel is due to its portrayal of important, recognizable Mexican political leaders of those times, leaders who were corrupt, hated, and feared but successful and, therefore, worthy of imitation. The narrator of the novel is a woman in her thirties who tells the story of her life with one of these leaders, from the time she married him at the age of sixteen until his death. Through skillful manipulation of dialogue combined with biting sarcasm and humor that demythify stereotypes and customs associated with women's traditional roles as virgin, wife, and mother, Mastretta presents Mexican machista society through the eyes of her narrator, who herself emerges as a complex character. The narrator, who understands that her well-being is tied to that of her husband, overlooks his extramarital affairs and becomes an accomplice in his unscrupulous quest for power. Thus, the novel raises questions about the narrator's individual integrity as well as about women's possibilities in a corrupt society dominated by men.

Mastretta's second book, *Mujeres de ojos grandes* (1991; Women With Large Eyes), is a series of vignettes about women during crucial moments of their lives. Mastretta's ability to depict Mexican cultural realities, especially gender relations, with a touch of humor is also apparent in this work. In 1993 she published *Puerto libre* (Open Port).

REFERENCES:

Danny J. Anderson, "Displacement Strategies of Transformation in *Arráncame la vida,*" *Journal of the Midwest Modern Language Association,* 21 (1988): 15–27;

Janet Gold, "*Arráncame la vida:* Textual Complicity and the Boundaries of Rebellion," *Chasqui,* 17 (1988): 35–40.

— M.E.S.

MEJORANA

Of Spanish origin, the *mejorana* may be sung or danced. In the sung version, performed by males only and never danced, the vocalist must negotiate as much as a two-octave melodic range in falsetto. The typically descending melodic contour features wide, disjunct intervals of sixths, sevenths, and ninths. The text is presented in two sections, the first a rhymed quatrain followed by a section resembling the **décima**. The sung version is also known as the *sovacón*. Accompaniment may be provided by a Spanish guitar or by the mejoranera, a Panamanian five-string guitar. The rhythm consists of duple and triple divisions of 6/8 meter. The mejorana is sung in both major and minor modes; its harmonic accompaniment is limited to pri-

Dancers performing the mejorana santeña, a form of the mejorana developed in the Los Santos province of Panama (Lila R. Cheville and Richard A. Cheville)

mary chords of tonic, subdominant, and dominant (I, IV, V). The danced version reflects the mejorana's Spanish heritage in its use of zapateado figures (see **zapateo**) and a paseo (promenade).

REFERENCE:

Gerard Béhague, "Latin American Folk Music," in *Folk and Traditional Music of the Western Continents,* by Bruno Nettl (Englewood Cliffs, N.J.: Prentice-Hall, 1990).

— R.L.S.

RIGOBERTA MENCHÚ

The best-known Central American **testimonial narrative** of the twentieth century is *Me llamo Rigoberta Menchú y así me nació la conciencia* (1984; translated as *I, Rigoberta Menchú: An Indian Woman in Guatemala*). Rigoberta Menchú (1960–), a Mayan woman from the Quiché highlands of Guatemala, gave testimony of her life and that of her community to the Venezuelan/French ethnographer Elisabeth Burgos in 1983. Menchú was twenty-three years old at the time

and was visiting Paris as a representative of a popular front organization fighting against government oppression. She met Burgos in Paris, and they subsequently spent eight days together, during which Burgos taped hours of Menchú's testimony in Spanish, a language that Menchú had only recently learned. Burgos later transcribed, organized, and edited the account, correcting some grammatical errors, to present it in narrative form. Burgos's intervention in Menchú's testimony has been the object of much criticism and theoretical debate centering on authorship, authenticity and the nature of representation in the text, and the value of the testimonial itself. This book has been translated into numerous languages and has received widespread international attention. Largely because of her testimonial, Menchú won the Nobel Peace Prize in 1992.

In *Me llamo Rigoberta Menchú,* Menchú describes the customs and practices of her Mayan community that have been handed down by generations of ancestors through a rich oral tradition and ritual daily activities. The importance of a communal spirit is underscored, as is the intimate connection with nature that is necessary for a harmonious balance. Some of the passages describing this relationship use lyrical language to compose vivid portraits of a Mayan way of coexisting with the earth. Menchú also describes the discrimination and harsh treatment of the Mayan peoples by the minority ladino (non-Indian) population of Guatemala. She focuses on the late 1970s and early 1980s, when dictatorial rule under generals Jorge Ubico and later Efraín Ríos Montt unleashed some of the worst repression of the Mayans. Determined to wipe out guerrilla insurgency in the highlands, the government allowed the army full rein in their genocidal campaign, which massacred tens of thousands of Indian civilians, burned down villages, and sent thousands more fleeing into the jungle and across the border into Mexico. Among the victims were Rigoberta Menchú's brother, mother, and father. The details of their tortured deaths and those of others are anguished portrayals of her people's pain in the face of brutal policies of extermination. Menchú also had to flee for her life and continues to live in exile for security reasons. Menchú and Burgos's text, then, functions on a cultural level to preserve in written form a Quiché Mayan way of life and on a political level to make the world aware of the genocide against the Mayans and thus motivate action to prevent it.

REFERENCES:

Maureen Shea, "Latin American Women and the Oral Tradition: Giving Voice to the Voiceless," *Critique,* 3 (Spring 1993): 139–153;

Marc Zimmerman, "Testimonio in Guatemala: Payeras, Rigoberta, and Beyond," *Latin American Perspectives,* 18 (Fall 1991): 22–47.

— M.E.S.

ANA MENDIETA

The Cuban American Ana Mendieta (1948–1985), one the most important contemporary Latin American artists, explored the relationship between women and nature as well as the awareness of roots and the displacement of exile. Mendieta, whose granduncle was Carlos Mendieta, president of Cuba in the 1930s, grew up in that country, but in 1961 she and her sister were sent to the United States by their parents, who, for political reasons, were unable to leave the island after the revolution. Following four or five difficult years living in orphanages, the sisters were finally joined by their mother. Some time later Mendieta began studying painting at the University of Iowa and later attended its Multimedia and Video Art Program.

Mendieta's work, influenced by feminist theory and later by anticolonialist politics, consists of performances and ephemeral pieces that were recorded in

Ana Mendieta (courtesy of Galerie Lelong)

photographs and on film (see **Conceptual Art, Installation Art, and Performance Art**). In the early 1970s Mendieta produced strong performances related to the themes of rape, death, and the return of the body to nature after death. Later, she began to explore the idea of becoming one with nature, as a way of achieving a sense of belonging to the earth and partaking of its creative forces and cyclical rhythms; it is a view of nature as sacred, and one characteristic of ancient matriarchal rites and the African Cuban religion of Santería. In Oaxaca, a city she visited several times during the 1970s, Mendieta created a series of earth sculptures called *Siluetas* (Silhouettes) by tracing the outline of her own body onto natural surfaces such as tree trunks and the earth itself, in an effort to symbolize her search for unity with the land. She also used unorthodox materials such as gunpowder and fire.

In the 1980s, after Mendieta moved to New York, she began to explore the sense of displacement she felt from the U.S. mainstream and from her Cuban roots, while making her art into subtle but effective statements against colonialism. In 1980 she returned to Cuba for the first time, acting as a mediator between the international art scene and the new generation of Cuban artists who emerged in the 1980s, all of whom, including **José Bedia,** favored radical new approaches to art and the exploration of ideological and cultural issues. During her trips to Cuba, Mendieta produced her series of *Esculturas rupestres* (1981; Rock Sculptures), simple archetypal female outlines carved on rock and cave walls at Jaruco, a hill near Havana. Through these pieces Mendieta established a link not only with the Rupestrian art and the fertility deities of the indigenous Cubans (the Taíno people) but also with spiritual healing processes practiced in Santería.

Mendieta's art received several important awards, including grants from the National Endowment for the Arts, a Guggenheim Fellowship, and an American Academy Fellowship in Italy. It was in Rome that she produced her first indoor earth and sand sculptures, such as *Nacida del Nilo* (1984; Nile-Born), which also reflected archetypal female figures. In 1985 she married well-known minimalist sculptor Carl André, but a few months later fell to her death from the window of their high-rise apartment building in New York. Her art was honored with a retrospective exhibition at the New Museum of Contemporary Art in New York.

REFERENCES:

Petra Barreras del Río and John Perreault, *Ana Mendieta: A Retrospective* (New York: New Museum of Contemporary Art, 1987);

Luis Camnitzer, "Ana Mendieta," *Third Text*, no. 7 (December 1989): 44–49.

— F.B.N.

MERENGUE

The merengue is the most popular song/dance of the Dominican Republic, and its infectious rhythms have transmitted new energy to Latin music throughout the world. The origin of the merengue is often disputed. The most reasonable explanation ascribes it to a fusion of three different but similar sources, all of which were imbued with African elements: the Dominican mangulina, the Cuban upa, and the Puerto Rican danza. Once a lascivious dance of the poor in rustic areas, the merengue was despised by the polite ruling and upper colonial classes. The suggestiveness of the provocative, sensuous movements of the dance, in which the couples were clasped closely together, was confirmed by the liberties taken in explicit lyrics that often featured double entendres. The status of the merengue was considerably improved when, following the war of independence from Haiti in 1844, it became a symbol of Dominican nationalism and patriotism. In that role the merengue began to serve as a form of oral history, for the texts that were sung documented important national events. Under the dictatorship of Gen. Rafael Leonidas Trujillo (1930–1961) the merengue was forced on polite society because it was Trujillo's favorite dance. After he ordered that it be played at formal dances, it not only became acceptable but was reinforced in its function as a national symbol.

To the early folk ensemble of string instruments (*bandurria*, **cuatro, tres, seis,** and *tiple*) were

A perico ripiao (ripped parrot) merengue group, led by José Quesada; members play the güira (metal scraper), saxophone, tambora drum, and accordion (copyright © Vicente Fernández/City Lore). Named after a popular bar in Santiago de los Caballeros, the perico ripiao is a form of merengue popular in the Cibao Valley region of the Dominican Republic.

added the **tambora** drum and the **güiro** (gourd scraper). The principal percussion instrument became the tambora. This instrumentation changed, however, when the accordion arrived from Germany in the late nineteenth century and replaced the stringed instruments. In addition, the gourd (**güiro**) was replaced by a handmade metal instrument, the güira, which provided a better acoustical balance with the accordion. Eventually the saxophone was added for sonorous purposes, and it continues to be a mainstay in the basic ensemble.

During the era of big bands the merengue became popular to the extent that at least one could be expected in each forty-five-minute set of dances, alternating with an assortment of **mambos, cha-cha-chas,** and **boleros.** As North American tourists flooded the Caribbean on tour boats from Miami, they were enchanted with the merengue and other dances of the region. The merengue, however, was danced in a fast duple (2/4) meter, and few northerners could move their feet fast enough. Dominican musicians, in their benevolence, slowed down the beat to accommodate them and called the new version "Pambiche," which represented a sincere effort to say the name of the place of origin of the tourists: Palm Beach. Currently the merengue resides under the generic umbrella of **salsa,** a term that covers many Afro-Caribbean genres.

REFERENCE:

José del Castillo and Manuel A. García Arévalo, *Antología del merengue (Anthology of the Merengue),* bilingual edition (Santo Domingo: Banco Antillano, S.A., 1989).

— R.L.S.

Jean Charlot and Carlos Mérida at the opening of a 1947 exhibition of Mérida's works at the Mont-Orendain Gallery, Mexico City

CARLOS MÉRIDA

The art of the Guatemalan Carlos Mérida (1891–1984), one of the most important Latin American artists, combines abstraction with pre-Columbian themes. During his youth Mérida studied art and music in Guatemala City, where he also frequented the avant-garde circles led by Jaime Sabartés and Carlos Valenti. In 1912 he left for Europe and met several vanguard artists, including the Mexicans **Diego Rivera** and Roberto Montenegro. Upon his return to Guatemala in 1914, he became a supporter of **Indigenism;** after a short period in New York, where he befriended Juan José Tablada, Mérida settled in Mexico. By then his paintings, such as *La muchacha del perico* (1917; Young Woman with Parrot), depicted indigenist themes with highly simplified forms and flat areas of color. During the early 1920s Mérida participated in Mexican **Muralism:** he assisted Rivera with his encaustic mural *La creación* (1922; Creation) at the Anfiteatro Bolívar of the Escuela Nacional Preparatoria, joined the Sindicato de Obreros Técnicos, Pintores, y Escultores

(Technicians' and Artists' Union), and later painted two murals at the children's library of the Secretaría de EducaciónPública.

While in Europe during the late 1920s, Mérida became interested in **Surrealism,** which had a crucial effect on his art. His work became increasingly abstract but remained concerned with indigenous themes. Paintings such as *Proyección de una cacería (Temas mayas)* (1938; Projection of a Hunt [Maya Themes]) feature curvilinear, simplified figures (inspired by Maya codices) floating in an ambiguous space, together with other abstract shapes. This turn toward abstraction intensified after a short period in the United States, as Mérida also introduced elements of Abstract Expressionism into his art. In the informal abstract painting *El oráculo* (1944; The Oracle) Mérida immerses his Maya-like figures in a background of strong colors applied with thick, expressive brush strokes.

During the 1950s Mérida began to integrate his art into the context of architecture, turning away from Informal Abstraction to a stronger use of geometry. He produced mural paintings, polychromed reliefs, and mosaics for numerous public buildings such as

Mexico's massive apartment complexes, the Multifamiliar Miguel Alemán (1950) and the Multifamiliar Presidente Juárez (1952, destroyed in the 1985 earthquake), as well as Guatemala's Palacio Municipal. For instance, in his series of painted reliefs *Antiguas leyendas precolombinas* (Ancient Pre-Columbian Legends) for the Multifamiliar Presidente Juárez, Mérida narrated indigenous themes through simplified human figures whose geometrized shapes and carefully selected colors interlocked to form an even, all-over pattern, an approach also seen in many of his canvases of the time, such as *Los hechiceros* (1958; The Wizards). After the 1960s Mérida also explored the use of lyrical colors and different textural qualities in paintings such as *El vendedor de pájaros* (1969; The Bird Vendor) and *Tiempo estático* (1979; Static Time).

Perhaps because Mérida was Guatemalan, he escaped the harsh criticisms issued by Rivera and **David Alfaro Siquieros** in condemnation of Mexican artists such as **Rufino Tamayo** and **José Luis Cuevas,** who, like Mérida, had rejected Muralism and wanted to explore more avant-garde forms of figuration. Mérida also published several books and articles about modern Mexican art and taught art in Mexico and the United States.

REFERENCE:

Luis Cardoza y Aragón, *Carlos Mérida: Color y forma* (Mexico City: Dirección General de Publicaciones, Consejo Nacional para la Cultura y las Artes, 1992).

— F.B.N.

MESTIZAJE

In the nineteenth century, as the newly independent Spanish American republics fell prey to dictatorial leaders, many people looked with envy on the democracy to the north. Hoping to find ways of establishing better governments at home and to "progress" toward modernized, developed societies, many intellectuals began a quest for an autonomous national identity and for the root causes of their national maladies. Various nineteenth-century writers offered explanations of the sources of their problems, often building on the positivist, scientifically based theories of race popular in Europe at the time. Such theories were much influenced by Darwinism, social organicism, and anthroposociology — all of which linked the social and cultural development of a people to its biological race. A common thread that ran through the writings of many Latin American intellectuals during the nineteenth century linked the "backwardness" of Latin American nations to what were considered the primitive elements in their societies, nonwhite populations of indigenous or African origins.

One of the most prominent of these thinkers was the Argentinean intellectual Domingo Faustino Sarmiento, president of his country from 1868 to 1874. Sarmiento's *Civilización y barbarie,* also known as *Facundo* (1848; translated as *Life in the Argentine Republic in the Days of the Tyrants*), is not without its internal contradictions and ambiguities, but it seems to divide Argentina into civilized urban elements and barbaric rural ones consisting primarily of the Indians and the gauchos (mestizo cowboys) living on the plains. Sarmiento advocated their extermination and the importation of more white Europeans to "improve" the racial mix in Argentina and thereby to better the economic, social, and cultural possibilities of that nation. Sarmiento had his critics, but his views were embraced by many nineteenth-century thinkers; generally it was held that *mestizaje* (racial miscegenation) had produced an inferior people and that with greater purity of blood would come civilization.

At the turn of the century, however, positivist thought began to lose popularity, and several Latin American writers reacted against the inferior status accorded nonwhites in their societies. Among them were the Peruvian Manuel González Prada, whose defense of the Indians and critique of Spanish oppressive legacies in America were presented in *Páginas libres* (1894; Autonomous Pages) and *Horas de lucha* (1908; Time of Struggle); the Cuban **José Martí,** whose essay "Nuestra América" (1891; translated as *Our America*) stood in stark contrast to an earlier one of the same title by Carlos Octavio Bunge (Martí called for equal treatment of all races, which, he wrote, in reality were only one); and the Mexican Justo Sierra, once a prominent advocate of scientism who later, in a speech delivered in 1908, reversed his way of thinking and exhorted Mexicans to reject the idea that scientism was the only way to improve society. Another extremely influential essay, *Ariel* (1900), by the young Uruguayan José Enrique Rodó, urged Latin Americans to reject the idea that science and utilitarianism were the solutions to all problems and called instead for a more humane and artistic approach. Rodó's essay also criticized the United States for sacrificing its spiritual values to material wealth.

In the twentieth century many Latin American writers began to reassess the racial question, viewing indigenous and African elements as positive rather than negative contributions to their societies. Although not quite escaping the racist stereotyping of some previous intellectuals, writers such as the Mexican **José Vasconcelos** and the Cuban **Fernando Ortiz** called for a positive revaluation of mestizaje.

Vasconcelos's well-known essay *La raza cósmica* (1925; The Cosmic Race) depicts the mestizo as a fifth race that brings together the most positive aspects of the white, black, red, and yellow races and that will ensure a dynamic future for mankind. Ortiz's *Contrapunteo cubano del tabaco y el azúcar* (1940; translated as *Cuban Counterpoint, Tobacco and Sugar*) explores the positive aspects of black and mulatto culture in Cuba. In promoting the values of nonwhite cultures, however, both of these writers used generalizations about racial differences that today might be considered racist. Two more recent approaches to hybridization in contemporary Latin American societies are *Transculturación narrativa en América Latina* (1982; Narrative Transculturation of Latin America), by the Uruguayan Angel Rama; and *Culturas híbridas, estrategias para entrar y salir de la modernidad* (1989; Hybrid Cultures, Strategies to Enter and Exit Modernity), by the Argentinean Nestor García Canclini. (See also **Indigenous Cultures, Criollismo and Costumbrismo**, and **Peoples and Races**.)

REFERENCE:

Martin Stabb, *In Quest of Identity* (Chapel Hill: University of North Carolina Press, 1967).

— M.E.S. & P.S.

MEXICAN MELODRAMAS

In Mexico melodrama became the central genre of the sound cinema after the success of the early sound feature *Santa* (1931), directed by Antonio Moreno, an adaptation of a well-known melodramatic novel by Federico Gamboa about an innocent girl from the provinces who is forced into prostitution in the big city and finds redemption only in death. Melodramatic movies were a staple in Mexico from the 1930s through the 1960s. However, the Mexican film industry did not take off until the international success of the *comedia ranchera* (ranch comedy) *Allá en el rancho grande* (1936; Out on the Big Ranch), directed by Fernando de Fuentes, a comedy that added a pastoral fantasy to the Gene Autry–Roy Rogers formula.

Aided by U.S. wartime policies, Mexican cinema thrived during World War II and the immediate postwar period. Whereas in 1941 Mexican cinema had only 6.2 percent of the domestic market, by 1945 it had claimed 18.4 percent, and by 1949 it had attracted 24.2 percent; a staggering 124 films were produced in 1950, most of them melodramas. In the sound period Mexican filmmakers became skilled generic "chemists," separating and mixing the imported Hollywood genres. The melodramas of the 1930s through the 1950s demonstrated two tendencies: the family melodrama focused on the problems of love, sexuality, and parenting, while the epic melodrama reworked national history, especially the events of the **Mexican Revolution**.

Juan Orol and the actress Sara García created the archetypal mother figure of the Mexican melodrama in *Madre querida* (1935; Dear Mother), the heart-wrenching story of a young boy who goes to a reformatory and whose mother dies of grief precisely on the tenth of May (Mother's Day in Mexico). In the following years García played suffering, self-sacrificing mothers in many films, such as *No basta ser madre* (1937; It's Not Enough to Be a Mother), *Mi madrecita* (1940; My Mom), and *Madre adorada* (1948; Beloved Mother). In *Una familia de tantas* (1948; A Family Among Many), directed by Alejandro Galindo, the threat against family values is linked to the clash between the family and modern life under capitalism. Rodrigo, a middle-class father (played by Fernando Soler, who became the prototypical father figure of the Mexican melodrama), maintains feudal control over his family to protect it from the turmoil of modern life. His tyranny crumbles when Roberto del Hierro (literally, "Iron Robert," played by David Silva), a vacuum-cleaner salesman representing "Bright O'Home" appliances, appears on his doorstep. Invaded by the American way of life, the patriarch is helpless: the family buys a vacuum cleaner and later a refrigerator. Worst of all, the teenage daughter and the aggressive young salesman fall in love against the father's wishes. Although the young couple pay a price for their disobedience — the father forbids the relationship and prevents the family from attending the wedding — the movie suggests that the couple will nevertheless lead a happy life.

The sexy temptress plays an important part in the Mexican melodrama. María Félix fulfilled this role admirably in various films, starring in movies such as *Doña Bárbara* (1943), directed by Fernando de Fuentes and based on the novel of the same title, by the Venezuelan Rómulo Gallegos; *La mujer de todos* (1946; Everyone's Woman), directed by Julio Braucho; *La devoradora* (1946; The Devourer), directed by de Fuentes), and *Doña Diabla* (1949; Devil Woman), directed by Tito Davison. A subgenre of Mexican melodrama was the *caberetera* (cabaret movie), in which the character of the prostitute achieves an almost iconic status. One of the best examples of this genre was *Aventurera* (1952; Adventuress), directed by Alberto Gout. The starring role was played by Ninón Sevilla, the Cuban equivalent of Marilyn Monroe, and the movie focuses on a happy bourgeois girl who is forced into a world of crime and prostitution after her mother dies. The plot is clearly inspired by the song

Pancho Villa

"Aventurera," sung in the movie by Pedro Vargas, which urges the adventuress to "sell your love expensively."

REFERENCE:

Latin American Cinema: Le Cinéma Latino-Américain, special issue of Iris: Revue de Théorie de l'image et du son. A Journal of Theory on Image and Sound, no. 13 (Summer 1991).
                                                    — S.M.H.

THE MEXICAN REVOLUTION

The Mexican Revolution (1910–1920) was one of the most violent and chaotic social upheavals in Latin America. Porfirio Díaz had ruled Mexico with an iron hand for thirty-five years (1876–1911). Although he did much to improve the economic infrastructure of his country, Díaz's regime was characterized by a concern for the wealthy and further disenfranchisement of the landless poor. The growing frustration of these people finally led to Díaz's overthrow in 1911, when he announced his plans to seek reelection. This date marked the beginning of ten years of turbulence that left few sectors of Mexican society unscathed.

Various leaders held power for short periods of time; all of them were eventually killed. The first to enter Mexico City triumphantly after Díaz was forced out of power was Francisco Madero, the son of wealthy landowners, an idealist with only a vague notion of how to govern. He, in turn, was overthrown in 1913 by his own commanding general, Victoriano Huerta, who imprisoned Madero and had him killed. Huerta was forced out of the country the following year, in part because of U.S. pressure, and the country became further divided into bands led by caudillos (popular strongmen) vying for power.

The principal regional leaders were Venustiano Carranza in the northeast, Alvaro Obregón in the northwest, Pancho Villa (his real name was Doroteo Arango) in the north, and Emiliano Zapata in the south. They led nomadic bands of men and women soldiers caught up in the whirlwind of violence, soldiers who often neither knew nor cared what they were fighting for. Carranza eventually took power in 1917 with the help of Obregón, who then turned against him. Carranza was put to death and Obregón took power in 1920, more or less signaling the end of the violent period of the revolution. Obregón was shot to death in 1928.

The notorious Villa, basically a bandit and a thug who sacked villages and raped and murdered as he made his way through the countryside, became famous largely because of his successful evasion of U.S. troops, who chased him throughout northern Mexico after he crossed into New Mexico on one of his raids. Villa became the subject of many popular folk tales and songs romanticizing his role as the man who had triumphed over the colossus to the north. Villa was shot by a band of men, presumed to have been under Obregón's command, in 1923.

Zapata was an Indian idealist who fought to gain control of the large haciendas (ranches) and to redistribute the land to the peasants. Of all the leaders, he was the only one (besides Madero) who was not motivated by personal gain but rather was committed to the revolutionary struggle as a means of bettering the lot of the landless peasants. He was killed by one of Carranza's officers in 1919.

Although the worst of the revolutionary violence ceased in 1920, the date serves more as an artificial marker of the end of the revolution. Some believe the revolution has never ended and that the same problems that plagued Mexicans in the early part of the century continue today. This argument accounts for the widespread disillusionment with the results of the revolution. The violent tumult of the revolution and its aftermath became a favorite subject for artists and writers.

REFERENCES:

Peter Calvert, *The Mexican Revolution* (Cambridge: Cambridge University Press, 1968);

Eduardo Galeano, *Memory of Fire / Century of the Wind* (New York: Pantheon, 1988);

John M. Hart, *Revolutionary Mexico* (Berkeley: University of California Press, 1987);

John Rutherford, *Mexican Society During the Revolution: A Literary Approach* (Oxford: Clarendon Press, 1971).

— M.E.S.

Pedro Mir

Pedro Mir (1913–), poet, novelist, short-story writer, and essayist, was born in 1913 at San Pedro de Macoris in the Dominican Republic. Both **Manuel del Cabral** and Pedro Mir were members of the literary group called *La Cueva,* begun by the poet Rafael Américo Henríquez. Exiled from his country during Rafael Trujillo's dictatorship (1947–1961), Mir lived in Cuba, where he wrote and published *Hay un país en el mundo* (1949; There is a Country in the World). In this extensive poem Mir delineates the history of the Dominican Republic and, like many others at that time, expresses

his concern about social injustice and poverty in the sugarcane mills. In Guatemala Mir published an even more extensive poem, *Contracanto a Walt Whitman* (1953; Countersong to Walt Whitman), in which the poet tries to respond to Whitman with the collective "we" of exploited workers. Back in his country in 1969, Mir assumed a position as professor at the Universidad Autónoma de Santo Domingo and published *Amén de mariposas* (Apart from Butterflies), a lengthy poem in which he describes the struggles against the Dominican dictator Trujillo. In the experimental novel *Cuando amaban las tierras comuneras* (1978; When They Loved the Communal Lands), written without punctuation, the action takes place during the period between the two American invasions of the Dominican Republic (1916–1965). Mir's political commitment is evident in his writing.

REFERENCE:

Doris Sommer, *One Master for Another: Populism as Patriarchal Rhetoric in Dominican Novels* (Lanham, Md.: University Press of America, 1983).

— F.V.

Modern Dance

Modern dance began in Germany in the 1910s. It stemmed from a desire to break with what some artists considered the out-of-date strictures of classical ballet, as well as a desire to express contemporary psychological, social, or other concerns arising from the turmoil of World War I. In the Hispanic Caribbean, Mexico, and Central America modern dance grew in the twentieth century with the same vigor as in many other areas of the world. Because it diversified so quickly into many forms of expression rather than a specific set of steps or movements, modern dance offered a new freedom; the choreographer could seek new means of expressing twentieth-century reality without utilizing either ballet, which was tied to Europe, or folk dance, which was tied to an indigenous or colonial past.

In Costa Rica the modern dance movement was founded by Margarita Esquivel, who had worked with Martha Graham in the 1940s to establish the Ballet Tico (a "Tico" is a Costa Rican). Before her untimely death at age twenty-four, Esquivel created "Plastic Technique," which combined classical ballet, the Graham technique, character dance, and drama; its goal was for the dance artist to use the body to express the tragedy of the human being and mankind's search for identity. Grace Lindo, a disciple of a disciple of Isadora Duncan, established a school in Costa Rica that trained, among others, Mireya Barboza, the great pioneer of Costa Rican modern dance. Barboza was especially active in the 1970s, a period when the government began to support the arts and in which there was obviously a "dance movement" rather than a few dance artists working in isolation. Active for ten years in Mexico and Europe, Barbosa is one of the few professional dancers trained by Grace Lindo to return to Costa Rica. Violent political upheavals in the 1970s led to residence in Costa Rica by exiled choreographers from Uruguay and Chile. A program of government scholarships for study abroad, exchanges, and international university connections brought to Costa Rica the techniques of Graham, Cunningham, Limón, and German Expressionist dance-theater, all of which had considerable effects on the development of Costa Rican choreography. A case in point is Rogelio López, a dancer dedicated to the German *Folkwangschule* style and one who directed the company of the Universidad de Costa Rica; other cases are Jorge Ramírez and Nandayure Harley, of the dance company of the Universidad Nacional, both of whom are faithful to their North American university dance training.

Government support for culture declined in the 1980s in Costa Rica, but dance continued to grow. Independent groups, often financing themselves by productions abroad, including Diquis Tiquis and Losdenmedium. Well trained technically, these groups are directed by dancers and choreographers who also know how to commission composers, design lighting, and arrange international tours. Collective choreography and social criticism have appeared with more frequency in Costa Rican modern dance since the late 1970s.

The Mexican modern dance movement can be traced to 1896, when the dancer Loie Fuller, known for her solo spectacles featuring enormous fabric costumes and elaborate lighting, visited the country. Soon thereafter, Mexican emulators were mounting similar spectacles. Such leading creators of modern dance in the United States as Martha Graham and Anna Sokolow became interested in Mexican culture, visiting the country and the Mexican-influenced southwestern United States in the 1930s. Their residencies and tours coincided with the beginning of a period called the Mexican Modern Dance Movement, which lasted from 1940 to 1960. In 1939 the first modern dance company in Mexico, the Ballet de Bellas Artes, was created by American dancer, teacher, and choreographer **Waldeen** at the invitation of Celestino Gorostiza, then director of the National Institute of Fine Arts. Waldeen introduced choreographic techniques based on combining modern dance with anthropological research into the rituals of pre-Columbian Mexico. Prior to Waldeen's work the only modern dance in Mexico was taught by Estrella Morales, a teacher inspired by Isadora Duncan.

There is a long tradition in Mexico of official dance companies connected with the National Institute of Fine Arts or government-run universities, as well as so-called independent groups, which also depend on state subsidies. Proliferating modern dance groups struggle with the tension between their desires for artistic autonomy and their financial dependence on the state — a central struggle in Mexican modern dance's search for authenticity.

Dance artists in Mexico were influenced by foreign ideas in ways similar to the experience of Mexican painters, who brought back techniques and aesthetic and political views learned in Paris and New York. The American company of Katherine Dunham visited the country in 1947, leaving behind impressions of African American dance and of performances derived from cultural anthropology. Rather than merely receiving teachers from abroad, in 1962 the **Ballet Nacional de México** began sending its dancers for ten-week residencies at the Martha Graham School in New York. Over the years, the dancers of the Ballet Nacional came to investigate other schools, theories, and tendencies in dance, bringing this knowledge back to the Ballet Nacional and provoking heated discussions about the training a dance artist should receive. The exchange of knowledge went in the other direction as well: a steady stream of teachers from the Graham school and company began to work in Mexico, among them David Wood, Yuriko, Kazuko Hirabayashi, Takako Asakawa, David Hatch Walker, Tim Wengerd, and Christine Dakin.

Although the **Ballet Nacional de Cuba** is a classical ballet company, it has encouraged the development of modern dance under its aegis since its founding in 1948. Apart from Loie Fuller's appearance in 1897, the first mention of modern dance in Cuba is a brief reference to a visit by Isadora Duncan in 1916. Duncan dance was not seen in Cuba, however, until her adopted daughters Ana and Irma performed there in 1930–1931. Ruth Page, who danced in Cuba with Pavlova's corps de ballet in 1918, returned in 1919 for a series of recitals accompanied on the piano by Martha Graham's collaborator, Louis Horst. In 1935 two Russian dancers billed as performing "abstract pantomime" brought their works to Cuba, and in 1937 Ted Shawn, the American modern dance pioneer and founder of the Jacob's Pillow Dance Festival in Massachusetts, brought his celebrated Men Dancers. The great German Expressionist dancer Harold Kreutzberg, a renowned disciple of Mary Wigman, appeared in 1938, and the Ballets Kurt Jooss appeared in 1940, the same year that Ruth Page returned, this time with a male partner. The Martha Graham Dance Company appeared in 1941. Miriam Winslow, a former dancer with Denishawn, the modern dance company created by Ted Shawn and Ruth St. Denis, came to Cuba in 1942 and taught some of the first principles of German and American modern dance.

The single most influential person in the establishment of Cuban modern dance was Ramiro Guerra, who, after touring with the Ballets Russes du Colonel de Basil, remained in New York in the late 1940s to study with Martha Graham, Doris Humphrey, Charles Weidman, and Katherine Dunham, all of whose techniques Guerra brought back to Cuba. **Alicia Alonso**'s support for Guerra while he was a professor in the Academia de Ballet Alicia Alonso (founded in 1950) allowed him to present the first Cuban modern dance recitals (which he performed solo throughout the 1950s) and to choreograph for the newly named Ballet Nacional. In 1959 the Department of Dance was founded within the National Theater of Cuba. Guerra began with thirty people imbued with a love of dance but trained only in cabarets or for television spectacles. Cuban modern dance was first officially presented in 1960 in the form of the Departamento de Danza Moderna, which was renamed the Conjunto Nacional de Danza Moderna in 1962, Danza Nacional de Cuba in 1974, and Danza Contemporánea de Cuba in 1988. The distinguishing characteristics of this company are the heterogeneity of its dancers and its assimilation into modern dance technique of Cuba's African heritage and of popular Cuban dance. Choreography by Doris Humphrey and other Americans, as well as by Mexican, Uruguayan, and Polish artists, has been included in the company's predominantly Cuban repertoire.

Independent Cuban modern dance groups include Así Somos (That's How We Are), formed in 1981 by U.S. choreographer Lorna Burdsall and following the Alwin Nikolais and Merce Cunningham lineage; Ballet Teatro de la Habana, founded in 1987 by Caridad Martínez, former principal dancer with the Ballet Nacional, and combining minimalism, irony, and a search for new means of communicating with the audience; Danza del Caribe, founded in 1988 and concentrating on Caribbean history, legends, and traditions; Danza Abierta (Open Dance), also founded in 1988, by Marianela Boán, formerly with the Ballet Nacional, and dedicated to postmodernism; Danza Combinatoria, founded in 1990 by Rosario Cárdenas, also formerly with the Ballet Nacional, and based on everyday movement; and Retazos, founded by Ecuadoran Isabel Bustos in 1987 and following a dance-theater line. In different ways these companies combine postmodernism, dance theater, new dance, and minimalism.

After World War II the U.S. Information Agency began sponsoring tours to Latin America by U.S. dance companies, choreographers, and teachers as well as residencies at U.S. universities by Latin American dance teachers, choreographers, administrators, and dancers. These initiatives have had an enormous influence on the development of modern dance in Latin America. Other strong influences have been such organizations as the French and the Goethe Institutes, which sponsor performances in Latin America by French and German or Swiss dance companies. The American Dance Festival, which takes place in Durham, North Carolina, has made a deliberate effort to bring choreographers from Latin America to the festival for residencies of varying duration, and the video revolution has greatly facilitated the exchange of dance knowledge. The development of postmodern dance is related to national characteristics, with the difference that choreographers working in a postmodern vein identify themselves by reference to multiple characteristics — as Latino and American, or Latino and postmodern, or political and artistic — characteristics that may at times seem contradictory. These choreographers include Viveca Vázquez, Merián Soto, Arthur Aviles, Karen Langevin, and Evelyn Vélez of Puerto Rico; Carmelita Tropicana and Ana Vega of Cuba; and Eva Gasteazoro of Nicaragua.

REFERENCE:

Sally Banes, "La Onda Próxima: Nuevo Latino Dance," in *Proceedings of the Society of Dance History Scholars: "Dance in Hispanic Cultures"* (Riverside, Cal.: Society of Dance History Scholars, 1991).

— J.M.H.

Modernismo

In conflict with the aesthetic principles of European realism and its Spanish American variants **criollismo, costumbrismo,** and **Indigenismo,** a Spanish American literary movement, known as Modernismo emerged simultaneously in Central America and the Caribbean around the turn of the twentieth century. Inspired by French Parnassianism, with its art for art's sake philosophy, and by French Symbolism, with its use of free verse, synesthesia, musical effects, references to colors, jewels, and precious stones, the Modernistas chose as their favorite symbol the swan, which stood for absolute beauty. Although the Modernistas retained certain preoccupations of European Romanticism — such as feelings of melancholy and discontent, a cult of death, and a fascination with the Far East — and included references and allusions to Greek mythology in their writings, Spanish America Modernismo sprang from American cultural, economic, and political concerns and was dominated by an American spirit that expanded the notion of nationalism to include all of Spanish America as a cultural unit. Cosmopolitan in concept, the Modernista movement sought to revitalize and transform expressive modes and was especially influential in poetry. (See **poetry.**)

Named by Nicaraguan **Rubén Darío,** the Modernista movement can be divided into two stages. The first generation, active in 1888–1896, included Cuban **José Martí,** the great writer of Modernista prose; Darío, who initiated the movement with the publication of his well-known book of lyrical prose and poetry *Azul* (1888; Blue); Mexican Manuel Gutiérrez Najera; and other writers associated with the journal *Revista Azul.* The second generation of the movement, also called Mundonovismo (New Worldism), followed the publication of Darío's *Prosas profanas* (1896; Profane Hymns) and included only Darío from the first group. Martí and Gutiérrez Najera — as well as Colombian José Asunción Silva, who was also part of the first generation — were dead by 1896. The second stage was dominated by American themes exalting the nature and history of Spanish America and was concerned about the future of the region in a world order dominated by the newly powerful United States. This generation included **Amado Nervo** and the writers associated with the journal *La Revista Moderna.* Critics put the end of the movement variously at the time of the publication of Darío's third major work, *Cantos de vida y esperanza* (1905; Songs of Life and Hope), or at the date of Darío's death in 1916, or at the symbolic death of the swan in Mexican Enrique González Martínez's well-known poem "Tuércele el cuello al cisne" (1911; Wring the Swan's Neck).

The Modernista movement successfully revitalized literary language in Spanish and helped to achieve cultural autonomy in a region that had previously imported literary movements and divided itself through regional representations. The movement had far-reaching consequences and continues to influence writers in all of Spanish America and Spain long after its supposed demise. (See also **Modernismo** in *Dictionary of Twentieth Century Culture: Hispanic Culture of South America*).

REFERENCES:

Aníbal González, *La crónica modernista hispanoamericana* (Madrid: Gredos, 1983);

Rafael Gutiérrez Girardot, *Modernismo: Supuestos históricos y culturales* (Mexico City: FCE, 1988);

Max Henríquez Ureña, *Breve historia del modernismo* (Mexico City: FCE, 1954);

Angel Rama, *Rubén Darío y el modernismo* (Caracas: Ediciones de la Biblioteca de la Universidad Central de Venezuela, 1970).

— A.G.

JOSÉ MOJICA

One of the most prominent artists of the lyric-romantic song in Latin America, José de Jesús Mojica (1896–1974) was born in San Gabriel, Jalisco, Mexico. It appears that his life was destined to be shaped by a series of unusual coincidences. His mother, victimized and abandoned by an already married doctor, increased their misery by marrying a destitute drunkard who ended up in prison for almost killing her. After moving to Mexico City, mother and son began a reconstructive and relatively happy period. José Mojica planned to return eventually to manage his grandfather's farms, but that plan was discarded when a volcano destroyed the farms.

José Mojica became fascinated with the artistic ambience of Mexico City, especially the performances of **zarzuela** and opera in the principal theaters. When classes at his school were suspended because of the **Mexican Revolution,** he studied painting in the mornings and music, French, Italian, and mime in the afternoons. While many of his classmates became celebrities in the theater and silent-movie industry, Mojica began serious study of vocal technique. After paying his dues as a member of the chorus in light productions, his solo debut was in the role of Count Almaviva in a Mexico City production of *The Barber of Seville* (1919); other operatic roles quickly followed. In 1919 Mojica won the role of Edmundo in a production of *Manon Lescaut* in which the great Italian tenor, Enrico Caruso, was featured. They became friends; Caruso recommended him for the role of Sposino, which he subsequently sang in the production of *Lucia* at the Chicago Opera later the same year. Mojica remained with the Chicago Opera for several years, appearing in productions with the great Russian bass Fyodor Chaliapin and the popular soprano Mary Garden.

In 1921, four years before regular radio broadcasts were established in Mexico, Mojica sang *Tango negro* (Black Tango) in the first experimental Mexican broadcast. In 1930 he went to Havana with **Ernesto Lecuona** to perform *María La O*. Later he was contracted by the Edison Recording Company to help publicize their new high-fidelity phonograph; the resulting recordings were a success, but even greater was the success of those made for the Victor "Red Label." Mojica's first hit recording was **María Grever**'s *Júrame* (1926; Promise Me), followed by an enviable succession of Latin American favorites in the romantic song tradition. Among them are: *Dime* (Tell Me), *¿En dónde estás?* (Where Are You), *Adiós mi amor* (Goodbye, My Love), *Gratia plena*, *Cuando me vaya* (When I Leave), and *Un beso loco* (A Crazy Kiss). Many of Mojica's recorded successes stemmed from his film career. The experience gained on the musical stage was propitious for the new "talking" film industry being developed in Los Angeles and Mexico City. Among his many film credits are: *El precio de un beso* (The Price of a Kiss), *Cuando el amor ríe* (When Love Laughs), *Melodía prohibida* (Forbidden Melody), *La ley del Harem* (The Law of the Harem), and *La cruz y la espada* (The Cross and the Sword).

In the late 1930s Mojica returned to the Chicago Opera for the last time to perform in *Salomé,* by Richard Strauss, and *Falstaff,* by Giuseppe Verdi. Upon completion of his last film, *Melodías de América* (1941; Melodies of America), with music by **Agustín Lara** that included one of the most enduring Latin favorites of all times, "Solamente una vez" (Only Once), Mojica announced that he was retiring from worldly life to enter the Franciscan order in Perú. He was ordained in 1947 at the age of fifty-one, but at the request of the Church, he continued evangelical performances in public, on radio, and in recordings. In 1956 he produced his biography, *Yo pecador* (I, a Sinner), which inspired a film starring Libertad Lamarque, with Pedro Geraldo playing the role of Mojica. In 1960 he toured, promoting his last film, *Seguiré tus pasos* (I Will Follow In Thy Footsteps). Fray José de Guadalupe died in his cell at the Convento de San Francisco de Asís in Lima, on 20 November 1974.

REFERENCES:

Cristobal Díaz Ayala, *Música cubana del Areyto a la Nueva Trova,* second edition (San Juan: Editorial Cubanacán, 1981);

Hernán Restrepo Duque, *Lo que cuentan los bolers* (Sante Fe de Bogotá: Centro Editorial de Estudios Musicales, 1992);

Jaime Rico Salazar, *Cien años de boleros* (Bogotá: Centro Editorial de Estudios Musicales, 1987).

— R.L.S.

CARLOS MONSIVÁIS

Carlos Monsiváis (1938–) is a Mexican essayist and novelist who established his reputation as a chronicler of the turbulent political years in Mexico during the 1960s and 1970s. As an adolescent Monsiváis became a political activist. Soon, fascinated by the arts, he began to participate in various cultural projects, becoming director of the university radio program of the Universidad Nacional Autónoma de México (National Autonomous University of Mexico), where he was a student. He studied in the United States in 1965, and there he witnessed the protests against the Vietnam War and was influenced by the countercultural student movement. Back in Mexico he wrote extensively for various journals, among them *Excélsior, Siempre,* and *Nexos;* these and other writings closely identified him with the student movement and the massacre of protesters at **Tlatelolco** in 1968. In his collection of essays *Días de*

guardar (1970; Days to Remember) he portrays the political discontent of students and workers in the late 1960s and early 1970s. In 1977 he published *Amor perdido* (Lost Love), a collection of essays dealing mostly with current Mexican personalities. His ironic and satirical way of describing Mexican society, combined with perceptive observations and caustic humor, led to its being received with wide acclaim. *A ustedes les consta* (1980; It's Up to You) underscores the importance of a writer's social and political commitment, while his first work of fiction, *Nuevo catecismo para indios remisos* (1982; New Catechism for Remiss Indians), consists of fables with varying messages.

REFERENCE:

Martin Stabb, *The Dissenting Voice* (Austin: University of Texas Press, 1994).

— M.E.S.

AUGUSTO MONTERROSO

If one were to try to characterize the literature of Augusto Monterroso (1921–) in a couple of words, they would surely be *conciseness* and *irony.* He is a master of economy (one of his stories is seven words long) whose output is correspondingly slim but of disproportionate value. Monterroso's efforts to contribute to cutting back the rhetorical jungle of the Latin American tradition puts him in company with writers such as the Mexican **Juan Rulfo** and the Argentineans Jorge Luis Borges and Julio Cortázar. Monterroso has the perfectionism and attention to detail of Rulfo and Borges, the readability of Cortázar, a formal inventiveness akin to that of Borges, and a sense of humor to compare with those of both the Argentineans. Indeed, Borges is one of Monterroso's preferred authors, along with Jonathan Swift (who also influenced the Argentinean master). Yet it is with Cortázar that Monterroso can better be compared on a personal level, for he is a man who has had a life of active commitment to democratic causes but one who has seen creative writing as an undertaking driven above all by aesthetic considerations. For example, Monterroso tells how — as he was in the process of writing one of his best-known stories, "Mr. Taylor" — he made strenuous efforts to set aside his political indignation at the U.S.-supported overthrow of a democratic regime in Guatemala. The end product does not lack political weight, but it acquires it through a subtle and accomplished use of irony, creating a farcical situation worthy of Swift. Although he is largely self-taught, Monterroso is one of the most polished writers of the century.

Augusto Monterroso (photograph by Efrén Figueredo)

Monterroso was born in Honduras and brought up in Guatemala. He had little schooling and worked first in a butcher's shop but had the good fortune of having a literate supervisor who encouraged him to read. In the 1940s Monterroso became associated with Guatemalan writers known as the "Generation of 1940" and cofounded an association of young artists and writers and a literary magazine called *Acento.* His first short story was published in the newspaper *El Imparcial* but was banned from being read on the national radio station. In 1944 he lost his job for inciting a strike among his coworkers. Later he participated in popular antigovernment uprisings and signed a petition that came to be known as the "Manifesto de los 311" (Declaration of the 311), demanding the resignation of the dictator Jorge Ubico. After Ubico's fall from power, his successor, Ponce Vaides, suppressed Monterroso's opposition newspaper *El Espectador* (of which Monterroso had been cofounder and editor). Eventually, Monterroso sought refuge in Mexico. He later served the short-lived democratic government of Jacobo Arbenz as a diplomat in Bolivia, but with Arbenz's overthrow in 1954 (the time of composition of "Mr. Taylor"), Monterroso fled to Chile. In Chile the newspaper *El Siglo* published his short story "El eclipse" (The Eclipse), and there Monterroso met and befriended the Chilean poet Pablo Neruda, who invited him to his home in Isla Negra and to collaborate on *La Gaceta de Chile.* After two years in Chile, Monterroso (still a citizen of Guatemala) returned to Mexico. He soon became associated with the university and literary scene, editing the *Revista de la universidad,* teaching at El Colegio de México and at the Universidad Nacional Autónoma de México (National Autonomous University of Mexico). He has been a

contributor to several publications and literary magazines and a recipient of many literary awards.

The fable has been a favorite form for Monterroso, as the titles of two of his few books reveal: *La oveja negra y demás fábulas* (1969; translated as *The Black Sheep and Other Fables*) and *Viaje al centro de la fábula* (1981; Voyage to the Center of the Fable). However, unlike the fables of Aesop and others, Monterroso's are often open to multiple interpretations. There is also an almost constant playfulness in his fiction, which, for all its accessibilty, flatters readers by assuming they are intelligent and perceptive enough to read between the lines. Beneath an apparent simplicity there lies a richness that comes with erudition, while humor is never far off. **Carlos Fuentes,** attempting to convey something of the flavor of Monterroso's *La oveja negra y demás fábulas,* invites one to imagine Borges's taking tea with Alice in Wonderland and Jonathan Swift and James Thurber exchanging notes.

Monterroso's other publications are *Obras completas y otros cuentos* (1959; Complete Works and Other Stories), *Movimiento perpetuo* (1972; Perpetual Motion), and *Lo demás es silencio* (1978; The Rest Is Silence). This last work is subtitled "The Life and Works of Eduardo Torres," referring to a figure invented by Monterroso, but one who had acquired a certain level of credibility in Mexico since his first appearance on the cultural scene some twenty years previously. In *Lo demás es silencio* other equally fictitious persons also bear witness to the character and activities of Torres, while some of his aphorisms help fill out the picture. Most engagingly (and somewhat in the vein of Luigi Pirandello), Torres reviews Monterroso's *La oveja negra y demás fábulas.*

REFERENCES:

Dolores M. Koch, "El micro-relato en México," *Hispamérica,* 10, no. 30 (1981): 123–130;

Juan Antonio Masoliver, "Augusto Monterroso o la tradición subversiva," *Cuadernos Hispanoamericanos,* 408 (1984);

Robert A. Parsons, "Self-Parody in *Lo demás es silencio," Hispania,* 72, no. 4 (1989): 938–945.

— P.S.

ARMANDO MORALES

The Nicaraguan Armando Morales (1927–), an important Latin American artist, studied art in Managua at the Escuela de Bellas Artes with Rodrigo Peñalba, whose expressionism helped renovate Nicaraguan art. In the early 1950s Morales depicted regional themes in a pervasive realist style that he — like many of his contemporaries — eventually found outmoded and rejected. In 1957 Morales exhibited at the Pan-American

Desnudo, caballo, incinerador (1974; Nude, Horse, Incinerator) by Armando Morales (Archer M. Huntington Art Gallery, The University of Texas at Austin, Barbara Duncan Fund, 1975 [G1975.33.1P])

Union in Washington, D.C. After receiving a Guggenheim Fellowship, he moved to New York. During this period Morales turned toward Informal Abstraction and became interested in the work of artists such as the Spanish informalist Antoni Tàpies and the American Abstract Expressionist Robert Motherwell (See **Abstract Art.**) Although Morales emphasized the use of broad areas of color and textural surfaces in his paintings, he never completely stopped referring to reality. In works such as *Paisaje marino* (1964; Seascape) he suggests nature by using a few simple geometric shapes with uneven borders and opaque colors: whites, blues, blacks, and earth tones.

In 1966 Morales visited Nicaragua, where the Praxis group had revolutionized the art scene by adopting avant-garde styles. He also traveled to Italy, where he admired the art of the Italian metaphysical painter Giorgio de Chirico. After returning to New York Morales gradually abandoned abstraction. During the 1970s and 1980s he formulated a kind of figuration that critics relate to **magical realism** and **Surrealism** because of the dreamlike atmosphere of works such as *Desnudo, caballo, incinerador* (1974; Nude, Horse, In-

cinerator), which features a statuesque female nude and a horse in a shallow, friezelike space, and *Bañistas y barca roja* (1986; Bathers and Red Boat), which shows nude women standing next to a lake with a steamboat in the background. Morales reflects his admiration for Renaissance anatomical studies in the classical three-dimensionality of his female figures, while their sometimes headless or fragmented bodies reveal his interest in Giorgio de Chirico's mannequins. At the same time, Morales worked with tightly controlled spaces surrounded by classical and Romanesque architecture, which he had seen not only in the paintings of Giotto di Bondone and de Chirico but also in his native city of Granada. His interest in texture continued during this period, but he achieved it illusionistically, by painting the surface of his canvasses with several coats of deep and neutral colors that were later partially shaved off in a crosshatching pattern. Although the surface is finished with smooth coats of varnish, the layering and soft modulation of the colors give the work tactile and abstract qualities.

In 1982 Morales was appointed the Nicaraguan delegate to UNESCO in Paris, where he has lived since

1987. While in Paris he also worked on a series of imaginary views of rain forests, such as *Selva tropical* (1987; Tropical Forest), inspired by memories of his childhood and of his 1959 trip to the Brazilian and Peruvian rain forests. Although the careful attention to minute details emphasizes the realism of these paintings, the lack of visual depth, the emphasis on vertical elements, and the contrast between concave and convex spaces lends them an abstract quality. Morales's most recent paintings, for instance *Adiós a Sandino* (1985; Farewell to Sandino), represent historical events in Nicaragua and emphasize a sense of cultural identity.

REFERENCE:
Celia S. de Birbragher, "Armando Morales," *Arte en Colombia,* no. 45 (October 1990): 33–41.

— F.B.N.

NANCY MOREJÓN

Nancy Morejón was born in Havana, Cuba, in 1944 and was a teenager at the time of the triumph of **Fidel Castro** in the Cuban Revolution. The effect of this transformation in 1959 is evident in her poems, which frequently explore themes of rebellion. Her poetry is marked by a commitment to examining cultural, political, and social issues, especially those issues dealing with blacks in Cuba. Her work also draws attention to the oppressed conditions of blacks in the United States. Many of her poems reflect a concern with female and black identity; her most recognized poem is "Mujer negra" (Black Woman), which speaks of the debasement of slavery but also demonstrates how black women are empowered by their attachment to each other throughout generations, an attachment that is reflected in their close relationship with the land. Her poem "Freedom Now" depicts the situation of blacks in the southern United States and is a harsh criticism of a society that enriches itself through cheap labor. Much of Morejón's poetry is highly ironic and scathing, yet subtle. Understatement is her forte. She presents her criticisms through a skillful use of imagery, suggesting condemnation rather than launching direct attacks on the objects of her anger, the exploiters of underprivileged, especially black women.

Morejón has published ten volumes of poetry. Among them are *Elogio de la danza* (1982; In Praise of Dance), *Cuaderno de Granada* (1984; Granada Notebook), *Where the Island Sleeps Like a Wing* (1985; a bilingual edition), and *Piedra pulida* (1986; Polished Stone).

REFERENCE:
Yvonne Captain-Hidalgo, *Nancy Morejón* (Westport, Conn.: Greenwood Press, 1990).

— M.E.S.

MOVIES FROM BOOKS

Although early adaptations of literary works for the cinema screen tended to be somewhat stiff, many important Spanish American books of the twentieth century have been successfully filmed. In 1944 Luis Buñuel made a film of **Rodolfo Usigli**'s *Ensayo de un crimen.* In 1964 the Mexican directors Alberto Isaac and García Riera adapted Gabriel García Márquez's short story *En este pueblo no hay ladrones* (translated as "In This Town There Are No Thieves") to create a screen version that was awarded second prize in a competition sponsored by the Sindicato de Trabajadores de la Industria Cinematográfica (Cinematic Industry Workers' Union). **Guillermo Cabrera Infante**'s *Tres tristes tigres* (1966; translated as *Three Trapped Tigers*), one of the major novels of the **Boom,** was transposed to the big screen by Chilean director Raúl Ruiz in 1968; the sad/trapped tigers of the title are the petty-bourgeois protagonists, who waste their time talking in bars, unable to relate to the changing realities of Cuban society. That same year saw the release of the celebrated Cuban director **Tomás Gutiérrez Alea**'s *Memorias del subdesarrollo,* based on the novel by Edmundo Desnoes. *Pantaleón y las visitadoras* (1973; translated as *Captain Pantoja and the Special Service*), a popular novel by another of the major Boom authors, the Peruvian Mario Vargas Llosa, was filmed in the Dominican Republic in 1976, with the author himself making a brief appearance. Jorge Fons made a 1976 film version of *Los albañiles* (1964; The Bricklayers), by **Vicente Leñero.** The Chilean director Miguel Littín made two coproductions of literary works in the late 1970s: *El recurso del método,* based on **Alejo Carpentier**'s novel of the same name (1977; translated as *Reasons of State*), and *La viuda de Montiel* (1979; Montiel's Widow), a rather drawn-out adaptation of one of García Márquez's short stories. García Márquez's active involvement with Cuban cinema through the **New Latin American Cinema Foundation** also led to the production of the much more successful *Letters from the Park,* released in 1988 and based on his novel *El amor en los tiempos del cólera* (1985; translated as *Love in the Time of Cholera*); it was directed by Tomás Gutiérrez Alea from a screenplay by Eliseo Alberto Diego and García Márquez, and it starred Víctor Laplace, Ivonne López, and Miguel Paneque. Another coproduction by the Cuban foundation (this time with Spanish rather than Italian television) was

Barroco (Paul Leduc, Mexico, 1989), based on Alejo Carpentier's short novel *Concierto barroco.* **Carlos Fuentes,** who had been involved as writer of the screenplay for Carlos Velo's 1966 movie based on **Juan Rulfo**'s *Pedro Páramo* (1955), also collaborated with Jane Fonda in 1989 to produce *Old Gringo,* the English-language film version of his own novel *Gringo viejo* (1985). The major success of the 1990s has been Mexican Alfonso Arau's *Como agua para chocolate,* which came out in 1993 and was based on the novel of the same name (translated as *Like Water for Chocolate*) by Laura Esquivel.

                                                              — P.S.

MUJER TRANSPARENTE

Mujer transparente (1990; Transparent Woman) comprises five dramatic short films, produced by teams led by the Cuban directors Hector Veitía, Mayra Segura, Mayra Vilasís, Mario Crespo, and Ana Rodríguez. Coordinated by **Humberto Solás,** who encouraged Cuban filmmakers to address socially sensitive issues, *Mujer transparente* had its origins in three creative groups set up at the **Cuban Film Institute** in 1987. The strength of *Mujer transparente* lies in its ability to present a variety of perspectives on the female experience in Cuba and in its balanced portrayal of the private and the social lives of the characters.

Through its main character each short examines a woman's struggle to express herself. Directed by Veitía, who wrote the script with Tina León, *Isabel* deals with a middle-aged woman (played by Isabel Moreno) who is promoted to a managerial position and must deal with established attitudes toward women at home as well as at work. *Adriana,* written and directed by Segura, takes the audience into the fantasy world of an older woman (Veronica Lynn). *Julia,* written and directed by Vilasís, focuses on a woman's recollections of her failed marriage and her divorce. *Zoé,* directed by Crespo with a script by Osvaldo Sánchez and Carlos Cedrán, compares the lives of a nonconformist young artist (Leonor Arocha) and a student leader (Leonardo Armas) sent to investigate her absences from the university. Finally, *Laura,* written and directed by Ana Rodríguez, explores a woman's uncertain feelings about a female friend who has come back to Cuba for a visit.

REFERENCE:

Zuzana M. Pick, *The New Latin American Cinema: A Continental Project* (Austin: University of Texas Press, 1993).

                                                              — S.M.H.

MURALISM

Mexican Muralism is one of the most important and influential avant-garde movements in the Americas. Mexico has a long history of mural painting that goes back to pre-Columbian and colonial times and includes the folk tradition of *pulquería* wall paintings as well (a *pulquería* is a bar that serves *pulque,* a fermented liquor from the maguey cactus). In the twentieth century the idea of creating a national school of public mural art was first posited by **Dr. Atl,** who in 1910 obtained a commission to decorate the walls of the Anfiteatro Bolívar at the Escuela Nacional Preparatoria (National Preparatory School); work on that commission, however, was interrupted by the outbreak of the **Mexican Revolution.**

Muralism was a state-supported movement. The postrevolutionary administration of Alvaro Obregón (1921–1926), a coalition of urban middle-class sectors, saw Muralism as an opportunity to reach the largely illiterate masses in order to gain broader support and legitimize state policies. Muralism also corrected the violent image of the Mexican Revolution by presenting to the outside world a new image of Mexico as a civilized nation, helping the new administration gain recognition from other countries. The minister of education, **José Vasconcelos,** wanted a national art based on idealized indigenous values; thus, in 1921 he offered walls in public buildings to any artist who requested them. Artists had artistic freedom as long as they depicted Mexican themes.

The first phase of Muralism was influenced by Vasconcelos's classical ideals. Among the earliest murals were those of Fernando Leal, Fermín Revueltas, Ramón Alva de la Canal, **Jean Charlot, José Clemente Orozco, Diego Rivera,** and **David Alfaro Siqueiros** at the Escuela Nacional Preparatoria. For instance, Rivera's encaustic wall painting *La creación* (1922; Creation) features allegories of the virtues and liberal arts, a theme inspired by Vasconcelos and **Symbolist Art.** Charlot, Orozco, Rivera, and Siqueiros had been abroad and worked with avant-garde styles connected to Expressionism and post-Cubist figuration. During the early 1920s many muralists were influenced by Manuel Gamio's writings on **Indigenism** and sought to define a new iconography that represented their view of Mexican identity and their political ideas. Following Obregón's rhetoric, in their early frescoes muralists glorified the concept of *el pueblo* (the people), which meant urban workers, peasants, and Indians, rather than historical heroes.

In the second phase of Muralism artists working at the Preparatoria began to depict radical political themes, as in Siqueiros's *El entierro del obrero* (1923;

Burial of a Worker) and Orozco's caricature-like fresco *Fuerzas reaccionarias* (1924; Reactionary Forces), which caused a scandal and the dismissal of the muralists. Simultaneously, Rivera and Siqueiros rose to the leadership of the mural movement, the Mexican intelligentsia, and the Mexican Communist Party. Muralists became important players in national politics and created the Sindicato de Obreros Técnicos, Pintores, y Escultores (Union of Technical Workers, Painters, and Sculptors), whose avant-garde manifesto outlined their political and artistic aims. During the administration of Plutarco Elías Calles, Rivera monopolized the massive commission that came from the Secretaría de Educación Pública (Ministry of Public Education), and he produced his most politically radical works, such as *La distribución de tierras* (1923–1924; Land Distribution). In 1926 Orozco was allowed to continue his frescoes at the Preparatoria, including his famous *La trinchera* (1926; The Trench) and *Cortés y Malintzín* (1926; Cortés and Malintzín).

The third phase of Muralism started in the late 1920s, when it began to achieve official status as the School of Mexico. During this period muralists focused on historical Mexican themes, often depicting specific revolutionary heroes, such as Miguel Hidalgo y Costilla and Emiliano Zapata. On occasion the strong political views of *los tres grandes* (the big three: Rivera, Siqueiros, and Orozco) conflicted with those of the Mexican government, which resulted in periods of exile during the 1930s. Siqueiros was even incarcerated during the 1950s.

The most important mural projects since the mid 1920s include the following: Rivera's allegorical frescoes at Chapingo's Escuela Nacional de Agricultura (1926; National School of Agriculture) and his monumental vision of Mexican history at Mexico City's Palacio Nacional (1929, 1942–1945; National Palace); Cuernavaca's Palacio de Cortés (1929; Palace of Cortés); Orozco's expressionist frescoes in Guadalajara, at the Universidad de Guadalajara (1936; University of Guadalajara), the Palacio de Gobierno (1937; Government Palace), and Hospicio Cabañas (1938–1939; Cabañas Orphanage); Siqueiros's formal experiments in his murals *Retrato de la burguesía* (1939–1940; Portrait of the Bourgeoisie) at the Sindicato de Electricistas Mexicanos (Mexican Electricians' Union) and *Marcha de la humanidad en Latinoamérica* (1966–1973; March of Humanity in Latin America) at the Poliforum Cultural (Cultural Polyforum); and **Juan O'Gorman**'s mosaic murals on the exterior of the Biblioteca Central building (1950; Main Library) of the Universidad Nacional Autónoma de México (National Autonomous University of Mexico).

The dominance of Muralism in Mexican art remained unchallenged until the 1950s, when **La Ruptura Generation** denounced the didactic, ideological, and stylistic limitations of the School of Mexico. Muralism was influential both in the United States and Latin America. Los tres grandes completed several well-known and often controversial murals in the United States, including Rivera's murals in the Detroit Institute of Fine Arts (1932–1933) and the now-destroyed fresco at the Rockefeller Center RCA Building (1933); Siqueiros's mural *Tropical America* (1932) in Los Angeles; and Orozco's frescoes at Pomona College (1930), the New School for Social Research (1930–1931), and Dartmouth College (1932–1934). Muralism also inspired the Works Progress Administration Federal Art Project, which supported artists during the Depression. Muralism's emphasis on Indigenism also exerted a considerable influence in the Andean and Central American countries, through the art of **Carlos Mérida** and Alfredo Gálvez Suárez. Later, Muralism's stress on leftist politics also attracted the interest of Puerto Rican, Cuban, Chilean, Nicaraguan, and Chicano artists, beginning in the 1950s. In Nicaragua an important mural movement during the 1980s was backed by official support from the Sandinista government, which provided public walls in easily accessible places. Many of these murals have now been destroyed.

REFERENCES:

Laurance P. Hurlburt, *The Mexican Muralists in the United States* (Albuquerque: University of New Mexico Press, 1989);

Desmond Rochfort, *The Mexican Muralists: Orozco, Rivera, Siqueiros* (London: Laurence King, 1993).

— F.B.N.

MUSIC

The phenomenal diversity of music in Mexico, Central America, and the Caribbean emerged from the forced coalescence of three principal cultural influences: European, indigenous, and African. There was no conquest but rather a monumental encounter in which there were musical gains as well as losses. Among the gains are the many exciting examples of syncretic musics, some reflecting the union of two of the cultures and others revealing influences from all three.

The most severe losses were indigenous and date from early colonial times; ritual musics of the Indians were summarily prohibited under penalty of death. Indigenous musics survived intact only in remote, inaccessible areas of Mexico and Central America. This surviving music would provide the indigenous sources to which composers would turn in the twentieth century (see **Nationalism in Music**). In the Hispanic Caribbean the indigenes themselves expired along with their musical cultures, reducing our present-day knowledge of them to archaeological and anthropological studies. Although such studies have produced evidence and descriptions of music in indigenous life, no sonorous evidence of this music can be identified in subsequent musical practice. Without immunity to European diseases and unable to withstand the harsh treatment of the Europeans, indigenes became the earliest American victims of racial and cultural genocide.

Although African rituals were also discouraged, if not prohibited entirely, the continuous influx of slaves, especially from West Africa, served as a constant source of cultural regeneration until the official ban on the importation of slaves in the nineteenth century. Similarly, the importation and renewal of European musical cultures continued almost without interruption from the colonial period to the present, prominent especially among people of European descent but also engaged in by the indigenous and African populations.

The process of musical acculturation began during the earliest days of colonization, the period often referred to now as El encuentro (The Encounter). The intention of the Spanish priests who accompanied the conquistadors was not simply to destroy indigenous musics and rituals because they were pagan practices but, more important, to replace them with Christian, Catholic music and ritual. There was sufficient interest in teaching and learning European religious music to warrant Pedro de Gante's founding a school of music in Texcoco in 1524, only three years after the occupation of the Aztec capital of Tenochtitlán; his students were aspiring indigenous musicians. More than a hundred years before the *Bay Psalm Book* appeared in New England (1698), various books of Catholic church music were published in Mexico, the earliest in 1556. Among less advanced and more remote indigenous groups in Mexico and Central America there existed neither the interest nor the effort to emulate the Europeans. As a consequence, remote musics tended to remain intact, serving as valuable sources for subsequent generations intent on developing distinctive cultural identities.

It soon became evident to many native Americans, as it had to musicians throughout the history of Europe, that music, albeit in the Church, provided a unique means of social and economic mobility. It also became apparent through the excellent examples of polyphonic music sent back to Spain that native composers could match European standards of composition.

It was only a matter of time and of continued growth of the mestizo population in Middle America

before musical acculturation became apparent in secular as well as sacred music. Secular musicians had accompanied the first explorations of Mexico, providing popular music for song and dance. The mestizo reality was important in the process of acculturation. It is recorded that the male child of Hernán Cortés and his native interpreter, **Malinche,** was the first mestizo, the first product of the union of European and native Americans. The vast majority of Europeans who colonized Mexico did so without the company of their families, pairing instead with indigenous partners. The mestizo population soon became the majority in several countries and was encouraged to preserve a measure of both inherited cultures, an inheritance that resulted in the syncretized musics of today.

Although similar social processes occurred in the Hispanic Caribbean, the demise of most indigenous populations by the sixteenth century produced a different result in that region. To replace the rapidly diminishing native population, slavery was introduced to furnish laborers for tobacco and sugarcane plantations. The subsequent growth of a large mulatto population produced a condition similar to that of Middle America. Slaves who learned how to play European instruments and music well received preferential treatment and better living conditions. The Spanish gentry gave strong support to this practice: to play music, even as a pseudo-professional, was beneath their station, but it was a service properly rendered by servants. Ironically, for Afro-Caribbean slaves, performing music as a profession became one of the few avenues to economic independence. As in Mexico, the full efflorescence of syncretic music in the Hispanic Caribbean occurred in secular genres.

Instruments brought from Europe, such as guitars, harps, rebecs (predecessors of the violin), trumpets, flutes, shawms (predecessors of oboes), and others were immediately accepted, and many were quickly modified. Some adaptations were due to idiosyncratic tastes; others were based on the availability of materials used in making them. Many variations of the guitar appeared, among them the **tres,** jarana, **guitarra de golpe, guitarrón,** jaranita, and **cuatro.** In addition, various versions of the harp were developed, especially in Mexico. Africans were not permitted to bring their instruments during the era of slavery, but that did not deter them from reconstructing them from materials found in the New World. Adaptations of African drums became especially important in the organology of the Americas. In the same manner, genres of music from the Iberian Peninsula such as the **romance,** seguidilla, fandango, zapateado, and jota served as antecedents for New World innovations such as the **corrido,** jarana, **jarabe, seis,** and **mariachi.**

The nineteenth-century wars of liberation, civil hostilities, and general political instability in Mexico and Central America delayed the growth and development of national musical identities. Shifting alliances, invasions, confederations, and partitions of territory tended to isolate the diverse musical cultures within the new republics. In the Hispanic Caribbean multinational struggles to exploit the islands, invasions, and military occupations resulted in a similar condition of insecurity. Although there were growing demands for autonomy, Cuba, the Dominican Republic, and Puerto Rico remained in the Spanish Empire until the end of the century, which helped foster cultural communication through the transmigration of musicians and other artists among the islands of the Greater Antilles. The anthropological and sociological kinship of the Hispanic islands and their propensity to share musical experiences eventually produced a Hispanic-Afro-Caribbean identity that would endure until the twentieth century, when each island came to feel impelled to focus on idiosyncratic differences. In one sense twentieth-century **nationalism in music** of the Caribbean basin represented a delayed response to nineteenth-century nationalism in European musics; in another it symbolized the necessity of establishing national identities that corresponded with new and, in most cases, more stable political identities.

The revolutionary process in Mexico produced a mass movement of people and military units to previously unfamiliar areas; the **mariachi,** corrido, **son,** and **canción mexicana** became nationally recognized genres rather than regional peculiarities. The establishment of regular radio broadcasts of Mexican music shortly after the **Mexican Revolution** not only reinforced a sense of national identity for Mexicans but exerted a predominant musical influence throughout Central America. Mexico also provided the leadership in classically oriented music through the works of **Manuel Ponce, Silvestre Revueltas,** and especially **Carlos Chávez.** Their musical intentions, strongly supported by the new government, focused on autochthonous sources in a movement popularly known as **Indigenismo.** As the century progressed, Mexico continued to consolidate and exert its cultural power and influence far beyond its borders through the establishment and support of national institutions and industries in which music was a primary concern or of critical importance. Strong government support of conservatories, symphony orchestras, and folkloric agencies has enabled them to provide training and performance venues for thousands of performers and creative artists. Export of Mexico's impressive cultural products was facilitated by the development of the film, recording, and television industries.

The Spanish-American War led to a close relationship between the United States and the Hispanic Caribbean. The migration of Dominicans, Cubans, and especially Puerto Ricans to urban centers such as New York and Chicago increased, while the Caribbean (particularly prerevolutionary Cuba) became a tourist playground for North Americans. As other immigrant groups in the United States had done, those from the Hispanic Caribbean brought their music, often at the request of emerging commercial recording companies. In the 1930s romantic **boleros** and **popular trios** were in great demand by Brunswick, RCA, Decca, and Columbia. By the 1940s the bolero was sharing popularity with the **mambo.** At the same time, the improvisational nature of their Spanish and African musical heritages attracted many of the Caribbean musicians into North American jazz groups, where their melodic and rhythmic innovations were welcomed by stars of the caliber of Dizzy Gillespie and Stan Kenton. Jazz had a reciprocal influence on Caribbean musics as well. In the 1940s Afro-Caribbean jazz musicians such as **Frank "Machito" Grillo**, Mario Bauzá, **Tito Puente,** and **Tito Rodríguez** combined big-band instrumentation with Latin percussion sections to produce new renditions of Caribbean music. Through recordings and radio broadcasts the Latin music of New York resonated in the urban centers of the Caribbean basin, creating additional reciprocal influences. Several factors in the 1960s temporarily suspended the proliferation and commercial success of Caribbean musics. The sudden international popularity of the Beatles consumed the interest of the public; the Cuban Revolution and subsequent U.S. blockade cut musical ties with the island; and the disintegration of big bands sent smaller combos back into neighborhood bars and cabarets. Not until the 1970s did a new convergence of Caribbean musics recapture the public's affection under the rubric of **salsa,** a multicultural, multiracial music that has garnered phenomenal popular and commercial success in the Caribbean as well as in Europe, Asia, and the United States.

REFERENCES:

Gerard Béhague, *Music in Latin America: An Introduction* (Englewood Cliffs, N.J.: Prentice-Hall, 1979);

Alejo Carpentier, *La música en Cuba,* second edition (Mexico City: Fondo de Cultura Económica, 1972);

Cristóbal Díaz Ayala, *Música cubana del Areyto a la Nueva Trova,* second edition (San Juan, Puerto Rico: Editorial Cubanacán, 1981);

Bernarda Jorge, *La música dominicana: Siglos XIX–XX* (Santo Domingo: Editora de la Universidad Autónoma de Santo Domingo, 1982);

Otto Mayer-Serra, *The Present State of Music in Mexico* (Washington, D.C.: Panamerican Union Music Division, 1946);

César Miguel Rondón, *El libro de la salsa; Crónica de la música del caribe urbano* (Caracas: Editorial Arte, 1980);

Robert Stevenson, *Music in Mexico: A Historical Survey* (New York: Crowell, 1952).

— R.L.S.

MUSICAL INSTRUMENTS

The contributions of the indigenous cultures of Spanish America to the body of contemporary musical instruments are related to the demographic strength, sociological organization, and technological achievements of these various groups during the colonial era. In Puerto Rico, for example, the practically defenseless indigenes were effectively extinct by the middle of the sixteenth century. By the end of the century the same was true for Santo Domingo (Hispaniola) and Cuba. Preconquest Antillean Indians employed a variety of drums, whistles, ocarinas, bone flutes, **maracas,** claves, and scrapers, few of which have survived into the modern era. Among those instruments that are still in existence, only the maracas, claves, and **güiro** have been incorporated into folk, popular, and commercial ensembles. Many instruments similar to those used during the pre-Columbian era in the Antilles, however, are still in use among indigenous groups living in isolated areas of Central America.

The most advanced pre-Columbian culture in Mesoamerica was that of the Aztec Empire of Mexico. Although this empire was destroyed, its musical instruments survived in the rituals and celebrations of isolated tribes despite vigorous efforts by the Catholic Church to abolish their use. After the **Mexican Revolution** supporters of **nationalism in music** turned to these instruments and the music associated with them. Aztec musicians employed a varied array of aerophones (wind instruments), including wooden, bone, and ceramic flutes; ocarinas; whistles; and wooden and conch-shell trumpets. Their principal percussion instruments were idiophones — maracas, scrapers, and various kinds of rattles — and membranophones — drums of various sizes and shapes. Chordophones (stringed instruments) were unknown to indigenous groups of the Americas prior to their encounter with Europeans.

Colonial efforts to abolish the use of pagan indigenous instruments were accompanied by a successful drive to replace them with European models. Over the centuries many amateur and professional European musicians migrated to the Americas, where they encountered eager natives who had observed the advantages of social mobility afforded to those who could master European instruments. The demands of the church for sacred music and those of the Spanish colonists for secular music caused a proliferation of European instruments throughout the hemisphere. Over time European instruments of every type were either brought to Latin America or duplicated there.

With the introduction of African slaves to the Americas in the sixteenth century the number and variety of instruments in Latin America increased enormously. Prohibited from bringing personal belongings or cultural artifacts to the New World, slaves re-created from memory an extensive array of primarily West African instruments, and these have remained in use throughout the centuries. The process of re-creation inevitably produced examples that were somewhat different from the original African instruments. Occasionally the differences between New World instruments and their African counterparts were attributable to the lack of traditional African materials and the use of American substitutes.

The most extensive category of African instruments in the Americas is that of membranophones: drums of all sizes and shapes, with differing construction and higher and lower tunings, are played with hands, fingers, or sticks in various combinations and are still prominent throughout middle America and the Caribbean. Perhaps the most ubiquitous of African drums throughout the world is the **conga** drum, which is often played in conjunction with its larger form, the tumbadora, and its smaller version, the quinto. Conga drums have only one skin, or head, but some drums, such as the **tambora** and the batá, have skins — and are played — on both ends of their frames. Conga and batá drums are played with the hands only, but tamboras and the large caja drums are played with a combination of hand and stick. The bincomé (or biancomé) drum is played only with the index finger, while yuka drums have two players: one hits the skin with hand and stick while the other strikes the wooden frame with sticks. Players of friction drums, such as the ekué, produce sound by rubbing the membrane rather than striking it. Metal bells (agógo), wooden sticks (claves), boxes (cajas), spoons, gourds (**güiros**), glass bottles, rattles (maracas), and any other material that produces sound when struck or shaken (as well as the clapping of hands) are examples of idiophones.

The intermingling of Indians, Europeans, and Africans produced new genres of music and new musical instruments. As the guitar, a European instrument, became omnipresent throughout Latin America, it inspired or was imitated by instruments created to achieve particular musical effects. In Mexico, for example, several instruments developed from the guitar model: the **jarana,** a small, simplified, strummed instrument, became a favorite of rural mestizos; the **guitarrón,** a large but portable bass version of the guitar, became a prominent member of the **mariachi** ensemble; the **guitarra de golpe,** also a member of the mariachi ensemble, was developed to provide a percussive accentuation of rhythm and harmony. In Cuba the **tres** was developed as a three-course guitar whose primary function is melodic. A similar melodic role is assigned to the Puerto Rican **cuatro.** The prominent use of these instrumental derivatives did not by any means eliminate the continued use of similar European instruments such as the bandurria, the tiple, and the laúd. Rather, they contributed to the rich timbral resources that has distinguished Latin American musics.

The largest and most diverse group of acculturated instruments in Latin America consists of the chordophones (stringed instruments). European, African, and indigenous aerophones, membranophones, and idiophones tended to preserve their original designs. In some cases, however, substituted materials created a superior quality of sound, as is the case with the **marimba,** the **marímbola,** and certain drums. The late twentieth century has produced new changes in traditional instruments and their uses. Electronic amplification has been widely accepted and has meant that traditional instruments once heard only in intimate acoustical environments now commonly have their sound reinforced for performances in larger settings.

REFERENCES:

Bernarda Jorge, *La música dominicana: Siglos XIX–XX* (Santo Domingo: Universidad Autónoma de Santo Domingo, 1982);

Léonie Rosentiel, "The New World," in *Schirmer History of Music* (New York: Schirmer, 1982);

Rodrigo Salazar Salvatierra, *Instrumentos musicales del folclor costarricense* (Cartago: Editorial tecnológica de Costa Rica, 1992);

Marcio Veloz Maggiolo, *Arqueología prehistórica de Santo Domingo* (Singapore: McGraw-Hill Far Eastern Publishers, 1972).

— R.L.S.

N

Carmen Naranjo

Born in Cartago, Costa Rica, in 1931, Carmen Naranjo has published numerous novels and collections of short stories. Of her three books of short stories, *Ondina* won the EDUCA (Editorial Universitaria Centroamericana) prize in 1982. Her most recent collection of short stories is *Nunca hubo alguna vez* (1989; *There Never Was a Once Upon a Time*). The narrative point of view is that of children and adolescents confronting realities in the here and now, realities that they would prefer to avoid. Her protagonists lose their innocence as they approach maturity and search for different ways of understanding the world. The disjointed sentences and fluctuating verb tenses reflect the children's way of thinking, in which the present predominates and all other time is relative. Four of her novels have won prizes that place her on an equal footing with some of the most respected Central American writers. Among her well-known novels are *Los perros no ladraron* (1966; The Dogs Did Not Bark), *Memorias de un hombre palabra* (1968; Memories of a Wordman), *Responso por el niño Juan Manuel* (A Prayer for the Child Juan Manuel), *Diario de una multitud* (1974; Diary of a Multitude), and *Sobrepunto* (1985; Overpoint). She has also written books of poetry, including *América* (1961), *Canción de la ternura* (1964; Song of Tenderness), *Idioma del invierno* (1967; Language of Winter), and *Mi guerilla* (1984; My Little War). Many of her works have been characterized as rebellious, impatient, and committed to revealing the social injustices of her country, one dominated by foreign interests. Naranjo served as ambassador of Costa Rica to Israel (1974–1976) and as minister of culture (1974–1976). She was also the director of EDUCA publishing house.

Carmen Naranjo, 1992 (photograph by Ardis L. Nelson)

REFERENCES:

Zoe Anglesey, ed., *Ixoc Amar Go: Central American Women's Poetry for Peace* (Penobscot, Maine: Granite Press, 1987);

Patricia Rubio, "Carmen Naranjo," in *Spanish American Women Writers*, edited by Diane Marting (Westport, Conn.: Greenwood Press, 1990).

                                                                    — M.E.S.

NATIONAL FOLKLORIC DANCE COMPANIES

Several countries have established official or government-sponsored dance companies whose mission is to preserve popular and folk dances and make them known abroad by translating them to the stage. The best known of these companies is the Ballet Folklórico de México, founded in 1959 by Amalia Hernández. Hernández studied ballet, folklore, and modern dance at the Escuela Nacional de Danza and performed with the Academia de la Danza Mexicana and the **Ballet Nacional de México.** The Ballet Folklórico is in residence at the Palacio de Bellas Artes in Mexico City, where since 1960 it has given four to five weekly performances that are widely advertised in campaigns designed to attract foreign visitors. The company has toured the world many times. The Ballet Folklórico quickly inspired other folkloric groups, created by governmental institutions, universities, elementary schools, and even trade unions.

Other examples of such companies are Cuba's Conjunto Nacional Folklórico, the Ballet del INGUAT (Ballet of the Guatemalan Tourism Institute), the Ballet del ISTU (Ballet of the Salvadoran Tourism Institute), and the Ballet Folklórico Dominicano. The dancers in these companies are usually urbanites trained in codified systems of classical ballet, modern dance, and folkloric styles. The Ballet Folklórico Dominicano, founded in 1975 and directed by Fradique Lizardo, has forty-five salaried dancers and fifteen unpaid singers. Lizardo, who had studied folkloric dance in Cuba and Venezuela, wanted 60 to 80 percent of his dancers' training to be in classical ballet.

In addition to official and professional dance activities, groups of unpaid aficionados from banks, schools, and professional associations perform theatrical versions of popular and folkloric dances. Discussions continue as to whether the research leading up to these performances and the performances themselves are authentic, with one writer going so far as to call folkloric dance learned in studios and performed in theaters *folkloroid,* in an attempt to distinguish legitimately between authentic folk dance and folk dance for the stage.

                                                                    — J.M.H.

NATIONALISM IN MUSIC

In the new Latin American republics the desire for political independence was mirrored in the aspirations of intellectuals and artists to pursue national cultural identities free of the hegemony of Spanish colonialism. It is in this context that nationalistic tendencies in the arts began to develop in the nineteenth century and reached their full realization during the first half of the twentieth century. In art and literature, regionalism, **criollismo,** and **Indigenismo** were manifestations of these tendencies. In music they are reflected in nationalism. Rather as European composers had reacted against German musical dominance in the earlier part of the century, composers of the Americas began to utilize folk songs, dances, regional rhythms, hybrid instruments, newly evolved genres, and characteristic themes to express distinctive national musical values.

Evidence of early nationalism in Cuba is found in the *Contradanzas* of Manuel Saumel (1817–1870) and the *Danzas cubanas* of Ignacio Cervantes Kawanagh (1847–1905). These works incorporated the essence of Cuban folklore while avoiding direct quotations of folk sources, and they served to motivate two outstanding nationalists of the twentieth century, **Amadeo Roldán** (1900–1939) and **Alejandro García Caturla** (1906–1940). Afro-Cubanism, the new direction of Cuban nationalism that appeared in 1925, was initiated in Roldán's *Obertura sobre temas cubanos* (Overture on Cuban Themes). Although African elements had long since had an important place in popular Cuban music, they were conspicuously absent in Cuban art music before Roldán's overture. His *Tres pequeños poemas* (Three Small Poems) of the following year focused on Cuban folk expressions: African songs and dances, street cries, and festivities. The ballet suite *La Rebambaramba* (1928) evoked scenes of colonial life that included both Creole and slave celebrations. García Caturla's *Bembé* (1930) is based on an Afro-Cuban Santería ritual. Among his other compositions of the period were *Yamba-O* (1928–1931), *La rumba* (1933), and the *Obertura cubana* (1937). Afro-Cubanism in the hands of García Caturla did not mean simply borrowing or quoting from Creole and African genres but rather effecting a true synthesis of multiple ingredients.

In Mexico, Tomás León (1826–1912) and Felipe Villanueva (1862–1893) had incorporated vernacular elements from popular songs and dances, such as the **jarabe** and *danza mexicana,* into the concert and salon repertoires. Nevertheless, musical nationalism in Mexico reached its zenith in the first half of the twentieth century. The **Mexican Revolution** spurred artists on to seek a cultural identity that owed a lesser debt to colonial and foreign influences. The first important twentieth-century Mexican composer to accommodate nationalistic tendencies within a Romantic musical environment was **Manuel Ponce** (1882–1948). Although still in the tradition of Romantic salon music, by simple, direct means his *Canciones mexicanas* captured the poetic character of Mexican folk songs, many of which had become popular during the revolution. Among his orchestral works, *Chapultepec* (three symphonic sketches that refer musically to a Mexico City park) and *Ferial* (a symphonic poem that includes references to and actual quotations from Mexican folk tunes) are prominent. Ponce's Piano Concerto No. 1, which had its premiere in 1912, was the first major composition to incorporate elements of Mexican folk music, inaugurating the ensuing era of overt musical nationalism.

Ponce's most prominent successors, **Carlos Chávez** (1899–1978) and **Silvestre Revueltas** (1899–1940), explored quite different avenues of expression. The compositions of Revueltas appear to form a stylistic link, though not a chronological one, between Ponce and Chávez. In spite of Revueltas's affinity for contemporary techniques, his works recall the Romantic interest in descriptive scenes, expressed through Mexican folk and popular musical sources; examples are the symphonic poems *Esquinas, Janitzio, Caminos, Sensemayá,* and *La noche de los mayas.* In addition to many songs and chamber works, Revueltas provided incidental music for several Mexican films. For his part Chávez, in response to what has been called the Aztec Renaissance, focused attention on the indigenous heritage in the context of a contemporary musical environment. Rather than simply reiterating Romantic settings of Indian music, he developed aesthetic theories on the properties and structure of preconquest music, its instrumentation, and, ultimately, its universality. Eventually, he applied the standard of universality to all aspects of Mexican music, including mestizo, folk, and popular music, as well as music inspired by foreign influences. Chávez was not an exclusively nationalist composer — elements of neoclassicism and primitivism are prominent in many of his works — but the number and intensity of compositions in the nationalist vein would be more than sufficient testament to his position as the most representative such composer in Mexico. His ballets *El fuego nuevo* (1921), *Los cuatro soles* (1926), and *Caballos de vapor* (1926–1927) — all later reframed as orchestral suites — refer to Aztec culture and Mexican folk sources. In *Sinfonía india* (1935–1936) he incorporates not only Indian music but also indigenous instruments, features that become even more prominent in *Xochipilli Macuilxochitl* (the Aztec god of love, dance, and flowers), an orchestral work employing copies of ancient instruments. Overt nationalism began to subside somewhat in the works of Mex-

ican composers in the 1930s and 1940s as contemporary European influences created interest in more-universal values.

Although nationalistic tendencies were typical of the early works of many twentieth-century Latin American composers, those who have achieved international recognition have generally transcended the narrow parameters of nationalism, without denying their own musical heritage, to arrive at more universal musical values.

REFERENCES:

Gerard Béhague, *Music in Latin America: An Introduction* (Englewood Cliffs, N.J.: Prentice-Hall, 1972);

Alejo Carpentier, *La música en Cuba,* second edition (Mexico City: Fondo Cultura Económica, 1972);

Otto Mayer-Serra, *The Present State of Music in Mexico,* translated by Frank Jellinek (Washington, D.C.: Pan American Union, 1946).

— R.L.S. & P.S.

LA NEGRA ANGUSTIAS

La negra Angustias (1949; Angustias the Black Woman) is the second feature-length motion picture directed by Matilde Landeta, one of the few women working in the Mexican film industry during the 1940s and 1950s. Angustias, the daughter of a famous revolutionary, is ostracized for her refusal to marry and her insistence on maintaining manly attributes long past adolescence. After the death of her father, she becomes a revolutionary in her own right. Unlike most films based on the **Mexican Revolution,** the true passion and drama of *La negra Angustias* occur not between revolutionary fighters and a corrupt government but in the battles between men and women. The most notable battle occurs in two parts: a would-be rapist assaults Angustias, and later she captures him and takes revenge by having him castrated. *La negra Angustias* is unusual for its ending, which leaves Angustias strong, active, and still fighting after her momentary surrender to romantic love. In its portrayal of a strong female figure, this movie made a radical break with the female stereotypes of Mexican cinema.

REFERENCES:

Julianne Burton, ed., *Cinema and Social Change in Latin America: Conversations with Filmmakers* (Austin: University of Texas Press, 1986);

John King, *Magic Reels: A History of Cinema in Latin America* (London: Verso, 1990);

Zuzana M. Pick, *The New Latin American Cinema: A Continental Project* (Austin: University of Texas Press, 1993).

— S.M.H.

NÉGRITUDE

Early in the twentieth century black intellectuals from the Caribbean and Africa reacted against assimilation into dominant white societies. In literature the movement to establish a black identity, uncover cultural traits rooted in Africa, and reject the emulation of literary trends of white European writers became associated with the French term *Négritude* and referred primarily to poetry. In Spanish variations are known as *negrismo* and *negritud.*

Négritude evolved through various stages after the 1930s, and the term has multiple meanings related to concepts of race, philosophical considerations of cultural roots, political practices, and artistic expression. In 1932 a manifesto by Etienne Léro, a black poet from Martinique living in Paris, was published in the journal *Légitime défense* (Justifiable Defense; only one issue was published). The manifesto condemned white exploitation of the black masses while criticizing the efforts of black writers to imitate their white counterparts and urging black poets to resist assimilation and to discover their personal voice. Shortly afterward, in that same vein, another journal, *L'Etudiant noir* (1934; The Black Student), was founded by Aimé Césaire from Martinique, Léon Damas from French Guiana, and Léopold Senghor from Senegal, all black students living in Paris. Its central focus revolved around three axioms: the construction of a black identity, the rejection of European cultural models, and a revolt against European colonialist practices. This first phase of Négritude lasted approximately until World War II. In 1948 Jean-Paul Sartre categorized Négritude into two tendencies: the tendency to deal with one's particular experiences of alienation as a black person living in white-dominated societies and the tendency to focus more generally on African cultural roots.

The second period of Négritude was characterized by an increasingly militant stance that vehemently attacked white racist beliefs and practices. The revolutionary ardor apparent in the poetry of this period, condemning colonial policies of forced assimilation, was much influenced by Marxist thought.

After Senegal's independence and with the ascension of Senghor to the presidency of Senegal (he would also become the first black member of the Académie Française), a third phase among the poets of Négritude emerged that reflects a more conciliatory trend and an attempt to discover ways of merging the different white and black cultural worlds. Some black poets, however, emphatically criticized and rejected this stance, preferring the more militant position.

Négritude in literature came to be associated largely with poetry from the Caribbean and Africa, much of it in French by black writers living in former or current French colonies, but it also refers to writers from Brazil. Hispanic poets who have been influenced by Négritude include **Luis Palés Matos** and **Nicolás Guillén.**

REFERENCES:

Between Négritude and Marvellous Realism, edited by Vere W. Knight, special issue of *Black Images,* 3, no. 1 (1974);

Edouard Glissant, *Caribbean Discourse* (Charlottesville: University Press of Virginia, 1989);

Norman R. Shapiro, *Négritude: Black Poetry from Africa and the Caribbean* (New York: October House, 1970).

— M.E.S.

NEOREALISM IN MOTION PICTURES

Neorealism, a cinematic style that originated in Italy in the late 1940s and 1950s, was adopted by several Latin American filmmakers in the 1950s and 1960s. The Cubans **Tomás Gutiérrez Alea** and **Julio García Espinosa** and the Argentinean Fernando Birri — all of whom studied at the Centro Sperimentale di Cinematografia (Center for Experimental Cinematography) at the University of Rome in the 1950s — were highly influenced by neorealism. According to one neorealist critic, neorealism "exposed — without pleasure, without exaggeration and without an evil taste for the picturesque — the human conditions which constituted *per se* both a condemnation of certain social systems and a warning against them." Neorealism was a revelation to those budding Latin American filmmakers who were striving to find a new cinematic language to express the reality of Latin America as it faced the challenge of underdevelopment. Neorealism represented the formerly unrepresented, explicitly rejecting the dominant Hollywood model. According to Gutiérrez Alea, neorealism emphasized the transparency of contemporary events, allowing the essence of reality to show through. For many years Italian neorealism was the dominant mode used in **Cuban Film Institute** movies because, when politicized, it offered a perfect means for exploring the reality of postrevolutionary Cuba. There the neorealist aesthetic became primarily concerned with history, memory, political action, and choice. This adaptation of neorealism in the Latin American cultural context demonstrates the process of convergence and synthesis of art and politics that is so common in Latin America.

REFERENCES:

Julianne Burton, ed., *Cinema and Social Change in Latin America: Conversations with Filmmakers* (Austin: University of Texas Press, 1986);

John King, Ana M. López, and Manuel Alvarado, eds., *Mediating Two Worlds: Cinematic Encounters in the Americas* (London: BFI, 1993).

— S.M.H.

AMADO NERVO

One of the most important writers associated with **Modernismo,** Amado Nervo (1870–1919) was born in Tepic, Mexico. As a youth he studied the Spanish and Latin classics; later he entered a seminary to study for the priesthood and became immersed in the writings of the mystics. Although he left to pursue a career as a journalist in Mazatlán, the influence of the mystics became evident in his later works. His first novel, *El bachiller* (1895; The Graduate), and his first book of poetry, *Místicas* (1897; Mystics), established his reputation as an important literary figure. In 1898 he and Jesús E. Valenzuela founded the Modernist journal *Revista moderna* (1898–1911). He later served as a diplomat in Spain (1905–1918), where he met **Rubén Darío** and other European and Latin American writers. He died in Montevideo in 1919.

Nervo's writings passed through various stages. His first works reveal the influence of the French Parnassians and emphasize formal perfection and exotic imagery with mystical overtones. *Místicas* (1897; Mystics), *Poemas* (1901; Poems), *Perlas negras* (1898; Black Pearls), *El éxodo y las flores del camino* (1902; The Exodus and the Flowers Along the Path), *Lira heroica* (1902; Heroic Lyre), and *Los jardines interiores* (1900; The Interior Gardens) belong to this first stage. Works of the second stage turned inward and explored religious themes, indicating that he was influenced by oriental philosophies, especially Buddhism. *En voz baja* (1909; In a Low Voice), *Serenidad* (1914; Serenity), *Elevación* (1917; Elevation), and *Plenitud* (1918; Plenitude) belong to this period, the last two especially influenced by his pantheistic view of nature and an all-encompassing love for humankind. The third stage is one of simplicity and a profound questioning of the meaning of life and death. One of his most famous works, *La amada inmóvil* (1920; The Motionless Beloved), appeared during this period, later becoming a film. One of his most prominent themes, love, dominates this work as well as *El arquero divino* (1922; The Divine Archer). The soothing purity of his verses reflects Nervo's perception of love in its various manifestations as wholesome and ideal. His poetry is subjective and sincere, exhibiting not only doubt and metaphysical anguish in a search for the divine but also a resigned attitude when facing the unknown. Along with poetry and novels, Nervo also published two

Amado Nervo (courtesy of the Organization of American States)

books of short stories, *Almas que pasan* (1906; Souls Passing By) and *El diablo desinteresado* (1916; The Disinterested Devil). Amado Nervo was internationally recognized and extremely popular during his lifetime, and today his works are still considered among the best in Latin American poetry.

REFERENCES:

Raúl Héctor Castagnino, *Imágenes modernistas: Rubén Darío, Rufino Blanco Fombona, Amado Nervo, R. M. del Valle Inclán* (Buenos Aires: Editorial Nova, 1967);

Esther Turner Wellman, *Amado Nervo: Mexico's Religious Poet* (New York: Instituto de España en los Estados Unidos, 1936).

— M.E.S.

NEW LATIN AMERICAN CINEMA

During the early 1950s, young directors in Latin America began exploring ways to express their political vision in a cinema rooted in the social reality of their region. They formed groups such as the Documentary Film School of Santa Fe in Argentina, the Ukumau group in Bolivia, and *cinema nôvo* in Brazil, as well as equivalent groups in Cuba, Colombia, Chile, Uruguay, and Venezuela. In 1967 many of these filmmakers came together at the historic first international festival of Latin American cinema, held in Viña del Mar, Chile, where the New Latin American Cinema movement was born. For the first time film directors from all parts of the region got together, exchanged ideas, and set up an agenda for future cooperation. The discussions focused mainly on sociocultural and political issues rather than cinematic techniques.

As the Cuban delegate, Alfredo Guevara, suggested, the Viña del Mar festival was significant because "we stopped being independent or marginal filmmakers, promising filmmakers or amateurs experimenting and searching, in order to discover what we were without yet knowing: a new cinema, a *movement*." Setting out an ambitious set of resolutions concerning future collaborative work, the participants agreed to reject imperialism in favor of the development of national cultures, to adopt a regional perspective that would further the formation of a Great Latin American Nation, and to make cinema a means of raising the consciousness of the masses. Not all of these grand designs materialized. The festival succeeded, however, in establishing personal contacts and in helping to attract attention to Latin American filmmakers by showing many of their movies. It was a significant first step toward the elusive goal of Pan-American solidarity, and Latin American motion pictures began gradually to receive more and more coverage at other international film festivals, especially in Europe.

In 1968 the First Convention of Latin American Documentary Film, a follow-up to the Viña del Mar meeting, was held in Mérida, Venezuela, and the following year, as a direct result of that second festival, the Universidad de los Andes in Venezuela founded a documentary film center, which went on to produce newsreels, documentaries, and feature films. That same year another film festival, held in Viña del Mar, was more extensive than the 1967 festival and entailed the showing of 110 short films and features by filmmakers from ten countries. Among the movies shown was Chilean director Raúl Ruiz's 1969 screen adaptation of **Guillermo Cabrera Infante**'s novel *Tres tristes tigres* (Three Trapped Tigers).

By 1970 the New Latin American Cinema, sometimes described as "Third Cinema," had established itself as a revolutionary film movement. In 1979 Fernando Solanas defined it as "the way the world is conceptualized and not the genre nor the explicitly political character of a film.... Third Cinema is an open category. It is a democratic, national, popular cinema." Other parallel initiatives carried on the good work

begun in Viña del Mar. In 1969 the Cinémathèque of the Third World in Montevideo, Uruguay, initiated the distribution and exhibition of films and joined the periodical *Marcha* in launching a film festival. The Committee of Latin American Filmmakers, founded in 1974 and expanded and reorganized as the New Latin American Cinema Foundation in 1985, and the International Festival of the New Latin American Cinema in Havana, founded in 1979, helped to support the work of up-and-coming film directors and to disseminate new ideas and strategies. The movement also attracted some outside sponsorship, notably from RAI, the Italian state-run media organization. (See also **Cuban Film Institute**.)

REFERENCES:

John King, *Magical Reels: A History of Cinema in Latin America* (London: Verso, 1990);

Zuzana M. Pick, *The New Latin American Cinema: A Continental Project* (Austin: University of Texas Press, 1993).
                                                              — S.M.H.

News Networks

The two most important news networks in Latin America are Associated Press (AP) and United Press International (UPI). AP maintains seventeen bureaus in Latin America. Most are small, but some cities, such as Mexico City and Buenos Aires, have large full-time staffs. The AP Miami and San Juan bureaus share responsibility for covering the Caribbean region. Of special interest to Latin Americans is La Prensa Española (PA), AP's Spanish-language news service, which serves five hundred clients, including fifty Spanish-language broadcasting stations and newspapers in the United States. PA claims that its news bulletins for Latin America offer not simply off-the-wire translations but also original news.

UPI, the second-largest news agency in the world, also has a powerful presence in Latin America, which has, in fact, been one of UPI's most successful and lucrative markets for many years. The UPI Latin American desk, LATAM, has been the preeminent international news service in South America and Central America for much of the twentieth century. Although UPI plays a secondary role to AP in the United States, UPI thinks of itself as the "General Motors of Latin American news services." Whereas AP is a media-based news service whose members share operation costs, UPI is a profit-making organization. The most important recent development in press agencies in Latin America was the purchase in 1986 of UPI, saddled at the time with huge debts, by Mexican media magnate Mario Vásquez-Rana for $41 million. He sold the news agency in 1988. (See also **CANA.**)

REFERENCE:

Michael B. Salwen and Bruce Garrison, *Latin American Journalism* (Hillsdale, N.J.: Lawrence Erlbaum, 1991).

— S.M.H.

THE NICARAGUAN REVOLUTION

In 1909 the president of Nicaragua, José Santos Zelaya, was deposed by a coalition of his enemies led by the United States. That year marked the beginning of U.S. intervention in the area, which continued throughout the century. In 1912 U.S. Marines occupied Nicaragua to protect U.S. economic interests; the occupation lasted, with a minor interlude, until 1933. In 1926 an impoverished peasant, Augusto César Sandino, began a guerrilla movement to remove the U.S. Marines from Nicaragua. His army consisted of ill-equipped, illiterate, barefoot campesinos (peasants). By 1933 their tactics had become so successful that the U.S. Marines withdrew; however, in their wake they left the Nicaraguan National Guard, an army unit trained by the marines and led by the American-educated Gen. Anastasio Somoza García. In 1934 Sandino laid down his arms; shortly afterward, however, he was murdered by Somoza's National Guard while trying to negotiate a settlement. Somoza seized the reins of the government, and he and his two sons ruled Nicaragua until 1979. During this time they concentrated wealth into the hands of the wealthy, especially their own close associates, and were indifferent to the plight of the impoverished, landless majority. Their dictatorship was marked by intolerance and a brutal suppression of human rights. Thousands of people were tortured, imprisoned, and murdered by Somoza's National Guard.

This repression led to the organization of a clandestine revolutionary movement to overthrow the Somozas. Taking its name from the peasant leader Sandino, the Frente Sandinista de Liberación Nacional (National Sandinista Liberation Front) gained widespread popular support, especially after the December 1972 earthquake that devastated the capital, Managua. The regime of Anastasio Somoza Debayle pocketed much of the international relief money and even sold donations of blood for profit. In 1978 the internationally respected journalist, José Joaquín Chamorro, an opponent of the regime, was assassinated on the streets of Managua by Somoza's National Guard. His murder served as a catalyst for the Frente Sandinista to mobilize the masses. After ferocious battles with severe casualties, the Sandinistas ousted Somoza and took over

Cero (Edén Pastora), the Sandinista who commanded the 22 August 1978 raid on the National Palace that toppled the Somoza regime in Nicaragua (photograph by Karen DeYoung/*The Washington Post*)

the government (19 July 1979). Somoza fled the country with most of the nation's treasury, and the Sandinistas were left to contend with the desperate economic situation at home.

Despite the initial idealistic agenda of the Sandinistas, many of the reforms they had promised failed to materialize. The principal obstacle was the U.S.-sponsored "Contra" war beginning in 1985, in which the U.S. government and various private factions funded former members of Somoza's National Guard in their attempt to overthrow the Sandinistas. As a result the Sandinistas were forced to pour money desperately needed for such things as health care and education into military defense. The war destroyed the remnants of the Nicaraguan economy and eroded popular support for the Sandinistas, who themselves became increasingly intransigent and dictatorial. In February 1990 the opposition led by Violeta Chamorro, a member of a family with a long tradition in public affairs in Nicaragua and widow of the assassinated José Joaquín Chamorro, was elected president. Nevertheless, many of the social advances brought about by the revolution, such as literacy campaigns, improvements in health care and in women's rights, and the abolition of the death penalty, remained in place. The

Sandinistas also retained a significant voice in Nicaragua.

REFERENCE:

Eduardo Galeano, *Memory of Fire/Century of the Wind* (New York: Pantheon, 1988).

— M.E.S.

NORTEÑO MUSIC

The term *norteño* refers to musical styles in the north of Mexico and along the border between Mexico and the United States. Also known as *Tex-Mex*, norteño music preserves vestiges of musical traditions that developed when the southwestern United States belonged to Mexico. Musics from the colonial period, such as the **jarabe,** the **jarana,** and the **romance,** were joined by the revolution-inspired **corrido,** the vals (waltz), and the Bohemian polka (polca in Spanish).

The nineteenth-century German and Czech immigration to Mexico brought about a profound change in the basic instrumentation and performance of borderland music. The introduction of the German accordion resulted in a new ensemble, the conjunto, consisting of a traditional guitar, a twelve-string guitar (bajo sexto), a double bass, and the bandoneón, an accordion-like instrument that features buttons instead of the accordion keyboard. The bajo sexto is an expanded guitar with twelve strings arranged in six courses of double strings tuned in unison and in octaves. Other instruments such as the violin, trap-set drums, and minor percussion instruments may be added to the ensemble. In the typical conjunto the singer plays the bandoneón. When the singer (typically male) sings the lyrics, simple chordal accompaniments are played, allowing concentration on the verses. Between the verses the bandoneón provides a florid, ornamental interlude.

The polca became the principal genre of the new conjunto ensemble, and its repertoire focused on border problems of the poor: crime, smuggling, and illegal entry into the United States. Millions of immigrant laborers have carried the conjunto and norteño music across the border through California and Texas to New York and Florida.

A star performer for more than fifty years in norteño music was Lidia Mendoza, an anomaly in the usually male-dominated tradition. Other popular stars include Flaco Jiménez, "El Rey de Texas" (The King of Texas); Narciso Martínez, "El Huracán del Valle" (Hurricane of the Valley); and Little Joe Hernández, who sings norteño themes accompanied by a big band ensemble.

Lino Novás Calvo

REFERENCES:

Peter Manuel, *Popular Music of the Non-Western World: An Introductory Survey* (Oxford: Oxford University Press, 1988);

Jeremy Marre and Hannah Charlton, *Beats of the Heart: Popular Music of the World* (New York: Pantheon, 1985).

— R.L.S.

LINO NOVÁS CALVO

Although born in Spain, Lino Novás Calvo (1905–1983) spent most of his life in Cuba, where he rapidly established a reputation as one of that country's best writers, mostly cultivating the genre of the short story while earning his living as a journalist. His fame began with the publication of two of his stories in the influential *Revista de Occidente*, directed by José Ortega y Gasset, and his reputation continued to grow as other stories were published in prestigious journals in Spain, Cuba, and Latin America. His novel *El negrero* (1933; The Slave Trader) describes the life of a famous slave trader; in it he depicts the greed, passions, and horrors that marked the commerce in human flesh. However, he is mostly known for the meticulous realism of his short stories as well as his penetration into the subconscious of characters who are frequently outcasts of society. His stories are collected in *La luna nona y otros cuentos* (1942; The Ninth Moon and Other

Stories), *No sé quién soy* (1945; I Don't Know Who I Am), *Cayo Canas* (1946; Smuggler's Key), and *En los traspatios* (1946; Between Neighbors). After 1959 Novás Calvo lived in exile in the United States.

REFERENCE:

Lorraine Elena Roses, *Voices of the Storyteller: Cuba's Lino Novás Calvo* (Westport, Conn.: Greenwood Press, 1986).

— M.E.S.

Novela Rosa

The sentimental romances known as novelas rosas (pink novels) are as much a part of Latin American mass culture as are Harlequin novels in the United States. An international genre, the novela rosa is also available in other forms of mass cultural production: illustrated **fotonovelas** and **telenovelas** (television soap operas). The most prolific author of such novels is the Spaniard María del Socorro Tellado López (1926–   ), better known to millions of readers as Corín Tellado, whose books began to appear in the 1940s and who remains highly popular today. The novela rosa predates Tellado's work by two decades, however.

The genre has evolved in accordance with the needs of its primarily female readership. Nevertheless, some elements remain constant: an exclusive focus on romantic love with a happy ending, a lack of social or historical analysis, an invocation of escapist or compensatory fantasies, and narrative techniques derived from rudimentary nineteenth-century realism.

REFERENCE:

José Luis Méndez, "The Novels of Corín Tellado," *Studies in Latin American Popular Culture,* 5 (1986): 31–40.

— R.G.M.

Salvador Novo

Salvador Novo (1904–1974), an important writer of prose, poetry, and theater in twentieth-century Mexico, is held in high esteem by contemporaries such as **Xavier Villaurrutia** and Celestino Gorostiza. Novo's poetry is best described as unique; his poetic techniques reflect a rebellion against academic norms. His intonation is often more reminiscent of his North American than of his Latin American contemporaries. The two major volumes of poetry produced by Novo are *Nuevo amor* (1933; New Love), considered his greatest poetic work, and *Espejo* (1933; Mirror).

Salvador Novo has often been referred to as "the chronicler of Mexico City," because of the pre-Hispanic historical dimension evident in most of his prose. Novo's thematic approach to his prose works frequently carried over into his theatrical endeavors, resulting in such plays as *Cuauhtémoc* (1962), which uses an original, modern dialogue to dramatize the predicament of the heroic Aztec leader. His other important pre-Hispanic historical drama is *La guerra de las gordas* (1963; *The War of the Fatties*), which dramatizes an episode recorded in the Aztec chronicles and dealing with the war between Tenochtitlán, the Aztec capital, and its vassal city, Tlatelolco. Not all of Novo's dramas concentrate on pre-Hispanic themes. In his play *A ocho columnas* (1956; In Eight Columns), whose title makes reference to a newspaper printing format, Novo severely criticizes the media for their destructive, as well as influential, capabilities. He also produced a theatrical adaptation of Miguel de Cervantes's famous novel, *Don Quijote* (1947), for the children's theater season in the National Palace of Arts. Salvador Novo's most impressive plays are contained in the collection *Diálogos* (1956; Dialogues). This collection contains eight dialogues between historical figures as diverse as Adam and Eve, Cuauhtémoc, Sor Juana (a seventeenth-century Mexican nun), and Pita (a contemporary author). Through their innovative theatrical techniques such as interior monologue, these plays display Novo's ability to create original work based on historical reality.

REFERENCE:

Antonio Magaña Esquivel, *Salvador Novo* (Mexico: Empresas Editoriales, 1971).

— M.T.

Nueva Presencia

Active from 1961 to 1963, the Nueva Presencia (New Presence) group, also known as Los Interioristas (The Insiders), included Arnold Belkin, Rafael Coronel, Francisco Corzas, **José Luis Cuevas, Alberto Gironella,** Leonel Góngora, Francisco Icaza, Ignacio "Nacho" López, and others. As part of **La Ruptura Generation**, the members of Nueva Presencia denounced the emphasis on social realism and didacticism of the dominant schools of **Muralism** and **indigenism** but, unlike their contemporaries, Los Interioristas rejected the use of abstract modes in favor of Neofiguration, becoming one of the most important neofigurative groups in the Americas. Neofiguration was part of a generalized trend toward the representation of the human figure that emerged in Europe, the United States, and Latin America during the 1950s.

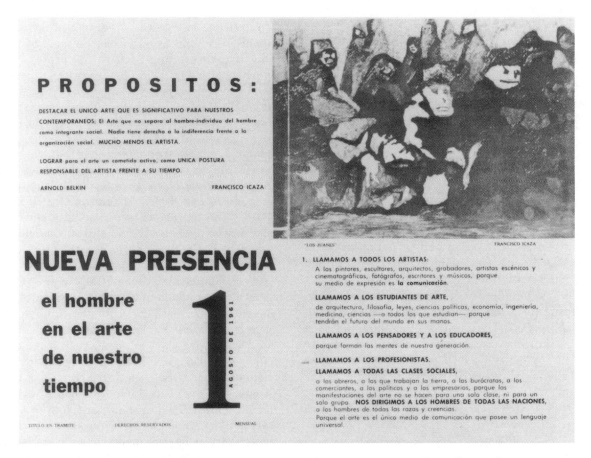

Cover for the first issue (August 1961) of the poster-magazine published by the Nueva Presencia group

Many of the European artists who worked in neofigurative styles, such as the COBRA (Copenhagen, Brussels, Amsterdam) group, as well as Jean Dubuffet and Francis Bacon, expressed existentialist concerns relating to the individual in the anxious context of postwar Europe. In Latin America the industrialization and urban growth of the 1940s and 1950s resulted in an increasingly alienating urban lifestyle that also made artists receptive to existentialist ideas. The members of Nueva Presencia became aware of existentialism through the writings of **Octavio Paz,** the Beat poets Allen Ginsberg and Lawrence Ferlinghetti, the European writers Albert Camus and Franz Kafka, and especially the United States author Selden Rodman, whose book *The Insiders: Rejection and Rediscovery of Man in the Arts of Our Time* (1960) explains the label "Los Interioristas" and influenced the group's philosophy.

Belkin's series *La guerra y la paz* (1963; War and Peace), Cuevas's series *Los mundos de Kafka* (1957; The Worlds of Kafka), and Icaza's series *Metamorfosis de un pájaro* (1961; Metamorphosis of a Bird) share not only a preference for an expressionism inspired by the works of Francisco de Goya and **José Clemente Orozco** but also the representation of marginal and alienated beings, a dark vision of humanity. In 1961 the Nueva Presencia group exhibited in Mexico for the first time under the name Los Interioristas and published the first of the five issues of the poster-magazine *Nueva Presencia,* which had begun as a newsletter in support of **David Alfar Siqueiros,** who was then in prison for political reasons. Many artists rallied to Siqueiros's defense, including Belkin, Cuevas, Coronel, and Icaza, in spite of their aesthetic differences and Cuevas's severe public attacks on Muralism. In 1962 Cuevas separated from Nueva Presencia, perhaps because of its support for Siqueiros or because the younger members of the group worked in a style Cuevas considered too close to his own. The group dissolved in 1964.

REFERENCE:

Shifra M. Goldman, *Contemporary Mexican Painting in a Time of Change* (Austin: University of Texas Press, 1981).

— F.B.N.

O

EUNICE ODIO

Eunice Odio (1922–1974) was born in San José, Costa Rica. Deploring the provincial attitude of many Costa Rican politicians and intellectuals, she moved to Guatemala and became a citizen of that country in 1948. Later she did the same in Mexico, living there from 1955 (interrupted by a two-and-a-half-year stay in New York) until her tragic death in 1974. (Her decomposed body was found in her bathtub many days after her death, and it is possible she committed suicide.) First and foremost a poet, Eunice Odio had to earn her living as a journalist in Mexico. She published her first poems at the age of twenty-three. In 1947 she received the Central American Award for Poetry for her book *Los elementos terrestres* (The Earthly Elements). An avid Bible reader, Odio injects into her work a religious and spiritual tone that is often similar to that of the poetry of the Spanish mystic Santa Teresa. Odio's erotic mysticism, however, goes beyond the spiritual; for her, poetry alludes to the supreme joy of corporal ecstasy with the loved one. Another book of poetry, *Zona en territorio del alba* (1953; Zone in the Land of the Dawn), is a series of short poems with a variety of themes, much influenced by the vanguardist techniques that became more fully developed in her later poetry. Her masterpiece, and perhaps one of the most challenging poems in the Spanish language, given its complex and hermetic style, *El tránsito de fuego* (1957; Journey of Fire), is a single poem of 456 pages. Taking several years to write, this metaphysical poem in the form of a dialogue examines the role of the creator, the creator's works, and the isolation suffered by him when dispersed among his own creations which, unlike him, are able to be whole. Odio preferred childhood and religious themes and opted for a dialogic and dramatized poetry that is personal and not easily understood.

REFERENCE:

Rima de Valbona, *La obra en prosa de Eunice Odio* (San José: Editorial Costa Rica, 1980).

— E.S.C.

JUAN O'GORMAN

Mexican painter and architect Juan O'Gorman (1905–1982) was a proponent of Functionalism in his early career and later worked to incorporate the visual arts into architectural designs. O'Gorman studied architecture in Mexico and was influenced by Le Corbusier. In the late 1920s he become one of the first Mexicans to embrace Functionalism. During the 1930s O'Gorman built several functional homes for members of Mexico's elite. His most famous was the house and studio of **Diego Rivera** (1931) at Pedregal San Angel. Employed as a professor of architecture at Mexico City's Instituto Nacional Politécnico (National Polytechnic Institute) in 1932, O'Gorman taught and designed twenty-eight schools for the Secretaría de Educación Pública (Ministry of Public Education). Throughout most of his career as an architect, he was interested in the need for mass urban housing. He was an active member of the leftist intelligentsia and often viewed architecture as a tool for social engineering.

In the mid 1930s O'Gorman, also a participant in **Muralism,** focused his energies on painting, producing both murals and easel paintings. His panel *La ciudad de México* (1942; Mexico City) depicts the modern urban city from the perspective of a Mexican architect standing on a building under construction. This work includes many symbols of Mexican identity: Quetzalcoatl (the plumed serpent), the eagle and the snake; the twin peaks of Popocatépetl and Ixtaccihuatl; and both pre-Columbian and modern walls in the foreground. Similar narrative and didactic themes continued throughout O'Gorman's murals, as can be seen in his frescoes *Retablo de la Independencia* (1960–1961; Retable of Independence) in the Chapultepec Castle and *El crédito transforma México* (1965; Credit Transforms Mexico) at the Banco Internacional in Mexico City.

In the 1950s O'Gorman decried Functionalism for its failure to take account of both nature and indigenous American architectural traditions. Instead, he adopted the style of organic architecture espoused by Frank Lloyd Wright, which he applied to the design of his own house at Pedregal San Angel (1956). Most of this house was built in a natural grotto and used the rough volcanic rock of Pedregal. Since he was interested in integrating painting and architecture, O'Gorman became involved in the designs for the campus of the Universidad Nacional Autónoma de México (UNAM). Together with the architects Juan Martínez de Velasco and Gustavo Saavedra, O'Gorman designed UNAM's main library (1949–1951). He was the sole designer of the exterior decoration of the central part of this building, a ten-story tower covered with monumental mosaics portraying scenes and figures from pre-Hispanic, colonial, and modern Mexico, together with allegorical scenes from the arts and sciences. After the 1950s O'Gorman worked mainly with mosaic and painted murals, including those in Chapultepec Castle (1961) and the Palacio de Bellas Artes (1968).

REFERENCE:

Ida Rodríguez Prampolini, *Juan O'Gorman: Arquitecto y pintor* (Mexico: Universidad Nacional Autónoma de México, 1982).
—C.M.

Old Gringo

The motion picture *Old Gringo* (1989) is based on the novel *Gringo viejo* (1985) by the celebrated Mexican novelist and cultural critic **Carlos Fuentes.** The director, Luis Puenzo, wrote the screenplay with Aida Bortnik; the producer was Lois Bonfiglio. *Old Gringo* was a Fonda Films production for Columbia Pictures, but the movie was in many ways a Fonda-Fuentes coproduction. Most of the movie was shot at Churubusco Studios in Mexico City and on location at an abandoned ranch outside the city. Fuentes has a small part in the movie, playing the role of Pancho Villa, a colorful military leaders of the **Mexican Revolution** (1911–1917), who in the scene in question is organizing an early-morning execution of prisoners of war.

The title character, played by Gregory Peck, is based on the well-known American journalist and fiction writer Ambrose Bierce, who disappeared in Mexico during the revolution and the movie offers a possible solution to the unsolved mystery of Bierce's fate. Jane Fonda plays Harriet Winslow, a frustrated spinster who flees her unrewarding life in America hoping to make a new life. Harriet is drawn together with Bierce and Arroyo (played by Jimmy Smits), a fiery young general driven by both the revolution and his love for Harriet. The microdrama of their relationships takes place within the macrodrama of the revolution, a theme that Carlos Fuentes has explored in his creative work on many occasions. The film is more or less faithful to the main theme of the novel: the interrelation between the national destinies of Mexico and the United States. Most of the scenes in the movie are not in the book, though the basic story and characters are retained. As a result of this foray into film, Fuentes was accused by the Mexican intellectual Enrique Krauze of having sold his soul to Hollywood.

REFERENCE:

Latin American Cinema: Le Cinéma Latino-Américain, special issue of *Iris: Revue de Théorie de l'Image et du Son. A Journal of Theory on Image and Sound,* no. 13 (Summer 1991).
—S.M.H.

Los olvidados

Made in Mexico, *Los olvidados* (1950; The Young and the Damned) is one of the milestones in the film career of the distinguished Spanish director Luis Buñuel (1900–1983), winning him the prize for best director at the Cannes Film Festival in 1951. In retrospect the motion picture can be seen as an important precursor of the **New Latin American Cinema** movement of the 1960s. Buñuel traveled to Mexico from the United States, where he had spent the years of World War II working in the Museum of Modern Art. Becoming a naturalized citizen of Mexico in 1949, he made eighteen "Mexican" films from 1946 until the mid 1960s.

Los olvidados is the story of some street urchins (with the protagonist, Jaibo, played by Roberto Cobo) who are prepared to steal, maim, and kill in order to survive in the poor neighborhoods of Mexico City. The movie focuses obsessively on the dispossessed of Mexico, the "real" life of the Third World, employing images that contrast violently with the glitzy Hollywood film rhetoric prevalent at that time. In particular the scene in which a blind old man is beaten by a gang aroused much controversy. The vision Buñuel sought to communicate is illustrated in an anecdote about the

Alfonso Mejía in *Los olvidados* (1950; The Young and the Damned), directed by Luis Buñuel

filming of another of his Mexican movies, Nazarín (1958). His cameraman, Gabriel Figueroa, prepared a beautiful shot of the countryside for Buñuel, but, after looking at the image, Buñuel asked him to turn the camera and film some goats on a desolate hillside instead. *Los olvidados* was not aimed at building a national Mexican identity or a Latin American aesthetic, but it did signal a rupture with the cinematic language of the past.

REFERENCE:

John King, Ana M. López, and Manuel Alvarado, eds., *Mediating Two Worlds: Cinematic Encounters in the Americas* (London: BFI, 1993).

— S.M.H.

La Onda

Between the 1960s and early 1970s a generation of young Mexican writers known as La Onda (the Wave) began to write and publish. Most of them were in their twenties at the start of their writing careers, and their personal, youthful vision of society is reflected in their narratives, which focus on the language and lifestyles of adolescents, chiefly in urban areas. The influence of previous writers such as Agustín Yáñez, Carlos Fuentes, and Juan Rulfo is apparent in the techniques they use, which include shifting points of view; fragmented, nonchronological time; multiple narrative voices; and the incorporation of other genres within the narrative. Their themes, however, do not generally reflect the nationalistic concerns of previous generations but rather represent a rebellion against conventions, treating formerly forbidden subjects such as drugs and heterosexual and homosexual sex and reflecting a taste for jazz, rock music, and hippie culture. In general, La Onda writers were interested in escaping a nationalistic orientation and attempted instead to place Mexican literature in a world context.

Many writers are associated with La Onda; some of the more prominent are Gustavo Sainz (1940–), José Agustín (1944–), María Luisa Puga (1944–), Salvador Elizondo (1932–), Fernando del Paso (1935–), Luis Zapata (1951–), and Parménides García Saldaña (1944–). Elizondo's acclaimed first novel, *Farabeuf* (1965), is experimental; in it he attempts to undermine chronology by a technique of repetition, to represent simultaneously orgasm, death, and suffering. Elizondo has said that the book is based on "methodical, irrational connectedness."

Gustavo Sainz's first novel, *Gazapo* (1965; Tall Tale), concentrates on the inconstant, conflicting world of adolescence, depicted through tape-recorded conversations, letters, diaries, and telephone dialogues. The adolescent protagonist reviews and reinvents the past through the use of the tape recorder, which to him and his friends represents an escape from the restrictions of the adult world and allows them to explore sexual fantasies and fantastic adventures. The fragmented structure of the novel represents the ambiguous lives of the adolescents, and the experimentation, involving various kinds of language from the colloquial to the flamboyant, reflects the quest for artistic as well as social freedom.

José Agustín mixes colloquial speech with descriptive prose in his novels *La tumba* (1964; The Tomb) and *De perfil* (1966; In Profile) to reflect the frustrations of youth while criticizing middle-class values. *La tumba* is the story of an adolescent whose wealthy family waxes indifferent toward him. He dedicates himself to a bohemian lifestyle, reading, drinking, and flirting; in the end he comes close to committing suicide. *De perfil* is also about the difficulties confronting an adolescent as he approaches maturity.

In *Las posibilidades del odio* (1978; The Possibilities of Hatred) María Luisa Puga offers a view of the effects of colonialism on Kenyan society, involving ethnocentric and racist attitudes and cultural and economic domination by so-called developed countries. The parallels with realities of life in Mexican society become apparent. In *Cuando el aire es azul* (1980; When the Air is Blue) Puga describes her vision of a utopian society living in spiritual peace and harmony. *Pánico y peligro* (1983; Panic and Danger) focuses on the lives of four adolescent males struggling to maintain their integrity in Mexico City during the corrupt and violent years of the 1960s and 1970s.

Fernando del Paso's novel *José Trigo* (1966) draws parallels between the conquest of the Aztec empire in 1521 and government suppression of a strike by railroad workers in 1960 in Tlatelolco. Tlatelolco had been the center of the Aztec empire, and at the time of the strike it was the center of Mexico's railway system. The brutality of the government's treatment of the strikers foreshadowed the events of October 1968, when hundreds of students were massacred by government troops. In the ambitious, voluminous, and comic *Palinuro de México* (1975; Palinuro of Mexico) Fernando del Paso uses the **Tlatelolco** events of 1968 as the climax of his narrative. The comprehensive ambi-

tions of del Paso's novels have been compared to those of Carlos Fuentes (particularly *Terra Nostra*), but del Paso's inclination toward a liberating and irreverent use of humor also recalls Julio Cortázar. Though del Paso's novels are huge, they are not ponderous. *Palinuro de México* is an episodic compendium of the comic and erotic, with fleeting appearances by a host of literary characters drawn from other writers' works. Del Paso's delight in language sometimes resembles that of the Cuban writer **Guillermo Cabrera Infante.**

Luis Zapata's novels frequently center on homosexual issues. *Hasta en las mejores familias* (1975; Even in the Best Families) is about a boy probing his family's background in search of his own identity. The discovery of his father's homosexuality allows him to free himself emotionally. *Melodrama* (1983; Melodrama) makes fun of the attitudes of a bourgeois world toward homosexuality, and *En jirones* (1985; In Shreds) deals with the destructive potential of passion, in this case of one man for another.

La Onda writers had a decisive impact on the next generation of Mexican writers, particularly in their incorporation of colloquial language into literary discourse and their efforts to open literature up to more varied themes, techniques, and personal styles.

REFERENCES:

David William Foster, *Mexican Literature: A History* (Austin: University of Texas Press, 1994);

Donald L. Shaw, *Nueva narrativa hispanoamericana* (Madrid: Cátedra, 1981);

Reinhard Teichmann, *De la onda en adelante* (Mexico: Editorial Posada, 1987).

                                       — M.E.S. & P.S.

YOLANDA OREAMUNO

Yolanda Oreamuno (1916–1956) was born in San José, Costa Rica, where she spent the first twenty years of her life in relative happiness, while the next twenty were tormented by the psychological trauma, tragedies, and loneliness that would surface in much of her writing and are reflected in the predominant theme of existential anguish. She began writing at an early age, and her first short stories were published when she was twenty years old. She married a Chilean diplomat and lived in Chile until he committed suicide in 1936. She returned to Costa Rica and in 1937 married again and bore a son. The marriage did not succeed; she divorced her husband, was separated from her son in 1945, and thereafter lived in a bitter, self-imposed exile in Mexico and Guatemala. She became seriously ill and had

Yolanda Oreamuno (courtesy of the Organization of American States)

numerous operations, all of which contributed to her deteriorating emotional state. She died in Guatemala at the home of her friend, the Costa Rican writer **Eunice Odio.**

Oreamuno's literary production consists of short stories, essays, and one published novel. Apparently she wrote several other novels that were lost or never finished. Her rich imagination and ability to explore the realms of the fantastic, blending reality with magic, lent her writings a distinctive quality. Her major themes are alienation, solitude, nature, the general indifference of society, the shallowness of sexual relationships, and death. Some of her short stories can be found collected in *A lo largo del corto camino* (1961; Along the Short Road) and *Relatos escogidos: Yolanda Oreamuno* (1977; Selected Stories: Yolanda Oreamuno). Her only novel, *La ruta de su evasión* (1949; The Path of Their Evasion), won a literary prize in Guatemala, where it was originally published. In it, Oreamuno employs avant-garde techniques, combining memories, physical sensations, and dreams, to explore rational and psychic dimensions of human beings who wish to escape their surrounding realities.

REFERENCE:

Arlene Schrade, "Yolanda Oreamuno," in *Spanish American Women Writers,* edited by Diane Marting (Westport, Conn.: Greenwood Press, 1990), pp. 394–406.

— M.E.S.

ORGANIZATION OF AMERICAN STATES

Originally known as the Pan American Union, the Organization of American States (OAS) — the Organización de los Estados Americanos (OEA) in Spanish — was founded in 1948 to increase mutual understanding, peace, and cooperation among the countries of the Americas. The OAS has an elaborate infrastructure, presided over by its General Assembly and including councils such as the Interamerican Council for Education, Science, and Culture. Article 101 of the revised OAS charter specifies that this council shall support increased availability of education and the integration of all sectors of the population into their national cultures; stimulate educational and technological research and exchange; encourage intellectual and artistic activity, including the exchange of cultural works and folklore; and foster the preservation of diverse cultural heritages.

The OAS magazine *Américas,* a bimonthly published in separate English and Spanish editions, is aimed at realizing these objectives, as were a series of Interamerican Music Festivals held in Washington, D.C., from 1958 to 1978 and more than one hundred world premieres of Latin American music.

The OAS also has several specialized organizations. Among them are the Pan American Institute of Geography and History and the Interamerican Indian Institute, both based in Mexico City, and the Interamerican Institute for Cooperation on Agriculture, located in San José, Costa Rica.

REFERENCES:

M. Margaret Ball, *The OAS in Transition* (Durham, N.C.: Duke University Press, 1969);

Viron P. Vaky and Heraldo Muñoz, *The Future of the Organization of American States* (New York: Twentieth Century Fund Press, 1993).

— P.S.

MARÍA CRISTINA ORIVE

The Guatemalan María Cristina Orive (1931–) was among the first Latin American photographers to be recognized and hired by international press organizations in the 1960s and 1970s (see **Photography**). Orive grew up in a French-Guatemalan family connected with intellectual circles in Central America. She studied French and communications at Smith College in the United States, specializing in radio journalism. From 1957 to 1973 Orive lived in Paris, where she worked for ORTF, the French Radio and Television Organization. Through her radio work she met and befriended numerous Latin American artists and writers. At the same time, she taught herself photography and began working for the Argentinean newsmagazine *Primera Plana,* for which she produced a series of photos to accompany articles written by her friend and collaborator, the Peruvian writer Mario Vargas Llosa. In the late 1960s Orive began working for international press agencies, such as ASA, SIPA, and GAMMA, which distributed her photographs to magazines such as *Paris Match, Stern, Newsweek,* and *L'Express,* reporting in both black-and-white and color photos about issues such as the Panama Canal and the election of Salvador Allende in Chile.

In 1973 Orive settled in Buenos Aires where, along with Argentinean photographers Sara Facio and Alicia D'Amico, she cofounded La Azotea Photographic Publishers, the first editorial company of its kind in Latin America. They introduced the work of other Latin American photographers into Argentina and Europe and actively supported the work of women photographers, who in general have found it hard to gain recognition and employment both nationally and internationally. Tired of the media manipulation of her photographs, in the early 1980s Orive began to work full-time for La Azotea, which organized exhibitions, published postcards and posters, and produced several books, including Orive and Facio's collaborative project *Actos de fe en Guatemala* (1980; Acts of Faith in Guatemala). This book of Orive's black-and-white photographs, including a text by **Miguel Angel Asturias,** documents important religious events on Good Friday in Guatemala, events that synthesize indigenous, Roman Catholic, and Spanish spiritual traditions.

REFERENCE:

María Cristina Orive, "Ways of the Cross in Guatemala," in *Desires and Disguises: Five Latin American Photographers,* translated and edited by Amanda Hopkinson (London & New York: Serpent's Tail, 1992), pp. 41–52.

— F.B.N.

JOSÉ CLEMENTE OROZCO

One of the leaders of **Muralism,** José Clemente Orozco (1883–1949) was an extremely influential Mexican artist. He studied at the Instituto Nacional de Bellas Artes (National Institute of Fine Arts), where he met **Dr. Atl,** who became his mentor. His early works focused on images of women, schoolgirls, and prostitutes. He also produced **editorial cartoons** for the political journal *El Ahuizote* (see **Graphic Art**). In 1914 Orozco and Dr. Atl, whom Venustiano Carranza had appointed chief of propaganda, fled to Orizaba when Mexico City was occupied by Pancho Villa's forces. At Orizaba, Dr. Atl published the pro-Carranza newspaper *La Vanguardia* with the collaboration of Orozco, **Francisco Goitia, David Alfaro Siqueiros,** and others. Orozco witnessed the violence of the **Mexican Revolution** and its effects on the poor, and from that time on he identified with the dispossessed. He frequently dealt with issues related to the war — political propaganda, the futility of violence, and sympathy for the suffering poor — issues that are evident in his illustrations for *La Vanguardia,* produced in a compelling expressionistic style inspired by **José Guadalupe Posada** and Francisco José de Goya y Lucientes. After Carranza became president, Orozco published *Cucaracha I* (1914–1915; Cockroach I), a caricature critical of the excesses of Carranza's forces, in *La Vanguardia.* Orozco fell out of favor with Carranza and was forced to live as an outcast in the poorest neighborhoods of Mexico City, where he produced a series of expressionist watercolors entitled *Los marginados* (circa 1915; The Outcasts). In 1916 Orozco had a large-scale exhibition of his work, which was savagely panned by critics unaccustomed to such avant-garde art. In 1917 Orozco left for California and later New York, where he made a living painting portraits and working as a commercial artist.

Orozco returned to Mexico in 1920, but his art was ignored until he received a commission for a mural at the Escuela Nacional Preparatoria (National Preparatory School) through the intercession of Juan José Tablada, who recommended him to the minister of education, **José Vasconcelos.** In 1923 Orozco began a series of experimental murals in which he tried various painting techniques, but none of these early murals survived. Orozco's first technically successful work is *Maternidad* (1923; Maternity), whose allegorical theme evokes the emphasis on classical ideals posited by Vasconcelos. During the early 1920s, Orozco and other muralists became increasingly involved in politics, helping to found the Sindicato de Obreros Técnicos, Pintores, y Escultores (Union of Technical Workers, Painters, and Sculptors). President Alvaro Obregón's selection of Plutarco Calles as his successor for the 1924 elections was perceived as a return to conservative policies. In reaction Orozco produced a series of biting, caricature-like murals at the Preparatoria, such as *Los ricos en banquete mientras los obreros pelean* (1923–1924; The Rich at Their Banquet While the Workers Quarrel), expressing his disillusionment

La trinchera (1926; The Trench) and *El franciscano y el indio* (1926; The Franciscan and the Indian), murals by José Clemente Orozco at the Escuela Nacional Preparatoria in Mexico City

with the state's betrayal of revolutionary ideals. The daring nature of these murals caused a riot at the Preparatoria, during which many of the works were damaged. Afterward all the muralists, except **Diego Rivera,** were dismissed. In 1926 Orozco was allowed to complete his commission at the Preparatoria, where he produced some of his best-known murals, such as *La trinchera* (1926; The Trench), *Cortés y Malintzín* (1926; Cortés and Malintzín), and *El franciscano y el indio* (1926; The Franciscan and the Indian). Although in general Orozco rejected indigenist themes, in some of these murals he presented a rather bleak view of the unbalanced exchange between European and Indian peoples.

In 1927 Orozco left for the United States, completing a series of remarkable murals at Pomona College in California (1930), at the New School for Social Research in New York (1930–1931), and at Dartmouth College in New Hampshire (1932–1934). After his return to Mexico in 1934, he produced expressionist frescoes in Guadalajara, at the Universidad de Guadalajara (1936; University of Guadalajara), the Palacio de Gobierno (1937; Government Palace), and Hospicio Cabañas (1938–1939; Cabañas Orphanage). Although the themes of some of these murals refer to specific histor-

ical events or peoples, he represented them as symbolic universal forces shaping the human condition. Such a universalistic approach later influenced the works of the members of **La Ruptura Generation,** such as **José Luis Cuevas.**

REFERENCES:

Teresa del Conde, ed., *José Clemente Orozco: Antología crítica* (Mexico City: Universidad Nacional Autónoma de México, 1983);

Laurance P. Hurlburt, *The Mexican Muralists in the United States* (Albuquerque: University of New Mexico Press, 1989).

— F.B.N.

FERNANDO ORTIZ

The Cuban intellectual Fernando Ortiz Fernández (1881–1969) invented the term *transculturation* to describe the influence of African and other cultures on the languages, folklore, music, history, and sociology of Latin America. The theory of transculturation is explained in his pioneer work *Contrapunteo cubano del tobaco y el azúcar* (1940; Cuban Counterpoint Between Tobacco and Sugar), which had a significant impact on theories of race and miscegenation. Ortiz continued in the antiracist vein of José Antonio Saco and **José Martí** (two progressive nineteenth-century Cuban intellectuals — Martí is considered the father of the Cuban nation), representing Cuba in numerous international congresses concerned with **Indigenist** and African themes. He was an active member of the Liberal Party of Cuba in the 1920s and 1930s but was forced into exile in 1930 because of his opposition to then-dictator Gerardo Machado. He stimulated interest in the study of Cuban national identity through his journal *Revista bimestre cubana* and such organizations as the Academy of History, the Society for Cuban Folklore, and the Society for Afro-American Studies. In 1943 he founded the International Insititute of Afro-American Studies in Mexico. He published books that focused on the idea of transculturation in various disciplines, ranging across history, biography, archaeology, lexicography, musicology, ethnography, and sociology. Among them are *Glosario de afronegrismos* (1924; Glossary of Black African Terms); *Las cuatro culturas indias de Cuba* (1943; The Four Indian Cultures of Cuba); *El huracán: Su mitología y sus símbolos* (1947; The Hurricane: Mythology and Symbols); *Los bailes y el teatro de los negros en el folklore de Cuba* (1951; Dance and Theater of Black Africans in the Folklore of Cuba); and *La música afrocubana* (1975; Afro-Cuban Music).

REFERENCES:

Diana Iznaga, *Transculturación en Fernando Ortiz* (Havana: Editorial de Ciencias Sociales, 1989);

Vera M. Kutzinski, *Sugar's Secrets: Race and the Erotics of Cuban Nationalism* (Charlottesville: University Press of Virginia, 1993).

                                                           — M.E.S.

P

JOSÉ EMILIO PACHECO

Considered one of the most significant writers of his generation, José Emilio Pacheco (1939–) has published books of poetry, novels, short stories, cultural and critical studies, screenplays, and translations. His principal themes include the ephemeral nature of life, the progressive erosion of the modern world, the devastation caused by hatred and war, nostalgia for the lost innocence of youth corrupted by an adult world, and current political, economic, and social crises in Mexico City, where he was born.

His first book of poetry, *Los elementos de la noche* (1963; The Elements of Night), uses classical and modern metrical forms, including sonnets and poems in prose. Pacheco's linguistic dexterity and his vast cultural knowledge are apparent in this first book, which was well received. Through lucid imagery he communicates themes of the temporality of human life surrounded by an exterior, seemingly more permanent world, and humanity's attempt to escape solitude. As in other works by Pacheco, the word, or poetry, serves not only as a way of revealing the anguish associated with the frailty of human existence but also as a means of confronting that anguish. His second book of poetry, *El reposo del fuego* (1966; The Repose of Fire), is divided into three parts that are concerned with destruction, temporality, and permanence. Here the poetic voice is frustrated by the impossibility of corresponding to the reality it is trying to express: the word always says something other than what is intended. Pacheco's other books of poetry include *No me preguntes cómo pasa el tiempo* (1969; Don't Ask Me How Time Passes), *Irás y no volverás* (1973; You Will Leave and Not Return), and *Los trabajos del mar* (1982; The Labors of the Sea).

José Emilio Pacheco (courtesy of the Organization of American States)

Pacheco's disillusionment with contemporary society is apparent in his novels as well. *Morirás lejos* (1967; You Will Die Far Away) is a complex work involving constant displacement and fragmentation of time and space, with seemingly meaningless inserts that nevertheless lend coherence to the narration as a whole. There is on the one hand the writer's commitment, and on the other the ineffectiveness of writing as a means of bringing about social change. The novel is a condemnation of the Holocaust. At the same time, it admits to the futility of communicating such horrors through language.

Another of Pacheco's important novels reveals a similar preoccupation with the corrupting and devas-

219

tating effects of the modern world. *Las batallas en el desierto* (1981; The Battles in the Desert) relates the story of a youth growing up in Mexico City, where the native culture is gradually being taken over by U.S. capitalist interests, while foreign leaders worldwide are using force to enhance their economic power. The disillusionment of youth confronted by adult cynicism and a disenchantment with the contemporary realities of Mexican society are the principal threads that weave through this well-structured, brief novel.

Pacheco also has several books of short stories, including *La sangre de Medusa* (1958; Medusa's Blood) and *El viento distante y otros relatos* (1963; Distant Wind and Other Stories). His list of publications of translations, criticism, journalistic articles, and film scripts is long and has earned him a reputation as a sharp and perceptive critic of society.

REFERENCE:

Hugo J. Verani, *José Emilio Pacheco ante la crítica* (Mexico City: Dirección de Difusión Cultural, Departmento Editorial, 1987).

— M.E.S.

THE PADILLA AFFAIR

In 1968 the Cuban poet Heberto Padilla was awarded a poetry prize by UNEAC (Union of Cuban Artists and Writers) with a disclaimer identifying the poet as a counterrevolutionary. In 1971 the Cuban authorities arrested Padilla and forced him to make a public confession of his politically incorrect views; he was even forced to denounce his wife. The "Padilla Affair," as the episode was subsequently called, marked a change in Cuba from the relatively autonomous status of the arts in the preceding decade to their stringent control by the Communist Party. European and Latin American intellectuals — including Jean-Paul Sartre, Simone de Beauvoir, Italo Calvino, **Octavio Paz, Carlos Fuentes,** and Julio Cortázar — signed a letter entreating Castro to review the situation created by the Padilla Affair and defending the intellectual's right to critical dissent. Castro's response was to break ranks with his former admirers. Four years later, in an address to the First Congress of the Communist Party, Castro proclaimed that writers and artists would no longer be the conscience of society but would instead base their legitimacy on their allegiance to the principles of Marxism-Leninism. The Ministry of Culture was created to direct and supervise artistic activities.

— R.G.M. & P.S.

LUIS PALÉS MATOS

Luis Palés Matos was born in Puerto Rico in 1898, the year his country became a territory of the United States. After passing from Spanish rule to the status of a United States possession, Puerto Rico lacked a clearly defined national identity. The death of Palés Matos, like his birth, occurred during an important year in the history of Latin America, 1959, the date of the **Cuban Revolution.**

During the years following 1898, characterized by a questioning of the nation's roots and loyalties, Palés Matos established himself as one of the writers who defined Puerto Rican culture as a synthesis of African and Spanish traits. For Palés Matos and other Afro-Antillean intellectuals, the nations of the Caribbean could only be conceived in terms of their shared mulatto tradition. Palés Matos turned to African folklore, mythology, superstitions, and rituals in an attempt to understand that part of his own cultural formation. This interest in what many Europeans termed the "primitive" cultural practices in Africa echoed the aims of the **Négritude** movement begun in Paris during the 1930s. Palés Matos differs, however, in that he does not value the "primitive" for the sake of its supposed purity, as did the members of the Négritude movement.

The poetry of Palés Matos displays the richness of African culture, but it does so in combination with Spanish traditions. The two heritages are contrasted in his poems as well as represented in a coming together of disparate customs. The place for this fusion of cultures is Puerto Rico, the land Palés Matos praises in his poetry for its varied landscape and for providing the poet with tangible proof of its difference. In his early collection of poetry *Azaleas. Poesías* (1915; Azaleas. Poems) Palés Matos introduces his unique approach. He manipulates vocabulary that is often borrowed and sometimes nonsensical to form tongue twisters and imitate animal sounds. His poetry is intended to be read aloud and listened to carefully. In addition to the difficult wordplays and strange sound combinations, Palés Matos includes a steady rhythmic pulse. The accents in each line are spaced evenly to imitate dance beats. Each line also ends on a stressed syllable in contrast to the typical second-to-last-syllable stress of most poetry in Spanish. These techniques in rhythm and vocabulary are repeated in the collection *Tuntún de pasa y grifería* (1937; the title suggests musical and other cultural practices among Antillean blacks). Palés Matos moved beyond technical and formal innovations to comment on racial issues in Puerto Rico. Not only did he provide a new perspective on Puerto Rico as a mulatto culture, but he also spoke out against the prevalent racism in his country.

REFERENCE:

Josemilio González, *La poesía contemporánea de Puerto Rico (1930–1960)* (San Juan: Instituto de Cultura Puertorriqueña, 1980).

— D.H.

MARIO PANI

Mexican architect Mario Pani (1911–) embraced the International Style more fully than most other Mexican architects of his time. Born into a Mexico City diplomatic family, Pani was raised in Europe and studied architecture in Paris at the Ecole des Beaux Arts. After returning to Mexico in 1934, Pani received a commission to design the Hotel La Reforma, which became the first leading tourist hotel in Mexico City and a precursor of modern architecture in Mexico. Over the following three decades Pani designed numerous buildings along major Mexico City thoroughfares. Most appear to be more significant in scale than in design, but, because of the use of structural steel, which had not been readily available in Mexico prior to World War II, Pani was instrumental in the incorporation of the modern skyscraper into the Mexico City skyline.

Like most of his contemporaries, Pani considered architecture and urban planning to be inseparable. Already concerned with Mexico City's growth rate in the 1930s, Pani's answer to the strain of rapid urbanization was to promote massive residential building programs. Tlatelolco, Pani's largest project, was begun in 1964. The 101-building complex provided space for seventy thousand residents and included 11,916 apartments, thirteen schools, three medical clinics, a movie theater, shops, and social gathering areas. Tlatelolco was successful in its mission to provide affordable housing, thanks to the sensitivity of preliminary sociological surveys and the experience gained by Pani in previous Mexico City complexes such as the Escuela Normal de Maestros (1945–1947; Normal School for Teachers), the Multifamiliar Presidente Juárez (1950, destroyed in the 1985 earthquake), and the Unidad de Servicios Sociales y Vivienda de Santa Fe (1954–1956; The Social Services and Housing Unit of Santa Fe).

During the 1950s Pani joined Carlos and Enrique del Moral as chief architects of the Ciudad Universitaria (University City) at the Universidad Nacional Autónoma de México (National Autonomous University of Mexico), one of the most important architectural projects in Latin America during this period, comparable to Caracas's Ciudad Universitaria (begun in 1950; University City) and the city of Brasilia. Although not as successful as the Caracas campus, the designs for UNAM's University City integrated visual arts with functionalist architecture. Several of the buildings were covered with large-scale mural mosaics, the most famous covering the central rectangular block of the main library, designed by **Juan O'Gorman.** The entire campus project covers an area of fifteen hundred acres and includes the work of more than one hundred architects.

REFERENCE:

Manuel Larrosa, *Mario Pani: Arquitecto de su época* (Mexico City: Universidad Nacional Autónoma de México, 1985).

— C.M.

PARALITERATURE

The term *paraliterature* refers to the reworking or incorporation in literature of other material, itself often literary. For example, the Mexican **Gustavo Sainz**'s *Gazapo* (1965) and the Puerto Rican **Luis Rafael Sánchez**'s *La guaracha del macho Camacho* (1976; translated as *Macho Camacho's Beat,* 1976) both make use of pop-music culture. In *La guaracha del macho Camacho* the title derives from a popular song whose lyrics promise that life is wonderful ("la vida es una cosa fenomenal") while the reality portrayed shows it to be empty, repetitive, dull, and unpromising. In *Gazapo* the sexual and criminal exploits of a group of Mexican adolescents are shared as they record them on tape, while the narrative is punctuated with passages from the narrator's diary and his tape recordings, all of which gives a "playback" feel to the novel. In *Fantomas contra los vampiros multinacionales* (1975; Fantomas against the Multinational Vampires), Julio Cortázar makes use of the comic-strip hero Fantomas, while Mario Vargas Llosa's *La tía Julia y el escribidor* (1981; translated as *Aunt Julia and the Scriptwriter*) is cast in the form of a parody of a soap opera (**telenovela**). The best-known examples of paraliterature are the works of Manuel Puig, especially *Traición de Rita Hayworth* (1968; translated as *Betrayed by Rita Hayworth*) and *Boquitas pintadas* (1973; translated as *Heartbreak Tango*), which incorporate various manifestations of mass culture, such as sentimental songs and elements drawn from Hollywood films.

REFERENCE:

Chuck Tatum, "Paraliterature," in *Handbook of Latin American Literature*, edited by David William Foster (New York & London: Garland, 1992), pp. 687–728.

— S.M.H.

OCTAVIO PAZ

Born in Mexico City, Octavio Paz (1914–) is Mexico's most respected poet and essayist. He spent his childhood years with his mother, aunt, and paternal grandfather in the small town of Mixcoac, where they were able to avoid most of the chaos generated by the **Mexican Revolution.** He later studied in Mexico City and published his first book of poems, *Luna silvestre* (Rustic Moon), in 1933. He married the writer **Elena Garro** in 1937 and then traveled to Republican Spain to participate in the Writers' Congress, which attracted important international figures in the midst of the Spanish Civil War. Witnessing this tragic period in Spanish history made a deep impression on him, evident in his long poem *¡No pasarán!* (1936; They Shall Not Pass!). It was with Spanish intellectuals exiled in Mexico that Paz collaborated during the late 1930s in literary journals, including *Taller.* After receiving a doctorate from the Universidad Nacional Autónoma de México (National Autonomous University of Mexico), Paz traveled throughout the United States on a Guggenheim Fellowship between 1943 and 1945. He then went to Paris as the Mexican cultural attaché from 1945 to 1951, and there became involved with André Breton and the surrealist writers and artists. During the next two decades he traveled extensively through Europe and Asia. He served as Mexican ambassador to India from 1962 to 1968, resigning in protest against the massacre of students at **Tlatelolco.** In 1990 he became the fifth Latin American writer to win the Nobel Prize for Literature.

Initially, Paz's poetry is marked by a reaction against the apolitical preferences of the **Contemporáneos,** but his most important work involves an exploration of human existential problems (whether personal or historical) and an investigation into language, the creative process, and the nature of poetry itself. His principal themes include alienation, solitude, anguish when confronting the limits of one's existence, poetry, love, communication, and an attempt to discover oneself through erotic experiences. A constant theme reflected in his poetry is the search for the meaning of poetry in relation to human existence in the midst of contemporary crises. Poetry and love become instruments to reestablish dialogue and communication in a world torn apart by violence and tyranny, and the role of the poet is to provide those instruments.

Paz's poetic technique was initially influenced by the surrealists and later by oriental philosophies, especially Hinduism. The principal Hispanic influences on Paz's style were the poetry of Pablo Neruda and the contemporary Spaniard Luis Cernuda. His

Octavio Paz, 1966

style is profoundly lyrical and original, revealing a preoccupation with language that can, for example, yield exceptional metaphors. His most important books of poetry are *Raíz del hombre* (1937; Root of Mankind), *Libertad bajo palabra* (1949; Liberty Under Parole), *Semillas para un himno* (1952; Seeds for a Hymn), *Piedra de sol* (1958; translated as *Sun Stone*) *La estación violenta* (1958; The Violent Season), *Salamandra* (1962; Salamander), and *Viento entero* (1965; Intact Wind). *Piedra de sol,* perhaps his most famous poem, is structured around the motif of the Aztec calendar stone, which spirals the reader through history back to the beginning of the poem, reflecting the Aztec concept of cyclical time. It is a lengthy poem composed of 584 uninterrupted hendecasyllabic lines, suggesting the 584 years of the indigenous cycle, after which there is a new beginning. Love is depicted as the redemption of man from the hell of history, and woman represents the other who completes the male poet's divided self. Central to the poem is the argument that the world can be changed through carnal love, overcoming alienation through ecstasy.

Paz is renowned for his essays, which frequently address the problems of poetics and aesthetics but also explore the various dimensions of Mexican identity. He established his reputation with the publication of *El laberinto de la soledad* (*The Labyrinth of Solitude*) in 1950, a book that has been widely read and translated into many languages. In it he examines aspects of the Mexican personality reflected in the traditions, language, folklore, and attitudes of the Mexican male, aspects which he traces to the conflict of cultures between the Aztecs and the Spanish conquerors in 1519. The alienation and solitude experienced by the Mexican is the result of what was considered a betrayal by the Aztec princess **Malinche,** who aided the Spanish conqueror Hernán Cortés in defeating the Aztecs and who bore his children. She is considered the mother of the Mexican race, and hence the vulnerability and shame associated with being the descendants of one who opened herself to the invader and betrayed her own people. Paz's controversial analysis of the attitude and sexual behavior of the Mexican male toward women is based on this initial betrayal: the openness of the female makes her suspect and vulnerable to attack. Therefore, the Mexican male must be self-contained (closed) to protect himself from outside penetration or he will be considered less than a man. This self-containment involves dissimulation to such a degree that he becomes alienated not only from society but also from himself.

Another controversial and famous essay is *El arco y la lira* (1956; translated as *The Bow and the Lyre*), which contains many of Paz's reflections on the nature of poetry and its relationship to people. In Paz's view the poet, shunned by those in power, represents a subversive minority who can reach into the innermost depths of people to reveal their true identity and save them from alienation. *Los signos en rotación* (1965; The Signs in Rotation) functioned as an epilogue to *El arco y la lira,* focusing on the power of the poet to create an inner language capable of subverting exterior reality. Other well-known essays by Paz are *Los hijos del limo* (1974; translated as *Children of the Mire*) and *El ogro filantrópico* (1979; The Philanthropic Ogre). The latter was written while Paz was in the United States. It analyzes the limitations on pleasure, gastronomic and sexual, that North Americans impose on themselves. Paz believes that a recognition of the importance of desire can lead to a better future.

Paz is also masterful at genre mixing, in the form of poetic prose. *El mono gramático* (1974; translated as *The Monkey Grammarian*), set in India, is a lyrical, circular, and complex treatise on language and poetics, one that reveals the nature and limitations of writing. In 1982 Paz published his long study of the life and works of the seventeenth-century Mexican nun and intellectual Sor Juana Inés de la Cruz. In *Sor Juana Inés de la Cruz o las trampas de la fe* (translated as *Sor Juana Inés de la Cruz or the Traps of Faith*) he details Sor Juana's struggle to assert her right as a woman to pursue her studies in the face of rigid opposition by the Catholic patriarchy.

REFERENCES:

Martin Stabb, *The Dissenting Voice* (Austin: University of Texas Press, 1994);

Jason Wilson, *Octavio Paz* (Boston: Twayne, 1986).
                                                                    — M.E.S.

Naturaleza muerta con piña (1967; Still Life with Pineapple) by Amelia Peláez (Museo Nacional de Bellas Artes, Havana)

AMELIA PELÁEZ

One of the pioneers of the introduction of modern art in Cuba, the painter Amelia Peláez (1896–1968) developed a personal variation of synthetic Cubism. Like most Cuban artists of her generation, she studied at the Academia San Alejandro under the progressive teaching of Romualdo Romañach and later went to Europe to continue her artistic training. She studied art in Paris during the late 1920s and early 1930s and came into contact with a variety of modern art movements. She admired the work of Henri Matisse, Georges Braque, and Pablo Picasso, all of whom had an impact on her art, but she was especially drawn to the work of the Russian constructivist Alexandra Exter, with whom she studied. Peláez's art during this period reflects her rejection of academic models and gradual adoption of avant-garde forms. For instance, in the painting *Gundinga* (1931), a portrait of a young woman, she works with a primitivizing realism of flat, simplified shapes.

Soon after her return to Havana in 1934, Peláez had an exhibition at a progressive cultural institution called the Lyceum, which turned her into one of the leading artistic forces of her generation. Although she worked in relative isolation, she joined the ranks of the artistic avant-garde; in fact, her neocolonial family home became a meeting place for members of the Cuban intelligentsia. Like them, Peláez supported *cubanismo,* a tendency to redefine the national culture of Cuba through art, literature, and, for some members, social and political activism. In Peláez's drawings of the 1930s, such as *Juego de cartas* (1936; Card Game) and *La siesta* (1936; The Siesta), she features images of *guajiros,* rural descendants of Spanish colonists and African slaves, who had become symbols of Cuban culture. While Peláez's style shows a tendency toward increasingly fluid and abstract compositions, her themes reflect the general identification of the vanguardists with the lower classes.

During the 1930s and 1940s, a period that saw an increase in international recognition of her work, Peláez pursued her vision of *cubanismo* in her paintings of still lifes, which reveal her thematic as well as stylistic interest in colonial ornamental designs and the flora of her native land; from these sources she formulates her characteristic, almost baroque style. In *Frutero* (1947; Fruit Dish), representing tropical fruits on a table top, she combines the simplified figuration of synthetic Cubism, the use of bright colors with heavy black outlines, and the arabesque, lacelike shapes of traditional Cuban stained-glass window and iron screen designs. In the 1950s Peláez's style became increasingly abstract as she concentrated on her work with ceramic decoration. She also produced two murals: the ceramic mural in the Tribunal de Cuentas and a mosaic mural, subsequently destroyed, for the Havana Hilton. She returned to oil painting in the 1960s.

REFERENCE:

Juan A. Martínez, *Cuban Art and National Identity: The Vanguardia Painters, 1927–1950* (Gainesville: University Press of Florida, 1994).

                                                                    — F.B.N.

CARLOS PELLICER

Associated with the Generation of the **Contemporáneos** (the contemporaries), the Mexican poet Carlos Pellicer (1899–1977) was born in Villahermosa, Tabasco. He studied in Mexico and Colombia, where he became a career diplomat, later serving in posts throughout Latin America and Europe. He worked as a literature and history teacher in secondary schools and at the university level, as well as serving in various other public offices, among them that of director of the National Palace of the Arts.

Very much influenced by **Ramón López Velarde,** Pellicer's poetry evolved through several stages. The first stage reveals strains of the **Modernista** style, with emphasis on vivid and colorful imagery of a sensual nature. Using innovative images, he describes Nature in a joyful, exuberant manner, appealing to the senses through a rich, metaphorical language, found in *Poemas en el mar y otros poemas* (1921; Poems At Sea and Other Poems) and *Piedra de sacrificios* (1924; Sacrificial Stone). His second stage, influenced by the vanguardist tendencies of the Ultraists, concentrated on a precise, metaphorical language, as seen in *Hora y 20* (1927; An Hour and 20 Minutes). Religious overtones are present in his third stage, as he ages and faces mortality; the poetry he wrote then is considered his best for its pure, unadorned lyricism. *Hora de junio* (1941; June Hour), *Discurso por las flores* (1946; Discourse for the Flowers), *Sonetos* (1950; Sonnets), and *Práctica de vuelo* (1956; Flying Practice) are some of his more-recognized works produced during this period. Almost all of Pellicer's poetry may be found in *Material poético* (1918–1961), published by the Universidad Nacional Autónoma de México (National Autonomous University of Mexico) in 1962.

REFERENCES:

Edward J. Mullen, *Carlos Pellicer* (Boston: Twayne, 1977);

José Prats Sariol, *Pellicer, río de voces* (Villahermosa, Tabasco: Gobierno del Estado de Tabasco, Instituto de Cultura de Tabasco, 1990).

                                                                    — M.E.S.

PEOPLES AND RACES

Although it is believed that at the time of conquest the indigenous population of the Caribbean islands was substantial (possibly as many as a million people on Hispaniola), within the first few decades of Spanish rule almost all of them had been wiped out by battle or disease. Furthermore, the European element was not confined to Spanish settlers alone; in time the French, British, and Dutch all laid claim to Caribbean territories. Once sugar cultivation became crucial in the drive for prosperity, African slaves were imported, and with the abolition of slavery came indentured laborers, primarily from India. The population of the Hispanic Caribbean is largely European or mulatto (a mixture of white and black). The same is not true for Mexico and the northern countries of Central America, where strong and populous indigenous civilizations and a long tradition of intermingling have led to a great many people being of mixed European and Indian racial heritage. In addition, African elements are significant along the Gulf of Mexico and Caribbean coastlines. As in other places in Latin America, there are some people of Arab and Oriental origins in Mexico, Central America, and the Caribbean.

The mingling of races is a widespread phenomenon in Latin America, dating back to the earliest colonial times. To have "mixed blood" can be a source of pride, despite nineteenth-century attitudes that saw mixed race as a factor explaining the anemia of the new republics (see **Mestizaje**). Several terms, of which *mulato* is one, have arisen to designate race and ethnicity. While these terms can be used pejoratively, it is important to note that they do not always have negative overtones. The term *criollo* technically refers to a person of European descent who was born in Latin America, but the designation is sometimes applied broadly to anyone born in the Americas. *Mestizo* usually refers to a mixture of criollo and indigenous peoples, but sometimes the term is used for other mixtures. The terms *zambo* and *cholo* are used in some places to designate a mixture of Negro and Indian. The Spanish American "Indians" sometimes prefer to be called *indígenas* rather than *indios,* and they use the term *ladinos* to refer to everyone else. The appellative *gringo,* whose origins are not wholly clear, may be applied to any foreigner, although it tends to refer to North Americans. (See also **Indigenous Peoples.**)

—P. S.

PEPATIÁN

Pepatián Inc. is an arts organization dedicated to creating, presenting, and supporting multidisciplinary Latino art. Founded in 1983 by the Puerto Rican choreographer Merián Soto, the Puerto Rican visual artist Pepón Osorio, and the U.S. choreographer Patti Bradshaw, Pepatián has increased networks of communication among Latino artists, providing new opportunities for dialogue, collaboration, creativity, and performance. Soto and Osorio create collaborative work born of the experience of cultural, geographic, and linguistic displacement that is characteristic of contemporary Puerto Rican society. Pepatián has initiated several touring and residency projects across Latin America and the United States, presenting work in Puerto Rico at such institutions as the Instituto de Cultura Puertorriqueña, the Teatro La Perla, and the Anfiteatro **Julia de Burgos,** as well as the Festival de Danza Postmoderna in Caracas, Venezuela. Choreographers, performance artists, visual artists, writers, and filmmakers promoted by Pepatián have come from Puerto Rico, Ecuador, Nicaragua, Peru, Venezuela, and Brazil.

—J.M.H.

PHOTOGRAPHY

Although in Latin America photography is sometimes regarded as a Brazilian invention, since a substantial body of evidence points to Hercules Florence's having used the camera obscura, glass negatives, and light-sensitive paper as early as 1833, it was the European-developed daguerreotype that became the most influential photographic technique. Revealed to the public in 1839 by its inventor, Louis-Jacques-Mandé Daguerre, the daguerreotype sparked commercial photography around the world through the invention of a process for capturing the image produced by a camera obscura on a silvered plate sensitized with iodine of bromine vapor. The daguerreotype arrived in Mexico, Cuba, and the countries of northern and eastern South America around 1840 and spread to Central America by the middle of the decade. Many of the professional photographers in Latin America in the 1840s and 1850s were temporary visitors from Europe and the United States. Some set up commercial studios to meet the upper-class demand for portraits, while others employed in scientific cataloguing and exploration produced photographs as an aid for the engravers who made book and journal illustrations.

While Matthew Brady's photographs depicting scenes from the U.S. Civil War (1861–1865) are often regarded as the world's first accurate photo-documentation of war, in fact other photographs taken by an anonymous Mexican photographer documented the horror and hardships of war between the United States and Mexico in 1847. Technical innovations made in Europe in the 1850s, which permitted smaller formats and reduced costs, made photographic portraits accessible across class lines in Latin America after 1860. Many studios were set up by local photographers in the 1860s and 1870s. Photographers continued to specialize in portraiture and also to produce large numbers of calling cards and postcards. The photographic journals, clubs, and exhibitions that proliferated in late-nineteenth-century Europe and the United States were formed later in Latin America, in part because of the lack of readily available photographic supplies. Nevertheless, even in Cuba and Mexico, where supplies were available, few such organizations were formed until the 1950s. In some ways this delay had a positive effect on photographers, some of whom became socially integrated into major artistic and intellectual circles and less isolated in photographic niches than were their European or U.S. contemporaries. One of the first to expand the artistic borders of photography was the Cuban photographer José María Mora. After immigrating to New York, he brought originality and a personal quality to his portraits of the late nineteenth century.

Bicicletas en domingo (1966; Bicycles on Sunday), photograph by Manuel Alvarez Bravo

At the beginning of the twentieth century Mexico and Central America turned away from the pictorialist trends of European photography. During the **Mexican Revolution** a strong documentary tradition of black-and-white photography was developed. The photojournalist Agustín Víctor Casasola, who worked in Mexico City, created numerous official portraits of figures such as Porfirio Díaz, Pancho Villa, and Emiliano Zapata. Such images acquired enormous historical value and influenced the work of several generations of artists and photographers. While many famous photographs of the Mexican Revolution were directly attributed to Casasola, they were, in fact, shot by others, by journalists and soldiers who were in the field. Casasola collected them and created an impressive archive, which later published several photographic albums, such as the ten-volume set *La historia gráfica de la revolución* (Graphic History of the Revolution). Foreign photographers working in Mexico in the late 1920s, such as Edward Weston and Tina Modotti, emphasized their interest both in modern forms and revolutionary themes. The Mexican photographer **Manuel Alvarez Bravo,** who, with his wife and fellow photographer, **Lola Alvarez Bravo,** had continued the documentary tradition of the traveler-reporter artists, used black-and-white photography to illustrate Oaxaca's landscape and people. Lola Alvarez Bravo rejected her husband's interest in lyricism and allegory and became instead a pioneer in both photojournalism and advertisement photography, beginning in the 1930s. These two photographers captured contradictory elements of Mexican life that were labeled surreal by people such as André Breton (see **Surrealism**). Considered the father of Latin American photography, Manuel Alvarez Bravo helped establish photography as a creative medium that was independent of the other arts. His im-

ages have greatly influenced the work of younger generations of Latin American photographers.

During the Great Depression the U.S. Farm Security Administration employed photographers such as Dorothea Lange and Walker Evans for public relations and propaganda purposes. Such use of photography became firmly established in Mexico and the Caribbean, which had previously produced few photojournals or newspapers incorporating photographs. From that time on, Latin American photojournalists produced remarkable documents of important events that were often disregarded by the rest of the world. They recorded the terrible effects of the economic depression of the 1930s in Latin America and the ensuing poverty and political instability: from Augusto César Sandino's rebellion in Nicaragua to Gerardo Machado's fall in Cuba. The images of Latin America seen worldwide in the 1940s and especially during the Cold War were not produced by local photographers but rather created by foreign professionals working for international press agencies, which presented a "sanitized" version of the social and political conditions as well as the regular military and economic penetrations by the United States into the area, especially Central America. In the 1950s press photography was skillfully manipulated during the **Cuban Revolution** by all parties involved, and it was used in the 1970s and 1980s as a tool for raising global awareness of the civil wars in El Salvador and Nicaragua. Latin American photojournalists, such as the Chileans Helen Hughes and Sergio Larraín and the Guatemalan **María Cristina Orive,** were among the first to be recognized and hired by international press organizations in the 1960s and 1970s.

Despite social upheaval and economic hardship in Mexico, Central America, and the Caribbean, photo documents of traditional ways of life continued to be made by photographers such as the Cuban Luis Castañeda, who began a career in photojournalism with the magazine *Cuba* in 1965, and the Panamanian **Sandra Eleta,** who produced a remarkable black-and-white photographic series about traditional life in the coastal town of Portobelo in the 1970s and 1980s. Similarly, since the 1960s Mexican photographers such as Lázaro Blanco, Ignacio "Nacho" López, and Pedro Meyer have documented a wide variety of themes, ranging from urban life and psychological interactions to the shocking effects of poverty and violence. At the same time, their work often goes beyond simple documentation to create images that can be poignantly dramatic or subtly poetic. Yolanda Andrade, a younger photographer, also focuses on depicting urban life, but her images have a more stark and gritty quality.

A renewed and more poetic version of **Indigenism** was proposed by the Mexicans Mariana Yampolsky, **Flor Garduño,** Gerardo Suter, and **Graciela Iturbide.** Yampolsky often works in the countryside documenting the difficult life of impoverished but tenacious and dignified indigenous people. Garduño has also taken photos of Indian groups in Mexico, Central America, and the Andes, charging her sometimes startling images with a sense of spirituality. Suter, one of the few Mexican professionals to use color photography, focuses on carefully composed, dramatic, and sometimes shocking images inspired by Mesoamerican rituals. Both Iturbide and Eleta have followed a more intimate approach in their work, photographing members of marginal groups with whom they have spent long periods of time and formed a more personal relationship. While Iturbide's main series is based on images of matriarchal Tehuantepec women, Eleta has concentrated on an African Panamanian community based in Portobelo.

Since the 1970s there have been several concerted efforts not only to determine the main issues involved in this medium, but also to establish a general, comparative history of Latin American photography, a research project that is still in its early stages. With the aim of giving photography due recognition and improving the general understanding of it, the Consejo Mexicano de Fotografía, founded in 1976, organized two important colloquia accompanied by the first continental exhibitions of Latin American photography (1978 and 1981). Since these conventions and others in Havana in 1984 and Quito in 1990, many photographers in Latin America have become more aware of the social and cultural importance of their work, and the result has been an increase in strategic agreements among them and greater international recognition.

REFERENCES:

Elizabeth Ferrer, "Masters of Modern Mexican Photography," *Latin American Art,* 2 (Fall 1990): 61–65;

María Eugenia Haya, "Photography in Latin America," *Aperture,* no. 109 (Winter 1987): 58–69;

Amanda Hopkinson, ed. and trans., *Desires and Disguises: Five Latin American Photographers* (London & New York: Serpent's Tail, 1992).

—C.M.

VIRGILIO PIÑERA

Poet, novelist, essayist, playwright, and short-story writer, Virgilio Piñera (1912–1979) was one of the most controversial Cuban writers. Born in Cárdenas, in the province of Matanzas, he studied philosophy and letters at the University of Havana. From the beginning of his career, Piñera established a reputation as a polemical writer. In 1941 he refused to defend his dissertation because he considered the committee to be a "bando de burros" (bunch of jackasses). That same year, he created a scandal because of his comments on the nineteenth-century Cuban writer Gertrudis Gómez de Avellaneda and immediately was labeled a "disrespectful writer," a title he adopted proudly. In 1942 Piñera refused to publish in the journal *Nadie parecía* because of its Catholic orientation and founded his own journal, *Poeta.* From 1944 on, he started publishing poems, short stories, and articles in *Orígenes,* a journal founded by **José Lezama Lima,** with whom he had a passionate relationship for many years. From 1946 to 1958 Piñera resided in Buenos Aires, where he had the opportunity to meet writers such as Jorge Luis Borges, Witold Gombrowicz, and José Bianco. Piñera established a cultural bridge between Buenos Aires and Havana by sending his manuscripts to and requesting other manuscripts from Cuba.

Although Piñera wrote a large number of poems, short stories, novels, essays, and plays, he is best known for his short stories, *Cuentos fríos* (1956; Cold Tales), in which he reveals his obsessive concern with style. In *Cuentos fríos* he portrays the absurd and grotesque side of modern life. In his first novel, *La carne de René* (1952; René's Flesh), the aesthetics of masochism govern the life of the characters. In one of his novels Piñera tells of a famous diamond that turns out to be a fake and gets thrown down the toilet; the diamond is called "Delfi," an anagram of "Fidel." Needless to say, Piñera was not popular with the Castro regime. Marginalized in the past not only in Cuba but also throughout Latin America, Piñera's work has been vindicated during the 1990s by many critics, writers, and readers.

REFERENCES:

Read Gilgen, "Virgilio Piñera and the Short Story of the Absurd," *Hispania*, 632 (1980): 348–355;

Dolores M. Koch, "Virgilio Piñera, Short Fiction Writer," *Folio*, 16 (1984): 80–88.

                      — F.V.

PLENA

The *plena* is an Afro–Puerto Rican song/dance folk genre characterized by simplicity and repetition. Its traditional social function has been to entertain and to inform. The plena has traditionally been the bearer of news, humor, and rumor. In that role it is similar to the Mexican **corrido**, the Dominican **merengue**, and the Spanish **romance**. Although its origins are disputed, its history is associated with the city of Ponce on the southern coast of Puerto Rico, where slaves gathered on Saturday nights to sing and dance plenas and **bombas**. Plenas were also popular in the neighboring Dominican Republic. The plena and bomba, often cited among the principal folk genres of Puerto Rico, enjoyed renewed popularity in the 1950s and 1960s, when they were included in performances of **salsa** by Frankie Malabe and Willie Colón.

The plena is performed by an improvising soloist and unison chorus in the call-and-response format common to much **Afro-Caribbean music**. It was originally accompanied by two tambourines, but eventually accordion, guitar, Puerto Rican **cuatro** (derived from the mandolin), and **güiro** (scraped gourd) were added. It is believed that originally couples were separated while dancing the plena, but that early in the twentieth century they began to dance together in a simple forward and backward step.

REFERENCES:

Charley Gerard, *Salsa! The Rhythm of Latin Music* (Crown Point, Ind.: White Cliffs Media Company, 1989);

Francisco López Cruz, *La música folklórica de Puerto Rico* (Sharon, Conn.: Troutman Press, 1967);

Rebecca Mauleón, *Salsa: Guidebook for Piano and Ensemble* (Petaluma, Cal.: Sher Music, 1993);

                      — R.L.S.

POETRY

Modern literature in Spanish America began with "modernista" poetry near the close of the nineteenth century. **Modernismo** (a movement not equivalent either chronologically or in terms of literary content to Anglo-American or European Modernism) was the Spanish American synthesis of the most innovative currents of French poetry — Romanticism, Parnassianism, and Symbolism — and represented a break with the civic and declamatory poetry written by Spanish American poets since independence from Spain in the early nineteeth century. The initial stage of Modernismo was programmatically aesthetic, emphasizing the cultivation of beauty for its own sake and the plastic and musical values of poetic language. The second stage, sometimes called "mundonovismo" ("New Worldism") and dating from the Spanish-American War of 1898, was characterized by a concern with the cultural identity of Spanish America. Both stages are present in the poetry of the Nicaraguan **Rubén Darío** (1867–1916), the greatest poet of the period and the founder of modern Spanish American poetry. His *Prosas profanas* (1896) marks the high point of aesthetic Modernismo, while his *Cantos de vida y esperanza* (1905) together with the Uruguayan José Enrique Rodó's essay *Ariel* (1900) are the most important examples of the later modernista style. Before coming to an end, Modernismo went through a final phase represented by the work of "mannerist" poets, who turned modernista style against itself through parody and exaggeration.

The years immediately following the death of Darío were characterized by the introduction of European avant-garde poetry into Spanish America, a process initiated in South America by Vicente Huidobro and Jorge Luis Borges. The formal tenets of Modernismo — rhyme, meter, ornamental descriptions, elaborate syntactic constructions, poetic structure, verbal melody, and display of a confessional persona — came under fire, but other aspects of Darío's movement were carried on, especially the claim that poetic discourse was autonomous and specific, and the cosmopolitan aura that enveloped modernista poetry. The avant-garde, after all, was merely an acceleration of the same modernizing impulse that had driven late-nineteenth-century poetry and the same imperative to insert Spanish American poetry into a "universal" framework. After 1924 (the date of André Breton's first manifesto) Surrealism was the most influential avant-garde movement in Spanish America and deeply affected writers such as **Octavio Paz,** one of the greatest poets and essayists twentieth-century Spanish America has produced.

Mexico produced many fine poets apart from Paz. During the period following the **Mexican Revolution,** for example, there was a short-lived movement led by Manuel Maples Arce known as "Estridentismo," influenced by Russian Futurism; **Alfonso Reyes** wrote erudite poetry reflecting his belief that communication with other cultures should be kept alive; the magazine *Los contemporáneos* (founded in 1928) brought together a cluster of talented younger poets who, like Reyes, were often concerned with archetypal themes. These poets wrote for a limited, well-educated public and were attacked by the Chilean poet and future Nobel laureate Pablo Neruda for that reason.

The period dominated by the avant-garde came to an end with the Spanish Civil War of 1936–1939, a conflagration that redefined the poetic orientation of some of the major figures of Spanish American poetry. Poets as dissimilar as Pablo Neruda, César Vallejo, Octavio Paz, and **Nicolás Guillén** wrote important works inspired by the Spanish war in a new, politically committed vein. The solidarity of these poets with the Republican cause and their forceful stance against fascism stood in contrast to the self-absorption that was typical of experimental poets and reconnected poetry with a wider reading public.

A related development of regional and often more popular poetry was "poesía negra" (black poetry), influenced by the **Négritude** movement. In the Caribbean, particularly in Cuba, poets such as Guillén, Emilio Ballagas, and **Luis Palés Matos** exploited the rhythms, sounds, and rituals associated with the strong African presence in Caribbean societies, not as outsiders observing the exotic but as participants in those societies who were expressing their own syncretic culture. In the case of Guillén, the picturesque gave way to the political, notably in *West Indies Limited* (1934). Guillén became a key player on the cultural stage in **Fidel Castro**'s Cuba, unlike **José Lezama Lima,** an immensely learned poet and one of several Cubans associated with the influential journal *Orígenes.*

Avant-garde poetry did not die out at the end of the 1930s. In subsequent decades groups of aesthetically (and often politically) militant poets kept popping up all over Spanish America, but their poetic models and objectives were no longer those that had inspired their predecessors. Among notable new influences was that of the American Beat poets. Leading poets to emerge in Spanish America following the heyday of the avant-garde include the Chilean Nicanor Parra and the Nicaraguan **Ernesto Cardenal.** The former demystifies the poetic myths of Surrealism and tones down the elevated rhetoric of his compatriot Pablo Neruda by means of an ironic style grounded in colloquial language. Colloquial language also characterizes the poetry of Ernesto Cardenal, who integrates traditional poetic forms (such as the epigrams of Roman poetry) with contemporary themes (political repression), and biblical language (derived from the Psalms or Revelation) with topics ranging from multinational capitalism to the hydrogen bomb and Marilyn Monroe.

REFERENCES:

Gordon Brotherston, *Latin American Poetry: Origins and Presence* (Cambridge: Cambridge University Press, 1975);

David William Foster, *Handbook of Latin American Literature,* second edition (New York & London: Garland, 1992);

Frederick S. Stimson, *The New Schools of Spanish American Poetry* (Madrid: Castalia, 1970);

Saúl Yurkievich, *Fundadores de la nueva poesía latinoamericana* (Barcelona: Seix Barral, 1971).

                                                                    — R.G.M. & P.S.

MANUEL PONCE

Manuel Ponce (1882–1948), known throughout the Western world as the composer of "Estrellita," was the first of three giants of twentieth-century Mexican music. Seventeen years senior to **Silvestre Revueltas** and **Carlos Chávez,** Ponce became the first outstanding figure of Mexican nationalism by applying the principles and techniques of nineteenth-century Romanticism to Mexican popular music in ballads, character pieces, and suites.

Ponce was born in Fresnillo, Zacatecas, while the Ponce family was temporarily away from its permanent home in Aguascalientes. He began piano lessons at the age of four with his older sister, Josephine. Continuing his studies with local teachers until the age of eighteen, he enrolled in the National Conservatory in Mexico City but was disappointed with the instruction he received there. He returned to Aguascalientes after only one year and began teaching piano. With savings from his teaching, he left Mexico for Europe in 1904 and studied at the Liceo Rossini in Bologna for two years and subsequently at the Stern'sches Konservatorium in Berlin. In Germany some of his fellow students were studying folk songs as source material for compositions: Ponce was inspired to do the same with Mexican folk music. Ponce's early Mexican output of songs and rhapsodies made him, as Otto Mayer-Serra put it, "the outstanding precursor of the new musical ideology of the Revolution." Trained in the European Romantic tradition, Ponce returned to Mexico in 1909 and was appointed professor of piano and music history at the National Conservatory. Active as a touring chamber musician, he also opened a private piano studio, in which for several years he had the opportunity to impress his Mexican musical interests on a talented young student, Carlos Chávez.

Ponce's Piano Concerto No. 1, which had its premiere in 1912, was the first major composition to incorporate elements of Mexican folk music, inaugurating the ensuing era of overt musical **nationalism.** Music of the concert hall had also become an unwitting ally of the **Mexican Revolution.** In 1912 Ponce also composed

"Estrellita" and the piano arrangements of folk songs gathered as *Canciones mexicanas*, including "La cucaracha" and "Valentina," two of the many songs that had become popularly identified with the revolution. Yet it appears that Ponce's paramount interests were more nationalistic than revolutionary. The titles of many of his more than a hundred piano works show that his purpose was to preserve and present Mexican folk elements as music rather than as revolutionary material: "Cuatro danzas mexicanas" (Four Mexican Dances), "Para los pequeños pianistas I" (For the Little Pianists), "Preludio mexicano" (Mexican Prelude-Cielito Lindo), and "Balada mexicana" (Mexican Ballad for Piano and Orchestra).

From the beginning of the revolution of 1910, resurgent violence disrupted the political and social environment in Mexico. In 1915, during the Venustiano Carranza revolution (1914–1917), Ponce left Mexico for Havana, where he worked as a music critic and studied Cuban folk music. During his two years there a concert appearance in New York performing his own music attracted a small audience and received a poor review. The new constitution of 1917, signed by rival groups in Mexico, gave promise of a new era of peace; Ponce returned to resume his position at the conservatory and to conduct the National Symphony Orchestra.

A concert in Mexico City by the great Spanish guitarist Andrés Segovia proved to be a propitious event for both Ponce and Segovia. To Segovia's request for an original work Ponce responded with *Serenade*, piece based on a popular Mexican folk song (**jarabe**). Segovia's enthusiastic approval resulted in its incorporation as a movement in the *Sonata mexicana,* the first of more than eighty works that Ponce wrote for guitar, many of which were premiered by Segovia and refined with his collaboration. Ponce's works for guitar constitute a major contribution to guitar literature of the twentieth century.

Seeking to rejuvenate his approach to composition, Ponce returned to Europe in 1925 to study with Paul Dukas at the Ecole Normale de Musique in Paris. In the company of classmates who were musical nationalists of their own cultures (Joaquín Rodrigo of Spain and Heitor Villa-Lobos of Brazil), Ponce's sense of nationalism was reinforced. There were also new aesthetics in vogue in Paris, aesthetics that were to exert a strong influence on his later compositional style: neoclassicism, impressionism, and neoromanticism. Ponce's most frequently played orchestral works were influenced by this stylistic renewal.

Ponce returned to Mexico in 1933 and was named interim director of the National Conservatory; he also held the chair in musical folklore at the Universidad

Nacional Autónoma. Following the eight years he had spent in Paris, he devoted more attention to orchestral composition: *Canto y danza de los antiguos mexicanos* (1933), *Chapultepec* (three symphonic sketches, 1929; revised, 1934), *Instantáneas mexicanas* (1938), and *Ferial* (tone poem, 1940).

Ponce was a prolific composer of songs—he wrote more than one hundred—the majority of which were in popular style, but he also composed songs in more formal style and song cycles, including works for voice and orchestra. In addition to the *Balada mexicana* for piano and orchestra, he composed two piano concertos, a violin concerto, and a guitar concerto (*Concierto del sur*). Ponce began work on the *Concierto del sur*, with Segovia's collaboration, in the late 1930s. They premiered the work in Montevideo in 1941. A Mexico City performance in 1947 was part of a festival organized by Carlos Chávez in honor of Manuel Ponce. That same year Ponce won the Mexican National Prize for Arts and Sciences. Following Ponce's death in 1948 an entire issue of *Guitar Review* was dedicated to his memory; in that issue Segovia credits him with having raised the status of the guitar, with saving it from being limited to music written only by guitarists.

REFERENCES:

Otto Mayer-Serra, *The Present State of Music in Mexico* (Washington, D.C.: Panamerican Union Music Division, 1946), p. 32;

Andrés Segovia, "Manuel Ponce: Sketches from the Heart and Memory," *Guitar Review*, 7 (July 1948): 4;

Robert Stevenson, *Music in Mexico: A Historical Survey* (New York: Crowell, 1952);

Leo Welch, "The First Movement Sonata Style of Manuel Ponce in His Sonatas for Solo Guitar," dissertation, Florida State University, 1995.

— R.L.S.

ELENA PONIATOWSKA

Elena Poniatowska (1933–   ), whose father was French with Polish ancestry and whose mother was Mexican, was born in Paris. When she was nine years old, the family moved to Mexico, where she was sent to British private schools. She then spent two years in a boarding school in the United States. Because of these circumstances Poniatowska spoke French and English before she spoke Spanish. She began to forge cultural and linguistic ties with the Mexican people through the servants in her parents' house and consequently became interested in the lives of the underprivileged. Since 1954 she has worked for several journals where she has focused on cultural issues and interviewed people from all sectors of society, many associated with the arts. Her journalistic style has influenced her writing of short stories and novels, which frequently are a combination of fact and fiction. Her habit of listening to and recording the voices of others has earned her a reputation as a witness for the people and defender of the most marginalized members of society.

Poniatowska's first book of short stories, *Lilus Kikus* (the name of the protagonist), was published in 1954, followed by a series of interviews published in *Palabras cruzadas* (1961; Crosswords) and *Todo empezó el domingo* (1963; It All Began On Sunday). With the publication of *Hasta no verte Jesús mío* (1969; translated as *Until We Meet Again*), Poniatowska began to establish her reputation as a **testimonial** writer. *Hasta no verte Jesús mío* is based on a series of long interviews between Poniatowska and Jesusa Palancares, an elderly, underprivileged woman who suffered severe economic, political, and sexual exploitation throughout her life. Palancares's life story includes her participation as a combatant in the **Mexican Revolution** and the gradual disillusionment of the lower classes with that revolution as the promised reforms did not materialize. Poniatowska cultivated the testimonial genre in several other works: *La noche de Tlatelolco* (1971; translated as *Massacre in Mexico*) documents the events that led up to the 1968 student movement and the subsequent massacre of hundreds of participants by the army on 2 October of that year. By incorporating testimonies of students, workers, professors, parents, police, soldiers, political prisoners, and others, Poniatowska conveys the multiple interpretations of the event. Weaving together various texts and important historical moments, Poniatowska issues a strong condemnation of the army's actions by equating them with the brutality of the Spaniards in their conquest in 1521 of the Mexicas (Aztecs), the predominant indigenous civilization in Mexico at that time. Other testimonial works are *Gaby Brimmer* (1979), *Fuerte es el silencio* (1980; Silence is Strong), and *Nada, nadie* (1988; Nothing, Nobody), which documents the experiences of the people who lived through the earthquake that devastated Mexico City in 1985. In the short stories collected in *La "Flor de Lis"* (1988), *Lilus Kikus,* and in the novel *Querido Diego, te abraza, Quiela* (1976; *Dear Diego*), Poniatowska uses some documentation to fictionalize the lives of various female protagonists from different sectors of a male-dominated society, most of whom are suffering some form of repression. Women's struggle against patriarchal domination is continued in her 1992 novel, *Tinísima,* a monumental effort documenting the life of the Italian-born photographer Tina Modotti through photographs, letters, court records, newspaper articles, and interviews with

Elena Poniatowska

people who knew her. The description of Modotti's experiences among the mostly Marxist artistic elite in Mexico during the 1920s is a fascinating portrait of this unique period of Mexican cultural history, and it is followed by a rendering of Modotti's experiences in the Stalinist Soviet Union and the Spanish Civil War in the 1930s. Though Poniatowska bases her novel on factual information, she combines it with a fictionalized narration, which adds to its appeal. She is especially successful in the interplay between visual and written narrative; the novel is punctuated by photographs, many taken by Modotti herself. Although it has been criticized for its length, some critics consider *Tinísima* to be the culmination of Poniatowska's literary and journalistic talents. Poniatowska is recognized as one of the most important Mexican writers of the end of the twentieth century, and her reputation as a Latin American writer continues to grow.

REFERENCES:

Maureen E. Shea, *Women as Outsiders: Undercurrents of Oppression in Latin American Women's Novels* (San Francisco: Austin & Winfield, 1993);

Elizabeth Starcevic, "Elena Poniatowska: Witness for the People," in *Contemporary Women Authors of Latin America,* edited by Doris Meyer and Margarite Fernández Olmos (New York: Brooklyn College Press, 1983), pp. 72–77.

— M.E.S.

Popular Dance

The great variety of popular dance forms in Mexico, Central America, and the Hispanic Caribbean results from an intermingling of indigenous, European, and African cultures. In the Caribbean the disappearance of indigenous peoples during the colonial era has led to an absence of an extant indigenous dance culture. Indigenous dances are found in Mexico and those neighboring countries of Central America with large Indian populations. Traditions sometimes survive unscathed because of the relative isolation of the communities involved, but more often dances display signs of syncretism, often deliberately brought about during the colonial era as a way of suppressing indigenous cultures.

In Guatemala research is under way (notably by the Grupo Cultural Uk'ux Pop Wuj and by the Grupo Gucumatz) with the purpose of unearthing authentic dance practices of the Quiché Mayans in the highland areas north of Guatemala City. Since the political power of the various Mayan groups has stabilized, there is now greater freedom to interview elders about their nearly forgotten dance history, to attempt reconstructions of ancient dances, to organize meetings and festivals, and to perform openly. The dances tend to be stylistically simple (for example, two steps and two tempi) and are related to rituals of courtship, sacrifice, healing, planting, and harvest. A typical Quiché dance is the one dedicated to Sijolaj, a king of the time before bad people existed and who is said to ride a horse and burn a basket of sugar cane, symbolizing the harvest. In order to escape colonial censorship, the figure of Sijolaj was disguised as Saint Thomas. Another example is the *Pop Wuj* (a name derived from the *Popol Vuh,* the sacred book of the Mayas), which represents the four stages of Man: the Man of Mud, who does not recognize the gods and is therefore destroyed; the Man of Wood, who is rigid and destroyed by fire; the Monkey Man, who is too playful; and Man proper, able to recognize, respect, and petition the gods.

The **Mexican Revolution** provided a stimulus for the identification and preservation of indigenous dance practices in that country, though there has been disagreement as to what is authentic. Among the many groups that have arisen with the mission of researching and performing indigenous dances are the Grupo Folklórico Huaxtecapan, the Grupo INDAMU (Investigación de Danza y Música), and the Corporación de Danza Azteca de la Gran Tenochtitlán.

Africa accounts for the vitality of certain genres that characterize popular dance in the Caribbean. **Salsa, merengue, seis, bomba,** and **plena** are music/dance forms that have spread through the Hispanic Caribbean territories, beginning in Puerto Rico. Another extremely popular and widespread Caribbean dance form is the Cuban **rumba,** of which the following three styles survive. In the yambu, the music is played on wooden boxes since the drums were banned in various periods of the colonial era, and in it the couple dance harmoniously, complementing one another. In the **guaguancó,** a modernized yambu, male and female dancers compete. Finally, the columbia is a rural dance in which men compete, showing off their virtuosity.

Other Cuban multinational dances are the **cha-cha-cha, mambo,** and pachanga. Three syntheses mark the development of these forms. Early mambo was created around 1939, when African dance music, the **son montuno,** was added to the **danzón** from Europe. Around 1948 the mambo was separated from the more delicate danzón: large choirs of saxophones and trumpets were added, and violins and flutes disappeared. Around 1953 the genteel danzón, replete with flutes, **güiros,** and unison vocals, emerged transformed into the easier-to-dance cha-cha-cha. Different instrumentation accompanied these forms, as well as varied responses from their audiences in Cuba and the United States; different degrees of influence from American jazz, swing, and bop; and different performance styles, from participatory to professional, from choreographed, samba-influenced arm movements to versions admitting natural improvisational grace or imagination. In 1959 a new dance form, the pachanga, was created by a young Irish-Jewish-Cuban composer; it linked Cuban-Yoruban secular bembé dance movements with a samba beat. All of these dance/music forms are in a continual state of evolution, eclipse, and revival, influenced by world travel, scholarship, mass media, and nationalism.

Spanish dances have naturally been popular throughout the Spanish-speaking countries of the Caribbean, Mexico, and Central America. They, too, have been adapted or syncretized in the American context. Examples of popular forms are the *fandango* and the *paso doble.* Other dances imported from European countries include the quadrille, the polka, the schottische, the waltz, and the mazurka, which continue as part of the **norteño** repertoire and form the nucleus of "bailes de salón" (ballroom dances). In Mexico during the colonial era these bailes de salón were divided into different groups, each regarded as appropriate for a certain social class. The social role of ballroom dances was also apparent in the 1930s, when it was considered de rigueur for young people of the rising middle class to attend ballroom dance sessions, organized in schools and in popular clubs. The ultimate objective of these gatherings was to attract a mate of equal or higher social class. Schools existed specifically to prepare young people for these balls, which were attended by both children and parents and sometimes lasted all night.

REFERENCE:

Meira Weinzweig, "A 'Heart of Darkness' in the New World: Carmen Amaya's Flamenco Dance in South American Vaudeville," in *Proceedings of the Society of Dance History Scholars: Dance in Hispanic Cultures* (Riverside, Cal.: Society of Dance History Scholars, 1991).

—J.M.H.

THE POPULAR TRIO

The popular, or romantic, trio continues to hold a prominent place among the musics of Latin America. Well-modulated voices accompanied by acoustic guitars harmonize the charm, passion, and nostalgia of life with picturesque lyrics and memorable melodies. A clear and precise account of the early history of the popular trio, during which voices and guitars were combined, has not yet been developed. The documented history of the genre in this century, however, is confirmed in the records of two closely related commercial enterprises: the broadcast and recording industries. Although the dissemination of the popular trio throughout the Caribbean basin was directly attributable to these industries, its popularity was ensured by Hispanic communities in search of new cultural identities. The Spanish-American War in 1898 and the **Mexican Revolution** in 1910 prompted a new awareness of self, accompanied by new expressions of national identity.

From the 1920s on, trios of voices and guitars began to appear in Mexico, Cuba, Puerto Rico, Colombia, and Spanish Harlem in New York City, where large populations of Hispanics, especially Puerto Ricans, had immigrated since the Spanish-American War. It was in New York, in fact, that one of the earliest documented popular trios was formed in 1925 by Puerto Rican immigrants: the *Trío Borinquen,* with **Rafael Hernández**. In the same year Miguel Matamoros founded the *Trío Matamoros* in Cuba. A year later the quintet *Trovadores Tamaulipecos* (Troubadors from the state of Tamaulipas, in northeastern Mexico) was performing occasionally as a trio. At times the term *trio* identified a duet of voices accompanied by a single

guitar; at others it was applied to an ensemble of three voices accompanied by one or more guitars. The *Trovadores Tamaulipecos* often performed with three voices in trio style, as did the *Trío Vegabajeño* (from Vega Baja in Puerto Rico). These early ensembles might more properly be referred to as precursors of the popular trio, an ensemble that gained more-precise definition in the 1940s with the most famous trio of all, *Los Panchos*. (*Pancho* was a popular and affectionate name in the United States for the increasing number of Mexican and other Hispanic immigrants; the revolutionary leader Pancho Villa had become a folk hero for many North Americans, including Mexican Americans).

Several distinguishing features of the *Trío Los Panchos* catapulted them to international stardom and effectively established their position as the most emulated popular trio in the world. Unlike previous trios, *Los Panchos* established a true trio of compatible voices consisting of a lead singer, supported by second and third vocally harmonized parts. The approach to the trio of guitars was equally revolutionary, consisting of separate accompanying parts for each guitar. The new format provided for a trio of voices and a trio of guitars, two different ensembles combined into one. An additional innovation affecting the construction and role of the first guitar was brought about by Alfredo Gil, a founder and lead guitarist of *Los Panchos*. Vicente Tatay, the famous Spanish luthier, constructed a special instrument, the *cuarterola* (a smaller, higher-pitched guitar) according to Gil's recommendations. Gil used the instrument to emulate the role of a violin, providing florid ornamentation of melodic lines. Both the instrument and its ornamental role soon became standard fare in popular trios throughout the hemisphere.

The *Trío Los Panchos* began in New York in 1944 with Alfredo Gil (born in 1915 in Tezaitlán, Puebla, Mexico), José de Jesús "Chucho" Navarro (born in 1913 in Iracuato, Guanajuato, Mexico), and Hernando Avilés (1914–1986, San Juan, Puerto Rico) as the lead singer. This trio enjoyed immediate success and laid claim to international fame through numerous tours, broadcasts, and recordings with Columbia Records of Mexico. Gil and Navarro remained in the trio for many years, with occasional replacements of the lead singer. Among the artists who have performed as lead singer are: Raúl Shaw Moreno, Jolito Rodríguez, Johnny Albino, Enrique Cáceres, Ovidio Hernández, and Rafael Basurto Lara. Over the years the *Trío Los Panchos* recorded more than 250 LPs, most of which are in Spanish but some of which also include numbers in Greek, Japanese, Arabic, and English. Among the international stars who appeared and recorded with *Los*

Panchos as guest artists were: Eydie Gormé (three LPs); Gigliola Cinquetti, Italian winner of various prizes in the European International Song Festival; Estela Raval, lead vocalist of *Los Cinco Latinos* (The Five Latins, a well-known Argentinean ensemble) and winner of the Martín Fierro Award in Argentina; María Martha Serra Lima, a classical vocalist from Argentina; and Javier Solís, the popular Mexican recording artist. The *Trío Los Panchos* also appeared in at least fifty motion pictures made by the Mexican film industry.

Among the more famous popular trios that were influenced by the innovations of *Los Panchos* are: from Puerto Rico, *Trío Vegabajeño, Johnny Albino y su Trío San Juan, Trío Johnny Rodríguez, Trío Julio Rodríguez, Trío Los Condes*; from Cuba, *Los Hermanos Rigual*; from Ecuador, *Trío Los Brillantes, Los Embajadores*; from Mexico, *Trío Los Delfines, Trío Los Tres Ases, Trío Los Tres Diamantes*; and from Colombia, *Trío Dalmar*.

REFERENCES:

Pablo Marcial Ortíz Ramos, *A tres voces y guitarras: Los tríos en Puerto Rico* (San Juan: Editora Corripio, 1992);

Edna Abruña Rodríguez, *Los Panchos: La mejor agrupación de voces y guitarras de todos los tiempos*, volume 1 (N.p.: Published by the author, 1991);

Hernán Restrepo Duque, *Lo que cuentan los boleros* (Bogotá: Centro Editorial de Estudios Musicales, 1992);

Jaime Rico Salazar, *Cien años de boleros* (Bogotá: Centro Editorial de Estudios Musicales, 1987).

— R.L.S.

JOSÉ GUADALUPE POSADA

The Mexican José Guadalupe Posada (1852–1913) created some of the most important and influential examples of **graphic art** in the Americas. He began drawing at an early age and also helped in his uncle's pottery workshop. He later studied at the Academia de Arte y Artesanía (Academy of Art and Handicrafts). During the 1860s Posada became an apprentice in lithography and intaglio at Trinidad Pedroza's graphic studio, and he published illustrations in popular magazines. In the late 1870s he took over Pedroza's workshop in León and produced lithographs for a variety of commercial products and books. His early illustrations and cartoons are characterized by their delicate drawing and halftones, comparable in style to French political cartoons of the 1860s. After the catastrophic flood of 1887 in which he lost part of his family, Posada left León and moved to Mexico City.

In 1888 Posada set up his own engraving workshop in a carriage entrance on Santa Inés Street. There passersby could observe him work. One of the art students from the nearby Academia de San Carlos (Academy of San Carlos) who watched him was **José Clemente Orozco,** whose cartoons of the 1920s reflect his admiration for the old master's work. Posada produced political cartoons for popular magazines and also illustrated thousands of pennysheets called the *Gaceta Callejera* (Street Gazette) for the Antonio Vanegas Arroyo Publishing House. These wood and metal cuts were made in a simplified expressionistic style and later hand-colored in garish tones by the women of the Arroyo family. Posada designed his prints to entice even the illiterate. By clearly stating the full story and its details, his dramatic images explained a text that the targeted audience, mostly the urban poor and Indian peasants, was sometimes unable to read in its entirety. Posada's themes were as enormously varied as the news itself and reflected the most sensational events in the life of the nation. Ranging from the horrific to the comic, from the edifying to the scandalous, his illustrations reached every corner of Mexico.

The speed with which Posada had to work forced him to reuse parts of his images, such as street demonstrations and houses on fire. *Llegada del cuerpo del General Manuel González* (1893; Arrival of the Corpse of General Manuel González), the first print — produced for the announcement of González's death — showed the dead general with a drapery in the background, while the revised version replaced the area of drapery above the body with a rendition of the funeral procession. Among Posada's best-known images, published on the Day of the Dead (an important day in the Mexican calendar), are the *calaveras* (skulls), which transform all kinds of public and powerful figures into skeletons. For instance, *Calaveras de periodistas* (1889–1894; Skulls of Journalists) shows a bony press group on bicycles trampling on a fallen skeleton, and the famous *Calavera Catrina* (1913) portrays a ladylike skeleton wearing a large hat, feathered boa, and fancy gown, a symbol of the deadly effects of the Porfiriato (the rule of Porfiro Díaz) that would ultimately result in the **Mexican Revolution.** Like his contemporaries **Francisco Goitia** and the anonymous photographers included in the Archivo Agustín Casasola, Posada created some of the most memorable images of the revolution. Working with the more flexible lines of relief etching, a technique he adopted during the last years of his life, he illustrated revolutionary ballads, battle scenes, and the hard life of the soldiers, as in *Despedida de un maderista y su triste amada* (1910s; The Farewell [The Kiss]), probably inspired by a photograph now in the Casasola Archive, showing a soldier kissing his sweetheart goodbye.

Chispeante y divertida de Doña Tomasa y Simón el aguador (Sparkling and Funny by Miz Tomasa and Simon the Waterman), engraving by José Guadalupe Posada (Collection of Manuel Alvarez Bravo)

Posada's art not only influenced the development of graphic art in Mexico during the twentieth century but also greatly inspired the interest in Mexican popular culture among artists such as **Jean Charlot,** Orozco, and **Diego Rivera.** Posada's printmaking tradition has also been continued by numerous Chicano artists.

REFERENCES:

Roberto Bedeceus and Stanley Appelbaum, *Posada's Popular Mexican Prints* (New York: Dover, 1972);

Jean Charlot, *Posada's Mexico,* edited by Ron Tyler (Fort Worth & Washington, D.C., 1972).

— F.B.N.

POST-BOOM

The heyday of the Latin American novel in the 1960s is referred to as the **Boom** period, and many critics use the term *Post-Boom* to refer to the period that followed it. Leftist critics have used the term to revalidate a type of populist fiction made unfashionable by the cosmopolitanism of the Boom; others point to formal simplicity as the hallmark of the Post-Boom novel, as evidenced by the restoration of linear narrative and the scaling down of the representation of authorial consciousness, which had played a central role in such modern novels as Julio Cortázar's *Rayuela* (1963; translated as *Hopscotch*) and **Carlos Fuentes**'s *Cambio de piel* (1967; translated as *A Change of Skin*). Still others posit a Latin American "minimalism" in opposition to the totalizing ambitions of the Boom novel. The term *Post-Boom* is further complicated by its relation to postmodernism, an overarching notion of cultural changes in Europe and in the United States, and one whose relevance to Latin American criticism is a matter of debate. What is clear is that the high-literary aesthetic of the modern novel underwent profound modifications in the last few decades of the century, as writers incorporated mass cultural forms (film, melodrama, thrillers, forensic journalism, and popular music) into their work.

REFERENCE:

Ricardo Gutiérrez Mouat, "La narrativa latinoamericana del posboom," *Revista Interamericana de Bibliografía,* 38, no. 1 (1988): 3–10.

— R.G.M.

POSTERS

Posters are one of the most public forms of popular culture in Mexico, the Caribbean, and Central America; often found on building walls and meant to be read by passersby, they are usually designed with a specific political message in mind. The first known posters in the New World were the anonymous messages called "pasquines," written on walls in Mexico during Hernán Cortés's military campaign there in 1519–1522. Highly critical of his actions, these pasquines are the distant antecedents of the political graffiti and posters that are prevalent in Latin American cities during the twentieth century. Revolutionary governments use posters to educate the public about government policy and to foster ideological unity. In Cuba, for example, posters sponsored by the government of **Fidel Castro** stress Latin American unity in resistance against imperialism. In Havana in 1989–1990 a long and narrow billboard featured at its center a youthful Fidel Castro and his brother Raúl striding toward the spectator, arm in arm with Camilo Cienfuegos, a young revolutionary hero who disappeared in 1960 and whose body was never found. On either side of these three, arm in arm in a line, are depicted groups of three or four students, police, and workers, all smiling and striding toward the spectator. Many of the details in the poster were, however, from a later era. The Nicaraguan revolutionary government also used posters but seemed to prefer large-format works in the tradition of Mexican **Muralism,** which were displayed on highway billboards where they could be seen by passing motorists and pedestrians.

REFERENCES:

John King, Ana M. López, and Manuel Alvarado, eds., *Mediating Two Worlds: Cinematic Encounters in the Americas* (London: BFI, 1993);

Chuck Tatum, "Paraliterature," in *Handbook of Latin American Literature,* edited by David William Foster (New York & London: Garland, 1992), pp. 687–728.

—S.M.H.

MIGUEL POU

The Puerto Rican painter Miguel Pou (1880–1968) belonged to a generation of artists who, during the first half of the twentieth century, effectively resisted the cultural hegemony of the United States, which had direct control of the island from 1898 to the 1950s. Pou was a follower of nineteenth-century Puerto Rican painter Francisco Oller. After Pou received artistic training in his native land, he became the first Puerto Rican artist also to study in the United States. In 1920 he founded the Academia Miguel Pou in Ponce, an art school he directed until 1950.

Pou's urban and rural landscapes, portraits of the well-to-do, and **costumbrista** scenes are painted in a realist style with signs of an interest in light effects characteristic of **Impressionism.** For instance, in *Los coches de Ponce* (1926; The Coaches of Ponce) Pou depicts stagecoaches waiting on a street with a city skyline in the background. The trees are in full bloom, and the brilliance of their colors shining under the tropical sun is painted with loose, impressionistic brush strokes. In other paintings, such as *Camino del pueblo* (undated; The Way of the People), Pou represented the nostalgic image of the jíbaro, the poor white peasant considered at the time a descendant of the Spanish colonizers and a symbol of Puerto Rican culture. Like his contemporary **Ramón Frade,** Pou rejected avant-garde style and also turned his back on the multiracial nature of Puerto Rican society by painting mostly whites. Pou's regionalist figuration had a considerable influence on the artistic generation of the 1960s.

REFERENCE:

Marimar Benítez, "The Special Case of Puerto Rico," in *The Latin American Spirit: Art and Artists in the United States, 1920–70* (New York: Bronx Museum of the Arts/Abrams, 1988), pp. 72–105.

—F.B.N.

PREMIO BIBLIOTECA BREVE DE NOVELA

Begun in 1957 by the Spanish publishing house Seix Barral and continued until 1972, this annual prize for unpublished novels played a crucial role in identifying and marketing the writers of the Latin American **Boom,** first heard in 1962, when the prize was awarded to Mario Vargas Llosa's first novel, *La ciudad y los perros* (translated as *The Time of the Hero*). Other Latin American novelists who won the Biblioteca Breve include the Cuban **Guillermo Cabrera Infante,** for *Tres tristes tigres* (1964; translated as *Three Trapped Tigers*), and the Mexican **Carlos Fuentes,** for *Cambio de piel* (1967; translated as *A Change of Skin*).

—R.G.M.

PREMIO MIGUEL DE CERVANTES DE LITERATURA

Established in Spain in 1975 and granted for the first time in 1976, the Premio Miguel de Cervantes is the most prestigious award for Spanish-language writers.

Tito Puente playing vibraphone (Jay Photography)

Awarded under the auspices of the Spanish Ministry of Culture, the prize is designed to recognize writers from Spain and the Spanish American countries as members of the same cultural community. It carries a large honorarium and is awarded yearly in a formal ceremony in Alcalá de Henares, the birthplace of Miguel de Cervantes; the king of Spain invariably attends the event. Candidates are nominated by the Spanish Royal Academy of Language, by corresponding national academies of Spanish-speaking countries, and by previous winners. Spanish American winners of the prize include **Alejo Carpentier** (1977), Jorge Luis Borges (1979), Juan Carlos Onetti (1980), **Octavio Paz** (1981), Ernesto Sábato (1984), **Carlos Fuentes** (1987), Augusto Roa Bastos (1989), Adolfo Bioy Casares (1990), **Dulce María Loynaz** (1992), and Mario Vargas Llosa (1994). The prize is not associated with the earlier and now defunct Premio Miguel de Cervantes.

— R.G.M.

PREMIO RÓMULO GALLEGOS DE NOVELA

The most prestigious Latin American prize awarded to novelists is named after the eminent Venezuelan writer and former president of the republic, Rómulo Gallegos, author of *Doña Bárbara* (1929) and *Canaima* (1935). Gallegos was still alive when the prize was instituted in 1964; it was originally intended as a quinquennial affair and was awarded for the first time in

1967 to Mario Vargas Llosa for *La casa verde.* In 1972 Gabriel García Márquez won the prize for *Cien años de soledad;* in 1977 the Mexican **Carlos Fuentes** received the award for his *Terra Nostra;* in 1982 Fernando del Paso's *Palinuro de México* was selected; and in 1987 Abel Posse won for his *Los perros del paraíso.* Subsequently the Premio Rómulo Gallegos has been awarded every two years. In 1989 it went to Manuel Mejía Vallejo for *La casa de dos palmas,* in 1991 to Arturo Uslar Pietri for *La visita en el tiempo,* and in 1993 to Mempo Giardinelli for *El santo oficio de la memoria.* In 1995 the prize carried an honorarium of $11,000 plus a guaranteed edition of twenty-five thousand copies of the winning novel.

— R.G.M.

TITO PUENTE

Following studies at the Juilliard School of Music in New York, Tito Puente (1923–) began to play professionally in New York. For a time he played *timbales* (drums) with various groups, including Fred Martin's Brazilian band in the Copacabana Club. Meanwhile, the audiences at the new Blen Blen Club formed by **Frank "Machito" Grillo** were clamoring for more-authentic Latin music. Puente and his group, the Picadilly Boys, joined Grillo at the Palladium, and he soon changed the name to the Tito Puente Orchestra. He became known as "King of the Timbales," a title that reflected his innovative use of the instrument in Latin music, especially in the **mambo,** a genre innovated by Israel "Cachao" López in 1937. The timbales had been traditionally associated with the Cuban **danzón** in a rather regimented rhythmic role. Puente used them for solos and as a lead instrument to coordinate the rhythmic precision of the entire ensemble and to inject figurations influenced by North American jazz techniques. His use of timbales within a Latin percussion section mirrored the role of the drum set in jazz ensembles and served to syncretize jazz and Afro-Cuban rhythmic elements in an east coast mambo style. In 1956 Puente released *Puente Goes Jazz*, the first of many such albums.

In the 1960s a new generic term, **salsa,** was coined to include the many styles and formats that had traditionally been included under the umbrella of "Latin music." Always abreast of new trends, Puente identified with the movement and for many years was introduced as "The King of Salsa," but in 1991 the title of his one hundredth album, claimed yet another crown, the name "The Mambo King".

Puente continues to appear regularly in performances focusing on the fusion of jazz and Latin musics. His 1994 album *Tito Puente's Golden Latin Jazz All Stars: In Session* featured outstanding players and band leaders of the genre, all selected by Puente: Mongo Santamaría and Giovanni Hidalgo (**congas**); Dave Valentín (flute); Hilton Ruiz (piano); Mario Rivera (tenor, soprano sax, and piccolo); Charlie Sepúlveda (trumpet); Ignacio Berroa (drums); Andy González (bass); special guest James Moody; and Tito Puente (timbales). Their special performances at New York's Blue Note Night Club and as part of the Salsa Meets Jazz series at the Village Gate, as well as a sold-out performance at the Lincoln Center, led to a three-week tour of the major jazz festivals in Europe and appearances at the Playboy Jazz Festival in the Hollywood Bowl, the New Orleans Jazz and Heritage Festival, Carnegie Hall, and the JVC Jazz Festival.

REFERENCES:
Vernon W. Boggs, *Salsiology: Afro-Cuban Music and the Evolution of Salsa in New York City* (New York: Excelsior Music Publishing Company, 1992);

John Storm Roberts, *The Many Worlds of Music*, issue 3 (New York: Broadcast Music, 1976);

César Miguel Rondón, *El libro de la salsa: Crónica de la música del caribe urbano* (Caracas: Editorial Arte, 1980).

— R.L.S.

PUNTO CUBANO

Punto cubano, punto guajiro (Cuban peasants are referred to as *guajiros*), *punto camagüeyano,* and *punto libre* are among various terms that identify rural Cuban folk songs whose origins reflect a Hispanic rather than African heritage. Characteristic is the use of the **décima,** a poetic form consisting of ten lines, each with a specified number of syllables. The verses may be read, memorized, or improvised, and often they alternate with a refrain (estribillo). These verses may be of a devotional nature (a lo divino) or may treat secular topics (a lo humano). In a modified form puntos may be performed by two singers in a simulated, humorous argument known as a controversia. Regional variations or differences in development and in performance styles are implied by the variety of names applied to this genre.

The punto is commonly accompanied by lute, guitar, **tres, güiro** (a gourd scraper), and claves (rhythm sticks). Occasionally additional instruments are added. The rather simple harmonic content is ornamented by rhythmic alternations between 3/4 and 6/8 meters. Melodic progressions tend to proceed with almost monotonous repetition, since the principal attention is devoted not to musical elements but to poetic form.

The origins of the punto can be traced to immigrants from Spain and the Canary Islands. Similar genres, although with different names, developed in the Dominican Republic, Puerto Rico, and Venezuela.

REFERENCE:
María Teresa Linares, "The *Décima* and *Punto* in Cuban Folklore," in *Essays on Cuban Music*, edited by Peter Manuel (Lanham, Md.: University Press of America, 1991).

— R.L.S.

R

RADIO AND TELEVISION

Latin America is one of the few regions of the world where privately controlled, commercially operated mass media predominate over other forms of media organization. In 1980 Latin America had 977 daily newspapers, almost 2,000 weekly newspapers, 2,987 AM (amplitude modulation) radio stations, 730 shortwave radio stations, 287 FM (frequency modulation) radio stations, and 538 television stations. In that same year eight of the twenty-three nations had video-cable systems that carried programs to communities marginally served by television stations. The total daily newspaper circulation in Latin America during 1980 reached 22.6 million copies, with 97 million radios and 49.3 million television sets in daily use. Each day Latin Americans use four times as many radios and twice as many television sets as there are daily newspapers sold.

Broadcasting in Mexico, Central America, and the Caribbean is relatively advanced compared to most developing regions of the world. Whereas printed media in Latin America have always been associated with serious political affairs, radio and television primarily serve entertainment and escapist functions. In some nations where literacy rates are low, radio is a popular source for news of current events and public affairs. Broadcasting in Latin America essentially began when small radio stations started scheduling programs during the late 1920s and early 1930s. Radio had arrived in Latin America by 1930, when two American radio networks, the National Broadcasting Company (NBC) and the Columbia Broadcasting System (CBS) extended their shortwave broadcast programming to the region. Along with their technologies, the U.S. networks brought their production and business practices to Latin America. The following table shows the numbers of radio stations in Mexico, Central America, and the Caribbean, as revealed in the results of a survey published in 1985:

Country	AM	FM	Total
Belize	3	2	5
Costa Rica	55	46	101
Dominican Rep.	122	62	184
El Salvador	76	9	85
Guatemala	98	20	118
Honduras	129	32	161
Mexico	630	110	740
Nicaragua	52	11	63
Panama	72	30	102

A form of popular culture present in all Spanish American nations, television is predominantly a commercial enterprise, run by private companies and supported by advertising revenue. As a result, television programming is most often oriented toward entertainment rather than education. Latin America was the first region outside North America and Europe where television was introduced on a large-scale level. When television came to Latin America in the early 1950s, some nations, such as Mexico and Cuba, were quick to adopt the new medium, while the small nations, particularly the Caribbean island nations, still receive substantial amounts of foreign programming.

The first television station in Latin America, XHTV (Channel 4), began broadcasting on 31 August 1950 from Mexico City, making Mexico the sixth nation in the world to have television. The station was owned by the newspaper *Novedades*. During its first several months it aired musical variety programs and government news. By the mid 1960s, Mexican television was well established, airing news and entertainment as well as covering special events. Cuba also took quickly to television, and Cuban entrepreneurs rapidly adopted television during the 1950s. In October 1950, after Brazil had officially introduced television, Cuba became the third Latin American nation to have television and began broadcasting on a regular basis during 1951. In prerevolutionary Cuba the brothers Goar and Abel Mestre built CMQ-TV into a network that rivaled stations in New York City for their technical quality. After the Cuban government took over their $25 million in assets in late 1960, Goar Mestre went on to establish stations or program-distribution centers in Argentina, Venezuela, and Peru. Television in Cuba after the revolution became state controlled and, since that time, has supported the party line in its coverage of worldwide news.

Unlike many of the larger Latin American nations, such as Mexico, which have witnessed decreased foreign dependence in programming and increased domestic production, the Caribbean nations and the smaller Central American nations are unable to afford domestic productions. They continue to rely on foreign technology and programming. In particular the proximity of the Caribbean nations to the United States contributes to the easy access to inexpensive U.S. programs. In the case of Mexico, however, proximity has not led to a dependence on U.S. programming. Indeed, the Mexican network **Televisa** has been successful in penetrating the U.S. market with its programs.

Apart from cable channels received from the United States, Mexico has four main television channels that are offered by Televisa. Channel 2 (XEWTV) combines news programs, comedy shows (such as *Papá soltero*), and soap operas (including *Sueño de amor, Los parientes pobres, Valentina,* and *Entre la vida y la muerte*) and audience-participation game shows (such as *Llévatelo*). Channel 4 (XHTV) combines international news with adventure programs and sports. Channel 5 (XHGC) is a children's channel that shows some feature films but mainly dubbed U.S. cartoons. Channel 9 (XEQ) combines news features with movies, comedy programs (such as *Mis huéspedes*), and soap operas (such as *Mundo de juguete, Amor en silencio, La pícara soñadora,* and *Cara sucia*). Finally, the cable channel 24 (GEMS) shows successive installments of seven soap operas each day. There are some other independent channels. Televisión Azteca (Channel 13), for example, has quiz programs such as *Gol, canasta y nocaut,* and audience-participation game shows. Channel 11

is Hoy en la Cultura (Culture Today), an arts channel run by the Instituto Politécnico Nacional of the Department of Public Education.

Despite the various regional differences, it is clear that an exponential growth in television has occurred in Mexico, Central America, and the Caribbean. The following chart illustrates the growth of television stations in various countries of the region between 1960 and 1982:

Country	1960	1982	% increase
Costa Rica	6	86	1,433
Cuba	74	164	227
Dominican Rep.	6	78	1,300
El Salvador	11	64	581
Guatemala	9	26	288
Haiti	1	4	400
Honduras	1	13	1,300
Mexico	19	111	584
Nicaragua	67		

REFERENCES:

Marvin Alisky, "Latin America," in *Global Journalism,* edited by John C. Merrill (New York: Longman, 1983), pp. 249–301;

Michael B. Salwen and Bruce Garrison, *Latin American Journalism* (Hillsdale, N.J.: Lawrence Erlbaum, 1991).

SERGIO RAMÍREZ

Sergio Ramírez Mercado (1942–), one of the most gifted novelists and essayists of Central America, was born in Masatepe, Nicaragua. During his adolescent years he studied law at the National University in León. In July 1959 Ramírez witnessed the student massacre perpetrated by Anastasio Somoza's National Guard, which was to be a decisive factor in influencing him to become a member of the Grupo de los Doce (Group of Twelve), the Sandinista opposition group organized to fight against the Somoza dictatorship. (See **Nicaraguan Revolution**). After the revolution of 1979, when the Sandinistas overthrew Somoza, Ramírez became a member of the Junta de Reconstrucción Nacional (the Board for National Reconstruction) and in 1984 he was elected vice president of Nicaragua. His successful political career parallels his success as a writer.

In 1960, along with Fernando Gordillo, he founded the journal *Ventana,* in which he published his first stories. In the late 1960s he lived in Costa Rica, where he held an important university post and founded the prestigious publishing house, EDUCA. Over a period of some thirty years he has published *Cuentos* (1963; Stories), *Mis días con el Rector* (1965; My Days with the Chancellor), *Nuevos cuentos* (1969; New Stories), *Tiempo de fulgor* (1970; Time of Resplendence), *De tropeles y tropelías* (1972; To Gallop and Trample), *El pensamiento vivo de Sandino* (1974; Sandino's Philosophies Today), *Balcanes y volcanes* (1974; Balkans and Volcanoes), *¿Te dio miedo la sangre?* (1976; translated as *Did the Blood Frighten You?*), *Charles Atlas también muere* (1976; translated as *Stories*), *Las armas del futuro* (1987; The Weapons of the Future), *Castigo divino* (1988; Divine Punishment), *Clave de sol* (1992; the title suggests the musical key of G, but also key in the sense of solution, and sun), and *Un baile de máscaras* (1995; A Masked Ball).

Politics predominate in almost all of Ramírez's literary creations. His narratives display multiple meanings stemming from an ingenious manipulation of popular language and, at times, humor, combined with a scathing critique of right-wing dictatorships. *Cuentos* (1963) underscores a profound pessimism when confronting the apathy and conformity of the Nicaraguan people, who accept misery and injustice without protest. In *Nuevos cuentos* the same themes are repeated in the depiction of a corrupt government and judicial system represented by the judge and the National Guard. The strongest condemnation is of the "ley fuga," a law that permits the killing of prisoners who attempt to escape (or who are given permission to escape). In his first novel, *Tiempo de fulgor,* Ramírez continues his criticism of the upper classes of León in the nineteenth century. The novel contains historical, psychological, and regional elements and interweaves historical moments, along with myths and miracles that reflect the influence of **magical realism.** *¿Te dio miedo la sangre?* depicts the inhumanity of the Somoza dictatorship as opponents of his regime are forced to dig their own graves after undergoing atrocious torture sessions. The narrative technique is complicated with verses, commercials, and popular songs interspersed throughout the narration, creating a kind of collage. *Castigo divino* is a suspense novel based on a famous murder that took place in León in 1933. Fiction and history in this book are interwoven, allowing the narrator to satirize the illicit love affairs, jealousies, and infidelities prevalent among the bourgeoisie of León. The narrative world is enriched by legal documents, letters, fragments from newspapers and testimonies from witnesses. In *Clave de sol,* a more recent collection of short stories, Ramírez again addresses the politi-

cal problems of his country. *Un baile de máscaras* is set in Masatepe, a Nicaraguan town, and on a single day; but in it Ramírez manages to sum up the history of the town, its people, and the family which is the prime focus. Once again, magical realism is in evidence.

REFERENCE:

John Beverley and Marc Zimmerman, *Literature and Politics in the Central American Republics* (Austin: University of Texas Press, 1990).

—N.P.

REDE LATINO AMERICANA DE PRODUCTORES INDEPENDENTES DE ARTE CONTEMPORÂNEA

The Rede Latino Americana de Productores Independentes de Arte Contemporânea (Network of Independent Producers of Contemporary Art; the name intentionally mixes Spanish and Portuguese) was set up to support touring by contemporary performing artists within Latin America. Aided by financing from the Rockefeller Foundation, the network has a central office in Paraty, Rio de Janeiro State, Brazil, and branches in Buenos Aires and Córdoba, Argentina; in six Brazilian cities; as well as in Bolivia, Chile, Colombia, Mexico, Paraguay, Peru, and Venezuela. There is also an office in the United States at Miami-Dade Community College in Florida. The purpose of the network is to create a touring circuit throughout Latin America, to help artists and artistic groups become stable by providing funds for rehearsals and performances, and to make possible enough touring to a sufficient variety of venues to ensure the acquisition of professional skills on all fronts.

—J.M.H.

RETRATO DE TERESA

Retrato de Teresa (1979; Teresa's Portrait), directed by Pastor Vega, is one of the classics of Cuban cinema. Somewhat documentary in style, the movie focuses on Teresa (played by Daisy Granados), a housewife and mother who works in a textile factory and who is torn between her involvement in political and cultural groups and the bond of sexual and emotional empathy she shares with her husband, Ramón (played by Adolfo Llaurado). Like some other important Latin American movies, including those directed by the Chilean Miguel Littín and the Bolivian Jorge Sanjinés, *Retrato de Teresa* deliberately avoids the glamorous Hollywood depiction of womanhood, concentrating instead on the less attractive aspects of Teresa's life, such as the grind of everyday life. For example, she has to feed and dress her children every morning, and her workdays, including union meetings and rehearsals for cultural activities, typically start at 8:00 A.M. and finish at 10:00 P.M.

The media, particularly television, play an important role in the movie. Teresa's success in a televised dancing competition is gauged by how she looks on television. Ramón is a television repairman and as a result has some social clout which he is not averse to using when it comes to his dealings with women. Having left Teresa, he decides to return to her when he sees her being interviewed on television after she has won the dance contest. There are several scenes in which individuals are "glued" to the television screen and seem to be unaware of what is going on around them.

Retrato de Teresa attempts to dismantle the stereotypical image of women conveyed in the media. Despite the new rhetoric of liberation in postrevolutionary Cuba, women are being obliged to shoulder the double burden of working and running the household as usual. Teresa's domestic situation, including verbal and physical abuse by her husband, seems intolerable. The movie ends with the "portrait" of Teresa walking away from Ramón, inviting the audience to infer that the only way out is by leaving domesticity behind. This interpretation makes *Retrato de Teresa* a feminist rather than a revolutionary motion picture.

REFERENCE:

John King, *Magical Reels: A History of Cinema in Latin America* (London: Verso, 1990).

                                — S.M.H.

SILVESTRE REVUELTAS

Silvestre Revueltas (1899–1940), born in Durango, Mexico, began studying the violin at age eight and continued with various local teachers until age fourteen, when he went to Mexico City to study composition. Later he attended Saint Edward College in Austin, Texas, for two years, and from 1918 to 1920 he studied violin and composition at the Chicago Musical College. He was active in orchestral studies in Chicago, as a recitalist of contemporary music with **Carlos Chávez** in Mexico, and as a violinist and conductor of light theater music in Texas and the southern United States. In 1929 Carlos Chávez called him to Mexico City to become his assistant conductor of the new Symphony Orchestra of Mexico, a post Revueltas retained until 1935. In addition, he taught violin and chamber

music at the National Conservatory of Music and conducted the student orchestra. After a tour of Europe, including concerts in Spain, he returned to Mexico to teach and to begin to focus on the production of lighter music for the Mexican film industry.

Although Revueltas consistently included studies in composition during his preparation as a violinist, he did not become active as a composer until the last ten years of his life. His total production is not large: a dozen symphonic poems that provide brief romantic descriptions of things, places, colors, and ambiences; three string quartets and other chamber pieces; some fifteen songs or song sets; and ballet music. His first major work, the symphonic poem *Cuauhnahuac*, was written in 1930 but did not have its premiere until 1933. Its title is the original name of the town of Cuernavaca. Perhaps more popular, or at least more widely performed, is the symphonic poem *Sensemayá* (1938), based on Afro-Cuban cult music and a text by the poet **Nicolás Guillén**. Both works reveal a masterful use of the orchestra and an exciting use of percussion and rhythmic drive.

Critics of Revueltas's works see little development of ideas and compositional technique between his early works and his later ones. Otto Mayer-Serra, however, credits him with providing an important step in the evolution of nationalism in Mexican music: his "picturesqueness," coming between the romantic salon music of **Manuel Ponce** and the transcendent universal ideals of **Carlos Chávez,** provided a logical progression to Chávez's overtly Indianist compositions. (See **Nationalism in Music.**)

The last five years of Revueltas's life produced incidental music for six Mexican movies: *Redes* (1935), *Vámonos con Pancho Villa* (1936), *El indio* and *Ferrocarriles de Baja California* (1938), and *Los de abajo* and *Bajo el signo de la muerte* (1939).

REFERENCES:

Gerard Béhague, *Music in Latin America: An Introduction* (Englewood Cliffs, N.J.: Prentice-Hall, 1979);

Julio Estrada, "Raíces y tradición en la música nueva de México y de América Latina," *Latin American Music Review*, 3 (Fall/Winter 1982): 188–205;

Otto Mayer-Serra, *The Present State of Music in Mexico* (Washington, D.C.: Panamerican Union Music Division, 1946).

                                — R.L.S.

ALFONSO REYES

The Mexican writer Alfonso Reyes (1889–1959) was an intellectual in every sense of the word. He combined critical studies with creative writing and based his career in letters on decades of meticulous study of Hispa-

Alfonso Reyes (courtesy of the Organization of American States)

nic classics. During his years studying law in Mexico City (1906–1913), Reyes befriended a group of revolutionary intellectuals who hoped to change the direction of Mexican culture. Together with Pedro Henríquez Ureña and **José Vasconcelos,** Reyes founded the Ateneo de la Juventud, a circle of intellectuals who shared common pedagogical and cultural goals. The members of the Ateneo shared an interest in reviving the study of the humanities, especially the classic works of world literature. They reacted against the positivist mode of thinking that dominated Mexico during the latter part of the nineteenth century and concentrated instead on more metaphysical and spiritual interpretations of human existence. They also attempted to transform the focus of advanced education in Mexico by revitalizing interest in European and ancient Greek cultures. Reyes looked to European authors such as Stéphane Mallarmé, Johann von Goethe, and Luis de Góngora y Argote as models of literary training.

During his university years Reyes published his first book of essays, *Cuestiones estéticas* (1911; Aesthetic Questions). This early work reflects the shared beliefs of the Ateneo group and points to Reyes's interest in world literature. In 1914 Reyes left Mexico for Spain, where he stayed for ten years. In Madrid he worked with the important Spanish essayist and literary critic José Ortega y Gasset on the journal *Sol;* Reyes contributed to its historical section. He also worked as a researcher in philology at the Center for Historical Studies. Reyes's work as a cultural historian brought him into contact with an array of Spanish writers; among others, he associated with Juan Ramón Jiménez, Azorín (José Martínez Ruiz), and Ramón del Valle Inclán. During his stay in Spain, Reyes published one of his best works, the lengthy and beautifully written essay *Visión de Anáhuac* (1914; translated as *Vision of Anahuac*). The Anahuac valley is the site of present-day Mexico City and was once that of the Aztec capital, Tenochtitlán. Reyes's essay is devoted to communicating the majesty of the Aztec empire just before the conquest of Mexico by Hernán Cortés. Through vivid imagery Reyes invokes the beauty and grandeur of what he terms "la región más transparente del aire" (the clearest region of the air), a description that **Carlos Fuentes** later used as the title of one of his novels. Reyes's essay describes Aztec society, the mythical founding of the city, and the majesty of the Aztec leader, Montezuma. To portray the Spaniards' reaction to the city he describes, Reyes uses the chronicles of the conquest — narratives written in the form of nov-

The Mother Country (1959) by Carlos Raquel Rivera (Collection of the Cooperativa de Seguros Múltiples, San Juan, Puerto Rico)

els, letters, and diaries by the early Spanish explorers of America. *Visión de Anáhuac* includes the words of some of the chroniclers, transformed into poetic expressions by being placed in the new text. Reyes captures the beauty of the Aztec city and the wonder of the Spanish explorers who encountered it in the early 1500s. He also emphasizes that Mexicans can arrive at their essential identity if they reach far enough into their past to discover their Aztec roots. For Reyes, Anahuac symbolizes a pure, forgotten place that must be rediscovered.

After his return to Mexico, Reyes served his country as a diplomat in Spain, France, Argentina, Brazil, Chile, and Uruguay. Among his other publications are the essays in *El cazador* (1921; The Hunter) and *Simpatías y diferencias* (1921–1926; Sympathies and Differences) and the short stories in *El plano oblicuo* (1924; The Oblique Plane). In 1939 Reyes abandoned his diplomatic career to dedicate himself exclusively to his writing and studies. The following year he opened the Colegio de Mexico, a major center for studies in the humanities and for a time a gathering place for exiled Spanish intellectuals.

REFERENCES:

Barbara B. Aponte, *Alfonso Reyes and Spain* (Austin: University of Texas Press, 1972);

Alfonso Reyes, *Mexico in a Nutshell and Other Essays,* translated by Charles Ramsdell (Berkeley: University of California Press, 1964);

Reyes, *The Position of America and Other Essays,* translated by Harriet de Onís (New York: Knopf, 1950).

                                                                    — D.H. & M.E.S.

CARLOS RIVERA

Carlos Raquel Rivera (1923–) is a member of the Generation of 1950 and a contributor to the development of **graphic arts** in his native Puerto Rico. After he studied art on the island and in the United States, he joined the Centro de Arte Puertorriqueño and later worked under the direction of **Lorenzo Homar** at the Taller de Arte Gráfica of the División de Educación de la Comunidad in the Departamento de Instrucción Pública. During the 1950s the Taller hired artists full-time to illustrate books and produce posters publicizing health, educational, and political issues. Like other artists of his generation, Rivera was an active sup-

Diego Rivera at work (courtesy of the Organization of American States)

porter of the independence movement. His figurative work presents national and political themes, and he often preferred print portfolios and posters as a way of reaching broad popular audiences, although he also produced important paintings.

In his linocut *La masacre de Ponce* (1956; The Massacre at Ponce), Rivera shows the negative effects of the United States, symbolized by a looming bald eagle, on Puerto Rico. The image commemorates a tragic event in 1936, when participants in a nationalist demonstration in Ponce were killed by the police. Similar political commentary also appears in Rivera's *Huracán del norte* (1955; Hurricane from the North), which shows people carried through the air by the northern wind, flying in pursuit of a figure of death clutching a money bag. Although the nightmarish quality of its imagery connects this work with **Surrealism,** its meaning is not surreal but rather allegorical.

REFERENCE:

Manuel Pérez-Lizano, *Arte contemporáneo de Puerto Rico 1950–1983: Cerámica, escultura, pintura* (Puerto Rico: Universidad Central de Bayamón, Ediciones Cruz Ansata, 1985).

— F.B.N.

DIEGO RIVERA

Diego Rivera (1886–1957), probably the best-known leader of the Mexican **Muralist** movement, is one of the most significant Latin American artists. Rivera, who had a precocious talent for art, studied in Mexico at the Academia de San Carlos and in Europe. After a time in Spain, Rivera settled in Paris during World War I, and there he met Pablo Picasso and Juan Gris. He soon joined the European avant-garde and produced remarkable cubist paintings such as *Paisaje zapatista — El guerrillero* (1915; Zapatista Landscape — The Guerrilla), which synthesized the cubist treatment of form with Rivera's renewed interest in Mexican themes. Like Picasso and other avant-garde artists in the late 1910s, Rivera abandoned Cubism and worked in a realist style that was considered radical at the time. While in Paris he came into contact with **Dr. Atl** (Gerardo Murillo) and **David Alfaro Siqueiros,** who made him aware of the changed conditions in Mexico following the **Mexican Revolution.** Rivera readily accepted an invitation from Minister of Education **José Vasconcelos** to participate in Muralism, and to that end in 1920 he spent several months in Italy studying Renaissance murals. Rivera returned from Europe in 1921 and began to work on his first mural, the encaustic painting *La creación* (1922; Creation) at the Anfiteatro Bolívar at the Escuela Nacional Preparatoria (National Preparatory School), with the assistance of **Carlos Mérida** and **Jean Charlot,** who had the practical knowledge of fresco technique Rivera lacked. Inspired by Vasconcelos's classical ideals, *La creación* features allegories of the virtues and liberal arts. Vasconcelos wanted muralists to create idealized images of different Mexican regions and peoples as a statement of national identity. For this reason he sent Rivera, who had been out of the country for more than twelve years, on a trip to study indigenous Mexican peoples and costumes. Rivera's first murals at the Secretaría de Educación Pública (Ministry of Public Education) depicted images of traditional life in Tehuantepec and other regions.

During the early 1920s, Rivera and other muralists became increasingly involved in politics. He and Siqueiros rose to the leadership not only of the mural movement but also of the Mexican intelligentsia and the Mexican Communist Party. The Muralists founded the Sindicato de Obreros Técnicos, Pintores, y Escultores (Union of Technical Workers, Painters, and Sculptors) and published an avant-garde manifesto. However, this union soon disintegrated, partially as a result of Rivera's appetite for publicity, which the other members resented. Rivera also succeeded in monopolizing the mural commissions at the Secretaría building, on which he worked until 1928. In his numerous frescoes for this project, such as *La distribución de tierras* (1923–1924; Land Distribution), one of his most politically radical paintings, Rivera defined a new Mexican iconography that synthesized his views on cultural identity, **Indigenism,** and leftist politics. Rivera became the most influential Mexican artist of his time. He received major mural commissions at Chapingo's Escuela Nacional de Agricultura (1924–1927; National School of Agriculture), at Mexico City's Palacio Nacional (1929; National Palace), where he created a monumental vision of Mexican history, and at Cuernavaca's Palacio de Cortés (1929; Cortés Palace). By then Muralism had acquired official status as the School of Mexico, and Rivera was appointed the director of the Instituto Nacional de Bellas Artes (National Institute of Fine Arts).

In 1929 Rivera married **Frida Kahlo,** and together they traveled to the United States. Rivera completed murals in California at the San Francisco Stock Exchange (1930–1931) and at the California School of Fine Arts (1931). He also painted the well-known fresco cycle at the Detroit Institute of Fine Arts (1932–1933) and a mural for the Rockefeller Center RCA

Building (1933) that caused an uproar because Rivera had included a portrait of Lenin. Although the Rockefellers ordered that the fresco be destroyed, when Rivera returned to Mexico he painted a similar work in the Palacio de Bellas Artes (Palace of Fine Arts). During the late 1930s, Rivera and Kahlo befriended Leon Trotsky and his wife as well as André Breton, who visited Mexico in 1938. Both Rivera and Breton signed Trotsky's "Manifesto: For a Free Revolutionary Art." At this time Rivera worked on a series of easel paintings that included portraits and indigenist images. He also briefly experimented with **Surrealism,** exhibiting surrealist paintings at the Exposición Internacional del Surrealismo (International Exhibition of Surrealism) organized by César Moro, Wolfgang Paalen, and Breton.

During the 1940s and early 1950s, Rivera completed murals at the Palacio Nacional (1942–1945), the Lerma Waterworks (1950–1951), the Estadio Olímpico of the Universidad Autónoma de México (1953; Olympic Stadium, National Autonomous University of Mexico), and the Hospital de la Raza (1953–1955), as well as his famous portable mural, *Sueño de una tarde de domingo en la Alameda Central* (1943; Dream of a Sunday Afternoon at the Central Alameda), which was housed in the now-destroyed Hotel del Prado. During his last years Rivera continued to be a strong supporter of the School of Mexico, a stand that placed him in opposition to artists such as **Rufino Tamayo.**

REFERENCES:
Diego Rivera: A Retrospective (New York: Norton / Detroit: Detroit Institute of Fine Arts, 1986);
Ramón Favela, *Rivera: The Cubist Years* (Phoenix: Phoenix Art Museum, 1984).
— F.B.N.

ARNALDO ROCHE RABELL

The Puerto Rican Arnaldo Roche Rabell (1955–) is an important member of the generation of Latin American artists that emerged in the 1980s. He began studying architecture at the University of Puerto Rico and during the early 1980s attended the Art Institute of Chicago. From early on, Roche worked in his Neo-Expressionist figurative paintings with a complex and ritualistic creative process he called "rubbing," a type of frottage. Through this technique he establishes an active psychological interaction with his models, while giving them a more dynamic role in generating the represented figure and thus helping dissolve the barriers between artist and subject. In this process Roche places the model, whether person or object, on the floor under a canvas previously prepared with one or two layers of paint. He then scrapes the model's outline on the fabric with a spoon or a spat-

Hay que soñar azul (1986; You Have to Dream in Blue) by
Arnaldo Roche Rabell (Collection of the Artist)

ula, which results in an expressionistic, flattened-out
image he then continues to transform. In *El deseo de ser
tormenta* (1986; The Desire to Become a Storm) the female model represented was Roche's own mother, a
strong, spiritual woman who raised her six children on
modest means and overcame the loss of two of them. The
artist considers this large painting an homage to his
mother and to motherhood in general, an idea reinforced
by the wide shape of the female figure (a result of the
rubbing process), reminiscent of the Venus of Willendorf.
A similar treatment of the figure appears in his painting
La expulsión y la entrega (1986; Expulsion and Surrender), where a male model was used to represent the figure
of fallen mankind. Inspired by *The Expulsion from Paradise,* by Masaccio, Roche included a rubbing of a rough
iron gate as the background to the scene, in which Adam
is expelled from heaven into the welcoming arms seen at
right, rubbed from those of the artist himself.

Like other Latin American painters such as **Luis
Cruz Azaceta** and **Nahum Zenil,** Roche has produced numerous self-portraits since the late 1980s, in his case as a
means of achieving self-awareness and confronting his bi-

cultural condition. In fact, most of Roche's themes are
based on autobiographical events, including dreams and
visions, as well as the feeling of displacement that comes
from living between two different cultures. Roche's self-
portraits are usually frontal views of his own face, its monumental size attenuated by a fragmentation of the image,
achieved by blending the face with vegetal or lacelike
decorative patterns that give it a kaleidoscopic or even
disturbing appearance. In *Hay que soñar azul* (1986; You
Have to Dream in Blue) the intensity of the hypnotic gaze
of Roche's face is emphasized by bold expressionistic
brush strokes and the stark contrast between the image's
dark, almost vegetal, skin and intense blue eyes. While the
rubbings of palm leaves included in the portrait suggest a
Puerto Rican context, the blue eyes, associated with the
wish expressed in the painting's title, reflect the pressure to
conform to mainstream U.S. culture.

REFERENCE:

Charles Merewether, *Arnaldo Roche: Los primeros díez años*
(Monterrey: Museo de Arte Contemporáneo, 1993).
— F.B.N.

FRANCISCO RODÓN

Francisco Rodón Elizalde (1934–), one of the most
important Puerto Rican painters, belonged to a generation of artists who came of age in the 1960s. Although
Rodón studied art in Costa Rica, Mexico City, Madrid,
Paris, and New York, his artistic formation was
brought about independently, since he never attended
any art school for more than a few months at a time. In
Puerto Rico he worked under **Lorenzo Homar** in the
Taller de Artes Gráficas of the Instituto de Cultura
Puertorriqueña and later taught art at the Universidad
de Puerto Rico. During the 1960s many of Rodón's
contemporaries adopted abstract styles, but he pre-
ferred figuration. Following the example of earlier
Puerto Rican artists such as **Miguel Pou** and **Carlos
Raquel Rivera,** Rodón rejected abstraction as a mani-
festation of U.S. cultural colonialism. However, unlike
Pou and Rivera, he did not paint nationalistic subjects.
The most important genre in Rodón's art is the portrait; his portraits reveal great psychological insight,
especially into famous people such as **Alicia Alonso,**
Luis Muñoz Marín, Jorge Luis Borges, and **Juan Rulfo.**

In Rodón's well-known painting *Estampa vigilante, Inés II* (circa 1969; Watchful Gaze, Inés II), the
artist depicts his young niece Inés lost in disquieting
thoughts in the middle of a luxuriant garden. Like most
of Rodón's paintings, this work reveals his interest in
emphasizing to the extreme the effects of light and
shadow. As a result his images become transformed

Estampa vigilante, Inés II (1968; Watchful Gaze, Inés II) by Francisco Rodón (Collection of Dr. and Mrs. Arsenio Comas)

into a fluid mosaiclike pattern of flat, simplified shapes and isolated areas of color, a pattern that gives his paintings a paradoxically abstract quality. Rodón worked on his pieces over long periods of time, often producing several versions of the same subject.

REFERENCE:

Marimar Benítez, "Viendo pintar a Francisco Rodón," *Campeche, Oller, Rodón: Tres siglos de pintura puertorriqueña,* edited by Francisco J. Barrenechea and Benítez (San Juan: Instituto de Cultura Puertorriqueña, 1992).

— F.B.N.

TITO RODRÍGUEZ

Pablo Tito Rodríguez Lozada (1923–1973) was born in Santurce, Puerto Rico, among the youngest of fourteen brothers and sisters. An extraordinary vocalist, he sang for a time in his brother's popular romantic trio, the Johnny Rodríguez Trio. He left Puerto Rico for New

York City at the age of sixteen and there completed the first of many recordings with RCA Victor. His first regular appearances in the United States were with the popular virtuoso pianist Noro Morales, with whom he perfected performance styles of the Cuban **son** and **guaracha**. He also sang with Xavier Cugat's orchestra. Later for a brief time he joined the José Curbelo Orchestra, in which **Tito Puente** was also performing. Eager to direct his own ensemble, he left Curbelo's orchestra and formed a septet that became the basis for the Tito Rodríguez Orchestra, which later became famous at the *Blen Blen* Club. Although Rodríguez had much less training and experience in music than Tito Puente and **"Machito" Grillo,** his persistent striving for perfection in performance equalized the competition when all three were performing at the Palladium. Many of the recordings of his live performances are still treasured by aficionados as classics.

In the late 1950s and early 1960s Rodríguez was at the height of his popularity, a condition enhanced by his willingness to satisfy audience tastes with the fashionable **mambo,** the **cha-cha-cha,** and the most recent innovation from Cuba, the *pachanga*. In the early years of the 1960s he became the undisputed leader of **Afro-Caribbean music.** A series of events, however, affected the remarkable flowering of music from the Hispanic Caribbean (see **Music**). In 1963 Rodríguez took his orchestra to Venezuela to play in concerts and at local carnivals. Realizing that musical tastes were changing and that the days of the big band were over, he disbanded the orchestra and returned to New York City to concentrate on recording **boleros.**

Tito Rodríguez became known as "El cantante del amor" (The Singer of Love) because of his many recordings of romantic boleros. Two albums that won Gold Record Awards head the list: *Inolvidable* (Unforgettable) and *La paloma* (The Dove). Others include *Llanto de luna* (Tears of the Moon), *Háblame, mi amor* (Speak to Me, My Love), *En mi soledad* (In My Solitude), and *Beso extraño* (Strange Kiss). His last concert was given in Madison Square Garden, where he received the greatest public tribute of his life. Afterward he was rushed to the hospital, where he died.

REFERENCES:

Pedro Malavet Vega, *Historia de la canción popular en Puerto Rico (1493–1898)* (Santo Domingo: Editora Corripio, C. por A., 1992);

César Miguel Rondón, *El libro de la salsa: Crónica de la música del caribe urbano* (Caracas: Editorial Arte, 1980);

Jaime Rico Salazar, *Cien años de boleros* (Bogotá: Centro Editorial de Estudios Musicales, 1987).

— R.L.S.

AMADEO ROLDÁN

Afro-Cubanism, the new direction of Cuban **nationalism in music** that appeared in 1925 (see also **Afro-Caribbean music**), was initiated in the *Obertura sobre temas cubanos* (Overture on Cuban Themes) by Amadeo Roldán (1900–1939). Although Afro-Cuban elements had long been ubiquitous in vernacular Cuban musics, African elements were conspicuously absent in Cuban art musics until Roldán's overture acknowledged their eminent potential in the concert hall. *Tres pequeños poemas* (Three Small Poems) of the following year focused on three Cuban folk expressions: *Oriental* (referring to Oriente, the eastern province), in which African songs and dances of the Dahomeyan tradition were featured; *Pregón* (Street Vendor's Cry); and *Fiesta negra* (Black Fiesta), which focused on the rhythmic aspect of Afro-Cuban music. The ballet suite *La Rebambaramba* in 1928 evoked scenes of colonial life that included both Creole and slave celebrations. This work received extensive international exposure through performances in Mexico, Paris, Berlin, Budapest, Los Angeles, and Bogotá.

Roldán's influence on Cuban contemporary music was considerably expanded through the many facets of his musical career. Born in Paris of Cuban parents, he was an outstanding concert violinist in Spain and later in Cuba (from 1919). He became concertmaster of the Philharmonic Orchestra of Havana, was violist for the Chamber Music Society, founded the Havana String Quartet (1927), and became a conductor at the Teatro Nacional of Havana in the early 1920s. His appointment as assistant conductor of the Philharmonic Orchestra of Havana (1925) led to his appointment as conductor (1932) until his death in 1939. As a music educator Roldán was active as cofounder of the Escuela Normal de Música (Normal School of Music, 1931), taught harmony and composition at the Philharmonic Conservatory, and occupied a similar position as professor (1935) and later director (1936–1938) at the Conservatorio Municipal de Música del Ayuntamiento de la Habana (Havana Municipal Conservatory). Now known as the Conservatorio Provincial Amadeo Roldán, the institution honors the memory of one of Cuba's most innovative composers.

Roldán's pursuit of an Afro-Cuban nationalism was carried on by several successors; **Argeliers León** is the best known.

REFERENCES:

Alejo Carpentier, *La música en Cuba,* second edition (México City: Fondo de Cultura Económica, 1972);

Cristóbal Díaz Ayala, *Música cubana del Areyto a la Nueva Trova,* second edition (San Juan: Editorial Cubanacán, 1981).

— R.L.S.

ROMANCE

Spanish ballads called *romances,* brought to the New World by the first explorers and conquistadors, were lengthy poems, usually put to music, that recounted stories from history and legend. Most often they were composed of four-line stanzas of eight-syllable lines. Romances were the precursors of and inspiration for popular music and stimulated the practice of improvising lyrics, an important feature in many Latin American folk and popular songs.

REFERENCE:

Gerard Béhague, "Latin American Folk Music," in *Folk and Traditional Music of the Western Continents,* by Bruno Nettl (Englewood Cliffs, N.J.: Prentice-Hall, 1990).

— R.L.S.

JUAN RULFO

Juan Rulfo (1918–1986) belongs among the later writers of the **Mexican Revolution,** the "generation of the 1940s" and is considered one of the precursors of the generation of the **Boom.** Rulfo's literary works are few but widely recognized as artistic masterpieces for their stark, direct style, their temporal and narrative daring, and for the dramatic and intense rendition of rural life during the first half of the twentieth century in Mexico. He was born in Apulco, in the state of Jalisco, where his father was a landowner. The **Cristero War** (1926–1928), a reaction against the anticlerical reforms of the Mexican Revolution, ruined his family: his father was killed; his mother died shortly thereafter; and Rulfo was sent to an orphanage. His experiences in the orphanage marked him with a profound sense of alienation and loneliness that later found resonance in his writings. He moved to Mexico City in 1934 and worked for the Immigration Department from 1945 to 1955, which sent him on travels throughout the rural areas of his youth. The harshness and poverty of the earth and the hopelessness and desolation of the peasant population inhabiting it became prominent themes in his narratives. His first publication, *El llano en llamas* (1953; *The Burning Plain and Other Stories*), consists of fifteen short stories in which he depicts the desperate plight of the rural peasants during the Cristero War and its aftermath. The stories are structurally simple, marked by descriptions of certain rural areas of Jalisco. The way of life and colloquialisms of the characters are clearly regional. However, the analysis of the characters reveals a deep interest in the subconscious as well as the anguished condition of human beings who are faced with an uncertain, solitary, and hopeless existence. In this

A 1962 writers' meeting: (standing) Juan Rulfo, José Emilio Pacheco, and Juan García Ponce; (seated) Carlos Valdés, Rosario Castellanos, and Alberto Dallal

sense the universal appeal of his stories transcends their regional nature. Also prevalent are themes of violence, lack of communication, misery, a strong sense of culpability, and a depiction of the Catholic religion as fanatical, superstitious, and useless.

These themes may be found in Rulfo's chef d'oeuvre, the short novel called *Pedro Páramo* (1955), which depicts the final violent years and the subsequent failure of the Mexican Revolution. Páramo is a rich and brutal landowner who manipulates the masses to enrich himself while pretending to support revolutionary activities. The various narrative levels break with conventional time; halfway through the book the reader becomes aware that all the characters are dead and that Comala, the town they inhabit, is populated by phantasms, many of them ánimas en pena (condemned souls) because they have sinned against their religion and died without being pardoned for their sins. The main characters either have little faith in religion (or the local priest) or believe it serves no purpose in helping them achieve salvation. The sense of guilt is pervasive, with allusions to hell, to a lost paradise, and to original sin. The evil title character's name simultaneously suggests the guardian of the gates of heaven

and a stony wasteland. In the closing words of the novel he disintegrates into a pile of stones. This novelistic world is one dominated by violence and death, alienation and solitude, one for which there is no possible solution (unless the occasional signs of rain are to be read as hints of optimism). Although there is no direct reference to an external reality, it is clear that on one level *Pedro Páramo* is a condemnation of the failure of a revolution fought mostly for land reforms that did not come about.

Rulfo's style is spare and sometimes elliptical, his imagery vivid, his language simple. The sense of suffering, hopelessness, and violence is powerful. Because of his innovative techniques and the demands he makes upon the reader (who must work at deciphering the text), Rulfo is considered a precursor of the novelists of the Boom. He uses juxtaposition of scenes, a complex of flashbacks, a mixture of images of daily living side by side with the otherworldly, multiple points of view, and leitmotivs, all of which establish his reputation as an important formal experimenter.

Rulfo also wrote the screenplays collected in *El gallo de oro y otros textos para cine* (The Golden Rooster and Other Cinematic Scripts), which finally appeared in 1980. Despite the urgings of his friends and fans, Rulfo never published his long awaited second novel, though he announced its title ("La cordillera"; The Mountain Range). Rulfo's works have been translated into many languages; (*Pedro Páramo* has been translated twice into English). **Carlos Fuentes,** who wrote the screenplay for a film version of *Pedro Páramo* directed by Carlos Velo (1966), thought the novel was "the highest expression" the Mexican novel had attained, and a book in which was to be found "the thread that leads us to the new Latin American novel."

Although Rulfo published so little, he gained an international reputation as one of the most important Mexican writers of the century. The hopes that a new novel would appear and the reclusiveness of the author no doubt added to the almost mythical aura that came to surround him. As the distinguished Chilean writer José Donoso wryly observed, "only the reputation of Rulfo grows with every book he doesn't write."

REFERENCES:

José C. González Boixo, *Claves narrativas de Juan Rulfo* (Spain: University of Leon, 1983);

Luis Leal, *Juan Rulfo* (Boston: Twayne, 1983);

William Rowe, *El llano en llamas* (London: Grant & Cutler, 1987).

— M.E.S. & P.S.

rhythms, and dance movements. The yambú, the slowest of the styles, is in 2/4 meter; the rhythms are played on packing crates of different sizes (often with spoons) and on a bottle tapped with a coin. The colombia and the guaguancó use **conga** drums of different sizes: the tumbadora (the largest conga drum), the segunda (middle-size conga), and the quinto (smallest). Typically, the larger drums concentrate on reiterated patterns while the smallest drum improvises and interacts with the solo singer. Claves accompany the drums, and small sticks are used to beat additional rhythms on the sides of the drums. The rumba is popular in urban and rural areas as an informal social event. The texts of the songs include commentary on daily life, rumors, and other topics, treated in an improvisational style.

REFERENCES:

Gerard Béhague, "Latin American Folk Music," in *Folk and Traditional Music of the Western Continents,* by Bruno Nettl (Englewood Cliffs, N.J.: Prentice-Hall, 1990);

Larry Crook, "The Form and Formation of the Rumba in Cuba," in *Salsiology: Afro-Cuban Music and the Evolution of Salsa in New York City*, edited by Vernon W. Boggs (New York: Excelsior Music Publishing Company, 1992);

Charley Gerard with Marty Sheller, *SALSA! The Rhythm of Latin Music* (Crown Point, Ind.: White Cliffs Media, 1989).

— R.L.S.

RUMBA

The Afro-Cuban rumba should not be confused with the 1930s-style rhumba in the United States that was intended for ballroom dancing and typically employed large orchestras (Xavier Cugat's, for example) that played undulating, accommodating, smooth rhythms. The *h* in *rhumba* is intended to distinguish the North American variety, which was intended for more modest, conservative audiences. The street-music variety of rumba in Latin America was the entertaining creation of working-class people: vibrant, erotic, energetic, and even acrobatic in its realization. The rumba quickly spread throughout the Antilles and especially to the southern rim of the Caribbean basin and even to the Pacific coast of Colombia.

Three styles of Cuban rumba developed as folk genres: the *yambú*, the *colombia*, and the **guaguancó.** The yambú and the guaguancó are couple dances that portray courtship, pursuit, and evasion. The colombia is primarily danced by men, often in competition. All rumba styles feature the African call-and-response format, that is, a soloist followed by a collective refrain. Each style, however, has distinguishing characteristics, including different meters, tempi,

LA RUPTURA GENERATION

The term *La Ruptura* (The Break) was first used by **Octavio Paz** as a label for several artists who were active during the 1920s, such as the members of **Estridentismo, Rufino Tamayo,** and **Carlos Mérida,** all of whom supported artistic alternatives to the increasingly dominant school of **Muralism.** The term was used again in the 1960s by art critic Luis Cardoza y Aragón to designate a group of young artists in Mexico who in the late 1950s demanded greater artistic freedom and denounced the rhetorical emptiness, outdated realism, and propagandistic bent of Muralism and **Indigenism.** As with Tamayo and other artists who broke from the official art of the School of Mexico, the members of La Ruptura were in turn strongly attacked by muralists such as **Diego Rivera** and **David Alfaro Siqueiros,** and the result was a heated public debate. The generation of "The Break" included artists working in a variety of styles and with differing aesthetic philosophies. Manuel Felguérez, Mathias Goeritz, Gabriel Aceves Navarro, Lilia Carrillo, Pedro Coronel, Fernando García Ponce, Gabriel Ramírez, Olivier Seguin, Vlady (Vladimir Kibalchich Rusakov), Vicente Rojo, and Gunther Gerzso all worked with different modes of

abstract art, including Geometric Abstraction and Informal Abstraction. On the other hand, Arnold Belkin, Rafael Coronel, Francisco Corzas, **José Luis Cuevas, Alberto Gironella,** Leonel Góngora, and Francisco Icaza, all members of the **Nueva Presencia** group, rejected abstraction in favor of Neofiguration, a type of expressionistic figurative mode inspired by the philosophy of existentialism.

The success achieved by these artists during this period was in part due to the creation in Mexico of new art galleries such as Prisse, Antonio Souza, Proteo, and Juan Martín, which provided a much-needed place for avant-garde artists to exhibit their work. The support they also received from Miguel Salas Anzures, director of the Departamento de Artes Plásticas (Department of Plastic Arts) of the Instituto Nacional de Bellas Artes (National Institute of Fine Arts), José Gómez Sicre, director of the Pan-American Union's Division of Visual Arts, and Latin American art critic Marta Traba, further facilitated their participation in international art exhibitions and helped many of them gain access to art galleries in the United States.

REFERENCE:

Shifra M. Goldman, *Contemporary Mexican Painting in a Time of Change* (Austin: University of Texas Press, 1981).

— F.B.N.

S

SALARRUÉ

Salvador Salazar Arrué (1899–1975), or Salarrué as he called himself, is perhaps El Salvador's best-known twentieth-century writer. His body of work includes novels, numerous essays, poetry, and theater, but he is most recognized for his short stories. Salarrué was also a prolific and highly praised painter and illustrator, exhibiting his artwork in El Salvador, Guatemala, Costa Rica, and the United States. Salarrué's literary work can be divided into two main modes that alternated throughout his career: the vernacular, or regional, novel and what has come to be called his cosmopolitan literature.

His first novel, *El señor de la burbuja* (1927, 1956; The Man in the Bubble), is part of his vernacular work and won first prize in a 1923 national fiction contest sponsored by the San Salvador newspaper *Diario Salvadoreño*. His regional literature often includes a poetic use of local Salvadoran dialects, most important that of the Izalco Indians of the Sonsonante region portrayed in his famous work *Cuentos de barro* (1933; Stories of the Earth), a collection of short stories written and published during a government campaign of oppression against the peasant population. While Salarrué's stories did not directly criticize the treatment the Indians received or their subaltern place in Salvadoran society, such criticism is certainly implied. The stories are brief, intense vignettes of the Izalcans' lives, clearly showing their misery, poverty, and ignorance, and, more subtly, implicating the Church, the military, and the system of land tenure in the maintenance of the Indians' condition. These stories and others, such as *Cuentos de cipotes* (1945, 1961; Children's Stories), reflect Salarrué's interest not only in Izalcan culture but also in the condition of children and the state of the nuclear family in Salvadoran society. He portrays intensely meaningful events in children's

lives, uses them as narrators in some cases, and also writes for children. His research for *Cuentos de barro* has been called "almost anthropological," stressing his concern for authenticity in his portrayal of customs and going beyond the nebulous, romantic inventions of other contemporary authors. Salarrué presented the Indians in a highly artistic manner, emphasizing their human dilemmas as well as communicating the social relationships of power that existed at the time. The content of Salarrué's vernacular literature is heavily influenced by such works as *El libro del trópico* (1915; The Book of the Tropics) by Arturo Ambrogui, as well as the Surrealism and the haiku poetry of such writers as Guatemala's Flavio Herrera. Salarrué's vernacular cycle closes with *La espada y otras narraciones* (1960; The Sword and Other Stories).

The author's interests in the Izalcans and in the plight of children are probably closely linked. His parents separated when he was a boy, at which time he went to live with an uncle in Santa Tecla. It was in his boyhood homes in the Sonsonante region that he came into contact with the Izalcans and also experienced life as an outsider, separated from his parents and enrolled in a new school. He quickly became known as a storyteller, and this talent, as well as his artistic tendencies, made him unusual and at times marginalized by other children, but it eventually earned him respect as well. He was awarded a scholarship to study art in the United States in 1917. He lived in Washington, D.C., and New York City, where much of his cosmopolitan literature is set. Less impressive than his regional writing, this part of Salarrué's work is closely linked to the author's interest in eastern philosophies. Along with his three books of philosophical essays, it reflects his preoccupation with the nature of good and evil, with the power of contemplation or meditation, and with what one critic has called his "resistance to death."

These works are filled with fantastic voyages into the future, reincarnations, supernatural coincidences, and long-lost cultures. Salarrué is influenced in this cycle of his work by **Modernismo** and later vanguard movements and by such writers as Guatemala's **Rafael Arévalo Martínez** and Panama's **Rogelio Sinán.** His best-known works in this cycle are perhaps his novel *O'Yarkandal* (1929), some of his stories from *Eso y más* (1940, 1962; That and More), and the third and final section of *La espada y otras narraciones.*

REFERENCES:

Richard Browning, "El niño excluido: Relaciones familiares en *Cuentos de barro de Salarrué," Journal of Interdisciplinary Literary Studies,* 4, nos. 1–2 (1992): 71–88;

Rafael Lara Martínez, *Salarrué o el mito de la creación de la sociedad mestiza salvadoreña* (San Salvador: Dirección de Publicaciones e Impresos, 1991).

— R.B.

SALSA

Salsa is a late-twentieth-century, urban, Latin music whose early development in the Hispanic barrio of New York City was based on Afro-Caribbean traditions that were strongly influenced by jazz. Accounting for its origin and development is a subject of controversy, with claims often based on nationalistic rivalries.

In the early decades of this century, large numbers of Puerto Ricans, Dominicans, and Cubans immigrated to the United States, many of them settling in New York City. While preserving their own characteristic musical traditions in small clubs and social groups of the barrio (neighborhood), many of the talented musicians also became cross-culturally active in jazz groups during the big-band era of the 1930s and 1940s. The Latin influence of Caribbean musicians such as Juan Tizol in Duke Ellington's band, Mario Bauzá in Cab Calloway's orchestra, and Chano Pozo in Dizzy Gillespie's orchestra precipitated the growth of jazz-latino styles, in which Caribbean genres and rhythms were combined with jazz techniques and procedures. The prominent use of trumpets, trombones, and saxophones in jazz influenced the gradual replacement of insular stringed-instrument ensembles, giving birth to a new sonority of Latin music in New York. Big bands in Latin style began to unite the Caribbean immigrants of Spanish Harlem in an explosion of Hispanic pride. In the late 1940s the Palladium became the centerpiece of their musical revolution, with resounding successes by orchestras led by **Frank "Machito" Grillo, Tito Puente,** and **Tito Rodríguez.** This new wave of Latin music, emanating from New York, resonated across the Spanish Caribbean via

radio, television, commercial recordings, and live performances. By the 1950s the recording industry created the market that ultimately forced a reinterpretation of Afro-Caribbean musics.

In the late 1960s the term *salsa* was employed by Fania Records to exploit the musical phenomenon that was born of the gradual mixture of Afro-Caribbean and North American jazz and popular musics. We are familiar with salsa as a spicy sauce to enrich the taste of food; applied to music, the term also implied a new, hot and spicy flavor. Many Cubans object to the term on the basis that it is simply a new word for older Cuban music. The **son** is certainly at the heart of **salsa,** as are the **son montuno** format and **mambo** solo improvisations; yet these procedures are not the exclusive cultural property of a single community, but rather are widespread in the Afro-Caribbean world. Salsa is not simply the restatement of son, montuno, and mambo; it is more accurately a reinterpretation of content, context, and performance practice. In sum, salsa is the urban offspring of a collective Afro-Caribbean–North American-jazz ancestry.

Salsa may be performed instrumentally, but its more typical format is based on song. Its formal organization is sectional, and in it the following order is normally observed: an instrumental introduction; a song verse (guía); a call-and-response (montuno) section; a mambo section (usually instrumental, introducing new material); and a coda. Some sections represent a specific cultural contribution; for example, the song verse derives from the European song tradition of copla and **romance.** Any topic may serve for the song section, but topics typically relate to current events and may take the form of social or political criticism or may refer to romantic and even lewd subjects. Rubén Blades, a major figure in salsa from Panama, often employs salsa verses to communicate political ideas that might otherwise be inaccessible to his large public. **Celia Cruz** often refers nostalgically in song to her homeland, Cuba. The call-and-response section following the verse identifies directly with African traditions of song, in which the leader reiterates and amplifies the song verse in alternation with a repeated choral response. The mambo section, not to be confused with the mambo genre, is normally an instrumental section, introducing new musical material in the form of solo improvisations over a repeated harmonic/rhythmic pattern or repeated patterns with orchestrated phrases by groups of instruments. The coda is the closing cadential progression. With the exception of the coda, any of the sections of salsa may be repeated at will, depending on the response of the audience.

The term salsa may be used to identify a specific rhythmic context, or it may be used generically to include any one of several popular Afro-Caribbean genres. Salsa ensembles often organize concerts and dances into sets (groups of musical numbers), in which case an evening of salsa might properly include **bolero, merengue,** mambo, **bomba, plena**, or the pre-salsa **danzón**.

The instrumentation of salsa ensembles is flexible and varied. The standard percussion section includes **conga drums**, **bongos**, *timbales*, cowbells, *tambora* (two-headed lap drum), **güiro** (gourd scraper), piano, and electric bass. Trumpets, trombones, saxophones, and flutes may be used singly, in pairs, or in any other combination. Decisions regarding the number and variety of players and singers are usually inspired more by economics than aesthetics.

REFERENCES:

Vernon W. Boggs, *Salsiology: Afro-Cuban Music and the Evolution of Salsa in New York City* (New York: Excelsior Music Publishing, 1992).

Charley Gerard and Marty Sheller, *Salsa! The Rhythm of Latin Music* (Crown Point, Ind.: White Cliffs Media, 1989);

Rebeca Mauleón, *Salsa: Guidebook for Piano and Ensemble* (Petaluma, Cal.: Sher Music, 1993);

César Miguel Rondón, *El libro de la salsa; Crónica de la música del Caribe urbano* (Caracas: Editorial Arte, 1980);

— R.L.S.

Luis Rafael Sánchez

LUIS RAFAEL SÁNCHEZ

Luis Rafael Sánchez (1936–) was born in Humacao, a community in the southeast region of Puerto Rico. His family joined the exodus of workers from the countryside to San Juan when he was twelve years old. There he became an actor and later a playwright, essayist, short-story writer, and novelist.

His first literary production was influenced by a previous generation of Puerto Rican writers, especially **René Marqués,** and presents the customs and traditions of the rural areas along with a defense of Puerto Rican nationalism and a nostalgic view of the colonial Spanish past. His style soon acquired its own particular characteristics, with an emphasis on reproducing the popular language spoken in marginalized sectors of society, such as drug addicts, homosexuals, and prostitutes, as well as a concentration on excavating the African presence in Puerto Rican history. The use of popular street language, or antilanguage, spoken by people generally ostracized by the Puerto Rican bourgeoisie, had a significant impact on Puerto Rican narrative and influenced a whole new generation of writers. This style became apparent with the publication of his book of short stories *En cuerpo de camisa* (1966; Dressed Up), replete with the characteristically musical inflec-

tions of black popular language and with sexual allusions, vulgarities, and colloquialisms particular to diverse members of underprivileged Puerto Rican society. The anguished world he depicts has little to do with the one traditionally presented in Puerto Rican literature.

Moral degradation, grotesque characterizations, graphic depictions of corporal functions, and carnivalesque descriptions anticipate Sánchez's first novel and masterpiece, *La guaracha del macho Camacho* (1976; translated as *Macho Camacho's Beat*). This novel has been considered a rewriting of an earlier essay by Antonio S. Pedreira, *Insularismo* (1934; Insularity), a national classic that examines Puerto Rican history and questions of identity. Nevertheless, with its use of street language, its irreverent humor, and its ridiculing of virtually all Puerto Rican traditional views through mock depictions of such things as sexual norms, accepted gender roles, political practices, and elitist culture, the novel breaks with Pedreira's text and presents a different vision. *La guaracha* is a celebration of Puerto Rican popular culture, while at the same time it laments the moral degradation of contemporary Puerto Rican society, a society portrayed as a social, political, and economic chaos generated by its colonial

Severo Sarduy (photograph by D. Roche, copyright © Seuil)

status and the corruption of its members by the colonial power, the United States. This first novel is considered one of the most important literary works of late-twentieth-century Puerto Rican literature. After a long gap Sánchez published his second novel, *La importancia de llamarse Daniel Santos* (1989; The Importance of Being Daniel Santos), based on the life of a popular singer.

REFERENCES:

Arnaldo Cruz, "Representation and the Language of the Mass Media in Luis Rafael Sánchez's *La guaracha del Macho Camacho*," *Latin American Literary Review*, 13, no. 26 (1985): 35–48;

Juan Gelpí, *Literatura y paternalismo en Puerto Rico* (San Juan: Editorial de la Universidad de Puerto Rico, 1993).

— M.E.S.

SEVERO SARDUY

The reputation of Severo Sarduy (1937–1993) is based primarily on his novels, though he also wrote in other forms and painted. He was born in Camagüey in Cuba and moved to Havana to be a medical student, but felt the calling to be a writer from an early age, writing poetry in elementary school. Some of his poetry was published in the literary journal *Ciclón*. Sarduy studied medicine for only a year at the University of Havana because under orders from the then-ruler of Cuba, Fulgencio Batista, the university was closed. Sarduy actively opposed the government of Batista and became one of the most prominent intellectuals of the **Cuban Revolution.** He collaborated in various journals, had an early short story published by **Guillermo Cabrera Infante** in *Carteles,* and above all, acted as art critic for *Lunes de Revolución.* He was also a member of the editorial committee on art and literature for the newspaper *Diario Libre.* In 1959 Sarduy won a scholarship from the new government to study art history in Europe. After a stay of a few months in Madrid, Sarduy moved to Paris, where he studied at the Ecole du Louvre (School of the Louvre) and stayed while Cuba entered an era of censorship. In Paris Sarduy became involved with the group associated with the journal *Tel Quel* and was influenced by the Structuralist and Poststructuralist movements. He also edited the Latin American collection of one of France's major publishing houses, Editions du Seuil, introducing several translations of Latin American literature, including Gabriel García Márquez's *Cien años de soledad* (1967; translated as *One Hundred Years of Solitude*). In the late 1960s Sarduy wrote for several important literary and intellectual journals, including *Mundo nuevo, Plural, Papeles de son armadans, Sur, La Quinzaine Littéraire*, and *Ruedo ibérico*. Estranged from the Castro government, Sarduy remained in Paris, where he died of AIDS.

Younger and more theoretically oriented than Latin American **Boom** novelists, Sarduy has much in common with other writers associated with *Tel Quel*. His work also reveals his acquaintance with the theories of Mikhail Bakhtin, especially in his mistrust of authorship and of the signifying powers of language. He particularly admired his fellow Cuban writer **José Lezama Lima.** Sarduy's novels are enigmatic, difficult, and laced with eroticism, often portraying the seamy side of life. According to his own description, Sarduy's style is "neobaroque." His first novel, *Gestos* (1963; Gestures), was originally published in French and is referred to as "action writing." A search for Cuban identity in the Batista era, the book moves away from realism and the dominance of plot and uses elements of popular culture that at once demonstrate the influence of Maurice Merleau-Ponty. *Gestos* was well received. The exploration of "Cubanness" reappears in the more experimental format of *De donde son los cantantes* (1967; translated as *From Cuba With a Song*), a parody of Cuban history. In this novel Cuba's racial diversity is represented by three groups: African, Chinese, and Spanish. Criticized for not including Cuba's indigenous groups, Sarduy commented that readers who try to find "meaning" in his work are *lectores babosos* (naive readers). In *De donde son los cantantes,* the theme of transvestitism surfaces, a theme that recurs throughout his later works. In the novel *Cobra* (1972) the protagonist, Cobra, is a transvestite, as are other characters, and Cobra is in a constant state of metamorphosis. *Cobra* is an experimental, often violent, nihilistic novel, which won the Prix Médicis. Sarduy's next novel, *Maitreya* (1977), continues the experimental approach of his previous work, with temporal and spatial superimpositions. The transvestite theme once more appears. Also evident is his interest in the Orient; (the title, for example, comes from the name for the future Buddha who will bring peace and truth, while the first part of the novel is set in the Orient). Sarduy is not alone in his focus on orientalism; the exploration of oriental cultures from a Latin American viewpoint also interested such writers as **Octavio Paz** and Lezama Lima, to whom *Maitreya* makes many literary references. (It is worth noting that the interest in orientalism also has a specific, Cuban dimension; Cuba has a significant population of Chinese origin,

and part of *Maitreya* is set in the Cuban town of El Dulce, where many Chinese Cubans live). In *Colibrí* (1984; Hummingbird), Sarduy breaks away from his Cuban orientation to deal more generally with the relationship between nature and culture in the New World.

Sarduy published several collections of essays, including *Escrito sobre un cuerpo* (1969; translated as *Written on a Body*) and *Barroco* (1974; Baroque). His poetry collection *Big Bang* (1974) is based on the big bang theory, which posits that the universe is in a constant state of growth. Using his own particular cosmology, Sarduy creates his own poetic form. Sarduy made his debut in radio with a play, *La Playa* (1971; The Beach), in Stuttgart, Germany. He also published two poetry collections in that same city, *Flamenco* (1971) and *Mood Indigo* (1971). Sarduy produced several other radio plays, which won prizes in France and Italy.

REFERENCES:

Roberto González Echevarría, *La ruta de Severo Sarduy* (Hanover, N.H.: Ediciones del Norte, 1987);

Rolando Pérez, *Severo Sarduy and the Religion of the Text* (Lanham, Md.: University Press of America, 1988).

— M.T. & P.S.

SEIS

Popular in the folk culture of Puerto Rico and the Dominican Republic, the seis is a song/dance genre based on the octosyllabic ten-line stanzas of the **décima.** When the seis is sung, an instrumental introduction of eight to sixteen measures is played before each verse. The verses, often improvised, tend to focus on a given topic. Folk festivals often include contests to determine who is the best improviser. In such contests the topic is usually not given to the singer until the ensemble has begun to play the introduction, thus taxing the singer's inventiveness. At times the last line of the refrain is given, requiring the singer to improvise an appropriate rhyme scheme to fit it. A popular variation features two singers, often of opposite sex, performing a controversia (controversy), a humorous confrontation. Although the seis is typically in 2/4 meter, triplet figures often appear in the vocal or melodic line. Both the style of the vocal performance (a high-pitched nasal sound) and the frequent use of the descending Andalusian cadence reflect the Spanish roots of the seis. The typical instrumentation of the accompaniment now includes a Puerto Rican **cuatro,** guitars, **güiro** and, when available, **marímbola,** but in times past the bordonúa, the tiple, and the requinto (all variations on the Spanish guitar) were also employed. The seis is popular as a couple dance.

REFERENCE:

Francisco López Cruz, *La música folklórica de Puerto Rico* (Sharon, Conn.: Troutman Press, 1967).

— R.L.S.

LAS SEIS

Rosario Murillo, Michelle Najlis, Yolanda Blanco, Vidaluz Meneses, Giaconda Belli, and Daisy Zamora form a group of Nicaraguan women poets, known as *Las seis* (The Six). Their work reflects the new women's poetry that evolved along with the revolutionary struggle that culminated in the overthrow of Anastasio Somoza. In general, their poetry is intertwined with their politics, although in their earlier works the political aspects were largely disguised in order to conceal their involvement with the Sandinistas and avoid repercussions from Somoza's National Guard. Although each woman has a distinct, individual style, the group's poetry may be jointly characterized by a commitment to revolutionary struggle, an effort to reveal and overcome patriarchal stereotypes, a demythification of sexual double standards, a concern for a better future for the children of their generation, a mourning for fallen comrades and other loved ones, and a conspicuously erotic use of language and imagery, all of which are reflected in many of the titles of their books. Among those published by Rosario Murillo are *Un deber de cantar* (1981; A Duty to Sing) and *Amar es combatir* (1983; To Love Is to Fight); Najlis' published books include *El viento armado* (1969; Armed Wind) and *Augurios* (1981; Auguries); Meneses has published *Llama guardada* (1974; Protected Flame) and *El aire que me llama* (1982; The Air That Calls Me); Blanco's books of poetry include *Así cuando la lluvia* (1974; When It Rains), *Cerámica sol* (1977; Sun Ceramics), and *Penqueo en Nicaragua* (1981; Insurrection in Nicaragua); Belli, who is perhaps the most well-known outside Nicaragua, has published *Línea de fuego* (1978; Line of Fire), for which she won a **Casa de las Américas Prize**, *Sobre la grama* (1974; On the Turf), and *Truenos y arco-iris* (1982; Thunder and Rainbows); Zamora's best-known book of poetry is *La violenta espuma* (1981; Violent Foam).

REFERENCES:

Zoé Anglesey, ed., *Ixok Amar Go: Central American Women's Poetry for Peace* (Penabscot, Maine: Granite Press, 1987);

John Beverley and Marc Zimmerman, *Literature and Politics in the Central American Revolutions* (Austin: University of Texas Press, 1990).

— M.E.S.

EL SILENCIO DE NETO

El silencio de Neto (1994; Neto's Silence) has the distinction of being the first feature-length movie to have come out of Guatemala. Its director is Luis Argueta, a native of Guatemala educated at the University of Michigan and resident, since 1977, in New York. According to him, the fact that the film was shown and won prizes at the **Huelva** and **Biarritz Festival**s in 1994 ensured that it did not go unseen in Guatemala. *El silencio de Neto* depicts the experiences of a young boy who is growing beyond the cocoon of childhood and beginning to face the complexities of the adult world at a moment in Guatemalan history (1954) when that country was to have its democratic government overthrown by a CIA-backed coup led by Carlos Castillo Armas, who was effectively under the control of Washington. In a newspaper interview Argueta admitted to a strong autobiographical influence, adding that Neto's silence stands for the silence that all Guatemalans learned to adopt, for to speak out was to be thought a subversive. While the film expresses nostalgia for a lost Guatemalan innocence, its main focus is on the child's personal transition to adulthood, and it is understated and poetic in quality.

— P.S.

ROGELIO SINÁN

Bernardo Domínguez Alba (1902–), born on the island of Taboga, in Panama, goes by the pen name Rogelio Sinán. Some critics consider him the most important author in twentieth-century Panama. He studied at the National Institute of Panama, and abroad in Chile, Italy, and Mexico. Sinán was a Panamanian diplomat who served as consul in Calcutta and as first secretary at the embassy in Mexico; he also taught literature at the National Institute of Panama and theater at the University of Panama. He directed a monthly literary publication, *Biblioteca selecta,* dealing mostly with Panamanian authors, although there was some participation by other Latin American authors. He also served as the director of the National Department of Culture of the Ministry of Education in Panama.

Rogelio Sinán began his literary career writing poetry. His earlier work reflects the vanguardist tendencies in vogue at the time, principally during the 1920s and 1930s. He published several collections of poetry, such as *Onda* (1929; Wave) and *Semana santa en la niebla* (1944; Holy Week in the Mist). From poetry Sinán shifted to short stories. *La*

Rogelio Sinán

boina roja (1954; The Red Beret), which won the Inter-American Short Story Prize presented by the Mexican newspaper *El Nacional,* reflects an ambiguous world of fantasy. In addition to poetry and short stories, however, Sinán has produced two notable novels: *Plenilunio* (1947; Full Moon) and *La isla mágica* (1979; The Magical Island). Each of these novels, as well as *Semana santa en la niebla,* won the Ricardo Miró National Literature Prize, the most prestigious literary prize presented in Panama. *La isla mágica,* Sinán's most highly acclaimed novel, is heavily influenced by **magical realist** style. Sinán has also produced children's theater, often betraying the influence of Luigi Pirandello.

REFERENCE:

Enrique Jaramillo Levi and others, *El mago de la isla: Reflexiones críticas en torno a la obra literaria de Rogelio Sinán* (Panama: Instituto Nacional de Cultura, 1992).

— M.T.

DAVID ALFARO SIQUEIROS

One of the leading and most artistically experimental members of Mexican **Muralism,** David Alfaro Siqueiros (1896–1974) was so committed to his political activities that they often took precedence over his work as an artist. He studied at the Escuela Nacional de Bellas Artes (National School of Fine Arts), where he met **Dr. Atl** (Gerardo Murillo), an early proponent of public murals. Siqueiros participated in the student strike of 1911 and later attended the newly established Escuela de Pintura al Aire Libre Barbizón (Barbizon Open-Air School of Painting) at Santa Anita (see **Impressionism**), where experimentation with impressionist techniques helped him become free of the academic tradition and more interested in indigenist themes. During the **Mexican Revolution** Siqueiros joined the Constitutionalist army and became the only major muralist who directly participated in the revolution. He also worked for Dr. Atl, who — as Venustiano Carranza's chief of propaganda — published the pro-Carranza newspaper *La Vanguardia,* with the collaboration of Siqueiros, **Francisco Goitia,** and **José Clemente Orozco.** In 1919 Siqueiros traveled to Europe with a state grant and met **Diego Rivera** in Paris. In 1921 he lived in Barcelona, where he edited the magazine *Vida Americana,* whose only issue included a manifesto: "Tres llamamientos de orientación actual a los pintores y escultores de la nueva generación americana" (Three Calls to the New Generation of American Painters and Sculptors for a Timely Orientation). In this influential document he proposed the creation of a public art movement which would synthesize **Indigenism,** universal values, and avant-garde forms and materials. During this early period he worked in a style related to Futurism and German New Objectivity, as seen in his drawing *Retrato de William Kennedy* (1920; Portrait of William Kennedy).

At the insistence of the then-minister of education, **José Vasconcelos,** Siqueiros returned from Europe in 1922 and joined the mural project already under way at the Escuela Nacional Preparatoria (National Preparatory School). He worked on a series of allegorical murals, such as *Los elementos* (1922–1923; The Elements), influenced by Vasconcelos's classical ideals and the emphasis on muscular figures of Italian Renaissance artist Michelangelo. Soon Rivera and Siqueiros rose to the leadership of the mural movement, the Mexican intelligentsia, and the Mexican Communist Party. Muralists joined the Sindicato de Obreros Técnicos, Pintores y Escultores (Union of Technical Workers, Painters, and Sculptors), which Siqueiros helped organize. Muralists began to reflect their increasing involvement in national politics in their works, such as Siqueiros's fresco *Entierro de un*

David Alfaro Siqueiros (photograph by Manuel Alvarez Bravo)

mártir obrero (1923–1924; Burial of a Martyred Worker), inspired by the execution of a liberal Yucatán governor named Felipe Carrillo Puerto by Huerta's reactionaries. In a simplified realism the mural features the communist symbols of hammer and sickle together with Aztec masklike faces. In 1924 riots broke out at the Preparatoria in reaction to the radical nature of Orozco's and Siqueiros's art; the result was the mutilation of some of their murals and the dismissal of all muralists except Rivera.

In the following years Siqueiros concentrated on politics, and in 1930 he was confined to the village of Taxco as punishment for his political activities. There he returned to depicting social and indigenist themes with a simplified, monumental treatment of form, as in *Madre campesina* (1930; Peasant Mother). In 1932 he went into exile in Los Angeles, where he produced his formally ambitious but thematically controversial mural *Tropical America* (1932, later whitewashed over) for the Plaza Art Center. This work featured an Indian crucified under the United States eagle in a jungle setting with preconquest ruins, all of which amounted to a critical statement against American imperialism; the following year Siqueiros was deported from the United States. He trav-

eled to Argentina, where he met Antonio Berni and Lino Eneas Spilimbergo, with whom he collaborated in an experimental mural at the private residence of Natalio Botana.

In 1936 Siqueiros settled in New York and founded the Siqueiros Experimental Workshop, attended by avant-garde artists such as Jackson Pollock, who was also interested in synthesizing radical content with unorthodox techniques and materials. Siqueiros used industrial pigments, spray paint, and the technique of dripping in semiabstract compositions such as *Birth of Fascism* (1936) and *Echo of a Scream* (1937). His political commitment moved him to participate in the Spanish Civil War until 1939, when he returned to Mexico and began working on his monumental *Retrato de la burguesía* (1939–1940; Portrait of the Bourgeoisie). In a cinematic way, this remarkable and formally complex mural at the Sindicato de Electricistas Mexicanos (1939; Mexican Electricians' Union) reflects an epic battle between imperialist capitalism and revolutionary socialism.

Implicated in an assassination attempt on Leon Trotsky, who was then living in Mexico, Siqueiros was forced once more into exile. He went to Chile, where he painted murals at Chillán, and also traveled to Cuba, Peru, Ecuador, and Panama. Back in Mexico once more, he was imprisoned in 1960, and the artists of **La Ruptura Generation** publicly demanded his release even though they condemned the propagandistic nature of his art. Released in 1964, Siqueiros received the government's National Prize in 1966. Among Siqueiros's last murals was one of his most formally ambitious and monumental works, the *Marcha de la humanidad en Latinoamérica* (March of Humanity in Latin America), later installed at the Poliforum Cultural (1966–1973; Cultural Polyforum).

REFERENCES:

Laurance P. Hurlburt, *The Mexican Muralists in the United States* (Albuquerque: University of New Mexico Press, 1989);

Antonio Rodríguez, *Siqueiros* (Mexico City: Fondo de Cultura Económica, 1974).

—F.B.N.

HUMBERTO SOLÁS

The Cuban film director Humberto Solás (1942–   ) joined the Instituto Cubano de Arte e Industria Cinematográficas (**Cuban Film Institute**), or ICAIC, in 1959, the year of its founding. He had begun studying architecture in 1957 but interrupted his studies to participate in the insurrectionary movement against the government of Fulgencio Batista, as a member of a group known as Acción y Sabotaje (Action and Sabotage). Solás's early films, such as *Minerva traduce el mar* (1962; Minerva Translates the Sea), are highly experimental and somewhat hermetic. In 1964 he went to Europe, spending most of his time in Italy, where he came under the influence of Italian **neorealism.** He was impressed by the early films of Luchino Visconti, such as *La terra trema* (1948; The Earthquake) and *Ossessione* (1942; Obsessions). Between 1968 and 1970 Solás's interest in European cinema was supplanted by an interest in the Cinema Nôvo of Brazil. His medium-length feature *Manuela* (1966) was based on the guerrilla struggle that led to the Cuban Revolution of 1959. During the filming Solás used improvisation in his work with the actors, only two of whom were professionals. *Manuela* was quite successful in Cuban circles and hinted at the talent Solás would unleash in his three-part *Lucía* (1968), one of the masterpieces of Latin American filmmaking.

   Lucía focuses on the lives of three women with the same name who exemplify the social tensions of three different times in Cuba. The first Lucía is an aristocrat living in 1895, during the struggle for Cuban independence from Spain (*Lucía 1895*); the second is a factory worker married to a revolutionary in 1933 during the dictatorship of Gerardo Machado (*Lucía 1933*); and the third, who lives in **Fidel Castro**'s Cuba, is a courageous, newly married peasant whose husband considers her his property (*Lucía 1959*). The casts of *Lucía 1933* and *Lucía 1959* were a mixture of professional and nonprofessional actors, but the cast of *Lucía 1895* was made up of highly professional actors and actresses, such as Raquel Revuelta, a theater-company director. Solás chose women as the subject of his film because, he has argued, "women are traditionally the number one victims in all social confrontations." Therefore, he adds, "The woman's role always lays bare the contradictions of a period and makes them explicit." Though social contexts may have changed over the years, women's struggle to establish independence from male domination continues. Yet, Solás adds, "*Lucía* is not a film about women; it's a film about society."

   Solás's *Un día de noviembre* (1972; A Day in November), in which an inexperienced actor (a university professor) played the leading role, was not as successful. In its experimentation with time and space the medium-length *Simparele* (1974), which Solás has called an "interpretative documentary about the people's struggle in Haiti," serves as a sort of prelude to his *Cantata de Chile* (1975), in which he combines political commentary with popular art forms. *Cecilia* (1982), his ambitious adaptation of the Cuban novel *Cecilia Valdés* (1882) by Cirilo Villaverde, met with a

A scene from *Lucía 1959* (1968), directed by Humberto Solás

lukewarm reception in Cuba and abroad. In Solás's view filmmaking should present a revolutionary ideology, with an eye to transforming reality; by avoiding defeatism, the revolutionary film should educate the people about how to change society.

REFERENCES:

Julianne Burton, ed., *Cinema and Social Change in Latin America: Conversations with Filmmakers* (Austin: University of Texas Press, 1986);

John King, *Magical Reels: A History of Cinema in Latin America* (London: Verso, 1990).

— S.M.H.

SON

Son simply means a sound with artistic merit, one that is agreeable to the ear. In musical terminology son refers to a variety of vernacular song/dance genres that reflect cultural characteristics particular to different regions or cultural groups. These characteristics are expressed musically through melodic, rhythmic, and harmonic configurations as well as through the selection of accompanying instruments.

   In the Cuban context *son* actually refers to several hybrid types; among them are Afro-son, guajira-son, **son montuno**, and son-pregón, all of which demonstrate prominent influences from African, Spanish, and native Creole sources. The basis of the Cuban son is found in the rhythmic progression, a two-measure pattern in duple meter that influences melodic and harmonic movement. Mauleón explains that it "consists of a 'strong' measure containing three notes (also called the tresillo [triplet]) and a 'weak' measure containing two notes." In musical notation this configuration amounts to an unequal triplet in the first measure followed by a two-note syncopated figure in the second measure. When syncopation is extended to accompanying parts, a complex rhythmic fabric is woven from the contrasts.

The son chapín, or son guatemalteco, from Guatemala, however, developed with characteristics inherited from European ballroom dances, practically devoid of African influence. The Mexican sonecitos regionales (regional sones) exhibit as much or more variety than does the son in the Caribbean. The son jorocho (rough, brusque), from the Veracruz region, reflects influences from Mexican Indians, Africans, and mestizos. Its tempo is quite fast, and it is sung in a very high vocal register. It is normally accompanied by the arpa jarocha (a diatonic harp), a requinto (a small four-stringed guitar), and a **jarana** jarocha, but a violin may occasionally be substituted for the requinto. The son jaliscience (from Jalisco) and the son huasteco (from the Huastecan mountain region) both feature sesquialtera, a cross-rhythm produced by the accented combination of 6/8 and 3/4 meters. Both also feature high vocal registers for the singer, but the huasteco is slower than the jaliscience and is accompanied by violin, jarana, and quinta (an eight-stringed low-pitched guitar) rather than harp, requinto, and jarana.

The common characteristic of the son, regardless of geographic location or ethnic identity, is its prominent role and acceptance in popular and folk culture. In addition to an instrumental introduction, the son typically features two sections: the first consists of rhymed couplets sung by a soloist; the second, referred to in the Caribbean as the montuno, is a responsorial refrain in which solo improvisations are answered by a coro, or group, in the style of the African call-and-response format. The textual topics may be picaresque, rude, or satiric.

REFERENCES:

José Blanco Aguilar, *Ochenta años del son y los soneros en el Caribe* (Caracas: Fondo Editorial Tropykos, 1992);

Rebeca Mauleón, *Salsa: Guidebook for Piano & Ensemble* (Petaluma, Cal.: Sher Music, 1993);

Steven Loza, "From Veracruz to Los Angeles: The Reinterpretation of the *Son jarocho*," *Latin American Music Review*, 13, no. 2 (Fall/Winter 1992): 179–194;

Gabriel Saldivar, *Historia de la música en Mexico* (Mexico City: Departamento de Bellas Artes, 1934).

— R.L.S.

SON MONTUNO

The son montuno is a genre derived from the Afro-Cuban **son** tradition, one that eventually became a standard in the **salsa** repertoire. It consists of two es-

sential structural elements: a verse section of composed melody or lyrics and a montuno section in which solo improvisation alternates with a choral/instrumental refrain in call-and-response format. The performance medium may be either vocal or instrumental. In the vocal version a soloist sings the verse accompanied by instruments, while in the montuno section a chorus of singers provides a refrain in alternation with the soloist's improvisations. In the instrumental version the composed melody is typically played by an instrumental soloist, and in the montuno section an instrumental refrain alternates with the improvisations of one or more instrumental soloists. To these basic structural units additional features may be added, such as an instrumental introduction, bridges between different sections, a closing section (coda), and a **mambo** section. If a mambo section is included, it usually presents new melodic and harmonic material, featuring trumpets and/or trombones and an enlivened rhythm.

The entire son montuno is set in 2/4 meter, but the different sections feature variations in the rhythmic scheme. Sectional rhythmic variations are reinforced by changing the percussion instruments employed. For example, the **bongos** and the bongo rhythmic pattern played in the song/verse section are replaced in the montuno section by cowbells, with a different rhythm pattern.

The precise origin of the Cuban son is unclear. It appears to have become popular in the nineteenth century among rural blacks in eastern Cuba. The early son ensemble consisted of guitars, percussion, singers, and a typical Cuban folk instrument, the **tres**. Upon its arrival in Havana in the early twentieth century, the early son ensemble was expanded to a sextet by the addition of string bass and a selection of additional percussion instruments (bongos, **maracas**, claves, **güiro**, **marímbula**). The septet ensemble, featuring the addition of a trumpet, also became popular in Havana. In the 1930s Arsenio Rodríguez added two more trumpets and a piano to the ensemble, which became known as the son conjunto. The son and the son montuno eventually made their way to New York, where emigrants from Cuba and Puerto Rico began to bring in the instrumentation of North American jazz bands.

REFERENCES:

Jesús Blanco, *80 años del son y soneros en el Caribe* (Caracas: Fondo Editorial Tropykos, 1992);

Charley Gerard and Marty Sheller, *Salsa! The Rhythm of Latin Music* (Crown Point, Ind.: White Cliffs Media, 1989);

Rebeca Mauleón, *Salsa: Guidebook for Piano and Ensemble* (Petaluma, Cal.: Sher Music, 1993);

Helio Orovio, *Diccionario de la música cubana: Biográfico y técnico* (Havana: Editorial Letras Cubanas, 1992).

— R.L.S.

Roberto Sosa

The Honduran poet Roberto Sosa (1930–) is a controversial figure in his country. Born in Yoro, Sosa comes from an impoverished family. His father died of blue lung disease from working as a fumigator on a Standard Fruit banana plantation. As a child of five or six Sosa resorted to selling bread on trains to help his family survive financially. His mother taught him how to read and write; however, he was also able to attend school for a period. Sosa's most formative reading was of works by Giovanni Papini. He also read many works by European philosophers and fiction writers such as Friedrich Nietzsche, Arthur Schopenhauer, Johann Wolfgang von Goethe, and Franz Kafka. Sosa held several prestigious positions, including the editorship of the magazine *Presente* (a review of Central American art and literature), the presidency of the Honduran Journalists' Union, and membership in the Honduran Academy of Letters. He also taught literature at the National Autonomous University of Honduras.

Sosa's literature is characterized by clarity of language and extreme social commitment. His earlier works include *Caligramas* (1959; Calligrams), *Muros* (1966; Walls) and *Mar interior* (1967; The Sea Inside), winner of the Juan Ramón Molinas Award in 1967 in Honduras. His later works became much more politically edged. *Los pobres* (1969; The Poor) was recognized in Spain with the awarding of the Adonais prize. *El mundo para todos dividido* (1971; A World Shared by All), for which he was awarded a **Casa de las Américas Prize** in 1971, is Sosa's key work, attacking Honduras as a class-ridden society. Because of this poetry collection Sosa was considered dangerously anti-militarist at home. His books were banned during the U.S. occupation beginning in 1984, which coincided with the U.S.–led Contra war against Nicaragua; he also lost his university position and received several death threats. Nevertheless, he is popularly regarded as a powerful voice of truth in Honduras.

REFERENCE:

Roberto Sosa, *The Difficult Days,* translated by Jim Lindsey (Princeton: Princeton University Press, 1983).

— M.T.

Surrealist Art

Surrealism in the art of Latin America did not develop as a unified or cohesive movement but rather as a series of isolated groups and artists who either used otherworldly images in their work for the purpose of constructing invented realities or followed the more characteristically Surrealist exploration of the unconscious through dream imagery and automatist techniques. During the 1940s there were important and complex developments in Mexico, where two different groups of artists were associated with Surrealism. One group included artists working independently, such as the Mexicans **Lola Alvarez Bravo, Mario Alvarez Bravo, María Izquierdo, Frida Kahlo,** Agustín Lazo, Guillermo Mesa, Roberto Montenegro, Antonio Ruiz, and the Guatemalan **Carlos Mérida.** The other group was formed by artists who had direct connections with Surrealism, including the exiled Europeans **Leonora Carrington,** José Horna, Kati Horna, Wolfgang Paalen, Alice Rahon, and **Remedios Varo;** the Peruvian César Moro (also a writer); and the Mexican Gunther Gerzso. Many of them arrived in Mexico in the late 1930s and early 1940s and eventually settled there.

European Surrealists had been interested in Mexico since the 1920s; their leader, André Breton, called Mexico the Surrealist country par excellence. In 1936 the French poet Antonin Artaud visited Mexico and claimed Izquierdo's art for Surrealism. Similarly, Breton traveled to Mexico in 1938 and declared Kahlo a Surrealist. Like many of the other artists mentioned above, both Izquierdo and Kahlo had developed their personal styles independently, which makes the use of the Surrealist label problematic. While their art often featured odd visual juxtapositions, an emphasis on fantasy, and dreamlike imagery, they did not call themselves Surrealists, even though most of them exhibited their work at the Exposición internacional del surrealismo (International Exhibition of Surrealism), organized by Moro, Paalen, and Breton in Mexico City in 1940.

Carrington and her Mexican husband, Renato LeDuc, arrived in Mexico City in 1942 and lived close to Remedios Varo and her husband, the surrealist poet Benjamín Péret. There were many other European artists living in Mexico at the time (including Luis Buñuel, Enrique "Chiqui" Weisz, Paalen, Rahon, Gerzso, and José and Kati Horna), but they tended to keep apart from their Mexican counterparts. In 1944 they collaborated on Paalen's magazine *Dyn.* In spite of the personal success of many of these artists during the 1950s, Surrealism was never a dominant style in Mexico.

In the Caribbean the Cuban **Wifredo Lam** became one of the main forces in the second generation of Surrealists. During the 1940s Lam formulated a masterly and personal synthesis of African and Cuban elements with modern styles, including Cubism and Surrealism. In 1940 he befriended several Surrealists, including Breton and Max Ernst, as they awaited passage from Marseilles to the Americas during World War II. Lam traveled to Martinique in the company of Breton and the anthropologist Claude Lévi-Strauss. There

Cover, with a photograph by Manuel Alvarez Bravo, for the catalogue of the international exhibition of Surrealist art held in Mexico City in 1940

REFERENCES:

Dawn Ades, *Art in Latin America: The Modern Era, 1820–1980* (New Haven & London: Yale University Press, 1989);

Dore Ashton, "Surrealism and Latin America," in *Latin American Artists of the Twentieth Century,* edited by Waldo Rasmussen, Fatima Bercht, and Elizabeth Ferrer (New York: Museum of Modern Art, 1993);

El surrealismo entre viejo y nuevo mundo (Madrid: Comisión Nacional Quinto Centenario, Fundación Cultural Mapfre Vida, 1989).

— F.B.N.

SYMBOLIST ART

Symbolist art was among the first modern styles adopted in Latin America. At the beginning of the twentieth century it became popular in several countries, including Brazil, Ecuador, Argentina, and especially Mexico. In Europe Symbolist art was influenced by Romanticism and was developed at the turn of the century by the French artists Gustave Moreau and Pierre Puvis de Chavannes, the Catalan Antoni Gaudí i Cornet, and the Uruguayan Joaquín Torres-García. This type of art also had many parallels in the poetry of the Nicaraguan **Rubén Darío** and the Cuban **José Martí** as well as the Symbolist poetry of the Frenchmen Arthur Rimbaud and Charles Baudelaire. During the last years of Porfirio Díaz's dictatorship, a group of Mexican authors and artists became associated with the publications *Revista moderna* (1897–1905) and *Savia moderna.* The group included writers interested in Spanish-American **Modernism,** such as Jesús Valenzuela, **Alfonso Reyes, Ramón López Velarde, José de Vasconcelos,** and Juan José Tablada, as well as the Symbolist artists **Saturnino Herrán,** Julio Ruelas, and Roberto Montenegro. These artists rejected the realism of academic art and proposed a new art based on subjectivity, fantasy, and imagination. Probably, they were also influenced by the emphasis on classical themes in **Vasconcelos**'s writings. In his painting *La iniciación de Don Jesús Luján a la Revista moderna* (1904; The Initiation of Don Jesús Luján to the *Revista moderna*), Ruelas presents the heads of the members of this avant-garde group attached to the bodies of different animals, including a satyr and centaurs. Similarly, Herrán used stylized classical proportions in his languid representations of indigenous peoples, such as *Nuestros dioses* (1918; Our Gods).

Symbolist art influenced the beginning of **Muralism** through Vasconcelos's writings, which inspired **Diego Rivera**'s first mural, *La creación* (1922; Creation), featuring symbolic representations of the virtues and liberal arts. Montenegro's symbolist mural *El cuento de Aladino* (1925; The Tale of Aladdin) at the

they met Eugenio F. Granell, a Spanish Surrealist artist who settled in Puerto Rico after a period in Guatemala, where he befriended Carlos Mérida. Breton and Lam were to form a lasting friendship and later visit Haiti together in 1945. Lam's illustrations for Breton's *Fata Morgana* (1940) include fantastic horned and masked beings that reveal his interest in Surrealism's use of automatist drawing, dreamlike configurations, archetypal symbols, and metamorphic imagery.

Later contemporary artists connected with Surrealism include the Nicaraguan **Rodolfo Abularach,** who from the 1960s worked with close-up images of the eye, understood as mandala-like archetypes with cosmic connotations, and **Alberto Gironella,** who participated in the **Nueva Presencia** group.

Centro Escolar Benito Juárez features a fantastic theme.

REFERENCE:

Ida Rodríguez Prampolini, *El surrealismo y el arte fantástico de México* (Mexico City: Universidad Nacional Autónoma de México, 1969).

—F.B.N.

SYMPHONY ORCHESTRAS

Vocal and instrumental music figured prominently in Mexico, Central America, and the Hispanic Caribbean from the earliest days of Spanish colonialism, but symphonic music did not begin to develop until the nineteenth century. During the colonial period Spanish regimental bands, municipal bands, chamber ensembles, and theater orchestras provided musical entertainment for the general public. Municipal bands are still very much a part of life in Latin America, especially in Central America, where professional musicians play regular, open-air concerts in town plazas. Theater orchestras have been popular since the colonial period to accompany Italian operas, Spanish **zarzuelas**, and other entertainments. An indication of the early interest in theatrical music was demonstrated by the composition in 1701 of the first opera in the New World (Tomás de Torrejón y Velasco's *La púrpura de la rosa*), and by Mexican-born Manuel Zumaya's composition of his first opera in Mexico (*La Parténope*) in 1711.

One of the earliest reports of a symphony orchestra in the New World describes the Sociedad Filarmónica Mexicana, founded in 1824 by José Mariano Elizaga, who reportedly also founded the first conservatory in America the following year (though Pedro de Gante is also known to have founded a school of music in the sixteenth century). Apparently it was easier to begin a symphony orchestra than to maintain one over long periods of time. The first symphony orchestra in El Salvador, for instance, was founded in 1860, and fifteen years later was replaced by a second orchestra, the Sociedad Filarmónica, only to be followed later by the Orquesta Sinfónica Salvadoreña. In some republics the church provided a measure of stability. In the Dominican Republic, for instance, the Cathedral of Santo Domingo organized a chamber orchestra in 1862, later expanded, to play for High Mass, certain holy days, and funerals. By the end of the century Puerto Rico boasted three such orchestras in San Juan. It was not uncommon for musicians to play for both sacred and profane functions, just as some do today. A second event appears to have accompanied each attempt to establish an orchestra: the opening of an academy of music to train future players. However, this pattern was not exclusive to the nineteenth century and has been repeated in the twentieth century.

Despite common histories of intense effort, only a few of the symphony orchestras in Central America have enjoyed economic and political stability in the twentieth century. Civil wars, revolutions, and economic difficulties have interrupted national orchestral traditions in El Salvador, Nicaragua, and Panama; Honduras and Guatemala have managed to maintain national symphony orchestras but have been forced to rely on young talent to preserve them. All of the Central American republics currently focus energies and scarce resources on the development of youth orchestras in an attempt to ensure a less tenuous future for their national ensembles.

Among middle and Central American republics, Mexico and Costa Rica have achieved the greatest stability and progress with their national symphony orchestras. The Orquesta Sinfónica Nacional de México (OSM) was founded in 1928 with **Carlos Chávez** as its first conductor and continues to hold a preeminent position among middle American orchestras. The programs of the OSM have consistently emphasized the values of Mexican music as well as international contemporary music. Costa Rican musicians formed symphony orchestras in 1910 and 1920, but, lacking government support, these orchestras did not survive. In 1941 the Costa Rican government began funding a national orchestra and created a fully professional ensemble with regular annual seasons. Mexico and Costa Rica also invest heavily in youth orchestras as training institutions. Carlos Chávez founded and became the first director of the Mexican Conservatory Orchestra. Costa Rica began its youth orchestra as part of a free music school in 1970, naming Gerald Brown from the United States as its director. The Costa Rican Youth Orchestra has distinguished itself in tours of Europe and the United States and in 1995 produced its first compact disc recording. To stimulate interest in the continuing development of orchestras in middle America, the School of Music of the University of Costa Rica sponsored a successful revival of the Central American Youth Orchestra in 1994 with participants from the various republics.

The history of the formation of orchestras in Cuba resembles that of its Hispanic Caribbean neighbors. The tradition of military and municipal bands was gradually replaced by the sporadic appearance of philharmonic societies, but not until the early twentieth century was any sense of permanency achieved. The Orquesta Sinfónica de la Habana, cofounded by **Ernesto Lecuona** and Gonzalo Roig in 1922, enjoyed early success but ceased to exist in 1940. Among its many guest conductors were **Pablo Casals** and Julián

Carillo. In 1924 Pedro San Juan founded the Orquesta Filarmónica de la Habana, an orchestra that was later conducted by **Amadeo Roldán** and Alberto Bolet, the brother of **Jorge Bolet**. The Filarmónica was closed in 1958 because of difficulties with the Fulgencio Batista dictatorship. Harold Gramatges founded and conducted the Havana Municipal Conservatory Orchestra in 1945 to provide orchestral experience for young players. The Orquesta Sinfónica Nacional was begun by the Cuban revolutionary government in 1960. Its first director was Enrique González, who was assisted and later succeeded by Manuel Duchesne Cuzán. As is the case with practically all symphony orchestras in Mexico, Central America, and the Caribbean, the Cuban orchestra has benefited from the participation of foreign players.

The Sociedad Sinfónica de Santo Domingo was formed in 1932 but for lack of instruments was unable to perform for several years. Petitions to the dictator, Gen. Rafael Trujillo, earned the institution minimal financial support, but without professional musicians there was little progress. In 1941 the name was changed to Orquesta Sinfónica Nacional de Santo Domingo, coinciding with the arrival of many talented musicians who had fled the armed conflict in Europe and provided, albeit temporarily, the nucleus of the new orchestra. Despite much hardship, the orchestra and its musicians survived and progressed, especially after the Trujillo assassination in 1961. The orchestra now plays a heavy schedule of concerts throughout the republic, but a depressed economy deprives it and the national conservatory of needed financial resources. Music academies and cultural centers in cities such as Santiago de los Caballeros and La Vega provide valuable support in the training of musicians.

In 1823 a Sociedad Filarmónica was formed in San Juan, Puerto Rico, by bringing together individual professionals and amateurs and existing orchestral groups. The organization was revived in 1845 and served as a stimulus for similar organizations and music schools. By the end of the nineteenth century major cities such as Ponce and Mayagüez were offering orchestral concerts, and San Juan, the capital city, boasted theater orchestras for opera and zarzuela in addition to the church orchestras. The first fifty years of the United States presence in Puerto Rico witnessed the demise of some local orchestras: the Sociedad de Conciertos, the Orquesta Sinfónica de Puerto Rico, the

Orquesta Filarmónica de Puerto Rico, and others. Various attempts were made to reestablish orchestras following World War II, but the Chamber Orchestra of the University of Puerto Rico, founded in 1956 by Donald Thompson, who became its director, prevailed and became the predecessor of the current Puerto Rico Symphony Orchestra. The Commonwealth Legislature of Puerto Rico founded the Puerto Rico Symphony Orchestra (PRSO) in 1957 and the Puerto Rico Conservatory of Music in 1958. Both became entities of the Casals Festival Corporation, subsidized by the Puerto Rico Industrial Development Corporation. Under the direction of **Pablo Casals**, a series of summer festival concerts was begun in 1957 to promote tourism and industrial development. A large number of musician/teachers, mainly from the United States, were brought to the island to bolster the small Puerto Rican membership. With time, island-based musicians began to protest against the domination by nonresidents of both the Festival Orchestra and the Puerto Rico Symphony Orchestra. Since 1963 several reorganizations and realignments of the PRSO have resulted in a new structure; the PRSO is now responsible to the Corporation for the Musical Arts. The results have been positive: the PRSO has been significantly enlarged and now plays a full season (forty-four weeks). The ratio of island residents to nonresidents is much improved. More compositions by Puerto Rican composers are programmed, and the PRSO is now the official resident orchestra for the annual Puerto Rico Casals Festival.

REFERENCES:

Charles T. Brown, "Music in Costa Rica," in *Inter American Music Bulletin*, no. 75/76 (1970);

Gilbert Chase, *A Guide to Music of Latin America* (Washington, D.C.: Joint Publication of the Pan American Union, General Secretariat, Organization of American States, 1958);

J. M. Coopersmith, *Music and Musicians of the Dominican Republic* (Washington, D.C.: Division of Music and Visual Arts, Department of Cultural Affairs, Pan American Union, 1949);

Barbara Aylor March, "Latin American Music Today," in *Inter American Music Bulletin*, no. 32 (1961);

Donald Thompson, "Puerto Rico Symphony Orchestra," in *Symphony Orchestras of the United States: Selected Profiles*, edited by Robert R. Craven (New York: Greenwood Press, 1986);

Kernan Turner, "Musical Revolution in Costa Rica," in *Inter American Music Bulletin*, no. 84 (1972).

—R.L.S.

T

Rufino Tamayo

Mexican artist Rufino Tamayo (1899–1991) synthesized modern and pre-Columbian sources in a non-narrative manner that provided an alternative to **Muralism.** Of Zapotec Indian ancestry, Tamayo was born in Oaxaca and later moved to Mexico City, where he attended the Instituto Nacional de Bellas Artes (National Institute of Fine Arts) from 1917 to 1921. He lived in New York during the 1920s and from 1936 until 1949, when he resided in Paris. He returned to Mexico in 1964.

Tamayo's paintings from the early stage in his career were influenced by a group of poets known as the **Contemporáneos.** They strove to remove anecdotal elements from Mexican poetry, just as Tamayo removed narrative elements from his art. He rarely incorporated Mesoamerican figures and symbols directly into his paintings, but the aesthetic of pre-Columbian art, which emphasized spatial definition by means of line and color, greatly influenced his art. Early in his career Tamayo was attacked by several of his compatriots, including **Diego Rivera** and **David Alfaro Siqueiros,** for not advancing the interests of the School of Mexico, namely **Indigenism** and Muralism. Although Tamayo was not apolitical — he associated with the leftist Liga de Escritores y Artistas Revolucionarios (League of Revolutionary Painters and Artists) at various stages in his career — he strongly rejected the political agenda of Muralism and the use of art as propaganda. In his works Tamayo evoked universal themes that generally transcended national boundaries. Even his paintings *Homenaje a Juárez* (1932; Homage to Juárez) and *Homenaje a Zapata* (1935; Homage to Zapata) represent those national heroes as painted sculpture busts rather than through direct portraiture. They are monuments that offer no overt interpretation of history beyond their mere existence.

In spite of his criticism of mural painting, Tamayo painted several murals himself at the Conservatorio Nacional de Música (1933; National Music Conservatory) and others in Massachusetts at Smith College (1943), in Mexico City at Museo Nacional de Antropología (1964; National Museum of Anthropology), and in the Mexican Pavilion at Expo '67 in Montreal.

Tamayo explored various media, including murals, printmaking, and sculpture, but his primary means of expression throughout his career remained oil on canvas. His canvases during the 1930s and 1940s continued to portray readily recognizable Mexican themes. *Vendedoras de frutas* (1938; Fruit Vendors) depicts two women in traditional white peasant costume standing behind a basket of fruit. Such a depiction of typical Mexican fruit was not only an autobiographical and cultural expression but also a vehicle for experimenting with bright colors within formally constructed compositions. During the 1940s Tamayo also produced an important series of expressionistic works, including images of animals, such as *Animales* (1941; Animals) and *Muchacha atacada por un extraño pájaro* (1947; Girl Attacked by a Strange Bird), which critics suggest express wartime concerns.

Influenced by art circles in New York and Europe, Tamayo's subject matter became increasingly abstract during the 1940s, 1950s, and 1960s as he achieved an even fuller definition of form by means of color alone. Such abstraction can be seen in *Sandías* (1968; Watermelons), in which the cross sections of melons are recognizable only by the layered colors of green skin, white rind, and red flesh. While Tamayo's mature style reveals his interest in the abstract expressionist treatment of color and texture, he never abandoned subject matter. Many of his works from the 1970s, such as *La playa* (1974; The Beach) or *El reloj olvidado*

Rufino Tamayo (center) and President José López Portillo (right) at the Rufino Tamayo International Museum of Contemporary Art in Mexico City

(1975; The Forgotten Clock), also visually explore the mysteries of time and space. In the 1980s, works such as *Torso rojo* (1981; Red Torso) reincorporated the subject into recognizable interior space. During this decade pastel colors took on a prominent role, often replacing the fully saturated colors long associated with Tamayo's art.

In addition to his own art, Tamayo left another great legacy by donating a museum of pre-Columbian art to the city of Oaxaca. Many consider him the first in the series of artists from the so-called School of Oaxaca, which includes **Francisco Toledo** and Rodolfo Nieto. In 1981 a museum in Tamayo's honor was opened in Mexico City.

REFERENCE:
Rufino Tamayo, *Rufino Tamayo: 70 años de creación* (Mexico City: Museo de Arte Contemporáneo Internacional Rufino Tamayo, Instituto Nacional de Bellas Artes, 1987).

— C.M.

TAMBORA

The tambora is considered the national instrument of the Dominican Republic because of its distinctive role in the performance of the **merengue.** It not only provides the basic rhythmic patterns of the merengue but

is also featured as a solo instrument. Folk tamboras are constructed from a section of hollowed tree trunk with a male goatskin on one end and a female goatskin on the other. The lower-pitched male side is played with the fingers of one hand, and the female-skin side is played with a short stick (*palito*). The sexual implications of this performance practice are obvious. The skins are held in place with bands (*aros*) made of vine and are tied to each other in a manner that permits tightening for higher-pitched tuning.

REFERENCE:
Bernarda Jorge, *La música dominicana: Siglos XIX–XX* (Santo Domingo: Publicaciones de la Universidad Autónoma de Santo Domingo, 1982).

— R.L.S.

TAMBORITO

Popularly known as the national dance of Panama, the tamborito is a courtship dance in which the men leap, crouch, and throw their hats in the direction of the women, who remain erect and dignified, swaying slightly, manipulating their skirts, and executing delicate walking or running steps. The music employs a call-and-response song format, drumming, dancing, and hand clapping. Its rhythms and structure reveal the

Dancers performing the tamborito, the national dance of Panama (photograph by George Archer)

strong African heritage of the Atlantic coastal region. The dance has five sections: la invitación (the invitation), el paseo (promenade), los tres golpes (three drumbeats), la vuelta (the circle), and el corrido. Sung by female voices only, with a syllabic text, the cantadora alante (lead singer) is answered by an unchanging choral refrain. One couple dances at a time inside a large circle formed by other dancing couples. These couples do not embrace, and their choreographies are individually improvised. At one end of the circle are three or four drummers, the singer(s), and other instrumentalists. Syncopated rhythms are reinforced by drums of various sizes played with the hands. If the **tambora** is used, it is played with sticks. The tamborito is in 2/4 meter, and its tempo is accelerated near the end to create an exciting climax.

REFERENCE:

Gerard Béhague, "Latin American Folk Music," in *Folk and Traditional Music of the Western Continents,* by Bruno Nettl (Englewood Cliffs, N.J.: Prentice-Hall, 1990).

— R.L.S. & J.M.H.

TELENOVELAS

Telenovelas, or television soap operas, are immensely popular and widely distributed throughout Latin America. Usually set in homes that could be anywhere in Latin America, they are paradigms of urban popular culture in the region, and though they often convey sociopolitical messages, telenovelas tend to legitimize the status quo rather than question it.

The first Latin American telenovela, *El derecho de nacer* (The Birthright), started in 1948 as a radio serial in Cuba and began appearing on Mexican television in the mid 1960s. Like many telenovelas, it is built around a protagonist searching for her true parents. Playing a major part in the intrigue is the struggle against a world of appearances and evil actions that prevents true identity from being recognized. During the 1960s this telenovela was extremely popular in Mexico and in other parts of Spanish America, such as Puerto Rico, Central America, and Peru. One of the most successful telenovelas was *Simplemente María,* a 1960s Peruvian telenovela about the upward mobility of the poor, which ran for more than four hundred

Alma Muriel as Bárbara, a teacher from humble origins, and
Juan Paláez as the upper-class Jorge in *Ven conmigo*
(Come with Me), a Mexican telenovela that stresses the
importance of literacy

episodes, making it the longest-running Latin American soap opera. A highly popular **fotonovela** was created to accompany the soap.

Mexico has exported many telenovelas to the
whole Spanish-speaking world. Its formulas have been
successfully imitated by Argentina, which ranks third
in production of telenovelas, after Mexico and Brazil.
Mexican soap operas normally focus on the trials and
tribulations of the rich. Interviewed for a British television program about their attitude to telenovelas, a
group of women in Mexico City said they preferred to
watch the lives of rich people because they have fewer
problems. *La vuelta extraña de Diana Salazar* (1988;
The Strange Return of Diana Salazar) and *Cuna de
lobos* (Cradle of Wolves), both produced by **Televisa,**
the Mexican national television monopoly, give an indication of the basic ingredients of the Mexican

telenovela. The first has as its plot the reincarnation in
the late twentieth century of a seventeenth-century
aristocratic woman, burned at the stake by the Inquisition as a witch. It includes the customary elements of
good and evil, plus a love story, but it also has the
special powers of the heroine transferred to computers,
thereby combining the erotics of melodrama with the
modern fascination with information technology. In
Cuna de lobos the heroine is the incarnation of evil;
she wears a black patch over one eye and ruthlessly
murders those who get in her way, in one instance by
putting sugar in an airplane engine. The director of
Cuna de lobos commented that people liked his soap
opera because, as a result of the contemporary crisis in
Latin America, people identified themselves with evil,
not with good. It was watched by the largest audience
ever known for a telenovela: forty million people, that
is, more than half the population of Mexico. When the

Cover for the testimonial narrative of a Cuban who was born into slavery and lived to see the Cuban Revolution of 1959

last episode was shown, Mexico City came to a standstill; many people refused to go to work. Televisa continues to produce soap operas at a rapid pace. The visitor to Mexico cannot fail to be struck by the number of telenovelas broadcast every day on television. Apart from the telenovelas on the various regular channels, there is also a channel that is dedicated exclusively to showing soap operas all day long.

REFERENCES:

Azriel Bibliowicz, "Be Happy Because Your Father Isn't Your Father: An Analysis of Colombian *Telenovelas*," *Journal of Popular Culture,* 14 (Winter 1980): 476–485;

William Rowe and Vivian Schelling, *Memory and Modernity: Popular Culture in Latin America* (London: Verso, 1991).

— S.M.H.

TELEVISA

One of the success stories of Latin American broadcasting is that of the Mexican network Televisa, one of the world's largest conglomerates. Dominating broadcasting in Mexico, Televisa is the primary source of news for most Mexicans and is the largest television producer in the Spanish-speaking world, producing about twenty-one million hours of programming worldwide each year. Televisa transmits about four hundred hours of television a week, more than any other company in the world. Much of the growth and success of Televisa stems from its close connection with the ruling political party, the Partido Revolucionario Institucional (Institutional Revolutionary Party), or PRI. Televisa's reputation has sometimes been damaged as a result; during the 1988 presidential election, for example, Televisa refrained from reporting campaign irregularities involving the PRI. It displayed less bias, however, during its coverage of the 1994 presidential election, in which Ernesto Zedillo came to power. Televisa's Univisión television-programming network has been broadcasting programs to Spanish-speaking audiences in the United States since 1961; it has grown into the fourth largest commercial network in the United States, reaching six million U.S. households, in what has been seen as an example of "reverse media imperialism."

REFERENCE:

Michael B. Salwen and Bruce Garrison, *Latin American Journalism* (Hillsdale, N.J.: Lawrence Erlbaum, 1991).

— S.M.H.

TESTIMONIAL NARRATIVE

Me llamo Rigoberta Menchú (1983; translated as *I, Rigoberta Menchú*), the personal story of a Guatemalan peasant (see **Rigoberta Menchú**) who went on to win a Nobel Prize for peace, is probably the most famous example of testimonial narrative. As that book's title suggests, the idea of bearing witness is at the heart of testimonial narrative. In Spanish this genre is called simply *testimonio*. Testimonial narrative was given formal recognition as a genre in 1970, when the **Casa de las Américas** — the main cultural institution of revolutionary Cuba — established a separate category for it in its annual competition. The rules for entries under the testimonial narrative rubric require that such literature document some aspect of Latin American or Caribbean reality, draw directly on that reality, and have appropriate literary merit. In establishing this prize category, the Cubans were giving recognition to a type of writing that had already acquired prominence in the Latin American literary context.

Testimonios generally are accounts "authored" by groups of people on the margins of society, often by people without access to traditional literary forms of expression: the illiterate, for example, or ethnic minorities, revolutionaries, or schizophrenics. The genre is formally characterized by the use of a first-person narrator, whose access to the reader is usually through a third-party scribe. The account given is generally of a significant experience in the narrator's (or narrators') life. Despite the fact that personal experience is at the root of testimonio, it is not simply autobiography or narrative of the Bildungsroman type. Its time span follows a different convention (that of bearing witness to the events recounted), and the interpretation of those events is collective.

Many antecedents of the genre may be found in Latin American culture, including **Ernesto "Che" Guevara**'s account of the Cuban guerrilla war, *Pasajes de la guerra revolucionaria* (1959; translated as *Reminiscences of the Cuban Revolutionary War*), but the first major testimonial narrative is **Miguel Barnet**'s *Biografía de un cimarrón* (1966; translated as *Autobiography of a Runaway Slave*), which transcribes several interviews between a Cuban ethnographer and a former Cuban slave who lived to see **Fidel Castro**'s revolution. Other well-known examples of the genre are Omar Cabezas's *La montaña es algo más que una inmensa estepa verde* (1985; translated as *Fire from the Mountain*) and **Elena Poniatowska**'s *Hasta no verte Jesús mío* (1969; translated as *Until I See You My Jesus*). Texts written by women and providing a gender-inflected view of political injustice and racial violence include *"Si me permiten hablar..."*: *Testimonio de Domitila, una mujer de las minas de Bolivia* (1977; translated as *Let Me Speak! Testimony of Domitila, a Woman of the Bolivian Mines*), by Domitila Barrios de Chungara. The Dirty War in Argentina and the oppressive regime of Gen. Augusto Pinochet in Chile also provided the impetus for many such narratives. An exception to the leftist bent of testimonial narrative is Armando Valladares's *Contra toda esperanza* (1985; translated as *Against All Hope*), an account of the author's experience in a Cuban prison.

Closely related to testimonial narrative is documentary narrative. Documentary narrative, like testimonio, is based on empirical historic events, normally of a political kind; however, unlike testimonio, it involves a conscious artistic re-creation of the events concerned. Examples are the Argentinean novelist and movie director Rodolfo Walsh's *Operación masacre* (1957; translated as *Operation Massacre*); Elena Poniatowska's *La noche de Tlatelolco* (1971; translated as *Massacre in Mexico*), which recounts the mass killing of students demonstrating in Mexico City on 2 October 1968; and the Chilean Hernán Valdés's *Tejas Verdes: diario de un campo de concentración* (1974; Tejas Verdes: Diary of a Concentration Camp), an artistic retelling of the author's imprisonment.

REFERENCES:

John Beverley, "The Margin at the Center: On Testimonio," in *Against Literature* (Minneapolis: University of Minnesota Press, 1993), pp. 69–86;

René Jara and Hernán Vidal, eds., *Testimonio y literatura* (Minneapolis: Institute for the Study of Ideologies and Literature, 1986);

Charles Tatum, "Paraliterature," in *Handbook of Latin American Literature*, edited by David William Foster (New York & London: Garland, 1992), pp. 687–728.

— R.G.M. & P.S.

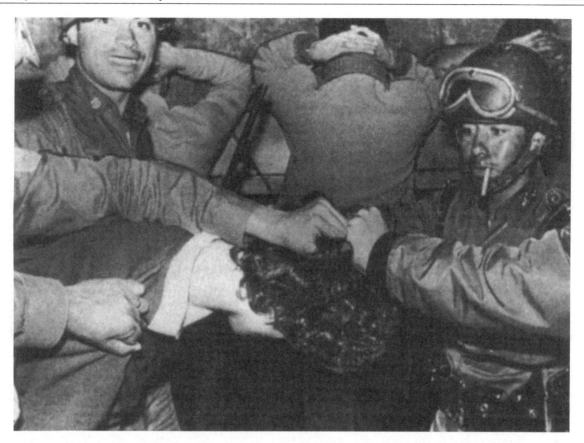

Police cutting a student activist's hair with a bayonet during the 2 October 1968 demonstration at Tlatelolco in Mexico City

THEATER

The theater in Spanish America has not reached the same levels of development as poetry and the novel. Only the largest capital cities (Buenos Aires and Mexico City first, Santiago and Caracas in more recent decades) have been able to support a theater establishment, but even there the predominance of commercial theater and cinema (feeding on foreign imports) has tended to suppress the evolution of a properly national and artistic theater. Actors are often amateurs, and many plays never reach the stage. Frequently playwrights themselves are "amateurs," that is, novelists or poets who make incursions into the theater and who have their works performed thanks, in part at least, to their reputations in the other genres; **Carlos Fuentes** may be cited as an example. The most successful Latin American play of recent times (*Death and the Maiden*) was in fact written by Ariel Dorfman, a Chilean essayist, poet, and novelist.

The individual achievements of several dramatists, however, have been noteworthy. As far as the countries covered in the present volume are concerned, Mexico clearly dominates. **Rodofo Usigli** (1905–1979)

is one of several important Mexican playwrights, a theater professional and critic whose own plays were sometimes seen as subversive and therefore suffered censorship. Henrik Ibsen and George Bernard Shaw are evident influences on Usigli. **Xavier Villaurrutia** (1902–1950), already known as a poet, emerged as a dramatist from the activities of a Mexican government-supported group called Teatro de Orientación (Theater of Orientation), founded by Celestino Gorostiza. Villaurrutia's theater reveals his lifelong obsession with solitude and death. The theater of his respected contemporary, **Salvador Novo** (1904–1974), is above all characterized by innovative modern dramatizations of pre-Hispanic themes of a kind also found in his prose works, but his theater also ranges over other historical periods. Another influential Mexican dramatist is **Emilio Carballido,** whose plays are varied in theme but often deliberately provincial and farcical. **Luisa Josefina Hernández** (1928–), who studied with Usigli, wrote many novels but is best known for her plays, many of which are about women struggling to understand their sexuality, their relationships, and their will or lack of will to overcome obstacles. Carlos Solórzano (1922–), whose plays address issues

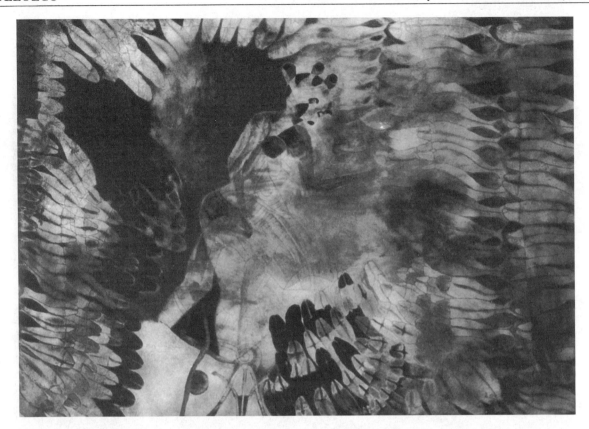

Mujer atacada por peces (1972; Woman Attacked by Fish) by Francisco Toledo (CNCA-INBA, Museo de Arte Contemporáneo Internacional Rufino Tamayo, Mexico City)

of personal freedom, is by far the most distinguished of Guatemalan dramatists, though his influence has been most felt in Mexico, where he has been a theater director and teacher. Cuban playwrights of note are **Virgilio Piñera,** Rolando Ferrer (1925–1976), **José Triana** (1932–), Anton Arrufat (1935–), and Julio Matas (1931–). Two tendencies can be observed in the postrevolutionary Cuban theater: one toward absurd, ritualistic drama and the other toward realistic theater with a message. **René Marqués** (1919–1979) is clearly the most famous of Puerto Rican dramatists; his dramatic style varies, but his themes of social protest often deal with the relationship of Puerto Rico and its people with the United States.

REFERENCES:

Frank Dauster, *Historia del teatro hispanoamericano* (Mexico City: Ediciones de Andrea, 1973);

Marina Gálvez Acero, *El teatro hispanoamericano* (Madrid: Taurus, 1988);

Leon F. Lyday and George W. Woodyard, eds., *Dramatists in Revolt: The New Latin American Theater* (Austin: University of Texas Press, 1975).

                                        — R.G.M & P.S.

Tlatelolco

Tlatelolco, an Aztec name, is the center of an enormous square in Mexico City, La Plaza de las Tres Culturas (Square of the Three Cultures), so called because it has architectural elements that represent the pre-Columbian, colonial, and modern periods. In 1968 it was the site of a demonstration organized by student activists unhappy with government economic and political policies who wanted to express the widespread discontent felt in various sectors of Mexican society. They chose 2 October 1968 as the date for their protest since Mexico was about to host the Olympic Games. The students believed that this event would focus international attention on the issues, thereby putting the Mexican government under pressure to enact reforms. Tens of thousands took part in the protest, which ended in tragedy when hundreds of armed police opened fire on the protesters, who became trapped in the square. Although the exact figure remains unclear, it is estimated that 350 were killed, with many more imprisoned and persecuted. Today, Tlatelolco stands as a symbol of the courage of Mexican students as well as a warning against repressive governments.

The tragedy of Tlatelolco, in part because it fell in the year of student rebellions in other parts of the world (notably Paris) and came in the wake of the Soviet invasion of Czechoslovakia, became a prominent topic in Mexican intellectual circles. An important contribution came from **Octavio Paz,** who in his essay "Posdata" analyzed the similarities between these various events and saw them all as heralding a new international alternative culture in which Mexico would play its part. In the context of Mexican national history the tragedy spoke of a tradition of repressive and centralized forms of control, dating back to before the arrival of the Spaniards. In protest against the authorities' reaction to Tlatelolco, Paz resigned as ambassador to India. A very different, less generalizing, less cohesive yet powerful interpretation of Tlatelolco was offered by **Elena Poniatowska** in her documentary novel *La noche de Tlatelolco* (1971; *Massacre in Mexico*). Another author who both participated in the events of Tlatelolco and wrote about them is José Revueltas. Other younger writers were present at Tlatelolco, and they generally have expressed condemnation of the massacre and disillusionment with progress since the **Mexican Revolution.** Indeed, the events of 1968 seemed to justify talk of a literature of Tlateloco, much as there had been a literature of the revolution. Some of the books published before 1968 and associated with **La Onda** were held in some way to anticipate the tragedy, while many published later clearly stemmed from it, works by authors such as **Carlos Monsiváis,** Luis Spota, Juan García Ponce, and Fernando del Paso.

REFERENCE:

Elena Poniatowska, *Massacre in Mexico* (Columbia: University of Missouri Press, 1971).

— M.E.S.& P.S.

FRANCISCO TOLEDO

One of the most important contemporary Latin American artists, the prolific Francisco Toledo (1940–) has excelled in different media, including printmaking, painting, sculpture, and ceramics. His art, together with that of his fellow Mexican **Rufino Tamayo,** has been considered the foundation of what came to be known as the School of Oaxaca. In the 1950s Toledo began to paint, studied printmaking in Oaxaca with a former student of **Frida Kahlo,** and later attended the graphic workshop at the Instituto Nacional de Bellas Artes (National Institute of Fine Arts) in Mexico City

(see **graphic art**). During the early 1960s Toledo lived in Paris, where he admired the works of Marc Chagall and Paul Klee and met the Mexican writers **Octavio Paz** and **Carlos Fuentes.** He returned to Mexico in 1965 and spent a short period in New York in 1977. He set up printmaking workshops in Cuernavaca and Paris and a painting studio in Oaxaca.

In his art Toledo evokes part of his Zapotec heritage through subjective allusions to the pre-Columbian myths and folk legends of Oaxaca. He deploys a startling menagerie of hybrid creatures — part animal, part human — which survive, change, and procreate in a metamorphic universe many critics have described as an example of **magical realism** and **Surrealism.** In *Mujer atacada por peces* (1972; Woman Attacked by Fish) a floating female figure is surrounded by subtle abstract patterns of translucent forms, suggesting violent and sexual interactions. In other works Toledo creates his hybrid beings through the use of unorthodox materials, as in his collage *Encacahuatado I* (1990; Peanutted I), in which he places an image of a grasshopper, a recurrent symbolic motif in his work, on an abstract field punctuated by peanut shells.

REFERENCE:

Teresa del Conde, "Francisco Toledo," *Art Nexus,* no. 2 (October 1991): 48–52.

— F.B.N.

TRES

Originally a homemade folk instrument from eastern Cuba, the tres is modeled on the guitar but with variant tuning of the strings. It is equipped with three courses of double strings, with each pair tuned in unison or in octaves. This arrangement makes it particularly useful for playing melodic parts. Typically used to accompany the Cuban **son,** it was often used in conjunction with **marímbula, güiro,** and **bongos** in small, informal groups but has also become popular as an instrument in larger ensembles.

REFERENCE:

Helio Orovio, *Diccionario de la música cubana: Biográfico y técnico* (Havana: Editorial Letras Cubanas, 1992).

— R.L.S.

JOSÉ TRIANA

The most distinguished of a group of dramatists who came to prominence at the time of the **Cuban Revolution,** José Triana (1932–) has said that the purpose of his theater is "to catch reality and raise it to a poetic level." Triana, a leading exponent of absurdist drama, attempts to find a meaning behind the often harsh realities of Cuban society, which for him lack coherence and sense. His one-act play *El mayor general hablará de teogonía* (The Major General Will Speak of Theogony), first performed in 1960 but written a few years before while the author was living in Spain, is an adventurous and ingenious parody of Christian myth but also a critique of another mass: the unthinking worshipers of the general, who, contrary to the title, has nothing to say. This play was brushed aside as unimportant by **Virgilio Piñera;** yet Piñera's own *Electra Garrigó* is thought to be the forerunner of another play by Triana, also premiered in 1960: *Medea en el espejo*. Euripides' characters are translated into typical, even stereotypical, Cubans: Medea becomes María in Triana's play, and Jason becomes Julián. Ordinary people in unpromising settings, Triana seems to say, can reach extraordinary heights. The verbal skill Triana deploys in this play is particularly striking.

Triana's best-known play is *La noche de los asesinos* (The Night of the Assassins), written in 1964, first performed at the Festival of Latin American Theater in Havana in 1966, and warmly received abroad thereafter. Set in a run-down basement or attic, the play quickly establishes itself as ambiguous, involving an absurd and disturbing ritual cycle in which the real cannot be separated from the fictitious, nor one "play" from another. A conflict of generations is portrayed, but the play is not a mere domestic drama. Triana is really creating an irrational and violent ritual that has mythical qualities that have been realized before and that are bound to be realized again. His play is a formal design in which, as one of the characters says, "todo está en juego" (everything is in play).

Among other works by Triana are *El incidente cotidiano* (1957; The Everyday Incident), *La casa ardiendo* (1962; The Burning House), and *La muerte del ñeque* (1963; The Death of the Strong Man). Triana is one of many writers who eventually left Cuba for a life in exile.

REFERENCES:

Edwin Twurbe Colón and José Antonio González, *Historia del teatro en la Habana* (Santa Clara, Cuba: Letras Cubanas, 1980);

Frank N. Dauster, "The Theater of José Triana," in *Dramatists in Revolt*, by Leon F. Lyday and George F. Woodyard (Austin: University of Texas Press, 1976), pp. 167–189.

— P.S.

U-V-W

RODOLFO USIGLI

A professional dramatist, Rodolfo Usigli (1905–1979) produced numerous theatrical works. *El apóstol* (The Apostle), his first play, dates from 1931. Usigli wrote one novel with a theatrical title: *Ensayo de un crimen* (1944; Rehearsal of a Crime), which was made into a movie by the renowned Spanish director Luis Buñuel. In addition to his distinguished career as a dramatist, Usigli was a theater critic and historian, producing two important critical works: *México en el teatro* (1932; translated as *Mexico in the Theater*) and *Itinerario de un autor dramático* (1941; The Development of a Dramatic Author). He held various positions as a theater professor and studied at a Yale drama workshop on a scholarship awarded in recognition of his efforts toward establishing a national theater in Mexico.

Usigli's style shows the clear influence of Henrik Ibsen, especially in his most famous play, *El gesticulador* (1937; The Impersonator), which was politically controversial at the time. This breakthrough drama, a satire on provincial Mexican politics, was not publicly performed for ten years. Because of the subversive nature of his plays, Usigli continued to have works censored throughout his lifetime.

Another important influence on Usigli's theater was the Irish playwright, George Bernard Shaw; Usigli was perhaps his closest follower in Spanish America. His play *La familia cena en casa* (1942; The Family Dines at Home) was criticized for being too much of an imitation of Shaw's *Pygmalion* (1913). Shaw's influence was probably because of Usigli's desire to stay abreast of European technical innovations inspired by the postsurrealist period following World War II. Nevertheless, Usigli always modified European theater to fit Spanish American reality. *Corona de sombra* (1943; translated as *Crown of Shadows*), generally acclaimed for its poetic quality and considered a classic of Spanish American theater, exploits modern theatrical techniques while underscoring the social commitment of

Rodolfo Usigli

the author. Shaw himself recognized the genius of Usigli's works after reading a translation of *Corona de sombra.*

REFERENCE:

Gerardo Luzuriaga, *Introducción a las teorías latinoamericanas del teatro* (Puebla: Universidad Autónoma de Puebla, Maestría en Ciencias del Lenguaje, 1990).

—M.T.

VALLENATO

Currently one of the most popular genres from Colombia, the *vallenato* has challenged the traditionally dominant popularity of the *cumbia* in Colombia, Panama, and Central America. From its past history as a song form emphasizing descriptive narrative, it has recently developed into a song/couple-dance genre serving popular and commercial venues.

Originally a folk genre from the northeastern sector of Colombia, the vallenato began as a descendant of the *galerón*, itself an Americanized version of the Spanish **romance.** The epic texts of these genres provided relief from the boredom of long sea voyages and lonely nights in sparsely populated rural areas. The unpretentious musical and literary properties of the vallenato were favored by working-class cowboys and laborers but held in disdain by sophisticated, urban colonials. Straightforward couplets set to simple melodies with a rustic accompaniment of accordion, stick scraper, and *caja de vallenato* (a small drum) became the musical fare of numerous taverns, cockfighting arenas, and public festivals. The common structural format consists of solo verses alternating with choral refrains.

Vallenato musicians and their audiences are emerging from a drug-related reputation that developed during the 1960s. Profits from marijuana and cocaine sales enabled drug lords to corrupt the economic, social, and political life of Colombia and, in the process, exercise considerable control over popular music by hiring vallenato musicians to sing their praises in public concerts and festivals. Record companies also contributed to the perversion of the tradition by financing and preselecting winners in so-called competitions. Many traditional vallenato bands have responded not by glorifying the perpetrators, but by supporting the victims of the drug trade: fatherless children, widowed mothers, and a destitute agricultural economy.

Another development has been a new approach to vallenato music in which electronic instruments and recording techniques have replaced the traditional trio of folk instruments. It is unlikely that contemporary young audiences, the new aficionados of vallenato, are aware of its sordid past, for at its best it is a lively and refreshing addition to the repertoire of Latin music.

REFERENCES:

Peter Manuel, *Popular Musics of the Non-Western World: An Introductory Survey* (New York: Oxford University Press, 1988);

Jeremy Marre and Hannah Charlton, *Beats of the Heart: Popular Music of the World* (New York: Pantheon, 1985);

Octavio Marulanda, *El folclor de Colombia: Práctica de la identidad cultural* (Bogotá: Artestudio Editores, 1984).

— R.L.S.

REMEDIOS VARO

The Spanish-born Remedios Varo (1908–1963) became one of the most important Mexican artists associated with **Surrealism.** As a child she traveled with her father, a hydraulic engineer, throughout Spain and North Africa, becoming interested in mathematics and mechanical drawings and devices. Varo studied art in Madrid at the Academia de San Fernando and was briefly married to a fellow student. She later moved to Barcelona, where she participated in avant-garde circles and met the surrealist poet Benjamín Péret. From 1936 to 1939 Varo and Péret lived together in Paris and actively participated in Surrealist circles. In France, Varo also began her lifelong friendship with fellow Surrealist **Leonora Carrington.** Like several other Surrealists, Varo and Péret left Europe at the beginning of World War II and went to Mexico.

Varo and Péret married in 1942 and lived near Carrington and her husband. The two women had a close and productive friendship; their works in the mid 1940s often show mutual influences. They became the center of a group of European Surrealist artists that included Luis Buñuel, Wolfgang Paalen, and Alice Rahon. Varo did not produce many works during the early 1940s. She supported herself and Péret by producing commercial dioramas, advertisements for Bayer, and even secretly restoring pre-Columbian pottery for Paalen. Varo's first exhibition in Mexico was not until 1954.

Like Carrington, Varo searched for self-knowledge and spiritual enlightenment through a personal iconography that included animated mechanisms such as engines and boats and alchemical devices, whimsical portraits of herself, and mysterious architectonic spaces reminiscent of those of the Italian painter Giorgio De Chirico. For instance, in her meticulously executed paintings *Harmonía* (1956; Harmony) and *La creación de los pájaros* (1958; The Creation of the Birds) Varo represents herself as a magical being working in isolated studio-like spaces that become transcendental sites where spiritual and creative energies are combined through the manipulation of hermetic secrets such as those of alchemy and Sufi mysticism.

REFERENCE:

Janet A. Kaplan, *Unexpected Journeys: The Art and Life of Remedios Varo* (London: Virago, 1988).

— F.B.N.

José Vasconcelos (courtesy of the Organization of American States)

JOSÉ VASCONCELOS

Fiery, contradictory, and controversial, Mexican writer José Vasconcelos (1882–1959) gained fame during the first decades of the century and became one of Latin America's most widely renowned essayists. Born in Oaxaca, Vasconcelos pursued his university studies in Mexico City, where he joined various writers and intellectuals in the Ateneo de la Juventud (Athenaeum of Youth), a group whose skepticism toward positivist thought and whose leaning toward a new humanism left its mark on the cultural life of Mexico. He participated actively in the **Mexican Revolution** and later became minister of education from 1920 to 1925. During those years he renovated the educational system, reformed rural education, built new schools, and fostered the arts, especially literature and painting. At that time Mexican painters such as the muralists **Diego Rivera** and **José Clemente Orozco** were gaining international recognition. When the government adopted

its anticlerical agenda in the mid 1920s, Vasconcelos left Mexico and lived in voluntary exile for many years, traveling and lecturing throughout Europe and Latin America. He returned to Mexico having become a fervent Catholic and distanced himself from previous revolutionary ideas and comrades.

Vasconcelos cultivated every genre, but he is best known for his essays covering a wide range of philosophical, historical, sociological, political, and cultural topics. In his best-known essay, *La raza cósmica* (1925; translated as *The Cosmic Race*) he analyzes the complex racial and cultural composition of the Latin American. In this essay he maintains that the combination of Spanish and Indian blood has produced a unique fifth race, that of the mestizo, which will confront the Anglo-Saxon race in the coming centuries. In the sequel *Indología* (1926; Indigenology) he affirms the superiority of this mestizo race, whose strength comes from the combination of different bloods. Vasconcelos

279

also wrote a series of semi-autobiographical novels; the most favorably received is *Ulises criollo* (1935; The Creole Ulysses), a novel of the Mexican Revolution. Vasconcelos wrote exhaustively while fighting for the ideals he believed in, which varied throughout his lifetime. He is known as one of the most powerful and original Latin American thinkers, one who addresses the vast and complex racial, ethnic, cultural, historical, and social problems of the continent.

REFERENCE:

Gabriella De Beer, *José Vasconcelos and His World* (New York: Las Américas Publishing, 1966).

           — M.E.S.

Ana Lydia Vega

Having published four collections of short stories, Ana Lydia Vega (1946–) is a best-selling author whose work is acclaimed in Puerto Rico and internationally by both literary critics and the general reading public. *Vírgenes y mártires* (1981; Virgins and Martyrs), her first book, written in collaboration with Carmen Lugo Filippi, chronicles the experiences of contemporary Puerto Rican women as they struggle with a social environment controlled by patriarchy and colonialism. Stories such as "Letra para salsa y tres soneos por encargo" (Salsa Lyrics and Three Soneos by Request) use humor and skillful representations of popular culture and popular language to provide striking portraits of urban Puerto Rico. Throughout her work, which includes *Encancaranublado* (1982; translated as *Cloud Over Caribbean*), *Pasión de historia* (1987; the title story has been translated both as "True Romances" and "Story-Bound"), and *Falsas crónicas del sur* (1991; False Chronicles of the South), Vega manipulates different literary genres — the murder mystery, the romantic novel, the political tract, the folktale, and the historical narrative — to weave her Caribbean tales. *Falsas crónicas del sur* can be described as a loving yet ironic collection of folktales and historical lore from the south of Puerto Rico, mimicking, mocking, and chronicling a historical trajectory that is both Puerto Rican and distinctly Caribbean. It has been argued that Vega, as one of a generation of Puerto Rican writers who set out to write against a paternalistic and insular literary tradition, has been particularly successful in her attempts to subvert limiting notions of national and literary identities predicated on hierarchies of race, gender, and class. Vega also contributed to and edited a collection of essays, *El tramo ancla: Ensayos puertorriqueños de hoy* (1988; Passing on the Baton), and an English translation of

selected stories by Vega, *True and False Romances,* was published in 1994. A collection of her essays, *Esperando a Loló y otros delirios generacionales* (Waiting for Loló and Other Generational Deliriums), was published in 1995.

REFERENCES:

Margarite Fernández-Olmos, "From a Woman's Perspective: The Short Stories of Rosario Ferré and Ana Lydia Vega" in *Contemporary Women Authors of Latin America,* edited by Doris Meyer and Margarite Fernández Olmos (New York: Brooklyn College Press, 1983), pp. 78–90;

Juan G. Gelpí, *Literatura y paternalismo en Puerto Rico* (San Juan: Editorial de la Universidad de Puerto Rico, 1993).

           — C.D.T.

Marcio Veloz Maggiolo

Born in Santo Domingo, Marcio Veloz Maggiolo (1936–) has worked as an archaeologist, professor, and journalist and has served as ambassador to Peru and Italy. As an archaeologist Veloz Maggiolo has traveled to many cities in the United States, giving papers and undertaking research commissioned by the Smithsonian Institution. His plays *Y después las cenizas* (And Later the Ashes) and *Creonte* have received much public attention; a third play, *El cáncer de cada día* (Our Daily Cancer) won an award in a literary contest sponsored by the Foundation for Fine Arts in the Dominican Republic. He has also published two books of poetry: *Intus* (1962) and *Transparencias: Poemas* (1971; Transparencies: Poems). His novel *El buen ladrón* (1960; The Good Robber), which won the National Book Award and also an award from the William Faulkner Foundation, belongs to a cycle of "biblical novels." It is an allegory of the social and political realities in the Dominican Republic during the decade of the 1950s. *De abril en adelante* (1976; From April On), his most acclaimed novel, narrates the historical events of the last years of Rafael Trujillo's dictatorship, the April Revolution, and the postrevolutionary period, through the discontented perspective of a group of intellectuals and bohemians. In 1980 Veloz Maggiolo published the novel *La biografía difusa de Sombra Castañeda* (The Diffuse Biography of Sombra Castañeda), the story of a dictator whose loneliness is seen as symptomatic of absolute power. In his latest novel, *Ritos de cabaret* (1991; Rites of Cabaret), Veloz Maggiolo uses the **bolero** to evoke nostalgia for the decades of the 1950s and 1960s. This novel also depicts the search for national and sexual identity during the final years of Trujillo's regime. Marcio Veloz Maggiolo is not only considered the most versatile Dominican writer but is also the most prolific.

REFERENCE:

Doris Sommer, *One Master for Another: Populism as Patriarchal Rhetoric in Dominican Novels* (Lanham, Md.: University Press of America, 1983).

— F.V.

VIHUELA

One of the original instruments of the **mariachi** ensemble, the *vihuela* of Mexico is an adaptation of earlier European guitarlike instruments. Unlike the flat back of the guitar, the Mexican vihuela has a vaulted, convex back; it is smaller than the acoustic guitar. Its size is not standardized but varies according to the individual tastes of different makers and according to regional preferences. Its five strings are tuned in descending order from the first string: E – B – E – D – G.

The vihuela is not plucked, but strummed, fulfilling an important rhythmic function by providing driving percussive patterns. The chordal harmony that it provides as an accompaniment to violin or trumpet melodies adds a crisp sound and brilliant color to the mellow sounds of the acoustic guitar and the **guitarrón.**

REFERENCE:

David Kilpatrick, *El Mariachi: Traditional Music of Mexico*, volume 1 (Pico Rivera, Cal.: Fiesta Publications, 1988).

— R.L.S.

VILLANCICO

Although *villancico*s come originally from Spain, they have also been produced in Latin America. Most Latin American villancicos are intended as Christmas songs; they are invariably religious, honoring saints, angels, souls, and Jesus. Most of the melodies resemble chants with syllabic settings of texts, requiring only narrow vocal ranges. Generally, there are no large or awkward intervals. In comparison with those of **aguinaldos,** which are also sung at Christmas, the rhythms are less syncopated and animated.

REFERENCES:

Isabel Aretz, *El folklore musical argentino* (Buenos Aires: Ricordi Americana S.A.E.C., 1952);

Gerard Béhague, "Latin American Folk Music," in *Folk and Traditional Music of the Western Continents,* by Bruno Nettl (Englewood Cliffs, N.J.: Prentice-Hall, 1990).

— R.L.S.

XAVIER VILLAURRUTIA

One of the few openly homosexual Latin American writers during the first half of the twentieth century, Xavier Villaurrutia (1902–1950) was an important Mexican poet and dramatist. He was born in Mexico City and died at a relatively young age. As a poet, Xavier Villaurrutia published three books of poetry: *Reflejos* (1926; Reflections), *Nostalgia de la muerte* (1938; definitive version in 1946; Nostalgia for Death), and *Canto a la primavera* (1948; Song to Spring). *Nostalgia de la muerte* inspired a whole generation of poets who followed, including the Nobel laureate **Octavio Paz.**

The poetry of Villaurrutia is passionate and sensual, appealing to the visual senses through concrete imagery and symbols. While exploring many themes characteristic of Spanish American **Modernismo,** Villaurrutia uses less flowery and elegant language than the *modernistas.* His natural affinity, however, lies with what has been described as verbal trickery, the use of rhetorical devices such as inversion and antithesis, to express his themes of anguished and solitary introspection. Influenced by the Surrealists, his poetry explores the parallels between dreaming and consciousness, love and hate, and the presence of death as mankind's constant companion. It can be described as poetry of desire.

Villaurrutia as dramatist emerged from the activities of a government-supported group called Teatro de Orientación (Theater of Orientation), founded by Celestino Gorostiza. Villaurrutia's theater follows the dark, passionate vein of his poetic works. His first play, *Parece mentira* (1934; Incredible), rehearses the existentialist themes that characterize his dramatic production. His play *El ausente* (The Absent One), published together with *Parece mentira* in a collection of one-act plays called *Autos profanos* (1943; Profane Acts), which the author calls a collection of mysteries, enigmas, and profane games, is the story of a wife who loses her husband to another woman. The play establishes the serious and often bitter tone of Vilaurrutia's future work. *Invitación a la muerte* (1940; translated as *Dancing with Death*) is perhaps Villaurrutia's most distinguished drama. The basis for the play is purely psychological: a boy creates an imaginary father after his real father abandons him. Yet *Invitación a la muerte* clearly speaks of Villaurrutia's lifelong obsession with solitude and death, themes that characterize both his poetry and his theater.

REFERENCE:

Frank Dauster, *Xavier Villaurrutia* (New York: Twayne, 1971).

— M.T.

WALDEEN

Waldeen Feldenkrais (1913–1993), a modern dancer from the United States, toured Mexico with the Japanese choreographer Michio Ito in 1939. She remained to teach **modern dance** and create the first offical modern dance group or company in Mexico, with full government support. This company lasted only a few years, although its students later formed a company called the Ballet Waldeen. Besides her pioneering teaching work in modern dance in Mexico, Waldeen is known for creating *La coronela,* a legendary and extremely successful piece of choreography about the **Mexican Revolution.** It was groundbreaking in the search for "Mexican dance," a form of national expression that would be neither folkloric nor indigenous. In Waldeen's workshops, dancers donned pre-Columbian masks — jaguars, Olmec heads, or devil masks — and used improvisation to investigate the earliest dance impulses of Mesoamerica.

— J.M.H

Y-Z

Agustín Yáñez

Today considered one of Mexico's most important novelists, Agustín Yáñez (1904–1980) was also an important lawyer, professor, and statesman. He was born and raised in Guadalajara, where he obtained a law degree; he then continued studying at the Universidad Nacional Autónoma de México (National Autonomous University of Mexico) in Mexico City. He was governor of Jalisco from 1953 to 1959 and served in several other important posts in the Mexican government. His most significant novels form a trilogy: *Al filo del agua* (1947; translated as *At the Edge of the Storm*), *La tierra pródiga* (1960; The Prodigal Land), and *Las tierras flacas* (1962; translated as *The Lean Lands*). Yáñez's style is influenced by various literary masters, among them James Joyce, William Faulkner, Marcel Proust, Virginia Woolf, and Aldous Huxley. Huxley's influence is especially evident when Yáñez is dealing with the world of the subconscious, notably in his most famous novel, *Al filo del agua,* a work which depicts the upheaval of the **Mexican Revolution.** Regarding that novel, Yáñez stated that his aim had been to apply to a Mexican pueblo the technique John Dos Passos had used in *Manhattan Transfer* (1900). The setting of *Al filo del agua* is a provincial town in rural Mexico. The stream-of-consciousness technique explores the inner, emotional worlds of characters who represent a collective subconsciousness; the inhabitants are obsessed with their sexual inhibitions, fears, frustrated desires, fantasies, and passions, which are labeled sinful and are stifled by the local patricians and matrons, whose lives are regimented by the tolling of the church bells. The reality behind the exterior world of appearances emerges with the oncoming revolution, symbolic of a liberating force for those compelled to live under domination and in stagnation. Some of Yáñez's other techniques involve the use of interior monologues, the jux-

Agustín Yáñez talking to villagers during his tenure as governor of the Mexican state of Jalisco

taposition of situations, the montage of simultaneous events, and fragmented time. His style is lyrical and rich in colloquialisms, as is also apparent in *La tierra pródiga,* a novel which presents an optimistic view of the economic and social transformations that shook Mexico after the revolution. The last novel of this cycle, *Las tierras flacas,* focuses on various aspects of society in the arid regions of northern Mexico. Yáñez's novels are regional; yet through his skillful techniques, his deep psychological analysis, and his accomplished prose style, they achieve universal dimensions, making him a writer who marks the transition from the novels of the revolution to the experimentalism of the **Boom.**

REFERENCES:

Helmy F. Giacoman, *Homenaje a Agustín Yáñez* (New York: Las Américas, 1973);

Joseph Sommers, *After the Storm: Landmarks of the Modern Mexican Novel* (Albuquerque: University of New Mexico Press, 1968).

— M.E.S. & P.S.

ZAPATEO

The rhythmic, staccato tapping produced by drumming the shoe (*zapato* in Spanish) on the floor is a recognized feature of flamenco dancing (used, for example, in the fandango and the seguidilla) and one that has been modified and incorporated into some dance forms in Spanish America. Another term that is sometimes used is *zapateado,* though technically it refers to a specific Spanish dance. *Taconeo* is derived from *tacón* (heel) and refers to similar percussive effects achieved with the heel of the shoe.

— P.S.

ZARZUELA

Among the many Spanish cultural traditions transplanted to the Americas is a form of light opera or operetta called *zarzuela,* whose origins date back to the seventeenth century. The earliest known Spanish composer of zarzuelas was Juan Hidalgo, while early librettos are credited to the two major playwrights of the time, Lope de Vega Carpio and Pedro Calderón de la Barca. The heyday of zarzuela came in the nineteenth century; Tomás Bretón (1850–1923) and Joaquín Valverde (1846–1910) each wrote more than fifty such operettas, while the individual most closely associated with the genre is probably Ruperto Chapí (1851–1900). The zarzuela is a popular, comic, and distinctly Hispanic form of operetta, generally in one act. Unlike grand opera, with its uninterrupted music and singing, zarzuela includes interludes of spoken dialogue and dances, and it can therefore be compared with Italian opera buffa, French opéra comique, English ballad opera, or the German Singspiel.

In colonial Latin America during the late seventeenth century, zarzuelas served a largely aristocratic audience. Later, as that audience became more attracted to Italian opera seria, the zarzuela fell somewhat out of fashion, and other forms of musical theater began to be produced in public venues. Toward the end of the nineteenth century there was a popular revival of the zarzuela in which the influence of Italian opera became apparent, for example in the way arias and recitatives were used.

Nostalgic and traditional, the zarzuela attracts the interest of few modern composers, but it continues to have a loyal following and is still regularly performed. Evidence of its vitality can be seen in the fact that in the 1990s **Plácido Domingo,** one of the world's leading tenors, participated in *Antología de la zarzuela,* a Spanish television production broadcast throughout the Americas and combined with an extensive tour.

REFERENCES:

Rodolfo Arizaga and Pompeyo Camps, *Historia de la música en la Argentina* (Buenos Aires: Ricordi Americana S.A.E.C., 1990);

Gerard Béhague, *Music in Latin America: An Introduction* (Englewood Cliffs, N.J.: Prentice-Hall, 1979).

— R.L.S. & P.S.

NAHUM ZENIL

Nahum Bernabé Zenil (1947–) is one of the most important young artists to have emerged in Mexico during the 1980s. First trained as an elementary school teacher, Zenil studied art at the Escuela Nacional de Pintura y Escultura (National School of Painting and Sculpture) during the 1970s and become a full-time painter in the 1980s. As in the case of the earlier Mexican artists **Frida Kahlo** and **José Luis Cuevas,** who produced numerous self-portraits, Zenil's principal theme is himself. Through this exploration of the self, Zenil also questions broader traditional cultural and sexual attitudes, a thematic approach that connects his art with the neo-Mexicanism of a loosely organized group of contemporary Mexican artists that includes **Rocío Maldonado** and Julio Galán.

In his startling works, most of them small, intimate mixed-media paintings, Zenil includes images of himself in religious and traditional contexts. In *Retrato de boda* (1988; Wedding Portrait) Zenil's self-representation reaches the narcissistic as he gives all members of the wedding party his own face. In *Bendiciones* (1987; Blessings) Zenil adopts the format of the exvoto, a type of popular Catholic painting featuring prayers and images of thanksgiving. In this case Zenil paints himself together with Gerardo, his look-alike, longtime companion and lover, standing below a well-known Mexican icon, the Virgin of Guadalupe, whose blessings in the form of roses (a flower traditionally associated with her) fall like rain over the two men. Zenil reinterprets and subverts established symbols in order to challenge sexual stereotypes and expose the homophobic prejudices prevalent in conservative Catholic society. The pain produced by such sexual intolerance becomes clear in examples such as *Esperar la hora que cambiará nuestra costumbre no es fácil* (1984; Waiting for the Time When Our Customs Will Change Is not Easy). In this work Zenil's nude and crouching self-portrait appears behind the crisscrossing strands of real rope attached to the frame, suggesting a sense of imprisonment. The art of Zenil and other members of the neo-Mexicanism group has signaled a return to ideological issues in Mexican art.

REFERENCE:

Edward J. Sullivan, "Nahum Zenil's 'Auto-Iconography,' " *Arts Magazine* (November 1988): 86–91.
                                                                        — F.B.N.

FRANCISCO ZÚÑIGA

The sculptor Francisco Zúñiga (1912–) is well known for his representations of indigenous peoples. Zúñiga, whose mother was Indian, began his art studies in his native Costa Rica with his father, Manuel M. Zúñiga, also a sculptor, and later attended the Escuela de Bellas Artes. He belonged to the artistic generation of the 1930s, which included artists such as **Manuel de la Cruz González** who worked with figuration and portrayed national or indigenist themes with modernized styles. Although Zúñiga's granite sculpture *Monumento a la madre* (1935; Monument to the Mother) was considered too modern by the conservative public of Costa Rica, it received first prize in an international competition, the Certamen Centroamericano de Escultura. This work shows his early preference for a simplified realism and bulky, blocklike, geometricized forms.

In 1936 Zúñiga settled in Mexico, became a student of Manuel Rodríguez Lozano and Guillermo Ruiz, and taught sculpture at the Escuela de Artes Plásticas La Esmeralda and other schools. In Mexico

Nuclear Physics (1964), fountain designed and executed by Francisco Zúñiga in Chapultepec Park, Mexico City

Zúñiga produced numerous indigenist works, such as *Mujer sentada* (1973; Seated Woman); this sculpture is typical of his compositions, which often combine the simplified pyramidal shapes of seated Indian women covered by mantles (large shawls) with a realistic rendition of faces and limbs. Zúñiga's sculptures have achieved great commercial success.

REFERENCE:

Sheldon Reich, *Francisco Zúñiga: Sculptor* (Tucson: University of Arizona Press, 1980).
                                                                        — F.B.N.

CONTRIBUTORS

J.F. ....Jacinto Fombona

A.G. ....Ann González

J.M.H. ....Jan Michael Hanvik

S.M.H. ....Stephen M. Hart

D.H. ....Deanna Hutson

C.M. ....Charles Maynard

R.G.M. ....Ricardo Gutiérrez Mouat

F.B.N. ....Florencia Bazzano Nelson

J.P. ....Julia Patiño

N.L.R. ....Nancy Lee Ruyter

E.S.C. ....Eduardo Santa Cruz

M.E.S. ....Maureen E. Shea

R.L.S. ....Robert L. Smith

P.S. ....Peter Standish

C.D.T. ....Cathy Den Tandt

M.T. ....Matthew Tremé

F.V. ....Fernando Valerio

DICTIONARY OF

TWENTIETH CENTURY CULTURE

Hispanic Culture of Mexico, Central America, and the Caribbean

PHOTO
INDEX

INDEX OF PHOTOGRAPHS

DICTIONARY OF

TWENTIETH CENTURY CULTURE

Hispanic Culture of
Mexico, Central America,
and the Caribbean

GENERAL INDEX

A

B

C

F

G

I

O

Los sordomudos (Hernández) 143
Sorolla, Joaquín 147
Sosa, Roberto 263
Soto, Jesús Rafael 92
Soto, Merián 189, 225
Souza, Antonio 23
Soy feliz (Tarraza) 51
Soy tuya (Tarraza) 51
Spanish Civil War 61, 130, 136, 141, 222, 229, 231, 260
Spanish Inquisition 270
Spanish Ministry of Culture 237
Spanish Royal Academy of Language 163, 237
Spanish-American War (1898) 52, 198, 233
Spilimbergo, Lino Eneas 260
Spirit of Panamá (Cordero) 87
Spota, Luis 275
Stalinism 231
Standard Fruit 263
Stern 216
Stern'sches Konservatorium, Berlin 229
Stockhausen, Karlheinz 159
Stokowski, Leopold 76, 122
Strand, Paul 29
Strauss, Richard 191
Stravinsky, Igor 66, 121
Streptomicyne (Aponte-Ledée) 31
String Quartet No. 1 (Chávez) 75
String Quartet No. 3 (Cordero) 88
Structuralism 238, 256
Suárez, Jaime 21
Suárez, Julio 21, 39
Subdirección General de Educación, Mexico 71
Sueño de amor 240
El sueño de Doña Marina 2 (Gironella) 126
El sueño de Santa María de las Piedras (Miguel Méndez M.) 77
Sueño de una tarde de domingo en la Alameda Central (Rivera) 246
Sueño y presentimiento (Izquierdo) 156
Sueños de papel (Iturbide) 155
Sufi mysticism 278
Suite para orquesta (García Caturla) 122, 141
Suite tropical sobre temas costarricenses (Fonseca) 116
Los supersabios (Butzo) 84
Sur 257
Surrealism 23–24, 30–31, 37, 39, 41–42, 65–67, 104, 108, 111, 113, 124, 151, 156, 158, 161, 172, 183, 193, 222, 226, 228–229, 235, 245–246, 253, 263–264, 278, 281
Suter, Gerardo 227
Swan Lake (Tchaikovsky) 28
Swift, Jonathan 191–192
Les Sylphides (Fokine) 28
Symbolist art 38, 145, 150, 189, 195, 264
Symbolist movement 172, 228
Symbolist poetry 101–102, 264
Symphony No. 1 (Flores) 115
Symphony Orchestra of Mexico. *See* Orquesta Sinfónica Nacional de México.

T

Taberna y otros lugares (Dalton) 98
Tabio, Juan Carlos 50, 82
Tablada, Juan José 183, 216, 264

Tableau (Ferrer) 112
Taibo, Paco Ignacio 103
Taino Indians 115, 143, 181
Un tal José Salomé (Azuela) 43
Taller 222
Taller de Artes Gráficas, Puerto Rico 39
Taller de Cine Super-8, Nicaragua 77
Taller de Gráfica Popular, Mexico 38, 74, 130, 150
El tamaño del infierno (Azuela) 43
Tamayo, Rufino 23, 39, 156, 184, 246, 251, 267–268, 275
Tambora 138, 182, 199, 268–269
Tamborito 268–269
Tango 61, 75, 98, 132, 141
Tango negro 190
Tapai Theatre, San Juan, Puerto Rico 143
Tapia Ruano, Juan 22
Tàpies, Antoni 193
Tarahumara Indians 110
La tarea 80
Tarraza, Juan Bruno 51
Tata Jesucristo (Goitia) 127
Tatay, Vicente 233
Tchaikovsky, Pyotr Ilich 28, 83
¿Te dio miedo la sangre? (Ramírez) 241
Te espero (Velásquez) 51
Te quiero, dijiste (Grever) 131
Teatro Campesino 77
Teatro de Orientación 273, 281
Teatro Fábrigas, Mexico City 141
Teatro Fausto Orchestra 143
Teatro Fedora de la Habana 165
— Department of Dance 189
Teatro La Perla, Puerto Rico 225
Teatro Martí, Cuba 165
Teatro Nacional, Havana 249
Teatro Nacional, Mexico 145
Teatro Nacional Popular, Venezuela 133
Teatro Puerto Rico 144
Tejas Verdes (Valdés) 272
Tel Quel 238, 256–257
Telenovelas 116, 209, 221, 269–271
Televisa 72, 110, 240, 270–272
Televisión Azteca 240
Televisión Española 93, 120
Televisión y Novelas 171
Tellado, Corín 209
Tellado López, María del Socorro. *See* Tellado, Corín.
Tema y seis diferencias (Aponte-Ledée) 31
Tiempo de audacia 78
Tengo (Guillén) 137
Tengo que acostumbrarme (Silva) 52
"Tengo un nuevo amor" (Lecuona) 165
Teotihuacán 145
Teresa of Avila, Saint 211
Termina el desfile (Arenas) 35
Terra Nostra (Fuentes) 119, 214, 237
La terra trema 261
El terror (Cardi) 104
Testimonial narrative 27–28, 36, 40, 48, 67, 71, 114, 153, 180, 231, 272
Los testimonios (Dalton) 98
Testimonios sobre Mariana (Garro) 125
Texera, Diego de la 77
Third Cinema. *See* New Latin American Cinema movement.
Third Festival of Latin American Music, Caracas (1966) 60
Third Piano Sonata (Halffter) 141

ISBN 0-8103-8484-1